Arizona FOR DUMMIES®

3RD EDITION

by Edie Jarolim

Wiley Publishing, Inc.

Arizona For Dummies®, 3rd Edition

Published by
Wiley Publishing, Inc.
111 River St.
Hoboken, NJ 07030-5774
www.wiley.com

For general information on our other products and services, please contact our Customer Care Department within the U.S. at 800-762-2974, outside the U.S. at 317-572-3993, or fax 317-572-4002.

For technical support, please visit www.wiley.com/techsupport.

Wiley also publishes its books in a variety of electronic formats. Some content that appears in print may not be available in electronic books.

Library of Congress Control Number: 2004114964

ISBN: 0-7645-6938-4

Manufactured in the United States of America

10 9 8 7 6 5 4 3 2 1

3B/RS/RR/QU/IN

Plan your trip with For Dummies

Covering the most popular destinations in North America and Europe, *For Dummies* travel guides are the ultimate user-friendly trip planners. Available wherever books are sold or go to www.dummies.com

And book it with our online partner, Frommers.com

- Book airfare, hotels and packages
- Find the hottest deals
- Get breaking travel news
- Enter to win vacations
- Share trip photos and stories
- And much more

Frommers.com, rated the #1 Travel Web Site by PC Magazine

About the Author

Edie Jarolim has worn many hats — not counting the sombrero she donned on a certain one-margarita-too-many night . . . . She has a Ph.D. in American literature from New York University and was a senior editor at Frommer's travel guides in New York before being lured by the warm sun and endless vistas — not to mention the inexpensive real estate — to Tucson, Arizona, in 1992. She has since written for a variety of national publications, from America West Airlines Magazine, Art & Antiques, and Brides to National Geographic Traveler, The New York Times Book Review, and The Wall Street Journal. She is also the author of Frommer's San Antonio & Austin.

Author's Acknowledgments

It has been more than a dozen years since Marjorie Magnusson and Leia James of the Arizona Office of Tourism (AOT) warmly welcomed a flustered, tardy travel writer who was new to the many mysteries of automobiles. My ability to judge driving distances between cities is a bit better these days, but the helpfulness and good spirits of everyone I've worked with at the AOT have remained unchanged. In addition to Marjorie — who continues to be an invaluable resource — I'd like to thank Laura McMurchie and Kristen Jarnagin for making my research so much fun. I'm pleased to see that Jacki Mieler is carrying on AOT's efficiency-plus-entertainment tradition.

If I could individually thank all the people who assisted me, this book would be twice the size, so I'll restrict myself to those that most directly helped to facilitate my research for the 3rd Edition. They are: Mike Finney (Arizona Rocks; northern Arizona and Grand Canyon tourism coalition); Luanne Matson (TMC Group, Inc., Bisbee); Ana Masterson (Flagstaff Convention and Visitors Bureau); Dwayne Cassidy and Joan Stavely (Page–Lake Powell Chamber of Commerce); Stacy Reading (Phoenix Convention & Visitors Bureau); Char Beltran, Sachiko Sado, and Jennifer Wesselhoff (Sedona–Oak Creek Chamber of Commerce); Kim Cole (and again, Laura McMurchie) (Scottsdale Convention & Visitors Bureau); Erika Breckel (Sierra Vista Convention & Visitors Bureau); Toni Graham (Tempe Convention & Visitors Bureau); Barbara MacDonald (Metropolitan Tucson Convention & Visitors Bureau); Donna Cochran (Williams–Grand Canyon Chamber of Commerce); and Julie Brooks (Wickenburg Chamber of Commerce).

Special thanks go to Nikki Buchanan, Phoenix Magazine's food critic, for her expert advice on Valley restaurants; to Vicki Rider, for her meticulous research; and to Jeff Kanonas, for his company and driving skills, which made my road trips at once enjoyable and efficient.

Publisher's Acknowledgments

We're proud of this book; please send us your comments through our Dummies online registration form located at www.dummies.com/register/.

Some of the people who helped bring this book to market include the following:

Editorial

Editors: Tere Stouffer Drenth, Alexis Lipsitz Flippin

(Previous edition: Jennifer Connolly, Lisa Torrance)

Cartographer: Anton Crane

Editorial Manager: Carmen Krikorian

Editorial Assistant: Nadine Bell

Senior Photo Editor: Richard Fox

Front Cover Photo: © Ed Gifford/ Masterfile

Back Cover Photo: © Steve Craft/ Masterfile

Cartoons: Rich Tennant, www.the5thwave.com

Composition

Project Coordinator: April Farling

Layout and Graphics: Lauren Goddard, Joyce Haughey, Michael Kruzil, Barry Offringa, Melanee Prendergast, Jacque Roth, Heather Ryan, Julie Trippetti

Proofreaders: David Faust, Carl William Pierce, TECHBOOKS Production Services

Indexer: TECHBOOKS Production Services

Publishing and Editorial for Consumer Dummies

Diane Graves Steele, Vice President and Publisher, Consumer Dummies

Joyce Pepple, Acquisitions Director, Consumer Dummies

Kristin A. Cocks, Product Development Director, Consumer Dummies

Michael Spring, Vice President and Publisher, Travel

Brice Gosnell, Associate Publisher, Travel

Kelly Regan, Editorial Director, Travel

Publishing for Technology Dummies

Andy Cummings, Vice President and Publisher, Dummies Technology/General User

Composition Services

Gerry Fahey, Vice President of Production Services

Debbie Stailey, Director of Composition Services

Contents at a Glance

Maps at a Glance

Table of Contents

Introduction

I always enjoy hearing friends who have never been to Arizona give their impressions of my adopted home state: "It's all desert, isn't it?" they say, or "It's all canyons," or "It's all Native Americans living on reservations," or "It's all fat cats playing golf."

Kind of reminds me of the story of the group of blindfolded men who, when asked to describe an elephant after having examined a small section of one, each come up with a completely different, fantastical description of it.

Like an elephant, Arizona is very large and can't be characterized by any one of its parts. But just because you haven't visited the state or have had only a limited experience with it, you don't have to take after those short-sighted pachyderm probers. With Arizona For Dummies, 3rd Edition, you see not only desert and canyons, American Indian reservations, and fat cats on golf courses, but also the best of the myriad sights and attractions that make the state such a popular destination.

About This Book

Forget all those other guidebooks, where you have to wade through a small forest's worth of paper to find out the one thing you wanted to know. Arizona For Dummies is a reference book as well as a guide, which means that you don't have to read it from cover to cover — or even from front to back. Each section and chapter is as self-contained as possible, so you can concentrate on what's important to you at the moment. You can always flip to a different section later if you feel like it. Just because the chapters are self-contained, though, doesn't mean that I keep repeating myself. I've been cornered at enough weddings by bores who want to keep telling me the same stories about their trip to Hawaii to know better (of course, trips to Arizona are endlessly fascinating). If I cover a topic that interests you in one section of the book, I refer you to that area rather than waste your time — and mine — by going over the information again.

Please be advised that travel information is subject to change at any time — especially prices. I therefore suggest that you write or call ahead for confirmation when making your travel plans. The authors, editors, and publisher can't be held responsible for the experiences of readers while traveling. Your safety is important to us, however, so we encourage you to stay alert and be aware of your surroundings. Keep a close eye on cameras, purses, and wallets — all favorite targets of thieves and pickpockets.

Dummies Post-it® Flags

As you're reading this book, you'll find information that you may want to reference as you plan or enjoy your trip — whether a new hotel, a must-see attraction, or a must-try walking tour. Mark these pages with the handy Post-it(r) Flags included in this book to help make your trip planning easier.

Conventions Used in This Book

In this book, in addition to lists of my favorite hotels and restaurants, I also include some general pricing information to help you as you decide where to unpack your bags or dine on the local cuisine. I use a system of dollar signs to show a range of costs for one night in a hotel (the price refers to a double-occupancy room) or a meal for one person at a restaurant (including appetizer, entree, and dessert). Check out the following table to decipher the dollar signs:

Cost	Hotel	Restaurant
$	$100 or less	$10 or less
$$	$101–$200	$11–$25
$$$	$201–$300	$26–$45
$$$$	$301–$400	$46–$60
$$$$$	$401 and more	$61 and more

Throughout the book, I also use abbreviations for credit cards. Sorry, I had room only for the biggies, so although your local discount club or gas card may well be accepted in Arizona, I couldn't include everything. The plastic that appears in these pages is:

AE: American Express

CB: Carte Blanche

DC: Diners Club

DISC: Discover Card

MC: MasterCard

V: Visa

To make pertinent information stand out, attractions and main telephone numbers (usually toll-free) are in bold typeface.

Foolish Assumptions

As I wrote this book, I made some assumptions about you and what your needs may be as a traveler. Here's what I assume:

- You're an experienced traveler who doesn't have much time to really get to know Arizona and wants expert advice when you finally do get a chance to further explore the state.
- You're not looking for a book that provides all the information available about Arizona or that lists every hotel, restaurant, or attraction available. Instead, you're looking for a book that focuses on the places that give you the best or most unique experiences in this beautiful state.

How This Book Is Organized

The information in this book is methodically arranged in an easy-to-use, logical fashion (I'm glad you can't see the stacks of paper piled on my home office floor). The book is divvied up into five parts, each one covering a major aspect of your trip. Those parts are then further subdivided into chapters that cover more specific topics, so you can zoom in on the one that interests you. The sections break down as follows.

Part I: Introducing Arizona

In this part, I introduce you to Arizona, past and present, as well as to some of the most outstanding experiences in the state. I also fill you in on what you need to consider when planning a trip to Arizona — everything from the dates of major festivals to the weather at different times of the year. I even offer you several possible itineraries based on your interests and traveling companions (well, if they're kids).

Part II: Planning Your Trip to Arizona

This nitty-gritty section walks you through those potentially difficult trip-planning stages. I cover the top ways to make travel arrangements, whether you decide to go it on your own, book an escorted tour, or do something in-between; the types of transportation you find in Arizona; your accommodation options; and the best way to deal with money matters and (heaven forbid) illness while you're on the road. I also devote a chapter to special interests, from seniors to families and astronomy geeks (sometimes those special interests overlap). This part also helps you wrap up those last-minute details — everything from buying travel insurance to finding the best cellphone.

Part III: Exploring the Big Cities

Here you find out all about Greater Phoenix and Tucson, including the lowdown on hotels, restaurants, sights, tours, activities, shops, and nightlife in Arizona's two major cities. I don't overload you with choices, though: I cut to the chase with the best options. I also explain why I think they're prime — that way, you can decide whether you agree (in other words, I can't make you like Garth Brooks, but I can tell you I think a bar is great because it plays his music all the time). Two additional chapters in this section give you the details on fun side trips you can take from each of the cities.

Part IV: Exploring the Regions

This part does for Arizona's top touring regions what Part III does for the cities, only on a larger scale. I pare down info even more than in the city chapters. For example, because the Grand Canyon has no nightlife to speak of, I don't include a section on nightlife. For details on the regions I chose and the reasons I chose them, see Chapter 3 (see, I told you I wasn't going to repeat myself).

Part V: The Part of Tens

No, this part isn't something out of Star Trek, although "Seven of Nine" may come to mind (if you're a bit of a Trekkie as — I confess — I am). Perhaps David Letterman's Top Ten list is somewhat closer to the mark. This fun section highlights characteristics of — some may say peculiarities of — Arizona, including the top crafts to buy, the prime desert animals for you to look (and look out) for, and ten quintessential Arizona foodstuffs.

You also find one other element near the back of this book. I include an appendix — your Quick Concierge — containing handy information about services in Arizona, such as phone numbers and Web sites for airlines, hotel chains, car rental agencies, local newspapers and magazines, and tourist information centers. You also find contact information for area hospitals, pharmacies, and police. Check out the appendix when searching for answers to little questions that may come up as you travel, or even before you leave.

Icons Used in This Book

You will notice the following icons sprinkled throughout the text. Think of them as signposts: I use them to highlight special tips, draw your attention to must-see destinations, and give you a heads-up on a variety of topics.

This icon alerts you to money-saving tips (like, "Never buy retail" — oops, that's another book) and/or great deals.

Not only does this book advise you on the top destinations, restaurants, and activities in the state, but Chapter 1 winnows down my picks even further, selecting the best in several categories. As you go through the various chapters, these icons remind you of what I've chosen as the crème de la crème.

Watch for this warning about rip-offs, tourist traps, and other details.

Although this entire book is devoted to giving you useful advice, this symbol lets you know when you should really pay attention if you want to make the most of your time and energy.

This icon is your green light for attractions, hotels, restaurants, and activities that are particularly family-friendly.

A gentle nudge in the ribs comes from this icon that points out sights, attractions, and things you're unlikely to see outside of the Southwest. These places tend to be historic, but some new attractions manage to achieve that ineffable Southwest-specific quality.

Where to Go from Here

As you read through this book and start to formulate your Arizona vacation, remember this: Planning really is half the fun. Don't think of choosing your destinations and solidifying the details as a chore. Make the homebound part of the process a voyage of discovery, and you'll end up with an entire vacation experience that is much more rewarding and enriching — really. Let your vacation begin right now.

Part I

Introducing Arizona

"Yeah, this is the Painted Desert. Try to stay on the drop cloths, okay?"

In this part . . .

So you think you want to go to Arizona — but what's the state really like, anyway? When's the best time to go? What are the top travel routes? What resources are available to you if you're single, traveling with a family, gay, or mobility impaired? So many questions — and so many answers. Think of this part as Arizona 101, a quick introduction to the state's geography, travel economics, and more.

Chapter 1

Discovering the Best of Arizona

In This Chapter

- Searching out the top historical sites and attractions
- Finding the best places to explore Native American culture
- Participating in Arizona's myriad activities
- Seeing glorious Western film–style landscapes
- Shopping for the top arts and crafts
- Discovering the best historic lodgings
- Dining at Arizona's top Southwest restaurants

Picture a land of silent, manly men and spirited, sun-worn women leaving clouds of dust in the wake of their pickups as they high-tail it through rugged canyon lands and parched deserts. Of noble braves in touch with Earth's ancient wisdom. Of lonely Mexican cantinas and rundown roadside cafes . . .

Then give it a name: Arizona.

Okay. You've obviously watched too many Westerns and pickup-truck commercials.

Me, too. Before I moved to Tucson, more than a dozen years ago, I had many of the same preconceptions about the state.

As it happens, the men in Arizona are far more likely to golf, hike, or mountain bike than to rope cattle, and the sassiest females are generally from New York City, like me. Women here know better than to go outdoors without slathering on sunscreen, and if their skin gets parched, they head for the nearest spa. More contrasts to your possible preconceived notions: Arizona's Sonoran Desert is lush with vegetation, much of the income of the southern Native American nations comes from casinos, and a long line often forms for the best Mexican restaurants, which tend to be in lively downtown barrios.

Arizona

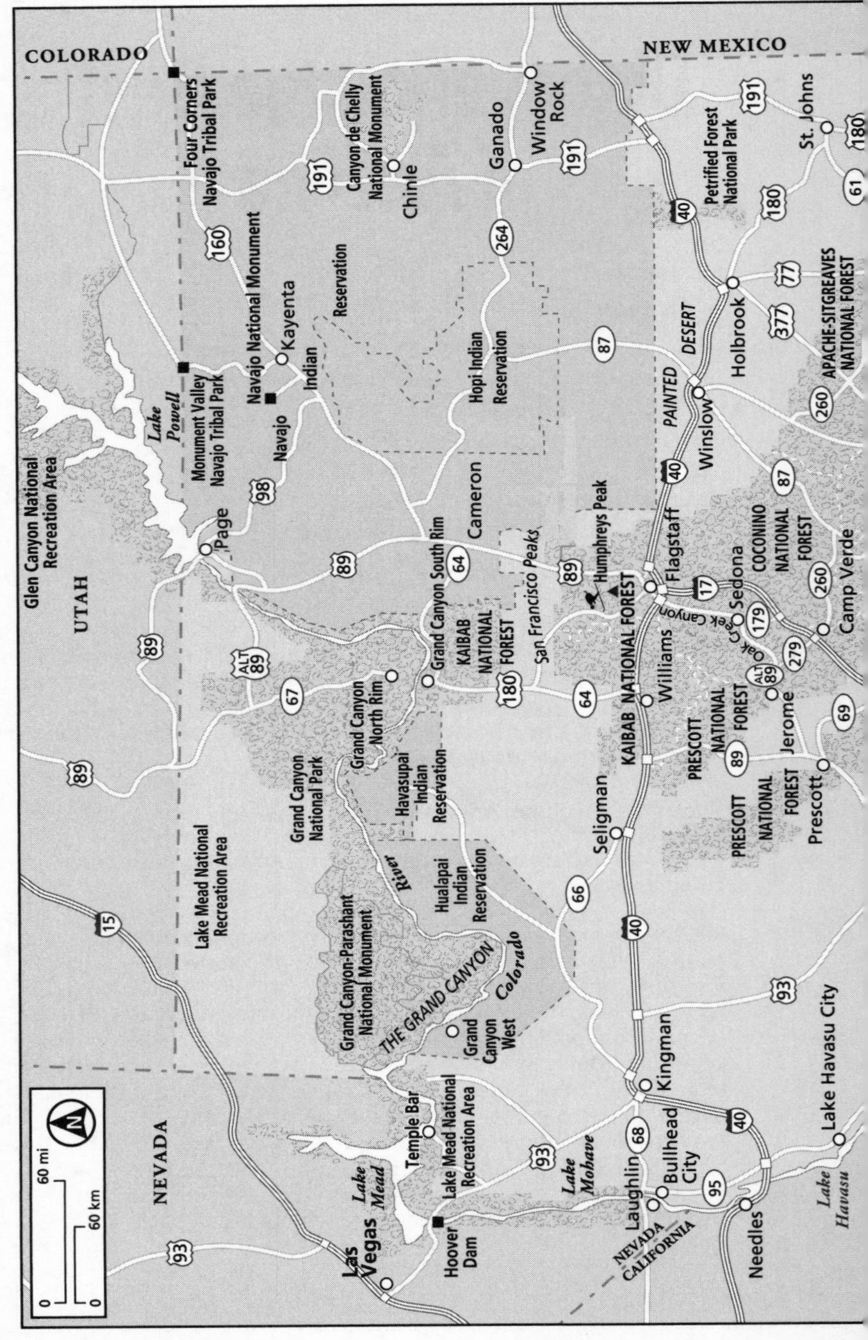

COLORADO
NEW MEXICO
UTAH
NEVADA
CALIFORNIA
NEVADA
Four Corners Navajo Tribal Park
Canyon de Chelly National Monument
Window Rock
Ganado
Chinle
St. Johns
Petrified Forest National Park
Navajo National Monument
Kayenta
Navajo Indian Reservation
Hopi Indian Reservation
Holbrook
APACHE-SITGREAVES NATIONAL FOREST
PAINTED DESERT
Winslow
Monument Valley Navajo Tribal Park
Lake Powell
Glen Canyon National Recreation Area
Page
Cameron
Humphreys Peak
San Francisco Peaks
Flagstaff
COCONINO NATIONAL FOREST
Sedona
Oak Creek Canyon
Camp Verde
Grand Canyon South Rim
KAIBAB NATIONAL FOREST
Grand Canyon North Rim
Grand Canyon National Park
Williams
Jerome
PRESCOTT NATIONAL FOREST
Prescott
Havasupai Indian Reservation
Seligman
Lake Mead National Recreation Area
Hualapai Indian Reservation
Grand Canyon-Parashant National Monument
THE GRAND CANYON
Colorado River
Grand Canyon West
Kingman
Lake Havasu City
Temple Bar
Lake Mead
Lake Mohave
Laughlin
Bullhead City
Needles
Lake Havasu
Hoover Dam
Las Vegas
60 mi
60 km

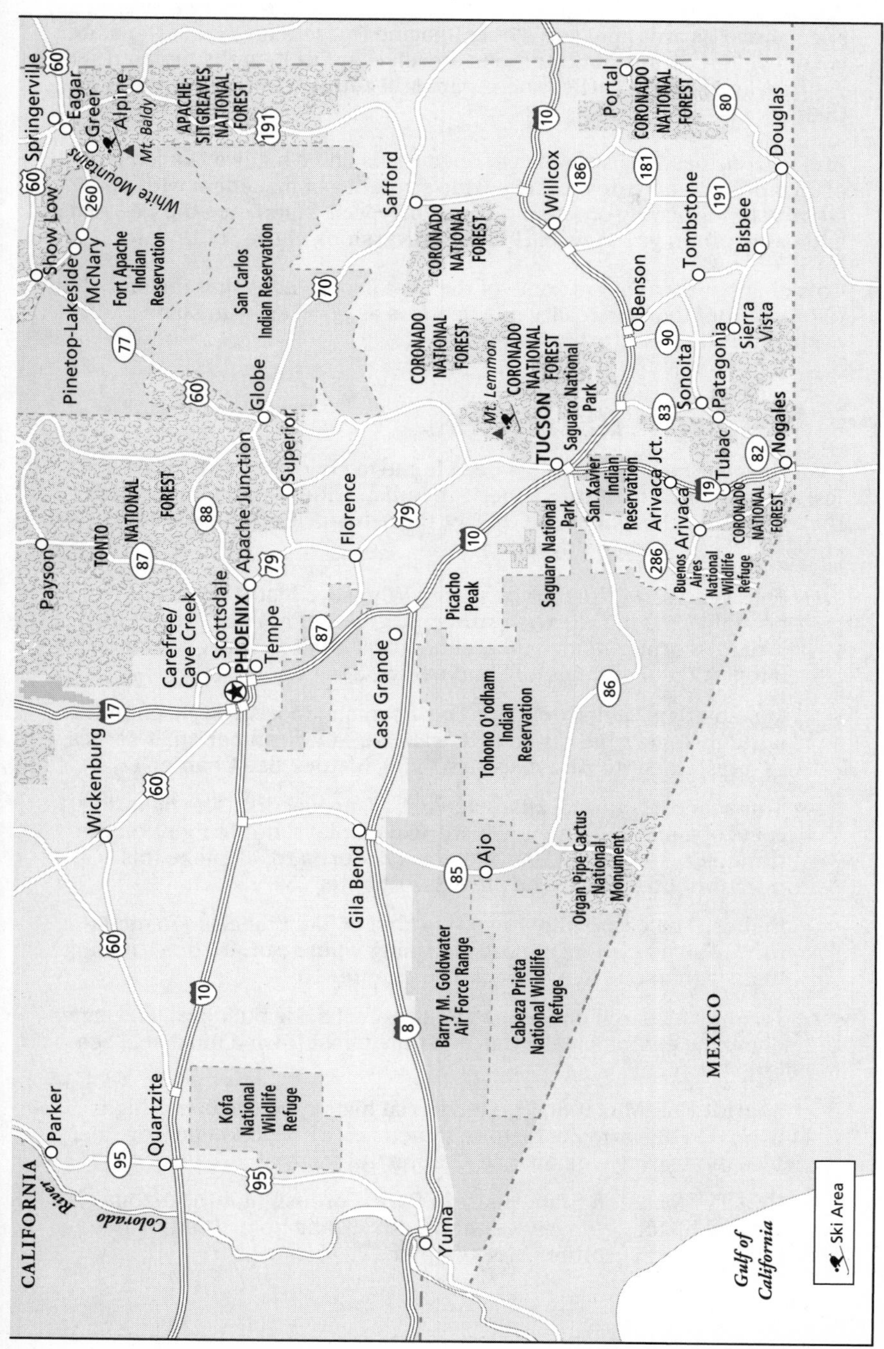
CALIFORNIA
Colorado River
Parker
Quartzite
Kofa National Wildlife Refuge
Yuma
Gila Bend
Wickenburg
Barry M. Goldwater Air Force Range
Cabeza Prieta National Wildlife Refuge
Ajo
Organ Pipe Cactus National Monument
MEXICO
Gulf of California
Ski Area
Casa Grande
Tohono O'odham Indian Reservation
PHOENIX
Carefree/ Cave Creek
Scottsdale
Tempe
Apache Junction
Payson
TONTO NATIONAL FOREST
Superior
Globe
Florence
Picacho Peak
Saguaro National Park
TUCSON
Mt. Lemmon
San Xavier Indian Reservation
Arivaca Jct.
Arivaca
Buenos Aires National Wildlife Refuge
Tubac
Nogales
Patagonia
Sonoita
Sierra Vista
Bisbee
Tombstone
Benson
Douglas
Willcox
Portal
CORONADO NATIONAL FOREST
Safford
San Carlos Indian Reservation
Fort Apache Indian Reservation
Pinetop-Lakeside
Show Low
McNary
White Mountains
Greer
Eagar
Springerville
Alpine
Mt. Baldy
APACHE-SITGREAVES NATIONAL FOREST

But back to those preconceived notions. The Arizona scenery is indeed as spectacular as anything you'd ever imagine (more than 80% of the state is undeveloped), ancient traditions are alive and well on the Indian reservations, and several cattle ranches are still active — some even rent out their rooms.

And Arizona has long stretches of open roads and a highway speed limit of 75 mph. Zooming down those wide stretches of macadam with your favorite tunes blaring on the radio, you may well experience the freedom and exhilaration you view in Hollywood versions of the Southwest.

This chapter, then, offers some of the best experiences that the state has to offer, proof that the reality of Arizona is as good as — in some places even better than — the fantasy.

Best Historic Attractions

Over the centuries, Arizona has been home to conquistadors, missionaries, miners, and a variety of American Indian tribes — all of whom left their marks on the landscape. Today, these historic sites are among the state's biggest tourism draws.

- Taliesen West (North Scottsdale): Who says historic sites have to be really old? In the urban sprawl of greater Phoenix, Frank Lloyd Wright's former home and architectural studio stands out for its integration of architecture and nature. See Chapter 11.
- Mission San Xavier del Bac: This Spanish Moorish–style church is not only lovely, but, as an active Native American parish, it serves as a testament to Arizona's rich living history. See Chapter 13.
- Tumacácori National Historic Park (Tumacácori): The haunting ruins of a mission, the fine historical displays, not to mention the tranquility of the gardens and grassy courtyard, all make this a prime spot to soak in the past. See Chapter 15.
- Bisbee: The entire hilly town — a kind of San Francisco in miniature — gives visitors a more charming glimpse of Arizona's mining history than one may expect. See Chapter 15.
- Jerome: Its perch on Cleopatra Hill, ramshackle buildings, and array of mining exhibits make this one-time ghost town a must-see. See Chapter 16.
- Sharlot Hall Museum: The territorial history of Arizona is highlighted in this array of historic structures, a collection put together by a pioneering woman. See Chapter 16.
- Riordan Mansion State Historic Park: For insight into Arizona's logging history, you can't beat this sprawling home built by two lumber-baron brothers. See Chapter 17.

- Grand Canyon Village Historical District: Tear your eyes away from nature for an hour or so to explore what man — and woman (architect Mary Colter, to be specific) — wrought at the edge of the abyss. See Chapter 17.
- Hubbell Trading Post National Historic Site: The former home of trader Lorenzo Hubbell is among the many lures of this still-active trading post. See Chapter 18.
- Holbrook: Dinosaurs, wigwams, neon signs . . . you won't find a better place in Arizona to view classic Route 66 kitsch. See Chapter 18.

Best Places to Explore Native American Culture

From 200 A.D. to 1300 A.D., Native American tribes had this country pretty much to themselves, sharing it only with the animals that freely roamed the land. The evidence of their civilizations is found throughout the state.

- The Heard Museum (Downtown Phoenix): Combining historic displays with exhibits of contemporary Native American works, this world-class museum is a must for anyone interested in Southwest Indian culture. See Chapter 11.
- Casa Grande Ruins National Monument: If not Arizona's largest Native American ruins, these are among the most elusive. What is that tall building anyway — and what's with all those fire pits? See Chapter 12.
- Amerind Foundation Museum (Dragoon): If you like your museums compact and in scenic settings, don't pass up this small collection of Native American artifacts. See Chapter 15.
- Montezuma Castle National Monument: An easy detour off Highway 17 is rewarded by the sight of a couple of well-preserved ancient apartment houses and, nearby, a dazzlingly blue, spring-fed pool. See Chapter 16.
- Museum of Northern Arizona: Find out about the native peoples of the Colorado Plateau in this historic building, which hosts a fine series of Native American markets in summer. See Chapter 17.
- Walnut Canyon National Monument: Here you have an opportunity to clamber among intact Sinagua ruins, nestled in a beautiful piney canyon. See Chapter 17.
- Navajo National Monument: A gorgeous, serene setting and dramatic cliff dwellings — Native American sites don't get much better than this. See Chapter 18.

- Hopi Mesas: Talk about living history. The Hopi people live on the three mesas that their ancestors settled centuries ago, and they still observe many of the same customs as their forebears. See Chapter 18.
- Canyon de Chelly National Monument: The Navajos have stewardship over — and dwell in — these spectacular canyons, which also host the former homes of ancestral Puebloans. See Chapter 18.

Best Activities

The state's warm, sunny climate is an outdoors-lover's dream. Even the winter cold in the northern regions of the state isn't all that cold — but it's cold enough to make Flagstaff a winter sports mecca.

- Golfing in Greater Phoenix: If you're a duffer, you won't find a better collection of challenging desert courses than in the Valley of the Sun. See Chapter 11.
- Driving the Apache Trail: Motoring through the long and winding — and oh-so-scenic — road that takes you through the Superstition Mountains is an adventure in itself. See Chapter 12.
- Horseback riding in Tucson: No other city affords so many opportunities to canter among lush stands of saguaro cacti. See Chapter 13.
- Stargazing at Kitt Peak National Observatory: Star light, star bright — Kitt Peak's dinner/observing program is heavenly. See Chapter 14.
- Observing hummingbirds in southern Arizona: Even those who find bird-watching tedious are enchanted by the tiny critters flitting around this region's nature preserves. See Chapter 15.
- Mountain biking in Sedona: Sedona's many bike-rental shops attest to the allure of fat-tiring among the red rocks. See Chapter 16.
- Riding the Verde Canyon Railroad: Eagles and wildflowers and canyons, oh my! You never know what kind of show Mother Nature will put on for you. See Chapter 16.
- Rafting the Colorado River in and around the Grand Canyon: The surrounding canyon walls are spectacular, and you don't have to white-knuckle it in whitewater — gentle float trips are also an option. See Chapter 17.
- Descending into one of the slot canyons near Page: Whether it's the popular Antelope Canyon or the more remote Canyon X, this region's skinny, dune-formed caves are a photographer's dream. See Chapter 18.

- Hiking Canyon de Chelly's White Horse Ruin Trail: The only trek into the canyon you can take without a Navajo guide rewards your (modest) efforts with an ancient cliff dwelling at the trail's end. See Chapter 18.

Best Places to See Western Film–Style Landscapes

The Westerns of film directors like John Ford are synonymous with the tumbleweed desert landscapes found in Arizona. See them for yourself at the following locations.

- Boyce Thompson Arboretum: The array of desert specimens in this off-the-beaten-path preserve is eye-popping, as are the sandstone boulders that serve as the plants' backdrop. See Chapter 12.
- Arizona Sonora-Desert Museum: You see impressive spreads of desert in many parts of southern Arizona, but you're never guaranteed a peek at the fauna that dwell in them — except in this wonderful zoo. See Chapter 13.
- Saguaro National Park: Gigantic saguaro cacti grow almost exclusively in Arizona and northern Mexico, and you find no better place to view them than in this prickly preserve. See Chapter 13.
- Organ Pipe Cactus National Monument: The skinny-armed cousin of the saguaro is the star of this desert park near the U.S./Mexico border and the Tohono O'odham Indian reservation. See Chapter 14.
- Chiricahua National Monument (Dos Cabezas Route): You'll be bowled over by the weirdly balanced boulders of the "Land of the Standing-Up Rocks," the rugged terrain where Cochise and his band of Apaches hid out from the U.S. cavalry. See Chapter 15.
- Red rocks of Sedona: The startlingly vermillion rocks and mesas around Sedona have inspired artists and filmakers from the 1930s on. See Chapter 16.
- The Grand Canyon: Celluloid can't fully capture this sight's gaping grandeur — probably for the best, because no actor could compete with this scene stealer. See Chapter 17.
- Monument Valley: The favorite "set" of filmmaker John Ford, these strangely shaped spires and mesas have come to symbolize the West for generations of cineastes. See Chapter 18.
- The Painted Desert: Petrified Forest National Park provides a good showcase for one of the West's softer landscapes, with its delicate shades of pink, dun, and sienna. See Chapter 18.

- Lake Powell: Adding water to Glen Canyon only enhanced its appeal, although the submerged rock formations seem a bit surreal. See Chapter 18.
- Canyon de Chelly: These sheer cliffs painted with "desert varnish"— a blue-black veneer formed by seeping water — are among the most awe-inspiring sights in the Southwest. See Chapter 18.

Best Places to Shop for Arts and Crafts

Artisans and craftspeople flock to Arizona as much for the quality of light and natural beauty as for the relatively inexpensive rents. Their wares, along with the distinctive crafts made by Native American tribes, make Arizona a rich source of original American artwork.

- Downtown Scottsdale: Fans of Western art, of both the cowboy and American Indian variety, won't find much better pickin's than on thoroughfares like 5th Avenue and Main Street. See Chapter 11.
- The Heard Museum gift shop (downtown Phoenix): Here you find an excellent selection of Native American crafts at reasonable prices (the artists aren't charged a gallery fee). See Chapter 11.
- The Lost Barrio: Southwest and ethnic furnishings and accessories are the focus of this collection of shops in an old warehouse district in Tucson. See Chapter 13.
- Old Town Artisans: The work of local, regional, and Latin American artists is showcased at these shops in a historic building occupying an entire city block in downtown Tucson. See Chapter 13.
- Kitt Peak National Observatory gift shop: Because the observatory is on land owned by the Tohono O'odham Indians, its visitor center carries many of the fine baskets made by tribal members. See Chapter 14.
- Tubac: Arizona's oldest European settlement is now a haven for local artists and crafters — as well as importers of wares from Mexico. See Chapter 15.
- Nogales: Bargaining is part of the adventure of shopping for crafts in this Mexican border town. See Chapter 15.
- Tlaquepaque Crafts Village: Practically all of Sedona is an arts and crafts zone, but you find the greatest concentration of high-quality boutiques in this charming Mexican-village replica. See Chapter 16.
- Jerome: The hippies who revived this one-time ghost town brought along their craftsy ways. Some of the shops lining Jerome's two main streets have gone upscale, but others retain an endearing quirkiness. See Chapter 16.

- Cameron Trading Post: You may be overwhelmed by the huge array of crafts at this Navajo-owned gift shop/grocery near the east entrance of the Grand Canyon's South Rim. See Chapter 17.
- Hubbell Trading Post: Come here for one of the best selections of antique Navajo rugs in the state; also watch new rugs being woven. See Chapter 18.
- Second Mesa: A smattering of crafts shops on Second Mesa, including the excellent Tsakurshovi, make this the prime place on the Hopi reservation to find katsina dolls and silver inlay jewelry. See Chapter 18.

Best Historic Lodgings

Many of the state's historic properties have survived and been reborn as vacation lodgings. The following are my picks for the best in the state.

- Arizona Biltmore Resort & Spa (Phoenix/Camelback Corner): This Frank Lloyd Wright–inspired resort, which celebrated its 75th birthday in 2004, continues to add amenities without subtracting character. See Chapter 11.
- Royal Palms Resort and Spa (Phoenix): Built as a winter getaway for a wealthy couple, this intimate property still fulfills that function, although now more upscale pairs can come to play. See Chapter 11.
- Camelback Inn, a JW Marriott Resort & Spa (Scottsdale): Scottsdale's first luxury resort has retained its old-fashioned appeal while keeping up with the times (most recently by rebuilding its excellent spa). See Chapter 11.
- Arizona Inn: Tucson was a desert outpost when the Arizona Inn opened in 1930. Although the city is no longer a primitive outpost, this charming property still provides the same civility it afforded weary travelers in the past. See Chapter 13.
- Hacienda del Sol Guest Ranch Resort: A girls school turned dude ranch to the stars in the 1940s, this is now a scenic mini-resort with artfully rustic rooms that offer all the creature comforts. See Chapter 13.
- Westward Look Resort: Among the legacies of this property's guest ranch past are spacious quarters designed for long-term stays, along with a generous spread of desert with great city views. See Chapter 13.
- The Royal Elizabeth B&B: Lovers of Victoriana will adore these downtown Tucson digs, with immaculately maintained fittings and gorgeous antique furnishings. See Chapter 13.

- Tubac Golf Resort: Founded in 1959 by a group of investors that included crooner Bing Crosby, this gracious property sits on Arizona's first Spanish land grant. Conferences are held in an 1880s hacienda. See Chapter 15.
- Copper Queen (Bisbee): A holdover from Arizona's days of mineral wealth, this hotel still offers lots of Old West charm. See Chapter 15.
- Hassayampa Inn: Prescott's premier historic hotel helped usher in Arizona's auto age with its modern covered driveway. Today's visitors like the fact that it's within easy walking distance of the town's Courthouse Square. See Chapter 16.
- Kay El Bar Ranch: This dude ranch remains faithful to its historic Western roots but offers a touch of Hollywood glamour, as well: Val Kilmer's family owned the ranch for a spell, and little Val used to hang out with the horses. See Chapter 16.
- Bright Angel Lodge & Cabins: It isn't the grandest of the Grand Canyon lodgings, but its genesis in 1896 as a hotel incorporating a log cabin — not to mention its proximity to the South Rim — make it the most appealing. See Chapter 17.
- Grand Canyon Lodge: It would be hard to find a better complement to the woodsy beauty of the North Rim than this impressive limestone-and-log structure flanked by rustic cabins. See Chapter 17.
- La Posada: Resuscitated in the 1990s, the hotel that architect Mary Colter created in Winslow in 1930 just keeps getting better, as the gardens mature and more original fittings are restored. See Chapter 18.
- Gouldings Lodge: Ever since Harry Goulding brought director John Ford out to his place, it has been a favorite of filmmakers, who like its proximity to Monument Valley as well as the modern conveniences subtly incorporated over the years. See Chapter 18.
- Thunderbird Lodge: This hotel, the only one inside Canyon de Chelly National Monument, features a dining room that used to be a trading post and cottonwoods planted in the 1930s by the Civilian Conservation Corps. See Chapter 18.

Best Places to Savor Southwest Flavors

New Southwestern cuisine is the nouveau cousin of the standard Mexican/cowboy fare traditionally found in these parts. But you won't have trouble finding standout versions of the latter in restaurants throughout the state. Here are my recommended places to dine.

- Roaring Fork (Scottsdale): Innovative takes on steak and other Western menu staples make chef Robert McGrath's restaurant a favorite with Valley foodies and meat-and-potato types alike. See Chapter 11.
- Los Sombreros (Scottsdale): This lively eatery departs from typical northern Mexico fare to range all over our southern neighbor's map. See Chapter 11.
- Kai (near Phoenix): Here, dazzling New Southwest recipes incorporate traditional ingredients grown on the reservation of the Pima and Maricopa Indians. See Chapter 11.
- Café Poca Cosa: For far-flung regional dishes not found in most of Arizona's Mexican restaurants, you can't beat this colorful downtown Tucson cafe. See Chapter 13.
- Café Terra Cotta: The creative recipes of Donna Nordin, one of the originators of New Southwest cuisine, are showcased in the art-filled dining rooms of this Tucson foothills restaurant. See Chapter 13.
- J Bar/Janos: The food at upscale Janos has a French accent, while that at more casual J Bar speaks with Mexican tones. These adjacent restaurants share the talents of Southwest cooking guru Janos Wilder. See Chapter 13.
- La Roca (Nogales, Mexico): Savory seafood and grilled meat dishes are among the offerings at this cavernous, romantic taverna. See Chapter 15.
- The Cowboy Club's Silver Saddle Room: The rattlesnake brochettes at this haute-rustic eatery in Uptown Sedona may be gimmicky, but the ribs, steak, seafood — and even buffalo cuts — are seriously good. See Chapter 16.
- El Tovar Restaurant: The Southwest-inspired fare in the fine dining room of the Grand Canyon's fanciest hotel competes with the view — which is saying a lot, because this is on the canyon rim. See Chapter 17.
- Cameron Trading Post dining room: Under the pressed tin roof of this historic dining room, you find the best Navajo taco in Arizona — huge and made with fresh hot fry bread. See Chapter 17.
- The Turquoise Room: Drawing on the menu of the Santa Fe railroad's luxury dining car and on Arizona regional specialties, the restaurant at La Posada in Winslow features everything from Hopi piki bread to chile-cherry duckling. See Chapter 18.
- Romo's: The New Mexican–style food at this low-key Holbrook cafe will bring happiness if you're a fan of sopaipillas (fried bread), red and green chile sauce, and other imports from the Land of Enchantment. See Chapter 18.

Chapter 2

Digging Deeper into Arizona

In This Chapter

- Uncovering Arizona's past
- Discovering Southwest architectural style
- Dining in the desert
- Talking the talk
- Previewing the state in books and films

Sure, Arizona has terrific weather and dozens of ways to play in it, but it also has a rich history, not to mention distinctive architecture and cuisine. You may have already developed a taste for Arizona's heritage, style, and way of life through the many books written and films made in which Arizona plays a prominent role. For more insight into what you'll be looking at, listening to, and ingesting when you visit, read on.

History 101: The Main Events

Once upon a time, before Sun City and other retirement communities went forth and multiplied, Arizona was a magnet for the young and the restless: conquistadors, missionaries, miners, and a variety of Native American tribes. The following sections give you, briefly, some of their stories.

Early arrivals

More than 15,000 years ago, the southern sector of the region now known as Arizona was the territory of mammoth hunters, but, hairy elephants aside, the action didn't pick up until about 200 A.D., when the Ancestral Puebloans (also called the Anasazi) arrived. After centuries of making baskets in modest pit houses, they started to build pueblos — see the "Building Blocks: Local Architecture" section later in this chapter — and carve homes out of cliffs at places like Canyon de Chelly and Navajo National Monument; no one is quite sure why they built these early "condos" so high. The Sinagua settled in the fertile plateau near Flagstaff (Walnut Canyon and Wupatki) and the Verde River valley (Tuzigoot and Montezuma Castle), while the Hohokam farmed the Gila and Salt river valleys between Phoenix and Casa Grande, leaving behind remnants of a huge irrigation system, as well as the Casa Grande ruin, and lots of petroglyphs (rock carvings). By 1300 A.D., most of these tribes had, literally, gone on to greener pastures: A major drought in the mid-1200s likely caused their mass migration out of the area.

The Spanish are coming (and the Native Americans are going)

Enter the Spanish conquistadors, who rode through Arizona in the early 16th century looking for gold but finding mostly trouble. Around 1600, in the Four Corners region, they clashed with the Navajo, themselves relative newcomers to the neighborhood. The conquistadors' religious brethren came out alright: Links in the chain of missions that the Jesuits established in the Sonoran Desert at the end of the 17th century included Tumacácori and San Xavier del Bac in southern Arizona. Still, not everyone was thrilled by the padres' presence. In 1751, in response to a Pima Indian uprising, the presidio (military post) of Tubac — Arizona's first permanent European settlement — was built to protect Tumacácori. After the presidio was moved north to Tucson in 1775, Tubac never recovered.

Mexico threw off the reign of Spain in 1821 but didn't hold on to most of Arizona for long, as a consequence of losing the Mexican-American War (1848). Five years later, General Santa Anna — yes, that Santa Anna of Alamo fame — sold off the state's remaining bits, including Tucson, in the Gadsden Purchase. Thus, America inherited the Indian wars. In 1864, the U.S. Army, under Colonel Kit Carson, defeated the Navajos in northeast Arizona. The Chiricahua Apaches, led by Cochise and Geronimo, held out against the Anglos in the southeast a little longer, but Cochise died in 1874, and Geronimo surrendered in 1886.

Mining the store

One of the reasons the U.S. Army tangled with the Apaches was to protect the region's mining interests. Many of the gold-rushing '49ers from the East never made it to California, instead lingering in the adjacent territory to try their luck. Silver and, eventually, copper turned out to be Arizona's mother lodes, and Tombstone and Bisbee became the largest — and wildest — towns in the state.

Things were a bit calmer to the north, where farmers in newly founded Phoenix irrigated fields using canals that had been dug by the Hohokam, and legislators argued over which town would be the capital of Arizona Territory (Prescott won). A major influx of cattle and their minders was followed in the 1880s by the arrival of the railroad, which made shipping both cows and copper far more efficient.

Dams, A/C, and microchips

Impressed by the 1911 debut of the Theodore Roosevelt Dam, which showed that it was possible to get water into the desert, the U.S. government made Arizona a state the following year. Over the next decades, Arizona continued to divert water for electrical and recreational purposes; Glen Canyon Dam and its offshoot, Lake Powell, are prime examples. Cotton became more popular, industrially speaking, than beef, and cattle ranches gave way to dude ranches and, eventually, resorts.

Desert combat training centers established during World War II inspired many servicemen to return to sunny Arizona after the conflict ended; the advent of air-conditioning in the 1950s clinched the deal. Motorola, Honeywell, McDonnell Douglas (now Boeing), and Hughes (now Raytheon) liked the (business) climate, too, and in the 1970s and 1980s, most of the copper mines closed. With computer chips replacing cow chips and good weather replacing subterranean treasure as incentives to come to Arizona, the transition from Old West territory to Sunbelt state was accomplished by the end of the 20th century.

Timeline

This section contains a brief timeline of the most momentous dates in Arizona history.

Ca. 9000 B.C.	Arizona's climate gets drier; most of the large animals die off or migrate.
500–1100 A.D.	Pueblos replace pithouses, and towns that likely served as trade centers begin to crop up.
Ca. 1300 A.D.	The Apaches and the Navajos migrate from Canada, becoming Arizona's first snow birds.
1539–1540	Spanish explorers, including Fray Marcos de Niza and Francisco Vasquez de Coronado, visit Arizona and claim it for Spain.
1691–1711	Father Eusebio Kino establishes 22 missions in northern Mexico and southern Arizona, including Tumacácori and San Xavier del Bac.
1863	Once part of New Mexico Territory, Arizona Territory is established as a separate entity.
1881	The Earps win the gunfight at Tombstone's OK Corral.
1901	Rail link to the Grand Canyon established.
1912	Arizona admitted to the union on Valentine's Day, the last of the 48 mainland states to join.

1960	Del E. Webb Inc.'s Sun City, one of the nation's first retirement communities, opens in the Valley of the Sun.
1988–1997	Governor Evan Mecham, charged with financial improprieties, is removed from office; financier Charles Keating is convicted of fraud in the Lincoln Savings & Loan scandal; Governor J. Fife Symington 3d, convicted on fraud charges, resigns.
1989	Rail link to the Grand Canyon reestablished.
1992	Faced with a Super Bowl and tourist boycott, Arizona becomes second-to-last state to establish a holiday honoring Martin Luther King, Jr.
1997	Women win the state's top five political positions, including governor (Jane Hull) and attorney general (Janel Napolitano).
2002	The final nail in the coffin of the cowboy era? Arizonans pass a proposition that requires the state to enter into gaming contracts with 17 of its 21 American Indian tribes.

Building Blocks: Local Architecture

The prototypes for many of the state's Southwestern-style structures lie north, at such archaeological sites as Wupatki, Navajo National Monument, Canyon de Chelly, and at the Hopi mesas, where you find traditional Native American pueblos, flat-roofed, multi-story adobe homes with ceilings made of heavy timbers (vigas) that protrude from the buildings' sides. But it took neighboring New Mexico, also home to many pueblos, to capitalize on American Indian architecture in what has come to be known as Santa Fe style, a style eventually imported to Arizona.

In addition to the original Native American pueblos (and the impressive hunting lodge–style structures that cropped during the turn of the-20th century; the Grand Canyon hotels are prime examples), you're most likely to come across the building types discussed in the following sections (although rarely in pure form; eclecticism is probably the most consistent element of Arizona's architecture).

The chronological list in the following sections omits the modernist style of Frank Lloyd Wright. Even though the architect built his influential Taliesen West in Scottsdale (see Chapter 11), Wright's organic form aesthetic had its roots not in the Southwest but in the Midwest.

Spanish colonial

The Spanish adapted many elements of the pueblos into their homes — as well as earlier Moorish influences — when they arrived in the new world, but retained their old-world architectural ways in the mission churches they built. The ultra-baroque mujedar style, with its domed roofs, inverted pyramids, and ornate plastered masonry, is exemplified at Mission San Xavier del Bac near Tucson (see Chapter 13), built between 1783 and 1797.

Sonoran

These modest, simple structures, characterized by thick adobe walls shared with the dwelling next door, small windows, flat roofs with drainpipes called canales, and ceilings that cross-hatch saguaro ribs with heavier timbers, were designed to offer shade to pedestrians strolling by. The Sonoran style, which arose in the 1850s, was particularly prevalent in Tucson — for example, the Edward Nye Fish House, part of the Tucson Museum of Art and Historic Block (see Chapter 13).

Territorial

Blending such traditional Sonoran features as clean lines and shared adobe walls with popular Greek Revival elements like wood trim, pediments, shutters, and pitched roofs covered in corrugated tin, this architectural style developed and flourished during Arizona's Territorial period (1863–1912), especially after the advent of the railroad. The storefronts of Tombstone, popularized in Old West film sets, are one version of this style. Other examples of Territorial architecture can be found in the towns of Tubac and Florence, and particularly in Prescott, Arizona's territorial capital.

Pueblo Revival or Santa Fe

This blend of Pueblo, Spanish, and Territorial styles that arose in New Mexico in the early 20th century is more evident today in Arizona's expensive homes (and in many of Sedona's celebrated bed-and-breakfasts) than in its public buildings. Characteristic features include rounded corners, protruding vigas (ceiling beams), flat roofs, thick walls suggestive of adobe, and exteriors of earth-colored stucco. Architect Mary Colter's Hopi House and the Watchtower at the South Rim of the Grand Canyon may be considered Pueblo Revival style, except that these buildings stem from Colter's attempt to re-create American Indian pueblos rather than adapt them to Anglo tastes.

Spanish Colonial Revival

The arches, stucco walls, patios, and courtyards identified with this style gained popularity in the 1920s. Related styles — Monterey, Mediterranean, and California Mission Revival, all imports from California — add the red-clay tile roofs that are ubiquitous in Arizona housing complexes. The main building of the Heard Museum in Phoenix (see Chapter 11), built in 1929, is a prime example of Spanish Colonial Revival architecture.

It's not a style, it's a building material

You're likely to come across buildings in Arizona described as "adobe style." That's the equivalent of calling a Georgian home a "brick style" structure — completely meaningless. Like brick, adobe is a building material, specifically, a mix of earth, water, and straw left to dry in the sun. The original Native American adobe blocks were shaped by hand; the Spanish introduced wooden molds to standardize the forms. To keep them from melting in the rain or crumbling back to their natural state, adobe structures were covered with nonpermeable plaster, whitewash, or cement stucco.

Early Arizona settlers used adobe because it was easy to make and because the thick walls it produced kept homes cool in summer and warm in winter. For the eco-conscious, construction with adobe — along with its cousins, straw bale and rammed earth — has made a comeback. Many like the soft lines and slight irregularities that the building material imparts, while others (generally of the New Age persuasion) believe that adobe brings to its users a spiritual connection with the earth.

Taste of Arizona: Local Cuisine

Arizona borders the northern Mexican state of Sonora, where beef is big, chiles aren't typically incendiary, and cheese is used liberally. Most of the Mexican food in Arizona's dining rooms fits this style, although you can find those that stray from it.

New Southwestern cuisine — so termed by chefs in order to distinguish it from the plainer Mexican and cowboy fare folks associate with the old Southwest — is known for its use of local ingredients like blue corn and (deprickled) cactus pads, its creative mélange of cooking styles, and its visually stimulating presentations.

On the opposite end of the spectrum is the food of Native America, which tends to marry nicely with Mexican cuisine. This fare tends to be heavy (one of its staples is fry bread, which is exactly what it sounds like) but can also produce something as light and flaky as piki bread, made with blue cornmeal. Cornmeal is a product of the New World staple corn, which also figures heavily in the cuisine.

For additional details on what you're likely to find on your plate in this state, see Chapter 21.

Word to the Wise: The Local Lingo

Passing for an Arizonan doesn't involve toning down that New Jersey or Louisiana accent; practically everyone who lives in the state is from somewhere else, anyway. You just need to master a bit of the lingo and determine which phrases and buzzwords can quickly blow your cover as a Zonie wannabe.

Speak a little Español

You hear and see plenty of Spanish in Arizona. Remember that the conquistadors, not the pilgrims, were the first real estate developers in these parts. (See the "History 101: The Main Events" section earlier in this chapter.) Arizona comes by its Iberian pretensions honestly.

Take street names, for example. Everything's "Cañon del Oro" (canyon of gold) this or "Via Linda" (pretty road) that — even if no canyon of gold exists within a hundred miles of the spot or if the road couldn't be less beautiful. Homes that no self-respecting horse would approach are often called "ranchos." (In fact, if you're acquainted with Spanish, you probably find the Housing Development dialect pretty amusing.)

On the other hand, Mexican-menu Spanish is not at all silly; it's extremely helpful, especially when it comes to getting fed throughout the state. See Chapter 21 for details.

In general, if a word seems to be of Spanish origin, watch your j's (sometimes pronounced h if at the beginning of a word, as in javelina [hav-uh-lee-nuh]); g's (sometimes pronounced like h, as in Gila monster [hee-la]); and n's that have funny squiggly things called tildes on top of them (always pronounced nyuh, as in the aforementioned Cañon del Oro [ca-nyuh-on del or-o]).

Never ask, "Where are the trees?"

Everyone knows that the real trees are in northern Arizona, decorating the area near the Grand Canyon (Mother Nature must have thought that big ole hole needed a little softening around the edges) or on top of mountains. You will quickly deduce that most of southern Arizona's plants (read: cacti) are unapproachable, after the hundredth time you've had to remove them from your person and clothing with tweezers if you got too close.

Do chant, "But it's a dry heat"

Everyone in southern Arizona becomes a pseudo-Buddhist in the hotter months, when this phrase is uttered continuously as a mantra.

Never say, "I'm looking for a shaded parking spot"

Oh, there's plenty of parking space, but shaded parking spots are as rare as hen's teeth. It just goes to show that Arizonans have more space than sense.

Never be put out if you're called a "Zonie"

Congratulations. You're not being accused of being a member of a cult; rather, you're accepted — and only slightly insulted — as an Arizonan. "Zonie" is probably one of the fonder names that Californians call residents of their next-door-neighbor state, partly because Arizonans tend to descend on cooler California en masse every summer.

Don't slip on slickrock

Unless you're a klutz who slips on everything, slickrock isn't slick, although it is bare of plants. The strikingly beautiful, eroded, rust-orange-and-buff sandstone of northern Arizona's Colorado Plateau got its name because it's often covered with a slightly shiny desert varnish (which isn't actually varnish but, rather, a thin blue-black veneer formed by seeping water, wind, and a variety of microbes). Slickrock served as the original Etch-a-Sketch for Native American artists, who pecked or scratched their designs onto the dark surface to reveal the lighter rock below (creating what are now called petroglyphs).

Background Check: Recommended Movies and Books

Get in the proper mood for your trip by checking out the following Arizona-centric movies and books.

Films

Arizona and the cinematic myth of the West found their apotheosis in Monument Valley, where John Wayne and director John Ford worked together on Stagecoach (1938), She Wore a Yellow Ribbon (1949), and The Searchers (1956). Old Tucson Studios — built in 1939 for the filming of Arizona, starring William Holden — was no slouch in the Western movie legends department, either. Classic shoot-'em-ups that came out of the studios include Rio Lobo (1970), also starring John Wayne; Hombre (1966) with Paul Newman (1966); and The Gunfight at the O.K. Corral (1957), featuring Kirk Douglas. In a more humorous Western vein, Old Tucson Studios also produced McClintock (John Wayne, 1962) and Three Amigos! (Steve Martin, Chevy Chase, Martin Short, 1986). B westerns too numerous to list were shot around the rest of the state, especially in Sedona. For more detail, check out John A. Murray's Cinema Southwest: An Illustrated Guide to the Movies and Their Locations (Northland; 2000).

Me? I like Westerns mainly for the good-looking guys in tight jeans — the 1994 Tombstone with Kurt Russell and Val Kilmer stands out in that category — but my favorite Arizona movies tend to be of the chick-flick variety: Boys on the Side (1994), filmed in Tucson and Tumacácori; Tin Cup (1995), shot in Tucson and Tubac; Waiting to Exhale (1995), panning across lots of Phoenix posh spots; and Thelma and Louise (1991) (do I care that Dead Horse Point in Utah stood in for the Grand Canyon at the end? Not a bit). I'm also fond of the goofy Harvey Girls (1946) because it highlights an interesting aspect of Arizona history and stars Angela Lansbury and Judy Garland (plus, I always find myself humming "On the Atchison, Topeka and the Santa Fe" afterward). Finally, there's the Coen brothers' unclassifiable Raising Arizona (1987), with lots of good shots of a less-developed Scottsdale, and of a young and very funny Nicholas Cage.

Books

I'm not going to pretend to be even close to comprehensive here. The following is a very eclectic, somewhat quirky cross-sampling from my bookshelves, including volumes that I found useful in researching this guide and ones that I just enjoyed reading. In the latter category — but otherwise hard to typecast — is the cautionary The Edge: Death in Grand Canyon, by Michael P. Ghiglieri and Thomas M. Myers (Puma Press; 2001). The book provides lots of horrified amusement as well as a sense of superiority ("I would never do anything as dumb as that," you assure yourself constantly).

On (and off) the road

If you like learning-as-you drive (well, as another person drives) guides, I recommend Travel Arizona: The Back Roads (Arizona Highway Press; 1999), by James Cook, Sam Negri, and Marshall Trimble, an illustrated volume focusing on the state's scenic byways. In addition to a road-marker-by-road-marker rundown of the sights, Fran Kusik's Native Roads: The Complete Motoring Guide to the Navajo and Hopi Nation (Treasure Chest; 1999) gives practical advice about visiting the reservations. If rocks rock your boat, you'll enjoy the Roadside Geology of Arizona by Halka Chronic (Mountain Press; 1983). Wonder about stuff like how Misery Fort got its name? Arizona Place Names by Will C. Barnes (University of Arizona Press; 1988) is for you. When you're ready to leave your car behind for a while, you'll find Scott S. Warren's 100 Hikes in Arizona (The Mountaineers; 1994) very useful.

Essays

The always cranky, always articulate Charles Bowden lashes out against the decline of the natural West, among other things, in Blue Desert (University of Arizona Press; 1986). Better known for her fiction, Barbara Kingsolver writes eloquently about Arizona, natural and unnatural, in High Tide in Tucson: Essays from Now and Never (Perennial; 1996). Cadillac Desert: The American West and Its Disappearing Water, by Mark Reisner (Penguin; 1993), will have you worrying about every fountain, swimming pool, and grassy golf course you see in the state. Alex Shoumatoff's Legends of the American Desert: Sojourns in the Greater Southwest (HarperPerennial; 1997) personalizes the exotic appeal of the region.

Death on the Grand Canyon Express

When I travel, I love to read mysteries set in the locales that I visit (I take it on faith that I won't come across any actual bodies). For northeast Arizona, you can't do better than Tony Hillerman, whose fictional detectives, Jim Chee and Joe Leaphorn, are Navajo and whose books are largely set on the "rez." If you visit southeast Arizona, try the J.A. Jance series, which features Joanna Barnes as the sheriff of Bisbee (for example, *Skeleton Canyon*). Most of Jake Page's books are set in and around Santa Fe, New Mexico, but *The Stolen Gods* uses the Hopi reservation and Tucson as its prime locations.

All these authors are also available in audiobook versions from either **Books on Tape** (☎ **800-88-BOOKS;** `www.booksontape.com`) or **Recorded Books, LLC** (☎ **800-638-1304;** `www.recordedbooks.com`). You can borrow them for free from many local libraries or, if you can't find them near you, order them directly from the companies. I especially recommend taking Hillerman tapes along with you if you're going to northeast Arizona. Listening to the books makes the longer legs of the trip zip by — and actually viewing the places Hillerman describes is a kick.

History

Environmental historian Stephen J. Pyne highlights the showcasing of the abyss in How the Canyon Became Grand: A Short History (Viking; 1998). In the richly illustrated Inventing the Southwest: The Fred Harvey Company and Native American Art (Northland; 1996), authors Kathleen L. Howard and Diana F. Pardue demonstrate how the Fred Harvey Company directed both Arizona's tourist history and Native American art. For a more general, and folksier, take on the state's past, try Marshall Trimble's Arizona: A Cavalcade of History (Treasure Chest; 1989).

Chapter 3

Deciding Where and When to Go

In This Chapter

- Discovering Arizona's different cities and regions
- Devising an itinerary
- Presenting the pros and cons of the different seasons
- Frolicking at Arizona's top festivals and events

I'm not going to try to fool you. I don't cover every inch of Arizona in this book. That would require a volume twice this size and half as useful. Besides, who has that much time? Instead, I select the top cities (luckily, Arizona only has two) and regions. Within these locations, I cover the best attractions and events Arizona has to offer. After you look it over, it's up to you to decide where you want to go and how to shape a vacation that's right for you.

Going Everywhere You Want to Be

Arizona offers you both big-city pleasures and real wilderness adventures. The following sections focus on destinations that offer the best sightseeing, attractions, and events in the state.

Introducing the cities

Be prepared: Arizona's major urban areas are not the compact, strollable spaces that most travelers associate with the term city. Both Phoenix and Tucson came of age when the United States was romancing the auto, and their original historic centers didn't hold. Take these two sprawling Sonoran Desert metropolises for what they are — the (heat) waves of the future. Incidentally, although Tucson is farther

Arizona Cities and Regions

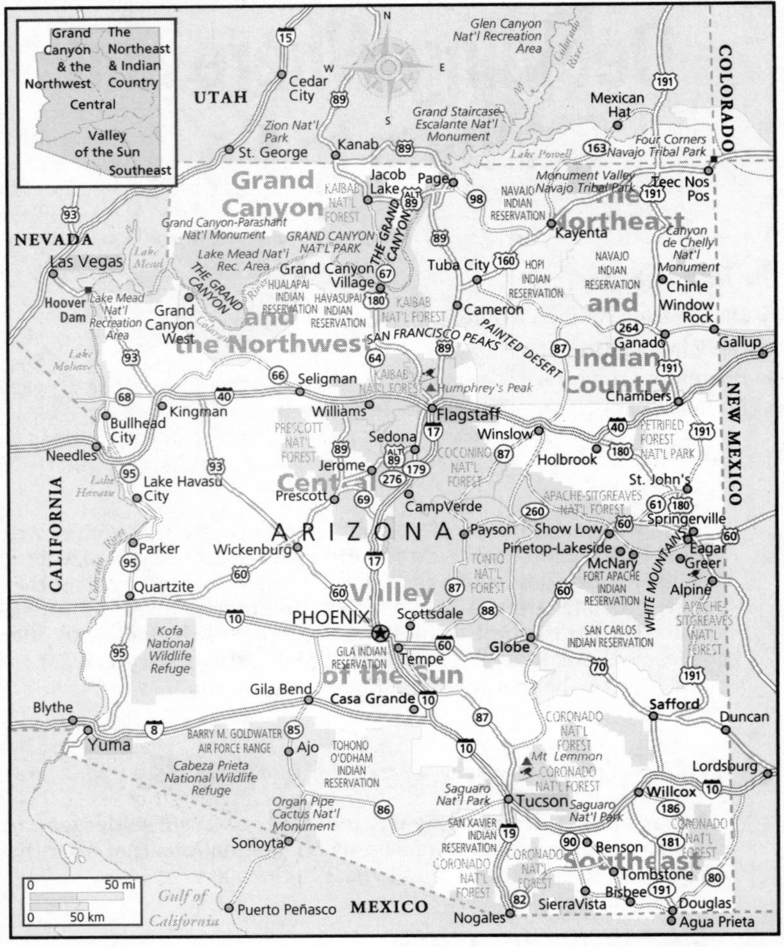

south than Phoenix, the temperature is generally about 5 degrees cooler, because its 2,100-foot elevation is 1,000 feet higher than Phoenix's and because it has less heat-retaining concrete.

The Valley of the Sun (also known as Greater Phoenix)

Arizona's largest, most populous city is actually a vast metropolitan complex. Phoenix, the state capital, and Scottsdale are its two best-known components. Growing rapidly and adding great restaurants, shopping centers, and resorts, but subtracting desert terrain, the Valley is quintessentially New West. Side trips from the Valley explore a far more pristine landscape (the Apache Trail), revisit Arizona's Hohokam past (Casa Grande), and provide a possible antidote against future shock (Arcosanti), among others.

Tucson

The state's second city is first in terms of history and culture. Established almost a century earlier than Phoenix, Tucson still has Old West and Spanish character. The city also has more protected land, including a national park devoted to cacti (Saguaro National Park). But urbanization has crept in here as well. Unbridled growth adds leisure amenities while diminishing natural beauty. Side trips from Tucson lead to an observatory (Kitt Peak), more cacti (Organ Pipe), and a place where people once lived in a glass house (Biosphere 2).

Dividing the regions

The east central, far northwestern, and far southwestern portions of the state have their appeal but don't significantly add to a first-time visitor's experience. You can break down the state's remaining areas into the following prime touring regions. The following sections start from the south.

The Southeast

The region southeast of Tucson has everything: Old West color, including the town of Tombstone and several remote guest ranches; venerable Spanish missions and new wineries; outdoor activities, from horseback riding to bird-watching; the state's latest underground attraction, Kartchner Caverns; and shopping down Mexico way.

Central

Within the up-and-down area northwest of Phoenix, renowned for its red rocks, granite dells, and spreading desert, Sedona vies with Scottsdale for the state's "ritziest little town" title; Prescott, the one-time territorial capital, is rich with Victoriana; and Wickenburg keeps its mining legends alive through its many dude ranches. Near Sedona, the Verde Valley offers a lively ghost town, a great train ride, and two well-preserved Indian ruins.

Grand Canyon and the Northwest

The Grand Canyon speaks for itself, but the rest of the northwest area may surprise you. For example, Flagstaff, Arizona's third-largest city, has a kickback college-town charm. Nearby, you can visit ancient dwellings that were left behind in a land that was ravaged by, and then fertilized by, some not-so-ancient volcanoes.

The Northeast and American Indian country

One of Arizona's most remote and intriguing regions encompasses landscapes that define the Southwest, including Monument Valley, Canyon de Chelly, and Petrified National Forest; the native cultures of the Navajo and the Hopi that keep its spiritual heart beating; splashy attractions like Lake Powell; and the kicky, kitschy Route 66.

Scheduling Your Time

If you're from a smaller, more urban-centric state, you may be tempted to plan a trip to Arizona based on more familiar travel experiences. Throw out those East Coast and Midwest touring models; they don't apply to the Southwest. Instead, when devising your Arizona adventure, keep in mind the rules discussed in the following sections.

More is less

Arizona is so large that, unless you have unlimited vacation time, you have to decide in advance which region(s) you plan to visit. Otherwise, you'll literally be spinning your wheels (see the following "Wheels win" section). Naturally, your specific choices depend on your interests and the time of year you travel. The information in the "Going Everywhere You Want to Be" section earlier in this chapter and in the "Revealing the Secrets of the Seasons" section later in this chapter should help you personalize an itinerary. In addition, Chapter 4 offers some sample itineraries that you can use or adapt.

Remember, too, that you can have too much of a good thing. Try to vary your terrain — literally and figuratively. For example, if you like the great outdoors, you'll be wowed by southern Arizona's cactus-laden landscape — but you don't need to go to Saguaro National Park in Tucson, take a side trip from Tucson to Organ Pipe National Monument, and then go to the Desert Botanical Gardens in Phoenix, all of which would leave you with no time to view the red rocks of Sedona or the strangely poised boulders of Chiricahua National Monument. Similarly, unless you're on a scholarly research mission, you can pass up the smaller museums of Native American culture if you've visited the Heard Museum in Phoenix. In fact, you don't really need to spend time in both Greater Phoenix and Tucson. The cities are sufficiently similar in their amenities and attractions that you won't gain much by dividing your time between them.

Because distances between Arizona's tourist attractions are so great, basing yourself in either major city may not be your best move. You wouldn't want to bed down in Phoenix, for example, and drive to the Grand Canyon and back in a single day. Getting away from the large metro areas and staying at smaller regional hotels or inns is fun — and often less expensive. On the other hand, if you want to relax in one place, Greater Phoenix and Tucson provide plenty for you to do. You can easily spend a week in either place and take some great side trips. You won't be bored, I promise.

Wheels win

Arizona is public transportation–challenged, so if you don't plan on driving, you either have to rely on escorted tours or spend huge amounts of time and/or money trying to get around independently. Yes, the major cities have bus systems, but they're slow and won't necessarily take you where you want to go; moreover, most bus lines shut down at ridiculously early hours. So, for example, if you didn't have a car and wanted to go out to dinner in most parts of Greater Phoenix, you'd have to phone in advance for a cab in both directions — and pay through the nose.

One exception to the you-can't-get-there-without-your-own-wheels rule is visiting the Grand Canyon, a site so popular that the state goes out of its way to transport people to it. You can catch a shuttle from Phoenix to Flagstaff — which, being a smallish college town has a pretty decent bus system, and a nice strollable downtown — then take another shuttle from Flag to the abyss, where, especially in summer, going carless is an asset.

Phoenix rising (and landing)

Don't assume that all parts of Arizona are equally accessible by air. You can fly directly into Tucson from some places — and, if you want to spend your time in that city and/or in southeast Arizona, I suggest you look into that option — but most airlines offer far more flights, especially economical ones, into Phoenix. Before spending time devising a vacation itinerary, check out flights to Arizona from your hometown. If all signs point to Phoenix, as is likely, plan your itinerary accordingly.

Of course, if you're driving into Arizona, ignore all of the preceding advice. You're probably already distance- and transportation-savvy.

Revealing the Secrets of the Seasons

Because of Arizona's size and its varied topography, vacationing in the northern part of the state on the Colorado Plateau is a completely different experience from touring the Sonoran Desert in the south. Because of the great temperature and altitude variations, the state's two sections are practically mirror opposites of each other — meaning Arizona always has great weather somewhere.

What is central Arizona's climate? Of the three towns covered in Chapter 16, Sedona and Prescott tend to follow the northern area's weather patterns (although these towns are a bit warmer), while Wickenburg's weather goes as the south goes. Tables 3-1 and 3-2 give you a month-by-month breakdown of average temperatures and rainfall for Phoenix and Flagstaff, respectively.

Table 3-1 Phoenix's Average Temperatures and Days of Rain

Month	*Average High °F/°C*	*Average Low °F/°C*	*Days of Rain*
January	65/18	38/3	4
February	69/21	41/5	4
March	75/24	45/7	3
April	84/29	52/11	2
May	93/34	60/16	1
June	102/39	68/20	1
July	105/41	78/26	4
August	102/39	76/24	5
September	98/37	69/21	3
October	88/31	57/14	3
November	75/24	45/7	2
December	66/19	39/4	4

Table 3-2 Flagstaff's Average Temperatures and Days of Rain

Month	*Average High °F/°C*	*Average Low °F/°C*	*Days of Rain*
January	41/5	14/–10	7
February	44/7	17/–8	6
March	48/9	20/–7	8
April	57/14	27/–3	6
May	67/19	34/1	3
June	76/24	40/4	3
July	81/27	50/10	12
August	78/26	49/9	11
September	74/23	41/5	6
October	63/17	31/–1	5
November	51/11	22/–6	5
December	43/6	16/–9	6

Southern Arizona

If you're like me and don't mind the heat — but, honey, when southern Arizona is hot, it's hot — you won't find a bad time of the year to visit. Spring — when the mercury hasn't peaked, but room prices have — is prime. Unless the winter's unusually dry, the desert blooms with wildflowers.

Winter

Winter is wonderful because . . .

- The weather's glorious — sunny and warm — and perfect for sightseeing and anything else you want to do.
- Everything's happening: events, festivals, music, and theater programs, you name it.

But keep in mind that . . .

- Room prices are at their highest.
- Crowds are at their largest, which means lots of traffic, too.

Spring

Spring is special because . . .

- The desert is usually a flowering wonderland.
- Room rates start to dip.

But keep in mind that . . .

- Temperatures begin to creep up; some days may be uncomfortably warm, and you may enjoy better weather in your hometown.
- Prices aren't as low as they're going to be in a few months.

Summer

Summer sizzles because . . .

- You can try the resort of your dreams for rock-bottom rates, and fancy restaurants run summer specials.
- The streets are uncrowded, thanks to the departure of students and snowbirds (long-term winter visitors).

But keep in mind that . . .

- The sizzling is literal.
- Desert tours, hikes, and other activities slow or cease; many restaurants in the southeast close when their owners head for the hills.

Fall

Fall is fabulous because . . .

- The room rates are still fairly low.
- Activities like concerts and shows come back on track.

But keep in mind that . . .

- It takes a while to cure that heat hangover; temperatures may still be uncomfortable.
- The University of Arizona and Arizona State University freshmen are beginners at driving around the streets of Tucson and Greater Phoenix.

Northern Arizona

Northern Arizona doesn't have any loser seasons — even the cold isn't very cold. The fall is prime because the crowds thin and the weather's crisp and comfortable. Stay away from the Grand Canyon in summer, though, unless you prefer to bond with a few thousand of your fellow human beings rather than with nature alone.

Summer

Summer sizzles because . . .

- The weather is great: sunny, warm, and clear.
- Everything's open and happening.

But keep in mind that . . .

- Everyone wants to visit in summer; the Grand Canyon is a zoo.
- The room rates are as high as the sun in the sky.

Fall

Fall is fabulous because . . .

- The crowds go back to school and work.
- The weather's still sunny and an actual autumn season begins with colorful leaves and all.

But keep in mind that . . .

- Many places begin observing shorter hours; some facilities start to close.
- The rates aren't at their lowest yet.

Winter

Winter is wonderful because . . .

- No scenery is prettier than the snow against the Grand Canyon (and Flagstaff is a winter sports mecca). Even if no snow is on the ground, the weather is crisp and clear.

- The room rates — and the crowds — bottom out; you enjoy your pick of lodgings.

But keep in mind that . . .

- The Grand Canyon's North Rim is closed, and you can't swim in Lake Powell without freezing your patooties off.
- Fewer services are offered than at any other time of year.

Spring

Spring is special because . . .

- Facilities reopen, but the crowds aren't present.
- The weather warms up.

But keep in mind that . . .

- Mother Nature is erratic; snow may fall, the roads may close, and the temperature's still not warm enough to dip into Lake Powell.
- The rates begin to warm up, too.

Checking Out the Calendar of Events

In addition to the typical U.S. holiday festivities and the events listed in the following sections, expect celebrations in southern Arizona for Cinco de Mayo (May 5), commemorating Mexico's victory over the French in an 1862 battle, and, to a lesser extent, for the Day of the Dead (or All Soul's Day), November 2. Christmas in the southern part of the state also has a Mexican accent, with luminarias (candles in small paper bags) lighting the paths to many churches and homes.

For more information about what's happening around the state, log on to www.arizonaguide.com and click on the "Calendar of Events" option.

January

You'll have a difficult time getting tickets for college football's biggest competition — and biggest post-game bash — the Tostitos Fiesta Bowl Football Classic, in Tempe's Sun Devil Stadium. Put yourself on the waiting list as soon as possible. Call ☎ 800-635-5748 or 480-350-0911 or log on to www.tostitosfiestabowl.com. January 1–4.

Scottsdale hosts horse roping, line dancing, live Country and Western music, a huge parade — the whole Western shebang — at Parada Del Sol Rodeo. Call ☎ 800-527-1880 or 480-990-3179, ext. 2 or visit www.scottsdalejaycees.com for details. Late January/early February.

February

Flagstaff's Winterfest features more than 100 events, including sled-dog races, llama games, skiing, sleigh rides, snow sculpture — pretty much any way you can think of to play in the snow (or, absent that, cold). To find out more, call ☎ 928-774-4505 or go to www.flagstaff.az.us. Entire month of February.

The convention center and downtown hotel rooms load up with fabulous stones, jewels, and fossils during the huge Tucson Gem and Mineral Show. Keep these dates in mind even if you don't care about crystals or dinosaurs (which are a big kiddie draw); hotel rooms are hard to nab. Call ☎ 520-322-5773 or log on to www.tgms.org for details. Early to mid-February.

Dozens of tribes gather in Casa Grande for arts and crafts exhibits, dance performances, and a huge rodeo at O'odham Tash, one of the country's largest annual Native American festivals. Get details by phoning ☎ 800-916-1515 or 520-836-4723. Presidents' Day weekend.

Tucson suspends all school classes for the kickoff of America's largest annual winter rodeo, La Fiesta De Los Vaqueros Rodeo & Parade, making the event a favorite with local kids. Visiting young 'uns also like the marching bands, floats, and one of the world's longest parades with horse-drawn floats. For additional information, phone ☎ 800-964-5662 or 520-741-2233 or visit www.tucsonrodeo.com. Final full week of February.

March

Talented Native American artists gather for a reception and juried competition, followed by sales at the Heard Museum's Guild Indian Fair and Market in Phoenix. Find out more by calling ☎ 602-252-8840 or clicking on www.heard.org. First weekend in March.

Scottsdale's Festival of the West features cowboy poets, Western films, shooting contests, chuck wagon cook-off . . . yee-HAW. For details, call ☎ 602-996-4387 or visit www.festivalofthewest.com. Mid-March.

April

Tucson's lively International Mariachi Conference, with folk dancers, workshops, and mariachi star-studded concerts, often gets hometown girl Linda Ronstadt up on stage. Call ☎ 520-838-3908, or log on to www.tucsonmariachi.org. Last or second-to-last weekend in April.

May

The Phippen Western Art Show and Sale in Prescott is a major Western art event, drawing talent from Canada, Mexico, and the United States. For more information, call ☎ 928-778-1385 or check the Web site at www.phippenartmuseum.org. Memorial Day weekend.

Rendezvous Days in Williams features a festive reenactment of the springtime regrouping of the trappers known as mountain men (but the actors are townsfolk who, presumably, take a few showers over the winter). Get details at ☎ 928-635-1418 or online at www.williamschamber.com. Memorial Day weekend.

Also see the Helldorado Days listing in the "October" section.

June

Celebrating the art of the cowboy — we're talking gorgeously crafted saddles, boots, spurs, bronze sculpture and more — the Trappings of the American West in Flagstaff is attended by serious collectors and tourists alike. Find out more by phoning ☎ 928-774-8861 or by logging on to www.drycreekarts.com. First through third weeks in June.

July

Proving the "world's oldest" claim is hard — who started keeping rodeo records, anyway? — but the parade, fireworks, melodramas, bands, and other activities held in Prescott during Frontier Days & World's Oldest Rodeo are rip roarin' fun. To learn more, call ☎ 800-358-1888 or 928-445-3103 or log on to www.worldsoldestrodeo.com. July 4th weekend.

The Museum of Northern Arizona kicks off its summer-long schedule of weekend events with early July's Hopi Marketplace, featuring sales of Native American artwork, crafts demonstrations, and tribal dances. The Navajo Marketplace is in early August, and the Native Artists Marketplace, celebrating the Colorado Plateau nations, including the Zuni and the Pai, takes place in early Sept. Call ☎ 928-774-5213 or check www.musnaz.org for information on all these events.

August

Hummingbirds rule, but bats and owls are among the other winged creatures touted on field trips, displays, and lectures during Bisbee's Southwest Wings Bird and Nature Festival. Phone ☎ 866-224-7233 or 520-432-5421 or check www.bisbeearizona.com for details. Early or mid-August.

September

The Navajo Nation Fair, held in Window Rock, is the tribe's prime powwow — literally — with arts and crafts demonstrations, horse racing, rodeo, traditional songs and dances, a fry bread contest, and more. For information, phone ☎ 928-871-7311 or visit www.navajonationfair.com. Early September (Thursday after Labor Day).

The Grand Canyon Music Festival, an annual series of evening concerts, ranging from classical to jazz, has excellent music — and an even better backdrop. Call ☎ 800-997-8285 or 928-638-9215 or log on to www.grandcanyonmusicfest.org for details. Two weeks in mid- to late September.

The red rocks — and attendant resorts and restaurants — are alive with the sounds of America's coolest music during Sedona's Jazz on the Rocks festival. This international event is popular, so you should buy your tickets up to two months in advance. Get information at ☎ 928-282-1985 or on the Internet at www.sedonajazz.com. Late September.

October

A chili cook-off, Country and Western bands, hangings, and general gunslinger-style rowdiness — along with the replay of a certain famous gunfight — are all a part of Tombstone's Helldorado Days, one of Arizona's oldest festivals (it celebrated its 75th anniversary in 2004). To find out more about this festival and the somewhat smaller but equally rowdy Wyatt Earp Days, held Memorial Day weekend, call ☎ 800-457-3423 or log on to www.tombstone.org/events. Third weekend in October.

Riders dressed as Spanish soldiers reenact the 1776 Juan Bautista expedition to California — at least the stretch of it between Nogales and Tubac (so, no, you don't end up at the Golden Gate Bridge) — during Anza Days. Food and entertainment celebrate the conquistadors'success. Get details by phoning ☎ 520-398-2252. Mid- to late October.

November

Twinkle, twinkle, little lights — more than a million of them go into creating 60 themed displays that you stroll among while enjoying classical holiday music at Sedona's Red Rock Fantasy of Lights. Find out more at ☎ 800-418-6499, 928-282-1777, or www.redrockfantasy.com. Late November through early January.

Fiddles, flat-pick guitars, banjos, and mandolins compete in 13 twangy categories at the Wickenburg Bluegrass Festival. This three-day event, the largest of its kind in the Southwest, includes arts and crafts and a kids' zone. To learn more, call ☎ 928-684-5479 or click on to www.wickenburgchamber.com. Mid-November.

Prescott has been dubbed Arizona's Official Christmas City, with its courthouse lighting and parade on the first Saturday of December. The city also hosts one of the tastiest festivals in the state. At Arizona's Largest Gingerbread Village, you can view more than 100 edible castles, estates, and houses. Cookie decorating (and nibbling) is involved, too.

Get details at ☎ 928-776-1666 or www.prescottresort.com. Late November through December.

December

Dock yourself at Wahweap Marina or anywhere on the 5-mile long Lakeshore Drive to watch a dazzling array of boats floating in formation on Lake Powell during the Festival of Lights Boat Parade, near Page. Kids find it mesmerizing. For details, call ☎ 928-645-1001. First Saturday in December.

La Fiesta de Tumacácori, held at a lovely Spanish mission south of Tucson, is a cultural heritage bash, with food, crafts, Native American folklore and dancing, and Mexican, Indian, and old-time Arizona music. Call ☎ 520-398-2341, ext. 0, for information or click on www.nps.gov/tuma/special_events.htm. First weekend in December.

Some 450 artists from 60 Native American tribes bring their wares to the Pueblo Grande Indian Market in Phoenix. Activities such as a "quick-draw" sketching contest and hands-on exhibits for kids add to the fun. To learn more, call ☎ 602-495-0901 or log on to www.pgmarket.org. Mid-December.

Chapter 4

Following an Itinerary: Five Great Options

In This Chapter

- Seeing Arizona's southern hot spots
- Traveling to northern Arizona's high (and low) points
- Mixing it up with a great Arizona combination plate
- Discovering Arizona for youngsters (and youngsters-at-heart)
- Mining the best of Arizona's Old West

You may already know exactly what you want to do in Arizona — park yourself at a Scottsdale resort and get spa treatments for the first week of your vacation and go white-water rafting on the Colorado River during the second week. But, if you're like most people, you may not have decided what you want out of your Arizona vacation, especially when faced with the terrific array of vacation opportunities. In this chapter, I present itineraries to help you hit the highlights — and forgo the rest.

For all these itineraries, I assume you're flying into Sky Harbor Airport in Phoenix, which has the greatest number of flights in the state (see Chapter 6 for information on which carriers fly to Phoenix). In addition, I assume that you're renting a car (see Chapter 7 for the lowdown on how to do that), which is really, the best way to tour the state.

Going North or South: Seeing Arizona's Highlights in One Week

Because you can't do the entire state in a single week — you just get super stressed if you try — I propose two weeklong "Greatest Hits" itineraries, one for the northern half of the state and one for the southern part. But which should you choose? Look at the information on Arizona's seasons in Chapter 3. If you're interested in beating the crowds and keeping your costs down, try the northern

Arizona itinerary in winter or the southern Arizona itinerary in summer. If you're dying for a winter getaway to a warm place and money isn't the main issue, go to southern Arizona in winter and . . . well, you get the picture.

Swinging through southern Arizona

Because the distances between attractions aren't as great as in the northern part of the state, during a one-week tour of the south you may even be able to fit in a little pool time. But you are still on the move. Part of the allure of southern Arizona is kicking back at a resort or a dude ranch, but if you follow my proposed schedule, you're not going to get much bang for your buck from these lodgings. If you opt for this itinerary, choose economical or historic digs, not ones with tons of built-in activities.

Assuming you're not completely wiped out on Day 1 when you arrive in Phoenix, spend the afternoon exploring Old Scottsdale's historic buildings and boutiques and visiting the Scottsdale Museum of Contemporary Art. If you're more interested in architecture than shops or contemporary art, head for Taliesen West, Frank Lloyd Wright's home and architecture school. (For information on all these sights, see Chapter 11.) In the evening, enjoy dinner at a Western steakhouse or a funky Mexican restaurant.

Spend Day 2 following the one-day Phoenix itinerary in Chapter 11 — but skip the Desert Botanical Gardens. You see plenty of cacti in Tucson during the next two or three days.

On Day 3, take the slow, scenic back route (Highway 87/287 to Highway 79 to Highway 77) down to Tucson, stopping at the Casa Grande Ruins National Monument, with its mysterious Hohokam structures, and in the town of Florence, which has the greatest number of homes on the National Historic Register — and the most prisons — in Arizona. (See Chapter 12 for information on both places.) Eat lunch in Florence, and then drive down to Biosphere 2, a big (and once very weird) science project in the desert (see Chapter 14). Spend the rest of the afternoon at the center. Then drive down to your Tucson hotel and eat dinner nearby; you may want to turn in early to prepare for a jam-packed Day 4.

On Day 4, follow the one-day itinerary for Tucson outlined in Chapter 13.

On Day 5, drive south from Tucson along I-19. Choose between the Titan Missile Museum, where you can descend into the former control center of a nuclear warhead, and the town of Tubac, with its historic fortress and myriad crafts shops. By choosing either the museum or a tour of Tubac, you may have time to stop at the moody, ruined mission at Tumacácori National Historical Park and get down to Nogales, Mexico, for lunch. Do a bit of bargaining and cross back over the border. Then take Highway 82 northeast to the sleepy one-time ranching town of Patagonia. If you're not shopped out, browse a few more crafts boutiques. Spend the night in Patagonia or in nearby Sonoita, which is even smaller — both have interesting lodgings and good restaurants, plus at least one cowboy bar. (See Chapter 15 for information on the attractions in this paragraph.)

Divide Day 6 between Bisbee, a Victorian-style mining town, and Tombstone (yes, that one, famous for the shootout at the OK Corral). Plan on spending the night in the last town you visit for the day. Bisbee and Tombstone aren't very far from each other, but why drive back to your hotel at night when you can walk, for a change? (See Chapter 15 for information on both towns.)

Spend the morning of Day 7 trekking among the strangely balanced boulders at Chiricahua National Monument. To get to the monument from Tombstone, take Highway 80 to I-10; then go east to Highway 186 south. From Bisbee, take Highway 90 east to Highway 191 north, and then go east on Highway 181. Head out early if you want to catch the daily hiking shuttle at 8:30 a.m. Enjoy a piece of apple pie for lunch in Willcox (you've earned it after all that exercise), and then visit the Rex Allen Cowboy Museum and Theater. In the afternoon, descend into Kartchner Caverns State Park near Benson, which puts you back on I-10 and in a position to zip back to Tucson where you can spend your last night if you don't have an early plane out the next day, or to Phoenix, if you do. (See Chapter 15 for the attractions mentioned in this paragraph. Note that you need to book tickets in advance for Kartchner Caverns.)

Traveling around northern Arizona

Pick up your rental car at the Phoenix airport on Day 1 and hit the road — I-17, that is — heading north. If you arrive reasonably early in the afternoon, stop for a half hour at the Indian cliff dwellings of Montezuma Castle National Monument en route to Sedona (see Chapter 16). Sedona is a good place to splurge on a really upscale dinner and room. You find that most of the meals and digs on the rest of the itinerary are not as swank.

Take a Jeep tour around the red rocks in the morning of Day 2, eat lunch at the lively ghost town of Jerome (see Chapter 16 for both), and enjoy a gorgeous mid-afternoon drive along Highway 89A through Oak Creek Canyon to Flagstaff (see Chapter 17). "Flag" is your last chance for anything resembling nightlife, so visit a brewpub or savor a hearty dinner, and then hit the Museum Club for some Country and Western music.

On Day 3, take the southwestern route from Flagstaff (via Williams and Highway 64) to the Grand Canyon's South Rim, where you spend the day and night. See Chapter 17 for ideas on how to organize your activities. Be sure to book a meal at the El Tovar, no matter where you stay.

Leave the Grand Canyon vicinity early in the morning on Day 4 and take the eastern route via Highway 64 out to Highway 89A, stopping at the Cameron Trading Post (see Chapter 17) to browse the Native American crafts — but don't spend too long. You want to be close to Monument Valley Navajo Tribal Park via Highway 160 to 163 by lunchtime. Eat a Navajo taco at Goulding's Lodge or at the visitor center's restaurant and tour the mesas and spires. Prepare to leave by late afternoon so that you can arrive at Canyon de Chelly (via Highway 191 south) in time to enjoy a leisurely dinner at the Thunderbird Lodge. (For the last four sights in bold, see Chapter 18.)

On the morning of Day 5, take the two Canyon de Chelly rim drives or hike down the White House Trail. Lunch near the canyon before heading east via Highway 191 to Highway 264 for the Hubbell Trading Post, where you can see Navajo rugs and, if you're lucky, catch the last tour of trader Lorenzo Hubbell's house. From there you have a choice: You can either head west along Highway 264 toward the Hopi Mesas and spend a quiet night on Second Mesa (one of the three mesas upon which most of the Hopi villages sit) at the Hopi Cultural Center or head south and hole up in either Holbrook or Winslow along I-40; these towns are very close to one another. Your evening's not going to be super exciting in these towns, but you have more restaurant choices — and you can enjoy a beer with dinner (the Indian reservations don't allow alcohol). If you opted for Holboork/Winslow, dine at the historic La Posada hotel in Winslow or at one of the Route 66 restaurants in Holbrook. (See Chapter 18 for the sights in this paragraph.)

If you wake up on Second Mesa on Day 6, explore the Hopi villages in the morning. Because you already enjoyed your Nöqkwivi (lamb and hominy stew) at the Hopi Cultural Center the night before, plan on lunch in either Winslow or Holbrook. Spend the rest of the afternoon browsing the kitschy Route 66 souvenir shops in and around Holbrook. Alternatively, if you start your day in Holbrook or Winslow, go to the Hopi mesas, have lunch at the Hopi Cultural Center, and return to the Route 66 area in time for dinner in Winslow or Holbrook. Spend the night in one of the two towns. (See Chapter 18 for all these sights.)

On Day 7, backtrack a little bit on I-40 to the Petrified National Forest and Painted Desert (see Chapter 18), where you can spend a nice leisurely morning and lunchtime among the dead wood. If your flight departs in the early morning from Phoenix the next day, you want to sleep in the Valley of the Sun. Take the scenic Highway 87 route back from Winslow to Highway 260 to Highway 17. If you haven't already done so on the way up, stop at Montezuma Castle (see Chapter 16) in the late afternoon. Enjoy a blowout farewell-to-Arizona dinner at a New Southwest or authentic Mexican restaurant in the Valley. Alternatively, if your flight leaves at noon or later the following day, after a morning at the Petrified National Forest, stop at Meteor Crater (see Chapter 18) and Walnut Canyon National Monument (see Chapter 17), off I-40, before retiring for dinner in Flagstaff (which may seem like a gourmet mecca by now). Get a good night's sleep in Flagstaff so you're refreshed for your morning drive to Phoenix and the flight back home.

Taking the Leisurely Route: Touring the Best of Arizona in Two Weeks

Have two weeks in Arizona? Sorry, but you can't just combine the one-week northern and southern Arizona itineraries to get a perfect two-week tour, because those itineraries are built around getting you back to the Phoenix airport, which you don't need to do in the middle of your two-week jaunt.

Follow the southern Arizona itinerary (see the "Swinging through southern Arizona" section earlier in this chapter) for the first six days. On Day 7, skip the detour to Chiricahua National Monument and Willcox and head to Prescott (Chapter 16) via I-10 to I-17 to Highway 69. (If you can get into Kartchner Caverns in the morning or still haven't toured Tombstone, fine, but don't go too far south or east.) It takes about five hours to get from Benson to Prescott, Arizona's one-time territorial capital, where you can spend the night at a historic hotel or B&B. If you need to stretch your legs en route, the Outlets at Casa Grande (off I-10) makes a useful — if potentially expensive — walkabout (see Chapter 12).

On Day 8, travel to Jerome, and spend the rest of the afternoon and evening in Sedona (see Chapter 16).

On the morning of Day 9, drive through Oak Creek Canyon (see Chapter 16) on Highway 89A and turn west on I-40, before you get to Flagstaff; then take Highway 64 north until you reach the Grand Canyon (see Chapter 17). From there, follow the itinerary from Days 3 through 7 from the "Traveling around northern Arizona" section earlier in this chapter.

Making It a Family Affair: Discovering Arizona with Kids

This itinerary assumes that you want to get in as many top sights as possible — without pushing your family's travel endurance to the limit — in a single week. If you don't feel compelled to see the Grand Canyon, you can spend a relaxing family vacation in southern Arizona. There, you can divide your time between a resort with a good kids' program in the Valley of the Sun (the Phoenix area — see Chapter 11) and a guest ranch in Tucson and take daily excursions to the top children's sights in those cities. When you stay in the Valley, visit all the attractions recommended in the following itinerary except the Desert Botanical Gardens, because Tucson's Arizona-Sonora Desert Museum covers the same territory, but better. Also, be sure your family doesn't miss Old Tucson Studios. So, for the state's "greatest family hits" tour, use the following agenda.

After you arrive in Phoenix, devote the afternoon of Day 1 to just one activity — either the Heard Museum or the Desert Botanical Garden, and eat dinner near your hotel. Alternatively, if you don't care about doing anything typically Southwestern but just want to show your kids that you aren't in the boonies, head over to GameWorks, an amazing two-story family fun center at the Arizona Mills mall. Naturally, the mall has a huge food court, too. (See Chapter 11 for the sights in this paragraph.)

On Day 2 in Phoenix, spend the morning at the Arizona Science Center. Chow down on a fast-food lunch at the center, and then spend the afternoon at the Desert Botanical Gardens if you haven't already. Time permitting, you can also visit the Phoenix Zoo, next door. Dine at a family steakhouse like Pinnacle Peak. (See Chapter 11 for this day's attractions.)

Hit the road on Day 3 by heading north on I-17. Stop off at the Deer Valley Rock Art Center, where you can view hundreds of petroglyphs (Native American rock art), or the Williamsburg-gone-West Pioneer Arizona Living History Museum. Both are close to the Rock Springs Café and Bakery, a former stagecoach stop with lots of kid-friendly lunch food (see Chapter 12 for these sights). Get up to Clarkdale on Highway 260 in time to board the Verde Canyon Railroad for a scenic afternoon train ride. If you visit from Wednesday to Sunday (any month except January and August, when the ranch is closed), go for the pony rides, a chuck-wagon supper, and a Western show at the Blazin' M Ranch in Cottonwood, which is, in any case, a convenient and economical place to spend the night. (See Chapter 16 for attractions in Clarkdale and Cottonwood.)

Spend Day 4 in Sedona. If the temperature is warm enough, swim at Slide Rock State Park in the morning before the crowds descend. If the weather is too cool for a dip, start the day with a Jeep tour, and then go fishing at the Rainbow Trout Farm in Oak Creek in the afternoon. The scenic drive north through Oak Creek Canyon on Highway 89A gets you to Flagstaff, which has loads of family restaurants and inexpensive chain hotels. (See Chapters 16 and 17 for information on Sedona and Flagstaff, respectively.)

On Day 5, drive to the Grand Canyon's South Rim (via I-40 and Highway 64) and spend the day and night. For suggestions on things to do at the canyon, see Chapter 17. Alternatively, if your kids get a kick out of the Verde Canyon train ride, consider reprising the event by using the Grand Canyon Railway as transport. You don't have to hassle with parking and you can stay overnight at Williams (also in Chapter 17), where the train depot sells railroad and forest toys (including cute Smokey Bear replicas).

Spend Day 6 and night six back in Flagstaff, where kid-friendly attractions include the Museum of Northern Arizona, which has a dinosaur exhibit (enough said); the Lowell Observatory, with lots of fun hands-on science displays (better still if you come at night when the observatory offers telescope viewing); and Snowbowl, a ski resort. If snow is on the ground, consider some family skiing; the slopes aren't very intimidating. In summer, take the ski lift to the top and walk around.

On Day 7, drive east on I-40 to Meteor Crater — not quite as deep as the Grand Canyon but created a lot more quickly — and Petrified Forest National Park, where dinosaur buffs can ogle more fossils (see Chapter 18 for both attractions). You can eat lunch at the national park or in Holbrook, where the retro Route 66 diners are the genuine items. If you're through early enough in the afternoon, take the scenic Highway 87 route from Winslow to Highway 260 to Highway 17. Stop at a not-very-taxing-on-the-weary Montezuma Castle (see Chapter 16). If it's late or you're all tuckered out, just drive straight east on I-40 to I-17 and zip down to Phoenix to spend the evening unwinding.

Digging In: Arizona's Old West History

This Old West itinerary provides a close-up look at Arizona's cowboy heritage and takes you around Arizona's former mining towns. If visiting what amounts to a few holes in the ground sounds like a yawn, think again. Most of the famous towns of the West rose and fell around mineral wealth. Greed, rowdiness, and, in southern Arizona, clashes with Native Americans are the stuff of America's legends and Hollywood Westerns. And Arizona's mines happen to be located in some mighty purty territory. You can also find plenty to admire here if your interests lie above ground.

On Day 1, head straight from the Phoenix airport (northwest on Highway 60) to Wickenburg (see Chapter 16), home to what was once the richest gold mine in the state. If it's still open, stop at the Desert Caballeros Western Museum for some town background (and art); if not, the Jail Tree and The Old Wishing Well never close, and you can stroll around Frontier Street, with its intact early 1900s buildings. Have dinner at the Rancho de Los Caballeros guest ranch or at a historic cowboy bar.

You spend a good part of Day 2 in Wickenburg. Visit the museum if you haven't already done so, and then drive to the Robson's Arizona Mining World, which re-creates an old mining camp. Take a Jeep tour into the surrounding mining territory or a self-guided tour of the Vulture Mine. Leave the Wickenburg area by late afternoon, so you can fully enjoy the scenery along the long, winding mountain roads (Highway 89 to 89A) up to Jerome (see Chapter 16) for the night.

Jerome isn't very large, but with such sights as the Jerome State Historic Park (a one-time mine-owner's mansion), the Jerome Historical Society and Mine Museum, and the Gold King Mine and Ghost Town — not to mention the streets lined with rows of crafts shops — you find plenty to fill the morning of Day 3. In the afternoon, come down from the mountain to nearby Clarkdale (see Chapter 16) and ride the Verde Canyon Railroad, which runs along tracks formerly used to haul minerals from Jerome (the haulers probably didn't appreciate the stunning vistas as much as you do). From here, drive back down along I-17 to the Valley of the Sun (Chapter 11), where you spend the night. You don't find much authentic Western history there, except in Old Scottsdale, but the area is the best jumping-off point for the next day. If you need a break from standard American fare, here is where you find some good, authentic Mexican food.

You have a choice for Day 4 on how you want to approach two sights east of Phoenix, the Apache Trail and Lost Dutchman Mine State Park, named for a world-famous gold mine that may never have existed. If you want to relax and enjoy the scenery and not drive along sometimes-harrowing mountain roads, book a full-day tour of the Apache Trail (see Chapter 12 for some options) and spend a second night in the Greater Phoenix area. If you don't mind a little adrenaline pumping, take the Apache Trail drive described in Chapter 12, only instead of going back to the Valley, bunk in the town of Globe, still an active mining area.

If, on Day 5, you wake up in Globe, take the scenic route (Highway 77, south toward I-10) and stop for lunch before you get to Tucson. You pass plenty of casual restaurants (try Cibaria if you're up for Italian). If you begin the day in the Phoenix area, pick up I-10 and, before you get to downtown Tucson, detour to the Arizona-Sonora Desert Museum, with its earth sciences center and mining display, and lunch among the desert flora and fauna (see Chapter 13). However you begin the day, eventually get back on I-10 and head southwest until you reach the turnoff for Tombstone (see Chapter 15), where you can spend the night.

On the morning of Day 6, explore Tombstone. The Tombstone Courthouse State Historic Park is the best place to get the truth behind the tourist hype. Next, head down to Bisbee (see Chapter 15), a mining mecca. Not only can you take a terrific miner-led tour of the defunct Copper Queen mine, but you can also gaze into the great gaping Lavender mine pit. The most obvious lodging choice is the Copper Queen Hotel, but several other hotels and B&Bs in town harken back to Bisbee's mining heyday.

On Day 7, take your pick of destinations. You can drive east from Bisbee to Douglas (which once hosted the smelters for Bisbee's mines) and visit the historic Gadsen Hotel. Afterward, go north along Highway 191 and tour the mining ghost towns of Gleeson, Pearce, and Courtland. Finally detour a short bit farther east on I-10 to explore the Rex Allen Cowboy Museum and Theater in downtown Willcox (which happens to be Arizona's apple pie capital). Or you can head west from Bisbee, stopping for lunch and a stroll in sleepy Patagonia (where silver was once transported from the railroad depot). Then, if your vehicle has good suspension, explore the ruins of Dusquesne. If you're not up for back-roading, pick up I-19 in Nogales and drive north to the Asarco Mineral Discovery Center, between Green Valley and Tucson, where you can see modern copper strip-mining in action. Either way, you end up close to Tucson, where you spend your last night — unless you have an early flight, in which case, you'd better hightail it back to Phoenix. (See Chapter 15 for the attractions.)

Part II
Planning Your Trip to Arizona

In this part . . .

You're Arizona bound, and you may even have an idea of which areas of the state you want to visit and when. This section deals with the ways to get there (with a group, on your own, by plane, by train, and so on); your means of transportation after you arrive; the types of rooms available and the rates you can expect to pay for them; methods of dealing with your finances while you're on the road; and assorted odds and ends from packing to planning for emergencies.

Chapter 5

Managing Your Money

In This Chapter

- Estimating your trip costs
- Ferreting out those sneaky charges
- Cutting expenses without cutting corners

You may dislike paying for fun you've already had — who doesn't? — but if you plan ahead, you can avoid going into credit card shock when you return from Arizona.

Planning Your Budget

To gauge how much your Arizona vacation will cost you, begin with transportation to the airport, and then add your flight costs (see Chapter 6 for tips on how to fly for less), car rental, gas, hotel rates, meals, admission prices to attractions, and the cost of the activities you're interested in (golf or Jeep tours, for example). To get an idea of what things cost in Arizona, see Tables 5-1 and 5-2. Consider the costs of souvenirs and only-in-Arizona items. After you do all that, add on another 15% to 20% to cover tips, taxes (if they're not included in flight or hotel rates), and miscellaneous costs.

Table 5-1 What Things Cost in Phoenix

Item	*Cost*
Double room at the Four Seasons Scottsdale resort in February ($$$$$)	$500
Double room at the Four Seasons Scottsdale resort in July ($$$$$)	$185
Double room at the all-suites Phoenix Inn in February ($$)	$139
Double room at the all-suites Phoenix Inn in July ($$)	$89

(continued)

Table 5-1 *(continued)*

Item	*Cost*
Dinner for two without drinks, tax, or tip at Micheal's at the Citadel ($$$$)	$120
Dinner for two without drinks, tax, or tip at San Carlos Bay ($–$$)	$25
Long-neck beer at Toolies	$3
Adult admission to the Heard Museum	$7
Greens fees at The Boulders golf course on a winter weekend	$250
Greens fees at the Papago Municipal golf course on a winter weekend	$57
Trail ride hourly rate at South Mountain Park	$23

Table 5-2 What Things Cost in Flagstaff

Item	*Cost*
Double room at the Little America Flagstaff in summer ($$)	$129
Double room at the Little America Flagstaff in winter ($$)	$99
Double room at The Inn at Northern Arizona University in summer ($)	$89
Double room at The Inn at Northern Arizona University in winter ($)	$69
Dinner for two without drinks, tax, or tip at Jackson's Grill at the Springs ($$–$$$)	$75
Dinner for two without brew, tax, or tip at Beaver Street Brewery ($–$$)	$25
Pint of pale ale at the Mogollon Brewing Co.	$4
Per person admission to both Sunset Crater Volcano and Wupatki National Monuments	$5
Weekend all-day ski lift ticket at Snowbowl (adult)	$42
Ski lift to the top of Mt. Agassiz (Snowbowl) when there's no snow (adult)	$10

Transportation

To the cost of your plane ticket (see Chapter 6 for tips on getting a low airfare), add your rental car costs, which include the rental fee, taxes, and approximate gas expenses. (Estimate your gas expenses as close to departure time as possible; your guess is as good as mine as to what the price of gas will be when you're traveling.) Of course, you may decide to fly from location to location within the state, in which case transportation costs become an even larger percentage of your total trip costs. Check out Chapter 7 for details about flying within Arizona and for ways to keep rental car charges down.

Lodging

The cost of your lodging really depends on the type of accommodations you prefer — and when you're traveling. A fancy resort in Scottsdale during high season is going to take a huge bite out of your budget (more than airfare, even). You pay considerably less for a stay at a chain motel or modest B&B off-season. In general, summer is high season in northern Arizona, while winter is high season in southern Arizona. See Chapter 3 for details on both. See Chapter 8 for specifics about lodging categories and costs.

Dining

You have a wide range of dining options in Arizona — everything from Navajo tacos to gourmet New Southwestern fare (for the highlights, see Chapters 2 and 21) — and thus a wide range of dining prices. If you're traveling with children, you'll have no problem finding plenty of kid-friendly chains and unique Old West spots with loads of character.

In this book, I use dollar signs, ranging from $ to $$$$$, to express the relative cost of a meal for one in a restaurant (including appetizer, entree, and dessert). Across Arizona, you can find a low-key (and low-cost) dinner, including, in some cases, authentic Mexican food, for $10 or under per person (the $ range). Move up to the $$ range, which runs you $25 or under per person, and you have an even wider choice of non-chain, non-pizza options. Outside of Greater Phoenix, Tucson, and Sedona, an evening meal at even the most expensive restaurants shouldn't run you more than $45 apiece ($$$), sans that bottle of Dom Perignon champagne. Even in the big cities, most good restaurants fall into that category. If you want to try the real upscale joints, the domains of cutting-edge chefs, you can expect to pay up to $60 ($$$$), and (rarely) more than $60 ($$$$$), which still isn't nearly as much as you'd pay for an equivalent meal in, say, New York City, Chicago, or San Francisco.

When budgeting for meals on an American Indian reservation, you don't need to include the cost of alcohol, because it isn't served.

Sightseeing

You won't break the bank visiting Arizona's top sights. Very few attractions in the state cost more than $10. (The Grand Canyon entry fee is $20 per vehicle, not per person, for example — and the price is good for one week.) You also find lots of free (or close to it) stuff to do in the state. Visiting Saguaro National Park West won't cost you a dime, nor will a trip to many of the museums on the University of Arizona campus — to offer just two Tucson examples.

Recreation and tours, on the other hand, can take you into rough financial terrain. Greens fees are very expensive at the top resort golf courses (as high as $250), spa treatments start at about $75 for 50 minutes, and a hot-air-balloon adventure in Sedona runs you $175 — to name just a few possibilities. Some activities, such as helicopter rides and Jeep tours, are never discounted, but prices for others, like golf, go way down in the off-season. And you can save on other items, such as spa treatments, if you book them as part of a hotel package (see Chapter 8 for details).

Shopping

Shopping is the real wild card in your vacation budget. Big-ticket items may include Western art and some Indian crafts. If you've always wanted a Navajo rug, you won't find a better place to buy one than in Arizona, but they can get pricey.

Rugs aside, you can find plenty to buy in Arizona that won't destroy your budget — pretty tinwork candlesticks from Mexico, for example (see Chapter 19). You can even consider a great pair of cowboy boots, which you may ultimately get a lot of use out of (I sure do out of mine).

Nightlife

Keeping your costs down when it comes to evening activities is no problem. Phoenix and Tucson have plenty of shows and concerts to see, and tickets won't cost you an arm and a leg (rarely above $45 for the best theater or ballet seats). In the same way, a couple of beers at a cowboy bar won't set you back a whole lot, and you can easily spend the entire evening in the big cities enjoying dinner in a celebrated restaurant. And gazing at all those wonderful stars up in the sky is absolutely free.

One-click bargain shopping

The Arizona Office of Tourism has set up a Web site to help you find bargains for everything from airfare to golf, restaurants, and lodging. Log on to `www.arizonavacationvalues.com` and — *ka-ching!* — start calculating those savings.

Cutting Costs — But Not the Fun

The destination chapters in Parts III and IV all include money-saving tips specific to those places. In this section, I give you some additional general advice — and it's free, too (talk about bargains!).

- Go off-season. Luckily, somewhere in Arizona is always off-season. If you visit southern Arizona in summer or northern Arizona in winter, you can cut room costs by as much as 50%; prices on activities like greens fees on golf courses go way down, too.
- Travel midweek. If you can travel on a Tuesday, Wednesday, or Thursday, you may find cheaper flights to your destination. When you ask about airfares, see if you can get a cheaper rate by flying on a different day. For more tips on getting a good fare, see Chapter 6.
- Check the package tours. Not many air/hotel/sightseeing bundlings exist for travelers to Arizona (see Chapter 6), but many resorts offer special packages that may include amenities like greens fees at their on-site courses, spa treatments, breakfast, champagne — you name it. Always ask when you're booking a room if the hotel has any deals; they may just fit your interests to a tee.
- Reserve a room with a refrigerator and coffeemaker. You don't have to slave over a hot stove to cut a few costs; several motels have minifridges and coffeemakers. Buying supplies for breakfast will save you money — and probably calories.
- Invest in a cheap cooler. You'll quickly recover the costs if you buy large bottles of water and 12-packs of soft drinks from a grocery store rather than buying individual drinks at more expensive roadside convenience stores or the hotel minibar. You may even give the cooler away to someone at the end of your trip — or to the clerk at the car rental company; most everyone in this state can use an extra ice chest.
- Always ask for discount rates. Membership in AAA, frequent-flier plans, trade unions, AARP, or other groups may qualify you for savings on car rentals, plane tickets, hotel rooms, and even meals. Ask about everything; you may be pleasantly surprised.
- Ask if your kids can stay in the room with you. A room with two double beds usually doesn't cost any more than one with a queen-size bed. And many hotels won't charge you the additional person rate if the additional person is pint-size and related to you. Even if you have to pay $10 or $15 extra for a rollaway bed, you'll save hundreds by not taking two rooms.
- Try expensive restaurants at lunch instead of dinner. In the Phoenix area and in Tucson, a lunch tab at a top restaurant is usually far lower than a dinner tab, although the menu often has many of the same specialties.

- Don't rent a gas guzzler. Renting a smaller car is cheaper, and you save on gas to boot. Unless you're traveling with kids and need lots of space, don't go beyond the economy size.
- Cut back on the costly activities and tours. If you're a golfer, eliminate one round — or try a municipal course instead of a resort course. If you're the independent type, buy a book about something you're interested in — Old West history, say, or desert plants — and devise a self-guided driving tour or a hike rather than paying for a guide or something expensive like a helicopter fly-by.
- Rein in the trinkets. As I discuss in the "Shopping" section earlier in this chapter, I wouldn't suggest you cut out consuming altogether; just be sure to plan for it and don't bother with items you can get anywhere, like key chains and T-shirts.

Handling Money

You're the best judge of how much cash you feel comfortable carrying or what alternative form of currency is your favorite. That's not going to change much on your vacation to Arizona. True, you probably are moving around more and incurring more expenses than you generally do (unless you happen to eat out every meal when you're at home), and you may let your mind slip into vacation gear and not be as vigilant about your safety as when you're in work mode. But, those factors aside, the only type of payment that won't be quite as available to you away from home is your personal checkbook.

The only parts of Arizona where the rules change slightly are on the American Indian reservations in the northeast, where not all the crafts vendors or tour operators take credit cards, and cash machines are fewer and farther between. If you travel to that part of the state, you may want to have more cash with you than in the other areas, especially if you plan to buy crafts.

Using ATMs and carrying cash

These days, far more people use ATMs than traveler's checks. Most cities have handy 24-hour cash machines linked to an international network that almost always includes your bank at home. Cirrus (☎ 800-424-7787; `www.mastercard.com`) and Plus (☎ 800-843-7587; `www.visa.com`) are the two most popular networks. Check the back of your ATM card to see which network your bank belongs to. The toll-free numbers and Web sites give specific locations of ATMs where you can withdraw money while on vacation. You can use them to withdraw just the money you need every couple of days, which eliminates the insecurity (and the pickpocketing threat) of carrying around a large green stash. Of course, many ATMs are little money managers (or dictators, depending on how you look at it), imposing limits on your spending by allowing you to withdraw only a certain amount of money — a maximum of $200, say — per day. Check with your bank before you leave to see if it has a maximum daily withdrawal limit.

Using ATMs in Arizona is as safe and convenient as can be. You find cash dispensers not only in banks, which are everywhere in the big cities, but also in shopping malls, in late- or all-night supermarkets, and even in bank drive-throughs. In short, the Grand Canyon state has no shortage of places to get the green stuff.

One important reminder before you go ATM crazy, however. Many banks now charge a fee ranging from 50¢ to $3 whenever nonaccount holders use their ATMs. Your own bank may also assess a fee for using an ATM that's not one of its branch locations. In some cases you get charged twice just for using your bankcard when you're on vacation. Reverting to traveler's checks may be cheaper (although certainly less convenient to obtain and use).

How do you decide whether ATMs are for you? Call your local bank and find out whether it has branches in Arizona. Many are represented in the state, especially in Greater Phoenix and Tucson. Bank of America, Bank One, and Wells Fargo are particularly ubiquitous.

Doting on debit cards

Another way of working with money you have — as opposed to the theoretical money of credit cards — is by using a debit card (an ATM card with a credit card logo). In many cases, your debit and ATM card are the same piece of plastic. Instead of getting cash, however, the debit card pays for purchases anywhere a credit card is accepted. The advantage? The money comes out of your checking account rather than pushing up against your credit card limit. Plus, you never pay an additional fee to use it, and you don't have to carry a lot of cash around.

Charging ahead with credit cards

Credit cards are a safe way to carry money, and they provide a convenient record of all your travel expenses when you arrive home. The disadvantage, of course, is that they're easy to overuse. Unlike ATM or debit cards, which are directly connected to the money you have in your checking account, credit cards can take you as far as your credit limit — which may not bear much relation to your actual financial resources — can go. Credit cards let you indulge in more impulse buying than any other form of payment.

You can also get cash advances off your credit card at any ATM if you know your Personal Identification Number (PIN). If you've forgotten it or didn't even know you had a PIN, call the phone number on the back of your credit card and ask the bank to send the number to you. You typically receive the number in about five to seven business days. Some banks can give you your PIN over the phone if you tell them your mother's maiden name or provide some other security clearance.

I never get a cash advance from my credit card except in emergencies. Interest rates for cash advances are often significantly higher than rates for credit-card purchases. More important, you start paying interest on the advance the moment you receive the cash. On airline-affiliated credit cards, a cash advance doesn't earn frequent-flier miles.

My personal travel strategy? I put as much money into my checking account as I can spare before I leave and use my ATM/debit card as much as possible. I save my credit card for planned purchases that I know I can pay off in full.

Toting traveler's checks

These days, traveler's checks are less necessary because most cities have 24-hour ATMs that allow you to withdraw small amounts of cash as needed. However, keep in mind that you will likely be charged an ATM withdrawal fee if the bank is not your own, so if you're withdrawing money every day, you may be better off with traveler's checks — provided that you don't mind showing identification every time you want to cash one.

You can get traveler's checks at almost any bank. American Express offers denominations of $20, $50, $100, $500, and (for cardholders only) $1,000. You'll pay a service charge ranging from 1% to 4%. You can also get American Express traveler's checks over the phone by calling ☎ 800-221-7282; Amex gold and platinum cardholders who use this number are exempt from the 1% fee.

Visa offers traveler's checks at Citibank locations nationwide, as well as at several other banks. The service charge ranges between 1.5% and 2%; checks come in denominations of $20, $50, $100, $500, and $1,000. Call ☎ 800-732-1322 for information. AAA members can obtain Visa checks without a fee at most AAA offices or by calling ☎ 866-339-3378. MasterCard also offers traveler's checks. Call ☎ 800-223-9920 for a location near you.

If you choose to carry traveler's checks, be sure to keep a record of their serial numbers separate from your checks in the event that they are stolen or lost. You'll get a refund faster if you know the numbers

Dealing with a Lost or Stolen Wallet

Be sure to contact all of your credit card companies the minute you discover your wallet has been lost or stolen and file a report at the nearest police precinct. Your credit card company or insurer may require a police report number or record of the loss. Most credit card companies have an emergency toll-free number to call if your card is lost or stolen; yours may be able to wire you a cash advance immediately or deliver an emergency credit card in a day or two. Call the following emergency numbers in the United States:

- American Express ☎ 800-221-7282 (for cardholders and traveler's check holders)
- MasterCard ☎ 800-307-7309 or 636-722-7111
- Visa ☎ 800-847-2911 or 410-581-9994

For other credit cards, call the toll-free number directory at ☎ 800-555-1212.

Chapter 6

Getting to Arizona

In This Chapter

- Winging it to Arizona
- Riding the wheels and rails
- Exploring package tours and escorted tours

Figuring out how to approach your Arizona vacation is one of the toughest — and earliest — decisions you need to make about your trip. You may want to be totally independent, reserving your own airfare and accommodations and plotting out your day-to-day itinerary. Or you may prefer to seek professional help, say, by going to a travel agent, or going on an escorted tour, where most of the decisions are made for you. Whatever the reason you want to make your own arrangements, this chapter supplies some basic transportation data.

Flying to Arizona

Flying in and out of Arizona couldn't be easier — international airports in both Phoenix and Tucson are served by numerous airlines. This section focuses on the best strategies for booking your flight to Arizona.

Finding out which airlines fly there

You won't have a problem flying into Arizona's capital: Phoenix Sky Harbor International Airport (www.phxskyharbor.com) is served by several major and commuter airlines (Table 6-1 lists them all), with nonstop service to and from nearly 100 cities in the United States and around the world. Phoenix is a hub for America West Airlines and Southwest Airlines. Nonstop international service is provided by Aeromexico (to and from Mexico), British Airways (to and from London-Gatwick Airport), Air Canada (to and from Toronto), and America West (to and from Calgary, Edmonton, Toronto, Vancouver, and destinations in Mexico).

You have fewer options if you want to fly directly to Tucson International Airport (www.tucsonairport.org). U.S. carriers serving this airport currently offer nonstop flights to only Albuquerque, Atlanta, Chicago, Dallas, Denver, Houston, Las Vegas, Los Angeles, Minneapolis, Newark, Phoenix, Salt Lake City, San Diego, and Seattle/Tacoma.

Table 6-1 Airlines That Fly into Arizona

Airline	*Web Site*	*Toll-Free Number*
Aeromexico	www.aeromexico.com	**800-237-6639**
Air Canada	www.aircanada.ca	**888-247-2262**
Alaska Airlines*	www.alaskaair.com	**800-426-0333**
Aloha Airlines	www.alohaairlines.com	**800-367-5250**
America West Airlines*	www.americawest.com	**800-235-9292**
American Airlines*	www.aa.com	**800-433-7300**
American Trans Air	www.ata.com	**800-225-2995**
Arizona Express	www.azxpress.com	**866-435-9872**
British Airways	www.british-airways.com	**800-247-9297**
Continental Airlines*	www.continental.com	**800-525-0280**
Delta Air Lines*	www.delta.com	**800-221-1212**
Frontier Airlines*	www.flyfrontier.com	**800-432-1359**
Great Lakes	www.greatlakesav.com	**800-554-5111**
Hawaiian Airlines	www.hawaiianair.com	**800-367-5320**
Midwest Airlines	www.midwestairlines.com	**800-452-2022**
Northwest Airlines*	www.nwa.com	**800-225-2525**
Southwest Airlines*	www.southwest.com	**800-435-9792**
Sun Country	www.suncountry.com	**800-359-6786**
United Airlines*	www.united.com	**800-241-6522**
US Airways	www.usairways.com	**800-428-4322**

**Offers service to both Phoenix and Tucson*

Getting the best deal on your airfare

Competition among the major U.S. airlines is unlike that of any other industry. Every airline offers virtually the same product (basically, a coach seat is a coach seat is a . . .), yet prices can vary by hundreds of dollars.

Business travelers who need the flexibility to buy their tickets at the last minute and change their itinerary at a moment's notice, and who want to get home before the weekend, pay (or at least their companies pay) the premium rate, known as the full fare. But if you can book your ticket well in advance, stay over Saturday night, or are willing to travel on a Tuesday, Wednesday, or Thursday, you can qualify for the least expensive price — usually a fraction of the full fare. On most flights, even the shortest hops within the United States, a 7- or 14-day advance purchase ticket may cost less than half of the full amount. Obviously, planning ahead pays.

The airlines also periodically hold sales in which they lower the prices on their most popular routes. These fares have advance purchase requirements and date-of-travel restrictions, but you can't beat the prices. As you plan your vacation, keep your eyes open for these sales, which tend to take place in seasons of low travel volume. You almost never see a sale around the peak summer vacation months of July and August, or around Thanksgiving or Christmas, when many people fly, regardless of the fare they have to pay.

Consolidators, also known as bucket shops, buy seats in bulk from the airlines and then sell them back to the public. Their prices are often lower than those your travel agent can get you. You see consolidators' ads in the small boxes at the bottom of the page in your Sunday-newspaper travel section.

Bucket shop tickets are usually nonrefundable or rigged with stiff cancellation penalties, often as high as 50% to 75% of the ticket price, and some put you on charter airlines with questionable safety records.

Several reliable consolidators are worldwide and available on the Net. STA Travel (☎ 800-781-4040; `www.statravel.com`), the world's leader in student travel, offers good fares for travelers of all ages. FlyCheap (☎ 800-FLY-CHEAP; `www.1800flycheap.com`) is owned by package-holiday megalith MyTravel and so has especially good access to fares for sunny destinations. Air Tickets Direct (☎ 800-778-3447; `www.airticketsdirect.com`) is based in Montreal and leverages the currently weak Canadian dollar for low fares; it'll also book trips to places that U.S. travel agents won't touch, such as Cuba.

Because competition among carriers for Phoenix air space is so much greater than for the sky above Tucson, you're most likely to get the lowest fares if you fly into Phoenix's Sky Harbor airport. If you're pressed for time, flying directly to Tucson may be worthwhile (if, of course, Tucson is your ultimate destination). But keep in mind that an hourly shuttle runs from Sky Harbor to Tucson. The trip takes about two hours each way and costs less than $45, round-trip (Chapter 13 has more info on the shuttle).

Booking your flight online

The "big three" online travel agencies, Expedia (www.expedia.com), Travelocity (www.travelocity.com), and Orbitz (www.orbitz.com) sell most of the air tickets bought on the Internet. (Canadian travelers should try www.expedia.ca and www.travelocity.ca; U.K. residents can go for expedia.co.uk and opodo.co.uk.) Each has different business deals with the airlines and may offer different fares on the same flights, so shopping around is wise. Expedia and Travelocity will also send you an e-mail notification when a cheap fare becomes available to your favorite destination. Of the smaller travel agency Web sites, SideStep (www.sidestep.com) receives good reviews from users. It's a browser add-on that purports to "search 140 sites at once," but in reality only beats competitors' fares as often as other sites do.

Great last-minute deals are available through free weekly e-mail services provided directly by the airlines. Most of these deals are announced on Tuesday or Wednesday and must be purchased online. Most are only valid for travel that weekend, but some (such as Southwest's) can be booked weeks or months in advance. Sign up for weekly e-mail alerts at airline Web sites or check mega-sites that compile comprehensive lists of last-minute specials, such as Smarter Living (smarterliving.com). For last-minute trips, **www.site59.com** in the United States and **www.lastminute.com** in Europe often have better deals than the major-label sites.

If you're willing to give up some control over your flight details, use an opaque fare service like Priceline (www.priceline.com) or Hotwire (www.hotwire.com). Both offer rock-bottom prices in exchange for travel on a "mystery airline" at a mysterious time of day, often with a mysterious change of planes en route. The mystery airlines are all major, well-known carriers — and the possibility of being sent from Philadelphia to Chicago via Tampa is remote. But your chances of getting a 6 a.m. or 11 p.m. flight are pretty high. Hotwire tells you flight prices before you buy; Priceline usually has better deals than Hotwire, but you have to play its name-our-price game. Note: In 2004, Priceline added non-opaque service to its roster. You now have the option to pick exact flights, times, and airlines from a list of offers — or opt to bid on opaque fares as before.

Driving to Arizona

Driving to Arizona is a fine idea if you live in the southern sections of California, Nevada, Utah, or Colorado, or in western New Mexico — or if you have a few weeks to spare for a major road trip. You can save money on car rental fees and throw everything you can possibly need into the trunk or the back of your van. You can definitely make good connections: I-40 runs through the state in the north, and I-10 traverses it (going through both Phoenix and Tucson) in the south. Phoenix is 369 miles from Los Angeles, 455 miles from Albuquerque, 660 miles from Salt Lake City, and 287 miles from Las Vegas.

Arriving by Train

Two Amtrak (☎ 800-USA-RAIL; `www.amtrak.com`) routes service Arizona. The Southwest Chief, which runs between Chicago and Los Angeles, stops in Flagstaff once a day from each direction, while the Sunset Limited from Orlando to Los Angeles stops in Tucson three days a week in each direction. Both routes offer shuttle buses to Phoenix, because no trains travel directly to the capital. You can tootle into Tucson or Flagstaff and rent a car there, or even continue on to the Grand Canyon from Flagstaff and explore the region via a bus tour (see Chapter 7). Riding the rails isn't the most time-effective method of travel, nor is it necessarily the most economical, but the train is relaxing (no need to worry about getting lost or experiencing air turbulence) and, for many folks, it's loads of fun.

Joining an Escorted Tour

You may be one of the many people who loves escorted tours. The tour company takes care of the details, and tells you what to expect at each leg of your journey. You know your costs up front and, in the case of the tamer trips, you don't get many surprises. Escorted tours can take you to the maximum number of sights in the minimum amount of time with the least amount of hassle.

If you decide to go with an escorted tour, consider buying travel insurance, especially if the tour operator asks you to pay up front. But don't buy insurance from the tour operator. You have no reason to expect that the operator will meet his or her insurance obligations if he or she can't even provide you with the vacation you paid for. Buy travel insurance through an independent agency. (I tell you more about the ins and outs of travel insurance in Chapter 10.)

When choosing an escorted tour, find out whether you have to put down a deposit and when a final payment is due. Then ask a few simple questions before you buy:

- What is the cancellation policy? Can the operator cancel the trip if it doesn't get enough people? How late can you cancel if you're unable to go? Do you get a refund if you cancel? If the operator cancels?

- How jam-packed is the schedule? Does the tour schedule try to fit 25 hours into a 24-hour day, or does it give you ample time to relax by the pool or shop? If getting up at 7 a.m. every day and not returning to your hotel until 6 or 7 p.m. at night sounds like a grind, certain escorted tours may not be for you.
- How large is the group? The smaller the group, the less time you spend waiting for people to get on and off the bus. Tour operators may be evasive about the group size, because they may not know the exact size until everybody has made reservations, but they can give you a rough estimate.
- Does the group have a minimum size? Some tours have a minimum group size and may cancel the tour if the company doesn't book enough people. If a quota exists, find out what it is and how close the operator is to reaching it. Again, tour operators may be evasive in their answers, but the information may help you select a tour that's sure to happen.
- What exactly is included? Don't assume anything. You may have to pay to get yourself to and from the airport. A box lunch may be included in an excursion, but drinks may be extra. Beer may be included but not wine. How much flexibility do you have? Can you opt out of certain activities, or does the bus leave once a day, with no exceptions? Are all your meals planned in advance? Can you choose your entree at dinner, or does everybody get the same chicken cutlet?

Depending on your recreational passions, I recommend one of the following tour companies:

- Maupintour (☎ 800-255-4266; www.maupintour.com), which has been in business since 1951, offers vacations for the general-interest traveler. Maupin offers an eight-day bus package that includes the Grand Canyon, Monument Valley, Lake Powell, Canyon de Chelly, Sedona, and a resort in Scottsdale, among other places. The price of $1,799 per person (based on double occupancy) includes transportation between sights, guides, food, and accommodations, but not airfare.
- GORPtravel (☎ 877-440-4677; http://gorptravel.away.com), on the other hand, specializes in adventure. You can choose anything from a three-day hiking, walking, mountain biking trip in northern Arizona ($600, including base-camp accommodations, equipment, local transportation, and camping meals) to a six-day hiking trip around southeast Arizona, with visits to the historic copper mining towns ($1,455, including all nights at inns or B&Bs, all meals, and guide service). Again, airfare is extra, and you usually pay an extra fee for single occupancy.

In addition, see Chapter 9, where I outline a few special-interest escorted tours.

Choosing a Package Tour

For many destinations, package tours can be a smart way to go. In many cases, a package tour that includes airfare, hotel, and transportation to and from the airport costs less than the hotel alone on a tour you book yourself. That's because packages are sold in bulk to tour operators, who resell them to the public. A package tour is kind of like buying your vacation at a buy-in-bulk store — except the tour operator is the one who buys the 1,000-count box of garbage bags and resells them ten at a time at a cost that undercuts the local supermarket.

Package tours can vary as much as those garbage bags, too. Some offer a better class of hotels than others, while some provide the same hotels for lower prices. Some book flights on scheduled airlines; others sell charters. In some packages, your choice of accommodations and travel days may be limited. Some let you choose between escorted vacations and independent vacations, while others allow you to add on just a few excursions or escorted day-trips (also at discounted prices) without booking an entirely escorted tour.

In Arizona, the resorts (see Chapter 8) tend to have good package deals, often throwing in activities, such as golf and spa treatments, with the room rates (especially during the off season). But for packages with more variety, your best options are from airlines: America West Vacations (☎ 800-TO-FLYAWV; www.americawestvacations.com) has the best selection, hands down, with a wide range of departure cities, hotel/rental car choices, and Arizona destinations to chose from, including the Grand Canyon Canyon, Sedona, Tucson, and the Valley of the Sun. American Airlines Vacations (☎ 800-321-2121; www.aavacations.com) comes in second, traveling to the same destinations but offering fewer hotel choices and rental car options.

If you live in or near Minneapolis/St.Paul, you may want to consider packages from Sun Country (☎ 800-FLY-N-SUN; www.suncountry.com), a small airline that runs vacations from Minnesota to Phoenix.

A good way to find package tours is to check the travel section of your local Sunday newspaper and the ads in the back of national travel magazines such as Travel & Leisure, National Geographic Traveler, and Condé Nast Traveler. Liberty Travel (call ☎ 888-271-1584 to find the store nearest you; www.libertytravel.com) is one of the biggest packagers in the Northeast and usually boasts a full-page ad in Sunday papers.

Chapter 7

Getting Around Arizona

In This Chapter

- Exploring the state by car
- Flying between destinations
- Taking the train
- Considering the bus

So what's the best way to see Arizona? That depends on your time frame, bank account, and interests. If you want to visit just the Grand Canyon in the north and Tucson in the south and are more strapped for time than funds, you may want to take to the skies. If you're like most people, however, you want to see more, and at eye level, which brings you to the most popular way to get around — the car. This chapter discusses all of your major options, including traveling by car, plane, train, and bus.

By Car

Wheels are by far the best way to tool around this large state. In Arizona, the car rules, which is why the longest section of this chapter is devoted to roadways and the wheelings and dealings of acquiring a rental car.

Navigating highways and byways

For the most part, Arizona roads are modern and well-maintained — just what you would expect in the wide-open Southwest. I-40 and I-10 are the main east-west thoroughfares, traversing the northern and southern portions of the state, respectively. They're linked between Phoenix and Flagstaff by I-17, which, despite the "I" in its name, isn't an interstate. The speed limit on these three arteries, all four- to six-lane divided highways, is 75 mph, except on curvy stretches and around towns and cities.

Be very careful when driving through Native American lands. Not all the livestock on the reservations is fenced in, and cows and goats often wander out on the road. Not only is hitting an animal dangerous and unpleasant (not to mention sad), but you also have to pay a hefty fee to the owner for destroying private property.

In desert areas, you may be surprised to see signs reading DO NOT ENTER WHEN FLOODED. Take them seriously. The area may be bone-dry 99% of the time, but flash floods occur, well, in a flash — as do drownings of people who drive into washes that suddenly fill up with water.

Other road hazards include dust storms, kicked up by fast-moving winds. Pull over if the visibility is too low.

Finally, fill 'er up often. Gas stations are as many as 60 miles apart in some places. Keep extra water in your car if you're traveling in the desert. You don't know when both you and your car may overheat.

Renting a car

The good news is that every car rental company you can think of — and some you've probably never heard of — is represented in Arizona, so rates are fairly competitive. Advantage, Alamo, Avis, Budget, Courtesy, Dollar, Enterprise, Hertz, and National (see the appendix for toll-free numbers and Web sites) all have rental counters in the terminals at Phoenix Sky Harbor Airport, and several others are on the airport's grounds.

Getting the best deal

Car rental rates vary even more than airline fares. The price depends on the size of the car, the length of time you keep it, where and when you pick it up and drop it off, where you take it, and a host of other factors. Asking a few key questions may save you hundreds of dollars.

- Weekend rates may be lower than weekday rates. If you're keeping the car five or more days, a weekly rate may be cheaper than the daily rate. Ask whether the rate is the same for pickup Friday morning as it is Thursday night.
- Many companies assess a drop-off charge if you don't return the car to the same rental location; others, notably National, don't do levy this fee.
- Check whether the rate is cheaper if you pick up the car at a location in town. Both Tucson and Phoenix add on a hefty concession recovery fee if you rent at the airport.
- Find out whether age is an issue. Many car rental companies add on a fee for drivers under 25, while some don't rent to them at all.
- If you see an advertised price in your local newspaper, ask for that specific rate; otherwise you may be charged the standard (higher) rate. Don't forget to mention membership in AAA, AARP, frequent-flier programs, and trade unions. These memberships usually entitle you to discounts ranging from 5% to 30%.

- Check your frequent-flier accounts. Your favorite (or at least most-used) airline is likely to have sent you discount coupons.
- As with other aspects of planning your trip, using the Internet can make comparison shopping for a car rental much easier. You can check rates at the major agencies' Web sites. Plus, all the major travel sites — Travelocity (`www.travelocity.com`), Expedia (`www.expedia.com`), Orbitz (`www.orbitz.com`), and Smarter Living (`www.smarterliving.com`), for example — have search engines that can dig up discounted car rental rates. Just enter the car size you want, the pickup and return dates, and location, and the server returns a price. You can even make the reservation through any of these sites.

In addition to the standard rental prices, other optional charges apply to most car rentals (and some not-so-optional charges, such as taxes). The Collision Damage Waiver (CDW), which requires you to pay for damage to the car in a collision, is covered by many credit card companies. Check with your credit card company before you go, so you can avoid paying this hefty fee (as much as $20 a day). CDWs are illegal in some states, but not in Arizona.

The car rental companies also offer additional liability insurance (if you harm others in an accident), personal accident insurance (if you harm yourself or your passengers), and personal effects insurance (if your luggage is stolen from your car). Your insurance policy on your car at home probably covers most of these unlikely occurrences. However, if your own insurance doesn't cover you for rentals or if you don't have auto insurance, definitely consider the additional coverage (ask your car rental agent for more information). Unless you're toting around the Hope Diamond, and you don't want to leave that in your car trunk anyway, you can probably skip the personal effects insurance, but driving around without liability or personal accident coverage is never a good idea. Even if you're a good driver, other people may not be, and liability claims can be complicated.

Some companies also offer refueling packages, in which you pay for your initial full tank of gas up front, and can return the car with an empty gas tank. The prices can be competitive with local gas prices, but you don't get credit for any gas remaining in the tank. If you reject this option, you pay only for the gas you use, but you have to return the car with a full tank or face charges of $3 to $4 a gallon for any shortfall. In my experience, gas prices in the refueling packages are at the high end, and I always find myself trying to drive the car in on fumes so I don't pay for an extra drop of fuel. So, I prefer to forgo the refueling package and always allow plenty of time for refueling en route to the car rental return. However, if you usually run late and a fueling stop may make you miss your plane, you're a perfect candidate for the fuel-purchase option.

The two most likely places to rent a car are Phoenix Sky Harbor Airport and Tucson International Airport. Additional costs include county tax

Comparing car costs

I made price-comparison calls to three rental companies for Phoenix and Tucson airports. Clearly, shopping around pays. Sample prices are weekly rates for an economy car with unlimited mileage and without taxes or special discounts. ***Note:*** None of the rental companies sampled accepted drivers under age 25.

Budget

- Phoenix: $238
- Tucson: $142

$25 per day per additional driver (other than spouse, for whom there is no extra charge)

Hertz

- Phoenix: $275
- Tucson: $265

$7 per day per additional driver (maximum $35)

Avis

- Phoenix: $229
- Tucson: $196

$25 one-time fee for additional driver (other than spouse)

(3.25% of the total in Phoenix and $3.50 per day in Tucson); city tax (15.1% in Phoenix, 10.6% in Tucson); customer facility fee ($4.50 per day in Phoenix, $3.50 per day in Tucson); and the aforementioned concession recovery fee — the extra charge for renting at the airport (11.11% in both Phoenix and Tucson).

If you plan to base yourself in either Phoenix or Tucson, renting a car at your hotel (if such an option exists), rather than at the airport, makes sense. The cost of a shuttle or cab to and from the airport may well be less than the extra tax on your rental car. Your hotel may even provide a free airport shuttle.

By Plane

America West Express (☎ 800-235-9292; `www.americawest.com`) offers most of the short hops around the state. Of the destinations I cover in this book, America West offers flights from Phoenix's Sky Harbor to Flagstaff, Lake Havasu, Prescott, Page, and Tucson. These flights rarely exceed $200 with a 21-day advance purchase and a Saturday night stay-over. Great Lakes Aviation (☎ 800-554-5111; `www.greatlakesav.com`)

services Page from Sky Harbor; flights cost roughly $165 round-trip with a 14-day advance purchase. Feeling flush? Westwind Aviation (☎ 888-869-0866; www.westwindaviation.com) runs charters from Phoenix's Deer Valley Airport to anywhere in Arizona and the Southwest.

Flying into Prescott or Flagstaff isn't an especially time- and cost-effective option. If you make good connections, these half-hour flights may be useful, but neither of these fairly scenic drives takes more than about 2½ hours. Plus, you don't have the hassle of changing planes. Whether the time you save is sufficient to warrant the extra expense is a toss-up.

If you're more time- than budget-conscious and are primarily interested in touring the Grand Canyon's North Rim and Native American country, I definitely recommend the Phoenix-Page hop. And if you're determined to see London Bridge in a time pinch, you might want to fly from Sky Harbor to Lake Havasu.

By Train

Although arriving by train is fine, riding the rails isn't a useful way to get around. The exception is the service to the Grand Canyon from Williams on the Grand Canyon Railway (☎ 800-THE-TRAIN; www.thetrain.com), which combines recreation with a very good means of transportation — you get the canyon without the parking hassle. For train schedules and fares, see Chapter 17.

By Bus

You can get to plenty of places in Arizona by bus — but you end up at a bus station without a car. The most useful buses are the various shuttle buses from the Phoenix airport to places where you can rent wheels, including Tucson, Sedona, Prescott, and Flagstaff (see the "Getting There" sections in Chapters 13, 15, and 17 for more on the shuttles).

Chapter 8

Booking Your Accommodations

In This Chapter

- Choosing an Arizona bunk
- Getting the best deal on your lodging

You don't often find a state with as wide a range of accommodations and with as many different price categories as Arizona. This chapter sketches your many lodging options, and then suggests ways for you to book them without paying top dollar.

Getting to Know Your Options

Arizona's wide range of room types gives the traveler plenty of options. The only types of Arizona accommodations I don't cover in this book are campsites — I assume you want a hard roof over your head — and youth hostels. If you're interested in details about where to pitch a tent or sleep dorm-style, consult a more comprehensive guide, such as Frommer's Arizona (Wiley Publishing, Inc.).

Also, except in B&Bs, most of which are totally nonsmoking, you can expect hotels and resorts in Arizona to offer smoking rooms (or rooms with balconies or patios that you can smoke on).

From the highest to the lowest prices, lodgings in Arizona include the following sections. Table 8-1 also gives a brief summation of what you can expect in each price category. Rates are based on double occupancy for one night during high season (see Chapter 3).

Table 8-1 Key to Hotel Dollar Signs

Dollar Sign(s)	*Price Range*	*What to Expect*
$	Less than $100	Many of the chain motels fall into this category. Expect decent amenities (often irons, coffeemakers, and even dataport phones) but basic decor. At historic lodgings in this price range, rooms tend to be small and, in some cases, TV- or phone-less. Baths will be in the room, but the plumbing may not be quiet.
$$	$101–$200	Mid-range chain hotels are likely to offer more convenient locations than those in the $ range, as well as slightly better in-room amenities (maybe microwaves) and outdoor recreation facilities (a larger pool). Expect TVs and nice bath products at the B&Bs and historic hotels that fall into this category.
$$$	$201–$300	Here, in the lower-end resort and higher-end inn range, accommodations begin to look plush. Think chocolates on your pillow, a decent restaurant, or an exercise room (or, in the case of B&Bs and historic hotels, privileges at a nearby health club).
$$$$	$301–$400	These top-rated — and top-priced — lodgings come with luxury amenities such as valet parking, major spa, golf and tennis courts, and a restaurant where the chef may have won a James Beard award.
$$$$$	More than $400	As with the properties in the previous categories, expect amenities out the wazoo. Add a staff that knows your name (and possibly birthday) and caters to your every whim.

Destination spas

These healthful retreats are where you go to have both mind and body attended to. Stay at a destination spa, and you don't have to pay for anything beyond what's included in your original room package: all meals and snacks (healthy, of course), classes, activities, and a certain number of spa treatments. No need to rent a car, because you have no reason to leave the premises. All the rooms at destination spas fall into the $$$$$ category.

Resorts

Most hotels and motels are designed to keep guests happy for a night or two, but resorts have a more ambitious mandate: They want to keep you playing — and paying — for more extended periods. Arizona's top resorts, primarily located in Scottsdale and Tucson, fulfill that role to a tee (literally). You can expect at least one great golf course on the premises (or, barring that, privileges at a few exclusive ones nearby), along with a pool complex, exercise facilities, tennis courts, spa — and some of the best restaurants and bars in the state.

Resorts also know that you may want to bring your family, so all have at least some kid-friendly recreational facilities. Many have elaborate children's programs as well. If they don't have baby-sitting or day-care facilities on the grounds, they can refer you to a place you can trust — after all, the resort's reputation is on the line.

Your room won't be anything to sneeze at, either. Accommodations and grounds are constantly being refreshed, and you can expect the latest in room decor and high-quality bath products. Standard amenities include room service (sometimes 24-hour), laundry/valet service (usually except for Sundays), minibars, hair dryers, irons/ironing boards, and dataports (often with a separate phone line). Robes and in-room wall safes are other semi-frequent features.

Naturally, none of these amenities comes cheap. Rack rates for most resort rooms are in the $$$$ to $$$$$ range, beginning about $250 in high season — at $400 in many Scottsdale locations. But almost every resort runs a variety of packages, throwing in spa treatments, golf, a bottle of champagne, breakfast in bed — pretty much any of the resort's services that you can think of, if you're willing to spend two nights or more. Because some resorts also cater to businesspeople, they may offer weekend specials.

Guest ranches

Once upon a time in the early 20th century, ranchers had the clever idea of renting out rooms to Easterners who were caught up in the romance of the West. These entrepreneurs got a bit of extra spending money, and the Easterners got fresh air and family fun. The heyday (or is that hay day?) of Arizona's dude ranches, now called guest ranches, may have passed, and many of the original ranches have shut down, but several remain, primarily around Tucson, southeast Arizona, and Wickenberg.

Guest ranches aren't as rustic as they used to be. You can expect private baths (not necessarily with bathtubs, but all have at least a shower) and basic bath amenities, such as soap and shampoo, but otherwise they vary widely. A few of the fancier ones may include hair dryers and irons, but they're very much the exception, not the rule. Similarly, a few guest ranches have added amenities like an exercise room or golf course, but far more typical are a swimming pool and low-tech recreation like volleyball, shuffleboard, and, of course, horseshoes. Kids always have plenty of stuff to do — everything from petting zoos to crafts centers to such activities as riding or roping contests. At night, expect cookouts, hayrides, singalongs, and other retro-Western activities.

Rates for a guest ranch stay are in the $$$$ to $$$$$ range, but they include three hearty, all-American meals (alcohol extra), two horseback rides a day (in most cases; a few ranches offer unlimited riding, while a few others charge extra for rides), and all other activities. Most charge lower rates for a full week, and if you're willing to stay put and relax, you won't have to shell out for a rental car.

Ranches often have a minimum stay, especially in high season, and many of them shut down for at least part of the summer, if not for all of June, July, and August. (Horses need a vacation, too, you know.)

Hotels, lodges, and inns

Arizona doesn't have many modern high-rise hotels, in part because new construction tends to go out (as in sprawling resorts or low-slung motels) rather than up. In the past, many hotels either tried to pretend they weren't in Arizona or got into the mood of their locales with a vengeance. As a result, you find a wonderful variety of historic lodgings in all shapes and sizes — everything from funky old Victorian mining hotels with no TVs in the rooms and, in some cases, shared baths, to rustic-elegant lodges that may no longer be luxurious but have the basics as well as loads of character, to once-chic hotels and inns with revamped rooms to include amenities matching the fanciest resorts.

That funky mining hotel is going to be in the $ category; the rustic, elegant lodge that provides, minimally, a private bath and TV, probably falls into the $$ or $$$ range; and the born-again chic inn or hotel that has been refitted with top-notch room amenities and modern on-site facilities, such as a spa, falls into the $$$$ or even $$$$$ price slot. The pricier hotels, like the resorts, do offer special packages.

Bed-and-breakfasts

If you automatically associate the words bed & breakfast with a certain British queen, you won't be entirely disappointed in Arizona B&Bs. But you can also find B&Bs far more characteristic of the state: one built of adobe in the Tucson desert, a former bordello that now rents rooms in Williams, even hogans (traditional Navajo homes) on the Navajo reservation. You find B&Bs scattered throughout the state, but the greatest concentrations are in Tucson and southeast Arizona and around Flagstaff, Prescott, and Sedona. The vast majority of Arizona's B&Bs tend to be comfortable but not luxurious. With a few exceptions, I don't recommend places with fewer than three rooms or ones that share baths (I specify where that's the case). You can expect full breakfasts — as opposed to continental spreads — at almost all of them, and prices are generally in the $$ category. The exception is Sedona, where the B&Bs tend to resemble small luxury inns. These boast high-tone touches — expensive bath toiletries, hair dryers, and individual breakfast menus — and rates to match: Most of Sedona's B&Bs fall into the $$$ to $$$$ slot.

In order to have room for the top choices in a variety of lodging categories, I don't include all the good B&Bs in the state, but if you're particularly interested in this type of lodging, contact the Arizona Association of Bed & Breakfast Inns (P.O. Box 22086, Flagstaff, AZ 86002, ☎ 800-284-2589; www.arizona-bed-breakfast.com), which has strict membership guidelines.

Chain hotels

You pretty much have your pick of chain lodgings throughout Arizona. I can't think of a single area that doesn't have at least a few links (and I don't mean golf courses). See the appendix for the toll-free numbers for those chains represented in the state. Rooms are generally in the $ or, at the most, $$ price range.

Remember that not all links of a chain are necessarily alike. In Arizona, for example, several Best Western hotels (including one in Tucson and one in Wickenburg) have loads of historic character. The granting of a franchise by a corporate office only means the franchisee has to live up to certain standards; it doesn't mean that the rooms have to be cookie-cutter alike. That cuts both ways, of course: If the corporate headquarters doesn't impose strict and frequent quality checks on its members, you may love the Hotel X in St. Louis, but be disappointed by the one in Phoenix. Bottom line: Ask to look at the room before you put your John Hancock on a credit card slip.

Finding the Best Room at the Best Rate

So, you have a general idea about what kind of room best suits you. Now you need to figure out how to nab it — and at the best price.

Finding the best rate

The rack rate is the maximum amount a hotel charges for a room. It's the rate you get if you walk in off the street and ask for a room for the night. You sometimes see these rates printed on the fire/emergency exit diagrams posted on the back of your door.

Hotels are happy to charge you the rack rate, but you can usually do better. Perhaps the best way to avoid paying the rack rate is surprisingly simple: Just ask for a cheaper or discounted rate. You may be pleasantly surprised.

In all but the smallest accommodations, the rate you pay for a room depends on many factors — chief among them being how you make your reservation. A travel agent may be able to negotiate a better price with certain hotels than you can get by yourself. (That's because the hotel often gives the agent a discount in exchange for steering his or her business toward that hotel.)

Reserving a room through the hotel's toll-free number may also result in a lower rate than calling the hotel directly. On the other hand, the central reservations number may not know about discount rates at specific locations. For example, local franchises may offer a special group rate for a wedding or family reunion, but they may neglect to tell the central booking line. Your best bet is to call both the local number and the toll-free number to see which one gives you a better deal.

Room rates (even rack rates) change with the season, as occupancy rates rise and fall. Chapter 3 gives you good general guidelines about what is defined as high season — the period when rooms are in most demand — in different parts of the state. Some destinations and accommodations types are busier than others in high season, however. For example, lodgings in Grand Canyon National Park of nearly every kind are at a premium in July (high season), while a room at a Scottsdale resort may be harder to book in February (high season) than, for example, one at a nearby chain motel. And few events listed in the calendar of events section in Chapter 3 have a significant impact on room occupancy (with the exception of the Gem and Mineral Show in Tucson). You never know when a huge convention is going to descend on a resort that you have your heart set on unless you call ahead.

For these and other reasons, even within a given season, room prices are subject to change without notice. Thus the rates quoted in this book may be different from the actual rate you receive when you make your reservation. Be sure to mention membership in AAA, AARP, frequent-flier programs, any other corporate rewards programs you can think of — or your Uncle Joe's Elks lodge in which you're an honorary inductee, for that matter — when you call to book. You never know when the affiliation may be worth a few dollars off your room rate.

Surfing the Web for hotel deals

Shopping online for hotels is generally done one of two ways: by booking through the hotel's own Web site or by going through an independent booking agency (or a fare-service agency like Priceline). These Internet hotel agencies have multiplied in mind-boggling numbers of late, competing for the business of millions of consumers surfing for accommodations around the world. This competitiveness can be a boon to you if you have the patience and time to shop and compare the online sites for good deals, but shop you must, because prices can vary considerably from site to site. And keep in mind that hotels at the top of a site's listing may be there for no other reason than that they paid money to get the placement.

Of the "big three" sites, Expedia offers a long list of special deals and "virtual tours" or photos of available rooms so you can see what you're paying for (a feature that helps counter the claims that the best rooms are often held back from bargain booking Web sites). Travelocity posts unvarnished customer reviews and ranks its properties according to the AAA rating system. Also reliable are Hotels.com and Quikbook.com. An excellent free program, TravelAxe (`www.travelaxe.net`), can help you search multiple hotel sites at once, even ones you may never have heard of, and it conveniently lists the total price of the room, including the taxes and service charges.

Another booking site, Travelweb (`www.travelweb`), is partly owned by the hotels it represents (including the Hilton, Hyatt, and Starwood chains) and is, therefore, plugged directly into the hotels' reservations systems — unlike independent online agencies, which have to fax or e-mail reservation requests to the hotel, a good portion of which get misplaced in the shuffle. More than once, travelers have arrived at the hotel, only to be told that they have no reservation. To be fair, many of the major sites are undergoing improvements in service and ease of use, and Expedia will soon be able to plug directly into the reservations systems of many hotels. In the meantime, it's a good idea to get a confirmation number and make a printout of any online booking transaction.

In the opaque Web site category, Priceline and Hotwire are even better for hotels than for airfares; with both, you're allowed to pick the neighborhood and quality level of your hotel before offering up your money. On the down side, many hotels stick Priceline guests in their least desirable rooms. Be sure to go to the BiddingforTravel Web site (`www.biddingfortravel.com`) before bidding on a hotel room on Priceline; it features a fairly up-to-date list of hotels that Priceline uses in major cities. For both Priceline and Hotwire, you pay up front, and the fee is nonrefundable. Note: Some hotels do not provide loyalty program credits or points or other frequent-stay amenities when you book a room through opaque online services.

Reserving the Best Room

After you make your reservation, asking one or two more pointed questions can go a long way toward making sure you get the best room in the house. Ask whether the hotel is renovating, and then request a room away from the renovation work. Inquire, too, about the location of the restaurants, bars, and clubs in the hotel — all sources of annoying noise. And if you aren't happy with your room when you arrive, talk to the front desk. If the hotel has another room available, the staff should be happy to accommodate you, within reason.

Chapter 9

Catering to Special Travel Needs or Interests

In This Chapter

- Touring with the junior and senior sets
- Rising above disabilities
- Locating resources for gays and lesbians
- Catering to your special interests

If you have special needs, interests, or concerns — and almost everyone does — this chapter may hold some answers for you. I may not be able to address every question you have on a particular topic, but I can at least help direct you to some additional information sources.

Traveling with the Brood: Advice for Families

Arizona is a great place for a family vacation, no matter what sort of travel you decide on. Just want to chill out at a resort? Most of the major ones have full menus of children's activities — fun for them and relaxing for you. Throughout this book, the Kid Friendly icon highlights places and activities particularly geared toward or welcoming to children, but when it comes to accommodations, even the cheapest motels in southern Arizona have swimming pools to keep kids happily splashing. Several places also let children as old as 18 stay in your room for free (depending on the hotel policy), so don't forget to ask when you're booking.

Food is no problem, either. Every chain restaurant you can think of is represented in the state. But chains are but one option: Nearly every city has Western steakhouses offering pint-size plates and a fun, rowdy atmosphere; friendly, inexpensive Mexican eateries that always include something on the menu for even the pickiest eater (including hamburgers); and casual roadside diners — you name it. Again, I use

Quick travel-with-kids tips

About to explore Arizona with a car full of kids? Use the following tips to increase their enjoyment and comfort while on the road.

In advance:

- Pack some of your youngest kids' **favorite books and toys,** even if they add bulk to your luggage. Going to unfamiliar places can be hard on even the most outgoing youngsters, and security blankets of all sorts help.
- Have your children **read up on Arizona.** If they're young, a book such as Susan Howell's *Three Little Javelinas* is great; older kids can go for Zane Grey's Western romances, nature books on the Sonoran Desert, or even corny films about Wyatt Earp and the OK Corral, of which 28 celluloid versions exist. Kids get a kick out of seeing the real thing later in Tombstone, where you can help them separate myth from fact.
- Bring along **protective gear** — hats, sunglasses, and sunscreen (although you won't have a hard time finding these items in Arizona). Kids' skin is super-sensitive to Arizona's powerful rays.
- Dig up **fun car games** from the recesses of your mind — or any other available sources (identifying license plates is always good in a pinch). You may be putting in lots of road time.
- If your kids are small, be sure to arrange with the car rental companies for **child-safety seats.**

When you're there:

- Don't let young children play in a pool unsupervised; tragedy can hit quickly.
- When in the desert, don't leave kids in a locked car for even two minutes to run in for a few items. Temperatures can rise to dangerously high levels before you know it.
- Don't overwhelm them with activities. Kids get sore muscles, too. Swimming, going on a tour, and having dinner at a Western restaurant may be too much. Gear activities to your child's age, physical condition, and attention span.

the handy icon to mark restaurants especially suited for children and, except for the really fancy places, you and your brood will be warmly welcomed nearly everywhere. When you're ready to hit the road, you can stock up on healthful snacks in the cities' huge supermarkets, and everywhere you go, you see convenience stores galore (where you can stock up on not-so-healthful supplies).

You can find the requisite water parks in and around the big cities and video arcades in nearly every mall. Arizona doesn't have a whole lot of theme parks per se; Old Tucson Studios — in Tucson, of course — is the only one that comes close. What Arizona does have, however, is far better: Tons of places where kids can engage with nature and history in a fun (but sneakily educational) way. Most are inexpensive to begin with and are even less costly when you subtract children's discounts. Chapter 3 offers an itinerary especially suited for families, but wherever you go, you can find activities to keep kids occupied, mind and body. (In this book, the especially appropriate activities are tagged with icons.) Also see the appendix.

A variety of resources exist on the Internet to help you plan family vacations. Familyhostel (☎ 800-733-9753; www.learn.unh.edu/familyhostel) takes the whole family, including kids ages 8 to 15, on moderately priced domestic and international learning vacations (in Arizona, for example, to the Grand Canyon and sights nearby). Lectures, fields trips, and sightseeing are guided by a team of academics. You find family-oriented vacation advice on the Internet from sites like Family Travel Forum (www.familytravelforum.com), a good resource for customizing trip planning; Family Travel Network (www.familytravelnetwork.com), an award-winning site with lots of travel features, deals, and tips; and Family Travel Files (www.thefamilytravelfiles.com), which offers an online magazine and a directory of off-the-beaten-path tours and tour operators for families.

The Phoenix-based monthly, Raising Arizona Kids (4545 E. Shea Blvd., Suite 201, Phoenix, AZ 85028; ☎ 602-953-KIDS; Internet: www.raisingarizonakids.com), concentrates on activities in the Valley of the Sun, but also includes a statewide calendar of events geared toward children. Copies are available at the Valley's major bookstores (and other locations specified on the Web site) for $2.95 per issue, and by subscription for $19.95 per year.

Making Age Work for You: Tips for Seniors

With its several huge Sun City retirement communities and cadres of retired snowbirds migrating down from colder climates come winter, Arizona is extremely senior friendly. The state caters to older travelers with everything from great golf courses to great medical facilities. The only thing missing is widespread early-bird specials for dinner — but that's probably because everyone in the state eats early, anyway. Most of the attractions in Arizona offer discounts to seniors. If available, these rates are indicated in this book with the other price listings.

You can make your gray hairs pay even before you arrive in Arizona: Mention the fact that you're a senior citizen when you make your travel reservations. Although all of the major U.S. airlines except America West — luckily, Arizona's major carrier — have cancelled their senior discount and coupon book programs, many hotels still offer discounts for seniors.

Not yet 60? You can still reap the benefits of maturity that your birth certificate indicates you've achieved. One of them is membership in AARP (formerly, the American Association of Retired Persons), 601 E St. NW, Washington, DC 20049 (☎ 888-687-2277 or 202-434-2277; www.aarp.org) — yes, first-wave baby boomers, you have to be only 50 to join. AARP offers members a wide range of benefits, including discounts on hotels, airfares, and car rentals, as well as AARP: The Magazine and a monthly newsletter.

The U.S. National Park Service offers a Golden Age Passport that gives seniors 62 years or older lifetime entrance to all properties administered by the National Park Service — national parks, monuments, historic sites, recreation areas, and national wildlife refuges — for a one-time processing fee of $10, which must be purchased in person at any NPS facility that charges an entrance fee. Besides free entry, a Golden Age Passport also offers a 50% discount on federal-use fees charged for such facilities as camping, swimming, parking, boat launching, and tours. For more information, go online to www.nps.gov/fees_passes.htm or call ☎ 888-467-2757.

Many reliable agencies and organizations target the 50-plus market. Elderhostel (☎ 877-426-8056; www.elderhostel.org) arranges study programs for people aged 55 and over (and a spouse or companion of any age) in the United States and in more than 80 countries around the world. Most courses last five to seven days in the United States (2–4 weeks abroad), and many include airfare, accommodations in university dormitories or modest inns, meals, and tuition. ElderTreks (☎ 800-741-7956; www.eldertreks.com) offers small-group tours to off-the-beaten-path or adventure-travel locations, restricted to travelers 50 and older. INTRAV (☎ 800-456-8100; www.intrav.com) is a high-end tour operator who caters to the mature, discerning traveler, although not specifically seniors, with trips around the world that include guided safaris, polar expeditions, private-jet adventures, and small-boat cruises down jungle rivers. In addition, Maupintour and GORPtravel, both discussed in Chapter 6, offer tours to Arizona for mature travelers.

Recommended publications offering travel resources and discounts for seniors include the quarterly magazine Travel 50 & Beyond (www.travel50andbeyond.com); Travel Unlimited: Uncommon Adventures for the Mature Traveler (Avalon); 101 Tips for Mature Travelers, available from Grand Circle Travel (☎ 800-221-2610 or 617-350-7500; www.gct.com); The 50+ Traveler's Guidebook (St. Martin's Press); and Unbelievably Good Deals and Great Adventures That You Absolutely Can't Get Unless You're Over 50 by Joann Rattner Heilman (McGraw-Hill).

Accessing Arizona: Advice for Travelers with Disabilities

Most disabilities shouldn't stop anyone from traveling, especially with more options and resources out there than ever before. Because of Arizona's aging population (resident and visitor), the state has good resources for the mobility impaired, as well as excellent medical facilities in the two big cities. The Arizona Office for Americans with Disabilities (100 N. 15th Ave., Suite 170, Phoenix; ☎ 800-358-3617 or 602-542-6276; TTY: 602-542-6686; www.know-the-ada.com) offers free statewide travel information and referrals.

The Golden Access Passport, a lifetime free-entry pass to all properties administered by the National Park Service — national parks, monuments, historic sites, recreation areas, and national wildlife refuges — is available free to any U.S. citizen or permanent resident who is medically certified as disabled or blind, regardless of age. To be issued a pass on the spot, go to one of the parks or monuments with proof of disability status and eligibility for receiving benefits under federal law. Besides free entry, the Golden Access Passport also offers a 50% discount on federal-use fees charged for such facilities as camping, swimming, parking, boat launching, and tours. For more information, go online to www.nps.gov/fees_passes.htm or call ☎ 888-467-2757.

Many travel agencies offer customized tours and itineraries for travelers with disabilities. Flying Wheels Travel (☎ 507-451-5005; www.flyingwheelstravel.com) operates escorted tours and cruises that emphasize sports and private tours in minivans with lifts. Access-Able Travel Source (☎ 303-232-2979; www.access-able.com) has extensive access information and advice for traveling around the world with disabilities.

Avis Rent a Car has an "Avis Access" program that provides such services as a dedicated 24-hour toll-free number (☎ 888-879-4273) for customers with special travel needs; special car features such as swivel seats, spinner knobs, and hand controls; and accessible bus service.

Organizations that offer assistance to disabled travelers include the MossRehab (www.mossresourcenet.org), which provides a library of accessible-travel resources online; SATH (Society for Accessible Travel and Hospitality) (☎ 212-447-7284; www.sath.org; annual membership fees: $45 adults, $30 seniors and students), which offers a wealth of travel resources for all types of disabilities and informed recommendations on destinations, access guides, travel agents, tour operators, vehicle rentals, and companion services; and the American Foundation for the Blind (AFB) (☎ 800-232-5463; www.afb.org), a referral resource for the blind or visually impaired that includes information on traveling with guide dogs.

For more information specifically targeted to travelers with disabilities, the community Web site iCan (www.icanonline.net/channels/travel/index.cfm) has destination guides and several regular columns on accessible travel. Also check out the quarterly magazine Emerging Horizons ($14.95 per year, $19.95 outside the U.S.; www.emerginghorizons.com); Twin Peaks Press (☎ 360-694-2462; http://disabilitybookshop.virtualave.net/blist84.htm), offering travel-related books for travelers with special needs; and Open World Magazine, published by SATH (subscription: $13 per year, $21 outside the U.S.).

Following the Rainbow: Resources for Gay and Lesbian Travelers

In most states, the cities with universities tend to have the most resources for gays and lesbians. In Arizona, these cities include Greater Phoenix (especially Tempe, home to Arizona State University) and Tucson and, to a lesser degree, Flagstaff and Prescott. Tucson, the most politically liberal city in a generally conservative state, is probably the gay-friendliest of the four. You don't find gay or lesbian residential neighborhoods or nightlife areas in any of these cities, just specific clubs.

In Phoenix, the best source of information is the Greater Phoenix Gay & Lesbian Chamber of Commerce (☎ 1-888-GAYAZ4U; www.gpglcc.org). 1N10 (☎ 602-234-2752; www.1n10.org) is another good resource for Greater Phoenix gays. The Tucson-based Wingspan (300 E. Sixth St.; ☎ 520-624-1779; www.wingspanaz.org) reaches out to Southern Arizona's gay, lesbian, bisexual, and transgender community. Also in Tucson, Antigone Bookstore (411 N. Fourth Ave.; ☎ 520-792-3715) is a good information source, especially for lesbians.

The International Gay and Lesbian Travel Association (IGLTA) (☎ 800-448-8550 or 954-776-2626; www.iglta.org) is the trade association for the gay and lesbian travel industry and offers an online directory of gay- and lesbian-friendly travel businesses; go to its Web site and click on Members. Many agencies offer tours and travel itineraries specifically for gay and lesbian travelers. Above and Beyond Tours (☎ 800-397-2681; www.abovebeyondtours.com) is the exclusive gay and lesbian tour operator for United Airlines. Now, Voyager (☎ 800-255-6951; www.nowvoyager.com) is a well-known San Francisco–based gay-owned and -operated travel service.

The following travel guides are available at most travel bookstores and gay and lesbian bookstores, or you can order them from Giovanni's Room bookstore, 1145 Pine St., Philadelphia, PA 19107 (☎ 215-923-2960; www.giovannisroom.com): Out and About (☎ 800-929-2268 or 415-644-8044; www.outandabout.com), which offers guidebooks and a newsletter ($20/yr; 10 issues) packed with solid information on the global gay and lesbian scene; Spartacus International Gay Guide (Bruno Gmünder Verlag; www.spartacusworld.com/gayguide/) and Odysseus, both good, annual English-language guidebooks focused on gay men; and the Damron guides (www.damron.com), with separate, annual books for gay men and lesbians.

Exploring Your Special Interests

Guest ranching (see Chapter 8) and golfing are just two of the state's specialties; other Arizona vacations cater to less obvious — but equally engaging — interests.

Astronomy

Several of the astronomical observatories that you can visit on a daily (or nightly) basis are detailed in Chapter 14. Want to extend your intergalactic adventure? The University of Arizona's Alumni Association and the Steward Observatory run a series of beginner and advanced astronomy camps each May, June, and October for adults and teens. Campers bunk on Mt. Lemmon, just north of Tucson, and have access to advanced telescopes. The price of $550 includes meals and lodging. For details, call ☎ 800-BEAT-ASU (outside Arizona), 520-621-4079, or 520-621-5233; or log on to http://ethel.as.arizona.edu/astro_camp.

Bird-watching

Chapter 15 details many of the excellent bird-watching spots in southeast Arizona and lists various local resources and festivals. If you want to take avian awareness even further, contact the southeast Arizona–based Hilonesome Bird Tours (570 S. Little Bar Trail, Sierra Vista, AZ 85635; ☎ 800-743-2668; www.hilonesome.com), which runs guided birding trips in the region. Several tours last about a week, but personalized single or half-day trips are options, too. You have to sign on for longer excursions if you go with the Tucson-based Borderland Tours (2550 W. Calle Padilla, AZ 85745; ☎ 800-525-7753 or 520-882-7650; www.borderland-tours.com) or with Field Guides (9433 Bee Cave Rd., Bldg. 1 Suite 150, Austin, TX 78733; ☎ 800-728-4953 or 512-263-7295; www.fieldguides.com), both of which run several southeast Arizona trips. None of the longer trips runs cheap. Expect to pay upward of $1,425, including food and nests for a week, but not including your flight.

Educational

The Ventures program of Flagstaff's Museum of Northern Arizona (☎ 928-774-5213; www.musnaz.org/education.ventures.html) offers a variety of educational vacations in the Four Corners area, with topics ranging from the archaeology of the Zuni to the geology of Escalante Canyon. The adventure level is wide-ranging, too. Encounters are day-trips with van support, Excursions are hotel-based, Explorations include moderate day hikes and camping, while the Expeditions generally involve kayaking and more rugged physical activities. Most programs depart from the museum.

If you think the Grand Canyon may be a cool place to go to school, check out the classes given by the Grand Canyon Field Institute (☎ 928-638-2485; www.grandcanyon.org/fieldinstitute) from March through November. Possibilities range from an introduction to backpacking and rim-to-rim hikes to watercolor classes to hands-on archaeology digs. Prices in 2004 start at $95 for an introductory day hike, going up to $1,200 for a four-day llama trek to Rainbow Bridge at Lake Powell.

See the information on Elderhostel in the "Making Age Work for You: Tips for Seniors" section earlier in this chapter.

Golf

Many resorts in Scottsdale and, to a lesser degree, Phoenix and Tucson, bundle golf deals in with their room rates. SGH Golf Inc. (☎ 800-284-8884; www.sghgolf.com) tends to specialize in European greens, but does offer several Scottsdale deals. If you're devoted to improving your game, check out Resort Golf Schools (☎ 888-373-7555; www.resortgolf.com), with programs in Scottsdale, Phoenix, and Tucson. Prices range widely depending on your point of departure, interest in upscale accommodations, and how much time you want to spend on the greens.

Photography

Arizona Highways magazine is renowned for its excellent photographs of the state's spectacular landscapes. If you go on one of the Friends of Arizona Highways photography trips (☎ 888-790-7042 or 602-712-2004; www.friendsofazhighways.com), you get some great photo tips and are guaranteed incredible scenery. Offered in different parts of the state, photo tours range from 3 to 11 days and cost from $895 to $3,325, including round-trip transportation from Phoenix and, in most cases, all meals and accommodations. Less extensive — and less expensive — one-day workshops are available, too.

Chapter 10

Taking Care of the Remaining Details

In This Chapter

- Managing your well-being: insurance and healthcare
- Reaching out by cellphone or e-mail
- Dealing with airport security

Okay, so you've decided when, where, and how you want to go to Arizona. Now the time has come for those last picky details that can make or break your trip.

Playing It Safe with Travel and Medical Insurance

Buying insurance is like carrying around an umbrella. If you have it, you won't need it. But insurance can be expensive. So, should you or shouldn't you buy it?

Three kinds of travel insurance are available: trip-cancellation, medical, and lost luggage. The cost of travel insurance varies widely, depending on the cost and length of your trip, your age and health, and the type of trip you're taking, but expect to pay between 5% and 8% of the vacation itself. The following is my advice on all three:

- Trip-cancellation insurance helps you get your money back if you have to back out of a trip, if you have to go home early, or if your travel supplier goes bankrupt. Allowed reasons for cancellation can range from sickness to natural disasters to the State Department declaring your destination unsafe for travel. (Insurers usually won't cover vague fears, though, as many travelers discovered who tried to cancel their trips in October 2001 because they were wary of flying.)

A good resource is "Travel Guard Alerts," a list of companies considered high-risk by Travel Guard International (www.travelinsured.com). Protect yourself further by paying for the insurance with a credit card — by law, consumers can get their money back on goods and services not received if they report the loss within 60 days after the charge is listed on their credit card statement. Note: Many tour operators, particularly those offering trips to remote or high-risk areas, include insurance in the cost of the trip or can arrange insurance policies through a partnering provider, a convenient and often cost-effective way for the traveler to obtain insurance. Make sure the tour company is a reputable one, however: Some experts suggest you avoid buying insurance from the tour or cruise company you're traveling with, saying it's better to buy from a third-party insurer than to put all your money in one place.

- For domestic travel, buying medical insurance for your trip doesn't make sense for most travelers. Most existing health policies cover you if you get sick away from home, but check before you go, particularly if you're insured by an HMO.

Staying Healthy When You Travel

Getting sick will ruin your vacation, so I strongly advise against it (of course, last time I checked, the bugs weren't listening to me any more than they probably listen to you).

For domestic trips, most reliable health-care plans provide coverage if you get sick away from home (see the preceding section for information on purchasing additional medical insurance for your trip).

Talk to your doctor before leaving on a trip if you have a serious and/or chronic illness. For conditions such as epilepsy, diabetes, or heart problems, wear a MedicAlert identification tag (☎ 888-633-4298; www.medicalert.org), which immediately alerts doctors to your condition and gives them access to your records through Medic Alert's 24-hour hotline.

If you fear that your medical condition may flare up, traveling to the more remote areas in northeastern Arizona isn't a good idea. The American Indian reservations have few modern hospitals, which are far apart.

If you do get sick in Arizona, try contacting your doctor back home to see whether he or she can refer you to someone local. (Greater Phoenix and Tucson have a large range of excellent medical facilities.) A friend of mine had a medical emergency — a detached retina — while she was visiting me in Tucson. When she phoned her eye doctor in Massachusetts, he recommended a physician at a nearby clinic that specialized in retinal surgery. Turned out, she felt she'd received better medical care and more personalized attention than she usually got back home.

Inventory your health

Although this chapter includes tips about health insurance, it doesn't take your machismo (or machisma) level into account. If you've never hiked a day in your life, don't plan on walking to the bottom of the Grand Canyon. And if your health is fragile, going to a remote Native American reservation isn't smart because you aren't near any contemporary medical facilities. Sticking near Phoenix or Tucson, both of which are chock-a-block with specialty hospitals, is a far better idea.

If you can't get in touch with your doctor or don't have one you can phone, ask the concierge at your hotel to recommend a local physician — even his or her own, if necessary. This recommendation is probably better than what you can get from any national consortium of doctors.

If you can't get a doctor to help you right away, try the emergency room at the local hospital. Many hospital emergency rooms have walk-in clinics for emergency cases that aren't life threatening. You may not get immediate attention, but you won't pay the high price of an emergency room visit (usually a minimum of $300 just for signing your name, on top of whatever treatment you receive).

The bottom line: Don't panic. Stress only compounds your symptoms.

Staying Connected by Cellphone or E-mail

Just because your cellphone works at home doesn't mean it'll work elsewhere in the country (thanks to our nation's fragmented cellphone system). It's a good bet that your phone will work in major cities. But take a look at your wireless company's coverage map on its Web site before heading out — T-Mobile, Sprint, and Nextel are particularly weak in rural areas. If you need to stay in touch at a destination where you know your phone won't work, rent a phone that does from InTouch USA (☎ 800-872-7626; www.intouchglobal.com) or a rental car location, but beware that you'll pay $1 a minute or more for airtime.

If you're venturing deep into national parks, you may want to consider renting a satellite phone (known as satphones), which are different from cellphones in that they connect to satellites rather than ground-based towers. A satphone is more costly than a cellphone but works where there's no cellular signal and no towers. Unfortunately, you'll pay at least $2 per minute to use the phone, and it works only where you can see the horizon (that is, usually not indoors). In North America, you can rent Iridium satellite phones from RoadPost (www.roadpost.com;

☎ 888-290-1606 or 905-272-5665). InTouch USA offers a wider range of satphones but at higher rates. As of this writing, satphones were very expensive to buy.

If you're not from the United States, you may be appalled at the poor reach of our GSM (Global System for Mobiles) wireless network, which is used by much of the rest of the world. Your phone will probably work in most major U.S. cities; it definitely won't work in many rural areas. (To see where GSM phones work in the United States, check out www.t-mobile.com/coverage/national_popup.asp.) And you may or may not be able to send SMS (text messaging) home — something Americans tend not to do anyway, for various cultural and technological reasons. (International budget travelers like to send text messages home because it's much cheaper than making international calls.) Assume nothing — call your wireless provider and get the full scoop. In a worst-case scenario, you can always rent a phone; InTouch USA delivers to hotels.

When traveling, you have any number of ways to check your e-mail and access the Internet on the road. Of course, using your own laptop — or even a PDA (personal digital assistant) or electronic organizer with a modem — gives you the most flexibility. But even if you don't have a computer, you can still access your e-mail and even your office computer from cybercafes.

The major cities in Arizona don't have cybercafes, but they do have branches of Kinko's, where you can access your e-mail. You find cybercafes in smaller Arizona towns like Flagstaff, Sedona, Prescott, and Page, but, at this writing, none exists on the Native Indian reservations. Although there's no definitive directory for cybercafes — these are independent businesses, after all — two places to start looking are at www.cybercaptive.com and www.cybercafe.com.

Aside from formal cybercafes, most youth hostels nowadays have at least one computer on which you can access the Internet. And most public libraries across the world offer Internet access free or for a small charge. Avoid hotel business centers, unless you're willing to pay exorbitant rates.

Most major airports now have Internet kiosks scattered throughout their gates. These kiosks, which you'll also see in shopping malls, hotel lobbies, and tourist information offices around the world, give you basic Web access for a per-minute fee that's usually higher than cybercafe prices. The kiosks' clunkiness and high price mean they should be avoided whenever possible.

To retrieve your e-mail, ask your Internet Service Provider (ISP) if it has a Web-based interface tied to your existing e-mail account. If your ISP doesn't have such an interface, you can use the free mail2web service (www.mail2web.com) to view and reply to your home e-mail. For more flexibility, you may want to open a free, Web-based e-mail account with Yahoo! Mail (http://mail.yahoo.com). (Microsoft's Hotmail is another popular option, but Hotmail has severe spam problems.) Your home ISP may be able to forward your e-mail to the Web-based account automatically.

If you need to access files on your office computer, look into a service called GoToMyPC (www.gotomypc.com). The service provides a Web-based interface for you to access and manipulate a distant PC from anywhere — even a cybercafe — provided your "target" PC is on and has an always-on connection to the Internet (such as with broadband cable). The service offers top-quality security, but if you're worried about hackers, use your own laptop rather than a cybercafe computer to access the GoToMyPC system.

If you are bringing your own computer, the buzzword in computer access to familiarize yourself with is Wi-fi (wireless fidelity), and more and more hotels, cafes, and retailers are signing on as wireless "hotspots," from where you can get high-speed connection without cable wires, networking hardware, or a phone line. You can get Wi-fi connection one of several ways. Many laptops sold in the last year have built-in Wi-fi capability (an 802.11b wireless Ethernet connection). Mac owners have their own networking technology, Apple AirPort. For those with older computers, an 802.11b/Wi-fi card (around $50) can be plugged into your laptop. You sign up for wireless access service much as you do cellphone service, through a plan offered by one of several commercial companies that have made wireless service available in airports, hotel lobbies, and coffee shops, primarily in the United States (followed by the U.K. and Japan). T-Mobile Hotspot (www.t-mobile.com/hotspot) serves up wireless connections at more than 1,000 Starbucks coffee shops nationwide. Boingo (www.boingo.com) and Wayport (www.wayport.com) have set up networks in airports and high-class hotel lobbies. IPass providers also give you access to a few hundred wireless hotel lobby setups. Best of all, you don't need to be staying at the Four Seasons to use the hotel's network; just set yourself up on a nice couch in the lobby. The companies' pricing policies can be byzantine, with a variety of monthly, per-connection, and per-minute plans, but in general you pay around $30 a month for limited access — and as more and more companies jump on the wireless bandwagon, prices are likely to get even more competitive.

There are also places that provide free wireless networks in cities around the world. To locate these free hotspots, go to **www.personaltelco.net/index.cgi/WirelessCommunities**.

If Wi-fi is not available at your destination, most business-class hotels throughout the world offer dataports for laptop modems, and a few thousand hotels in the United States and Europe now offer free high-speed Internet access using an Ethernet network cable. You can bring your own cables, but most hotels rent them for around $10. Call your hotel in advance to see what your options are.

In addition, major Internet Service Providers (ISP) have local access numbers around the world, allowing you to go online by simply placing a local call. Check your ISP's Web site or call its toll-free number and ask how you can use your current account away from home, and how much it will cost. If you're traveling outside the reach of your ISP, the iPass network has dial-up numbers in most of the world's countries. You'll have to sign up with an iPass provider, who will then tell you how to set up your computer for your destination(s). For a list of iPass providers, go to `www.ipass.com` and click on "Individual Purchase." One solid provider is i2roam (`www.i2roam.com`; ☎ 866-811-6209 or 920-235-0475).

Wherever you go, bring a connection kit of the right power and phone adapters, a spare phone cord, and a spare Ethernet network cable — or find out whether your hotel supplies them to guests.

Keeping Up with Airline Security Measures

With the federalization of airport security, security procedures at U.S. airports are more stable and consistent than ever. Generally, you'll be fine if you arrive at the airport 1 hour before a domestic flight and 2 hours before an international flight; if you show up late, tell an airline employee, and she'll probably whisk you to the front of the line.

Bring a current, government-issued photo ID such as a driver's license or passport. Keep your ID at the ready to show at check-in, the security checkpoint, and sometimes even the gate. (Children under 18 do not need government-issued photo IDs for domestic flights, but they do for international flights to most countries.)

In 2003, the TSA phased out gate check-in at all U.S. airports. And e-tickets have made paper tickets nearly obsolete. Passengers with e-tickets can beat the ticket-counter lines by using airport electronic kiosks or even online check-in from your home computer. Online check-in involves logging on to your airline's Web site, accessing your reservation, and printing out your boarding pass — and the airline may even offer you bonus miles to do so! If you're using a kiosk at the airport, bring the credit card you used to book the ticket or your frequent-flier card. Print out your boarding pass from the kiosk and simply proceed to the security checkpoint with your pass and a photo ID. If you're checking bags or looking to snag an exit-row seat, you will be able to do so using most airline kiosks. Even the smaller airlines are employing the kiosk system, but always call your airline to make sure these alternatives are available. Curbside check-in is also a good way to avoid lines, although a few airlines still ban curbside check-in; call before you go.

Security checkpoint lines are getting shorter than they were during 2001 and 2002, but some doozies remain. If you have trouble standing for long periods of time, tell an airline employee; the airline will provide a wheelchair. Speed up security by not wearing metal objects such as big belt buckles. If you've got metallic body parts, a note from your doctor can prevent a long chat with the security screeners. Keep in mind that only ticketed passengers are allowed past security, except for folks escorting disabled passengers or children.

Federalization has stabilized what you can carry on and what you can't. The general rule is that sharp things are out, nail clippers are okay, and food and beverages must be passed through the X-ray machine, but security screeners can't make you drink from your coffee cup. Bring food in your carry-on rather than checking it, because explosive-detection machines used on checked luggage have been known to mistake food (especially chocolate, for some reason) for bombs. Travelers in the United States are allowed one carry-on bag, plus a "personal item," such as a purse, briefcase, or laptop bag. Carry-on hoarders can stuff all sorts of things into a laptop bag; as long as it has a laptop in it, it's still considered a personal item. The Transportation Security Administration (TSA) has issued a list of restricted items; check its Web site (`www.tsa.gov/public/index.jsp`) for details.

Airport screeners may decide that your checked luggage needs to be searched by hand. You can now purchase luggage locks that allow screeners to open and re-lock a checked bag if hand-searching is necessary. Look for Travel Sentry–certified locks at luggage or travel shops and Brookstone stores (you can buy them online at `www.brookstone.com`). These locks, approved by the TSA, can be opened by luggage inspectors with a special code or key. For more information on the locks, visit `www.travelsentry.org`. If you use something other than TSA-approved locks, your lock will be cut off your suitcase if a TSA agent needs to hand-search your luggage.

Part III

Exploring the Big Cities

"Oh, it's okay if you're into neo-romanticist art. Personally, I prefer the soaring perspectives of David Hockney or the controlled frenzy of Gerhard Richter."

In this part . . .

Meet Arizona's two sprawling major cities, the metropolitan area known as Greater Phoenix or the Valley of the Sun, and its southern rival, Tucson. In this part, I give you everything you need to know about both of them, from boring nitty-gritty details, such as how to get from the airport to your hotel, to far more interesting info, like the best places to boogie after dark. When you're ready for some great day (or overnight) escapes from the cities, I have some terrific ones lined up for you, too.

Chapter 11

Phoenix, Scottsdale, and the Valley of the Sun

In This Chapter

- Getting the scoop on Greater Phoenix
- Bunking in the best places in the Valley
- Discovering the top restaurants
- Seeing the prime sights and diversions
- Shopping till you drop
- Kicking up your heels after dark

Los Angeles without water, except for its oceans of swimming pools, Phoenix epitomizes the new urban Southwest — leisure bent and car obsessed. This northern Sonoran Desert city is only part, albeit a major one, of a complex of satellites known collectively as the Valley of the Sun, which includes the tourist destinations of Scottsdale and Tempe.

For visitors, the region is the Valley of the Fun. Great museums and sports — of both the watching and doing variety — are Phoenix's prime arenas, while Scottsdale specializes in ritzy resorts, lush golf courses, chic boutiques, and posh spas. Tempe, home to Arizona State University, competes for tourist attention with a youthful personality, strollable streets, and a town lake that was created in 1999 and has quickly become a recreational haven for urbanites. But all the Valley towns share one key asset: plenty of year-round sunshine and endless ways to play in it.

Getting There

Phoenix is Arizona's prime transportation hub, receiving more flights than anywhere else in the state and linking to all major highways — but you can't get there by train.

Flying in

More major airlines fly into Phoenix Sky Harbor International Airport, 3 miles east of downtown Phoenix (☎ 602-273-3321; `www.phxskyharbor.com`), than into any other city in the state (see Chapter 6 for details). More than 37 million visitors pass through here annually — which means that baggage retrieval can be a slow process. Phoenix is the place where you're likely to begin your Arizona trip, even if you're not staying in the Valley.

Some hotels and resorts offer free shuttle service. Ask before you leave home if — and precisely where — you can expect to be picked up. Other options for getting from the airport to your lodging include:

- Renting a car: Several rental car companies operate out of Sky Harbor airport, so you're bound to find your favorites here — or at least those for which you have discount coupons. The major players — Advantage Alamo, Avis, Budget, Dollar, Enterprise, Hertz, National, and Thrifty — all operate out of Sky Harbor; see the Appendix for the toll-free numbers. Note: All the car rental companies currently have service counters at the individual terminals, but by the end of 2005, car rental operations will be consolidated into a single, separate building to which car renters will be shuttled.

  If you're headed to central or west Phoenix, you want to leave the airport by the west (24th Street/Piestewa Peak Parkway) exit and continue west on 24th Street to Washington Street or whatever street is closest to your destination. For east Phoenix and south and central Scottsdale, take the eastern (44th Street) exit and go north on 44th Street to the street most convenient to your resort (generally Indian School or Camelback roads or Lincoln Drive). To get to north Scottsdale, take the 44th Street exit and follow the signs to Highway 202 east (it comes up quickly, so keep an eye out) Go east on 202 until you reach Highway 101 north, which you should take to the exit closest to your resort. To reach Tempe, take the 44th Street exit to the Hohokam Expressway (Highway 143), and drive south one exit to University Avenue, which goes straight into town.

  Construction at Sky Harbor is a constant, so look out for detour signs. I've frequently ended up circling the airport, trying to find my exit.

- Hailing a taxi or hopping a shuttle: Outside the baggage claim area, you see queues of taxis from the only three companies licensed for airport pickup: AAA Cab (☎ 602-437-4000), Allstate Cab (☎ 602-275-8888), and Discount Cab (☎ 602-200-2000). AAA charges $2.50 for pickup, and $1.50 per mile ($5 minimum); Allstate cabs cost $1.50 for pickup, and $1.75 per mile; at Discount Cab, the pickup fee is $2.50, then it's $4.15 for the first mile, $1.65 for each additional mile.

SuperShuttle (☎ 800-BLUE VAN or 602-244-9000; www.supershuttle.com) vans provide reliable door-to-door service Valleywide, 24/7. The "Ground Transportation" signs in each terminal direct you to the pickup areas. A company agent stationed on the center island outside the baggage claim area calls a van for you when you've retrieved your luggage and are ready to hit the road. Fares are based on the zip code of your destination. If you're heading to central or downtown Phoenix, you pay about $7 for the first person, and $7 for each additional person. Trips to surrounding areas, such as Scottsdale, cost close to $16 for the first person and $7 for each additional person; children ages 3 and under ride free. Credit cards are accepted, and tips are expected.

The farther from the airport you're headed, the more sense it makes to use the shuttle. If, on the other hand, you're traveling a shorter distance to downtown Phoenix or Tempe, a cab is likely to be quicker (no stops for other passengers) and cost about the same (or less). The shuttle operates on an as-needed basis, so you don't need to make reservations before you arrive in town. When returning to the airport, however, call a day in advance to arrange a pickup from your hotel.

- Taking the bus: Valley Metro (see the "Getting around Phoenix" section later in this chapter) offers daily direct bus service from terminals 2, 3, and 4 of Sky Harbor Airport to downtown Phoenix and to central Tempe. If you don't have much luggage, the bus is a good deal: For $1.25, you can get to Tempe and downtown Phoenix in about 20 minutes. Although free transfers to Scottsdale and other Valley destinations are available, the savings isn't generally worth the chunk of time this form of transit carves from your vacation (and if you're staying in Scottsdale, you're probably not on a really tight budget).

  To reach downtown Phoenix, take the Red Line westbound. Buses run run about every 15 minutes Monday through Friday from 5:03 a.m. to 12:35 a.m.; Saturday and Sunday they start at 5:27 a.m. and stop at 12:57 a.m. and 10:27 p.m., respectively. To reach Tempe, catch the Red Line eastbound. Buses run about every 15 minutes from 3:36 a.m. to 12:05 a.m. weekdays, 5:21 a.m. to 12:21 a.m. Saturdays, and 4:51 a.m. to 10:21 p.m. Sundays. The Bus Book, which lists schedules, is sometimes available at the airport tourist information desk, but don't count on it; call ☎ 602-253-5000 or log on to www.valleymetro.org to check the times.

Driving in

Two interstates run into and through Phoenix — I-10, which extends from Florida to southern California, and I-17, which, despite its name, isn't really an interstate because it only goes north to Flagstaff, where it turns into Arizona Highway 89. This road does, however, hook up at Flagstaff with I-40, a genuine interstate that stretches from North

> ### Orienting yourself
>
> Don't be surprised if you find the Valley a bit daunting; I still do after years of driving up from Tucson. Here's what helps me find my way. I picture the entire Valley as a donut clock — what can I say? I have a vivid imagination that usually involves food — with Sky Harbor Airport as its more-or-less empty center; aside from the runways and the old railroad tracks, not much else is in this area. Starting from 12:00 where Phoenix's **Camelback Corridor** district lies, you move around this junk food timepiece to **Paradise Valley** (1:00), **East Phoenix and Scottsdale** (1:00–3:00), **Mesa** and **Tempe** (4:00–5:00), **South Phoenix** (6:00), and **downtown Phoenix** (9:00). Beyond the more remote sections of Phoenix that run along I-17 from 9:00–12:00 is what's called the **West Valley**, a largely suburban and residential region; its best-known towns are **Glendale, Peoria,** and the two **Sun City** planned retirement communities. You're likely to spend most of your visit in Phoenix and the East Valley, where generally the farther north and east you go of downtown Phoenix, the ritzier it gets.

Carolina to California. See the "Getting around Phoenix" section later in this chapter, for descriptions of some of the more minor arteries into town.

Riding in (no, not on horseback)

If you're riding Greyhound (☎ 800-231-2222; `www.greyhound.com`), you can roll into one of several area stations, including Phoenix, Tempe, and Mesa. The main terminal is in Phoenix at 2115 E. Buckeye Rd. (☎ 602-389-4200), near Sky Harbor Airport.

Amtrak (☎ 800-872-7245; `www.amtrak.com`) doesn't offer train service to Phoenix. The closest depot is in Maricopa, 30 miles to the south, and the railway doesn't provide bus transportation to any part of the Valley.

Introducing the Neighborhoods

The Valley is made up of a series of cities and towns. Getting to know their names can make getting around a lot easier on yourself. Within these cities and towns are smaller geographical sub-units, but, don't forget, you're not in Kansas (or, better for this example, Boston) anymore: With few exceptions, these sprawling new western towns don't divvy up into neighborhoods in the traditional sense of the term.

Phoenix

Most of Phoenix's attractions are in the downtown and Camelback Corridor areas, but South Mountain and the Papago Salado regions have a few tourist hooks, too.

Phoenix, Scottsdale, and the Valley of the Sun Orientation

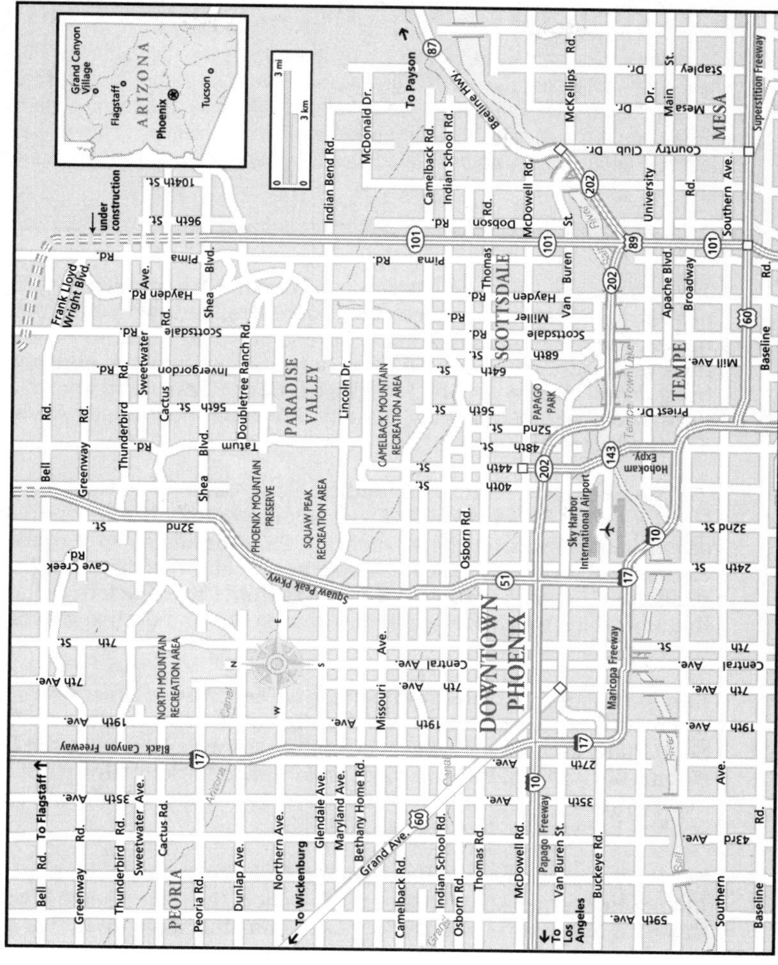

In the throes of a building frenzy, the formerly seedy southern sector of downtown, roughly bounded by Fillmore Street (north), Jefferson Street (south), 1st Avenue (west), and 7th Street (east), embraces several high- and low-tone tourist zones. Within downtown, the 90-square-block area dubbed Copper Square includes two major sports stadiums — America West Arena and Bank One Ballpark ("BOB") — both directly south of Jefferson; Heritage Square and the adjacent museum complex, including the Arizona Science Center; the glitzy Arizona Center entertainment/dining/office complex; and the nearby cultural hub of the Herberger, Dodge and Orpheum theaters.

The fabulous resorts of . . . Pumpkinville?

The Mormons who settled in the Valley of the Sun in the 1860s called Phoenix "Pumpkinville" after the gourds that grew along the canals built by the Hohokam Indians. Englishman Darrell Dupa's proclaimed in 1868 that "a new city will spring phoenix-like upon the ruins of a former civilization." This statement inspired the state legislature to adopt the city's more romantic, if less colorful (well, at least not orange) moniker.

The northern edge of downtown is where you'll find mostly older businesses, some newer corporate headquarters, and two actual neighborhoods: the ritzy Encanto/Palmcroft enclave near Encanto Park and, to the east, Willo, more middle class but artsy, with lots of appealing old bungalows. Nearby are the Margaret T. Hance Park (also known as Deck Park), the Arizona Historical Society Museum, the Phoenix Art Museum, and the Heard Museum.

The Camelback Corridor, extending along Camelback Road through North Central Phoenix toward Scottsdale (roughly from 20th to 44th streets), has fewer tourist attractions; its gleaming rows of office towers are interspersed with upscale shops, hotels, and restaurants. The wealthy residential Arcadia (44th to 68th streets from Camelback to Indian School Roads), which was once swathed with ranches and orange groves, abuts the corridor.

Papago Salado, named for Phoenix's earliest Native American settlers, is a mostly faceless, freeway-ridden area at the conjunction of Phoenix, Scottsdale, and Tempe. However, calling the area home are the Desert Botanical Gardens, Phoenix Zoo, and Papago Park northwest of Highway 202, and the Pueblo Grande Museum and Archaeological Park, sandwiched between Highways 143 and 153.

South Phoenix, which is slowly being revitalized, hosts the huge South Mountain Park and, just before its entrance, the fortress-like Mystery Castle. A few resorts and the large Arizona Mills mall are in this area, too.

Scottsdale

Arizona's answer to Palm Springs, Scottsdale is a newer, hipper version of the California town that coined the concept of wealthy desert chic. The long, skinny city of about 217,000 people stretches some 31 miles from Tempe in the south to Carefree in the north. Not very long ago, you could see endless stretches of empty desert along the northern part of Scottsdale Road, the town's main drag, but now you're hard pressed to guess where Scottsdale ends and the manicured planned community of Carefree starts (okay, the intersecting Carefree Road is a dead giveaway).

Not surprisingly, the town tends to be divided into shopping and arts districts (see the "Shopping the Local Stores" section later in this chapter for more details). Downtown Scottsdale, near Tempe, runs roughly between Osborn Road (south), Camelback Road (north), 68th Street (west), and Drinkwater Boulevard (east); within that area, the four square blocks of now touristy Old Town have authentic historic cachet. Scottsdale Road between Indian School Road and Shea Boulevard has been dubbed Resort Row because of — you guessed it — its abundance of large, upscale lodgings.

Paradise Valley

Nestled just west of central Scottsdale, Paradise Valley may be the most exclusive stretch of real estate in the Valley. The almost entirely residential area holds large, desert-embracing estates. A few hotels and resorts may bring you here if you don't happen to have rich relatives.

Tempe

Home to Arizona State University, Tempe comes closest to what is traditionally considered a town. You can stroll along its main drag, Mill Avenue, and actually see other people. Tempe has always had a thriving, student-driven nightlife, but aside from the museums and the Sun Devil Stadium on the ASU campus, tourists used to find little here during the day. That changed with the opening in 1999 of the man-made Tempe Town Lake, which flows between the Rio Salado Parkway and Highway 202 along a formerly dry bed of the Salt River. Although it quickly became a center for aquatic activities, Tempe Town Lake hasn't yet developed a waterfront restaurant and retail scene. That's likely to change, especially when the $65-million Tempe Center for the Arts, which broke ground in 2004, opens in 2006.

Glendale

Of all the West Valley towns, Glendale is one that out-of-towners are most likely to visit. Not only is Glendale the closest to downtown and central Phoenix, but it also has a strollable downtown with lots of historic buildings, a plethora of antiques shops, and the charming Bead Museum.

Finding Information after You Arrive

The bilingual — that's Spanish and English — staff at the information booths in each of the airport terminals dispenses tour brochures, city maps, and other introductory information.

The Greater Phoenix Convention and Visitors Bureau has two walk-in centers: 50 N. 2nd St. at Adams, downtown (☎ 602-452-6268; open Mon–Fri 8 a.m.–5 p.m.), and Biltmore Fashion Park, 24th Street and Camelback Road (☎ 602-452-6281; open Mon–Fri 10 a.m.–7 p.m., Sat 10 a.m.–6 p.m., and Sun noon–6 p.m.). (You find the second location between Macy's and Christofle, if you don't get sidetracked.)

Whoa, there!

Phoenix vies with Las Vegas as America's fastest-growing large (population of more than 1 million) city, boasting a growth rate of 40% during the 1990s. It overtook Philadelphia as the country's fifth-largest city in 2004.

The Scottsdale Area Chamber of Commerce/Convention and Visitors Bureau, 4343 N. Scottsdale Rd., Ste. 170, inside the Galleria Corporate Center (☎ 480-421-1004) is open Monday through Friday 8:30 a.m. to 6 p.m. The Scottsdale CVB also has staff at the concierge desk in Scottsdale Fashion Square Mall, at the corner of Scottsdale and Camelback roads (open Tues–Fri 1 p.m.–6 p.m., and Sat 11 a.m.–4 p.m.).

Getting around Phoenix

Greater Phoenix practically defines the term urban sprawl, and it's severely public-transportation-challenged to boot. Unless you're checking out a concentrated area like downtown Phoenix, Old Scottsdale, or Mill Avenue in Tempe, you need wheels if you want to see anything. Interested in exploring with just two of them? See the "Staying Active" section later in this chapter for the best urban and rural biking routes.

Exploring by car

Because of multiple mergings and name metamorphoses, the many highways that thread through the Valley aren't always easy to navigate. I-17, which leads north to Flagstaff, is the Valley's main north-south thoroughfare. Just south of downtown Phoenix, I-17 veers east and merges with I-10, at which point the road becomes the Maricopa Freeway. I-10 snakes through the Valley in a variety of directions, but in the west Valley and downtown Phoenix, where it's called the Papago Freeway, I-10 generally runs from east to west. North of the airport, I-10 connects with Highway 202 (almost always called Loop 202, though its official name is the Red Mountain Freeway). If you head east on 202, you get to downtown Tempe. Continue east along Loop 202 past Tempe to Highway 101 (a.k.a. Loop 101) north if you want to get to north Scottsdale. From the east, the best route is Loop 101, which connects with Loop 202 and Highway 60, the Superstition Freeway. Highway 60 leads east through Tempe and Mesa toward Apache Junction and the Superstition Mountains (see Chapter 12). In the other direction, when Highway 60 gets beyond I-10, it becomes Grand Avenue and then merges with Highway 89 as it winds its way northwest through Glendale, Peoria, and Sun City toward Wickenburg.

Three roads you have less need to think about are Highway 51 or Piestewa Peak Parkway, mostly useful for traveling from central Phoenix to north Phoenix, though it also connects to Loop 101 and Loop

202 (see above); Highway 143, the short Hohokam Expressway, which connects Loop 202 with I-10 on the east side of the airport; and Highway 87, the Beeline Highway, which starts in Mesa and heads northeast.

Make sure you have your directions planned out before you hit the road. You and your navigator aren't going to have much map-consulting time while you're freeway-switching.

Driving the streets is less confusing, if more time consuming: Phoenix, Scottsdale, and Tempe all operate pretty much on grids. The address nexus of the Valley is the intersection of Washington Street and Central Avenue in downtown Phoenix. Running north and south to the west of Washington are numbered avenues (they go from 1st Avenue up to 107th Avenue and higher in such West Valley cities as Glendale, Peoria, and Sun City); east of Washington are the numbered streets. The east-west thoroughfares have names; Camelback, Indian School, and McDowell roads are major routes across central Phoenix.

In Scottsdale, as opposed to the rest of the Valley, the left-turn arrows appear at the end of the light, not at the beginning. If you don't know the precise boundaries between Scottsdale, Phoenix, and Tempe — and most Valley residents don't — assuming you can turn left can be dangerous. Always wait until you see the green arrow before moving into an intersection.

The Valley of the Sun is so large — 9,127 square miles if you include all 22 incorporated cities — that AAA has three maps available for Greater Phoenix: The Phoenix/Arizona Vicinity map covers the entire Valley and includes all the new freeways. The one whose folds you'll probably wear out is called Phoenix/East Arizona. Phoenix/West Arizona is the third one. For information on the locations of AAA offices, see the Appendix.

Traveling by taxi

Unless you're on a company expense account or traveling within a very limited area, taking taxis isn't a great way to get around. Don't expect to be able to hail a cab on the street, even in downtown Phoenix (the exception is when a sports or concert event is taking place). You have to phone for your wheels and not on the spur of the moment, either. If you're on a tight schedule, book at least an hour in advance. The Greater Phoenix area has more than 40 taxi companies, but some of the more reliable ones include Yellow Cab (☎ 602-252-5252), Allstate Cab (☎ 602-275-8888), and Scottsdale Taxi (☎ 480-994-4567). Keep in mind, however, that you're likely to go a far stretch and that taxi fares are unregulated. Always ask ahead of time how much the fare will be and confirm before stepping into the cab.

Riding a bus or trolley

The Valley Metro Bus System (☎ 602-253-5000; `www.valleymetro.org`) services Phoenix, Scottsdale, Tempe, Mesa, and Gilbert, but coverage

Free-for-all

Although bussing around the Valley isn't generally the best way to go, you can't lose by taking advantage of three Valley transit freebies. Call **Valley Metro (☎ 602-253-5000)** or log on to `www.valleymetro.org` for exact schedules.

- **DASH** (Downtown Area Shuttle) makes frequent daily runs around Copper Square in downtown Phoenix. Look for the DASH stop sign at any one of the 29 stops between 18th Avenue and 5th Street within the boundaries of Jefferson and Van Buren streets.
- **FLASH** (Free Local Area Shuttle) loops around the areas surrounding Arizona State University in Tempe every day.
- **The Scottsale Trolley** provides free rides in downtown Scottsdale, Monday through Saturday (except from June–Oct). Look for the bright yellow and purple signs.

isn't exactly comprehensive, although it's improved in the last few years. You can sometimes find a copy of the Bus Book at the airport, at Central Station on Van Buren Street and Central Avenue, and at any Fry's or Safeway supermarket, but taking advantage of the telephone trip-planning service (available through the main number) is far easier. Fares are $1.25 for adults, 60¢ for ages 6 to 18 and seniors over 65, and free for children under 6 accompanied by an adult. Buses are equipped to accept dollar bills, but you need exact change. You can get free transfers between routes — they're good for an hour to 1½ hours after your bus reaches its final destination — but you need to ask for one when you pay your fare.

Staying in Style

Economic slowdown? No one seems to have told the Valley's hospitality industry, which has rarely skipped a beat since the turn of the 20th century and continues to grow as quickly as the Phoenix metro area itself — maybe even faster. Although no major new resorts have opened in the last year, the existing properties are in an intense competition to outdo one another with new facilities, especially spas. These mini leisure worlds are a prime reason to visit Arizona, so I devote the following section to them; see Chapter 8 for details on what you can expect for resort amenities. And don't forget to ask about special packages, also described in Chapter 8.

The second lodging section covers hotels and inns. The Valley has some dazzlers in this category, but because of complicated zoning practices, few bed and breakfasts. Again, make sure to ask about special packages when you call; many hotels offer them. The vast majority of listings in both sections are for lodgings in Scottsdale and Phoenix, the most visitor-friendly locations, but I also include two in Tempe — not only a nice place to wake up, but also extremely convenient to Sky Harbor airport.

Because of its appeal as a winter escape, the Valley is one of the most expensive places in the United States for a vacation. A standard room at a resort in Phoenix or Scottsdale usually falls into the $$$$ ($301–$400) category, with many rooms listed for $401 and beyond ($$$$$) in high season. If you're looking to save a few bucks, you may want to consider a B&B or even a mid-price chain (see the Appendix for the toll-free numbers). Predicting precisely when the hotels will be busy is difficult (major sports events are a factor, as are major snowstorms in the rest of the country), but the area is popular from mid-December through March — which is also when (surprise, surprise) the rates are highest. See Chapter 3 for more details on seasonal and monthly happenings. And check the Arizona Office of Tourism's Vacation Values Web site, `www.arizonavacationvalues.com`, to find out what rooms are on sale during your visit.

Resorts

Arizona Biltmore Resort & Spa

$$$$–$$$$$ Phoenix/Camelback Corridor

A local favorite since opening its Southwest Art Deco doors — designed, like the rest of the resort, by one of Frank Lloyd Wright's colleagues — in 1929, the Biltmore stays at the leisure-cutting edge with such amenities as guided mountain biking excursions and the latest spa treatments, while maintaining such gracious old-style features as croquet and high tea (in high season). Rooms are understatedly elegant, and the grounds are gorgeous, acres of rolling lawns poised against craggy Camelback Mountain. The Biltmore was the spur for Phoenix's thriving Camelback (or Biltmore) Corridor of restaurants and shops and remains its anchor, so you're close to some of the Valley's top retail and dining. You're not far, either, from many of Phoenix's top tourist sights, so this place makes a very convenient base.

See map p. 116. 2400 E. Missouri (at 24th Street). ☎ ***800-950-0086*** *or 602-955-6600. Fax: 602-381-7600.* `www.arizonabiltmore.com`*. Self-parking $5; valet $18. Rack rates: Jan–mid-May $375–$575 double; late May–Sept $325–$525; Oct–Dec $195–$275; suites from $650 in high season. AE, DC, DISC, MC, V.*

The Boulders Resort & Golden Door Spa

$$$$$ Carefree

No other resort even came close to maximizing a rugged desert setting as stunningly as the Boulders until the Four Seasons debuted in the new millennium. This resort's other advantages include a branch of the famed southern California pamper palace, the Golden Door Spa; superlative Southwest-design casitas (literally, "little houses"); two excellent golf courses; top-notch dining facilities; the on-site El Pedregal shopping

Phoenix, Scottsdale, and the Valley of the Sun Accommodations

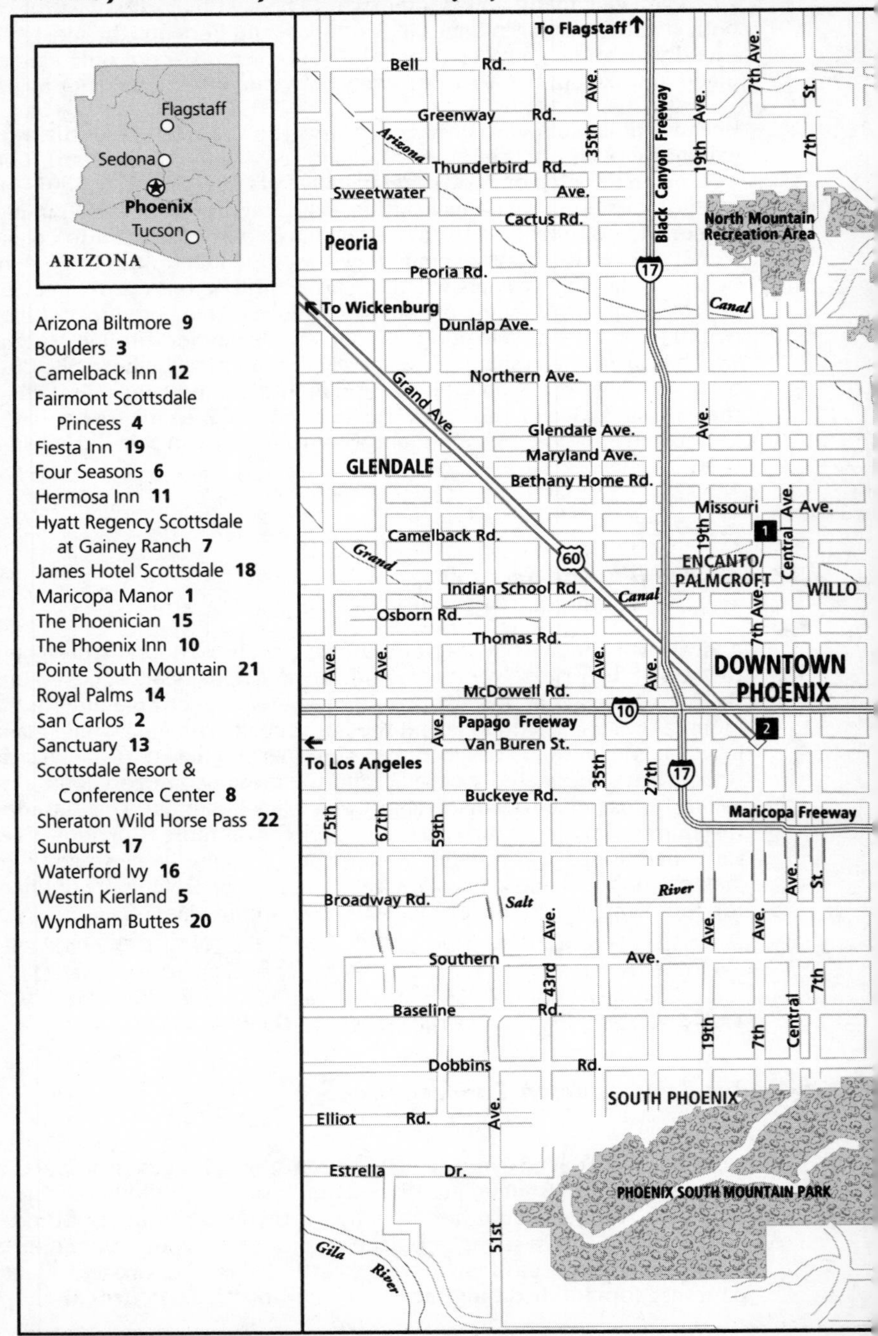

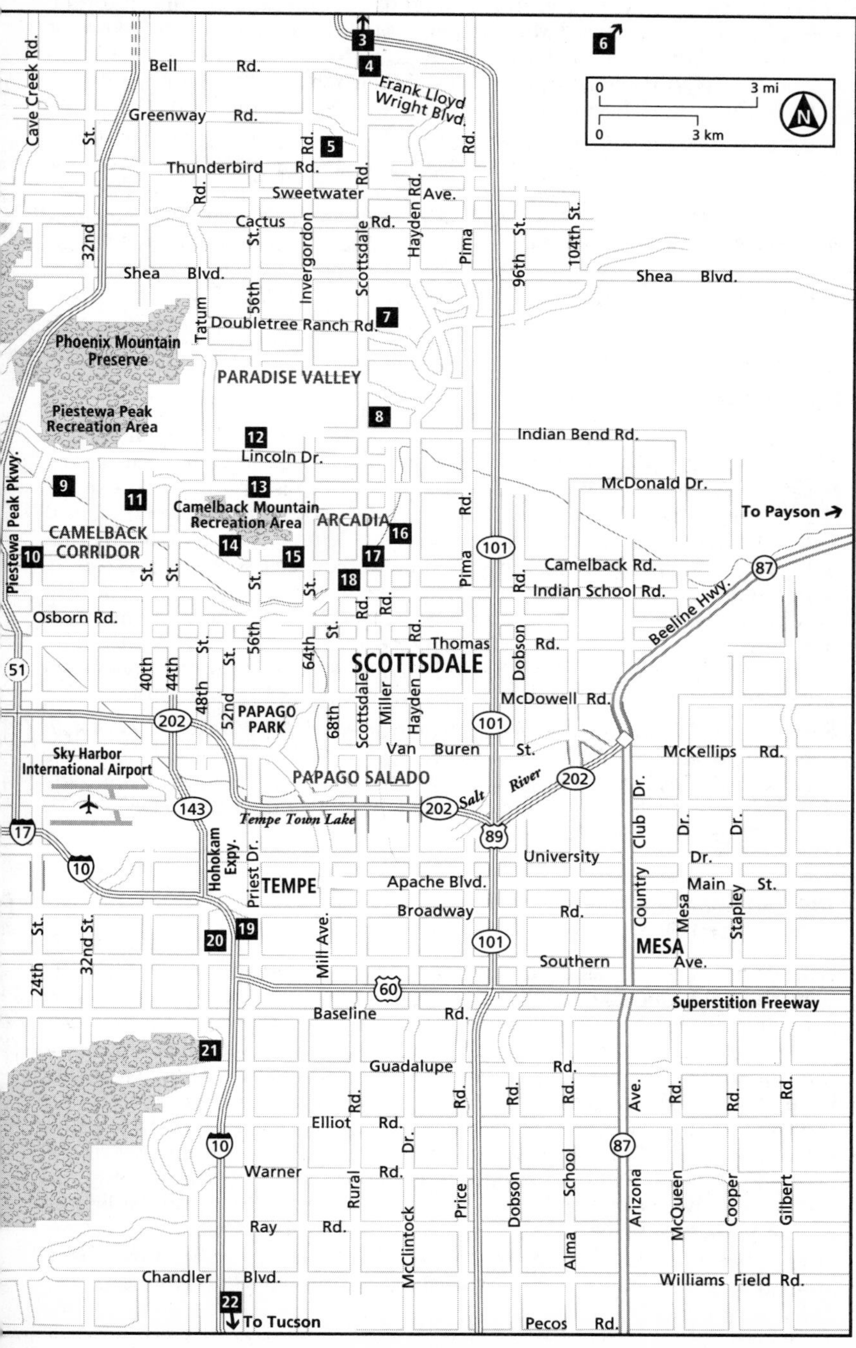
Bell Rd.
Greenway Rd.
Thunderbird Rd.
Sweetwater Ave.
Cactus Rd.
Shea Blvd.
Frank Lloyd Wright Blvd.
Doubletree Ranch Rd.
Phoenix Mountain Preserve
Piestewa Peak Recreation Area
PARADISE VALLEY
Indian Bend Rd.
Lincoln Dr.
McDonald Dr.
To Payson
Camelback Mountain Recreation Area
ARCADIA
CAMELBACK CORRIDOR
Camelback Rd.
Indian School Rd.
Osborn Rd.
Thomas Rd.
SCOTTSDALE
McDowell Rd.
PAPAGO PARK
Van Buren St.
McKellips Rd.
Sky Harbor International Airport
PAPAGO SALADO
Salt River
Tempe Town Lake
University Dr.
TEMPE
Apache Blvd.
Main St.
Broadway Rd.
MESA
Southern Ave.
Superstition Freeway
Baseline Rd.
Guadalupe Rd.
Elliot Rd.
Warner Rd.
Ray Rd.
Chandler Blvd.
Williams Field Rd.
Pecos Rd.
To Tucson
Beeline Hwy.
Hohokam Expy.
Priest Dr.
Mill Ave.
Cave Creek Rd.
Piestewa Peak Pkwy.
Tatum
Invergordon
Scottsdale Rd.
Hayden Rd.
Pima Rd.
96th St.
104th St.
32nd St.
56th St.
40th St.
44th St.
48th St.
52nd St.
64th St.
68th St.
Miller Rd.
Dobson Rd.
Country Club Dr.
Mesa Dr.
Stapley Dr.
24th St.
Rural Rd.
McClintock Dr.
Price Rd.
School Rd.
Alma
Arizona Ave.
McQueen Rd.
Cooper Rd.
Gilbert Rd.
0 3 mi
0 3 km
N
1 2 3 4 5 6 7 8 9 10 11 12 13 14 15 16 17 18 19 20 21 22
51
17
10
60
87
89
101
143
202

center (see the "Getting [boutique] mall'd" section later in this chapter), with a branch of the Heard Museum, no less. If you're planning to take a lot of day-trips north from the Valley — say, to Sedona — you're also well positioned here. If, however, you want to sightsee in the Valley, you're going to have to do a lot of driving to get to most local attractions.

See map p. 116. 34631 N. Tom Darlington Dr. (just north of the Scottsdale Road/ Carefree Highway intersection). ☎ ***800-553-1717*** *or 480-488-9009. Fax: 480-488-4118.* `www.wyndhamboulders.com`. *Self-parking and valet free. Rack rates: Jan–Apr doubles from $625; May and late Sept–Dec doubles from $495; June–mid-Sept doubles from $225; call for holiday rates. 1-, 2-, and 3-bedroom villas available. A $29 per casita service charge is added per night (no tips accepted except in the restaurants and spa). Kids under 16 stay free with adult. AE, CB, DC, DISC, MC, V.*

Camelback Inn, a JW Marriott Resort & Spa

$$$$–$$$$$$ Scottsdale

J.W. Marriott, who had been vacationing here with his family since the 1940s, liked this place so well that he decided to buy it as his first resort. Seeing the appeal is still easy. The Camelback Inn is as laid-back as ever, the newer casitas blend in beautifully with the original adobe units, and kids still happily graduate from the Hopalong College of fun. But such gradually added pleasure-enchancers as the golf courses, a huge spa (totally revamped in 2003–2004), and splashy pool complex take up space, so you may have a tough time finding parking near your stylish, home-away-from-home casita — or finding the casita, period. That said, this is one of my personal favorites, both for its Old Arizona style and its (relative) convenience to New Scottsdale amenities like shops and restaurants.

See map p. 116. 5402 E. Lincoln Dr. (at Tatum Boulevard). ☎ ***800-24-CAMEL*** *or 480-948-1700. Fax: 480-951-5452.* `www.camelbackinn.com`. *Self-parking free; valet is gratuities only. Rack rates: Jan–May $369–$410 double, suites from $750; June–early Sept $129–$189 double, suites from $350; early Sept–Dec $299–$359 double, suites from $525. AE, DC, DISC, MC, V.*

The Fairmont Scottsdale Princess

$$$$$ North Scottsdale

With its red-tile-roof casitas and hacienda-style dining and recreation complex, the Fairmont takes full advantage of its place in the Sonoran Desert sun. Dining rooms like the Marquesa and the Hacienda (see "A Mexican lexicon" sidebar later in this chapter) are a tad more formal than is typical for the Valley, but then the guests here tend to be a tad older. Younger people have plenty of facilities to enjoy, however, including the huge, spectacular Willow Stream spa, great tennis (unusual in this area), and tee-time priority at the adjacent Tournament Players Club of Scottsdale. Rooms are as elegantly Southwest as you'd expect, but the grounds are spread out, and they're not always easy to locate. This place used to be way off the beaten tourist path, but the city has grown up to meet it, so you won't be far from lots of good dining and shopping in north Scottsdale if you bed down here. You will have a bit of a car trek to most major tourists sights, though.

Razing Arizona?

If the scenery at the Four Seasons Resort Scottsdale at Troon North looks familiar, it's because the Coen brothers filmed *Raising Arizona* on this site, pre–Four Seasons, of course.

See map p. 116. 7575 E. Princess Dr. (off Scottsdale Road, north of Frank Lloyd Wright Boulevard). ☎ ***800-344-4758*** *or 480-585-4848. Fax: 480-585-9895.* `www.fairmont.com`. *Self-parking free; valet $18. Rack rates: Jan–Mar 23 $399–$769 double, suites from $769; Mar 24–late May $299–$699 double, suites from $669; May 26–Sept 15 $139–$389 double, suites from $379; Sept 16–Dec $269 –$559 double, suites from $569. Children 17 and under stay free with parents. AE, CB, DC, DISC, MC, V.*

Four Seasons Resort Scottsdale at Troon North

$$$$$ Northeast Scottsdale

The stylish Four Seasons chain pulled out all the stops with its first Arizona link, nabbing a beautiful, still more-or-less remote location; taking advantage of its unusual rock formations; and creating stunning, quintessential Southwest rooms and public areas. The two adjacent Troon North golf courses are as challenging as they come, and the views of the Valley from the Acacia dining room are awesome (its steaks are nothing to sneeze at, either). This property would be among my top picks if I wanted an idyllic desert getaway, but not if I was planning to do a lot of sightseeing (that's the downside of the still more-or-less remote location).

See map p. 116. 10600 E. Crescent Moon Dr. (from North Scottsdale or North Pima take Happy Valley Road east to Alma School Parkway and go north [left]; turn west [left] onto E. Crescent Moon Drive). ☎ ***888-207-9696*** *or 480-515-5700. Fax: 480-515-5599.* `www.fourseasons.com/scottsdale`. *Self-parking free; valet $18. Rack rates: Jan–May $500–$650 double, suites from $795; June–Sept 8 $185–$275 double, suites from $395; Sept 9–Dec $475–$545 double, suites from $795. Two kids under 17 per room stay free with adult. AE, DC, DISC, MC, V.*

Hyatt Regency Scottsdale at Gainey Ranch

$$$$$ North Scottsdale

Water, water everywhere. You'd hardly know you were in arid Arizona, what with the ten pools, waterslides, waterfalls, koi ponds, and even lagoons serviced by gondolas. All this moisture — not to mention a great kids' camp — makes the Hyatt wildly popular with families. Besides, you have the unique Native American and Environmental Learning Center and Southwest flora and fauna tours on the grounds to remind you of where you are. Rooms are decorated in subtle Southwest style (think earth tones) and are well-equipped and comfortable, but try to get one as far from the central lobby's bustle as possible.

*See map p. 116. 7500 E. Doubletree Ranch Rd. (east at Scottsdale Road; you're 6 miles north of McDonald Dr.). ☎ **800-233-1234** or 480-991-3388. Fax: 480-483-5550.* `www.scottsdale.hyatt.com`. *Self-parking free; valet $18. Rack rates: Feb–Apr $400–$580 double; suites from $960; May $340–$450; suites from $780; Jun–Aug $200–$340; suites from $470; Sept–early Dec $220–$430; suites from $510; Dec 7–Dec 23 $280–$390; suites from $660; Dec 24–Jan $340–$520; suites from $840. Kids under 18 stay free with adult, excluding some packages. AE, CB, DC, DISC, MC, V.*

The Phoenician

$$$$$ Scottsdale

This is where people come when they want to enjoy Arizona's desert weather without being subjected to any of the state's rusticity. In addition to all the requisite resort amenities — top-notch golf; a great spa — this place has lots of features you don't usually find in the Valley: Underground parking, acres of grassy lawns, rooms that don't hint of the Southwest (although they're airy and understatedly elegant), as well as what may be Arizona's most formal restaurant, Mary Elaine's (see the "Dining Out" section later in this chapter). Attentive service wins the resort top rankings in all the glossy travel mag polls. For such a posh place, it's surprisingly kid-friendly, with a super water slide and the Funicians Kids Club, a supervised activities program for children ages 5 to 12.

*See map p. 116. 6000 E. Camelback Rd. (between 44th Street and Scottsdale Road). ☎ **800-888-8234** or 480-941-8200. Fax: 480-947-4311.* `www.thephoenician.com`. *Self-parking free; valet $26. Rack rates: Jan–May $625–$725 double, suites from $1,550; Jun–mid-Sept $295–$355 double, suites from $995; mid-Sept–Dec $525–$585 double, suites from $1,450; villas also available. Children under 17 stay free with adults. AE, CB, DC, DISC, MC, V.*

Pointe South Mountain Resort

$$$$ South Phoenix

The ultimate jock retreat. We're talking two 18-hole golf courses plus an indoor, 3D golf trainer; 10 tennis courts; 5 racquetball courts; 2 volleyball courts; a basketball court; a fitness center the size of an airport hangar with a sports medicine clinic, plus Arizona's largest resort water park, with a river ride, giant wave pool, and three water slides. You're also next door to the hiking and horseback riding trails of South Mountain Park. You'll enjoy your attractive Southwest-chic room — should you ever find yourself in it. Dining options include the Western-themed Rustler's Roost, the prime magnet for the play-hard, party-harder guests.

*See map p. 116. 7777 S. Pointe Pkwy. (south of Baseline Road, between S. 48th Street and I-10). ☎ **877-800-4888** or 602-438-9000. Fax: 602-431-6535.* `www.pointesouthmtn.com`. *Parking free. Rack rates: Jan–April $329 double; May $296; June–Sept 5 $169; Sept 6–Dec $309. Children under 12 stay free with adult. AE, CB, DC, DISC, MC, V.*

Sanctuary on Camelback Mountain

$$$$$ Paradise Valley

Since its extreme makeover in the early 2000s from what used to be a tennis resort, Sanctuary has become a magnet for the monied young and restless (and sometimes famous to boot). This intimate property nestled against Camelback Mountain has a dual personality: part gracious Mediterranean getaway, part Zen chic retreat. The newer rooms, spa, and elements restaurant, clustered lower on the mountain, are stunningly pared down, while the less austere red-tile-roof casitas higher up feature gracious Mission-style furniture and bathtubs surrounded by votive candles. Both types are beautiful, and all offer luxurious touches, such as 300-thread-count sheets and Frette robes. And no matter where you stay, you have sweeping vistas of the Valley and of Mummy Mountain and Piestewa Peak.

See map p. 116. 5700 E. McDonald Dr. (at North 56th Street). ☎ ***800-245-2051*** *or 480-948-2100. Fax: 480-483-7314.* `www.sanctuaryaz.com`*. Parking free. Rack rates: Jan 4–Jan 21, May 3–Jun 5, and Sept 9–Sept 30 $345–$395 spa casitas, $295–$345 mountain casitas; Jan 22–May2, Oct–Dec 12, and Dec 26–Jan 1 $445–$495 spa, $395–$445 mountain; Jun 6–Sept 8 and Dec 13–Dec 25 $235–295 spa, $155–$225 mountain. 1- and 2-bedroom casitas from $495 in high season. AE, DC, DISC, MC, V.*

Scottsdale Resort & Conference Center

$$$ Scottsdale

A good bet if you're seeking resort facilities without paying mega-resort prices. Lush grounds, a location in a quiet residential area convenient to all parts of Scottsdale, and access to two adjacent 18-hole golf courses are among the leisure perks of this Spanish hacienda–style complex; on the other hand, you don't get a major spa. The large, attractive rooms have a Spanish old-world air (studded-leather headboards, dark wood armoires), but because this place was almost exclusively geared toward conferences in the past, all offer high-speed Internet access and other business-friendly features. Wireless Internet access is also available in many public areas.

See map p. 116. 7700 E. McCormick Pkwy. (between Scottsdale and Hayden roads); ☎ ***800-528-0293*** *or 480-991-9000. Fax: 480-596-7425.* `www.thescottsdaleresort.com`*. Valet and self-parking free. Rack rates Jan–May $249 double; June–Sept 6 $99 double; Sept 7–Dec $199 double. Children under 12 stay free with an adult. AE, CB, DC, DISC, MC, V.*

Sheraton Wild Horse Pass Resort & Spa

$$$–$$$$ Gila River Indian Reservation, near Chandler

A river runs through it, and wild horses roam around it. And those are only two of the things that make this Native American resort, the offspring of a marriage between the Maricopa and Pima Indians and the corporate American Sheraton, unique. The elders of the two tribes that coexist on the huge Gila River Indian reservation, just off I-10 south of Phoenix, oversaw all the resort's details — golf club, spa, equestrian center, and fine-dining restaurant, Kai (see "A taste of Native America" sidebar later in this chapter). Activities for kids — gourd decorating, nature observing, even whooshing down a water slide shaped like Casa Grande (see Chapter 12) — are painlessly educational. Freeway proximity makes the resort fairly convenient to the airport and Valley attractions, but unlike many other resorts in its price range, this place is so interesting you may not want to leave the premises.

See map p. 116. 5594 W. Wild Horse Pass Blvd., off Exit 162 of I-10. ☎ ***800-325-3535*** *or 602-225-0100. Fax: 602-225-0300.* `www.wildhorsepassresort.com`*. Self-parking free; valet $10. Rack rates: Jan 1–May 24 $289–$389double, suites from $480; May 25–Sept 9 $129–$189 double, suites from $245; Sept 10–Dec 31 $189–$299 double; suites from $450. Children 17 and under stay free with an adult. AE, DC, DISC, MC, V.*

The Westin Kierland Resort & Spa

$$$$$ North Phoenix

Although the Westin has a Phoenix address, that's just a technicality: You're right across the road from Scottsdale, the resort's spiritual (or should I say materialist) home. This place debuted in late 2002, and has all the latest recreational facilities, and it's on the doorstep of the equally new and still expanding Kierland Commons retail and restaurant complex. The Westin takes advantage of its gorgeous desert setting with striking architecture and (gracefully) themed areas that allude to Arizona's history. And the fine dining room, Deseo (see the "Dining Out" section later in this chapter), adds a touch of Latin spice.

See map p. 116. 6902 E. Greenway Pkwy. (just west of Scottsdale Road); ☎ ***800-625-5144*** *or 480-624-1000. Fax 480-624-1001.* `www.kierlandresort.com`*. Self-parking free; valet $18. Rack rates: Jan through May $399–$549 double, suites from $649, casitas from $749; Jun–Sept $139–$289, suites from $409, casitas from $459; Oct–Dec $348–$498, suites from $509, casitas from $609. AE, CB, DC, DISC, MC, V.*

Wyndham Buttes

$$$ Tempe

The good news is that this resort sits atop a mountain overlooking Phoenix and the Valley. The bad news is that its great views are fronted by a freeway. Similarly, the resort's dramatic design and landscaping — the lobby incorporates a cliff — are undercut by the motel-like guest rooms. Still, you have all the leisure facilities (except on-site golf) you could want, you can't beat the convenience to Sky Harbor Airport, and rates are quite reasonable for this high-rent district.

See map p. 116. 2000 Westcourt Way (north of Alameda Dr., west of I-10). ☎ ***800-WYNDHAM*** *or 602-225-9000. Fax: 602-431-2422.* `www.wyndham.com`*. Parking free. Rack rates: Jan–mid-April and mid-Sept–Dec $229 double; mid-April–May $199 double, June–mid-Sept $129 double; suites $475 year-round. Children 17 and under stay free with adult. AE, DC, DISC, MC, V.*

Hotels and inns

Fiesta Inn Resort

$$ Tempe

In Tempe, where the open wallets of separation anxiety–prone parents with kids at Arizona State University tend to jack up room rates, the Fiesta Inn Resort is a great deal. Cost-savers at this appealing independent property, built in the 1970s by a protégé of Frank Lloyd Wright, include complimentary local phone calls, free transfers to the airport, and in-room refrigerators, but you never think discount when you're lounging around the lushly landscaped pool, playing tennis, or enjoying the deck of your airy, Desert Deco–style room.

See map p. 116. 2100 S. Priest Dr. (SW corner of Priest Dr. and Broadway). ☎ ***800-528-6481*** *or 480-967-1441. Fax: 480-967-0224.* `www.fiestainnresort.com`. *Parking free. Jan–mid-April $189 doubles, mid-April–May $149, June–Sept $95, Oct–Dec $165. AE, CB, DC, DISC, MC, V.*

Hermosa Inn

$$$–$$$$ Paradise Valley

Built by cowboy artist Lon Megargee as a home and studio in 1930 and later run by him as an inn, this boutique lodging speaks far more of the artist than of the cowboy. True, the inn is as Western as all get out, with stuccoed adobe walls and rough-hewn beams, but the gardens are lovely and the rooms were stylishly and comfortably updated when the inn was refurbished in the late 1980s. Lon's (see the "Dining Out" section later in this chapter) is hugely popular Valleywide, but guests get first dibs on tables. Located in a posh town between Phoenix and Scottsdale, this place offers convenience as well as local color.

See map p. 116. 5532 N. Palo Cristi Rd. (east of 32nd Street at Stanford). ☎ ***800-241-1210*** *or 602-955-8614. Fax: 602-955-8299.* `www.hermosainn.com`. *Parking free. Rack rates: Jan–Apr $290 double, $340 casita, suites from $490; May $190 double, $240 casita, suites from $390; June–Sept 12 $110 double, $160 casita, suites from $310; Sept 13–Dec $250 double, $300 casita, suites from $590. Specials include discounts for reservations made online. AE, CB, DC, DISC, MC, V.*

Hotel San Carlos

$$ Downtown Phoenix

Resurging right along with downtown, this 1928 high-rise got a millennial makeover that lightened up its rooms and added amenities like coffeemakers, hidden minifridges, irons, and hair dryers, while holding on to the cool octogonal-tile bath floors. The gorgeously opulent lobby was spiffed up too, as was the rooftop pool. The place still needs a bit more work, but the staff is very accommodating, and the location and price are right. A variety of creative tour packages — including one to Sedona and the Verde Valley, another along the Apache Trail, and still another that snags you Diamondback seats — are not only money- but time-saving if you have a limited stay in the Valley.

*See map p. 116. 202 N. Central Ave. at Monroe Street. ☎ **866-253-4121** or 602-253-4121. Fax: 602-253-6668.* `www.hotelsancarlos.com`. *Self-parking $5 at nearby garage. Rack rates: Jan–April $159 double, $220 suite; May–Sept $119 double, $159 suite; Oct–Dec $135 double, $219 suite. Rates include a continental breakfast from the on-premises bakery/cafe. AE, DC, DISC, MC, V.*

Hotel Waterfront Ivy

$$ Downtown Scottsdale

The "waterfront" in the Hotel Waterfront Ivy's name is a not-so-aesthetic canal, but no matter: Five indoor pools with misting and sound systems, as well as a hot tub, provide all the moisture you may want. This all-suites property, part of the Hawthorn Suites chain, also includes tennis courts, a children's play area, a coin-op laundry, and a fitness room. In addition, the rooms are a cut above typical midrange chain accommodations (for example, all offer robes and nonallergenic feather pillows). All in all, for a hotel in the heart of Scottsdale's top shopping and gallery district, this is a great deal.

*See map p. 116. 7445 E. Chaparral Rd., Scottsdale (just east of Scottsdale Rd.) ☎ **888-770-7772** or 480-994-5282. Fax: 480-994-5625.* `www.hotelwaterfrontivy.com`. *Self-parking free. Rack rates: Jan–April 10 $129–$199 suites; April 11–May 22 $99–$149 suites; May 23–Sept. 11 $79–$109 suites; Sept. 12–Dec $109–$159. Rates include breakfast buffet, afternoon happy hour (Mon–Thurs). AE, CB, DC, DISC, MC, V.*

James Hotel Scottsdale

$$–$$$ Old Town Scottsdale

You can't miss this complex of blazing purple, red, and fuschia buildings near the Scottsdale Center of the Arts — and if you're seeking the hippest new (opened early 2004) place in the Valley to lay your head, you won't want to. Designed on the pared-down, industrial-chic model of the W hotels — only less pricey — the James has everything a trendy traveler could desire: 42-inch plasma-screen TV and broadband access in your room, a well-equipped gym, and an outdoor yoga space. Other assets: the sizzling-hot Fiamma Trattoria and J Bar in the main lobby; wi-fi by the pool and pretty much everywhere else on the grounds; and, within walking distance, the abundant shops, restaurants, and nightspots of Old Town Scottsdale.

*See map p. 116. 7353 E. Indian School Rd. (at Drinkwater Boulevard); ☎ **866-50-JAMES** or 480-308-1100. Fax: 480-308-1200.* `www.jameshotels.com`. *Self-parking free; valet $5. Rack rates: Jan–mid-April $175–$285 double, mid-April–mid-May and Sept–Dec $145–$215 double, mid-May–Aug $95–$165 double; suites $325–$425 year-round. Children under 17 stay free with an adult. AE, DC, DISC, MC, V.*

Maricopa Manor B&B Inn

$$ Central Phoenix

More inn than B&B, the Maricopa Manor draws business types and allergic-to-bonding-with-stranger vacationers with amenities such as portable phones with modem jacks, in-suite refrigerators, microwaves, coffeemakers, private entrances and decks, and baskets of breakfast goodies delivered directly to your door. All the spacious suites are individually — and attractively — decorated, so choose your mood. You can happily hang around the pool and hot tub of the pretty Spanish Colonial–style estate (built in 1928), but you're also a hop from the main attractions in Phoenix and Scottsdale.

See map p. 116. 15 W. Pasadena Ave. (one block north of Camelback Road, just west of Central Avenue). ☎ ***800-292-6403*** *or 602-274-6302. Fax: 602-266-3904.* `www.maricopamanor.com`. *Parking free. Rack rates: Jan–Mar $139–$199 double; Apr, Nov, and Dec $129–$179; May and Oct $109–$159; June–Sept $99–$109. AE, CB, DC, DISC, MC, V.*

The Phoenix Inn Suites

$$ Phoenix/Camelback Corridor

Location, location, location — in this case, right near the Camelback Corridor — and reasonable rates draw those in the know to this friendly all-suites property, part of a small western chain. Other pluses: free airport transport, free local phone calls, complimentary wireless Internet, in-room coffeemakers, microwaves, refrigerators, an outdoor pool and Jacuzzi, a fitness center, and guest laundry. All in all, this is a great deal for families as well as for business travelers.

See map p. 116. 2310 E. Highland Ave. (west of 24th Street and south of Camelback Road). ☎ ***800-956-5221*** *or 602-956-5221. Fax: 602-468-7220.* `www.phoenixinnsuites.com`. *Parking free. Rack rates Jan–April $129–$164 double; May–Sept 15 $79–$139 double, Sept 16–Dec $109–$149 double. Continental breakfast buffet included in room rates. Children under 17 stay free with parents. AE, DC, DISC, MC, V.*

Royal Palms Resort and Spa

$$$$$ Phoenix, between the Camelback Corridor and Scottsdale

A perfect spot for a special-occasion vacation, this resort is situated in a 1926 Spanish Colonial Revival mansion turned posh getaway in the late 1940s and architectural showcase in the late 1990s. Gorgeous landscaping, including the Egyptian palms for which it's named, vie for your attention with the stunning Mediterranean-by-way-of-Mexico rooms. T Cook's (see the "Dining Out" section later in this chapter) has some of the most coveted tables in town, as does the adjacent lounge. To remain competetitive in its price category, the Royal Palms recently opened a new spa, but (name notwithstanding) that didn't turn this property into a resort with a capital R — which I consider a good thing. This is a place where you won't get lost, literally or figuratively, something that can't be said for many of the larger properties.

See map p. 116. 5200 E. Camelback Rd. (between 56th Street and Arcadia Drive). ☎ ***800-672-6011*** *or 602-840-3610. Fax: 602-840-6927.* www.royalpalmsresortandspa.com. *Self-parking free; valet is gratuities only. Rack rates: Jan–May $375–$395 double, suites from $415; June–Sept 9 $179–$189 double, suites from $199; Sept 10–Dec $355–$375 double, suites from $385; casitas from $475, villas from $900 in high season. Children 17 and under stay free with adult. AE, CB, DC, DISC, MC, V.*

SunBurst Resort

$$$–$$$$ Downtown Scottsdale

A great downtown Scottsdale location, lushly landscaped grounds — including a very inviting lagoon-style pool complex — and comparatively low rates make this friendly mini-resort a local favorite. SunBurst recently underwent an $8-million renovation, adding an intimate spa with a large menu of treatments, and installing such luxe features as marble sinks and large screen TVs in the guest quarters, all of which have balconies or terraces. Being able to park right near your room is another perk, as is the free shuttle service to and from nearby shops and nightspots (it's nice to know your vehicle is close by — and even nicer to know you don't have to use it). Frequent specials add to the savings.

See map p. 116. 4925 Scottsdale Rd. at N. Chaparral Road. ☎ ***800-528-7867*** *or 480-945-7666. Fax: 480-946-4056.* www.sunburstresort.com. *Parking free. Rack rates: Jan–Mar $309 double, suites $595; Apr–June $139–$259 double, suites $400; July–Sept $139–$239 double, suites $295; Oct–Dec $239 double, suites $400. AE, CB, DC, MC, V.*

Dining Out

Greater Phoenix has grown both up and out in recent years, making this former cowtown a now town, replete with trendy restaurants of every stripe and watering holes for bucks-up tourists, local glitterati, and nationally known celebrities, who — like many average folk — can't get enough of the golf courses and great weather.

When you come, leave behind any preconceptions you may have about hotel dining rooms. A large part of the Valley's economy is driven by the influx of visitors from all over the country — make that, the world. To compete for business in this heated market, the major hotels and resorts have scrambled to create top-notch dining experiences, including drop-dead-gorgeous rooms presided over by celebrity chefs. In addition to the resort and hotel restaurants listed in the following reviews, I also recommend the Golden Swan at the Hyatt Regency Scottsdale at Gainey Ranch, elements at Sanctuary, and the Marquesa at the Fairmont Scottsdale Princess, three romantic dining rooms with very good — and pricey — food. For make-the-scene dining (and outrageously good desserts), consider Fiamma Trattoria, at the James Hotel Scottsdale.

(See the "Staying in Style" section earlier in this chapter for the locations of these properties.)

Forget, too, the idea that malls are bereft of restaurants with character. You can find some of the Valley's best food in strip malls and upscale retail emporia. Of course, Greater Phoenix also abounds with chain restaurants, ranging from fast-food drive-ups to tony steakhouses, with pseudo-ethnic eateries like the homegrown P.F. Chang's and Kona Grill in between. If you have favorites, chances are good you can find them in the Valley. My personal picks in the mid-range chain category are Sam's Café, with three Valley locations, including at the Arizona Center and Biltmore Fashion Park in Phoenix; and Z' Tejas Grill in Scottsdale Fashion Square (see the "Shopping the Local Stores" section later in this chapter, for all three). These two chains serve zesty Southwestern food in a casual atmosphere, and both are Texas imports — so at least they come by their Southwestern culinary credentials honestly.

A gourmet meal around Phoenix isn't exactly cheap. On the other hand, the bill is a bargain compared to the cost of similar restaurants in other major cities, and you can get just about everything here that you can there — except during late-night hours. Prime table time is about 7:30 p.m. If you want to eat at 8:30 or 9 p.m., you should have no trouble getting a reservation, but many restaurants close by 10:30 p.m. For some that don't, see the "Wine bars" section in the "Living It Up After Dark" section of this chapter.

Bloom

$$$ North Scottsdale NEW AMERICAN

A light, contemporary-chic room serving light, contemporary-chic food. Sure, you can get well-prepared hearty fare such as roasted rack of lamb, but this place really shines with salads such as the spinach with glazed pecans and Stilton cheese, appetizers like smoked salmon on a warm potato galette, and entrees such as ahi tuna with bok choy. The wine list is excellent, too. Wa rning: Any virtue you might display in your choice of main course is likely to disappear when you're faced with the triple-chocolate Bars of Sin. Go ahead; desserts here are worth every calorie.

See map p. 128. 8877 N.Scottsdale Rd. (at Doubletree Road in The Shops at Gainey Village). ☎ ***480-922-5666.*** *Reservations recommended for dinner. Main courses: $8–$12 lunch, $15–$24 dinner. Open: Lunch and dinner daily. AE, MC, V.*

Carlsbad Tavern

$$–$$$ Scottsdale NEW MEXICAN/SOUTHWESTERN

A casual, wide-ranging menu and late-night hours (until 1 a.m. nightly) are among the reasons to come to this colorful neighborhood favorite in south Scottsdale. Other reasons include a patio with a stream and fireplace, and spicy fare that's as characteristic of New Mexico as the underground attraction the restaurant's name and bat decor punningly allude to. My

Phoenix, Scottsdale, and the Valley of the Sun Dining

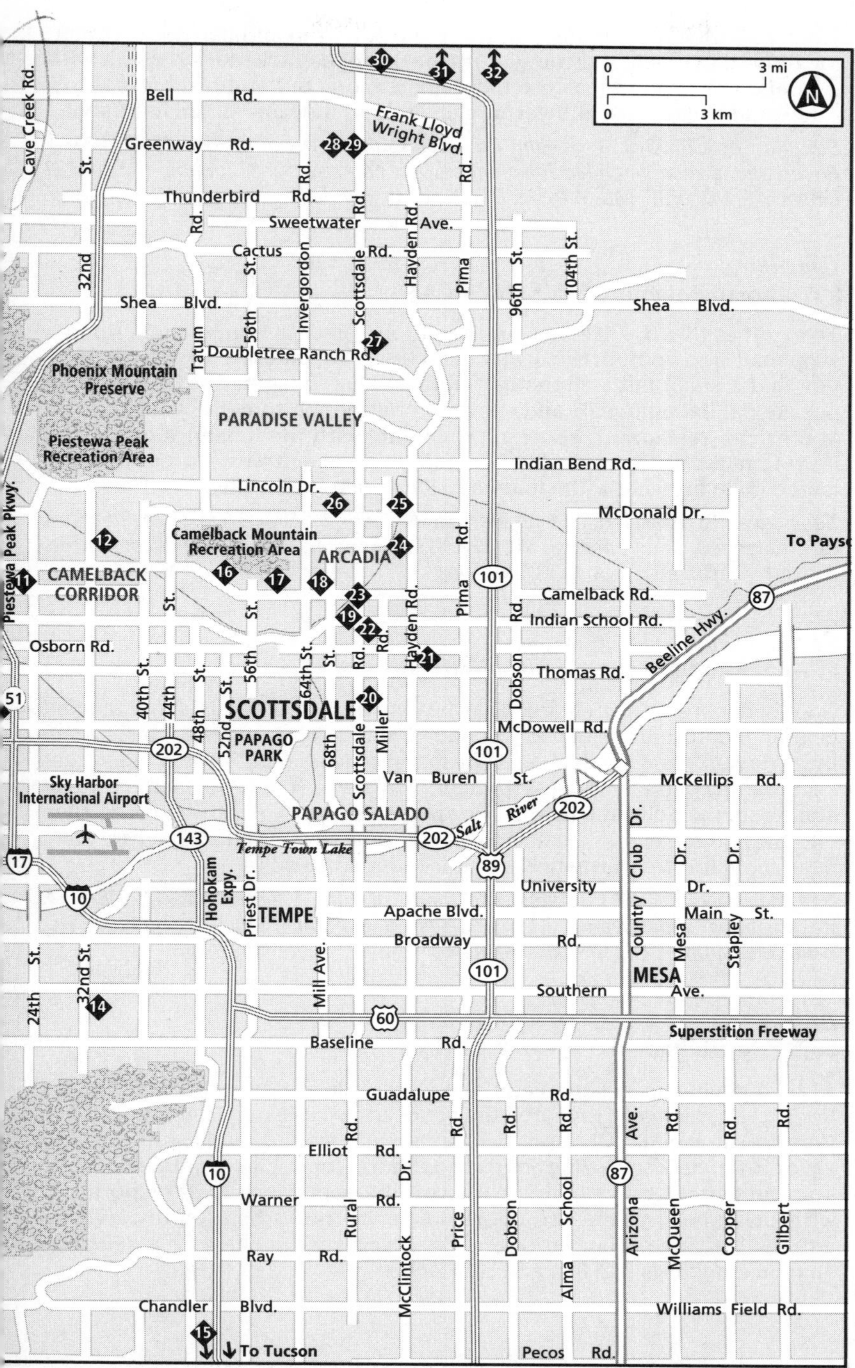

0 3 mi
0 3 km
N
Bell Rd.
Greenway Rd.
Frank Lloyd Wright Blvd.
Thunderbird Rd.
Sweetwater Ave.
Cactus Rd.
Shea Blvd.
Cave Creek Rd.
32nd St.
Tatum Rd.
56th St.
Invergordon Rd.
Scottsdale Rd.
Hayden Rd.
Pima Rd.
96th St.
104th St.
Doubletree Ranch Rd.
Phoenix Mountain Preserve
PARADISE VALLEY
Piestewa Peak Recreation Area
Indian Bend Rd.
Lincoln Dr.
McDonald Dr.
Camelback Mountain Recreation Area
ARCADIA
To Payso
Piestewa Peak Pkwy.
CAMELBACK CORRIDOR
Camelback Rd.
Indian School Rd.
Beeline Hwy.
Osborn Rd.
Thomas Rd.
40th St.
44th St.
48th St.
52nd St.
64th St.
68th St.
Miller Rd.
Dobson Rd.
SCOTTSDALE
McDowell Rd.
PAPAGO PARK
Sky Harbor International Airport
Van Buren St.
McKellips Rd.
PAPAGO SALADO
Salt River
Tempe Town Lake
Hohokam Expy.
Priest Dr.
University Dr.
Country Club Dr.
TEMPE
Apache Blvd.
Main St.
Broadway Rd.
Mill Ave.
Mesa Dr.
Stapley Dr.
MESA
Southern Ave.
24th St.
32nd St.
Superstition Freeway
Baseline Rd.
Guadalupe Rd.
Elliot Rd.
Warner Rd.
Ray Rd.
Chandler Blvd.
Williams Field Rd.
Rural Rd.
McClintock Dr.
Price Rd.
Dobson Rd.
Alma School Rd.
Arizona Ave.
McQueen Rd.
Cooper Rd.
Gilbert Rd.
To Tucson
Pecos Rd.
51
202
143
17
10
101
87
89
60

lunch favorites include the Southwest turkey wrap and habeñero burger; for dinner, I've enjoyed the go-for-(diet)-broke chicken-fried steak with jalapeño gravy, as well as the more abstemious but still tasty fish tacos. Add some margaritas, and you're definitely in the Land of Enchantment.

See map p. 128. 3313 N. Hayden Rd. (just south of Osborne). ☎ ***480-970-8164.*** *Reservations recommended for dinner. Main courses: $7–$12 lunch; $12.50–$20 dinner. AE, DC, DISC, MC, V. Open: Lunch and dinner daily.*

Convivo

$$$ North Phoenix NEW AMERICAN

To say that this upscale but unpretentious place is a mom-and-pop in a strip mall is to do both the owners and their customers a disservice. Here you find a small but well-thought-out wine list, imaginative food with an occasional Italian tweak, and the kind of attention to detail you'd expect at a pricier restaurant. You can't go wrong with the lobster and roasted corn tamales or the macademia-crusted ono as entrees; for dessert, the ancho chile brownie with cinammon ice cream is amazing.

See map p. 128. 7000 N. 16th St. (at Glendale Avenue). ☎ ***602-997-7676.*** *Reservations recommended. Main courses: $19–$22; $29.95 specials include appetizer, entrée, dessert. AE, DC, MC, V. Open: Dinner Tues–Sun Oct–Apr; closed Sun May–Sept.*

Cowboy Ciao

$$$–$$$$ Scottsdale SOUTHWESTERN/ITALIAN

Goofily decorated with Mardi Gras beads and a bright blue star-spangled ceiling, this former art gallery is one of Scottsdale's hippest (and friendliest) downtown retreats. Locals drop by for wine flights and a menu that successfully pairs Southwestern ingredients with Italian specialties. Menu standouts include the Stetson chopped salad, pork rib stuffed with blue cheese, and the exotic mushroom pan fry, the restaurant's signature dish. Save room for the warm, praline-sauced bread pudding.

See map p. 128. 7133 E. Stetson Dr. (north of Fifth Avenue). ☎ ***480-946-3111.*** *Reservations recommended. Main courses: $8–$14 lunch, $20–$32 dinner. AE, DC, DISC, MC, V. Open: Lunch Tues–Sat; dinner nightly.*

Deseo

$$$$ North Phoenix NUEVO LATINO

At his hugely successful Miami and New York restaurants, chef Douglas Rodriguez practically invented the genre known as Nuevo Latino. Now visitors to the Westin Kierland Resort's stylish main dining room can also savor Rodriguez's dazzling South and Central American–inspired cooking. You can't go wrong with any of the ceviche appetizers, and the pork loin with black bean puree and chorizo sausage ranks high on my favorite entrees list. Save room for one of the desserts; the chefs do a delicious spin on standards like flan and tres leches cake.

A taste of Native America

Two Valley restaurants on opposite ends of the price, ambience, and gourmet-aspiration spectrum have one thing in common: They give you a chance to sample the cuisine of Arizona' s first residents, or at least a version of it. After you get a taste of the specialty that gives the Tohono O'odham–owned **Fry Bread House** ($) 4140 N. Seventh Ave., Phoenix (☎ **602-351-2345**) its name, you won't care that you're sitting in a Formica booth under fluorescent lights. You'll be too busy savoring the huge piece of fresh-out-of-the-fryer dough, topped with everything from powdered sugar or honey to chopped beef, cheese, and lettuce. See map p. 128.

In contrast, **Kai** ($$$$), the fine-dining room at Sheraton Wildhorse Pass Resort (see the "Staying in Style" section earlier in this chapter), applies the talents of a James Beard award-winner (Janos Wilder, who created the menu) and a Native American graduate of the Culinary Institute of America (Sandy Garcia, the chef de cuisine) to food raised by the Pima and Maricopa tribes, who own the restaurant and the resort that hosts it. You'll be dining on the likes of rack of lamb with cornbread pudding or pecan-crusted chicken with chayote squash in the stylish dining room or on the chic mountain-view patio. See map p. 128.

*See map p. 128. 6902 E. Greenway Pkwy. (just west of Scottsdale Road) in the Westin Kierland Resort & Spa. ☎ **480-624-1000.** Reservations recommended. Main courses: $26–$32. AE, MC, V, DISC, DC. Dinner Mon–Sat.*

The Farm at South Mountain

$–$$$ South Phoenix ORGANIC

This 12-acre organic farm complex in South Phoenix — on land originally owned by the Heards of Heard Museum fame — offers a veritable cornucopia of dining experiences — all with an emphasis on fresh, local, organic ingredients. Munch out on a picnic table under spreading pecan trees at the Morning Glory Café ($) or The Farm Kitchen ($–$$); the former is known for its omelets and baked goods, the latter for creative salads and sandwiches. Or go gourmet indoors at Quiessence Restaurant and Wine Bar ($$$), where seasonally changing lunches and dinners are prepared in the open kitchen of a wonderful old farm house. A recent spring menu offered such items as hazelnut pesto, ravioli of spring vegetables, and beef tenderloin served with lemon aparagus risotto.

*See map p. 128. 6106 S. 32nd St. (just south of Southern Avenue). ☎ **602-276-6360.*** `www.thefarmatsouthmountain.com`. *Reservations recommended for Quiessence. AE, DC, MC, V. Open: Morning Glory Tues–Fri 8 a.m.–11 a.m., Sat and Sun 8 a.m.–noon. Farm Kitchen Tues–Sun 8 a.m.–3 p.m.; Quiessence 11 a.m.–2 p.m. and 5 p.m.–10 p.m. Tues–Fri.*

Franco's Italian Caffe

$$–$$$ Phoenix NORTHERN ITALIAN

If you're shopping at Biltmore Fashion Park, consider crossing the road to this appealing Art Moderne–style dining room in the smaller Esplanade mall. Tuscan-born chef Franco Fazzuoli makes a mean chilled seafood salad, and is also a whiz at pastas and thin-crust pizzas (you can sample the margherita version for free at happy hour during the week). Come here, too, for the novelty factor: The part owner and pastry chef at Franco's is Arizona's former governor Fife Symington, who attended the Scottsdale Culinary Institute after he left office under a cloud in 1997 (he was convicted of fraud but later pardoned by President Clinton). His signature chocolate cake, "The Governor," is above reproach.

See map p. 128. 2501 E. Camelback Rd. at 26th Street in The Esplanade. ☎ ***602-381-1155.*** `www.francositaliancaffe.com`. *Pastas $12–$18; main courses: $16–$20, AE, MC, V. Open: Mon–Fri lunch, Mon–Sat dinner.*

Lon's at the Hermosa Inn

$$$$ Paradise Valley NEW AMERICAN

Named for cowboy artist Lon Megargee, who built an adobe ranch house on this spot in the 1930s (see the "Staying in Style" section earlier in this chapter), this low-ceilinged, Southwestern artifact–furnished restaurant is a perfect example of rustic Arizona charm. But the sophisticated menu, boasting a robust New American cuisine, wasn't designed with the cowboy set in mind. Leave your Stetson at home and try the signature wood-grilled filet mignon or Oaxacan vegetable ragout. Be sure to snag a table on one of two fabulous patios for lunch or Sunday brunch.

See map p. 128. Hermosa Inn, 5532 N. Palo Cristi Rd. (east of 32nd Street at Stanford). ☎ ***602-955-7878.*** *Reservations recommended. Main courses: $8–$18 lunch; $19–$34 dinner. AE, DC, MC, V. Open: Lunch Mon–Fri; dinner nightly; brunch Sun.*

Mary Elaine's

$$$$$ Scottsdale CONTEMPORARY FRENCH/AMERICAN

A sumptuous decor, elegant service, and twinkling views of the city lights by night make this high-up haute spot tops for a money-is-no-object special occasion. Come here to remember why lobster, foie gras, truffles, caviar, and the like, all of which turn up on the weekly changing tasting menu, became hallmarks of fine dining in the first place. Expect to spend a small fortune but leave completely wowed. Incredible wine list, too, thanks to a $3-million inventory.

See map p. 128. The Phoenician Resort, 6000 E. Camelback Rd. (at 60th Street). ☎ ***480-423-2530.*** *Reservations required. Main courses a la carte: $42–$47; three-course tasting menu $87 per person; six courses $120; five courses with wine $395. AE, DC, DISC, MC, V. Open: Dinner Tues–Sat.*

A Mexican lexicon

Phoenix has more Mexican restaurants than you can shake a taco at, which makes selecting just one a difficult task. You find upscale dining rooms, featuring cuisine from all parts of Mexico; old-fashioned local standbys, serving down-home dishes from Sonora (Mexico's northernmost state, which borders Arizona); and corporate operations geared toward gringos (skip those). Here are some of my favorite places to savor south-of-the-border fare.

- **Carolina's** ($), 1202 E. Mohave St. at 12th Street (South Phoenix) (☎ **602-252-1503**), has locals lining up by 11:30 on any weekday morning, waiting patiently for a crack at the simple Sonoran food. Ambiance is nonexistent, but who cares when you can eat homemade tortillas still warm from the griddle? See map p. 128.
- **La Hacienda** ($$$), Fairmont Scottsdale Princess Resort, 7575 E. Princess Dr., north of Bell Road, east of Scottsdale Road (North Scottsdale) (☎ **480-585-4848**), is sumptuously decorated and decidedly expensive, but you won't find its regional Mexican specialties anywhere else. Roast suckling pig (carved tableside) and the mushroom and goat cheese quesadilla filled with glistening *huitlacoche* (the Mexican equivalent of truffles) are just two exotic examples. See map p. 128.
- **Los Dos Molinos** ($), 8646 S. Central Ave., one block north of E. Euclid (South Phoenix) (☎ **602-243-9113**), housed in the former stable of cowboy star Tom Mix, dishes up delicious New Mexican–style fare. The hot, hot, hot salsas will have you grabbing for the cold brews advertised on its funky neon signs. See map p. 128.
- **Los Olivos** ($$), 7328 E. Second St. at Scottsdale Road (☎ **480-946-2256**), has been around since the art in the nearby downtown Scottsdale galleries was affordable. Come to enjoy not only a slice of history but also dependably good Sonoran-style staples: green corn tamales, chicken enchiladas, and the like. See map p. 128.
- **Los Sombreros** ($$), 2534 N. Scottsdale Rd., south of Thomas (south Scottsdale) (☎ **480-994-1799**), ranges all over the map of Mexico for such savory dishes as *mole poblano* and Yucatan-style slow-roasted pork with tomatillo-chipotle sauce. Other pluses: a kicked-back patio and a nice list of mezcals (not one with a worm in it!). See map p. 128.
- **The New El Portal** ($–$$), 117 W. Grant St., near 2nd Avenue (Phoenix) (☎ **602-271-0521**), is a magnet for local movers and shakers, who come more for the great *carne asada* (grilled meat) tacos and red chile burritors than for the atmosphere. Get here before 2:15 p.m. or get shut out. See map p. 128.
- **Pepe's Taco Villa** ($–$$), 2108 W. Camelback Rd. at 21st Street, east of Highway 51 (Phoenix) (☎ **602-242-0379**), run by a family from Monterrey, dishes up *albondigas* (meatballs), *carnitas* (braised pork), and short ribs just like the Mexican grandma you never had used to make. See map p. 128.
- **San Carlos Bay** ($–$$), 1901 E. McDowell Rd, west of Highway 51 (Central Phoenix) (☎ **602-340-0892**), is the place for cool seafood cocktails, incendiary shrimp *endiablados* (named for the devil himself), and whole crisp snapper served Veracruz-style — it's all here and it's all good, including great chips, addictive salsa, and creamy refried beans. See map p. 128.

Michael's at the Citadel

$$$$ North Scottsdale NEW AMERICAN/NORTHERN ITALIAN

The long drive to this lovely restaurant, which boasts a romantic patio and a spectacular indoor waterfall, not to mention memorable food prepared by chef/owner Michael DeMaria, is worth your time. Customers ooh and ahh over the edible spoon hors d'oeuvres (the spoon is made of puff pastry) as well as over menu favorites such as rosemary-scented lamb chops with goat cheese lasagne and pesto-glazed salmon. The Sunday brunch is super.

*See map p. 128. 8700 E. Pinnacle Peak Rd. (at Pima Road).☎ **480-515-2575.** Reservations recommended. Main courses: $12–$16 lunch; $22–$29 dinner. AE, DC, MC, V. Open: Lunch Mon–Sat (closed for lunch Memorial Day to Labor Day); Sun brunch; dinner nightly (closed Mondays Memorial Day–Labor Day).*

Pizzeria Bianco

$$ Downtown Phoenix PIZZA

Sure it's just a pizza place, but it's a cut — make that a slice — above the rest. Chef-proprietor Chris Bianco combines the street cred of being from the Bronx with the gourmet chops of having won a James Beard award. The terrific wood-fired pizzas and salads are all made with top-notch, often organic, ingredients. The bad news: Proximity to Bank One Ballpark means that the teeny pizzeria, lodged in a 1927 house, is particularly packed on game nights. The good news: You can wait at the recently open beer-and-wine bar in the restored historic house next door. More good news: You can now enjoy the chef's creative wood-fired focaccia sandwiches at the takeout-only Pane Bianco ($), 4404 N.Central Ave. (☎ 602-234-2100), open for lunch Tuesday to Saturday.

*See map p. 128. 623 E. Adams St. in Heritage Square just west of 7th Street. ☎ **602-258-8300.** Pizzas $9–13; antipastos and salads $6–$11. MC, V. Open: Dinner Tues–Sat.*

Rancho Pinot Grill

$$$ Scottsdale NEW AMERICAN

What do you get when you cross funky cowboy-kitsch decor with a menu that's hip but homey? This warm, inviting place, which is booked solid in the winter months, and for good reason. Chef/owner Chrysa Kaufman's exotic mesquite-grilled shrimp with Thai slaw and mango relish is justifiably famous, and the strip steak with portobellas and pancetta is equally delicious. Check out the great wine list, and don't skip dessert.

*See map p. 128. 6208 N. Scottsdale Rd. in Lincoln Village (south of Lincoln Dr.). ☎ **480-367-8030.** Reservations essential in high season. Main courses: $16–$29. AE, DC, DISC, MC, V. Open: Dinner Tues–Sun Oct–Apr, Tues–Sat May–Sept.*

Roaring Fork

$$$ Scottsdale WESTERN AMERICAN

Chef/owner and ex-Texan Robert McGrath dishes up his own brand of hearty but haute Western American cuisine to urbane cowfolk. Patrons come to the airy, light dining rooms for the crab-stuffed catfish, chile-cured duck breast, and terrific short ribs (served with cheese grits). Be prepared to do battle to get a table in the more casual "saloon" ($$) section during weekday happy hours; this is a favorite spot to meet after work for a huckleberry margarita and green chile pork stew or a "Big-Ass" burger.

*See map p. 128. 4800 N. Scottsdale Rd. at Chaparral. ☎ **480-947-0795.** Reservations for main dining room recommended on weekends. Main courses: $16–$29. AE, DC, DISC, MC, V. Open: Dinner nightly; happy hour Mon–Sat 4–7 p.m.*

Sea Saw

$$–$$$$ Downtown Scottsdale SUSHI

A whiz with both wine and raw fish, Nobu Fukuda has Scottsdale's glitterati huddling around the sushi bar in a tiny (26-seat), stylishly pared-down room, nibbling seared tuna tataki and talking wine vintages. Even those who don't like fish in any form will find plenty to savor here, including a dazzling creamy edamame soup. Dishes are reasonably priced but fairly small, so the tab can add up quickly; if you plan to splurge anyway, go for the tasting menu ($100), which pairs Fukuda's fish and wine selections.

*See map p. 128. 7133 E. Stetson Dr., just north of Sixth Avenue. ☎ **480-481-WINE.** www.seasaw.net. Reservations strongly advised. Dishes: $10–$16. AE, DC, DISC, MC, V. Open: Dinner nightly.*

T Cook's

$$$$ Central Phoenix MEDITERRANEAN

For both comfort and elegance, nobody does it better than T Cook's, a lush hideaway with Mediterranean accents. I admit I always liked the atmosphere a bit more than the food, but the addition of Gregory Casale — whose Gregory's World Bistro won reams of accolades over the years — to the kitchen in 2004 put the menu in competition with the setting. Mussels with garlic saffron sauce or black truffle gnocchi with wild mushrooms make great starters; for an entree, try scallops with minted gratin potatoes or spit-roasted chicken with couscous. Finish off your evening with port and piano music in the cozy adjoining lounge.

*See map p. 128. 5200 E. Camelback Rd. at The Royal Palms Resort (between 56th Street and Arcadia Drive). ☎ **602-808-0766.** Reservations recommended. Main courses: $24–$32 dinner. AE, DC, DISC, MC, V. Open: Breakfast, lunch, and dinner daily, Sunday brunch.*

Welcome Diner

$ Phoenix AMERICAN

If you want food that harkens back to the days before anything was prepackaged or tasted like plastic, don't miss this tiny refurbished 1930s diner. The hot dogs, BLTs, grilled cheese sandwiches, and root beer floats are all made with fresh, frequently organic ingredients. Soup and sandwich specials are a bit more gourmet — and you can always get delicious sliced

Great cowtown steaks

Greater Phoenix may have shed many of its (literal) cowtown ways — back in the old days you could smell the stockyards from the airport — but its residents are still serious carnivores. High-end steakhouses abound in the Valley. In addition to corporate favorites like Ruth's Chris and Morton's, you find many independents that are capable of properly aging, cutting, and cooking USDA prime. Nor has the town lost its fondness for cowboy steaks, grilled over a mesquite fire and arriving with nothing fancier than a foil-wrapped baked potato and an iceberg-lettuce salad. Bottom line: If it's meat and it's cooked properly, they will come.

Here's one meat-lover's vote for the top spots to wield a steak knife:

- **Durant's** ($$$$), 2611 N. Central Ave. just south of Thomas (Central Phoenix) (☎ **602-264-5967**), is Phoenix's favorite old-timer, where local movers and shakers come for martinis, great steaks, and a look at each other. See map p. 128.
- **Drinkwater's City Hall Steakhouse** ($$$$), 6991 E. Camelback Rd. (at Goldwater Rd.) (Downtown Scottsdale) (☎ **480-941-4700**), is a swanky spot to swill some single malts and tuck into a filet mignon — and maybe make some business or romantic contacts. The service and food quality are commensurate with the prices. See map p. 128.
- **Fleming's Prime Steakhouse & Wine Bar** ($$$$), 6333 N. Scottsdale Rd. at Lincoln in the Scottsdale Hilton (Scottsdale) (☎ **480-596-8265**), offers prime steaks and great spuds remarkably similar to but slightly less expensive than matching selections at Ruth's Chris. See map p. 128.
- **Pinnacle Peak Patio** ($$–$$$), 10426 E. Jomax Rd. (North Scottsdale) (☎ **480-585-1599**), is, after 50 years, still the No.1 tourist destination for greenhorns hungry for mesquite-grilled steak and a taste of the cowboy life. Wear boots and dance to country bands; wear a necktie and the staff cuts it off and hangs it on the wall with your business card. And don't hesitate to bring the kids. See map p. 128.
- **The Rokerij ($$$)**, 6335 N. 16th St. (Phoenix) (☎ **602-287-8900**), may have a strange name — it's Dutch for "smokehouse," and pronounced *roe*-ker-ee — but the array of well-prepared meat dishes, smoked on a pecan grill or done to a T on a gigantic rotisserie, won't cause any culture shock. Perhaps more alien to early-to-bed Phoenix is that this local favorite is open until midnight, seven nights a week. See map p. 128.

tomatoes drizzled with olive oil — but forget your diet (and/or snooty ways) and go for the super-crunchy fritters. Need a diner fix at night? Come for Thursday dinner ($$$), and bring your own bottle — a Schlitz or Pabst Blue Ribbon, perhaps?

See map p. 128. 928 E. Roosevelt St. (at 10th Street). ☎ ***602-253-7799.*** *Breakfast and lunch from $1.75–$7; three- to four-course dinner Thurs. night $35. MC, V. Open: Breakfast and lunch Mon–Sat.*

Zinc Bistro

$$–$$$ North Scottsdale FRENCH

What a neat trick, transporting an authentic French bistro to a North Scottsdale mall. The details are perfect, from the etched-glass windows and brass wall sconces in the bustling, airy dining rooms right down to menu items like the onion soup gratinée and the tarte Tatin (upside-down apple tart). You can easily make a meal of those two, with a side of knockout pomme frites (french fries). Slaves to nutrition may want to try the wine-steamed mussels or the deliciously simple roast chicken. Now if only the view from the pretty terrace was of the Champs d'Elysee rather than of yet another Scottsdale megaboutique.

See map p. 128. 15034 N. Scottsdale Rd. (at Greenway), in Kierland Commons Mall. ☎ ***480-603-0922.*** *Reservations recommended. Main courses: $15–$22. AE, CB, DC, MC, V. Open: Lunch and dinner (including late-night menu) daily.*

Exploring Phoenix, Scottsdale, and the Valley of the Sun

The Valley generally enjoys such pleasant weather that many of the best ways to spend your days are listed in this chapter's "Staying Active" section. What follows are the top indoor diversions and ways to play outdoors that don't (deliberately) involve sweat.

The top attractions

Arizona Science Center

Downtown Phoenix

The ultimate kids' playscape, with two floors of supercool exhibits, includes a giant sneezing nose and a Fab Lab where you can shoot paper airplanes. You also find a state-of-the-art planetarium and a large-screen Iwerks theater. But you don't have to be pint-size — or a geek — to get a kick out of this place. Valley grown-ups liked it so much that they demanded — and got — their own time here in a series of adults-only evening classes. If you're doing the whole shebang — planetarium + film + exhibits — allot a full morning or afternoon. If not, allow at least two hours anyway; this place is tough to tear your kids (and yourself) away from.

Instead of trolling around for parking, pull into the Heritage and Science Park garage on the corner of Fifth and Monroe streets, where fees are discounted if you get your ticket validated at the science center.

See map p. 138. 600 E. Washington St. (at 7th Street). ☎ ***602-716-2000.*** `www.azscience.org`. *Exhibits admission: $9 adults, $7 ages 3–12 and seniors over 65. Planetarium admission: $5 adults, $4 children and seniors. Theater admission: $5 adults, $4 seniors. Open: Daily 10 a.m.–5 p.m.; closed Thanksgiving and Christmas.*

Phoenix, Scottsdale, and the Valley of the Sun Attractions

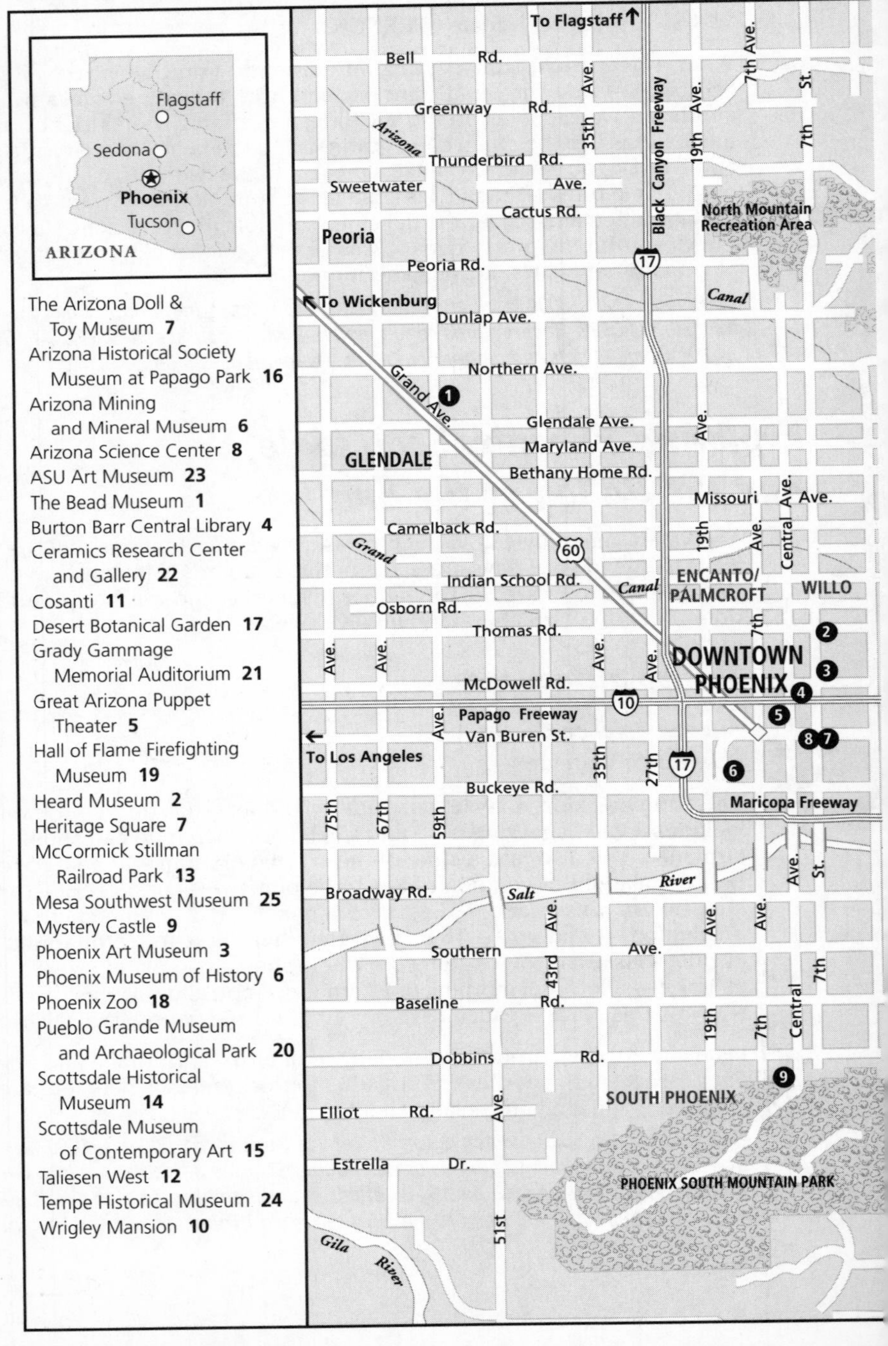

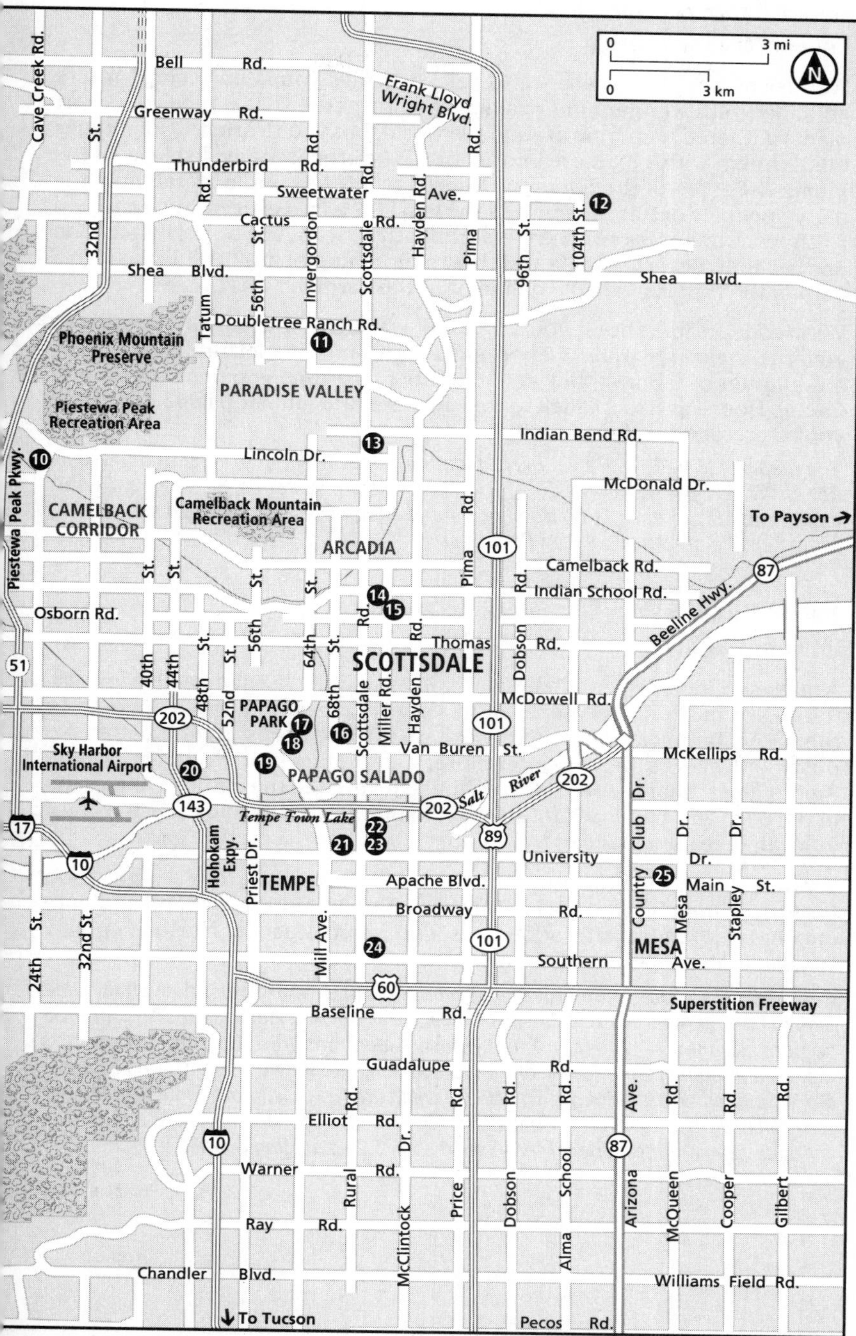
0
3 mi
0
3 km
N
Bell Rd.
Cave Creek Rd.
Frank Lloyd Wright Blvd.
Greenway Rd.
Thunderbird Rd.
Sweetwater Ave.
Cactus Rd.
Shea Blvd.
Shea Blvd.
Doubletree Ranch Rd.
Phoenix Mountain Preserve
Piestewa Peak Recreation Area
PARADISE VALLEY
Indian Bend Rd.
Lincoln Dr.
McDonald Dr.
CAMELBACK CORRIDOR
Camelback Mountain Recreation Area
To Payson →
ARCADIA
Camelback Rd.
Indian School Rd.
Osborn Rd.
Beeline Hwy.
Thomas Rd.
SCOTTSDALE
McDowell Rd.
PAPAGO PARK
Van Buren St.
McKellips Rd.
Sky Harbor International Airport
PAPAGO SALADO
Salt River
Tempe Town Lake
University Dr.
TEMPE
Apache Blvd.
Main St.
Broadway Rd.
Southern Ave.
MESA
Superstition Freeway
Baseline Rd.
Guadalupe Rd.
Elliot Rd.
Warner Rd.
Ray Rd.
Chandler Blvd.
Williams Field Rd.
Pecos Rd.
↓ To Tucson
Piestewa Peak Pkwy.
32nd St.
Tatum Rd.
56th St.
Invergordon Rd.
Scottsdale Rd.
Hayden Rd.
Pima Rd.
96th St.
104th St.
40th St.
44th St.
48th St.
52nd St.
56th St.
64th St.
68th St.
Scottsdale Rd.
Miller Rd.
Hayden Rd.
Dobson Rd.
Hohokam Expy.
Priest Dr.
Mill Ave.
24th St.
32nd St.
Country Club Dr.
Mesa Dr.
Stapley Dr.
Rural Rd.
McClintock Dr.
Price Rd.
Dobson Rd.
Alma School Rd.
Arizona Ave.
McQueen Rd.
Cooper Rd.
Gilbert Rd.
17
10
51
202
143
101
89
87
60
10
10
11
12
13
14
15
16
17
18
19
20
21
22
23
24
25

Desert Botanical Garden

Phoenix (Papago Park)

Wondering about all those weird prickly things you keep seeing? You're still filled with wonder after examining some of the 20,000 types of desert plants gathered here from around the world, but you're armed (sometimes multiarmed) with a lot more information. The ethnobotany displays on the Plants & People of the Sonoran Desert Trail, for example, detail how the native peoples of this area turned the local flora into everything from food to shoes. Don't miss two very colorful, attractions: the butterfly pavilion and a ⅓-mile desert wildlife trail that's blooming beautiful (in season); a map of the trail is available online or at the garden.

Wear comfortable shoes; you do a lot of walking, especially if you want to cover the two side trails. Wandering the grounds at a leisurely pace takes a minimum of 2 hours, but you can duck into the Succulent House and Cactus House and loop back to the entrance and gift shop in 45 minutes if you're pressed for time.

*See map p. 138. 1201 N. Galvin Pkwy. (south of McDowell Road, west of Scottsdale Road). ☎ **480-941-1225.*** `www.dbg.org`. *Admission: $9 adults, $8 seniors, $5 students with I.D., $4 ages 5–12, free ages 4 and under. Open: Oct–April 8 a.m.–8 p.m., May–Sept 7 a.m.–8 p.m.; closed Christmas.*

Heard Museum

Downtown Phoenix

A must-see. Established in a gracious Spanish Colonial–style house in 1929, the Heard has long been one of the country's best museums devoted to the native peoples of the Southwest, and it just keeps getting better. No dusty pot shards here: Contemporary, sometimes provocative, Native American art shares space with exhibits devoted to the cultures and crafts of the past, and hands-on, interactive displays entertain kids. On fine days, you can take advantage of the wonderful outdoor sculpture garden.

If you factor in time for browsing the huge, impossible-to-resist gift shop (see the "Shopping the Local Stores" section later in this chapter), figure on a full morning or afternoon here. The Heard Museum North is equally terrific, if on a much smaller scale.

*See map p. 138. 2301 N. Central Ave. (4 blocks north of McDowell Road, on the east side of Central Ave.). ☎ **602-252-8848.*** `www.heard.org`. *Admission: $7 general, $6 seniors, $3 ages 4–12, under 4 and Native Americans free. Guided docent tours included in admission price given noon, 1:30 p.m. and 3 p.m. Open: Daily 9:30 a.m.–5 p.m.; closed major holidays. The Heard Museum North is in the El Pedregal complex, 34505 N. Scottsdale Rd., Scottsdale. ☎ **480-488-9817.** Admission: $3 adults. free for ages 12 and under. Open: Mon–Sat 10 a.m.–5:30 p.m., Sun noon–5 p.m.*

Cafe culture

Three of Phoenix's top attractions, the Desert Botanical Garden, the Heard Museum, and the Phoenix Art Museum, feature Arcadia Farms cafes, branches of a Scottsdale restaurant known for its creative salads and sandwiches. So you won't go wrong, food-wise, if you plan your museum visit to overlap with lunchtime. These restaurants are very popular, though, so you may have a wait on weekends.

Phoenix Art Museum

Downtown Phoenix (North)

One of the Southwest's largest art museums, this is the venue that hosts all the major shows from out of town. The two low-slung boxes and a connecting patio that comprise the museum complex are open and attractive, and the permanent collection is strong in modern and Western art; the miniatures are a particular treat. To be honest, aside from special shows and events (such as the annual Cowboy Artists of America exhibition and sale in the fall), this museum isn't really a must-see unless you're visiting from an art-deprived city or experiencing culture shock. Still, you find plenty here to hold your attention for a few hours or so.

*See map p. 138. 1625 N. Central Ave. (at Coronado Road). ☎ **602-257-1222.*** www.phxart.org. *Admission: $9 adults, $7 students and seniors, $3 ages 6–17, free ages 5 and under. Free admission on Thursdays. Open: Tues, Wed, Fri–Sun 10 a.m.–5 p.m.; Thurs 10 a.m.–9 p.m.; closed Mon and major holidays.*

Pueblo Grande Museum and Archaelogical Park

Phoenix (Papago Salado area)

This prehistoric Hohokam village and associated museum, sandwiched between several freeways and in full view of Sky Harbor Airport, may not be Arizona's most impressive Native American site, but you won't find a more graphic contrast between the city's past and its present. Materials uncovered during Phoenix's various excavations — many done in order to build highways — are on display, so you get a fascinating record of the city's early dwellers, as well as some rare insight into the archaeological process. The real draw, however, is the ruins, which include an ancient ball court.

The ⅔-mile trail through the Hohokam village isn't a loop. If the day is hot or you're tired, you don't need to go beyond the platform mound to see the ball court at the far end of the complex (the perspective is better from on high anyway). The museum is small and the ruin trail relatively short; you can cover both in about an hour.

*See map p. 138. 4619 E. Washington St. (at 44th Street). ☎ **877-706-4408** or 602-495-0900.* www.ci.phoenix.az.us/PARKS/pueblo.html. *Admission: $2 adults, $1.50 ages 55 and over, $1 ages 6–17, free ages 5 and under; Sun free. Open: Mon–Sat 9 a.m.–4:45 p.m., Sun 1–4:45 p.m.*

Scottsdale Museum of Contemporary Art

Scottsdale (near Old Town)

For an "outpost" art museum to impress an ex-Manhattanite like me isn't easy, but I'm crazy about this place. It's fun and provocative, and it has a great venue, a former discount movie theater that artist Will Bruder creatively converted into an art space (see the "Architect trek: The next generation[s]" sidebar in this chapter). Rotating exhibits highlight architecture and design along with painting, sculpture, and things less classifiable — for example, preview exhibits from Roden Crater, an extinct volcano being turned into artwork by James Turrell. The museum isn't all that large; you can see everything in an hour or so. One bonus: Just across Drinkwater Bouleverd, at Scottsdale Civic Center Mall, you can view 13 modern sculptures, including Robert Indiana's red LOVE, an icon of the 1960s.

See map p. 138. 7374 E 2nd St. (at Drinkwater Boulevard). ☎ ***480-994-2787.*** www.scottsdalearts.org. ***Admission: $7 adults, $5 students, free ages 14 and under;*** *Thurs free. Open: Fall/winter spring Tues, Wed, Fri, Sat 10 a.m.–5 p.m., Thurs 10 a.m.–8 p.m., Sun noon–5 p.m.; Mon closed. Summer Wed and Sun. noon–5 p.m., Thurs 10 a.m.–8 p.m., Fri and Sat 10 a.m.–5 p.m., closed major holidays.*

Taliesen West

North Scottsdale

You don't have to be an architecture buff to want to head out to the winter home, studio, and architectural "laboratory" that were the domain of America's master builder, Frank Lloyd Wright, from 1937 until his death in 1959. Often ranked among Wright's top designs, Taliesen West is now a National Historic Landmark. From the early days, showing the public around the grounds was part of the training program for the apprentices at the (still operating) Frank Lloyd Wright School of Architecture. The desert may not be as pristine as it was when Wright ruled here — he was so irate over the few power lines that went up in the 1950s that he built his living room to face away from them — but as the excellent architectural tours

From gum to Spam

The **Wrigley Mansion,** 2501 E. Telawa Tr., Camelback Corridor (☎ **602-955-4079;** www.wrigleymansionclub.com), a huge Mediterranean residence built between 1929 and 1931 by chewing-gum king William Wrigley Jr., is now owned by Geordie Hormel, whose family made its fortune with Spam. A professional entertainer — in the 1950s and 1960s, he composed and performed TV themes, from shows such as *Ozzie & Harriet* to *The Untouchables* — Hormel now plays the piano at the elaborate Sunday champagne brunch. If you don't want to come for brunch, lunch (Tues–Fri), or dinner (Wed–Sat), you can take a fascinating tour Tuesday through Friday at 10 a.m. and 2 p.m. for $11 per person. (To find Telawa, turn into the Arizona Biltmore Circle, off 24th Street, between Missouri and Lincoln.) See map p. 138.

Architect trek: The next generation(s)

Frank Lloyd Wright put his mark on the Valley. In this chapter, you can find information on his best-known local projects: Scottsdale's **Taliesen West** (see the "Exploring Phoenix, Scottsdale, and the Valley of the Sun" section); Phoenix's **Arizona Biltmore Hotel** (see the "Spending the Night" section), for which Wright was a design consultant; and Tempe's **Grady Gammage Memorial Auditorium** at Arizona State University (see the "More cool things to see and do" section). But Wright also inspired two more generations of Greater Phoenix space-building pioneers.

You can tour the famed desert community of Wright protégé Paolo Soleri called **Arcosanti** (see Chapter 12) and its smaller, Scottsdale prototype, **Cosanti** (see "The tintinnabulation of the bells, bells, bells" sidebar in this chapter). And Soleri student Will Bruder not only created the **Scottsdale Museum of Contemporary Art** (see the "Exploring Phoenix, Scottsdale, and the Valley of the Sun" section), he's also responsible for downtown Phoenix's **Burton Barr Central Library,** 1221 N. Central Ave. south of Culver Street (☎ **602-262-4636;** www.phoenixpubliclibrary.org/web/ec.central.html), a 5-story cube partially covered in copper that's a real dazzler at sunset. For a closer look at some of its more unusual features — for example, the suspended ceiling in the huge reading room — stop at the directions desk at the foot of the stairs when you enter and ask for the self-guided tour pamphlet. See map p. 138.

and the Wright-o-bilia sold at the gift shop attest, the architect's work and principles are as vital as ever.

See map p. 138. 12621 Frank Lloyd Wright Blvd. (approximately 114th Street at Cactus Road). ☎ ***480-860-8810*** *(tour information) or 480-860-2700 (general information and directions).* www.franklloydwright.org. *Admission: Taliesen West offers five different guided tours (the only way to see the grounds), which vary depending on the season: They range from the 1-hour standard ("Panorama") tours, offered year-round (Oct–May $17.50 adults, $15 seniors and students, $5 ages 4–12; June–Sept $14 adults, $12 seniors/students, $4.50 ages 4–12) to a 3-hour "Behind the Scenes" tour ($45 per person in winter; $25 in summer). If you're in town on Fri night, May–Sept, don't miss the 2-hour "Night Lights on the Desert" tour ($22.50 person). Open: The visitor center/gift shop daily 8:30 a.m.–5:30 p.m Sept–June; closed Tues and Wed July–Aug and Easter. Tour times and frequency depend on season. Call ahead — but you can expect something every day starting at 9 a.m.*

More cool things to see and do

Additional attractions in Greater Phoenix range from a gem of a museum good for whittling away an hour or two to a city where you can easily devote several days.

- Mine the state's past: The early adventurers and investors who came to Arizona in droves learned the hard way that all that glitters isn't gold; you get a far less stressful version of that lesson at the small Arizona Mining and Mineral Museum, 1502 W. Washington

St. at 15th Avenue (☎ 602-255-3791; www.admmr.state.az.us). Whether you're interested in mines or mining, these rocks and gemstones are mighty pretty. Admission: $2, under 18 free. Open: Mon–Fri 8 a.m.–5 p.m., Sat 11 a.m.–4 p.m. Closed state holidays. See map p. 138.

- Get strung along: The Bead Museum, 5754 W. Glenn Dr. at 58th Avenue, Glendale (☎ 623-931-2737), is no mere ode to adornment. Beads had — and still have — commercial, ceremonial, and religious purposes, detailed through a variety of beautiful objects from around the world. You see everything from elaborate headdresses to beads that were traded for slaves. Crafters can learn the latest techniques, too. Admission: $4 adults, $2 ages 12 and under; free Thurs 5:30 p.m.–8 p.m. Open: Mon–Sat 10 a.m.–5 p.m., Thurs 10 a.m.–8 p.m., Sun 11 a.m.–4 p.m. See map p. 138.

- Explore Phoenix's heritage: Heritage Square, 115 N. 6th St. at Monroe, downtown Phoenix (☎ 602-262-5029, ext. 1 or 602-262-5071; www.ci.phoenix.az.us/PARKS/heritage.html), a group of Victorian-era structures listed on the National Register of Historic Places, gives a glimpse of an architectural style not generally associated with Arizona. The Rosson House is furnished with period antiques. The Stevens House hosts the Arizona Doll and Toy Museum (for details, see "The kids' corner" sidebar in this chapter). A tearoom/cafe/gift shop (☎ 602-252-4682) and Pizzeria Bianco (see the "Dining Out" section earlier in this chapter) are also in the complex. Admission: Complex, free; Rosson House, $4 adults, $3 seniors, $1 ages 6–12, free ages 5 and under. Open: Complex, always open; Rosson House, 30-min. tours Wed–Sat 10 a.m.–4 p.m. and Sun noon–4 p.m., last tour at 3:30 p.m.; closed mid-Aug–Labor Day, major holidays; tearoom/cafe/gift shop, Tues–Sat 11 a.m.–4 p.m. and Sun noon–4 p.m. See map p. 138.

- Imagine the past: Mystery Castle, 800 E. Mineral Rd. (take Central Avenue south to the entrance to South Mountain Park; ☎ 602-268-1581), created by Boyce Gulley in the 1930s and 1940s from local stones and unusual materials from all around Arizona, is part medieval fortress, part Old West town. Gulley's daughter, for whom the castle was built, still conducts tours of this folk-art phantasmagoria. Admission: $5 adults, $2 ages 6–15, ages 5 and under free. Open: Thurs–Sun 11 a.m.–4 p.m.; closed July–Sept. See map p. 138.

- Talk to the animals: The 125-acre Phoenix Zoo, 455 Galvin Pkwy., in Papago Park (☎ 602-273-1341; www.phoenixzoo.org), stars the usual animal suspects in their usual re-created habitats. Kids can get up close and personal with chickens, goats, sheep, and mules at the four-acre Harmony Farm. This fine zoo isn't distinctive enough to go on the top of a Phoenix tour list. Admission: $12 adults, $9 seniors (Jun–Aug $9 adults, $7 seniors), $5 ages 3–12, free ages 2 and under. Open: Sept–May daily 9 a.m.–5 p.m.; June–Aug 7 a.m.–4 p.m.; closed Christmas. See map p. 138.

The kids' corner

Phoenix has much to offer to keep the prepubescent set entertained. In addition to the attractions listed in this sidebar, also check out the Desert Botanical Garden and the Heard Museum (listed in the "Seeing the Sights" section in this chapter), the Phoenix Zoo (see the "More cool things to see and do" section), and the Phoenix Museum of History and Arizona Historical Society Museum (in the "It's history" sidebar).

- **The Arizona Doll & Toy Museum,** 602 E. Adams St., Heritage Square, downtown Phoenix (☎ **602-253-9337**), has something for all ages and genders, including an antique, miniature millinery store and candy store with ice cream counter; and an action-figure exhibit starring GI Joe. Admission: $3 adults, $1 children 12 and under. Open: Tues–Sat 10 a.m.–4 p.m., Sun noon–4 p.m.; closed Aug–Labor Day. See map p. 138.
- **Hall of Flame Firefighting Museum,** 6101 E. Van Buren St. in Papago Park, Phoenix (☎ **602-275-3473**; `www.hallofflame.org`), the world's largest of its type, features more than 90 gleaming pieces of fire equipment dating back to 1725. Retired firefighters often regale visitors with gripping tales of rescue, and kids get to climb on some of the equipment and (yikes!) even ring alarm bells. Admission: $5.50 adults, $4.50 seniors, $3 ages 6–17, $1.50 ages 3–5, free ages 2 and under. Open: Mon–Sat 9 a.m.–5 p.m., Sun noon–4 p.m.; closed New Year's Day, Thanksgiving, and Christmas. See map p. 138.
- **Mesa Southwest Museum,** 53 N. MacDonald St. at 1st Street, Mesa (☎ **480-644-2230**; `www.mesasouthwestmuseum.com`), wraps its learning in a very entertaining package, using everything from animated dinosaurs to hands-on gold panning to teach kids the history of the Southwest. Rotating exhibits on history and art cater to adults. Admission: $6 adults, $5 seniors and students with ID, $3 ages 3–12, free ages 2 and under. Open: Tues–Sat 10 a.m.–5 p.m., Sun 1–5 p.m.; closed Mon and major holidays. See map p. 138.
- **McCormick Stillman Railroad Park,** 7301 E. Indian Bend Rd. at Scottsdale Road, Scottsdale (☎ **480-312-2312**; `www.therailroadpark.com`), is a kick for both kids and adult rail buffs, who can tootle around the park on a 5/12 scale model train. Two railroad depots and several model trains add to the fun. You also find a 1929 carousel and a general store, where you can buy snacks and souvenirs. Admission: $1 for train and carousel rides, children under 3 free with a paying adult. Hours vary with the season, so call or visit the Web site for schedules. See map p. 138.

- Take a trip to Tempe: In this pleasant town just east of Phoenix, you can check out the various attractions on the campus of Arizona State University. These include the ASU Art Museum, Nelson Fine Arts Center, 10th Street and Mill Avenue (☎ 480-965-ARTS; `www.asuartmuseum.asu.edu`), where striking, subterranean galleries display contemporary and Latin American art and some modern

American masters (admission free; open Tues 10 a.m.–9 p.m. during the school year, 10 a.m.–5 p.m. in summer, Wed–Sat 10 a.m.–5 p.m.); the Ceramics Research Center and Gallery, just north of the art museum (☎ 480-965-2787; www.asuartmuseum.asu.edu/ceramicsresearchcenter), an airy, open space featuring contemporary and antique creations of clay and glaze; and the Grady Gammage Memorial Auditorium, Gammage Parkway and Mill Avenue (☎ 480-965-4050; www.asu.edu/it/museums/gammage.html), one of Frank Lloyd Wright's last creations, which offers free tours from 1 to 3:30 p.m. during the school year (may be closed during performance days). For other Tempe attractions, see the "It's history" sidebar and sections on shopping, guided tours, and keeping active — all in this chapter. The Tempe Convention and Visitors Bureau, 51 W. 3rd St., #105 (☎ 800-283-6734 or 480-894-8158 ; www.tempecvb.com; open: Mon–Fri 8 a.m.–5 p.m.), can give you additional information, such as how to pronounce the town's name (okay, I'll tell you myself: It's tem-pee). For all locations in Tempe, see map p. 138.

It's history

Right next to the Arizona Science Center, the **Phoenix Museum of History,** 105 N. 5th St., between Monroe and Washington streets (**☎ 602-253-2734;** www.pmoh.org), gives a far from old-fashioned peek into the city's past. Exhibits include everything from a replica of the beer-bottle sidewalk that fronted one of the city's saloons to the ultimate cheap hoosegow (a knee-high rock to which prisoners were chained). Admission: $5 adults; $3.50 seniors, students, military; $2.50 ages 7–12; free ages 6 and under, free on Wed from 2–5 p.m. Open: Tues–Sat 10 a.m.–5 p.m. See map p. 138.

In Tempe, the **Arizona Historical Society Museum at Papago Park,** 1300 N. College Ave. (**☎ 480-929-0292;** www.arizonahistoricalsociety.org), covers the entire state via excellent displays ranging from a reproduction World War II canteen to a room devoted to Wallace & Ladmo, a popular Phoenix children's show. (Admission: $5 adults, $4 seniors 60 and up and ages 12–18, free for children under 12, free first Sat of the month.) Open: Tues–Sat 10 a.m.–4 p.m., Sun noon–4 p.m.) See map p. 138. The smaller **Tempe Historical Museum,** 809 E. Southern Ave. at Rural Road (**☎ 480-350-5100;** www.tempe.gov/museum), has hands-on activities that include diverting the Salt River into canals and fields. Admission: Free. Open: Mon–Thurs and Sat 10 a.m.–5 p.m., Sun 1–5 p.m.; closed Fri and major holidays. See map p. 138.

Stop in at the 1910 schoolhouse that houses the **Scottsdale Historical Museum,** 7333 E. Scottsdale Mall (**☎ 480-945-4499;** www.scottsdalemuseum.com), to view the town B.C.C. (Before Conspicuous Consumption) and to pick up a map for a self-guided walking tour highlighting 13 historic locations of the 1894 town site now called Old Town Scottsdale. Admission: Free. Open: Wed–Sat 10 a.m.–5 p.m., Sun noon–4 p.m., closed July–Aug. See map p. 138.

Staying Active

From serene golfing greens to extreme biking terrain, Greater Phoenix has the means to keep you happily playing outside. But, in case you hadn't noticed, Phoenix is in a desert. Bring plenty of water and keep on drinking it, even if you don't think you're thirsty, and even if you don't realize you're sweating. Water evaporates quickly in this dry air. Keeping hydrated is important for any sport in which you participate, but especially for the more strenuous ones like hiking and biking.

Biking

Thanks in good part to a large student population, Tempe has more than 150 miles of urban bike paths, making it the Valley's best — really the only — in-city biking territory. In addition, a paved, off-street bike path, as well as a gravel mountain biking path, surround Tempe Town Lake. You can view a bikeway map on the Web site of the City of Tempe's Transit office, 20 E. Sixth St. at Mill Avenue, 3rd floor (☎ 480-350-2775; www.tempe.gov/tim), or request to have it mailed to you. You can also pick up a bikeway map at the transit office or at any bike shop in Tempe, including Tempe Bicycle, 330 W. University and Farmer, three blocks west of Mill Avenue (☎ 480-966-6896; www.tempebicycle.com), which has a great selection of road and mountain bikes for rent. Rates range between $15 and $40 for 1e day, $25 and $55 for 2 to 3 days, and $45 and $75 for a week. In Scottsdale, the Indian Bend Wash Greenbelt, covering more than 26 miles along Hayden Road from Shea to where it meets Tempe Town Lake's bike path, is popular with pavement-happy bicyclists, as well as with joggers and in-line skaters. You can enter the path from several spots off Hayden Road.

Desert-bound mountain bikers have their pick of dramatic Valley trails. Arizona Mountain Bike Guide: Fat Tire Tales and Trails, published by Cosmic Ray in Flagstaff, has the lowdown on the best ones. Order a copy ($11.95) online at www.amazon.com or pick one up at any local bike or outdoor shop; a good one in Scottsdale is REI, 12634 N. Paradise Village Pkwy. W. (☎ 602-996-5400; www.rei.com). Beginners often dust their wheels on the trail starting at Dynamite Road and Pima, 8 miles north of Bell Road in Scottsdale; the desert blooms are gorgeous here in spring. South Mountain Park, 10919 S. Central Ave. (☎ 602-495-0222; http://phoenix.gov/PARKS/hikesoth.html), and Papago Park, 625 N. Galvin Pkwy. (☎ 602-256-3220; http://phoenix.gov/PARKS/hikepapa.html), in south and east Phoenix, respectively, have plenty of trails to keep all levels happily shifting gears.

Boating

Spend a sunny afternoon on the Tempe Town Lake by renting a kayak or pedal boat ($12 for the first hour), or four- to six-person electric boat ($35 or $55 for the first hour) from the RioLago Cruise kiosk near the

Careful of those cacti: Tips for desert golfers

If you're used to teeing off onto wide, rolling greens, desert golf — also known as target golf — can be an entirely new ball game. To master these prickly courses:

- **Concentrate on aim rather than distance.** Fairways are narrow and frequently broken up by desert, so you have to hit the ball straight off the tee to get to the greens, even if that means not using a driver right away. (Get it? That's why they call it "target" golf.)
- **Bring lots of balls.** On desert courses, the rough is really rough — as in prickly and spiny. You're not going to want to go poking around in that stuff.
- **If you do go searching for a ball, take a club with you** so you can clobber the rattlesnakes (just kidding about the clobbering — slow but steady retreat is a much better strategy — but not kidding about snakes. Use the club to make sure any underbrush where your ball is hiding out is critter-clear).
- **Bring lots of water and keep drinking it,** even if you don't think you're thirsty. You don't always realize when you're getting dehydrated.
- **Don't forget sunscreen and a hat.**
- **If you see wildlife about to carry your ball off the fairway, yell loudly** — or take a mulligan.

Mill Avenue bridge at Tempe Beach Park, 55 W. Rio Salado Pkwy. (☎ 480-517-4050; www.riolagocruise.com); be prepared to leave a driver's license and credit card as a deposit.

Golfing

No doubt about it: In the Valley, golf rules. With more than 200 courses, Greater Phoenix consistently ranks among the world's top-five golf destinations. You're never much more than a putt away from some major greens action. The Official Arizona Golf Guide and Directory, available free at most local hotels, resorts, and golf courses, or in advance from the Valley visitor bureaus (see the "Finding Information after You Arrive" section earlier in this chapter), gives a general wrap up of the local courses. See Chapter 5 to find out about golf schools and golf-vacation packages.

Want to try some different courses but don't feel like juggling tee times? Stand-by Golf (☎ 480-874-3133) is a good, well, standby for last-minute reservations. Call between 6 and 9 p.m. the night before you want to hit the links to see what's available.

Unless I say otherwise, greens fees for the following recommended courses — arranged roughly in ascending budget-destroying order — include a cart. You find the best deals on weekday summer afternoons, usually the timeframe represented by the lowest prices in the following info.

Municipal courses

You can pay through the nose to play the Valley in high season — which is why people actually camp out for tee times at Papago Golf Course, 5595 E. Moreland St., south of McDowell and 52nd Street, Phoenix (☎ 602-275-8428; `http://phoenix.gov/SPORTS/papago.html`), surrounded by stunning red rock buttes and costing just $7 to $35 (plus $22 for a cart). The scenery isn't as dramatic but, then, the wait isn't nearly as long at Encanto Park, 2775 N. 15th Ave., two blocks south of Thomas, Phoenix (☎ 602-253-3963; `http://phoenix.gov/PARKS/park25.html`) ($7–$35, plus $18 for a cart). See also the listing for the Tournament Players Club in the "Resort courses" section, for details on a municipal course there.

Public courses

Arizona State alum Phil Mickelson studied his swing at the challenging Pete Dye–designed ASU-Karsten Golf Course, 1125 E. Rio Salado Pkwy. at Rural Road, Tempe (☎ 480-921-8070; www.asukarsten.com) ($25–$89). Tom Fazio's Raptor course at Grayhawk Golf Club, 8620 E. Thompson Peak Pkwy, 3 miles north of Frank Lloyd Wright Boulevard, Scottsdale (☎ 480-502-1800; `www.grayhawk.com`), is one of the toughest — and most gorgeous — in the Valley, with thick desert, deep fairway bunkers, and a 2-degree slope that can make your ball do funny things ($75–$225). McCormick Ranch Golf Club, 7505 E. McCormick Pkwy. at Scottsdale Road, Scottsdale (☎ 480-948-0260; `www.mccormickranchgolf.com`), is older but impeccably maintained; this course was designed in an age when landscapers were encouraged to have water and trees, now restricted on the newer, desert-conscious courses ($34–$150). Raven Golf Club at South Mountain, 3636 E. Baseline Rd., Phoenix (☎ 602-243-3636; `www.ravenatsouthmountain.com`), features lush, green fairways bordered by more than 7,000 pine trees, so you never have to hit into dirt ($59–$169). Dramatic elevation changes and deep sand bunkers challenge players at the Superstition Springs Golf Course, 6542 E. Baseline Rd. at Power Road, Mesa (☎ 480-985-5555; `www.superstitionspringsgc.com`), used in the past as a PGA Qualifying Site ($45–$109). The Scottish-style links laid out by Ben Crenshaw and Bill Coore at the Talking Stick Golf Club, 9998 E. Indian Bend Rd., 1 mile east of Loop 101, Scottsdale (☎ 480-860-2221; `www.talkingstickgolfclub.com`), are some of the best bunkered in Arizona ($60–$160). We-ko-pa Golf Club, 18200 E. Toh Vee Circle, 1½ miles north of the intersection of Beeline Highway and Shea Boulevard, Fountain Hills (☎ 480-836-9000; `www.wekopa.com`), on the Fort McDowell Yavapai Nation reservation, affords spectacular views of the Four Peaks mountain range and the surrounding desert — no residential development is allowed on the reservation ($65–$180).

Mercury up, golf prices down

Golf courses practically give away golf in the Valley in summer. If you're willing to hit the links in the hot months — and especially during the week after 2 p.m. — you can get great deals on some of the Valley's most exclusive courses. And while they don't have scantily clad maidens and lads with fans following you around, some resorts, like the Boulders, do the next best thing. They give you golf carts with built-in misters.

Resort courses

The perks of staying at a resort include discounted greens fees and first dibs on tee times at their golf courses, which consistently rank among the Valley's best — the better to lure guests. The rates listed here assume you won't have these resorts' room keys among your possessions. All the resort courses have different reservation policies for nonguests, so ask how far in advance you need to reserve (requirements range from 1–30 days).

Jay Moorish incorporated the astonishing scenery at the Boulders, 34831 N. Tom Darlington Dr., Carefree (☎ 480-488-9028; www.thebouldersclub.com) into the two courses he designed, with eye-popping effect. If you have to choose one, go South ($50–$250). The 27 beautifully landscaped holes at The Phoenician, 6000 E. Camelback Rd. at 64th Street, Scottsdale (☎ 480-423-2449; www.thephoenician.com), mix traditional and target styles. Camelback Mountain serves as a major distraction ($40–$180). If you've watched the FBR Open, formerly the Phoenix Open, you've already eyeballed the Tournament Players Club (TPC) of Scottsdale, 17020 N. Hayden Rd. at Bell Road (☎ 480-585-3939; www.tpc.com/daily/scottsdale), the Scottsdale Fairmont's fairways. The TPC's Stadium course is longer $87–$218), but the tighter, shorter Desert is a bargain municipal course ($27–$54). The Jay Moorish–designed Monument course at Troon North Golf Club, 10320 E. Dynamite Blvd., North Scottsdale (☎ 480-585-5300; www.troongolf.com) — the new Four Seasons' green stomping grounds — is peerless for desert beauty and, according to many, difficulty. Some veteran golfers prefer the sister Pinnacle course, which Tom Weiskopf had a hand in; it's no slouch in either category ($75–$275). Always in impeccable condition, Marriott's Wildfire Golf Club, 5350 E. Marriott Dr. at Tatum Road, Phoenix (☎ 480-473-0205; www.wildfiregolf.com), is desert style but user friendly, with wide fairways and big, multilevel greens ($45–$175). Of the 54 holes of championship golf at the luxurious Wigwam Resort, 451 N.Litchfield Rd., Litchfield Park (☎ 800-909-4224 or 623-935-9414; www.wigwamresort.com), the award-winning Gold course, designed by Robert Trent Jones, Sr., in 1961, welcomes duffers with its mature pines and palms and well-bunkered greens ($24–$120).

Hiking

The Valley has numerous places to hike, and some of the best trails and views are just minutes from the asphalt. Get the big picture from Day Hikes and Trail Rides in and around Phoenix, by Roger and Ethel Freeman, available in most Valley sporting goods stores and online at www.amazon.com ($14.95).

Straddling the border between Phoenix and Scottsdale, Camelback Mountain (http://phoenix.gov/PARKS/hikecmlb.html) has two 2- to 2.5-mile round-trip trails guaranteed to work your legs and your heart. They're nearly all uphill and pretty rocky in places — you see lots of rock climbers hanging out (and off) — but the payoff is amazing views from the top. The north side trail begins at the Echo Canyon parking lot east of McDonald Drive and Tatum. You can find the east side trail by hiking west on Cholla Lane off Invergordon Drive (you can park only on Invergordon, though, so be prepared to hike another half mile to the trailhead). Both trails are busiest in the morning and early evening — for a good reason: Don't even think about trying these hikes in the midday heat.

Also challenging and popular because it leads to one of the best panoramas of the city is the 1.2-mile Piestewa Peak Summit Trail in the Phoenix Mountains Preserve (☎ 602-262-7901; http://phoenix.gov/PARKS/hikesqua.html); be prepared for lots of switchbacks toward the top. Take Lincoln Drive between 22nd and 23rd streets to Piestewa Peak Drive.

The largest municipal park in the country, South Mountain Park, South Phoenix (☎ 602-495-0222; http://phoenix.gov/PARKS/hikesoth.html), is honeycombed with dramatic desert-and-mountain trails. To get there, take Central Avenue south until you can't go any farther (about 2 miles past Baseline). Monday through Saturday from 9 a.m. to 5 p.m., you can pick up a trail map at the visitor center, or on the weekend, from the ranger station at the park's entrance. The Summit National Trail, a 14-mile workout (for the very fit only, please), takes you past Indian petroglyphs as well as amazing scenery; follow the signs to the end of San Juan Road inside the park.

Want to know precisely what prickly plants you're coming up against — I hope not literally — on the trail? See the "Ecotours" section later in this chapter for naturalist-led hikes.

Horsing around

Come out West to see a horse, of course? The 400-acre **WestWorld of Scottsdale,** 16601 N. Pima Rd., Scottsdale (☎ **480-312-6801;** www.ci.scottsdale.az.us/westworld/), hosts a variety of equine-related events — everything from rodeos and polo matches to Arabian horse shows. Call to hear a recorded schedule of events and directions to the center.

It's a new (spa) age

The desert has long been considered a healing — as well as skin-drying — place, so don't be surprised to find Phoenix and Scottsdale at the forefront of the latest spiritual-sybarite trends. Forget Swedish massage. These days, Far Eastern rituals are meeting Native American remedies in aromatherapy-scented rooms presided over by body workers who can unblock your chakras faster than you can say Deepak Chopra. At the Valley's poshest spas, expect everything from rubdowns with heated stones that have been "re-charged" in the moonlight to treatments that involve oils being dripped onto your back — or your third eye.

The resorts generally have the best-equipped pleasure centers. Those spas at the Boulders, the Phoenician, the Arizona Biltmore, The Fairmont Scottsdale Princess, and Marriott's Camelback Inn, all detailed in the "Staying in Style" section earlier in this chapter, happily accept day guests. Prices start from around $75 for a 50-minute treatment and go up to about $325 for a full day of indulgence, including the use of the resort's fitness facilities and, often, lunch. Sure the spas are pricey, but, hey, where else can you find bliss in a dimly lit room with a stranger — guilt free?

Horseback riding

Saddle up in South Mountain Park with Ponderosa Stables, 10215 S. Central Ave., south of Baseline (☎ 602-268-1261). Prices start at $23 an hour for scenic trail rides; an early morning breakfast trot sets you back $27. D-Spur Ranch, Peralta Road, Gold Canyon (☎ 602-810-702 about 20 minutes southeast of Phoenix via Highway 60, offers one-ho ($26), two-hour ($50), four-hour ($90), and full-day ($150) rides into t Superstition Mountains. The Koli Equestrian Center at the Sheraton Wild Horse Pass (see the "Staying in Style" section earlier in this chap-ter), offering lessons, trail rides, and cattle drives, is open to nongue

River rafting and tubing

River rafting is as reliable as the rainfall in Arizona — that is, not very - but in a good year, the section of the Salt River that runs northeast of Phoenix can get pretty wet 'n' wild. If the nearby White Mountains hav enough snowmelt, you can ride class III and IV rapids through starkly matic, ancient granite gorges from late February to late May. Outfitte running Salt River raft trips include Wilderness Aware Rafting (☎ 231-7238; www.inaraft.com), with prices ranging from $90 per pe (including permit) for a five-hour trip to $775 for a five-day advent Mild to Wild Rafting (☎ 800-567-6745; www.mild2wildrafting. where you pay $105 for a full day on the river, $275 for a two-day/ one-night trip.

Tennis

Most all the big resorts offer top-notch tennis facilities, but few to outsiders. If you're not staying at a resort, you still have a f

Ouch — that ticket price hurts!

If you can't score any seats through the usual means, you have another option: Phoenix is one of the few cities where scalping is legal. Just be sure to check your tickets carefully before handing over the cash and make your deal off the venue's grounds, where scalping is illegal — although just a few yards away is okay.

Hockey

Hockey is showing up in the strangest places these days (the Tampa Bay Lightning won the 2004 Stanley Cup), and Phoenix is no exception. The Arizona Coyotes (☎ 480-473-5600; www.phoenixcoyotes.com) are now ensconced in the brand-new Glendale Arena, at the intersection of the Loop 101 freeway and Glendale Avenue, in Glendale (30 min. from downtown Phoenix). Hockey great Wayne Gretzky is a managing partner. Single-game tickets are available at the Coyotes' Web site and cost $15 to $100.

Seeing the Valley by Guided Tour

In addition to the tours listing in this section, see the "Biking" and "River-rafting and tubing" sections of the "Staying Active" section earlier in this chapter.

General bus tours

Gray Line Tours of Phoenix (☎ 800-732-0327 or 602-495-9100; www.graylinearizona.com) traces the city's history from its Hohokam Indian past during a four-hour tour ($40 adults, $20 children under 12). Stops include the state capitol, Heritage Square, Old Town Scottsdale, celebrity homes in Paradise Valley, and the Arizona State University campus in Tempe. The more intimate Vaughan's Southwest Custom Tours, Inc. (☎ 800-513-1381 or 602-971-1381; www.southwesttours.com) are a bit longer and have smaller groups (12 people maximum), which cost $45 per adult (children 12 and under are half price) and cover a variety of downtown sites and the Pueblo Grande Museum. Both companies provide hotel pickups in Phoenix and Scottsdale.

Ecotours

The earth-friendly excursions offered by Windwalker Expeditions (☎ 888-785-3382 or 480-585-3382; www.windwalkerexpeditions.
include a three- to four-hour Botanical Jeep Tour ($100 per pers
explores geological rock formations and slot canyons in the P
Mountains, and an all-day Archaeology Ecotour ($150, inc
which adds an exploration of the area's ruins to the Bota
hiking/four-wheeling agenda.

Four-wheel adventure tours

Climb aboard the most powerful 4x4 for a fun four-hour excursion through the Four Peaks wilderness with Desert Storm Hummer Tours, 15525 N. 83rd Way, Ste. 8, Scottsdale (☎ 800-374-8637 or 480-922-0020; www.dshummer.com). Both daytime ($95 adults, $75 ages 12 and under) and nighttime ($125/$100) tours afford up close looks at denizens of the desert; after dark, peering through night-vision goggles at glowing scorpions and jumping cacti adds to the adventure.

Lake tours

Float down Tempe Town Lake on a half-hour RioLago Cruise (☎ 480-517-4050) as you're regaled with amusing tales of Tempe's past. The tours ($6 adults, $5 seniors 65 and older and ages 6–12, $4 ages 5 and under) run Sat and Sun 1 p.m., 3 p.m. and 5 p.m., but not on days on which there are special events on the lake; best to call first. Buy your tickets from the same kiosk that rents the lake's water toys (see the "Boating" section earlier in this chapter).

Stadium tour

Want to get up close and personal with BOB — as Bank One Ballpark, 401 E. Jefferson St. at 7th Street (☎ 602-462-6799; www.bankoneballpark.com), is affectionately known — without several other people around or any Diamondback action to distract you? Terrific 1¼-hour behind-the-scenes tours take you to see everything from the private pool area near third base to the National Baseball Hall of Fame memorabilia. (Sorry, they won't retract the famous ceiling for you.) Outside of baseball season, tours depart Monday through Saturday at

Some BOB stats

Bank One Ballpark, known as BOB, was the world's first sports facility to combine a retractable roof, air-conditioning, and a natural turf playing field.

The roof is made up of 9 million pounds of structural steel. Using the technology found in drawbridges and cranes, a pair of 200-horsepower motors can zip the roof open or close it in under 5 minutes.

Because grass gets confused when it's subjected to both sun and air-conditioning, a whole new strain had to be developed for BOB. Steve Cockerham, one of the nation's leading turf agronomists — bet you didn't even know that was a job description — and head of the Department of Agricultural Operations at the University of California at Riverside, eventually came up with a hardy hybrid.

Note: As this edition was going to press, Bank One and J.P. Morgan Chase announced plans to merge, and as a result, BOB will get a new name, to be announced prior to the opening of the 2005 season.

10:30 a.m., noon, 1:30 p.m., and 3 p.m. In season — but only when the D-backs play at night — tours are offered Monday through Saturday at 10:30 a.m. and noon. The stadium doesn't offer tours on day games or during holidays and special events. Tickets, sold at the Tour Window at the main box office, cost $6 for adults, $4 for ages 7 to 12 and seniors over 60, $2 for ages 4 to 6, and free for ages 3 and under.

Following an Itinerary

I have plenty of ideas about the best ways for you to arrange your days (and, unlike my family and friends, you may even pay attention to them), but the Valley is very spread out. If you're sequestered away in a North Scottsdale resort, you drive a lot more on these itineraries than if you're holed up in central Phoenix. Similarly, many of the best activities are outdoors. Most people visit in winter, when the weather is great. The heat can get unbearable between May and October (and especially in June, July, and August), especially midday. (For details on the attractions, restaurants, and activities mentioned in these itineraries, see the corresponding sections earlier in this chapter.)

One-day itinerary

If you have only one day in the Valley, concentrate your time in downtown and central Phoenix, where you can get in a good dose of nature and Native American culture — as well as a little retailing. Start out at the Pueblo Grand Museum and Cultural Center, easy to reach by freeway from pretty much anywhere, and then head over to the Desert Botanical Gardens; both are in the Papago Salado part of town. Lunch is easy: You can dine at either the Arcadia Café at the gardens or at the clone of this restaurant at your next stop, the Heard Museum. Spend the afternoon perusing the exhibits and great gift shop, and then head a short way north to the beautiful Art Deco Arizona Biltmore resort, and kick back with a cocktail on the terrace. If you haven't satisfied your acquisitive urges at the Heard, you're right near Biltmore Fashion Park, where you can drop some more dollars and then have dinner across the street at Franco's Trattoria. Not completely done in? Boogie over to Old Town Scottsdale. You should plan to dress the part (drop-dead dramatic) if you want to check out the Valley's see-and-be-seen clubs; if you prefer not to get all gussied up, simply duck in to one of the more casual watering holes, such as the Rusty Spur Saloon. (Note: If you think this itinerary will send you into overdrive, cut out the Pueblo Grand Museum; it's a great place, but the Heard Museum covers some of the same cultural territory.)

Two-day itinerary

If you have two days, you can take a more leisurely approach sights covered on the one-day itinerary and add a few mo quick swim at your hotel, and then spend the morning at Museum. In the afternoon, head over to downtown Scottsa didn't already have lunch at the Heard, chow down at Cowboy Ciao before browsing the Fifth Avenue shops and Main Street galleries. The nearby Scottsdale Museum of Contemporary Art and the boutiques and galleries of Old Scottsdale should keep you happy the rest of the afternoon. If you want to stick around for the nightlife, you can eat at Los Olivos (or save Cowboy Ciao for dinner).

On day two, visit the Pueblo Grand Museum and Cultural Park and the Desert Botanical Gardens in the morning. In the afternoon, head to northern Scottsdale to tour Taliesen West and visit Cosanti. If you didn't eat at the Desert Botanical gardens, have lunch at Lon's at the Hermosa Inn, close to Cosanti. Still have plastic burning a hole in your pocket? Make a beeline for Kierland Commons mall, where you can follow up more shopping with dinner at Zinc Bistro or Deseo (make reservations for both).

If you're traveling with kids (or want to get in touch with your inner child), skip Taliesen West and Cosanti, and instead add the Arizona Science Center and either the Phoenix Museum of History and the Arizona Doll & Toy Museum or a tour of the Bank One Ballpark, all close to the science center. You can also substitute the Phoenix Zoo for the Pueblo Grande Museum and Cultural Park.

Three-day itinerary

Follow the two-day itinerary until the afternoon of the second day, and then head over from the Papago Salado area (locations of the Pueblo Grand Museum and the Desert Botanical Gardens) to nearby Tempe. Spend the afternoon kayaking, lake touring, strolling along Mill Avenue, checking out the sights on the Arizona State University campus, or any combination thereof; Four Peaks Brewing Co. is a good place to refuel. On day three, head up to Cosanti so you can watch the bronze bells being cast, and then go over to Taliesen West. The drive north along Scottsdale Road to the towns of Carefree and Cave Creek (see Chapter 12) isn't long. Either have a Southwest-chic lunch at the Palo Verde Room at the Boulders and then hit the ritzy boutiques and the Heard Museum's northern branch at El Pedregal, or go the wilder west route with chili beer at Crazy Ed's Satisfied Frog and the more down home shops of Cave Creek.

Shopping the Local Stores

Shopping in the Valley tends to be an all-mall affair — with several notable exceptions, detailed in the "What to look for and where to find it" section later in this chapter. Don't judge Valley shops by their locations: You sometimes find highly original, individual stores in faceless retail strips.

Best shopping areas

You can drop your dough at plenty of places throughout the Valley, but downtown Scottsdale has the most concentrated doses of retail activity per square block. The main indulgence districts here include, from north to south: 5th Avenue, angling diagonally between Indian School and Scottsdale roads, where Native American arts and jewelry shops and Western galleries number among the one-of-a-kind boutiques; the intersecting Marshall Way Arts District, roughly between Indian School Road and 3rd Avenue, lined with (mostly) contemporary art galleries; Old Town Scottsdale (see the "More cool things to see and do" section earlier in this chapter), featuring several Old West curio shops; and the adjacent Main Street Arts & Antiques district, Main Street and 1st Avenue between Scottsdale Road and Goldwater Boulevard, where the galleries tend toward the traditional and the Western, and boutiques sell a wide range of stuff that's been around long enough to get expensive.

Park your car in the free lot on the corner of 2nd Street and Wells Fargo Avenue near Old Scottsdale and explore the shopping areas by foot or trolley (see the "Free-for-all" sidebar near the beginning of this chapter). Some spaces in the lot have a three-hour limit (and those are marked), but the rest are completely off the meter.

In Tempe, Mill Avenue, from University Drive near the Arizona State University campus to Rio Salado Parkway, is less granola-y than it used to be — chains like Abercrombie & Fitch have largely replaced the independents — but the retail scene is still young, hip, and strollable.

Getting mall'd

Sometimes I feel like a new mall opens in the Valley every month (five more are slated to break ground by 2008). The most recent major arrivals are far-flung: Kierland Commons, at Scottsdale Road and Greenway Parkway in North Phoenix (but bordering on Scottsdale) (☎ 480-348-1577; `www.kierlandcommons.com`), appeals to the usual upscale suspects with its array of boutiques; Desert Ridge Market Place, Tatum Boulevard and Loop 101, north Phoenix (☎ 480-513-7586; `www.nextbigazthing.com`), features separate "districts" catering to the young and (retail) restless; while Chandler Fashion Center, Chandler Boulevard and Loop 101 (☎ 480-812-8488; `www.westcor.com`) in

Antiques alert

If you have a fondness for vintage stuff, check out the Midwest-meets-the-desert town of **Glendale,** about 20 minutes west of Sky Harbor Airport, with more than 90 antiques emporiums. The best pickings are in Old Towne Glendale, on Glendale Avenue between 57th Avenue and 58th Drive, but be sure to meander a few blocks to the north to the beautiful converted bungalows in the historic Catlin Court district. The **Glendale Office of Tourism and Visitor Center,** 5800 W. Glenn Dr., near 58th and Glendale avenues (☎ **877-800-2601** or 623-930-4500; `www.visitglendale.com`), open Monday through Saturday from 10 a.m. to 5 p.m., has maps of both areas.

Chandler, southeast of Phoenix, almost as large as Scottsdale Fashion Square (discussed in this section), has anchor stores such as Nordstrom and Sears.

A few central standbys are good options, too. The Arizona Center, Van Buren between 3rd and 5th streets, downtown Phoenix (☎ 602-271-4000; www.arizonacenter.com), is more outdoor entertainment complex than mall, with lushly landscaped courtyards, restaurants and bars, a 24-screen movie theater, and some 30 small shops and retail carts. Come here to pick up Southwestern-themed gifts or anything you can think of that bears a Phoenix sports team logo. In nice weather, Native American musicians often play in the center courtyard at lunchtime.

Arizona Mills, 5000 Arizona Mills Circle, Tempe (southeast quadrant of I-10 and U.S. Highway 60) (☎ 480-491-9700; www.arizonamills.com), is bargain and big-store central, featuring leading discount outlets like Last Call Neiman Marcus, Marshall's, and Burlington Coat Factory, and oversize retailers such as Virgin Megastore and Linens-n-Things; the smaller stores tend toward the lower end of the retail spectrum. An IMAX theater, a 24-plex cinema, a branch of Steven Spielberg's super high-tech GameWorks play center (☎ 480-839-4263; www.gameworks.com); and theme eateries, such as the Rainforest Café, mean you won't have any problem dragging the kids along (although getting them out may be difficult).

Biltmore Fashion Park, Camelback and 24th Street, Phoenix (☎ 602-955-8400; www.westcor.com), is the Camelback Corridor's retail and restaurant hub, where seriously upscale shops — we're talking Saks, Williams Sonoma, Gucci — mingle among bricked paths and lush greenery with middle-of-the-roaders such as Macy's and Pottery Barn. Suffering from shopper's fatigue? Stop in at Elizabeth Arden's Red Door Salon for a pedicure.

If you're in town on any Friday between October and early May, don't miss the farmer's market held here from 11 a.m. to 4 p.m., with everything from gorgeous produce, baked goods, and exotic Southwest products (prickly-pear jam anyone?) to locally produced jewelry and imported Italian leather briefcases.

Scottsdale Fashion Square, Camelback and Scottsdale roads (☎ 480-990-7800; www.westcor.com), is the undisputed queen of upscale Arizona malls, with 1.8-million square feet of retail space, retractable skylights, and the likes of Nordstrom, Neiman Marcus, Dana Buchman, and Tiffany & Co. singing siren songs to your credit cards. When you're ready to give the plastic a break — or at least a change of pace — a movie theater and panoply of restaurants await (I think a state law must mandate a minimum number of movie screens and feeding stations per mall).

In Chapter 12, see Day-Trip #2 for the Outlets at Casa Grande.

At the (art) hop

On Thursday nights from 7 to 9 p.m. year-round (except Thanksgiving), take part in the Scottsdale Gallery Association's self-guided **ArtWalks** (☎ **480-990-3939;** www.scottsdalegalleries.com), with cocktail receptions, live entertainment, and artist appearances designed to put you in an art-buying mood. Phoenix gets into the art action each month with **First Fridays** (☎ **602-256-7539;** www.artlinkphoenix.com). (I don't have to tell you which day of the week and which part of the month they take place, do I?) Park downtown in the lot of the Burton Barr Central Library, 1221 N. Central Ave., south of Culver Street, and, from 6 to 10 p.m., hop an ArtLink shuttle that loops around the 60-odd participating galleries, studios, and businesses (check the art listings in the local papers).

Getting (boutique) mall'd

The Borgata of Scottsdale, 6166 N. Scottsdale Rd. between Lincoln and McDonald drives (☎ 480-998-1822), looks like a Tuscan village, replete with courtyards, fountains, and (maybe not so Tuscan) upscale specialty shops, selling everything from Southwest art to silver jewelry and resort apparel.

El Pedregal Festival Marketplace at the Boulders, 34505 N. Scottsdale Rd., just north of Carefree Highway (☎ 480-488-1072; www.elpedregal.com), may just be Arizona's most scenic place to shop, its low-slung Pueblo architecture blending (almost) organically with the surrounding desert and rocks.

Although not as quaint as the other two, Shops at Gainey Village, Scottsdale Road and Doubletree Ranch Road, Scottsdale (☎ 480-948-5586, pays homage to its site on a former horse farm with faux-rustic linked outdoor plazas. Visit Two Plates Full, selling wonderful, whimsical Southwestern kitchen accessories.

What to look for and where to find it

Whether your tastes run to golf gear or high art, you can find something to satisfy them in the Valley.

Art

True, the Valley may have one of the highest rates per capita of canvasses filled with lonesome cowboys, but you find a whole lot more in town than Western art. In fact, Scottsdale is second only to Santa Fe as a Southwest-art destination. With more than 125 galleries and studios from which to choose, you can see everything from hand-blown glass and Native American abstracts to contemporary mixed-media pieces — and even plenty of non-cliché Western art.

- Eclectic: Art One, 4120 N. Marshall Way, Scottsdale (☎ 480-946-5076), is the place to see the up-and-comers and maybe get some art bargains. Most of the work by the young art students (the majority from Arizona) represented doesn't run higher than $1,000. One of the most dynamic galleries in the Valley, the 5,000-square-foot Gallery Materia, 4222 N. Marshall Way, Scottsdale (☎ 480-949-1262), showcases the high-end crafts of some 95 artists from the Americas, Asias, and Europe; media range from the traditional to fiber and wood. At the Work of Artists Gallery, 10835 N. Tatum Blvd., Suite 101, Phoenix (☎ 480-596-0304), you find wood carvings, paintings, pottery, furniture, and Native American crafts by more than 200 artists, costing anywhere from $1 to $5,000.
- Contemporary: Chiaroscuro, 7160 Main St., Scottsdale (☎ 480-429-0711), a clone from Sante Fe, puts on shows by major contemporary artists like Ricardo Mazal and Howard Ben Tre. The talent represented by Lisa Sette Gallery, 4142 N. Marshall Way, Scottsdale (☎ 480-990-7342), is a little less established but well known enough to command high prices for their work, which includes photography and sculpture as well as painting.
- Regional/Western: Open for more than 30 years, the Meyer Gallery, 7173 E. Main St., Scottsdale (☎ 877-947-6372 or 480-947-6372), sells high-quality Western and Native American art in the realist/Impressionist tradition. Faust Gallery, 7103 E. Main St., Scottsdale (☎ 480-946-6345) carries Native American work in a variety of genres, from jewelry to contemporary painting, as well as Mata Ortiz's pottery. Trailside Galleries, 7330 Scottsdale Mall (☎ 480-945-7751), showcases several members of the Cowboy Artists of America, including founder Joe Beeler, as well as other high-end Western painters. Riva Yares, 3625 N. Bishop Ln. (☎ 480-947-3251), is renowned for its contemporary Mexican, South American, and Native American collection, although aesthetically compatible Anglos such as Milton Avery turn up here, too. The work tends to be exciting but not inaccessible (except maybe in price).
- Architecture: You no longer have to go all the way up to Taliesen West for some Wright-eous shopping. At Wright Downtown, 7079 E. 5th Ave. Scottsdale (☎ 480-990-7710), you find clocks, scarves, bookends, and other items designed by Frank Lloyd Wright and his authorized imitators — as well as Wright-designed furniture not available at Taliesen's gift shop.

Golf supplies

The Valley definitely has the golf goods — everything from antique clubs to discounted state-of-the-art carts. You may like the putting green, personalized service, and Knuckles, the friendly bulldog, at Hornacek's House of Golf, 23369 N. Pima Rd., south of Pinnacle Peak Road, Scottsdale (☎ 480-502-0555). Hornacek's other Scottsdale location, 6107 N. Scottsdale Rd., Ste. 114 (☎ 480-948-5011), has everything the other store has — except Knuckles. A duffer's fantasy, In Celebration of

The tintinnabulation of the bells, bells, bells

You can tour **Cosanti,** 6433 E. Doubletree Ranch Rd. at Invergorden, Paradise Valley (☎ **800-752-3187** or 480-948-6145; `www.cosanti.com`), the architectural prototype for Arcosanti (see Chapter 12) and an Arizona State Historic Site, if you book ahead. Most people, though, just come for the wonderful ceramic and bronze Soleri windbells (prices start at about $25 and $50, respectively). Arrive early, and you can watch them being cast. The majority of the proceeds go to the Arcosanti project, but if you buy a bell from the "Cause" collection, you can contribute to your favorite participating nonprofit. Open Mon–Sat 9 a.m.–5 p.m., Sun 11 a.m.–5 p.m.

Golf, 7001 N. Scottsdale Rd. at E. Indian Bend Road, Scottsdale (☎ 480-951-4444), is part golf museum, part golf-art gallery (the country's largest), and part upscale golf retail store. Play (virtually) 18 holes at Pebble Beach in a simulation room, browse 800 pairs of shoes, or just munch free cookies while watching the Golf Channel. The warehouse-size Golfsmith, 15452 N. Pima Rd. at Frank Lloyd Wright Blvd., Scottsdale (☎ 480-607-9449), carries a mind-boggling amount of golf supplies while catering to your every golf quirk.

Native American crafts

Street vendors may try to sell you Native American jewelry and other crafts. Don't bite; it's the Arizona version of the Rolex watch scam. Only buy from reputable dealers who can guarantee the goods (see Chapter 19).

For the best one-stop Native American crafts shopping, head straight to the gift shop at the Heard Museum (see the "Exploring Phoenix, Scottsdale, and the Valley of the Sun" section earlier in this chapter). Here, you can get high-quality weavings, rugs, jewelry, pottery, baskets — you name it — at fair prices. Better yet, the profits go to the people who create the crafts rather than to store owners, traders, or other middle people. The downtown Phoenix store has the best variety, but you also find a decent selection in the El Pedregal branch in Carefree (see the "Getting [boutique] mall'd" section earlier in this chapter).

Western wear

Az-Tex Hat Company, 3903 N. Scottsdale Rd. between Main and 1st streets, Old Town Scottsdale (☎ 800-972-2116 or 480-481-9900), goes to the head of the tailoring class, carefully suiting its headgear to your cranium. Buy a hatband or get your old Stetson reblocked here. The specialty at Porters, 3944 N. Brown off Main Street, Old Town Scottsdale (☎ 800-279-3093 or 480-945-6182), is boots, the pointier-toed the better. Saba's Western Wear, 7254 Main St. at Brown Avenue, Old Town

Scottsdale (☎ 480-949-7404), has catered to local cowpokes and cowpoke wannabes since 1927. Still in the same family, Saba's expanded to nine stores around the Valley, including one in Old Town Scottsdale (3965 N. Brown Ave. at First Avenue; ☎ 480-947-7664). Another retail pioneer, Stockman's Westernwear, 23587 N. Scottsdale Rd. at Pinnacle Peak Rd., Scottsdale (☎ 480-585-6142), has been in business since 1953. If you're in North Scottsdale, this is the place to get your dude ranch duds.

Living It Up after Dark

You won't have a hard time finding something to do in the Valley after dark. However, unless you stay within walking distance of the areas where the clubs and concert halls are concentrated, you'll need wheels to get wherever you're going, whether your own car or a taxi.

The best source of listings for clubs and alternative arts events is the free Phoenix New Times, which comes out on Wednesday. The Rep weekend entertainment guide, included with the Arizona Republic on Thursday, but also available for free around town, is good for the more mainstream arts and nightlife listings. You can also search for Valley events by date, type, and city on the Republic's on-line calendar (`www.azcentral.com/ent/calendar`).

Nightlife

Downtown Scottsdale is the prime destination for see-and-be-seen partiers. Expect to dispense a little cash in this neck of the night owls' woods — both for covers ($5–$10) and for valet parking (about $5 plus tip), as regular parking is hard to come by and you can club-hop by foot (if your heels aren't too high) around here. Similarly, the clubs and pubs on Mill Avenue, near Arizona State University in Tempe, are generally just a sneaker hop away from one another (covers here range from zero to about $5). Phoenix's clubs, which tend to be a bit less collegiate than those in Tempe and less pretentious than those in downtown Scottsdale, aren't conveniently clustered. The exception: downtown Phoenix near Bank One Ballpark, where you find several spots to hoist a few post-game cold ones. Expect cover charges in Phoenix to be between nada and $6 or $7.

A lot of the bars that also serve food open their doors at midday. Most nightclubs generally open at 8 p.m. Since Arizona law extended bar hours to 2:30 a.m. in 2004, many places now have a 2 a.m. last call.

Country and Western

Two-step to live sounds any night of the week at Handlebar-J, 7116 E. Becker Ln., Scottsdale (☎ 480-948-0110; `www.handlebarj.com`), but come on Wednesday, Thursday, and Sundays if you want to learn how (for free). Vince Gill and Willie Nelson have dropped in to the Rusty Spur

Saloon, 7245 E. Main St., Old Town Scottsdale (☎ 480-425-7787; www.rustyspursaloon.com), where a band gets the crowd boot scootin' six nights a week. The saloon opened its doors in 1922 as Scottsdale's first bank; the safe now serves as a walk-in cooler. At Mr. Lucky's, 3660 N.W. Grand Ave., Phoenix (☎ 602-246-0687; www.mrluckys.com), you can line dance to the house band Wednesday through Saturday — except for Thursday, when free dance lessons are offered — ride a live bull (honest). Scarier for some is the kids' talent contest, held every Friday night at 7:45 p.m.

Rock and alternative

A former hair salon, the tiny Mason Jar, 2303 E. Indian School Rd., Phoenix (☎ 602-954-0455; www.masonjarlive.com), has hosted top talent rock for 25 years — from Kid Rock and Megadeth to Stone Temple Pilots and Jane's Addiction. Don't let the name of the Martini Ranch & Shaker Room, 7295 E. Stetson Dr. (☎ 480-970-0500), an Old Town Scottsdale staple, fool you. The club's better known for its live rock acts, DJs, and frat-type crowd than for its martinis. The Old Brickhouse Grill, 1 E. Jackson St., Phoenix, one block west of Bank One Ballpark (☎ 602-258-7888), serves up the newest in live hip-hop, goth, and heavy metal along with its burgers, beer, and signature caramel apples. A young crowd squeezes into a space the size of a living room to see live indy rock at Modified Arts, 407 E. Roosevelt St., downtown Phoenix (☎ 602-462-5516), an alcohol-free venue.

Jazz, blues, and R&B

Char's Has The Blues, 4631 N. 7th Ave., Phoenix (☎ 602-230-0205; www.charshastheblues.com), gets constant nods from the local press as Arizona's best blues club. One of the hottest blues, funk, and R&B clubs to hit town, Sugar Daddy's, 3102 N. Scottsdale Rd., downtown Scottsdale (☎ 480-970-6556; www.sugardaddysaz.com), hosts national acts as well as local ones, including Arizona blues legend Hans Olsen. At the distinctively nonglitzy, nonglamorous Rhythm Room, 1019 E Indian School Rd., Phoenix (☎ 602-265-4842; www.rhythmroom.com), some of the country's best jazz and blues musicians bring it on home. For relaxing vibes with Old Town Scottsdale ambience, come to J. Chew & Co., 7320 Scottsdale Mall (☎ 480-946-2733), where smooth jazz, blues, and soul is played inside or out on the patio.

For a complete listing of blues events, call the Phoenix Blues Society (☎ 602-252-0599) or log on to www.phoenixblues.org.

DJ and dance

George Clooney, Rod Stewart, and Michael Jordan have all made the scene at sister clubs Axis/Radius, 7340 E. Indian Plaza, Scottsdale (☎ 480-970-1112; www.axis-radius.com), still wildly stylish after several years in business. Most of the footwork action is at Radius, where the bands range from house and techno to salsa. Other clubs that have lasted more than 15 minutes in the wildly volatile downtown Scottsdale club scene include Suede Restaurant and Lounge, 7333 E. Indian Plaza (☎ 480-970-6969; www.suedeaz.com), a plush, laid-back club with Art Deco design and outdoor seating; Devil's Martini, 4175 N. Goldwater Blvd. (☎ 480-947-7171; www.devilsmartini.com), with three bars, dance floors and a killer courtyard; and Six, 7316 Stetson Dr., (☎ 480-663-6620; www.sixaz.com), an ultra-hip lounge that was named one of the 50 best night spots by In Style magazine Pepin, 7363 Scottsdale Mall, Scottsdale (☎ 480-990-9026), a small Spanish restaurant, has some of the steamiest Latin dancing in the Valley; Saturdays are especially hot. I can't guarantee they'll be around by the time you read this, but the hottest clubs when we went to press included Myst, 7340 E. Shoeman Lane (☎ 480-970-5000; www.mystaz.com), a high-energy dance club and lounge; and Next (☎ 480-970-NEXT; www.nextscottsdale.com), open for dinner, drinks, and dancing Tuesday through Sunday, both in downtown Scottsdale.

Pubs and sports bars

Many of the hopping hops spots are in collegiate Tempe, home to Arizona State University. For a bit 'o' the Blarney — not to mention the best-pulled Guinness in the Valley — you can't beat Rúla Búla, 401 S. Mill Ave. (☎ 480-929-9500; www.rulabula.com), which re-creates an Irish pub down to its last imported brick and boxty (potato pancake). Four Peaks Brewing Co.,1340 E. Eighth St., #103 (☎ 480-303-9967; www.fourpeaks.com), in a roomy converted creamery, has some of the finest home suds in the state — my favorite is the 8th Street Ale — not to mention an Elvis shrine. A newer north Scottsdale location, 15730 N. Pima Rd., D5-7 (☎ 480-991-1795), feels more suburban than collegiate — no Elvis shrine — but the beer's just as good. Prefer your quaffs even more upscale? Not a chicken wing or nacho is in sight at The Grill, 7575 E. Princess Dr. (☎ 480-585-4848, ext. 7330; www.thegrillattpc.com), at the Tournament Players Club golf course in Scottsdale. The atmosphere's swell, but prepare to shell out bucks if you want food with your drinks. On the opposite end of the sedateness scale is the shock-rock-meets-jock Alice Cooper'stown, 101 E. Jackson St., Phoenix (☎ 602-253-7337; www.alicecooperstown.com), owned by the Valley-dwelling Cooper. Come to this bar and grill, near both Bank One Ballpark and America West Arena, for a gigantic video wall, huge outdoor scoreboard, and tasty barbecue, served by staff in full makeup.

A great tequila hour — or several

About 90 kinds of tequila go down at the gazebo-bar of the **Old Town Tortilla Factory**, 6910 E. Main St., Scottsdale (**☎ 480-945-4567;** www.oldtowntortillafactory.com), as well as several types of margaritas. Perch on the patio and gaze out at the orange trees, night-lit fountain, and, in winter, a blazing fire pit; you'll soon be channeling Jimmy Buffett.

Lounges and wine bars

The Valley's hotels and resorts are chock-a-block with romantic spots to cozy up with a cocktail. Topping my list are the Arizona Biltmore's swank Squaw Peak bar (if it looks familiar, that's because Angela Bassett and her gal pals did some serious bonding here in Waiting to Exhale); the Mediterranean-chic Bar at T. Cook's at the Royal Palms Hotel, with its oversize floral arrays and cushy couches; and the lobby bar at the Hyatt Regency Scottsdale, where fire pits on the patio serve as a dramatic backdrop for nightly live music (see the "Staying in Style" section earlier in this chapter, for all three). Among my favorite places to get a light, late-night bite with a glass of Merlot are Postino, 3939 E. Campbell Ave., central Phoenix (☎ 602-852-3939), a former post office with a nice list of wines by the glass and good Italian sandwiches and salads; the speakeasy-style Kazmiriez, 7137 E. Stetson Dr., downtown Scottsdale (☎ 480-946-3004), where you can nibble Egyptian flatbread pizzas while sampling wine flights; and Cheuvront, 1326 N. Central Ave., downtown Phoenix (☎ 602-307-0222), an airy space that offers a great array of fresh gourmet cheeses to go along with a bit o' the grape.

The arts

Most Broadway road shows and national concert tours swing through the Valley. For tickets to almost any event or for a listing of what's on in town, contact Ticketmaster (☎ 480-784-4444; www.ticketmaster.com). If your chosen event is sold out, try calling Tickets Unlimited (☎ 800-289-8497 or 602-840-2340; www.ticketsunlimitedinc.com), Western States Ticket Services (☎ 800-326-0331 or 602-254-3300; www.wstickets.com), or The Ticket Company (☎ 800-279-4444 or 602-279-4444; www.tickco.com); one of them may have the coveted tickets tucked away.

Top arts venues

Downtown Phoenix is home to most of the Valley's cultural venues. The Dodge Theatre, 400 W. Washington St. (☎ 602-379-2888 or 480-784-4444; www.dodgetheatre.com), features concerts, Broadway shows, stage shows, family entertainment, specialty sporting events, and top national acts such as Chris Rock, Johnny Mathis, and the cast of Chicago, in person and projected onto the state-of-the-art video screens. The Dodge will also host some performances of the Phoenix Symphony during the 2005 season, while its home at Symphony Hall (see next listing) is being renovated. Phoenix Symphony Hall, 225 E. Adams St. (☎ 602-262-7272), home to the Phoenix Symphony, also hosts performances by Ballet Arizona, the Arizona Opera Company, and more; during renovations, slated to be completed in the fall of 2005, its resident companies will perform elsewhere. The Orpheum Theatre, 203 W. Adams St. at Second Avenue (☎ 602-262-7272), is an elegant 1929 structure with a colorful, wonderfully ornate facade. It will be filling in for Phoenix Symphony Hall during the 2005 season, after which it will return to its usual roster of Broadway shows, and international music and dance performances. The Arizona Theater Company, the Actors Theater of Phoenix, Center Dance

Ensemble, and Childsplay all share the Herberger Theater Center, 222 E. Monroe St. (☎ 602-252-8497; www.herbergertheater.org), a Spanish-style complex that stages more than 450 performances a year. In central Phoenix, the recently renovated Celebrity Theatre, 440 N. 32nd St., four blocks south of the Loop 202 freeway (☎ 602-267-1600; www.celebritythreatre.com), hosts headliners — everyone from George Carlin and Joan Rivers to B.B. King, Loretta Lynn, and Julio Iglesias — in an intimate theater in the round, with no seat farther than 75 feet from the revolving stage.

The lobby of the Scottsdale Center for the Arts, 7380 E. Second St. in the Scottsdale Mall (☎ 480-994-2787; www.scottsdaleperformingarts.org), doubles as an art gallery. The center hosts some of the best modern dance, jazz, and theater in town. When the weather is nice, part of the action moves outside to the Scottsdale Amphitheater.

The Grady Gammage Memorial Auditorium in Tempe, Gammage Parkway and Mill Avenue (☎ 480-965-3434; www.asu.edu/it/museums/gammage.html), wows not only with the quality of its Broadway performances, but also with its Frank Lloyd Wright design (see the "More cool things to see and do" section earlier in this chapter).

Classical music

The Arizona Opera Company, 4600 N. 12 St., Phoenix (☎ 602-266-7464 or 480-784-4444; www.azopera.org), shared by Phoenix and Tucson, hits the high notes about five times a year from October through April (ticket prices $25–$115). Members of the top-ranked Phoenix Symphony Orchestra, 455 N. 3rd St., Suite 390, Phoenix (☎ 602-495-1999; www.phoenixsymphony.org), arguably the best strings and brass in the Southwest, make beautiful music indoors when they're not doing outdoor pops ($10–$58).

Out-going entertainment

An outdoor concert on one of the Valley's balmy nights is amazing. From April through June, the **Desert Botanical Garden** (see the "Seeing the Sights" section earlier in this chapter) stays open late for its "Jazz in the Garden" series on Friday nights at 7 p.m. in April and May, 7:30 p.m. in June (a buffet is available one hour before the concert); the program changes, but you can expect the sounds to be mellow. Tickets cost $16 for adults, $8 for ages 3–12, free for children under 3; the buffet is an extra $7 to $9. The **El Pedregal Festival Marketplace** (see the "Getting [boutique] mall'd" section earlier in this chapter) tunes in from April through early July with the "Music by Moonlight" jazz, blues, and rock series on Thursday nights. All shows begin at 7 p.m., and tickets cost $10. Check what's happening, too, at the amphitheater of the Scottsdale Center for the Arts (see "The arts" section earlier in this chapter).

Baby bards

Childsplay, Tempe Performing Arts Center, 132 E. 6th St., Tempe (☎ **480-350-8101;** www.childsplayaz.org), puts on performances that range from the classic *(The Velveteen Rabbit)* to the thought-provoking *(The True Confessions of Charlotte Doyle).* Venues through the 2005 season include the Herberger Theater Center, the Scottsdale Center for the Arts, and the Tempe Performing Arts Center; the company will be moving into the new Tempe Center for the Arts for 2006. The **Great Arizona Puppet Theater,** 302 W. Latham St. at 3rd Avenue, Phoenix (☎ **602-262-2050;** www.azpuppets.org), pulls lots of strings in a historic theater; call ahead regarding puppet classes during your visit.

Dance

Ballet Arizona, 3645 E. Indian School Rd., Phoenix (☎ 888-3 BALLET or 602-381-1096; www.balletaz.org), pliés at the Orpheum and Phoenix Symphony Hall, when the dancers aren't making their graceful moves in Tucson ($12–$102). The Center Dance Ensemble (☎ 602-252-8497; www.centerdance.com) takes a turn in another direction, staging contemporary dance at the Herberger ($9–$20).

Theater

Almost two dozen professional and nonprofessional theater companies perform in the Valley. The major players include the Actors Theatre of Phoenix, the resident troupe at the Herberger Theater (☎ 602-252-8497; www.atphx.org), putting on a full range of drama, comedy, and musicals, and the Arizona Theatre Company, 502 W. Roosevelt, Phoenix (☎ 602-256-6995; www.arizonatheatre.org), which performs at the Herberger Theater September through May when the company isn't shuttling off to Tucson. Tickets for both range from $20 to $58.

Fast Facts: Phoenix, Scottsdale, and the Valley of the Sun

Area Code

Greater Phoenix is divided into three area codes that require ten-digit dialing (that is, the number and area code not preceded by a 1); you don't pay any long-distance charge when dialing between Valley area codes. Phoenix's area code is **602.** For East Valley cities such as Scottsdale, Tempe, and Mesa, use **480.** For the West Valley towns such as Glendale and Peoria, dial **623.**

Doctors

To find a local doctor, call the Banner 230 CARE Physician Referral and Resource Line (☎ **602-230-2273;** www.bannerhealth.com/230care). Also try the American Board of Medical Specialties

(☎ **866-275-2267;** www.abms.org) or the Maricopa County Medical Society (☎ **602-252-2844;** www.medical-society.com).

Emergencies

For fire, police, or medical emergencies, dial ☎ **911.** Phoenix Police (☎ **602-262-6151**); Phoenix Fire (☎ **602-262-6297**); Rural Metro Fire (☎ **480-627-6900**).

Hospitals

The reputable St. Luke's has locations in Phoenix, 1800 E. Van Buren at 18th Avenue (☎ 602-251-8100; www.stlukesmedcenter.com), and in Tempe, 1500 S. Mill Ave. south of E. Parkway Blvd. (☎ 480-784-5500; www.tempestlukeshospital.com). Branches of the Scottsdale Healthcare system (www.shc.org) are at 9003 E. Shea Blvd. (☎ 480-860-3000) and 7400 E. Osborn Rd. (☎ 480-675-4000. For kids, Phoenix Children's Hospital, 1919 E.Thomas Rd. (☎ 602-546-1000; www.phoenixchildrenshospital.com), is the best. The famous Mayo Clinic has a branch in Scottsdale at 13400 E. Shea Blvd. (☎ 480-301-8000) and a Mayo Clinic Hospital at 5777 E. Mayo Blvd. (☎ 480-515-6296). Both can be found on the Web at www.mayoclinic.org/scottsdale.

Information

Local sources include: The Phoenix Convention and Visitors Bureau (50 N. 2nd St. at Adams; ☎ **602-452-6268;** www.phoenixcvb.com; open: Mon–Fri 8 a.m.–5 p.m.; and Biltmore Fashion Park, 24th St. and Camelback Rd.; ☎ **602-452-6281;** open: Mon–Fri 10 a.m.–7 p.m., Sat 10 a.m.–6 p.m., and Sun noon–6 p.m.); The Scottsdale Chamber of Commerce/Convention and Visitors Bureau (4343 N. Scottsdale Rd., Ste. 170, in the Galleria Corporate Center; ☎ **480-421-1004;** www.scottsdalecvb.com; open: Mon–Fri 8:30 a.m.–6 p.m.; and at the concierge desk at Scottsdale Fashion Square Mall, at the northeast corner of Scottsdale and Camelback roads; open: Tues–Fri 1 p.m.–6 p.m. and Sat 11 a.m.–4 p.m.); The Tempe Convention and Visitors Bureau (51 W. 3rd St., #105; ☎ **480-894-8158;** www.tempecvb.com; open Mon–Fri 8 a.m.–5 p.m.); and, finally, the Glendale Office of Tourism and Visitor Center (5800 W. Glenn Dr.; ☎ **623-930-2955;** www.visitglendale.com; open 10 a.m.–5 p.m. Mon–Sat).

Internet Access

Kinko's provides high-speed Internet access in eight cities throughout the Valley. Three of the most convenient locations are: in downtown Phoenix, 3801 N. Central Ave. (☎ **602-241-9440**); in Scottsdale, 4150 N. Drinkwater Blvd. (☎ **480-946-0500**); and in Tempe, 933 E. University Dr. (☎ **480-894-1797**). The only Internet café in the Valley is Jamaican Blue, 4017 N. Scottsdale Rd., downtown Scottsdale (☎ **480-947-2160**); it's open every day from 6 a.m.–1 a.m.

Maps

Because Greater Phoenix is so spread out, any single map is either going to be sketchy or unwieldy. That's why I suggest having two: one to put the Valley in geographical perspective — get this map from any car rental company or tourist bureau — and another map with real detail. The H.M. Gousha map, sold at most gas stations, supermarkets, and convenience stores, is as good as any in the latter category. If you're a AAA member, you can ask for the double-your-fun Phoenix maps in advance or pick them up in Phoenix at 3144 N. 7th Ave. (☎ **602-274-1116**) or in Scottsdale at 701 N. Scottsdale Rd. (☎ **480-949-7993**). Serious map buffs might like the Wide World of Maps with two Valley locations: 2626 W. Indian School Rd., Phoenix (☎ **800-279-7654** or 602-279-2323), and

1444 W. Southern Ave., Mesa (☎ **480-433-0606**). Whatever you get, make sure it's current; the streets in the Valley shift far faster than its weather.

Newspapers/Magazines

The *Arizona Republic* is Phoenix's largest daily newspaper, with the *Tribune* coming in second in Scottsdale and Tempe. You can find the excellent free alternative weekly, the *Phoenix New Times,* at corner dispensers, coffeehouses, supermarkets, and many other places around the Valley. The monthly *Phoenix Magazine* covers Valleywide topics of interest, including up-to-date restaurant reviews. The glossy *Valley Guide,* published quarterly, is another good source of visitor-friendly articles and information.

Pharmacies

Walgreens has 24 Valley pharmacies that never close; call ☎ **800-WALGREENS** for the location nearest you. Two Phoenix branches of Fry's Pharmacy are also open 24 hours a day: at 59th Avenue and Thunderbird (☎ **602-978-4998**) and at Tatum and Bell (☎ **602-867-4060**).

Post Office

The Phoenix main post office is at 4949 E. Van Buren St., east of North 48th Street (☎ **800-275-8777**).

Restrooms

In downtown Scottsdale, where merchants want to be sure that shoppers are comfortable, you find four nice, clean public restrooms: off Marshall Way, between 1st and 2nd streets; on the east and west ends in the Scottsdale Civic Center; north of 2nd Street, between Brown and Drinkwater Boulevard; and at 5th Avenue, between Marshall Way and Craftsman Court. Otherwise, you have to do what you have to do everywhere else in Arizona: duck into a restaurant, hotel, or shopping mall.

Safety

Phoenix's violent crime rate has been on the decrease in the last decade — and it wasn't especially high to begin with — but the usual rules apply. Stick to crowded public areas at night, especially in downtown Phoenix. On the nights of sports events or concerts, stay with the rest of the crowd when walking to and from your parking spot. In contrast to violent crimes, Arizona has the highest rate of car theft in the country, with the majority of auto larcenies occurring in Maricopa County, where Greater Phoenix is located. The city also has a high rate of car break-ins, even in the more established areas. In short, leave your valuables in your hotel safe (and never on your front or back seat).

Smoking

Several Greater Phoenix cities passed ordinances in the1980s and 1990s that outlawed smoking in designated public places and in all areas of government buildings. Private businesses, however, can set their own rules. The great majority — including malls, sports facilities, and cultural venues — don't allow indoor smoking, but many restaurants, especially those with bars, still have designated smoking and nonsmoking sections. The only exceptions are the cities of Mesa, which outlawed puffing in all public places, including restaurants, and Tempe, where smoke is forbidden even in bars.

Taxes

State sales tax plus the sales tax in Maricopa County — where Greater Phoenix is located — adds up to 6.3%, but variable local taxes are also included. You can expect to be taxed a total of 7% on purchases and restaurant tabs in Phoenix, 7.7% in Scottsdale. Hotel room tariffs add up to 11.1% in Tempe, 11.67% in Scottsdale and Paradise Valley, and 12.07% in Phoenix. See Chapter 7 for information on car rental taxes at Sky Harbor airport.

Taxis

AAA Cab (☎ **602-437-4000**), Allstate Cab (☎ **602-275-8888**), Courier Cab (☎ **602-232-2222**), Scottsdale Taxi (☎ **480-994-4567**), and Yellow Cab (☎ **602-252-5252**).

Time Zone

Phoenix is in the Mountain time zone. The state doesn't observe daylight saving time.

Transit Info

For Valley Metro Transit, call ☎ **602-253-5000** or log on to www.valleymetro.org.

Weather Updates

Call ☎ **602-275-0073** for the National Weather Service; www.wrh.noaa.gov/phoenix.

Chapter 12

Going Beyond Greater Phoenix: Three Day-Trips

In This Chapter

- Traveling I-17 north
- Exploring along the Apache Trail
- Visiting old houses and big houses (prisons, that is)

You can visit the future and the past on these side trips from the Valley, with sights that include everything from Arcosanti, a vision — or is that mirage? — in the desert of cities to come (Day-Trip #1), to Casa Grande, impressive Native American ruins dating to the 1200s (Day-Trip #3). All these trips are a mixed bag, combining a variety of attractions from which you can pick and choose.

Day-Trip #1: From Rocks to Arcosanti

You don't have to leave the Valley to begin this tour north along I-17, which starts at the Deer Valley Rock Art Center, continues north to Cave Creek and the Pioneer Arizona Living History Museum, and finishes at Arcosanti, some 65 miles from central Phoenix. If you're traveling with kids, you may want to skip Arcosanti, an experimental desert community that's probably of limited interest to them.

Getting there

I-17 intersects I-10 in central Phoenix. Take I-17 north and exit from the highway as directed for each attraction. Unfortunately, no back roads or convenient loops connect the sights on this trip; you must return to the freeway to move on to the next location. The good news is, that for a major highway, I-17 is fairly scenic and quick (75 mph speed limit).

Taking a tour

You can't wander freely around Arcosanti. Aside from the bakery and the bell shop, most of the site is accessible only by guided tour. Tours are an option at the Deer Valley Rock Art Center; see the following section for schedules. If you want to see Cave Creek from the back of a horse, contact Cave Creek Outfitters (☎ 800-921-0040 or 480-471-4635; www.cavecreekoutfitters.com) for a two-hour ride for $60.

Seeing the sights

Close to the city (about 15 miles north of downtown Phoenix) and the freeway is the ❶ Deer Valley Rock Art Center, 3711 W. Deer Valley Rd. (2.5 miles west of I-17 via Exit 215B; ☎ 623-582-8007; www.asu.edu/clas/anthropology/dvrac; open: Oct–Apr Tues–Sat 9 a.m.–5 p.m., Sun noon–5 p.m., guided tour every Tues and Thurs 1 p.m. and Sat 10 a.m.; May–Sept Tues–Fri 8 a.m.–2 p.m., Sat 7 a.m.–5 p.m., Sun noon–5 p.m., guided tour every Sat 7:30 a.m.; admission: $5 adults, $3 seniors and students, $2 ages 6–12, 5 and under free). Although not especially rustic, the center has a large concentration of ancient petroglyphs (rock paintings). Some of the 1,500 images made by the region's earliest settlers may date back as far as 5,000 years. Kid-friendly activities include story time, art projects, games for ages 2–6, and identifying petroglyphs.

Return to I-17 and take Exit 223 east to reach Cave Creek, founded as a mining camp in the 1870s and still capitalizing on its Old West roots, as well as on the striking volcanic rock formations in the area. Wander around and browse the crafts, souvenir, and antiques shops, soak in the atmosphere at one of the Western saloons (see the "Dining locally" section for this day-trip), or stop in at the ❷ Cave Creek Museum, 6140 E. Skyline Dr. and Basin Road (☎ 480-488-2764; www.cavecreekmuseum.org; open: Oct–May Wed–Sun 1–4:30 p.m.; closed holidays; admission: $3 adults, $2 seniors, and students, 12 and under free). The small museum, which includes archaeological and pioneer displays, is in a historic complex with the town's first church, a tuberculosis quarantine cabin, and the remains of a mill. Head east on Cave Creek Road, and you soon come to the manicured community of Carefree, home to the Boulders Resort and the El Pedregal shopping center (see Chapter 11 for both), as well as a huge sundial and a strollable downtown with several upscale boutiques.

Another 2 miles north on I-17 is the Williamsburg-gone-West ❸ Pioneer Arizona Living History Museum, 3901 W. Pioneer Rd., just off Exit 225 (☎ 623-465-1052; www.pioneerarizona.com; open: mid-Sept–May Wed–Sun 9 a.m.–5 p.m.; June–mid-Sept Fri–Sun 9 a.m.–2 p.m.; admission: $7 adults, $6 seniors, $5 ages 5–18; children under 5 free. The museum has 28 original and reconstructed buildings — everything from a sheriff's office to a Victorian mansion. The costumed staff demonstrates frontier activities, such as blacksmithing; highlights include staged shoot-'em-ups and a petting zoo.

Don't visit Pioneer Arizona Living History Museum in summer, when all that's involved is a long, dusty walk around the grounds. Even during high season, if volunteers don't show up, the museum can be mighty slow going. Phone ahead to find out what, if anything, is happening on the day you plan to visit.

Side Trips from Greater Phoenix

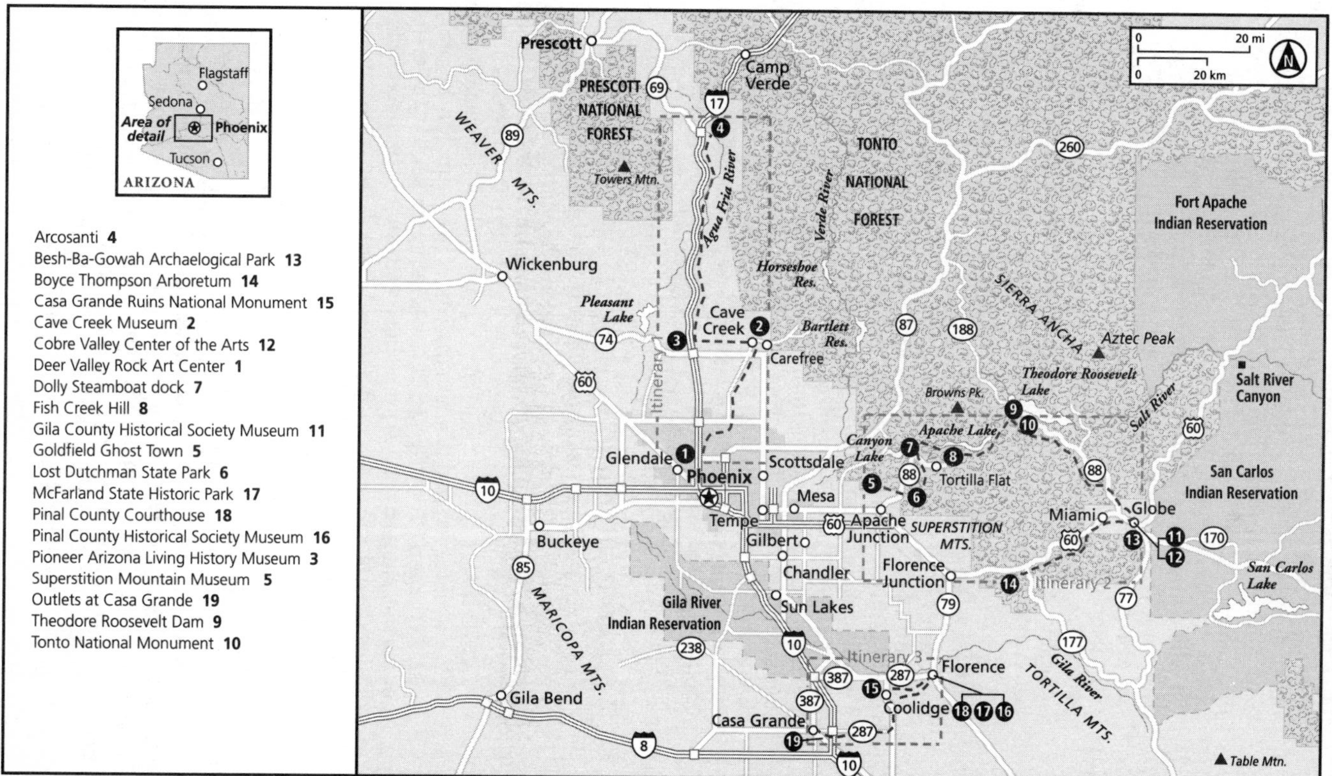

From the Pioneer Museum along I-17, drive 37 miles to Exit 262 (follow the signs) to ❹ Arcosanti (☎ 928-632-6217; www.arcosanti.org; open: daily 9 a.m.–5 p.m., closed Thanksgiving, Christmas, and New Year's; tours every hour on the hour 10 a.m.–4 p.m.; admission: $8, children under 18 accompanied by adult free). This drive involves about 1½ miles on a dusty, bumpy dirt road. Close your windows and go slowly. Arcosanti started in 1970 and is far from completed; this desert community embodies architect Paolo Soleri's vision of a world without suburban sprawl. Whether you come away convinced that you've seen the future and that Soleri's vision could, in fact, work, or you think Arcosanti is New Age hokum, the guided tours give you food for thought. Get more substantial fare at Arcosanti's excellent bakery/cafe, and then browse among the Soleri windbells and other crafts created on-site.

Dining locally

In Cave Creek, Crazy Ed's Satisfied Frog ($$), 6245 E. Cave Creek Rd. (☎ 480-488-3317), is renowned for its fried chicken and barbecued ribs — and for the incendiary beer that's brewed on the premises. Feeling more civilized? In neighboring Carefree, the veddy Victorian English Rose Tea Room ($–$$), 201 E. Easy St., #103 (☎ 480-488-4812), includes crumpets and cucumber sandwiches on the menu. My favorite lunch stop en route north from Tucson is the Rock Springs Café and Bakery ($–$$), 34900 N. Old Black Canyon Hwy. (☎ 623-374-5063), on the site of a former stagecoach stop. Take Exit 242 off I-17, between the Pioneer Living Museum and Arcosanti, and follow the signs. Just two words of menu advice: barbecue and pie.

Spending the night

You can return to the Valley on this easy day-trip, but if you want a change of venue, a few interesting options are available to you. Find creature comforts in the desert at the Full Circle Ranch Bed and Breakfast Inn ($$$), 40205 N. 26th St., between Cave Creek and I-17 (☎ 877-465-7570 or 623-465-7570; www.fullcircleranch.com), a secluded hacienda-style complex. You can even bed down in the city of the future for the prices of the past. Arcosanti (☎ 928-632-6217; www.arcosanti.org) offers basic rooms that range from $20 for a single with shared bath to $30 for a double (two single beds) with a private bath. A two-bedroom suite with stellar views ($75) is also available.

Day-Trip #2: Around the Apache Trail

The Apache Trail's 120-mile loop starts and ends at Apache Junction and passes through one of the country's most awe-inspiring landscapes. The loop's beginning stretch is a 48-mile trail created between 1906 and 1911 to haul construction materials to the site of the Theodore Roosevelt Dam. The dam's namesake said of the trail that it "combines the grandeur of the Alps, the glory of the Rockies, [and] the magnificence of the Grand Canyon" — and he said this even before they named the dam after him.

Part of the road (along Fish Creek Canyon) is unpaved and narrow, and even the paved sections are two-lane and, in many spots, loaded with switchbacks. In short, much of the trail isn't for the faint of heart or the afeard of heights. Consider taking a tour if you fit into either category — or if you just want to sit back and enjoy the scenery.

The route offers loads to do and is beautiful at both ends. You can do it in a full day, but, unless you have the leisure to stay overnight, you're better off doing just the half that appeals to you (Apache Junction to Roosevelt Lake via Highway 88 or Apache Junction to Globe/Miami via Highway 60 east).

Getting there

Take Highway 60 east from Phoenix to Apache Junction, and then get on Highway 88 east. Highway 88 east loops north and back south; follow it until you again reach Highway 60 (near Globe/Miami), which takes you west, back to Apache Junction.

You won't find gas stations along the trail, so fill up at Apache Junction.

Taking a tour

True to its name, Apache Trail Tours & Superstition Mountain Adventures (☎ 480-982-7661; www.apachetrailtours.com) specializes in this area. An 8-hour Jeep jaunt begins at Goldfield Ghost Town (where the company is located) and includes stops at Tortilla Flat, lunch at Apache Lake, and a hike through Tonto National Monument ($145). Among its many tours, the company also offers two-hour off-road trips into the Lost Dutchman mine terrain ($70), plus a variety of guided hikes into the Superstition Mountains and several hike/Jeep combinations.

Want to horse around in the mountains? Rides offered by Apache Lake Ranch, Highway 88 at mile marker 227.5, 2.5 miles west of Apache Lake Marina (☎ 928-467-2822), go into the spectacular northern Superstition Wilderness ($35 for 2 hours, $45 for 3 hours). See Chapter 11 for info on the D Spur Ranch, which also offers rides into the southern Superstitions.

Once a month from October through April, about two days before the full moon (call for exact dates), the rangers at Lost Dutchman State Park lead two-hour moonlit hikes — sometimes as many as 250 people show up.

Seeing the sights

This trip begins some 2.5 miles east of Apache Junction on Highway 88 at the ❺ Superstition Mountain Museum, 4087 N. Apache Tr. (☎ 480-983-4888; www.superstitionmountainmuseum.org; open: daily 9 a.m.–4 p.m.; closed Christmas; admission: $4 adults, $3 seniors, $2 ages 6–12; 5 and under free). The museum details the area's Native American, mining, and military histories Exhibits include 23 maps of the Lost Dutchman mine. About a half mile east of the museum, the touristy

Goldfield Ghost Town (☎ 480-983-0333; www.goldfieldghosttown.com; open: daily 10 a.m.–5 p.m.) is a reconstruction of the 1890s mining boomtown that once stood on the site. Admission to the town complex is free. However, you must pay to descend into a replica gold mine ($6 adults, $5 seniors, $3 ages 6–12); ride on Arizona's only narrow-gauge railroad ($5 adults, $4.50 seniors, $3 ages 5–12); and gawk at live rattlesnakes, Gila monsters, and scorpions ($3 adults, $2.50 seniors, $2 children under 18).

Today, the ❻ Lost Dutchman State Park, 6109 N. Apache Tr., one mile past Goldfield (☎ 480-982-4485; www.pr.state.az.us/Parks/parkhtml/dutchman.html; open: daily sunrise to 10 p.m.; admission $6 per vehicle, up to 4 passengers), attracts people more interested in hiking the hills — the volcanically formed Superstition Mountains — than in finding the gold reputed to be there.

As you leave the park and enter Tonto National Forest, you're officially on the Apache Trail, designated as Arizona's first historic and scenic highway in 1987. Drive 11 miles to get to Canyon Lake, popular for fishing, boating, and swimming and for boarding the ❼ Dolly Steamboat (☎ 480-827-9144 for reservations; www.dollysteamboat.com), a replica of a 100-foot double-deck sternwheeler. (Note: Advance reservations are suggested, but walk-ons are also accepted if there's room.) The 90-minute narrated nature cruise departs daily at noon and 2 p.m. (depending on the season and demand; call to check the day's schedule) and costs $16 adults, $9 ages 6–12, 5 and under free; twilight dinner cruises run Friday through Sunday (advance reservations required).

Two miles farther down the road, Tortilla Flat (☎ 480-984-1776; www.tortillaflataz.com) looks like a Western film set. This 1904 stagecoach stop, seriously damaged in a 1987 fire, was rebuilt with the help of local volunteers and today consists of a post office, ice cream shop (renowned for its fruity and not at all spiny prickly-pear ice cream), and restaurant/saloon/gift shop (see the "Dining Locally" section for this day-trip). All are generally open Monday through Friday from 9 a.m.–6 p.m., and weekends from 8 a.m.–7 p.m.; closed Thanksgiving and Christmas.

The pavement ends after about 5 miles as you begin a precarious (1,500 feet in 3 miles) descent down ❽ Fish Creek Hill — one of the most breathtaking rides you're likely to ever take. By the time you reach the marina at Apache Lake (☎ 928-467-2511; www.apachelake.com), some 9 miles away, you may be ready to spend the afternoon decompressing on the water. Pontoon boating ($25 per hour, minimum of 2 hours) and fishing (if you pick up an Arizona fishing license, and bring your own gear; $10 per hour, minimum 2 hours) are two fine ways to do so.

Drive another 14 miles to see the impressive ❾ Theodore Roosevelt Dam, the world's highest masonry dam. You can also view it from the 1,080-foot-long steel arch bridge that sits about a quarter mile upstream from the dam or from the back patio of the Roosevelt Lake Visitor Center, another mile up the road (☎ 928-467-3200; open: daily 7:45 a.m.–4:30 p.m.). Roosevelt Lake, the largest body of water contained within the state borders — don't you love these carefully qualified statistics? — is another get-wet-in-the-desert mecca.

The Apache Trail ends at the dam, returning you to paved road for the 5-mile trip to ⑩ Tonto National Monument (☎ 928-467-2241; `http://nps.gov/tont/`; open: daily 8 a.m.–5 p.m. [Lower Cliff Dwelling trail closes at 4 p.m.], closed Christmas; admission: $3 per adult, 16 and under free), a well-preserved complex of cliff dwellings built by the Salado people between 1100 and 1400 A.D. You can hike a mile (round-trip) up the hill to the Lower Cliff Dwelling on your own, but call as far in advance as you can if you want a place on the (free) three- to four-hour ranger-led hikes to the more extensive Upper Cliff Dwelling (Nov–Apr).

As you drive the 25 miles from Tonto National Monument to the Highway 60 junction, you know you're in mining country by the vast mesas of tailings (bleached-out remains of extracted rock) that you begin to see. From the junction, head east on Highway 60 for 3 miles to the Greater Globe-Miami Chamber of Commerce, 1360 N. Broad St. (☎ 800-804-5623 or 928-425-4495; `www.globemiamichamber.com`), where you can pick up a walking tour map of historic downtown Globe. Next door, the ⑪ Gila County Historical Society Museum, 1330 N. Broad St. (☎ 928-425-7385), gives you the lowdown on the area's mines. For a more elevating perspective, stop downtown at the ⑫ Cobre Valley Center of the Arts, 101 N. Broad St. (☎ 928-425-0884), an artist's co-op housed in the 1907 Gila County Courthouse. On the southeast side of town, the excellent ⑬ Besh-Ba-Gowah Archaelogical Park, 1100 Jess Hayes Rd. (☎ 928-425-0320; open: daily 9 a.m.–5 p.m.; closed Thanksgiving, Christmas, and New Year's; admission: $3 adults, $2 seniors, under 11 free), makes the ancient Salado Indian culture come alive. Kids enjoy climbing the ladders into the upper stories of the ancient pueblos, where pottery and tools excavated at the site are laid out as if they're waiting to be used.

As you head west on Highway 60 toward Apache Junction, you wind your way through the magnificent Devil's and Queen Creek canyons (not nearly as white-knuckle scary as the Fish Creek Hill descent, but not exactly relaxing, either). In contrast, the ⑭ Boyce Thompson Arboretum, 37615 Hwy. 60 (☎ 520-689-2811; `www.ag.arizona.edu/BTA/`; open: daily 8 a.m.–5 p.m., closed Christmas; admission: $6 adults, $3 ages 5–12, under 5 free), created between 1923 and 1929, is a picture of tranquility. If you think you're cactus-ed out by now, think again. You see rare desert specimens from around the world here, including the bizarre Boojum tree featured in Lewis Carroll's poem, "The Hunting of the Snark."

Dining locally

The Mining Camp Restaurant ($$), 6100 E. Mining Camp St., off Highway 88 about a half mile past Goldfield (☎ 480-982-3181), serves hearty all-you-can-eat family-style dinners in a place designed to look like a miner's shanty. The Superstition Saloon ($) at Tortilla Flat is as well known for its wallpaper — business cards and dollar bills lining every available inch of space — as for its chili, burgers, and biscuits and gravy. The restaurant at the Apache Lake Marina and Resort ($–$$) (see the following section) serves up good seafood and daily specials and an even better view of Apache Lake. Globe's Java Junction ($–$$), corner of Broad and Cedar streets (☎ 928-402-8926), housed in a 1906 building, has good sandwiches, pasta salads, Italian sodas, and, of course, coffee.

Spending the night

Whether your interests tend toward the nautical, historical, or golfical, the Apache Trail has a place for you. The rooms at the Apache Lake Marina and Resort ($–$$), Apache Lake (☎ 928-467-2511; `www.apachelake.com`), aren't particularly exciting, but their proximity to great watersports and to the surrounding rugged wilderness is. The Noftsger Hill Inn ($–$$), 425 North St. (☎ 877-780-2479 or 928-425-2260; `www.noftsgerhillinn.com`) offers sweeping views of the Pinal Mountains, mining-era antiques, and huge breakfasts. At Gold Canyon Golf Resort ($$$$–$$$$$), 6100 S. Kings Ranch Rd., Gold Canyon (☎ 800-624-6445 or 480-982-9090; `www.gcgr.com`), you can bunk in an upscale Southwestern-style casita and tee off on two gorgeous mountainside courses. Gold Canyon is only about 20 minutes from Phoenix, but the canyon is still very deserted.

Day-Trip #3: Casa Grande and Florence

This quick foray from the Valley, about 60 miles, takes you to southern Arizona's most interesting archaeological site and to a town that time — but not the state prison system — forgot. You can return from this day-trip via the scenic or the shopping route.

Getting there

To reach Casa Grande Ruins National Monument, take I-10 south to Exit 185 and head east on Highway 387, which turns into Highway 87/287; when you get off I-10, you'll be enjoying a gorgeous stretch of lush desert, especially stunning when the wildflowers bloom in spring. After exploring the ruins, continue 9 miles east to Florence on Highway 287. If you want to take the same basic return route but stop off to shop, go back to I-10 and head about 10 miles south to Exit 198 and the Outlets at Casa Grande. For a longer but more scenic loop return, go north on Highway 79 from Florence to Florence Junction and Highway 60. Highway 60 west returns you to I-10 and to various other Valley freeways. If you have time, detour east 12 miles on Highway 60 to the Boyce Thompson Arboretum (see the "Day-Trip #2: Around the Apache Trail" section earlier in this chapter).

Taking a tour

From December through March, rangers give 30-minute guided tours of the Casa Grande Ruins at regular intervals during the day. A tour of some of the 139 buildings in Florence listed on the National Register of Historic Places is offered only on the first Saturday in February. However, you can pick up a map from the Florence Chamber of Commerce, 291 N. Bailey St. (☎ 800-437-9433 or 520-868-9433; www.florenceaz.org; open: Oct–Apr Mon–Sat 9 a.m.–4 p.m., May–Sept Mon–Fri 10 a.m.–4 p.m.), and tour the homes on your own.

Seeing the sights

Although ⓯ Casa Grande Ruins National Monument, 1100 Ruins Dr., Coolidge (☎ 520-723-3172; nps.gov/cagr; open: daily 8 a.m.–5 p.m., closed Christmas; admission: $3 per adult, ages 16 and under free), became the nation's first prehistoric cultural site in 1892, the monument remains somewhat of a mystery. Archaeologists are fairly certain that the four-story big house, or casa grande — named by the Spanish missionaries who stumbled across it in the late 17th century — was built by the Hohokam people in the 13th or 14th century, but no one is exactly sure why. Some signs, for example, seem to indicate astronomical practices — walls that face the compass points, openings that align with heavenly bodies — but no real evidence proves that the structure was an observatory. The remains of the 25 ovens found near one of the site's ball courts are equally elusive. Archaeologists think the Hohokam people used them to cook ceremonial mescal roots.

The nearby town of Florence, founded in 1866, is home to another big house: the state prison. Moved here from Yuma in 1909, the prison is still the site of all of Arizona's executions. You won't see signs of this grisly legacy while strolling the town's sleepy main street, a throwback to the 1950s, but the ⓰ Pinal County Historical Society Museum, 715 S. Main St. (☎ 520-868-4382; open: Sept to mid-July Wed–Sat 11 a.m.–4 p.m., Sun noon–4 p.m.; admission by donation), has a collection of death-house paraphernalia, including hangman's nooses and the wooden chairs on which the condemned sat in the gas chamber. The ⓱ McFarland State Historic Park, Main and Ruggles (☎ 520-868-5216; open: Thurs–Mon 8 a.m.–5 p.m.; closed Christmas; admission: $3 adults, $1 ages 12–17, under 12 free), consists of a striking adobe building that served as the town's first (1878) courthouse. Inside are displays of some scary antique medical instruments and screens videos of World War II's largest POW camp, located near Florence. The clean-lined courthouse was replaced in 1891 by the ornate ⓲ Pinal County Courthouse, at Pinal and 12th street, the oldest public building still in daily use in Arizona. The courthouse is impressive, but chronometrically challenged: To save money on repairs, four clocks, all perpetually reading 11:44 (or 8:58), were painted on the tower.

For shopping, take Exit 198 off I-10 to reach the ⓳ Outlets at Casa Grande (☎ 800-405-5016 or 520-836-9663; www.outletsatcasagrande.com), with more than 30 stores, including Liz Claiborne, Guess, Reebok, and Samsonite.

Dining locally

The Italian-born owners of A&M Pizza ($–$$), 445 W. Hwy. 287 (☎ 520-868-0170), just outside Florence on the Casa Grande Ruins approach, dish out terrific pastas, calzones, and subs, as well as pizzas. In Florence's 1890 general store, Christina's Tea and Coffee Emporium ($), 110 N. Main St. (☎ 520-868-5748), offers quiches, scones, and other light fare. For something more substantial, savor the great fish tacos and green-chile burros at Luis & Bertha's Inn ($), 695 S. Main St., Florence (☎ 520-868-9981).

Spending the night

If you're interested in baseball history, consider bedding down at the Francisco Grande Hotel & Golf Resort ($–$$), 2600 Gila Bend Hwy, 5 miles west of the town of Casa Grande (☎ 800-237-4238 or 520-836-6444; www.franciscogrande.com), built in 1961 as a training and relaxation facility for the San Francisco Giants. A baseball bat–shaped pool and ball-shaped Jacuzzi are just two of the appealing features of this recently refurbished property; a quiet location, an 18-hole golf course (where Willie Mays played), and low room rates are others. In Florence, the sleeping standout is Florence's Inn at Rancho Sonora ($$), 9198 North Hwy. 79 (☎ 800-205-6817 or 520-868-8000; www.ranchosonora.com). Adjacent to an RV park, this converted 1930s adobe guest ranch is in a walled courtyard with lush desert landscaping. Cottages with kitchenettes are available, too. If you take the scenic Highway 60 route, consider bunking at the Gold Canyon Golf Resort (see the "Day-Trip #2: Around the Apache Trail" section earlier in this chapter).

Chapter 13

Tucson

In This Chapter

- Getting the lowdown on Tucson
- Scoping out the best Tucson bunks
- Chowing down on the city's top grub — Southwestern, Mexican, and more
- Checking out the best attractions and activities
- Shopping for crafts, Western gear, and more
- Finding prime after-dark diversions

Tucson, Arizona's second-largest city, combines New West urban savvy with Old West kicked-back attitude. Far older than Phoenix, Tucson was outpaced by its more development-happy rival after World War II. You find natural attractions here — two sections of Saguaro National Park sandwich the city, which is ringed by craggy mountain ranges and shot through with swathes of pristine desert — but also thriving dining, shopping, and cultural scenes, sparked by University of Arizona–inspired energy and anchored by rich Native American and Hispanic heritages. Add Sun Belt leisure staples, such as have-it-all resorts, world-class spas, and manicured golf courses, and you're talking a major crowd-pleaser of a metropolis.

Author bias alert: Tucson has been my home since 1992, when I moved here from Manhattan.

Getting There

Chapter 6 gives you the lowdown on the airlines that fly into Tucson. As I mention, more carriers serve Phoenix, so, depending on your departure location, the total cost may be cheaper for you to land in the capital and drive or shuttle down to Tucson (see the "Riding in" section later in this chapter). Railing and bussing it into town are other possibilities, although if you don't eventually get your own wheels, sightseeing isn't easy.

Cancel that camel — hump(h)

Tucson sits smack in the middle of the Sonoran Desert, which also sweeps across northern Mexico, but don't start thinking *Lawrence of Arabia.* This high desert region, as it's technically known, gets 11 to 12 inches of rain a year and is lush with flora and fauna. But the temperature does occasionally get very high (105° at times in summer) — and it's a dry heat (the Tucson mantra).

Flying in

The Tucson International Airport, 8½ miles south of downtown (☎ 520-573-8000; `www.tucsonairport.org`), is fairly easy to negotiate: It has only one terminal, with two concourses. The baggage carousels are on the lower level, where you also find the tourist information desks. However, a variety of expansion and improvement projects — everything from creating larger departure lounges to building a 2,000-space rental car parking structure — can complicate retrieving your luggage and renting a car.

You have several options for getting from the airport to wherever you plan to lay your head.

- Renting a car: You need a car in Tucson, so rent one as soon as you fly in — even though you'll pay higher taxes on the rental at the airport. Reserving a car in advance is always a good idea, and doing so during the busy winter season is essential. The major car rental companies line up in the baggage claim area. The nearby courtesy phones, across from the tourist information desk, connect you to agencies without booths in the airport. (See Chapter 7 for tips on renting a car.)
- Hailing a taxi or hopping a shuttle: Many of the airport-area hotels run free shuttles — you can contact them via courtesy phones in the baggage claim areas — and the two major spas and some ranches provide transportation, but as far as the majority of Tucson's far-flung lodgings are concerned, you're on your own. The taxi queue is across the street from the main airport terminal exit. Rates for taxi service, provided by three companies under contract with the Tucson Airport Authority, are $4.50 flagdrop (the cost at the start of the meter) and $1.80 each additional mile. Figure on paying about $22 to $26 for trips to central Tucson, and from $40 to $55 for outlying properties.
- Boarding the Arizona Stagecoach: Shuttle booths for the van service (☎ 520-889-1000) are located at both concourses, near the baggage claim area. For most of the downtown and central Tucson hotels, rates are $17 per person or $20 per couple one way, or $29 per person or $35 per couple round-trip. To get to the hinterlands (where many of the resorts are), you pay $30 per person one way,

$48 round-trip, or $38 per couple each way. The fare for children ages 6 to 12 is $2; children 5 and under ride free when traveling with an adult (or a reasonable facsimile thereof). You don't have to reserve in advance when you arrive, but you need to call at least 24 hours ahead to get a van back to the airport.

If more than two people over age 12 are heading to central Tucson together, taking a taxi rather than the shuttle generally makes sense. Prices are comparable when you add up the cost of the individual shuttle fares, and a cab takes you straight to your destination — do not pass go, do not drop anyone else off.

- Taking the bus: If you're traveling light and have plenty of time (but not much money) to spare, catch the city Sun Tran (☎ 520-792-9222; `www.suntran.com`), bus number 11. The stop is just to the left of the lower level as you leave the terminal. Buses run every half hour Monday through Friday from about 6 a.m. to 6:45 p.m., Saturday from a little before 8 a.m. to approximately 6:45 p.m., and Sunday from 8:45 a.m. to 6:45 p.m., heading north on Alvernon Way, one of the town's main north-south thoroughfares. From this route, you can transfer to most east-west bus lines. If you ask the driver nicely, he or she can tell you the bus that gets you closest to where you're staying. You can also transfer to a variety of lines via bus number 6, which leaves every half hour Monday through Friday from approximately 4:45 a.m. to 7:15 p.m., Saturday from 7:15 a.m. to 6:15 p.m., and Sunday 6:15 a.m. to 5:15 p.m. from the same airport location and heads to the Roy Laos transportation center south of town. To find out about fares and transfers, see the "Getting around Tucson" section later in this chapter.

Driving in

I-10, the main entryway into Tucson from practically everywhere, snakes around town, so find out in advance what exit is closest to your hotel. (Another freeway, I-19, connects with I-10 in Tucson, but this "interstate" goes only to Nogales, Arizona, just across the border from Nogales, Mexico.) Most people who drive down from Phoenix take the quick I-10 route. Unless you hit traffic (or stop at the discount outlet in Casa Grande; see Chapter 12), it shouldn't take you more than 1½ hours to drive the 111 miles from Phoenix's Sky Harbor airport to Tucson — the

North or west?

Signs on freeway entrances in Tucson read "West-Phoenix" — which is confusing, if you assume (correctly) that Phoenix is north. In fact, Phoenix is due northwest of Tucson. If you keep driving on I-10 past Arizona's capital, you eventually hit the beach at Santa Monica, California.

Address-ing a few issues

Central Tucson runs pretty much on a grid system, with Stone (north-south) and Broadway (east-west) as the starting points. Addresses on these two streets and the streets parallel to Stone and Broadway theoretically increase by 100 for every block you go from the Stone/Broadway intersection, so that 1820 E. Speedway is 18 blocks east of Stone — you get the idea. In theory, too, the odd addresses are on the north side of the street and the even numbers on the south — but sometimes (on Grant Road, for example) they switch when you cross Stone. And when you get to downtown, the Foothills, or any of the other outlying areas, all address-predicting bets are off.

And then Tucson has some invisible addresses: Seeing the numbers on most Tucson houses and businesses is hard, especially when you're zipping by in a car. If you're heading into unfamiliar territory — and you probably are — call ahead or ask at your hotel for helpful landmarks.

speed limit is 75 miles per hour most of the way. The views, however, are pretty boring and deceptively ugly; I'd hate for you to think it's a preview of what Tucson looks like. If you have time (about 2½ hours), and especially if you're staying in one of the resorts on the far north side of town, take Highway 60 from Phoenix to Highway 79 to Highway 77, both scenic. The latter turns into Oracle Road, a major north-south thoroughfare into Tucson.

Riding in

Although most people fly or drive to Tucson, some choose other means, one of which may appeal to you:

- Shuttling in from Phoenix: Phone Arizona Shuttle (☎ 800-888-2479 or 520-795-6771; `www.arizonashuttle.com`) and tell the representative what flight you're taking into Phoenix's Sky Harbor Airport so they can save you a seat. Shuttles leave from the terminal (ask where, exactly, when you book your seat) every hour on the half hour from 6:30 a.m. until 11:30 p.m. (fare: $27 one way if you book 24 hours in advance, $35 for same-day reservations, $52/$60 round trip). The vans drop you off at (and depart from) three convenient Tucson locations. Because airfare to Phoenix is often less expensive than airfare to Tucson, this is frequently a good option (you save additional money by renting a car someplace other than either the Phoenix or Tucson airport, where taxes are highest).
- Riding the rails: Amtrak's (☎ 800-872-7245 or 520-623-4442) Sunset Limited tootles into the newly revamped terminal at 400 E. Toole Ave. three times a week on its Orlando/Los Angeles run. You need to take a taxi to your hotel (cabs are usually waiting at the station when trains arrive).

- Taking the bus: If you decide to go Greyhound (☎ 800-231-2222 or 520-792-3475), you arrive in downtown Tucson at 2 S. 4th Ave. — just across from the Hotel Congress — a good place to bunk if you're traveling on a tight budget (see the "Staying in Style" section later in this chapter).

Introducing the Neighborhoods

Like many auto-dependent western cities, Tucson is divided into geographical regions rather than neighborhoods. Well, okay, some neighborhoods do exist, but they're mostly in the older areas. The newer parts (the majority) of town are larger and definitely not strollable, and have uninspiring designations like Northwest and Eastside. The following areas are arranged, roughly, from oldest to newest (and thus from most central to farthest from the city limits).

Downtown

Although no longer the city's commercial hub, the area where the Spanish soldiers planted their flag in 1775 still oozes character. Many of the city's architectural treasures are concentrated in three downtown historic districts. El Presidio, site of the city's original walled fortress, has some of the city's most opulent early homes, as well as the Tucson Museum of Art and Historic Block and the gorgeous mosaic Pima County Courthouse. The Tucson Convention Center complex is a bridge to Barrio Historico, where many of the city's more modest early adobes still stand. This area borders Armory Park, home to the ornate Temple of Music and Art and the Tucson Children's Museum. Downtown's boundaries are — very roughly — I-10 on the west, Toole (which curves around the railroad tracks and turns into Third Avenue) to the north and east, and Kennedy/ E. 16th Street (they switch names at Stone) on the south. The face of downtown is likely to change dramatically with the progression of Rio Nuevo, a massive development project designed to reclaim the Santa Cruz River and other natural habitats around "A" Mountain, and to highlight the area's past through tourist-friendly historic and archaeological complexes. Groundbreaking on Rio Nuevo isn't expected until 2006, however, so downtown still looks as though it's in decline.

The University of Arizona/Fourth Avenue

The West University Historic District developed just east of El Presidio after the University of Arizona was established in 1891. Bounded to the north and south by Speedway Boulevard and Sixth Street, respectively, and east and west by Euclid and Stone avenues, the district includes several beautiful turn-of-the-19th-century homes as well as the northern section of the Fourth Avenue shopping district (which extends roughly from University to Ninth Street). The University of Arizona campus adjoins the historic district on the east side of Euclid.

Central

Most real estate agents consider central Tucson's boundaries to be 22nd Street on the south, Oracle Road on the west, Wilmot Road on the east, and Prince Road or (pushing it) River Road on the north. The town conducts most of its business here, and many of the hotels and restaurants — but not most of the tourist attractions — are located in this area. You come across older, ritzy neighborhoods like Sam Hughes, east of the University of Arizona; El Encanto, near El Con Mall; and Winterhaven, on north Tucson Boulevard (renowned for its elaborate displays of Christmas lights), but strip malls, fast-food restaurants, and low-key homes and apartment complexes predominate. Be on the lookout for some great old neon signs between bouts of golden arches.

South Tucson

This separately incorporated, largely Mexican-American city doesn't get much Chamber of Commerce hype, but South Tucson is a magnet for Mexican food lovers, who flock to the down-home restaurants that line Fourth Avenue south of 12th Street, and to shoppers who frequent "the Lost Barrio" strip (see the "Decorator fever: The other South Park" sidebar in this chapter).

Eastside

After central Tucson was settled, much of the city's development moved east toward Colossal Cave and the Rincon district of Saguaro National Park. The majority of the housing complexes here are nothing to write home about (although many visitors do, which is why more are continually cropping up). You still find a bit of desert at far reaches of Speedway Boulevard, but, sadly, strip shopping centers have metastasized in much of this area.

Foothills

East of First Avenue and north of Ina/Skyline, expensive homes and upscale restaurants dot the lower reaches of the Santa Catalina Mountains (saying people live in the Foothills is code for "they're loaded"). Lots of chic resorts have staked a claim to this territory, too.

So why isn't it O'Tucson?

A former captain in the Spanish army, Irishman Hugo O'Conor, founded Tucson — which explains why St. Patrick's Day is a big deal here. But the name Tucson comes from the Indian word *stjukshon (stuck-shahn),* "spring at the foot of a black mountain." (That mountain is now "A" mountain, its landmark letter whitewashed by University of Arizona students annually.) The city often calls itself the "Old Pueblo," referring to the adobe barricades, or presidio, built under O'Conor's watch.

Tucson Orientation

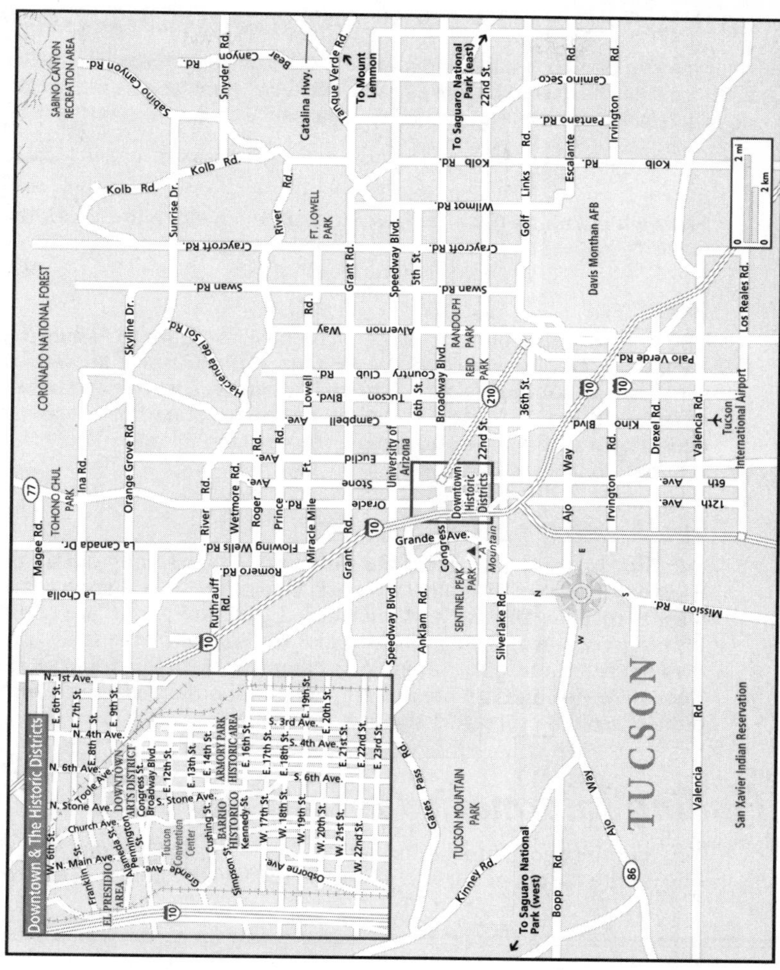

Sabino Canyon and Mount Lemmon are the main outdoor visitor magnets, but locals hike other parts of them thar hills, too.

Northwest

New development is rampant in this part of town, which extends to the northern reaches of Saguaro National Park West and the Tucson and Tortolita mountain ranges; many consider its eastern sections to be the Foothills. Two of Tucson's most popular malls, Tucson Mall and Foothills

Education — second only to incarceration

When the 13th Territorial Legislature voted to fund a university in Tucson in 1891, much of the local populace was annoyed. They wanted an insane asylum and prison, the more lucrative institutions that rival Phoenix nabbed.

Mall (which, name notwithstanding, isn't even close to the Foothills), are in the Northwest, as are several resorts and guest ranches.

Westside

The once-pristine patch of desert you pass en route to Saguaro National Park West, Old Tucson, and the Arizona-Sonora Desert Museum is slated for the next building frenzy. A huge Marriott resort opened in late 2004 at the east end of Tucson Mountain Park near Starr Pass; it was preceded by a golf course and smaller resort, and a large residential development continues to grow.

The Northern Satellites

Catalina, Marana, Casas Adobes, and Oro Valley, strung out along Highway 77 near Catalina State Park, Biosphere 2, and such far northwest resorts as Miraval and the Hilton El Conquistador, are constantly battling Tucson and each other about their legal status (they want their own services and governments; Tucson wants its tax dollars). Part of Tucson or not, they're here to stay and expanding, as leisure and residential growth creeps northward.

Finding Information after You Arrive

You find the two Airport Information Centers in the baggage claim areas, one on the east concourse and one on the west; both are open from 7 a.m.

Who's calling whom a dim bulb?

If you think Tucson's streets seem darker than those in most other cities, you're not imagining it. The many astronomical observatories in and around town — more in a 50-mile radius than anywhere else in the world (see Chapter 14) — have inspired ordinances to help prevent light pollution. For example, lights have to be aimed downward, rather than up beyond the horizon, and athletic fields have to call lights-out by 10:30 p.m. The **International Dark-Sky Association** (`www.darksky.org`) is headquartered in Tucson. Check out the site if you want to find out how good being kept in the dark can be.

Some Tucson driving oddities — and tips

Come winter, tourists, UA students, and *snowbirds* (northern retirees down for the season), all converge (well, with luck, not literally) on Tucson's roads, which makes for some interesting traffic interactions. Other quirks to watch out for:

- The left-turn arrow appears at the end of the green light, not the beginning.
- To find north, look for the Santa Catalina Mountains, the largest and most looming of the ranges that surround the city. You can see them from almost everywhere in central Tucson. Of course, you're out of luck at night, unless you know how to navigate by the constellations — which, as it happens, are terrifically visible most evenings (see the "Who's calling whom a dim bulb?" sidebar, in this chapter).
- No matter how ludicrous the "DO NOT ENTER WHEN FLOODED" signs look most of the year, when it rains, it pours, and Tucson has little in the way of drainage. Take those signs seriously. Every year, at least one person who ignored them makes the 10 o'clock news — as a drowning victim.

to 11 p.m. (☎ 520-573-8000). In addition to paging people and helping with directions around the airport, the volunteers answer questions about Tucson and distribute tourist brochures. If you haven't booked a room (bad! bad! — except in summer), the volunteers can call around and make reservations for you.

The Metropolitan Tucson Convention and Visitors Bureau, open Monday through Friday 8 a.m. to 5 p.m., Saturday and Sunday 9 a.m. to 4 p.m., is located downtown in the colorful La Placita Village, 110 S. Church St. (corner of Broadway), Ste. 7199 (☎ 520-624-1817; `www.visittucson.org`).

Getting around Tucson

Tucson is v-e-r-y s-p-r-e-a-d o-u-t (we're talking a metropolitan area of almost 500 square miles), and its public transportation system is limited. Unless you can afford a private chauffeur or want to rely on tour companies, you need to drive to the city's prime attractions.

Exploring by car

If the bad news is that you need to rent a car in Tucson, the good news is that, unless you're in a rush, driving around town is relatively low stress. Unlike Phoenix and the Valley of the Sun, which are loop-de-loop with raised asphalt, Tucson has only I-10 as a freeway and, because I-10 runs on the west side of a town that's spreading east, this interstate is used more as an escape route than as a way of getting around. As a result, you actually get to see the city when you drive here (okay, maybe more slowly than you may want to). And, except in downtown, where roads tend toward the one-way and narrow, Tucson's streets are generally wide, well marked, and dual-direction. On the largest streets, center turn lanes help ease the traffic flow. The main east-west thoroughfares in central Tucson are, from north to south: River, Ft. Lowell, Grant, Speedway, Broadway, and 22nd Street. Popular north-south streets (from the west) are Oracle, Stone, Campbell, Alvernon, Swan, Craycroft, and Wilmot/Tanque Verde.

Traveling by taxi

Don't even think about trying to hail a cab on the street; the coverage area is too vast to have much success hailing one. If you want a ride, always phone ahead for a taxi. And because the town is so spread out, you're not likely to get away cheap. Taxi rates vary, so ask in advance about the fare to your destination. Some of the more reliable cab companies include Allstate (☎ 520-798-1111), Orange Cab (☎ 520-624-4747), and Yellow Cab (☎ 520-624-6611). The drivers of Fiesta Taxi (☎ 520-622-7777) speak both English and Spanish.

Riding a bus

Tucson's public bus system, Sun Tran (☎ 520-792-9222 or 520-628-1565 (TDD); www.suntran.com), is clean and pleasant, but its hours of operation and routes don't cut it for most tourist purposes (for example, many lines stop running after 6:30 or 7 p.m. on weekends). The system gets you around central Tucson, though, which includes several of the sights and shops detailed in this chapter. Fares run $1, 40¢ for seniors and citizens with ADA eligibility cards, and children 5 and under are free. You need exact change. If you need a (free) transfer (good for two hours and two rides), request one as soon as you board the bus. Day passes cost $2.

Moving your own two feet

The downtown historic neighborhoods and the University of Arizona/Fourth Avenue areas are really the only desirable strolling spots. Most of the other walking you can do is around malls or in the desert — where it's called hiking.

Staying in Style

Tucson has been in the hospitality business for a long time — dudes started coming to the ranches in the 1920s — and the experience shows. These days the city has something to suit every lodging taste and budget, from inexpensive chain motels and historic B&Bs to guest ranches and some of the country's ritziest resorts and destination spas (Tucson is home to the world-famous Canyon Ranch and Miraval). The following are my favorite Tucson accommodations.

Christmas to mid-March is called high season for a reason — the room rates go through the roof. Still, prices for resorts and hotels in Tucson are generally lower than those prices in other leisure-bent Southwest cities — Scottsdale, for example — and, in the general scheme of things, are a deal. But for the real bargains, visit in summer: Room prices dip drastically when the mercury rises. Summer rates are sometimes as much as 70% lower than winter ones.

Don't be surprised if you have a hard time finding a room, at whatever price, during the Tucson Gem and Mineral Show in the first two weeks of February (see Chapter 3). You may not have heard of the show, but dealers and buyers from all over the world have. The events take place downtown, so during those weeks, look for accommodations in the Foothills or other resort-filled outskirts, rather than in the central area.

When calling the resorts and hotels, don't forget to inquire about package deals — too numerous to include here. Also, weekend rates are often lower than weekday rates and holidays tend to be unpredictable.

Tucson also has plenty of chain properties that are conveniently located and, in many cases, economical. Among the chains, I recommend the centrally located Clarion Hotel Randolph Park, which affords easy access to the airport and is near the excellent Randolph North golf course; the Clarion Hotel & Suites Santa Rita, close to the convention center and home to the terrific Café Poca Cosa (see the "Dining Out" section later in this chapter); and the Marriott University Park Hotel, practically on the University of Arizona campus and near all 4th Avenue's shops and restaurants. Because of its interesting history, I also include one motel with a familiar franchise tag. See the Appendix for 800 numbers and Web sites for these and other chains represented in town.

Spas

Canyon Ranch

$$$$$ Foothills

Another resort spa in the Berkshires and spa clubs in Florida, Las Vegas, and on the Queen Mary 2 share this high-cachet name, but this location is the original, opened in 1979 on the site of the historic Double U Guest Ranch. The city has grown up around the facility in the last two decades, so the grounds aren't as isolated as they used to be, but this resort is still a darned pretty desert getaway. And Canyon Ranch is still hot (and I don't mean the weather), with the latest sports equipment, spa treatments, and medical programs, everything from sleep therapy to Chinese herbal consultation and body-fat measuring. If you want to be prodded into making a major life change, Canyon Ranch remains the place to come.

See map p. 194. 8600 E. Rockcliff Rd. (take Sabino Canyon Road to Snyder, turn right, then look out for Rockcliff on the right; you see signs for the resort). ☎ ***800-742-9000*** *or 520-749-9000. Fax: 520-749-1646.* `www.canyonranch.com`. *Rack rates: Prices per person for a 4-night (minimum) stay, based on double occupancy Sept 26–June 4*

Tucson Accommodations

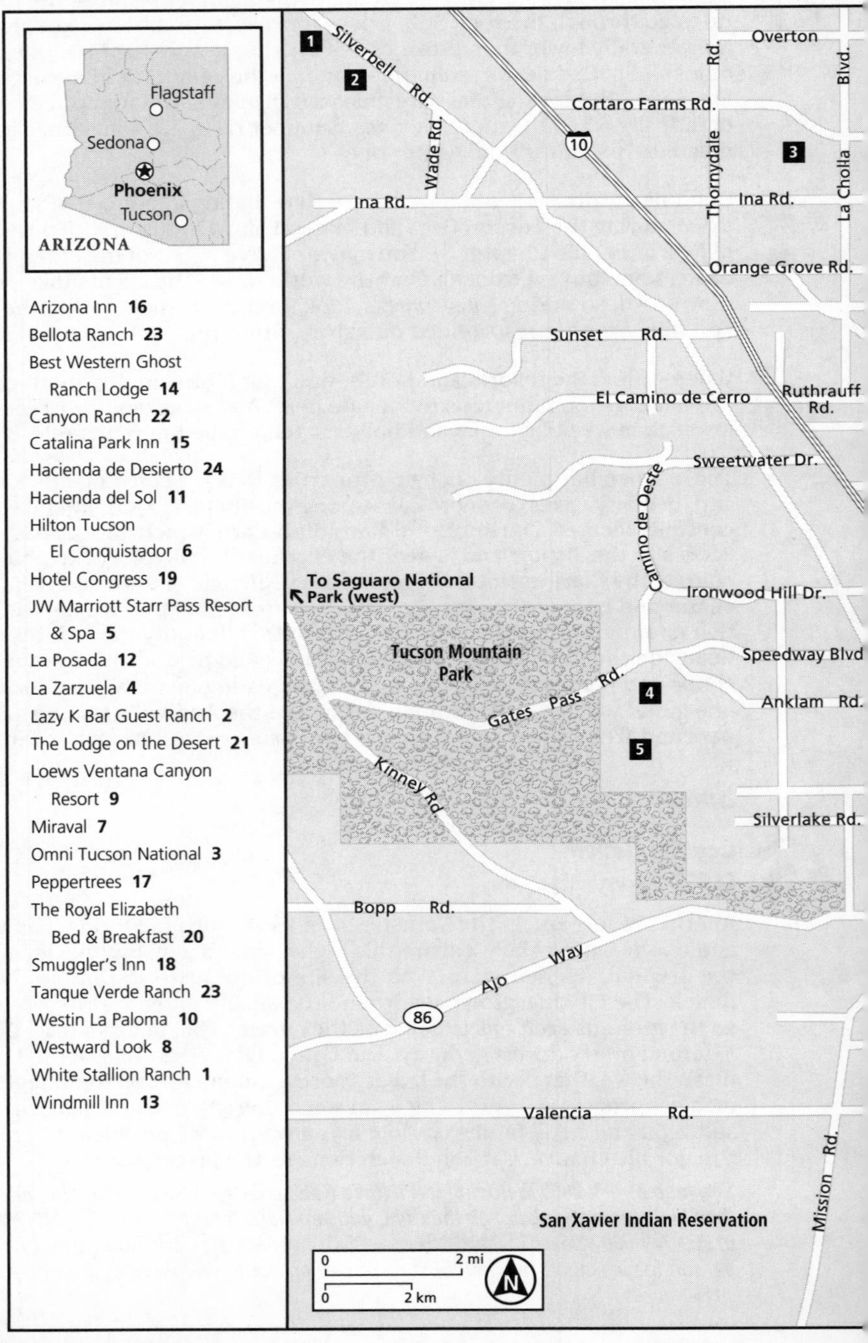

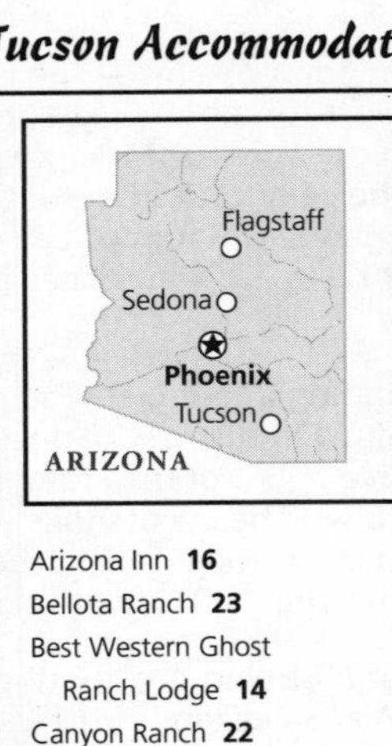

Arizona Inn **16**
Bellota Ranch **23**
Best Western Ghost Ranch Lodge **14**
Canyon Ranch **22**
Catalina Park Inn **15**
Hacienda de Desierto **24**
Hacienda del Sol **11**
Hilton Tucson El Conquistador **6**
Hotel Congress **19**
JW Marriott Starr Pass Resort & Spa **5**
La Posada **12**
La Zarzuela **4**
Lazy K Bar Guest Ranch **2**
The Lodge on the Desert **21**
Loews Ventana Canyon Resort **9**
Miraval **7**
Omni Tucson National **3**
Peppertrees **17**
The Royal Elizabeth Bed & Breakfast **20**
Smuggler's Inn **18**
Tanque Verde Ranch **23**
Westin La Paloma **10**
Westward Look **8**
White Stallion Ranch **1**
Windmill Inn **13**

1
2
Silverbell Rd.
Overton Rd.
Blvd.
Cortaro Farms Rd.
Wade Rd.
10
Thornydale
3
La Cholla
Ina Rd.
Ina Rd.
Orange Grove Rd.
Sunset Rd.
El Camino de Cerro
Ruthrauff Rd.
Sweetwater Dr.
Camino de Oeste
To Saguaro National Park (west)
Ironwood Hill Dr.
Tucson Mountain Park
Speedway Blvd
Gates Pass Rd.
4
Anklam Rd.
5
Kinney Rd.
Silverlake Rd.
Bopp Rd.
Ajo Way
86
Valencia Rd.
Mission Rd.
San Xavier Indian Reservation
0 2 mi
0 2 km
N

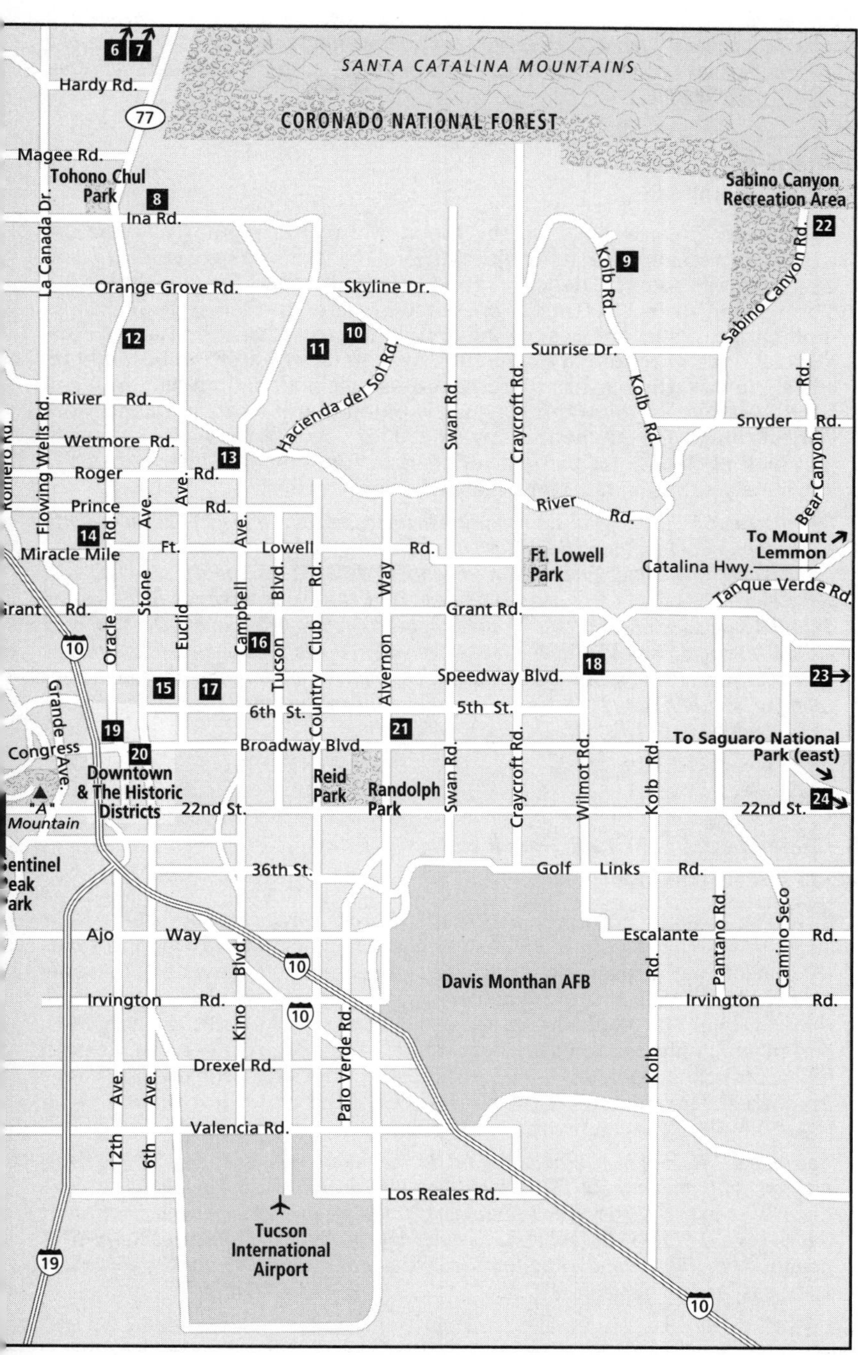

SANTA CATALINA MOUNTAINS
CORONADO NATIONAL FOREST
Hardy Rd.
77
Magee Rd.
Tohono Chul Park
Ina Rd.
La Canada Dr.
Orange Grove Rd.
Skyline Dr.
Sabino Canyon Recreation Area
Sabino Canyon Rd.
Kolb Rd.
Sunrise Dr.
Hacienda del Sol Rd.
River Rd.
Wetmore Rd.
Roger Rd.
Prince Rd.
Flowing Wells Rd.
Swan Rd.
Craycroft Rd.
Snyder Rd.
Bear Canyon Rd.
River Rd.
To Mount Lemmon
Catalina Hwy.
Tanque Verde Rd.
Miracle Mile
Ft. Lowell Rd.
Ft. Lowell Park
Grant Rd.
Oracle Rd.
Stone Ave.
Euclid Ave.
Campbell Ave.
Tucson Blvd.
Country Club Rd.
Alvernon Way
Speedway Blvd.
5th St.
6th St.
Grande Ave.
Congress
Broadway Blvd.
To Saguaro National Park (east)
Downtown & The Historic Districts
Reid Park
Randolph Park
22nd St.
Wilmot Rd.
"A" Mountain
Sentinel Peak Park
36th St.
Golf Links Rd.
Ajo Way
Escalante Rd.
Pantano Rd.
Camino Seco
Kino Blvd.
Davis Monthan AFB
Irvington Rd.
Drexel Rd.
Palo Verde Rd.
12th Ave.
6th Ave.
Valencia Rd.
Los Reales Rd.
Tucson International Airport
10
19

$2,840; June 5–Sept 25 $2030. Rates include all meals, use of facilities, classes and activities, unlimited local calls, Tucson airport transfers, sales tax, gratuities, and a selection of spa and health services based on length of stay. 4-night minimum stay. AE, DC, DISC, MC, V.

Miraval

$$$$$ Catalina

The newer (healthy) kid on the block, Miraval is regularly voted the world's top spa by readers of glossy travel mags. It's easy to see why. You won't believe that the delicious food is actually good for you (but it is). The remote desert setting is spectacular; and the Zen-style be-in-the-moment programs are less regimented than those at Canyon Ranch. Plus, Miraval doesn't require a minimum stay. You don't find Prohibition here, either (in fact, the bar has a pretty good single-malt scotch list). You can be as New Age as you wanna be, but you don't have to go in for the more offbeat things like equine therapy (that's for you, not the horse); you can just kick back and get pampered, head to toe. This spa introduced the supremely soothing hot stone massage; don't miss it.

*See map p. 194. 5000 E. Via Estancia Miraval (take Oracle/Highway 77 20 miles north of Tucson to Golden Ranch Road, turn left, go 2 miles to Lago de Oro, turn right; you see the gates in another 2 miles on your right). ☎ **800-232-3969** or 520-825-4000. Fax: 520-825-5163.* `www.miravalresort.com`. *Rack rates: per person May 16–Sept 30 $420–$465 single, $385–$415 double; suites from $605 single, $535 double; Oct 1–May 15 $625–$675 single, $525–$575 double; suites from $835 single, $735 double. Rates include all meals and activities, one spa treatment per night/or one-on-one-consultation/or round of golf, and round trip airport transfers (doesn't include tax or 17.5% service charge added to all bills). AE, DC, DISC, MC, V.*

Resorts

Hacienda del Sol Guest Ranch Resort

$$$–$$$$ Foothills

If you're looking for a getaway with more character than glitz — or amenities — this is your place. A movie-star magnet in the 1940s and 1950s (Katharine Hepburn and Spencer Tracy were among its devotees), this one-time dude ranch is now more resorty than horsy, but with an understated, relaxed tone. The 32 old-growth desert acres in the foothills are gorgeous, and the main-house rooms are decorated in rich, deep tones, with Mexican folk-art touches; some of the separate casitas (literally, "little houses") have fireplaces. The romantic Grill boasts a cool bar and a hot (if somewhat pricey) New American menu. Sunday brunches here are excellent.

*See map p. 194. 5601 N. Hacienda del Sol Rd. (between River Road and Skyline Road, just east of Campbell). ☎ **800-728-6514** or 520-299-1501. Fax: 520-299-5554.* `www.haciendadelsol.com`. *Free self-parking; gratuities-only valet parking. Rack rates: Jan 6–May 31 $155–$245 double, $335 suite, casitas from $375; June–Sept $79–$119 double, $145–165 suite, casitas from $165; Oct–Jan 5 $135–215 double, $300–$310 suite, casitas from $340. AE, MC, V.*

Hilton Tucson El Conquistador Golf & Tennis Resort

$$$$ Oro Valley (Northern satellite)

With a spread up north near Biosphere 2, the Hilton is a bit farther from the center of town than Tucson's other top resorts — but, then, why would you ever want to leave when you've got 45 holes of great golf, 31 tennis courts, an up-to-date wellness center, basketball, horseback riding, racquetball, volleyball, a dramatic new water feature . . . plus knockout Santa Catalina views? The rooms (separate casitas or main building units) define Southwest chic, and the staff is super friendly. Locals flock up to the Western can-can show put on at the casual Last Territory steakhouse on Friday and Saturday nights.

*See map p. 194. 10000 N. Oracle Rd. (about 10 miles north of Tucson; turn east off Oracle onto El Conquistador Way). ☎ **800-325-7832** or 520-544-5000. Fax: 520-544-1228.* `www.hiltonelconquistador.com`. *Free self-parking; $11 valet parking. Rack rates: Jan–May $215–$295 double, Jun–Aug $89–$139 double, Sept–Dec $189–$259 double. AE, DC, DISC, MC, V.*

Loews Ventana Canyon Resort

$$$$–$$$$$ Foothills

The most architecturally dramatic of Tucson's resorts — the style is a low-slung modernist tribute to sand and stone — Ventana Canyon is also a bit more formal than the others. That's not to suggest you'll have a problem relaxing on these 93 acres with an eye-popping Santa Catalina backdrop, and two top-rated golf courses — plus a place where you can drop the kids off guilt-free, while you indulge. Oh-so-tasteful, subtly desert-tone rooms are about the size of a small apartment, and they even have TVs in the marble bathrooms. Dining options include the swank Ventana Room, serving excellent (and commensurately pricey) nouvelle Continental cuisine, and the Flying V, where you can sample the Southwest/Latin American fare on a patio while gazing out at the 18th hole.

*See map p. 194. 7000 N. Resort Dr. (at N. Kolb and E. Sunrise Drive) ☎ **800-234-5117** or 520-299-2020. Fax: 520-299-6832.* `www.loewshotels.com`. *Self- or valet parking $9. Rack rates: Jan to mid-May $325–$445 double, mid-May to mid-Sept $115–$260 double, mid Sept–Dec $295–$385 double. AE, DC, DISC, MC, V.*

JW Marriott Starr Pass Resort & Spa

$$$$$ Westside

A dearth of good westside restaurants and of lodgings with top-notch amenities made bunking near premiere sights like the Desert Museum and Saguaro National Park inconvenient — until the Marriott debuted at the end of 2004. The first major resort to open in Tucson in nearly two decades, and the largest in this part of Arizona, this place has all the requisites: 27-hole Arnold Palmer signature golf facility, huge spa and fitness room, four pools, seven restaurants, and more. Other not-so-standard advantages include three trailheads into Tucson Mountain Park and underground parking so as not to spoil the views from any of the guest rooms.

*See map p. 194. 3800 W. Starr Pass Blvd. (west of E. 22nd St.).☎ **800-627-7468** or 520-792-3500; fax 520-792-3351;* `www.jwmarriottstarrpass.com`*. Valet parking for a fee. Rack rates: Jan–Mar from $399, Apr–May, from $250, Jun–Labor Day, from $175. Sept–Dec. $295. AE, DC, DISC, MC, V.*

Omni Tucson National Golf Resort & Spa

$$$–$$$$ Northwest

The Omni doesn't have the Southwest character, history, or glamour of Tucson's other major resorts, but if you're looking for great golf (the annual Tucson PGA Open is held here) and a top-notch spa, you've come to the right place. And although the public areas are a bit blah, the rooms successfully blend Mediterranean and Mexican design details to pleasing effect. Other pluses: proximity to Foothills Mall, where you can shop, eat, and watch movies 'til you drop — and, at the Catalina Grille, one of the best Sunday brunches in town (see the "Dining Out" section later in this chapter).

See map p. 194. 2727 W. Club Dr. (off Shannon, near Cortaro Farms Rd.). ☎ ***800-528-4856*** *or 520-297-2271. Fax: 520-297-7544.* `www.tucsoninternational.com`*. Free self-parking. $8 valet. Rack rates: Jan–early Apr $275–$375 double, suites from $295; mid-Apr–mid-May $125 to $250 double, suites from $220, late May–early Sept. $89 to $149 double, suites from 175; mid-Sept–Dec. $169 to $279 double, suites from $210. Rates do not include $7 nightly service charge. AE, DC, DISC, MC, V.*

The top bunks for cowpoke-wannabes

They're no longer called "dude" ranches (hey, should we blame the surfers for that, man?), but by any name, guest ranches are a great experience, offering hayrides, cookouts, and singalongs in some cases, and, in others, a chance to do some serious bonding with an equine pal. At the following top horsy hangouts, all meals, activities, and rides are included in the rates, which are per room, based on double occupancy; rates for singles are higher. With the exception of the Bellota Ranch, all these places offer plenty of activities for kids.

Bellota Ranch

$$$$ Eastside Ideal for serious riders — or for A-types seeking the ultimate desert getaway — this working cattle ranch features only eight rooms on 65,000 acres between the Santa Catalina and Rincon Mountains. You're a long and bumpy dirt road away from civilization, with only a hot tub, swimming pool (a converted cattle tank), board games (okay, and a computer and plasma-screen TV in the lounge) to divert you from the main event: riding. At various times of the year, skilled-with-equine guests can participate in cattle drives and round-ups. Contact Tanque Verde Ranch (see below), which owns and operates Bellota, for additional information. Rack rates: Dec 16–Apr $300–$325; May–Sept $330–$350; Oct–Dec 15 $345–$365. See map p. 194.

Lazy K Bar Guest Ranch

$$$$–$$$$$ Northwest A major upgrade of the facilities for the new millennium didn't eliminate any of the Lazy K's considerable color. Organized activities include cantering among the cacti in Saguaro National Park West and cattle penning, along with more tenderfoot activities, such as volleyball, mountain climbing/rappelling, and guided nature walks. If the bad news is that the city has begun to intrude on this once-remote property, the good news is you can easily access lots of shops and restaurants if you tire of the Western shtick. 8401 N. Scenic Dr. (from I-10, take W. Cortaro to N. Silverbell, then take West Pima Farms Road). ☎ **800-321-7018** or 520-744-3050. Fax: 520-744-7628. `www.lazykbar.com`. Rack rates: Dec 20–Apr $340–$485; May–June and Sept $230–$325; Oct–Dec 19 $320–$425. All-women "cowgirl camps" available. 5-night minimum stays during major holidays. AE, DISC, MC, V. Closed July and Aug. (maybe also June and Sept in 2005; check ahead). See map p. 194.

Tanque Verde Ranch

$$$$–$$$$$ Eastside Opened in the 1880s and one of the country's oldest guest ranches, the Tanque Verde has gone upscale, with tennis courts, a sauna, indoor and outdoor pools, relatively posh accommodations, seriously good food — even a new spa. But with 600 acres between Saguaro National Park East and Coronado National Forest, this ranch is definitely still the real deal. 14301 E. Speedway Blvd. (far east end of Speedway). ☎ **800-234-DUDE** or 520-296-6275. Fax: 520-721-9426. `www.tanqueverderanch.com`. Rack rates: Dec 16–Apr $370–$495, May–Sept $290–$375, Oct–Dec 15 $305–$390. AE, DISC, MC, V. See map p. 194.

White Stallion Ranch

$$$–$$$$ Northwest The same family has owned and run this spectacular 3,000-acre spread since 1965. If you actually know what you're doing on a horse, this ranch is your place, although greenhorns are equally happy to kick back and watch the weekly rodeos, and kids are crazy for the petting zoo and the many other activities organized for them. 9251 W. Twin Peaks Rd. (from I-10 take West Cortaro to North Silverbell, which turns into West Twin Peaks Road). ☎ **888-WSRANCH** or 520-297-0252. Fax: 520-744-2786. `www.wsranch.com`. Rack rates: Oct 3–Dec 15 and May $262–$370, $1,742–$2460 (per week for two people); Dec 16–May $288–$422, $1916–$2806, Sept–Oct. 2 about 10% less than Oct 3 –Dec 15 rates. Closed June–Aug. No credit cards. See map p. 194.

Westin La Paloma Resort & Spa

$$$–$$$$$ Foothills

A conventioneer magnet (most of Tucson's resorts are), this sprawling pink Westin also gets plenty of repeat family business, with its huge water-slide and separate children's pool. Grown-ups don't mind the extra time to relax by the swim-up bar, play a few sets of tennis, tee off, and get pampered in the resort's posh Red Door spa by Elizabeth Arden. The mutedly elegant guest rooms all have private balconies that look out on the city lights, the golf course, or the lush grounds. The usual array of on-site eateries are fine, but Janos and J Bar — on the property, but not part of the resort — kick culinary butt (see the "Dining Out" section later in this chapter). The service consistently gets raves, too.

See map p. 194. 3800 E. Sunrise Dr. (at Swan). ☎ ***800-WESTIN1*** *or 520-742-6000. Fax: 520-577-5878.* `www.westinlapalomaresort.com`. *Free self-parking; valet parking $12. Rack rates: Jan to mid-May $259–$449 double, mid-May to mid-Sept $99–$249 double, mid-Sept–Dec $209–$369 double. AE, CB, DC, DISC, MC, V.*

Westward Look Resort

$$–$$$$ Northwest

The New Age meets the Old West at Westward Look. Built as a private residence in 1912, turned guest ranch in the 1920s, and morphed into a resort in 1943, the facility opened a wellness center in the 1990s, and keeps up with current trends by offering nature walks and star-gazing programs. Other on-site stress-reducers include the standard resort amenities — pretty much everything except golf — and soothing earth-tone rooms, with Mexican tile and (on the upper floor) beamed ceilings. You can tell that the Westward Look was a guest ranch because, in most cases, you can drive right up to your door — a nice perk. Rates are often Old West, too, and the Gold Room has a creative New American menu and knockout city views (I highly recommend the wine-tasting dinners).

See map p. 194. 245 E. Ina Rd. (between Oracle Road and First Avenue). ☎ ***800-722-2500*** *or 520-297-1151. Fax: 520-297-9023.* `www.westwardlook.com`. *Free self-parking; gratuities-only valet parking. Rack rates: Jan–Apr $119–$309 double, May–Sept $89–$179 double, Oct–Dec $99–$209 double. AE, DC, DISC, MC, V.*

Hotels and inns

Arizona Inn

$$$–$$$$$ Central

High tea, anyone? Croquet? Such civilized rituals plus the superb service of an earlier era have kept the Arizona Inn Tucson's lodging darling since its 1930 debut. Some of the rooms, arranged in pink stucco casitas around a perfectly manicured lawn, have gotten bland with frequent upgrades, but the tradeoff is a state-of-the-art exercise room. The fine dining room is worth visiting for all those massive wood beams alone, and the swank piano lounge is a local favorite for a romantic aperitif.

See map p. 194. 2200 E. Elm St. (between Campbell and Tucson Boulevard). ☎ ***800-933-1093*** *or 520-325-1541. Fax: 520-881-5830.* `www.arizonainn.com`. *Free parking. Rack rates: Dec 27–Apr 18 $239–$399 double, Apr 19–May, $199–$329, Jun–Sept $139–$299 (including breakfast and nightly ice cream). Oct–Dec. 26 $169–$339. AE, DC, MC, V.*

Best Western Ghost Ranch Lodge

$–$$ Central

Not your average chain hotel: Georgia O'Keeffe designed the logo in 1936 as a wedding gift for the motel's original owner. The 8-acre grounds include an orange grove and one of the largest cactus gardens in the Southwest, and the guest units with their red-tile roofs have plenty of old Tucson charm. Sadly, the once-rural area is now on a semi-seedy motel row. The compensations include great rates and easy access to the freeway — and, when you're on the property, your next-door neighbors don't much matter.

See map p. 194. 801 W. Miracle Mile (just off the I-10 Miracle Mile exit, and west of Oracle between Glenn and Fort Lowell). ☎ ***800-456-7565*** *or 520-791-7565. Fax: 520-791-3898.* `www.ghostranchlodge.com`. *Free parking. Rack rates: Dec. 20–Mar $86–$106, Apr–May $56–$80; June–Sept $46–$60 double. Oct–Dec 19 $56–$70. Cottages from $115, suites from $125 in high season. AE, DISC, MC, V.*

Hotel Congress

$ Downtown

Fun and funky, with its Western Art Deco decor and gunslinger history (members of John Dillinger's gang holed up here for a while), the Congress is definitely not for everyone; it helps to be under 30 and a heavy sleeper. The rooms are pretty basic and the rocking Club Congress is a literal blast, especially on the weekends. But the price is right, the location is public-transport-friendly (you're right near the Greyhound and Amtrak stations and the main Sun Tran terminal), and the hotel's Cup Cafe is the hip downtown hangout (the food's reasonably priced and good, too).

See map p. 194. 311 E. Congress St. (between Toole and Sixth streets). ☎ ***520-622-8848.*** *Fax: 520-792-6366.* `www.hotcong.com`. *Free parking. Rack rates: Jan–May $69–$99 double, Jun–Aug $59–$79 double; Sept–Dec $69–$89 double. Youth hostel rooms from $20. AE, DISC, MC, V.*

La Posada Lodge and Casitas

$$ Northwest

Don't be put off by the location, on one of Tucson's busiest roads, or by the rather bland Southwest facade. Beyond the leather-and-tile lobby of this revamped 1956 property, you find grounds laced with palms, palo verde trees, and fountains, as well as outstanding views of the Santa Catalina mountains. Most of the guest rooms feature handmade furnishings from Mexico; a few are done up in 1950s retro style, replete with lava lamps. In-room kitchenettes, a small spa, and the excellent Miguel's restaurant (see the "Dining Out" section later in this chapter) also help make La Posada a standout.

See map p. 194. 5900 N. Oracle Rd. (just south of Rudasill Rd.). ☎ ***800-810-2808*** *or 520-887-4800. Fax 520-293-7543.* `www.laposadalodge.com`. *Free parking. Rack rates: Jan–Mar $109–$129 doubles, $139–$169 casitas (rates higher for both during*

Location, location, location — and breakfast, too

Tucson has the best selection of B&Bs in the state, hands down. They range in style from ornate and (for Tucson) formal to kicked back and low key, in locale from remote to central. My favorites, divided between town (well, okay, city) and country (well, okay, desert) follow. Check the Tucson listings of The Arizona Association of Bed and Breakfast Inns (☎ 800-284-2589; www.arizona-bed-breakfast.com) for other good options.

Town

Catalina Park Inn ($$), 309 E. First St. (at North Fifth Ave.), Central (☎ **800-792-4885** or 520-792-4541; www.catalinaparkinn.com), has the dual advantage of being close to the University of Arizona and Fourth Avenue's shops as well as to a quiet city park. The impeccably restored 1927 neoclassical home is high tone without being stuffy. See map p. 194.

The Royal Elizabeth ($$), 204 Scott Ave. (one block south of Broadway), downtown (☎ **877-670-9022** or 520-670-9022. Fax: 520-629-9710; www.royalelizabeth.com), built in 1878, is one of the few remaining Victorian adobe homes, anywhere. Satellite TVs and VCRs are discreetly tucked into antique armoires, so you don't have to abandon this century's comforts for the sake of period atmosphere. See map p. 194.

Peppertrees ($$), 724 E. University Blvd., University of Arizona/Fourth Ave. (☎ **800-348-5763** or 520-622-7167 [tel and fax]; www.bbonline.com/az/peppertrees), offers pretty, antiques-filled rooms in a Victorian main house as well as more contemporary units (some with kitchens and washer/dryers) in a separate building. You can't get closer to the University of Arizona campus without enrolling in classes. See map p. 194.

Country

Casa Tierra ($$), 11555 W. Calle Pima, Westside (☎ **866-254-0006** or 520-578-3058; www.casatierratucson.com), has a prime location near Saguaro National Park West and the Arizona-Sonora Desert Museum. You have to drive down a dirt road to get to this lovely hacienda-style house, but rooms all have kitchenettes, and the stars look mighty nice from the hot tub.

Hacienda del Desierto ($$), 11770 E. Rambling Tr., Eastside (☎ **800-982-1795** or 520-298-1764; www.tucson-bed-breakfast.com), counts lush desert gardens, nature trails, graceful architecture, and proximity to Saguaro National Park East among its lures. Serenity seekers will find their bliss here. See map p. 194.

La Zarzuela ($$$), 455 N. Camino de Oeste, Westside (☎ **888-848-8225**; 520-884-4824; www.zarzuela-az.com), provides proof that the desert can provide creature comforts as well as creatures. The ultimate in Southwest chic, the inn's five romantic casitas come fully equipped with the latest amenities — and offer drop-dead views of nature to boot. See map p. 194.

the Gem and Mineral Show, first two weeks of Feb); Apr–May 15 $99–$109 doubles, $129 casitas, May 16–Sept 15 $89 doubles, $109 casitas; Sept. 16–Dec $109; AE, DC, DISC, MC, V.

The Lodge on the Desert

$$–$$$ Central

The Mexican hacienda–style Lodge, opened in 1936, has mature citrus, winding paths, a central location — easy access to the airport and freeway as well as to restaurants on both the east and west sides of town — and (relatively) reasonable rates. A late 1990s revamp stripped the rooms of some character, but they still have beehive fireplaces and wood-beamed ceilings. Ask for one as far away from the main road as possible; the walls aren't especially thick.

See map p. 194. 306 N. Alvernon Way (just north of Broadway). ☎ ***800-456-5634*** *or 520-325-3366. Fax: 520-327-5834.* `www.lodgeonthedesert.com`. *Free parking. Rack rates: Jan 16–Apr 15 $189–$219 double, $269 suites; Apr 16–May 15 $129–$139 double, $149 suites; May 16–Sept $79–$109 double, $119 suites, Oct–Jan 15 $129–$149, suites $169. AE, DC, DISC, MC, V.*

Smuggler's Inn

$$ Central

A local favorite for its live music and happy-hour buffets, this low-key hotel has a lot to offer visitors, including proximity to Tucson's Restaurant Row and to the Dorado Golf Course; cheery tropical landscaping; a nice pool and hot tub; spacious, well-equipped rooms; a coin-op laundry; and economical rates. Room service is another perk you don't usually find at hotels in this price range.

See map p. 194. 6350 E. Speedway Blvd. (at Wilmot). ☎ ***800-525-8852*** *or 520-296-3292. Fax: 520-722-3713.* `www.smugglersinn.com`. *Free parking. Jan–Mar $99–$119 double, $125–$135 suites; Apr–Dec $59–$99 double, $99–$125 suites. Rates include continental breakfast. AE, DC, DISC, MC, V.*

Windmill Inn

$$ Central/Foothills

This all-suites hotel, part of a small chain, gives you a lot of bang for the buck, especially considering its location in a ritzy shopping complex that straddles the Foothills and central Tucson and hosts Vivace (see the "Dining Out" section later in this chapter). Extras include free local calls, complimentary Continental breakfast, gratis guest use of bicycles, and the use of two PCs in the business center. A coin-op laundry on the premises, as well as a microwave, refrigerator, two TVs, and a foldout couch in the separate living room of the roomy guest quarters make this place particularly convenient for families. Kids under 18 stay free in parents' rooms, and Fido can freeload, too.

See map p. 194 4250 N. Campbell Ave. in St. Phillips Plaza (just south of River Road). ☎ ***800-547-4747*** *or 520-577-0007. Fax: 520-577-0045.* www.windmillinns.com. *Free parking. Rack rates: Mid-Jan–mid-Mar $149–$169 double, Apr–May $99–$129 double, Jun–Aug $69–$189 double; Sept–mid-Jan $79–$109 double. AE, DC, DISC, MC, V.*

Dining Out

Going out to eat in my adopted hometown has taught me two things: You can enjoy seafood in the desert — as one of my new friends put it when I balked upon moving here, "So I suppose all the fish you ate in New York came out of the Hudson River?" — and you can find great food in a strip mall. Tucson has a surprising number of top-rate places to eat for a city of its size and chain orientation. But that's a relatively recent development. When I moved here from Manhattan in the early 1990s, modest Mexican tacquerias (loose translation: taco joints) and cowboy steakhouses were the local mainstays. Happily, they're still thriving, but they've also been joined in the last decade by far more sophisticated eateries, including many in the resorts.

Although its cuisine may be more sophisticated, Tucson is still backwoods in many ways — that is, the town shuts down seriously early. Prime dining time is 7 p.m. If you like to eat after 8 p.m. — but not too much later, as many restaurants shut their doors by 9:30 or 10 p.m. — you won't have trouble getting a table (even a good one) at the most popular spots. Keep in mind, too, that many of Tucson's top dining rooms shut their doors on Sundays. To avoid driving around, ready to eat your arm, call ahead; the resort restaurants and the ethnic eateries are your best bets.

Fourth and University avenues, near the University of Arizona, are really the only two areas where you can find decent food (mostly of the casual, college-budget persuasion) just by strolling around; I like the retro-chic B Line Café ($–$$), 621 N. Fourth Ave. (☎ 520-882-7575), for its casual Italian-ish fare. If you're on dinner patrol, two other stretches are worth checking out. Tanque Verde, between Grant and Sabino Canyon roads, is considered Tucson's Restaurant Row. My top pick there for a salad or sandwich is the Dakota Café ($$), 6541 E. Tanque Verde Rd. (☎ 520-298-7188), a nice anomaly in touristy Trail Dust Town. And Campbell Avenue, between Grant and Fort Lowell, near the university, is lined with low-key restaurants. My favorites are Yoshimatsu ($), 2660 N. Campbell (☎ 520-320-1574), serving authentic and health-conscious Japanese food; and Beyond Bread ($), 3026 N. Campbell (☎ 520-322-9965), with a wide range of gourmet sandwiches.

Leave that little black dress at home (though no one will stare if you wear it). Standard attire in even the most upscale restaurants tends to be "resort casual": a nice shirt and slacks or skirt, no visible stains.

Penny wise and pound(s) foolish: Some Tucson food bargains

Not only can you eat well and inexpensively at many of Tucson's casual cafes and ethnic restaurants, but you can also enjoy some of Tucson's top eateries at reduced prices. Here's how:

Come in summer. If you can stand the heat, summer is a great time to get into the city's top kitchens. Barrio, Bistro Zin, Cafe Terra Cotta, Janos, Kingfisher, Pastiche, and Wildflower are among the fine dining rooms listed in this section that hawk summer specials, such as bargain-price sampler plates or half-price bottles of wine.

Try happy hour. Several places attract the after-work crowds with cut-rate appetizers and cocktails from 5 p.m. to 7 p.m. At Firecracker, for example, all appetizers are half off and all drinks cost a dollar less than they do during regular hours.

Do brunch. Come Sunday, many major hotels and resorts lay on lavish spreads for not so lavish prices. We're talking seafood stations with shrimp, lobster tails, and sushi; carving stations with roast beef and pastrami; personalize-your-own-omelet stations; dessert bars with do-it-yourself-sundae fixings; Bloody Mary bars, and so on. My top picks are the brunches at the Arizona Inn, Hacienda del Sol, Loews Ventana Canyon, Omni Tucson National, and Westward Look (see the "Staying in Style" section in this chapter, for their addresses). Prices range from about $20 to $35 for all you can eat and (generally) at least one drink; most places have reduced rates for kids.

Barrio

$$–$$$ Downtown NEW AMERICAN

A perfect spot for a post-theater or pre-opera bite. Barrio is cool to the core, with a stylishly eclectic menu, sleek Art Nouveau–meets-the-Southwest decor, and a great bar. I go for the upbeat tostadas — whole-wheat tortillas stuffed with grilled chicken and white cheddar cheese — when I'm planning on an evening of light comedy, the deeply satisfying pork chop with Jamaican jerk sauce when I'm in Gotterdammerung mode.

See map p. 206. 135 S. 6th Ave. (just south of Broadway). ☎ ***520-629-0191.*** *Reservations recommended. Main courses: $12–$26. AE, DC, MC, V. Open: Lunch and dinner Tues–Fri, dinner only Sat and Sun.*

Bistro Zin

$$$ Central NEW AMERICAN

With its cushy banquettes, sparkly mosaic columns, tufted-leather bar, and black-and-white photos of jazz greats, Bistro Zin (as in "zinfandel") taps into a taste for nostalgia while toasting the latest fashions. The menu of this French-inspired American bistro also blends old and new: You find such inventive appetizers as beef carpaccio with arugula and shaved

Tucson Dining

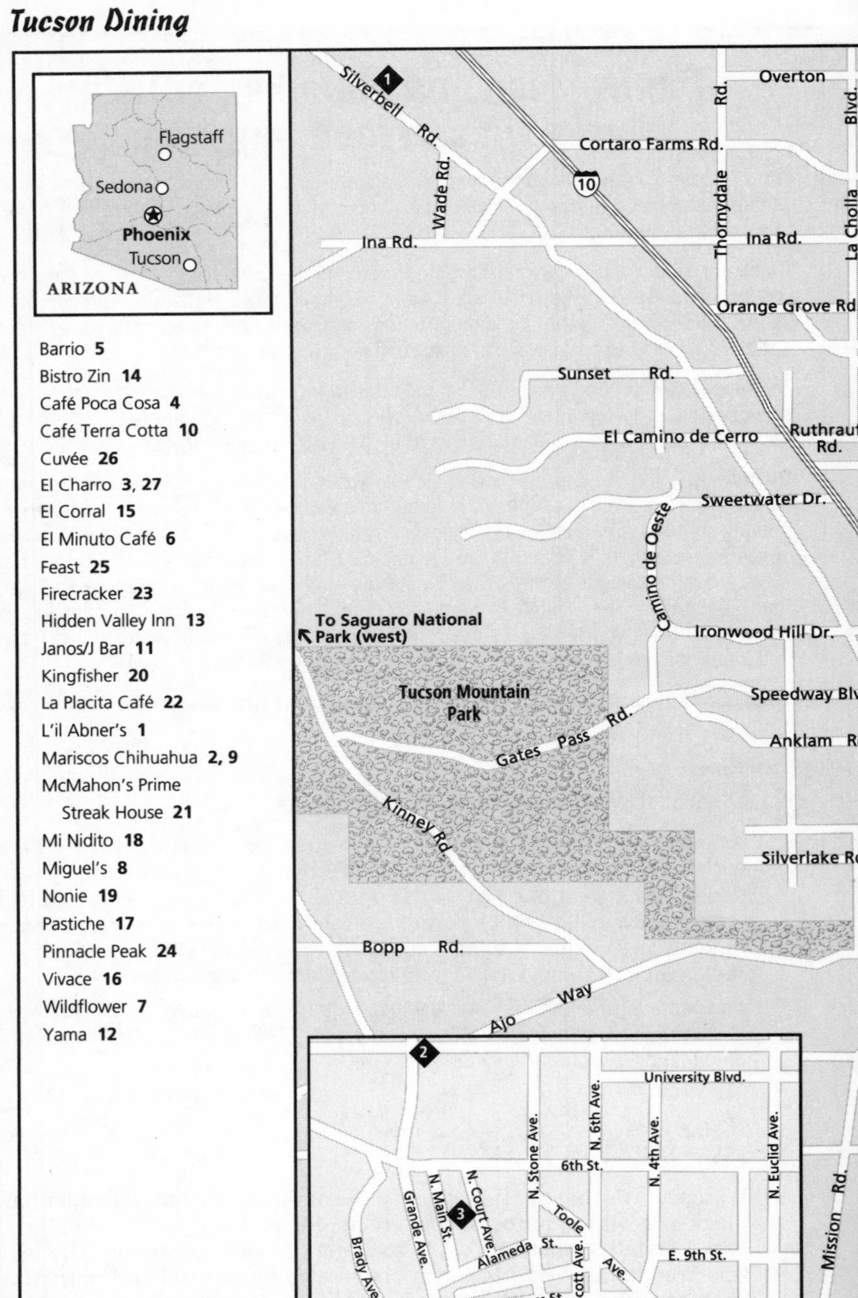

SANTA CATALINA MOUNTAINS
CORONADO NATIONAL FOREST
Hardy Rd.
77
Magee Rd.
Tohono Chul Park
Ina Rd.
La Canada Dr.
Orange Grove Rd.
Skyline Dr.
Sabino Canyon Recreation Area
Sabino Canyon Rd.
Kolb Rd.
Sunrise Dr.
River Rd.
Hacienda del Sol Rd.
Swan Rd.
Craycroft Rd.
Snyder Rd.
Bear Canyon Rd.
Flowing Wells Rd.
Wetmore Rd.
Roger Rd.
Prince Rd.
Stone Ave.
Ave.
Campbell Ave.
Miracle Mile
Ft. Lowell Rd.
River Rd.
To Mount Lemmon
Ft. Lowell Park
Catalina Hwy.
Tanque Verde Rd.
Oracle Rd.
Euclid
Tucson Blvd.
Country Club Rd.
Alvernon Way
Grant Rd.
10
see inset
Speedway Blvd.
6th St.
5th St.
Grande Ave.
Congress
Downtown & The Historic Districts
Broadway Blvd.
To Saguaro National Park (east)
Reid Park
Randolph Park
Swan Rd.
Craycroft Rd.
Wilmot Rd.
Kolb Rd.
"A" Mountain
22nd St.
22nd St.
entinel eak ark
36th St.
Golf Links Rd.
Ajo Way
Escalante Rd.
Pantano Rd.
Camino Seco
Kino Blvd.
Davis Monthan AFB
Irvington Rd.
Irvington Rd.
Drexel Rd.
Palo Verde Rd.
12th Ave.
6th Ave.
Valencia Rd.
Los Reales Rd.
Tucson International Airport
19
0 2 mi
0 2 km

parmesan mixing it up with familiar favorite entrees like roasted chicken sided by mac and cheese. Many just come to this retro-chic dining room — or its cozy back patio — to sample wine flights (trios of 2-ounce tasting portions). I sometimes just drop in for the amazing desserts.

*See map p. 206. 1865 E. River Rd. (at Campbell Avenue). ☎ **520-299-7799.** Reservations recommended. Main courses: $14–$23. AE, MC, V. Open: Lunch Mon–Sat; dinner nightly.*

Café Terra Cotta

$$–$$$ Foothills SOUTHWESTERN

The dazzling food created by Donna Nordin, one of the originators of New Southwest cuisine, gets a fitting setting in a dramatic pueblo-style building in the Foothills, featuring art-filled dining rooms and terraces with views of the Santa Catalinas. Don't miss the macadamia nut–laden, garlic custard appetizer, served with salsa and hot crusty French bread; shrimp stuffed with goat cheese on a tomato coulis; and any of the designer pizzas. A nice by-the-glass wine list and a loyal local clientele always keep things lively. Note: A July 2004 fire put the Terra Cotta out of business for several months, but it should be back up and running by the time you read this book. Call in advance to be sure.

*See map p. 206. 3500 E. Sunrise (at Campo Abierto, between First Avenue and Campbell). ☎ **520-577-8100.** Reservations recommended. Lunch: $7.75–$11; main courses: $15–$24. AE, DC, DISC, MC, V. Open: Lunch and dinner daily.*

Cuvée

$$$ Central NEW AMERICAN

A location across the street from the Loft, the city's main art cinema, as well as a setting and food fit for contemplating (or attempting to forget) the film you just viewed make the white-clothed tables of this eatery fill up fast. The airy, high-ceiling room is stylish without being pretentious, and that's true, too, of the menu. Consider a shrimp and scallop ceviche starter, followed by roast duck with port wine and cherry sauce. Suggestions of wine to complement each dish, including appetizers, are great if you can't tell your chardonnays from your chenin blancs — and even if you can.

*See map p. 206. 3352 E. Speedway Blvd. (east of Country Club Road in El Rancho Shopping Center). ☎ **520-881-7577.** Reservations recommended. Main courses: $15–$19. AE, MC, V. Open: Lunch and dinner Mon–Sat.*

Feast

$–$$ Central DELI

This European-style deli bills itself as a purveyor of "Tasteful Takeout," but I never feel like leaving the cheerful dining room, all blonde wood and flattering light fixtures. The food mixes and matches culinary styles — everything from Belgian endive salad with seafood sausage and Texas

A taste of Mexico

A great way to start a conversation with locals is to ask us for our favorite Mexican restaurant. Chances are no two lists are the same, although a few entries on them are likely to be in the same neighborhood, South Fourth Avenue in South Tucson. ***Warning:*** People tend to defend our choices to the death (at least of our appetites). Here are mine. Wanna make something of it?

- **Café Poca Cosa** ($$–$$$), 88 E. Broadway Blvd. at Scott Avenue in the Clarion Santa Rita (Downtown) (☎ **520-622-6400**), is my all-time favorite for its amazing Mexican regional cuisine — featuring dishes from across Mexico, not just the neighboring state of Sonora — and for its bustling, colorful atmosphere. Chef/owner Suzana Dávila proves that "south-of-the-border" and "gourmet" are not mutually exclusive terms. See map p. 206.
- **El Charro** ($$), 311 N. Court Ave. between Franklin and Washington streets (Downtown) (☎ **520-622-1922**), opened in 1922 by the current owner's great aunt, who laid claim to the invention of the chimichanga. Don't miss the *carne seca,* made with meat smoked on the roof, and the great margaritas. A time- (and tummy-) filling bonus is the branch at the airport (central terminal, ☎ **520-573-8225**). El Charro also has an east side location: 6310 E. Broadway at Wilmot Road (☎ **520-745-1922**), and a faster-food version, Charro Grill, 1765 E. River Rd. at Campbell (☎ **520-615-1922**). See map p. 206.
- **El Minuto Café** ($–$$), 354 S. Main Ave. at Cushing Street (Downtown) (☎ **520-882-4145**), near the Tucson Convention Center, has a tourist-friendly staff that serves up barrio-authentic food. Other pluses: Late hours and a great beer selection. See map p. 206.
- **La Placita Café** ($$), 2950 N. Swan Rd. in Plaza Palomino at Fort Lowell (Central) (☎ **520-881-1150**), is as up-market as its chic shopping center home, but the excellent food and soothing atmosphere are worth the (slight) extra expense. See map p. 206.
- **Mariscos Chihuahua** ($–$$), 1009 N. Grande Ave. at Speedway (Downtown) (☎ **520-623-3563**), may look plain and simple, but serves up some of the best Mexican seafood in town. You also find a location at 356 E. Grant Rd. near Stone Avenue (☎ **520-884-3457**). See map p. 206.
- **Mi Nidito** ($–$$), 1813 S. 4th Ave., at E. 28th Street (South Tucson) (☎ **520-622-5081**), is where the local Democratic politicos brought President Clinton when they wanted to show him some down-home South Tucson cooking. Republicans don't mind the generous portions, either. See map p. 206.

barbecued brisket sandwich to a chicken masala bowl — and sizes. Many items come by the pint and half pint, and, if you like, you can order a single smoked salmon cake ($2). Seating is mix and match, too. Opt for a romantic table for two, a solitary perch at the sleek bar, or a place at the community table. Menus change monthly, and the staff is very knowledgeable about wine.

*See map p. 206. 4122 E. Speedway Blvd. (west of Alvernon). ☎ **520-326-9363.** Main courses: $7.25–$14.50. AE, DISC, MC, V. Open: Lunch and dinner Tues–Sat.*

Firecracker

$$ Central PACIFIC RIM

Tucson's homegrown contribution to the Asia-lite culinary trend — food that does a spin on Japanese and Chinese food without getting overly ethnic — is among the best I've tried in that genre. The tongue-in-cheek decor, including tiki torches outside and harlequin-pattern banquettes amidst a birch grove inside, also helps draw a trendy crowd. I usually start with the lettuce cups, a kind of do-it-yourself eggroll, move on to the sesame-seared ahi or wasabi chicken, and (always) finish with the coconut crême brûlée. Pretend you're in the Asian tropics by booking a seat on the misted patio.

*See map p. 206. 2990 N. Swan Rd. (at Ft. Lowell in Plaza Palomino). ☎ **520-318-1118.** Reservations essential on weekends. Main courses: $12–$17. AE, DC, DISC, MC, V. Open: Lunch and dinner daily.*

Janos/J Bar

$$$–$$$$ Foothills SOUTHWESTERN/NUEVO LATINO

Janos Wilder, winner of the James Beard award for Best Chef in the Southwest, is Tucson's blue corn king, and he reigns over these two different, equally dazzling domains. An elegant, soaring-ceiling dining room is the setting for his formal, French-inspired Southwest cuisine. Options may include seared lamb tenderloin with marscarpone polenta or garlic shrimp with saffron risotto. Right across the reception area, at the more casual J Bar, you can enjoy Janos' high-class cooking without the high-class prices. My favorites are the spicy jerked pork and Yucatan-style plantain-crusted chicken. One common menu item: the chocolate jalapeño ice cream (trust me, it's amazing).

*See map p. 206. 3770 E. Sunrise Rd. (at The Westin La Paloma). ☎ **520-615-6100.** Reservations strongly recommended. Main courses: Janos: $26–$42; nightly prix-fixe dinners $75, with matching wine $110. J Bar: $12.50–$16. AE, DC, DISC, MC, V. Open: Dinner Mon–Sat.*

Kingfisher

$$$–$$$$ Central NEW AMERICAN/SEAFOOD

Tucson's hippest roadhouse, with large, cushy booths, plenty of neon, brick, and contemporary art, a terrific bar — and atypically late hours. The seasonally changing menu is a map of the current state of American regional cooking, with an emphasis on the two coasts. Kingfisher spearheaded (as it were) the drive to bring good fish to the desert. The fresh oyster selection is always awesome; order some, and then use your saved-calorie allotment on the warm cabbage salad with bacon and blue cheese.

See map p. 206. 2564 E. Grant Rd. (one block east of Tucson Boulevard). ☎ ***520-323-7739.*** *Reservations recommended. Main courses: $15–$21. AE, CB, DC, DISC, MC, V. Open: Lunch Mon–Fri, dinner and late-night menu nightly.*

Miguel's

$$$–$$$$ Northwest NUEVO LATINO

A bit of the tropics in Tucson, what with its swirling ceiling fans, rattan chairs, and colorful artwork, Miguel's is a relative newcomer to the local dining scene, but with food this good it's bound to become a fixture. To call the menu "Mexican" would be misleading — no mere tacos allowed here — but many dishes do a delicious spin on south-of-the-border seafood. Start with the fresh ahi ceviche or the crusty, piquante crab cake, followed by bacon-wrapped prawns daubed with horseradish and brown sugar. Want a soothing sip? The bar pours more than 100 types of tequila, all available in sampler trios.

See map p. 206. 5900 N. Oracle Rd. (just south of Rudasill Rd.). ☎ ***520-887-3777.*** *Main courses: $16–$28. AE, DC, DISC, MC, V. Open: lunch and dinner daily.*

Nonie

$$ Central CAJUN/CREOLE

One of my favorite local hangouts. Not only does Nonie cook up kickin' Cajun and Creole dishes — fried pickles and crawfish étouffée, washed down with Black Voodoo beer, and chased with espresso and a hot beignet is one of my fantasy last meals — but it also has literary cachet: The owner's father is mystery writer Elmore Leonard. Prices are reasonable, too.

See map p. 206. 2526 E. Grant Rd. (just east of Tucson Boulevard). ☎ ***520-319-1965.*** *Main courses: $12–$15. AE, DC, DISC, MC, V. Open: Lunch and dinner Tues–Fri, dinner only Sat and Sun.*

Pastiche

$$–$$$ Central NEW AMERICAN

Because Pastiche knows that not everyone wants to hold back at lunch or pig out at dinner, the same sophisticated but not overpriced New American menu turns up at both meals; smaller bistro portions of several dishes are available, too. I often order the smaller-size plate of Tennessee bourbon salmon or thyme-crusted sea bass; it's more than enough food, and leaves me room for the yummy cookie collage in a warm chocolate dipping sauce. Sometimes, after the movies — Pastiche stays open until midnight every night — I just drop in for a draft and an order of tasty margarita fries: lightly fried corn meal chips with a chile dipping sauce.

See map p. 206. 3025 N. Campbell Ave. (just south of Fort Lowell). ☎ ***520-325-3333.*** *Main courses $16–$26 ($12–$18 bistro size). AE, DC, DISC, MC, V. Open: lunch and dinner Mon–Fri, dinner only Sat and Sun.*

Vivace

$$$ Central NORTHERN ITALIAN

Vivace has long been Tucson's best upscale Italian eatery, and it never seems to get tired. I never tire, either, of the restaurant's perfectly prepared pastas and risottos — perhaps penne with roasted red peppers, sausage and Fontina cheese — and main dishes, including pork Sorrentino, baked with parmesan in a white wine sauce. The setting, a series of Tuscan yellow dining rooms with a pretty patio, is invigorating, too. Viva, Vivace!

See map p. 206. 4310 N. Campbell Ave. (just south of River Road) in St. Phillip's Plaza. ☎ ***520-795-7221.*** *Reservations essential on high season weekends. Pastas: $12.50–19; main courses: $14–$25. AE, DC, DISC, MC, V. Open: Lunch and dinner Mon–Sat.*

Wildflower

$$$ Northwest NEW AMERICAN

Everything's coming up roses for Wildflower, a chic contemporary dining room that looks more California than Arizona (check out the clever trompe l'oeil ceiling). Standouts include the spinach, stilton, pecan, and apple salad; the smoked salmon on a crisp potato pancake; and the grilled ahi with bok choy and wasabi mashed potatoes (be careful: they bite back). Desserts are knockout, so be sure to save room. Snag a seat on the outdoor patio for great lunchtime views of the Santa Catalinas.

Note: Just a few doors from Wildflower is the same restaurateurs' Sauce ($–$$), 7117 N. Oracle, (☎ 520-297-8575) a designer pizza/pasta place with great salads. Another Sauce opened in 2004 at 5285 E. Broadway (☎ 520-514-1122). For casual Italian fare, either location is tops.

See map p. 206. 7037 N. Oracle Rd., Casas Adobes shopping center (off the SW corner of Ina Road). ☎ ***520-219-4230.*** *Reservations highly recommended. Main courses: $13–$24. AE, MC, V. Open: Lunch Mon–Fri; dinner nightly.*

Yama

$$–$$$$ Foothills JAPANESE

Yama means mountain and you get an eyeful of them — the Santa Catalinas, to be precise — from the terrace of this Zen-chic eatery. Tucson's got lots of good sushi joints (go figure) but this one stands out not only for its stunning setting but also for the quality and variety of its dishes. Along with raw fish, you find such entrees as "baked ocean" — scallops, shrimp, and mushrooms in a delicate briny sauce — and kobe beef. This place has the largest selection of sake in town, and you can get yours served in a cedar box, overflowing onto your plate in traditional style. Wa rning: The menu is so large and, in many cases, so unfamiliar, that it's easy to get confused and overorder. Start with a few dishes; you can always get more.

See map p. 206. 5435 N. Kolb Rd. #115 (south of Sunrise Dr.). ☎ ***520-615-1031.*** *Main courses: $13–$22 (kobe beef selections higher). AE, CB, DC, DISC, MC, V. Open: Dinner nightly (call to find out about lunch schedule, which is in flux).*

Keep them doggies . . . smokin': A steakhouse sampler

Most of the high-end big meat chains haven't yet arrived in Tucson (the exceptions are Sullivan's and Fleming's). If you're looking for low-key cowboy steakhouses, however — places from which you depart stuffed, relaxed, and financially sound — you've come to the right city. With the exception of the upscale McMahon's ($$$$–$$$$$), all the following are in the $$–$$$ price range.

- **El Corral,** 2201 E. River Rd., just east of Campbell Avenue (Foothills) (☎ **520-299-6092**), has been roping in Tucsonans since 1936. As the town grew, so did the original adobe ranch house. If you're primed for prime rib, don't miss it. See map p. 206.
- **Hidden Valley Inn,** 4825 N. Sabino Canyon Rd. at Snyder Road (Foothills) (☎ **520-299-4941**), piles busloads of tourists into its fake, Old West saloon — and they always have a blast. Expect your basic steak and cowboy beans. See map p. 206.
- **L'il Abner's,** 8501 N. Silverbell Rd., between Cortaro and W. Ina (Northwest) (☎ **520-744-2800**), a former Butterfield stagecoach stop, has great mesquite-grilled steaks (or chicken, if you insist) and gen-u-ine cowboy cachet going for it. This place is so untrendy, the menu still includes a 2-pound porterhouse. See map p. 206.
- **McMahon's Prime Steak House,** 2959 N. Swan Rd., south of Ft. Lowell Road (Central) (☎ **520-327-7463**), is Tucson's swankiest big-meat palace — and the most expensive. The surf (terrific Alaskan King crab legs) is as good as the turf, and the wine list is massive. See map p. 206.
- **Pinnacle Peak,** 6541 E. Tanque Verde Rd. in Trail Dust Town (Central) (☎ **520-296-0911**), is renowned as much for its tie-clipping ways — the crowd just waits for a city slicker to come in wearing one — as for its large cuts of steaks and generous sides. See map p. 206.

Zona 78

$$ Northwest ITALIAN/PIZZA

Dishes made with super-fresh ingredients — locally grown and organic, whenever possible — emerge from the stone oven of this airy, friendly restaurant. More than just pizza gets the hot stone treatment, although thin-crust pies, topped with anything from mozzarella and parmesan to fennel, bacon, and kalamata olives, are definitely a specialty; steak, salmon, and even an apple tart share space in the oven. When the weather's hot, I just sit out on the misted terrace and enjoy a chopped salad — smoked turkey, pears, jicama, and pine nuts, among other yummy ingredients — or an antipasto with a nice glass of Chianti.

78 W. River Rd. (at N. Stone). ☎ ***520-888-7878.*** *Sandwiches, salads, pizzas: $6.50–$9; main courses: $7–$13. AE, DISC, MC, V. Open: Lunch and dinner daily.*

Seeing the Sights

East side, west side, all around the town . . . Tucson's attractions are as spread out as the city itself — more so, in fact, because some of the top touring spots lie beyond the city's borders. Check out the "Following an Itinerary" section later in this chapter for ideas on how to arrange your days so as to minimize what can otherwise be major road time. And remember, temperatures rise around noon. If you're in town from mid-March to mid-October, try to be outdoors only in the early morning and late afternoon, and save the indoor, air-conditioned stuff for midday.

The top attractions

Arizona-Sonora Desert Museum

Westside

My top pick for Tucson. Don't let the name scare you; this isn't a museum, but a terrific zoo and desert botanical garden (with proceeds going to desert conservation). I love coming here with visiting friends' kids to watch them check out all the strange desert critters, from Gila monsters to stinky javalinas (okay, so I'm usually the one that has to be pulled away from the adorable prairie dogs). Most of the displays are outdoors, but a great caving/mineralogical display, creepy snake and bug house, and good gift shop can keep you indoors for a while. All in all, this place is BIG: Wear comfortable shoes and plan on spending an entire morning or afternoon here. At the minimum, allot two hours.

The general advice to come early applies double here. This place gets very crowded, and parking spots fill up fast. Call in advance to see whether the Ocotillo Cafe is open, as hours are limited (Jan–Apr lunch 11 a.m.–3 p.m.; June–Sept dinner Sat); I recommend planning your day around having lunch on its terrace. The salads use herbs grown at the Desert Museum — and you may find prickly pear sorbet on the dessert menu.

See map p. 216. 2021 N. Kinney Rd. (14 miles west of downtown Tucson via Speedway Boulevard and Gates Pass Road; you see signs as you head west). ☎ ***520-883-2702;*** `www.desertmuseum.org`*. Admission: Nov–Apr $12 adults, $4 ages 6–12; May–Oct*

Don't pass on this passport

A version of the discount entertainment booklet, the Tucson Attractions Passport gives you lots of bang for your 15 bucks. You get two-for-one admissions to a variety of top sights, sporting events, and arts performances in Tucson and Southern Arizona — everything from the Arizona-Sonora Desert Museum to the Sidewinders baseball games and the Tucson Symphony — as well as discounts at several area malls. The Passport is available at the Tucson Visitors Center (see the "Finding Information after You Arrive" section earlier in this chapter), among other places. Call 800-638-8350 or log on to `www.TucsonPassport.com` for details.

Lunch with a mission

The **snack shop** (no telephone) at the back of San Xavier Plaza is a great place to try Indian fry bread — fresh hot dough topped with anything from honey or powdered sugar to meat, lettuce, and cheese. Just looking at the stuff raises your cholesterol 20 points — but every point is worth it.

$9 adults, $2 ages 6–12, free 5 and under. Open: Oct–Feb daily 8:30 a.m.–5 p.m.; Mar–Sept daily 7:30 a.m.–5 p.m.; open until 10 p.m. Sat nights Jun–Aug, until 9 p.m. Sat nights in Sept. Last tickets sold 1 hr. before closing.

Mission San Xavier del Bac

San Xavier Reservation

Even if religious buildings aren't usually your thing, don't miss this mission. One of the most beautifully preserved of the churches built in New Spain, this graceful white Moorish/Spanish structure is set dramatically against the desert. The Tohono O'odham Indians, for whom Jesuit father Eusebio Francisco Kino founded the mission in 1692, still worship here, and the wooden statue of Saint Francis Xavier that lies in the west chapel is pinned with photographs of loved ones and small tin milagros (literally "miracles," which represent parts of the body or psyche that the supplicant prays to the saint to heal). The religious folk art alone is worth the trip; one of the members of the team, who finished a restoration of the mission in the 1990s, called San Xavier the "Sistine Chapel of the United States" (and he should know — he worked on Michelangelo's original in Rome).

See map p. 216. San Xavier Road, 9 miles southwest of Tucson (take the Mission Road exit 92 on I-19 south). ☎ ***520-294-2624;*** `www.sanxaviermission.org`. *Admission: Free. Open: Daily 8 a.m.–5 p.m. (gift shop closed Easter Sunday and Christmas Day). Phone ahead for times of daily Masses.*

Mount Lemmon

Foothills (more or less)

Mount Lemmon, a 9,157-foot-high peak in the Coronado National Forest, was much in the news in 2003, when the huge Aspen fire destroyed thousands of trees and decimated much of the tiny alpine village of Summerhaven. But the mountain — and the village — are recovering: Almost all hiking trails are open to the public again, and many of Summerhaven's tourist-oriented businesses have been rebuilt. Rarely does Mount Lemmon have enough white stuff on the ground for you to schuss down it (see the "Skiing" section later in this chapter), but driving to the top is a peak experience any time. As you wind your way 8 miles to the mountain's summit, the terrain changes from desert to pine forest and the temperature drops about 20 degrees. You pass plenty of places to picnic

Tucson Attractions

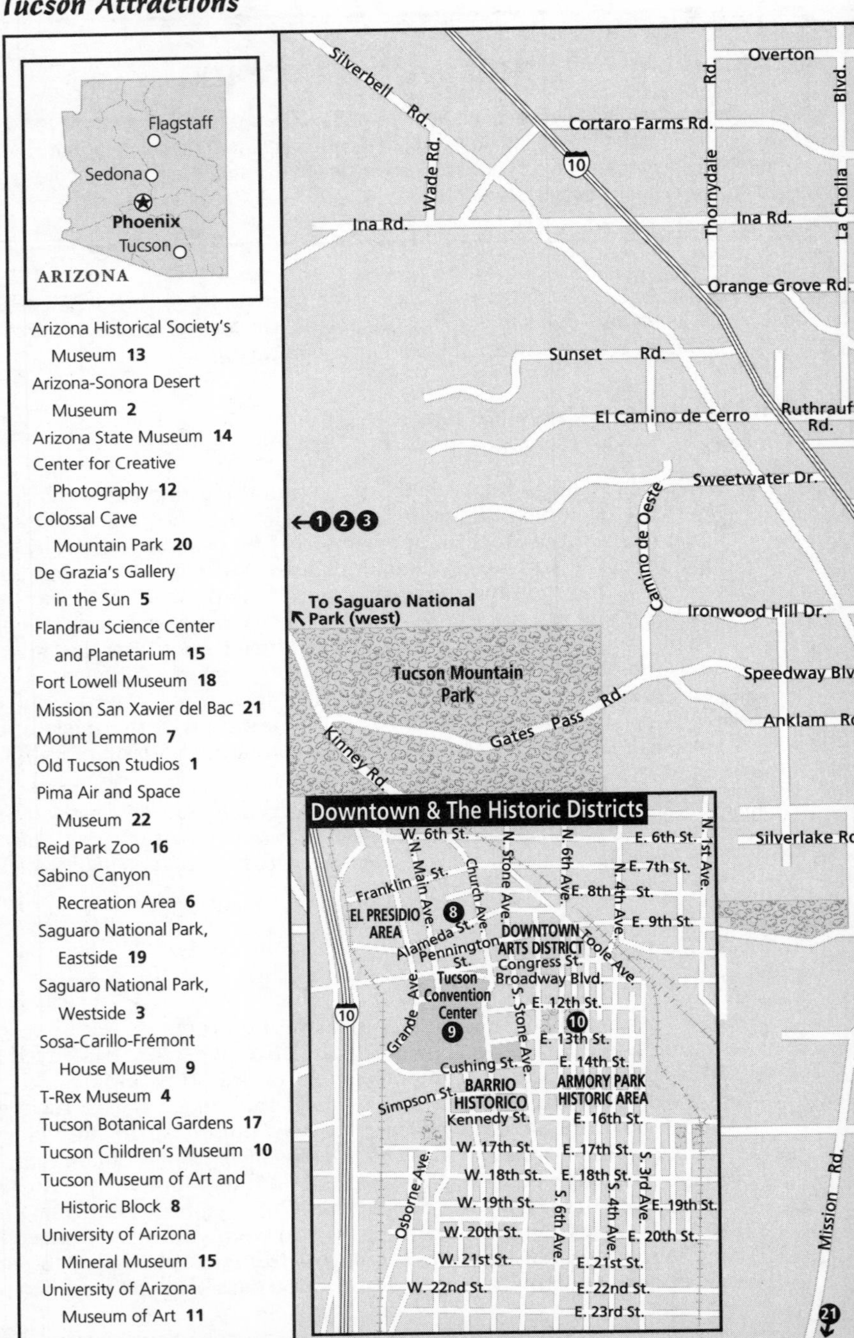

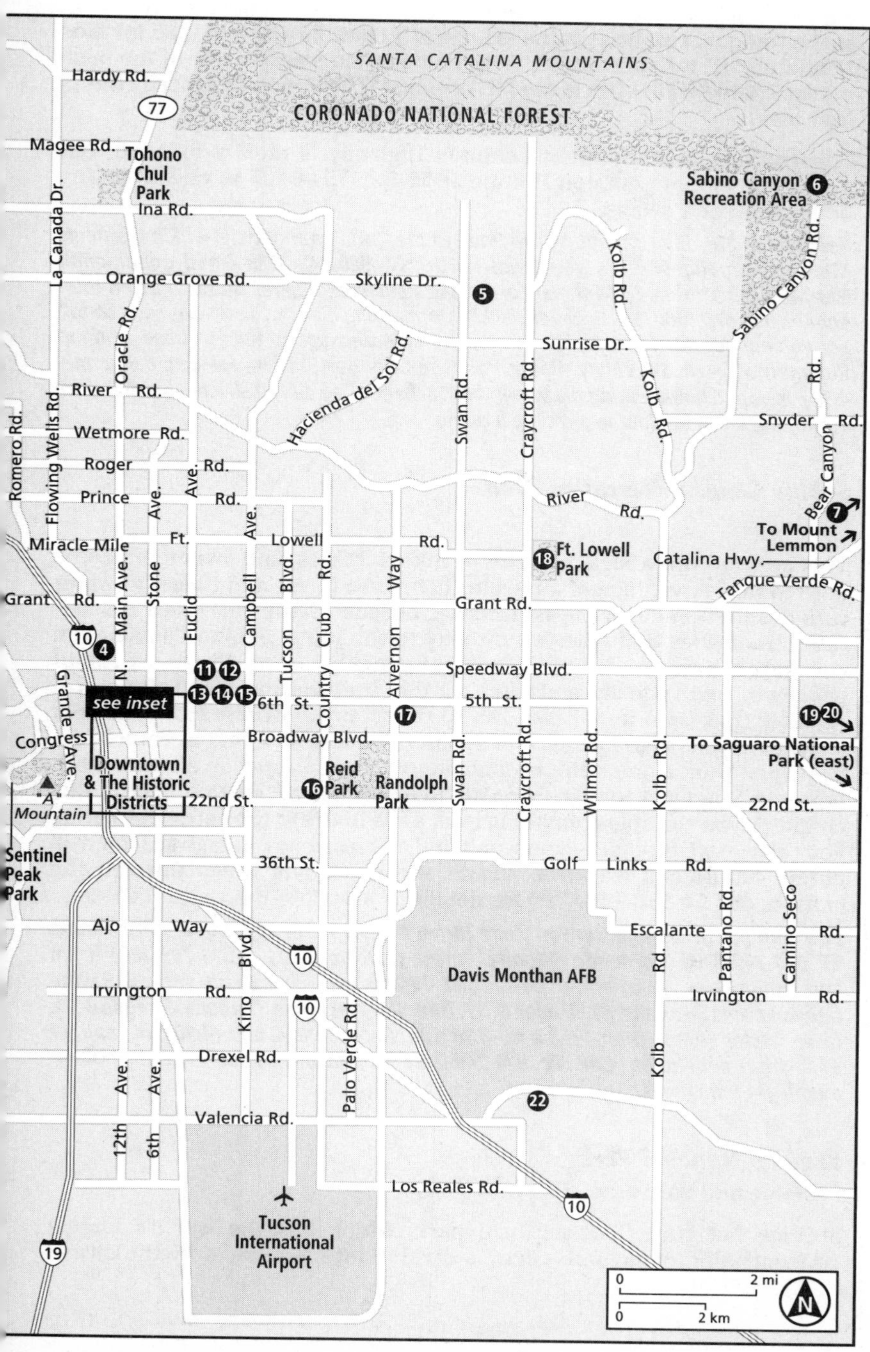
SANTA CATALINA MOUNTAINS
CORONADO NATIONAL FOREST
Hardy Rd.
77
Magee Rd.
Tohono Chul Park
Ina Rd.
La Canada Dr.
Orange Grove Rd.
Skyline Dr.
5
Sabino Canyon Recreation Area
6
Sabino Canyon Rd.
Kolb Rd.
Sunrise Dr.
Oracle Rd.
River Rd.
Hacienda del Sol Rd.
Swan Rd.
Craycroft Rd.
Snyder Rd.
Bear Canyon Rd.
Romero Rd.
Flowing Wells Rd.
Wetmore Rd.
Roger Rd.
Prince Rd.
Stone Ave.
Campbell Ave.
River Rd.
7
To Mount Lemmon
Miracle Mile
Ft. Lowell Rd.
Ft. Lowell Park
18
Catalina Hwy.
Tanque Verde Rd.
Grant Rd.
N. Main Ave.
Euclid
Tucson Blvd.
Country Club Rd.
Alvernon Way
Grant Rd.
10
4
11
12
Speedway Blvd.
Grande Ave.
see inset
13
14
15
6th St.
5th St.
17
19
20
Congress
Broadway Blvd.
To Saguaro National Park (east)
Downtown & The Historic Districts
Reid Park
16
Randolph Park
Swan Rd.
Craycroft Rd.
Wilmot Rd.
Kolb Rd.
"A" Mountain
22nd St.
22nd St.
Sentinel Peak Park
36th St.
Golf Links Rd.
Pantano Rd.
Camino Seco
Ajo Way
Escalante Rd.
10
Davis Monthan AFB
Irvington Rd.
Irvington Rd.
Kino Blvd.
10
Palo Verde Rd.
Drexel Rd.
12th Ave.
6th Ave.
22
Valencia Rd.
Los Reales Rd.
10
Tucson International Airport
19
0
2 mi
0
2 km
N

and hike (ask at milepost 19.9, the Palisades Ranger Station, for info) and, at the top, you can hop on the ski resort's chair lift ($9 adult, $5 for kids 12 and under) for spectacular views. Also at the summit, one of the businesses spared by the fire is the Mt. Lemmon Café, renowned locally for its fruit pies.

Construction on the Mount Lemmon Highway is mostly finished, but phone the Mount Lemmon Hotline at ☎ 520-751-9405 to check for any building-related delays.

See map p. 216. Take Tanque Verde Road to the Catalina Highway, which becomes Mt. Lemmon Highway as you head north. ☎ ***520-749-3329*** *(road conditions); 520-749-8700 (Coronado National Forest; the Palisades Ranger Station has no telephone); 520-576-1400 (Mt. Lemmon ski lift information);* `www.mtlemmon.com`*.* ***$5 toll*** *per vehicle per day for vehicles not going all the way up; no toll for those going to Summerhaven or Ski Valley. Open: Palisades Ranger Station, Fri–Sun 8:30 a.m.–4:30 p.m., open hours during the week. Apr 12–Labor Day daily 8:30 a.m.–5 p.m.; hours during the week subject to pending funding.*

Sabino Canyon Recreation Area

Foothills

This area is both a local favorite — hikers, bikers, and swimmers come here to take advantage of a terrain that mixes forest and (usually) water with desert — and a prime visitor stop, because of the fun Desert 101 narrated tram rides that take you directly to the top of Sabino Canyon. You can walk the entire way back — it's all downhill — or design a stroll of whatever length you like and catch another tram back at one of nine stops. Another (talk-free) tram heads out to Bear Canyon, where a popular trek leads to Seven Falls. The narrated tram ride takes 45 minutes, round-trip. If you just want a quick zip through nature, you can stay on all the way. If, however, you want to hike (see the "Keeping Active" section later in this chapter), you can spend anything from a few hours to the entire day (bring your own food, though — you won't find concessions). In high season, volunteer naturalists lead free nature and geological walks through the canyon; call ☎ 520-749-8700 for details or stop into the visitor center.

See map p. 216. Sabino Canyon Road (drive 4 miles north of Tanque Verde Road). ☎ ***520-749-8700*** *(Coronado National Forest visitor center) or 520-749-2861 (tram information;* `www.sabinocanyon.com`*). Canyon admission* ***$5*** *per vehicle. Sabino Canyon trams* ***$6*** *adults,* ***$2.50*** *ages 3–12; Bear Canyon trams* ***$3*** *adults,* ***$1*** *ages 3–12. Open: Vistor center, Mon–Fri 8 a.m.–4:30 p.m., Sat–Sun 8:30 a.m.–4:30 p.m.; call for daily tram schedules. Call* ☎ *520-749-2327 to find out about — and book — moonlight tram tours.*

Saguaro National Park

Eastside and Westside

Strange but true: This national park, which has the world's largest concentration of saguaro cacti, is divided into two parts by the city of

Tucson — which means you can pick and choose the side you want to visit, depending on where you're staying. The western section, or Tucson Mountain District, is smaller (24,000 acres) and more popular, in part because it adjoins the Arizona-Sonora Desert Museum (see the listing earlier in this section). Combining the two is a great way to spend the day. This side also has the newer visitor center, which gives a great introduction to the desert, and easily visited Hohokam petroglyphs (rock art) at Signal Hill. The eastern Rincon Mountain District looks a little less dramatic at first, but its 67,000 acres cross five climate zones. You can also mountain bike on the dirt hiking trails there (not so on the other side). Hiking/driving maps are available in the visitor centers in both districts, along with plenty of excellent literature on the desert. You can do a loop drive in an hour or spend all day hiking or biking around. Neither park section has snack bars or restaurants, so come prepared to picnic.

See map p. 216. Western District: 2700 N. Kinney Rd. (15 miles west of Tucson via Speedway Boulevard and Gates Pass Road). ☎ ***520-733-5158;*** `www.nps.gov/sagu`*. Admission: Free (what a deal!). Eastern District: Old Spanish Trail (take Speedway Boulevard or 22nd St. east)* ☎ ***520-733-5153****. Admission: $6 per vehicle, $3 individuals entering by bicycle or on foot. Visitor centers for both districts are open daily 9 a.m.–5 p.m.; closed Christmas Day, Thanksgiving, New Year's Day; paved park drives are open 6 a.m.–sunset.*

Tucson Museum of Art and Historic Block

Downtown

The Tucson Museum of Art doesn't have the most exciting collection of contemporary work, but the institution is on the site of the town's original 1775 presidio (fortress) and part of a fascinating art and historic complex. The modern main building is adjoined via a courtyard to the John K. Goodman Pavilion of Western Art, housed in an 1868 adobe home. Connected to the main building by a breezeway, another 19th-century adobe displays the museum's excellent world folk art, pre-Columbian, and Spanish Colonial holdings. The Spanish Mediterranean–style J. Knox Corbett House, to the north, is a showcase for the Arts and Crafts period, and across the Plaza of the Pioneers, on the east side of the complex, La Casa Cordova's two small rooms show how Tucsonans lived before the railroad — not to mention air conditioning — arrived (don't miss these rooms). Depending on your artistic tastes and historic interests, you may want to linger in some galleries and houses longer than others, but allow at least 1½ hours to do the whole complex justice.

See map p. 216. 140 N. Main Ave. (between Alameda and Washington). ☎ ***520-624-2333;*** `www.tucsonarts.com`*. Admission: $5 adults, $4 seniors, $2 students, 13 and under free; Sun free; Oct–May free docent-led tours of the historic block depart most days; phone in advance for specifics). Open: Mon–Sat 10 a.m.–4 p.m., Sun noon–4 p.m.; closed: major holidays, and on Mondays Memorial Day–Labor Day.*

University of Arizona Museums

University of Arizona/Fourth Avenue

Okay, I know, the University of Arizona museums aren't a single sight, but I always think of these museums collectively. All are interesting, but if I had to choose only two, I'd go for the Center for Creative Photography and the Arizona State Museum (newer north building). The Flandrau would top my list if I were traveling with kids. The Center for Creative Photography and the University of Arizona Museum of Art are right across from one another, and the Arizona Historical Society's Museum isn't far from the Arizona State Museum. If you're determined, you can visit all four on foot. The Flandrau, however, is on the other side of the campus. You really have to be an atypically fit museum buff to trek over there and back.

You're best off visiting the museums on weekends or during the summer (for a heat escape), when the students aren't on campus and parking's not a problem. The most convenient garage to the Arizona Historical Society's Museum and the Arizona State Museum is at Euclid and Second Street; the one most convenient to the Center for Creative Photography and to the Museum of Art is at Park and Speedway (an underpass leads from there to the campus). A visitor parking lot is just south of the Flandrau building. The garage charge is $2 for the first hour, $1 for each additional hour (free on weekends). Get validated at the Arizona Historical Society's Museum, and you can park for free during the week, too.

Arizona Historical Society's Museum, 949 E. Second St. at Park Avenue (☎ 520-628-5774; www.arizonahistoricalsociety.org), explores the state's past beginning with the Hohokam Indians. Temporary exhibits treat topics from medicine to fashion. Although basically an adult-oriented museum, kids like the replica of a mine shaft. The museum hosts an interesting lecture series in the evenings during high season; call to find out the topics. Admission: $5 adults, $4 seniors and students, under 12 free. Open: Mon–Sat 10 a.m.–4 p.m. See map p. 216.

The Arizona State Museum, just inside the main gate, near Park Avenue at University Boulevard (☎ 520-621-6302; www.statemuseum.arizona.edu), is the Southwest's oldest (established 1893) and largest anthropology museum. The permanent "Paths of Life: American Indians of the Southwest" showcases ten American Indian cultures via excellent multi-media exhibits, while temporary installations go into depth on particular subjects, such as Navajo textiles (through May 2005). Admission: $3 suggested donation. Open: Mon–Sat 10 a.m.–5 p.m., Sun noon–5 p.m. See map p. 216.

Center for Creative Photography, 1030 N. Olive Rd., just south of Speedway Blvd. (☎ 520-621-7968; http://dizzy.library.arizona.edu/branches/ccp), is a must-see for fans of modern and contemporary photography in general and of Ansel Adams, who first conceived of this place and is well represented here, in particular. Under the aegis of the unique PrintViewing program, anyone can call and make an appointment to spend an hour viewing original prints from the museum's collection of some 60,000 images, gratis. Admission: $2 suggested donation. Open: Mon–Fri 9 a.m.–5 p.m., Sat–Sun noon–5 p.m. See map p. 216.

Saguaro savvy

Pronounce the word suh-*wah*-roh. Say the "g" and everyone will instantly peg you as a tourist. Here are some additional facts:

- This type of cactus grows only in the western Sonoran Desert, that is, northern Mexico and Arizona and small sections of California. Don't be taken in by those saguaro shots in films supposedly set in Texas or Wyoming.
- An interior skeleton supports the saguaro. The Spanish made furniture and roof cross beams from its woody ribs.
- The saguaro grows very slowly — only about an inch a year.
- Those holes you see on its surface aren't potshots taken by drunken rednecks; birds, especially gila woodpeckers, that call the cacti home, peck them out. When the holes are large enough, they harden into cactus boots (not to be confused with cowboy boots, which are usually a little bigger).
- The saguaro is the country's largest cactus, sometimes growing to 60 feet or higher. Specimens can weigh 5 tons or more, sprout more than 50 arms, and live more than 150 years.
- It blossoms once a year, usually in June. The white saguaro blossom is Arizona's state flower.
- Damaging or stealing a saguaro is illegal. Plow into one or stick one in your suitcase, and you could get fined $250 or more.

Flandrau Science Center and Planetarium, 1601 E. University Blvd. at Cherry Avenue (☎ 520-621-STAR [recorded information]; www.flandrau.org), is a terrific introduction to astronomy and more earthly sciences. The Flandrau has all kinds of cool stuff, including an exploding asteroid exhibit that teaches about space debris (and you thought you had trash!); planetarium shows; and a 16-inch telescope through which visitors can peer the early evening. Included in the admission price to the Flandrau and on the lower level of the same building, the University of Arizona Mineral Museum (☎ 520-621-4227; www.geo.arizona.edu/minmus) has a terrific collection of gems and minerals, some of which glow in the dark. Admission: Exhibits, $3 for adults, $2 children, 2 and under free; exhibits' admission free with tickets to planetarium shows: $5.50 adults, $4.50 seniors and military, $3.50 ages $3–13 (under 3 not admitted to Planetarium). Open: Exhibits, Mon–Sat 9 a.m.–5 p.m., Sun 1–5 p.m. and Thurs–Sat 7–9 p.m. (the Mineral Museum doesn't observe evening hours); telescope open clear nights from dusk to 10 p.m. Wed–Sat. Planetarium show schedules vary. See map p. 216.

University of Arizona Museum of Art, Fine Arts Complex, Building 2, southeast corner of Speedway Boulevard and Park Avenue (☎ 520-621-7567; http://artmuseum.arizona.edu), makes up in quality what it lacks in size. Highlights include Fernando Gallego's 1488 Ciudad Rodrigo altar piece and one of the best sculpture collections in the Southwest, including works by Rodin, Noguchi, Moore, and Lipschitz. Admission: Free. Open: Sept to mid-May Mon–Fri 9 a.m.–5 p.m., Sat and Sun noon–4 p.m.; mid-May to Aug Tues–Fri 10 a.m.–3:30 p.m., Sat and Sun noon–4 p.m. See map p. 216.

More cool things to see and do

Not seen enough yet? Tucson offers everything from endless caverns and more cactus to art and outer-space exhibits.

- Get flighty. You don't have to be aviation crazy to be riveted by the Pima Air and Space Museum, 6000 E. Valencia Rd. (I-10 Exit 267), Southside (☎ 520-574-0462; www.pimaair.org), where one of the world's largest private collections of historic aircraft is displayed in 80 outdoor acres and 5 indoor hangars. The more than 250 flying machines include the surprisingly low-key Air Force One plane used by presidents John F. Kennedy and Lyndon Johnson and NASA's Super Guppy. See the "Aviation tours" section later in this chapter for information about the Davis Monthan Air Force tours that leave from this facility, and Chapter 15 for details of the Titan Missile Museum, also operated by the Arizona Aerospace Foundation. If you plan to visit more than one location, check into buying a combination ticket. Admission: $9.75 adults, $8.75 seniors and active military, $6 ages 7–12, 6 and under free. Combination Pima Air and Space/Titan Missile museums: $16. Open: Daily 9 a.m.–5 p.m. (last admission at 4 p.m.); closed Thanksgiving and Christmas. See map p. 216.

KID FRIENDLY

- Go underground. Colossal Cave Mountain Park, 16721 E. Old Spanish Tr., Eastside (☎ 520-647-7275; www.colssalcave.com) is home to the world's largest dry cavern — so big that parts of it still haven't been explored. Guides on the 45–50 minute tours regale you with cave facts and romantic legends — like the one about the stagecoach robbery booty that's reputedly hidden here. Note: Colossal Cave may be large, but ceilings are often quite low; this site isn't a good bet if you're claustrophobic. If you don't want to plumb the park's depths, you can still find plenty to do, including visiting a desert tortoise display, a butterfly garden, and a museum that explores the history of the cave. Located near the intersection of Colossal Cave and Old Spanish Trail roads, the cave is about 20 miles east of Tucson (take Broadway Blvd. or East 22nd St. to Old Spanish Trail, turn right to Colossal Cave Road or take I-10 to the Vail-Wentworth exit, # 279, and follow signs). Admission: Cave tours $7.50 adults, $4 ages 6–12, 5 and under 3; park entry $3 per car (plus $1 per person over 6 per car); $1 per bicycle; $ 2 motorcycle. Open: mid-Sept to mid-Mar Mon–Sat 9 a.m.–5 p.m., Sun and holidays 9 a.m.–6 p.m.; mid-Mar to mid-Sept Mon–Sat 8 a.m.–6 p.m., Sun and holidays 8 a.m.–7 p.m. See map p. 216.
- Explore more of Tucson's past. In addition to the Arizona Historical Society's museum/headquarters at the UA (see "The top attractions"

section earlier in this chapter), two more branches should appeal to history buffs. The Fort Lowell Museum, Fort Lowell Park, 2900 N. Craycroft Rd., Central (☎ 520-885-3832), once the digs of the commanding officer of a military installation built to protect Tucson from Apache attacks, highlights life on the base from 1873 to 1891. Artifacts from the Hohokam Indian village that predate the fortress are also on view in Fort Lowell Park. Civilian life — and attempts to live civilly on the frontier — are the focus of the Sosa-Carillo-Frémont House Museum, 151 N. Granada Ave., Downtown (☎ 520-622-0956). The Sonoran-style adobe home, built in 1858 with saguaro-rib ceiling crossbeams, was rented out to territorial Governor John Fremont in 1878. Admission: Both museums $3 adults, $2 students, 12 and under free. Open: both museums Wed–Sat 10 a.m.–4 p.m. See map p. 216.

- Discover where the West was filmed. You'll enjoy the Old Tucson Studios, 201 S. Kinney Rd., inside Tucson Mountain Park (☎ 520-883-0100; www.oldtucson.com), if you're old enough to remember the movies shot here when this was a functioning film studio — it was built in 1939 for the motion picture Arizona, starring William Holden, Rita Hayworth, and Glenn Ford — or young enough to get a kick out of the simulated shootouts and assorted rides added later. Even if you're an in-betweener and don't mind corny, you may like the production shows, the (very interactive) actors strolling around in Western gear, and the film clips of classic Westerns. Admission: Sat $12.95 adults, $7.95 ages 4–11, free 3 and under; Sun–Fri $9.95 adults, $6.95 children. Open: Sat 10 a.m.–4 p.m., Sun–Fri 10 a.m.–3 p.m. See map p. 216.
- Get artsy. The sentimental depictions of Native American and Mexican life by Arizona artist Ted De Grazia at De Grazia's Gallery in the Sun, 6300 N. Swan Rd. (1 mile north of Sunrise), Foothills (☎ 520-299-9191; www.degrazia.org), may not be to your taste, but the artist's former home, gallery, and gravesite, built of materials from the surrounding desert — and especially the small mission-style church where De Grazia is buried — are appealing. No original artwork is for sale, but you can get good reproductions in the gift shop. Admission: Free. Open: Daily 10 a.m.–3:45 p.m. (gift shop open until 4 p.m.) See map p. 216.

Neophyte neck kneaders

One of the most prestigious massage schools in the country, Tucson's Desert Institute of the Healing Arts, 140 E. Fourth St. (☎ **520-882-0899** [information] or **520-792-1191** [appointments]; http://desertinstitute.org), offers hour-long Swedish massages for $25 if you're willing to serve as a student guinea pig, er, subject (it's $50 if you go with one of the pros). These cut-rate pummeling sessions are available Monday through Thursday afternoons and evenings.

Also getting kudos from kids . . .

Along with the other kid-friendly spots that I describe in this chapter, families have a few more options.

Ideal for a central city afternoon outing, **Reid Park Zoo,** Reid Park, Lake Shore Lane, entrance off 22nd Street just east of Country Club Road, Central (☎ **520-791-4022;** www.tucsonzoo.org), is just big enough to keep kids occupied for an hour or two, but not too large to tire them (or you). The baby animal displays always score major points. Admission: $5 adults, $4 seniors, $2 ages 2–14 accompanied by an adult, under 2 free. Open: Daily 9 a.m.–4 p.m.; closed Christmas. See map p. 216.

At the **Tucson Children's Museum,** 200 S. Sixth Ave. at 13th St., Downtown (☎ **520-792-9985;** www.tucsonchildrensmuseum.org), your energetic offspring can work off excess juice while finding out everything from the human body to electricity. The "Take a Hike" program lets kids explore career choices. Admission: $5.50 adults, $4.50 seniors, $3.50 ages 2–16; free for everyone third Sun of each month. Open: Tues–Sat 10 a.m.–5 p.m., Sun noon–5 p.m.; closed New Year's Day, Easter, Thanksgiving, Christmas. See map p. 216.

Real and re-created fossils, artwork, dioramas, and other "touch and learn" exhibits fill the **T-Rex Museum,** 1202 N. Main Ave., downtown (☎ **520-792-2884;** www.trexmuseum.org), a converted warehouse with dinosaurs on the brain. For an extra fee, kids can dig in the Paleo Pit and take home what they unearth. Admission: $2. Open: Tues–Sat 10 a.m.–5 p.m., Sun noon–5 p.m., closed all major holidays. See map p. 216.

- Check out some more cacti. Saguaro National Park isn't the only patch with prickly plants in town. You can stroll along nature trails and wander through demonstration gardens at Tohono Chul Park, 7366 N. Paseo del Norte, 1 block west of Ina Road, Northwest (☎ 520-742-6455; www.tohonochulpark.org). The lovely 48-acre desert preserve also includes a greenhouse, a small art gallery, two excellent gift shops, and a tearoom/restaurant (☎ 520-797-1222). Sunday brunch is especially big; come early to avoid long waits. Admission: $5 adults, $4 seniors 62 and over, $3 students with valid ID, $2 ages 5–12, under 5 free. Open: Park daily 8 a.m.–5 p.m., buildings daily 9 a.m.–5 p.m.

  Smack in the center of town, the Tucson Botanical Gardens, 2150 N. Alvernon Way just south of Grant (☎ 520-326-9686; www.tucsonbotanical.org), has plantings that date back to the 1930s. A garden designed to attract birds and an area for carefully touching plants are part of the instruction — and fun. Bird and gardening tours begin at 9 a.m. every Tuesday, and docent-led botanical garden tours start at 10 a.m. Wednesday through Friday. Call to find out about additional garden talks and classes. Admission: $5 adults, $2.50 ages 6–11, ages 5 and under free. Open: Daily 8:30 a.m.–4:30 p.m. See map p. 216.

- Spa down. Although capable of doing a number on you skin, the desert is also considered a spiritual place (hey, if you're going to look like an alligator, you'd better have an attractive aura). The area's many spas tend to both body and soul with an array of soothing — and sometimes far out — treatments. Most of the spas at Tucson's resorts have day-visit options; my top picks are the spas at Miraval, Westin La Paloma (an Elizabeth Arden Red Door spa), Omni Tucson National, and Westward Look (all listed in the "Staying in Style" section earlier in this chapter). Of the independent day spas, Gadabout has the most facilities and locations (six, including one for men at 2951 N. Swan, ☎ 520-325-3300). The one in St. Phillips Plaza, 1990 E. River Rd. at Campbell (☎ 520-577-2000), is the largest day spa in central Tucson, but other branches may be more convenient to your hotel, so check the Yellow Pages. Treatments range from $20 for a basic manicure at Gadabout to $375 for five hours — including aromatherapy message, Dead Sea body masque, facial, manicure, pedicure, and lunch — at Omni Tucson National. A full day at Miraval can run you more than a grand. See map p. 216.

Keeping Active

Ways to play in Tucson's balmy weather abound — but don't play too long or too hard without the proper precautions, such as hydration and sun protection.

Biking

The best of Tucson's many bicycle-friendly areas include Sabino Canyon with a paved path to the top — uphill, but very scenic (☎ 520-749-8700; the path is open to bicyclists only from 5 p.m. to 9 a.m., except Wednesdays and Saturday, when bikers are not permitted) and Saguaro National Park East, where hikers share several trails with mountain bikers. See "The top attractions" section earlier in this chapter for both locations. Another option is Rillito River Park, a level, 4-mile trail that runs parallel to River Road between Campbell Avenue and La Cholla Boulevard along a (usually dry) riverbed. The Tucson Transportation Department (☎ 520-791-4372; `http://dot.ci.tucson.az.us`) can mail you a city bike map, or you can also pick one up at the downtown office of the Pima Association of Governments, 177 N. Church Ave., Ste. 405 (☎ 520-792-1093; `www.pagnet.org`). Reliable, centrally located bike stores include Fair Wheel Bikes, 1110 E. Sixth St., east of Euclid (☎ 520-884-9018), which loans mountain bikes for $20 for the first day, $10 for each additional day. Rentals at Bargain Basement Bikes, 428 N. Fremont, off Sixth Street (☎ 520-624-9673), start at $30 a day, going down to $15 for each following day. Want company on your cycling excursion? The Southern Arizona Mountain Biking Association `http://sambabike.org`), organizes frequent group rides to which visitors are welcome.

Bird-watching

Southern Arizona is a bird-lover's mecca. Although the greatest concentrations of birds flock to areas southeast of Tucson (see Chapter 15), the feathered ones also take to more citified spots. The best source for local birding information is the Tucson Audubon Society, which has an office and nature shop near the UA at 300 E. University Blvd., Ste. 120 (☎ 520-629-0510; www.tucsonaudubon.org). The society's publication, Finding Birds in Southeast Arizona, includes two chapters on urban bird hangouts and, during high season, members run field trips in and around Tucson and southeastern Arizona.

Golfing

Desert, traditional, resort, municipal — Tucson has golf courses to satisfy every duffer's taste and pocketbook. To get the lowdown on the local courses, get a free copy of The Official Arizona Golf Guide and Directory in advance from the Tucson Convention and Visitors' Bureau (see the "Fast Facts: Tuscon" section later in this chapter). The guides are also available at resorts, golf courses, and the Tucson Visitors Center (see the "Finding Information after You Arrive" section earlier in this chapter).

For last-minute reservations in high season, contact Standby Golf (☎ 520-882-2665), where your procrastination doesn't cost you anything (the golf courses pick up the tab). The service is closed in summer, when getting tee times is no problem.

Speaking of which, if you're an early riser or don't mind teeing off in the late afternoon (the periods of the day when the heat is bearable), consider traveling to Tucson from June through August. During these months, greens fees and room rates at the golf resorts dip drastically. I give you brief rundowns of the types of courses in the following list. See also my tips for desert golf, often called target golf, in Chapter 11.

- Municipal courses: Tucson's five municipal courses are far-from-seedy (although they're often seeded) city greens. In fact, the flagship of these bargain courses, Randolph North, hosts the annual LPGA tours, while Fred Enke stands out for being an urban target course. For locations, greens fees (which range from $45–$65 in high season, with cart, $23–$25 in summer), and reservations, contact the Tucson Parks and Recreation Department (☎ 520-791-4653 or 520-791-4336 [recorded information only]; www.tucsoncitygolf.com). To avoid disappointment, book the municipal courses at least a week in advance.

  If you play the municipal courses after 3 p.m. from November through January, for as many holes as you can see until it gets dark (generally about 7 or 7:30 p.m. — Arizona doesn't go on daylight savings time), fees are greatly reduced. And the summer specials, after Memorial Day, are outstanding.

- Public courses: A couple of Tucson's newer nonresort courses, both desert track and extremely scenic, are already among its most popular public places to get teed off. Arizona National Golf Club, 9777 E. Sabino Greens Dr., Foothills (☎ 520-749-3636; www.arizonanationalgolfclub.com), designed by Robert Trent Jones, is the most convenient to town of the two. The club's green fees are $165 in winter, $65 in summer. The Golf Club at Vistoso, 955 W. Vistoso Highlands Dr., Oro Valley, north of Tucson (☎ 520-797-9900; www.vistosogolf.com), a Tom Weiskopf creation, was selected as No. 1 in Tucson by Golf Digest. In winter you pay from $136 to $159 to play at Vistoso, in summer from $45 to $55. In Green Valley, a (largely) retirement community south of Tucson, The Haven Public Golf Course, 110 N. Abrego Dr. (☎ 520-625-4281), has a good, traditional layout that's very playable for all levels, not to mention reasonable: Green fees are only $39 in high season, $19 in summer.
- Resort courses: The Westin La Paloma has a guests-only policy for its greens, but you can play at all the other resorts even if you're not staying there. Remember, however, that guests get first dibs on the prime tee times. The two Tom Fazio-designed Ventana Canyon courses at 6200 N. Clubhouse Lane, Foothills (☎ 520-577-4015; www.ventanacanyonclub.com), renowned for their spectacular scenery, are the most popular of the resort desert target courses. Green fees: $199 in winter, $79 in summer. Prefer traditional Midwestern links? Go for the mix-and-match 27-hole greens at Omni Tucson National Golf Resort and Spa, 2727 W. Club Dr., Northwest (☎ 520-297-2271; www.tucsonnational.com), site of the annual PGA Tour. Rates for nonguests range from $80 in summer to $115 in the shoulder seasons (May and fall) and $200 in high season.

Hiking

Saguaro National Park, Sabino Canyon, and Mount Lemmon (see "The top attractions" section earlier in this chapter for all three) are Tucson trekker favorites. If you're seeking (relative) solitude, the Eastern district of the national park is your best bet. Other options include Catalina State Park, 11570 N. Oracle Rd., 9 miles north of the city (☎ 520-628-5798; admission: $5) and Tucson Mountain Park, 8451 W. McCain Loop Rd. (☎ 520-883-4200), which has no visitor center (or fee). You see signs for Tucson Mountain Park just before you come to Saguaro National Park West. You can usually hitch a hike with the local chapter of the Sierra Club (☎ 520-620-6401; http://arizona.sierraclub.org), which tends to head for the (foot)hills most weekends in high season (if you want to go on your own, log on to http://Arizona.sierraclub.org/trail_guide, which details a variety of Tucson hikes. The best all-around trail resource is the Tucson Hiking Guide by Betty Leavengood, which rates hikes by difficulty and discusses details such as terrain. You can pick up a copy at either branch of the Summit Hut, 5045 E. Speedway Blvd. (☎ 520-325-1554) or 605 E. Wetmore Rd. (☎ 520-888-1000), also a good source for hiking equipment.

Tucson's super dry air is deceptive; just because you're not sweating doesn't mean you're not getting dehydrated. Take plenty of water with you — about 2 to 4 quarts for a standard day hike, double that on really hot days — and keep on drinking, even when you don't think you're thirsty. Try to down about 20 ounces of fluids — nothing carbonated, caffeinated, or alcoholic, please — two hours before you get started and then take a hearty swig from your water bottle every 15 minutes.

Horseback riding

No matter if the closest you've come to a horse is watching Mr. Ed reruns on TV, this town has a mount with your brand on it. Pusch Ridge Stables, 13700 N. Oracle Rd. (☎ 520-825-1664), backed dramatically up against the Santa Catalinas north of Tucson, offers everything from easy group trots through the desert ($25 for 1 hour, $40 for 2 hours, $30 for 1½-hour sunset rides) to advanced private rides ($45 per hour). You can find your bliss — or at least have fun — at Cocaraque Ranch, 6255 Diamond Hills Ln. (☎ 520-682-8594; www.cocoraque.com), a working cattle ranch on the west side of town near Old Tucson Studios. You have to gather together a group of at least ten if you want to take part in a cattle drive (rates, from about $95 per person, depend on group size; Sept–May), but you can ride around with a guide until the cows come home — or until your money runs out (trail rides cost $20 for 1 hour, $25 for 1½ hours, $30 for 2 hours, or $80 for a 4½ to 5 hour ranch house ride). Follow an old stagecoach route from the historic ranch in Colossal Cave Mountain Park Stables 16721 E. Old Spanish Tr. (☎ 520-647-3450; www.colossalsave.com/explore.html). You pay $27 for the first hour, and $20 for each additional hour, up to four. Breakfast or lunch runs you $15 more, dinner another $20. Overnight camping trips on the ranch ($225) are available too. See the "More cool things to see and do" section earlier in this chapter, for directions to the park, on the far east side of town.

Skiing

Yes, Virginia, there is snow in southern Arizona — sometimes. But because the Mt. Lemmon Ski Valley, at the top of Mt. Lemmon (see "The top attractions" section earlier in this chapter), has no machines to help Mother Nature along with the white stuff, chances are good that you may not be able to do any schussing during your visit. (Call ☎ 520-576-1321 to see if a live person answers the phone — a good sign — or 520-576-1400 for a recorded snow report.) When the ski area is open, lift tickets cost $35 for an adult's all-day pass, $27 for an adult half-day pass starting at 12:30 p.m.; and $16 for an all-day pass for ages 12 and under ($11 after 12:30 p.m.). Instruction starts at $50 an hour for private lessons, and $18 for a 1½-hour group lesson. A $55 first-time skier's package ($31 for under 12) includes equipment rental, a lesson, and a lift pass upon completion of the lesson. The Valley offers 18 runs, ranging from beginner to advanced. And this mountain isn't a snowboard-free zone; you can rent them here as well as use them.

Mount Lemmon isn't the place for serious skiers; you'll be disappointed if you want expert slopes. If you just want a quick downhill fix, however, you can't beat going swimming in the morning and then hitting the slopes in the afternoon.

Tennis

Although the resort courts are restricted to hotel guests — you find the most courts at Loews Ventana Canyon, Sheraton Tucson El Conquistador, Westin La Paloma, Westward Look, and Canyon Ranch (see the "Staying in Style" section earlier in this chapter) — good public courts abound. The king of the city park tennis scene is Randolph Tennis Center, 50 S. Alvernon Way (☎ 520-791-4896; www.randolphtenniscenter.com), with 25 courts, 11 of them night lit. Fort Lowell Park, 2900 N. Craycroft Rd. (☎ 520-791-2584), and Himmel Park, 1000 N. Tucson Blvd. (☎ 520-791-3276), offer eight lighted courts each. All are in central Tucson and all charge ridiculously reasonable fees: $2.50 per adult per 1½ hours, plus $6 per court for night lighting. Ft. Lowell reduces the fees to $1 for ages 16 and under and seniors; Himmel's cost for seniors is $1, too. Neither place takes reservations: First come, first served (or serving). The least crowded times to play are from about 10 a.m. to 3 p.m., which is, of course, when the temperature is the most uncomfortably warm.

Rooting for the Home Team: Spectator Sports

Put some spring (training) into your step. Tucson is the only city in the country to host three major-league baseball teams for spring training. The Chicago White Sox and the Arizona Diamondbacks go to bat during the month of March at the Tucson Electric Park, 2500 E. Ajo Way, near the airport (☎ 866-672-1343 or 520-434-1111; www.tucsonbaseball.com). Tickets ($3–$14) became harder to get after the D-backs won the World Series in 2001 and Randy Johnson pitched a perfect game in 2004. Try to nab seats as soon as you know when you'll be in town.

Vying for fans of America's favorite pastime in March, the Colorado Rockies (☎ 520-327-9467 in season, or 800-303-ROCKIES otherwise; http://colorado.rockies.mlb.com) perfect their pitch at Hi-Corbett Field, 3400 E. Camino Campestre in Reid Park (S. Country Club and E. 22nd St.). Prices range from $4 to $45.

The Cactus Leaguers turn over the mound from April through August to the Tucson Sidewinders (☎ 520-434-1021; www.tucsonsidewinders.com), the Diamondbacks' AAA team (clearly, this franchise assumes that reptilian names won't rattle the fans). Ticket prices ($4–$8) include discounts for seniors, active military, and children under 16.

Seeing Tucson by Guided Tour

If you don't drive or just don't want the hassle of trying to find your way around a large, new city, you have some good general sightseeing options. Want to focus on some special interests? In addition to these tours, you can find more in this chapter's listings for Sabino Canyon and Tucson Museum of Art (see "The top attractions" section), Tucson Botanical Gardens (see the "More cool things to see and do" section), and Tucson Audubon Society (see the "Keeping Active" section).

General bus tours

Great Western Tours (☎ 520-572-1660; www.gwtours.net) offers the most Tucson excursions, ranging from three-hour city tours for $45 per person to all-day trips to Tombstone and Bisbee (see Chapter 15) for $100.

Archaeology tours

Enjoy channeling ancient civilizations (if only on the Discovery channel)? Dig in! Old Pueblo Archaeology (☎ 520-798-1201; www.oldpueblo.org) lets you discover the ropes — or the rocks — on an ancient Indian village in Marana, north of Tucson. Participants in the Dig for a Day program must be at least 12 years old, and the fee is $38. Advance reservations are required.

Aviation tours

Get on a higher plane with a bus tour of AMARC (Aerospace Maintenance and Regeneration Center), a 2,700-acre facility at the Davis Monthan Air Force base, which hosts more than 4,000 aircraft. Departure times for the tours, which take about an hour and depart from the Pima Air & Space Museum (see the "More cool things to see and do" section earlier in this chapter), vary seasonally, but tours are offered Monday through Friday, excluding holidays. Phone ahead to get information and to make reservations (☎ 520-574-0462, ext. 2), which are required at least a day in advance. Cost is $6 for adults and $3 for ages 12 and under.

Desert tours

Sunshine Jeep Tours, 9040 N. Oracle Rd., Ste. D (☎ 520-742-1943; www.sunshinejeeptours.com), gives you a great introduction to the desert in the Tortolita Mountains northwest of Tucson. You're off-roaded to an archaeological site with ancient petroglyphs, and you get the dirt on all the local flora and fauna (snake handling optional). A 3 to 3½-hour tour costs $55 for adults, $35 for ages 11 to 15, $25 for ages 6 to 10, 5 and under free. The higher Santa Catalina Mountains are the setting for the 3½-hour forays into the desert led by Trail Dust Adventures, 1665 S. Craycroft Rd. (☎ 520-747-0323; www.traildustadventures.com). The price is $54 for adults, half price for 12 and under.

History tours

Arrange for walking tours of the historic El Presidio district by calling the Arizona Historical Society at ☎ 520-622-0956 ($10 per person, under 12 free; Nov–March only Thurs and Sat at 10 a.m.). You can get a free self-guided tour map of the district from the Tucson Museum of Art (see "The top attractions" section earlier in this chapter) or the Metropolitan Tucson Convention & Visitors Bureau (see the "Fast Facts: Tucson" section at the end of this chapter).

Space mirror tours

The University of Arizona has some BMOC (Big Mirrors on Campus). Beneath the east wing of the UA's football stadium, the Steward Observatory Mirror Laboratory houses some of the largest and lightest mirrors in the world — ideal for collecting light from faint astronomical objects. The lab participated in several NASA projects and created the two 8.4-meter mirrors for Mt. Graham's Large Binocular Telescope (see Chapter 14). With 10 days' advance notice, the university offers free tours of the mirror lab on Monday through Friday from 9 a.m. to 3:30 p.m. Contact Ann Klocko at ☎ 520-621-1022 or by e-mail at `aklocko@as.arizona.edu`. Maximum group size of 15 (no minimum) and participants need to be at least high school age (photo I.D. required).

Following an Itinerary

When planning your perfect Tucson itinerary, factor in two variables: the weather and your hotel's location. Many of Tucson's attractions are outdoors and the city is very spread out, so if you visit in summer (or during one of our brief winter rainy bouts) and stay in an outlying resort, you may not be able to follow these itineraries as well as, say, someone who bunks in central Tucson on sunshiny winter days. These sketches are rough, and directions aren't set in stone or — in local lingo — petroglyphs. For details on all the sights and restaurants mentioned in these itineraries, see the relevant sections of this chapter.

One-day itinerary

If you have just a single day in Tucson, start out early and hit the Arizona-Sonora Desert Museum as soon as it opens. Spend a few hours, and then drive over to Saguaro National Park West visitor center about 10 minutes away. Look out at the amazing vistas, maybe view the introductory film, and browse the bookstore; you don't have time for much else before you head downtown to the Tucson Museum of Art and Historic Block. At lunchtime, grab a sandwich or salad at the museum's Café á la C'Art (if you have a sweet tooth, order dessert first — they sell out fast), and then wander through the various galleries and historic houses. The museum's gift shop is good, but if you want a larger selection of things Southwestern, head for the 1850s Old Town Artisans complex, just across the street. You aren't far from I-10. Drive a few exits east to I-19 and zip down to the Mission San Xavier del Bac. When you get your fill of all the wonderful religious folk art, walk across the courtyard to San Xavier Plaza, where you can (again) satisfy your more material urges with Native American arts and crafts (check out the friendship bowls made by the Tohono O'odham people). I'm not going to tell you to resist the Indian fry bread (I hardly ever can myself), but unless you share, you'll ruin your appetite for dinner (book a table at a restaurant near your hotel). If you're revived by food, go for some Country and Western sounds — and maybe dancing — at the Maverick: King of Clubs.

Two-day itinerary

On day one, take a more kicked-back approach to the morning part of the one-day itinerary: You still want to arrive early at the Arizona-Sonora Desert Museum to avoid taking your first Tucson hike in its large parking lot. When you get there, spend a little more time hanging out with the snakes and the hummingbirds (no, they're not in the same enclosure). If you're visiting in high season, have lunch in the Ocotillo Café; if not, or if you're traveling with kids, the Ironwood Cafeteria is fine for a midday meal. Then head over to Saguaro National Park West and get directions to Signal Hill, where you can take a short hike to some Hohokam petroglyphs. Pack lunch in a cooler before you head out in the morning and you can picnic here. Head back to your hotel and relax by the pool before dinner — an essential part of the Tucson experience, too. (If you're traveling with kids, substitute Old Tucson Studios for Saguaro National Park West, and expect to spend the entire afternoon there.) Unless you spend the afternoon at Old Tucson Studios, you should have energy for a night out at the Maverick after dinner.

On day two, go to the Tucson Museum of Art and Historic Block and Old Town Artisans in the morning. Afterward, you may want to wander over to the ornate Spanish-Moorish style Pima County Courthouse (on Church, between Alameda and Pennington), and then continue south on Church to Congress and east to Fifth Avenue, where you can get lunch at the hip Cup Café in the historic Hotel Congress. (If that looks like your scene, check out the Club Congress schedule and come back at night.) Alternatively, after looking at the Pima County Courthouse, you can eat at Café Poca Cosa, my favorite Mexican restaurant (take Church to Broadway, then head east 2½ blocks). Gallery hopping in this area or touring the Tucson Museum of Art is another possibility. Etherton Gallery and Barrio, which share the same building, make a good art-lunch combo. In the afternoon, drive to the San Xavier Mission and San Xavier Plaza. Who knows? You may be able to put in more swim time before dinner.

Three-day itinerary

For the first two days, follow the two-day itinerary. Start your third day at Sabino Canyon, catching the tram tour up, and taking a nice, easy walk down. Have lunch in one of the restaurants on Tanque Verde's restaurant row — maybe on the terrace of the Dakota Café. Interested in Western art? El Presidio gallery and Venture Fine Art are in this area. In the afternoon, head over to the University of Arizona Museums, where you can further your education in photography, history, ethnology, fine art, astronomy — or any combination thereof. After the museums, you can browse on nearby Fourth Avenue and then have dinner in one of the low-key restaurants there, or head for the restaurant strip on Campbell north of Grant. Don't worry if you haven't changed your clothes from the morning walk through Sabino Canyon (unless you're smelly from hiking — in which case go back to your hotel and shower immediately!). Casual is fine for any of the restaurants around here.

Shopping for Local Treasures

The shopping scene, which runs the gamut from Western kitsch-carrying thrift stores to sky's-the-limit native crafts boutiques, mirrors Tucson's ethnic and economic diversity. As in most western cities, mall-sprawl is more characteristic than eastern urban-style retail concentrations, but several good the-buck-drops-here enclaves do exist.

Tucson's malls tend to be open from 10 a.m. to 9 p.m. Monday through Saturday, from 11 a.m. or noon to 6 p.m. on Sunday, and with longer hours around the winter holidays. Many shops in other areas open at 8 or 9 a.m. and shut their doors at 6 p.m. Monday through Saturday, while others don't close until later. You can expect Sunday hours to be shorter (say, 11 a.m.–5 p.m.) or nonexistent.

Best shopping areas

Much of Tucson's retail is conducted in the strip malls along Speedway, Broadway, Grant, and Ina roads (east/west), and Oracle, Campbell, and Tanque Verde (north/south). Two of the best shopping stops, Tubac and Nogales, Mexico, lie just south of Tucson along I-19 (see Chapter 15).

Strolling Fourth Avenue

Fourth Avenue, between University Avenue and Ninth Street, is really Tucson's only shop 'n' stroll strip, with a few cafes to rev you up and

> **Music to downtown's ears**
>
> Opened in 1919 and still in the same family, the **Chicago Music Store,** 130 E. Congress St., at Sixth Avenue (☎ **520-622-3341;** `www.chicagomusic-musicland.com`), strikes the right note with nearly every musician who blows through Tucson. Johnny Cash, ZZ Top's Billy Gibbons, and Jackson Browne have all dropped in. The place claims the largest selection of new and used musical instruments and sheet music in the Southwest, and the building also has a great neon storefront.

some good bars to wind you down. Baby boomer alert: You may have flashbacks on this neo-hippie drag near the University of Arizona, lined with secondhand clothing stores and bead boutiques, along with some more upscale Southwestern wear shops and galleries.

Getting mall'd

The most popular shopping complex on the west side of town is the Tucson Mall, 4470 N. Oracle Rd. at Wetmore, Northwest (☎ 520-293-7330, ext. 4; www.tucsonmall.com), with more than 200 stores, including Dillard's, Macy's, Robinson-May, and Sears department stores; the Arizona Avenue section specializes in things Southwestern. On the east side, Tucson Mall gets a run for its money (or yours) from Park Place Mall, 5870 E. Broadway Blvd. at Wilmot, Central (☎ 520-748-1222; www.parkplacemall), a low-slung indoor-outdoor complex anchored by Dillard's, Macy's, Sears, and featuring plenty of upscale retailers; finding parking isn't always easy. Tucson's first enclosed shopping center, El Con, 3601 Broadway Blvd. at Dodge, Central (☎ 520-327-8767; www.elconmall.com), has been undergoing a major revitalization. The mall is still fairly low key, with Robinson-May, J.C. Penney, Home Depot, and Target as its main stores, but stay tuned. With luck, El Con will do as well as the Foothills Mall, 7401 North La Cholla at Ina, Northwest (☎ 520-219-0650; www.shopfoothillsmall.com), a once languishing collection of shops that was resuscitated by the addition of various upscale outlets (including Off-Saks Fifth Avenue) as well as a Barnes & Noble Superstore and several good refreshment stops.

Getting (boutique) mall'd

For the arty and upscale, try St. Philip's Plaza, 4280 N. Campbell Ave. at River, Central (☎ 520-529-2775; www.stphilipsplaza.com), which includes several galleries, a couple of high-end eateries, and plenty of stylish clothing stores. The plaza hosts a farmer's market every Sunday and, often, outdoor concerts. Plaza Palomino, 2970 N. Swan at Fort Lowell, Central (☎ 520-795-3516), is similarly decked out in neo-Spanish hacienda style and also has plenty of expensive galleries and home-furnishing and clothing boutiques. The latest arrival on the pseudo-village, semi-outdoor mall scene is La Encantada, 2905 E. Skyline Dr. at Campbell, Foothills (☎ 520-299-3556; http://laencantadashoppingcenter.westcor.com). Still a work in progress, this complex features familiar

Spiny souvenirs

You won't want to stuff any cacti in your suitcase, but you can get them shipped by **B&B Cactus Farms,** 11550 E. Speedway Blvd., 1.5 miles past Houghton Road, Eastside (**☎ 520-721-4687**), the town's top prickly plant connection. The farm is far out on the eastside, but the drive is beautiful and, if you're going to Saguaro National Park East or Colossal Cave, not out of the way.

names like Ann Taylor and Crate & Barrel as well as some Tucson originals, along with AJ's, a gourmet grocery, and several trendy restaurants.

What to look for and where to find it

As you may have guessed, things Southwest — everything from Western wear to Native American crafts — should top your Tucson shopping list. The good news: Although Tucson gets its fair share of tourists, this big city caters to local pocketbooks — which means you can often get better deals on Southwest goods here than you can in more high-rent towns like $cottsdale, $edona, or $anta Fe.

Art

The clarity of light, the beauty of the desert, and, no doubt, the relatively low cost of living have all made Tucson an artist magnet. If you want to invest in an as-yet undiscovered Picasso, Tucson may just be the place. On Thursday evenings from September through May, you can survey the downtown/Fourth Avenue scene by taking a free ArtWalk (Thurs Oct–May; call the Tucson Arts District Partnership [☎ 520-624-9977] for details). ArtLife Arizona, found in the lobbies of major hotels, resorts, and home decorating stores around town, covers the entire city, with an emphasis on the more established galleries. If you can't find a copy, phone the publisher at ☎ 520-797-1271.

Dinnerware, 210 N. 4th Ave. at 9th St., downtown (☎ 520-792-4503), veering strongly toward the avant-garde, is a good starting point for a budding art star search. Also downtown, Etherton, 135 S. Sixth Ave., a half block south of Broadway (☎ 520-624-7370), focuses on photography, historic as well as contemporary, although painting has a strong presence, too. Philabaum Glass Gallery, 4280 N. Campbell, Ste. 105, in St. Philip's Plaza (☎ 520-299-1939), and Philabaum Glass Gallery & Studios, 711S. 6th Ave., just south of downtown (☎ 520-884-7404), feature the work of world-renowned glass artist Tom Philabaum and other outstanding practitioners of the fragile art. Don't miss these galleries, even if you can't afford to buy anything. El Presidio, with branches at 3001 E. Skyline Dr. at Campbell, Foothills (☎ 520-299-1414), and at 7000 E. Tanque Verde Rd. #16 at Sabino Canyon Road, Central (☎ 520-733-0388), is a prime source for Western painting and bronze sculpture, as is the nearby Venture Fine Arts, 6541 E. Tanque Verde Rd. between, Kolb and Wilmot (☎ 520-298-2258), which also has a branch at 3001 E. Skyline Dr., Ste. 127 (☎ 520-298-2258). Medicine Man Gallery, 7000 E. Tanque Verde Rd. #7 (☎ 520-722-7798), specializes in Native American art; the adjacent Conley Museum of the West traces both cowboy and Indian traditions. Other galleries congregate at St. Philip's Plaza and Plaza Palamino (see the "Getting boutique mall'd" section earlier in this chapter for both); at Joesler Village, at River Road and Campbell Avenue (northwest corner); and at El Cortijo, at Skyline Boulevard and Campbell (northeast corner).

Clothing

If your tastes tend toward the colorful and flowing, Maya Palace, 6332 E. Broadway at Wilmot (☎ 520-748-0817) and in Plaza Palamino (☎ 520-325-6411), should suit you. Del Sol, 435 N. 4th Ave. at Sixth St., 4th Avenue/University of Arizona (☎ 520-628-8765), sells similarly attractive, loose-fitting clothing. (Just a coincidence that many of the styles have elastic waists and this is a city where large quantities of Mexican food are consumed? I think not.) Sorry, guys, women only for both stores — see the "Western wear" section later in this chapter for men's fashions.

Gems and minerals

Tucson's obsession with underground stuff, which comes to a head at the huge annual Gem and Mineral Show (see Chapter 3), manifests year 'round at such shops at the Discount Agate House, 3401 N. Dodge Blvd. (☎ 520-323-0781), a one-stop rock shopping center, where you can buy everything from semi-precious stones to coprolites (that's solidified dinosaur poop). At Enchanted Earthworks, 2980 N. Swan Rd. in Plaza Palomino (☎ 520-327-7007), the stones and crystals — many of the metaphysical sort — come already set in jewelry and sculptures. If you want to make a major rock statement, go to Zee's Gallery, 1 E. Toole Ave., downtown (☎ 520-624-2081; in summer, by appointment only at ☎ 520-294-9316), which specializes in the large and exotic — say, a triptych of fish fossils embedded in slabs of slate from an ancient sea bed.

Native American and Mexican crafts

Tucson is a prime gathering ground for Native American crafts, including Navajo rugs, Hopi katsinas, Zuni fetishes, and Tohono O'odham baskets, and for artistic items from neighboring Mexico (see Chapter 19 for explanations of these crafts). Anglo crafters in the Southwest tend to be influenced by both Indian and Mexican designs. Expect to find many interesting interpretations thereof in creative Tucson galleries like Pink Adobe, 6538 E. Tanque Verde Rd., #160, Central (☎ 520-298-5995). Picante, 2932 E. Broadway, Central (☎ 520-320-5699), is chock-a-block with whimsical, colorful items from Mexico. At Dry Heat Trading Co., 532 N. 4th Ave., University/4th Ave. (☎ 520-670-1700), work by local artists mingle with south-of-the-border imports. Bahti Indian Arts, 4300 N. Campbell in St. Philip's Plaza (☎ 520-577-0290), is a great place to buy — and find out about — Navajo rugs and other traditional crafts. Owner Mark Bahti has been a trader for a long time and is the author of several books on the Southwest. The Kaibab Courtyard Shops, 2837–41 N. Campbell Ave. just north of Glenn, Central (☎ 520-795-6905), which have been around since the 1940s, offer a wide-ranging, high-quality selection of Native American and Mexican crafts. For fine Native American jewelry, don't miss Desert Son, 4759 E. Sunrise Dr., Foothills (☎ 520-299-0818).

Decorator fever: The other South Park

South Park Avenue between 12th and 13th streets in South Tucson, known as "The Lost Barrio," boasts a row of stores specializing in ethnic home decoration and furnishings. At **¡Aquí Está!**, 204 S. Park Ave. (☎ **520-798-3605**), you can buy the Mexican goods ready made or tailor the tile work, fabrics, and woodwork to your tastes. **Rústica,** 200 S. Park Ave. (☎ 520-623-4435), also goes beyond the border for its vibrantly colored wares. Prices at both stores are probably the best you find north of Nogales — and you don't have to bargain here. **Dante Fraboni Studios,** 299 S. Park Ave. (☎ **520-624-61612**), can help you fill those empty spots in your garden with weird and wonderful metal sculptures.

If you head south on Park Avenue from central Tucson, you get stuck in the middle of the University of Arizona campus; instead, take Euclid Avenue south to 12th street (one block beyond Broadway) and go left two blocks.

The two gift shops at Tohono Chul Park (see the "More cool things to see and do" section earlier in this chapter) sell an outstanding array of contemporary Mexican and Southwestern crafts at very reasonable prices (If you're traveling with kids, I dare you to try to leave without buying a stuffed javalina or other cool Southwest nature toy.) A little on the pricier side but of consistently high quality, the shops at Old Town Artisans, 201 N. Court at Alameda, in downtown's El Presidio Historic District (☎ 520-623-6024), sells the works of some 100 regional crafters as well as Latin American imports.

Western wear

Rarin' to dress Western? Take it from the top with Arizona Hatters, 3600 N. First Ave. at Prince, Central (☎ 520-292-1320), with a huge selection of wrangler headgear, both ready-to-ride and customized. Corral West, 4525 E. Broadway between Swan and Columbus, Central (☎ 520-322-6001), which first opened its doors in 1945, carries everything the style-conscious cowboy or girl could want, from tight-fitting jeans and gaudily embroidered shirts to spur-stud earrings. The goods at Western Warehouse aren't quite as exciting, but the selection is huge and you're bound to find a branch near you (check `http://westernwarehouse.com`. Central Tucson stores are located on 3030 E. Speedway Blvd. at Country Club (☎ 520-327-8005); 3719 N. Oracle Rd., one block north of Prince (☎ 520-293-1808); and 6701 E. Broadway Blvd. between Wilmot and Kolb (☎ 520-885-4385). Corral and Western Warehouse both carry footwear, but if you're not a perfectionist, head for Stewart Boot Mfg. Co., 30 W. 28th St. between S. Sixth and Seventh streets, South Tucson (☎ 520-622-2706); only you and your pocketbook will know your boots are slightly flawed.

Living It Up after Dark

You probably didn't come to Tucson to attend the opera, but if you get a diva urge, you can indulge it here. In fact, this former desert outpost is one of only 14 U.S. cities that has opera, symphony, theater, and ballet companies (okay, it shares a couple of them with Phoenix). As for its low places . . . well, Tucson doesn't exactly rock after dark, but you can find some decent spots to hit when the sun sets.

Consult the Arizona Daily Star's "Caliente" section, published with the paper on Friday, for arts events (you can find the section on line at `www.azstarnet.com/caliente`). The paper also has club listings, but the free Tucson Weekly (`www.tucsonweekly.com`), distributed Thursday, is better in that department.

Nightlife

Although most major music acts that tour this part of the Southwest tend to bypass Tucson for Phoenix or Las Vegas, the city sometimes draws top-notch Country and Western talent to the Tucson Convention Center (see "The Arts" section later in this section) or, occasionally, to the Pima County Fairgrounds, 11300 S. Houghton Rd., east of town (☎ 520-792-3930; `www.swfair.com/concerts`). Tex-Mex-inspired tejano and Tohono O'odham waila ("chicken scratch") bands also turn up in the Old Pueblo, and the annual Tucson International Mariachi Conference (see Chapter 3) often gets hometown girl Linda Ronstadt up on stage in April. Major retro performers — everyone from the Temptations to Cyndi Lauper — perform at the Desert Diamond Casino, 1100 W. Pima Mine Rd., Exit 80 of I-19, about 10 miles south of Tucson (☎ 886-DDC-WINS or 520-294-7777; `www.desertdiamond.com`), run by the Tohono O'odham tribe.

In summer, a free concert series in the casino's courtyard is designed to lure locals down to the slot machines. The Marshall Tucker Band was among those who turned up in 2004.

Up-and-coming indie bands regularly mosey down to Tucson, usually stopping first at Club Congress, 311 E. Congress at Fifth Avenue, Hotel Congress (☎ 520-622-8848; `www.hotelcongress.com`). The alternative alternative venue is the Rialto Theatre, 318 E. Congress St. between South Fourth and Fifth streets (☎ 520-740-0126; `www.rialtotheatre.com`), which also presents good mid-range pop, jazz, Latin, and blues acts.

Unlike in many cities, Tucson's clubs aren't all age segregated. Sure, college hangouts exist, but many venues get a surprising inter-generational mix. Bars close at 2:30 a.m. (last call is usually at 2 p.m.), and covers for music typically range from nonexistent to about $5.

Bars

Good bars are interspersed around Tucson, but downtown stands out for its local color, the Foothills for its views.

The colorful ¡Toma!, 311 N. Court Ave. at Franklin (☎ 520-622-1922), joined at the hip with El Charro Mexican restaurant (see the "Dining Out" section), has the best margarita list in town and, possibly, the liveliest crowd. An artsy downtown crowd likes Vaudeville, 110 E. Congress St. at Scott (☎ 520-622-3535), for its laid-back atmosphere and live cabaret. Near the Convention Center, Cushing Street Café and Bar, 198 W. Cushing St. (☎ 520-622-7984), has a historic building, as well as good food, going for it.

Blues, rock, and reggae

Berky's, 5769 E. Speedway Blvd., between Craycroft and Wilmot, Central (☎ 520-296-1981) lays on live R&B, blues, or retro rock nightly. The large Chianti bottle that lets you know you've arrived at The Boondocks, 3306 N. First Ave. just north of Fort Lowell, Central (☎ 520-690-0991), may be fake, but the blues are for real. The Chicago Bar, 5954 E. Speedway Blvd. between Craycroft and Wilmot, Central (☎ 520-748-8169), has eclectic tastes (er, sounds), but you can expect whatever bands are brought in to rock. On the Fourth Avenue entertainment strip near the University of Arizona, Plush, 340 E. Sixth St. (☎ 520-798-1302), draw collegiate rockers of the hipster variety. (See also the Nimbus Brewing Co. in the "Microbreweries" section later in this chapter.)

Country & Western

The two major venues to listen to country music in central Tucson are the Cactus Moon Cafe, 5470 E. Broadway Blvd. at Craycroft (☎ 520-748-0049), where the crowd gets younger (and hipper) as the night wears on; and Maverick: King of Clubs, 6622 E. Tanque Verde Rd. near Pima (☎ 520-298-0430), with live sounds on the weekends. You have to travel a ways north to get to the Lariat Steakhouse & Saloon, 16666 N. Oracle Rd., Catalina (☎ 520-825-9907), but the trip is worth it for the historic venue — this is the oldest continuously operating country western club in the Tucson area — and the twangy house band.

Dance

Spice it up with salsa at El Parador Restaurant & Cantina, 2744 E. Broadway Blvd., between Tucson Boulevard and Country Club, Central (☎ 520-881-2808), or Irene's Peruvian Restaurant, 254 E. Congress St., between Fifth and Sixth avenues, Downtown (☎ 520-206-9385), featuring tango on Thursday nights, salsa-meringue on Saturdays. Heart-Five, 61 E. Congress St., downtown (☎ 520-903-0911), varies the sounds you can shuffle to, from progressive and techno-house to hip hop and funk. Club Miami at The Keys, 445 W. Wetmore Rd. at Oracle, Northwest (☎ 520-888-8084), lays on techno and top 40 tracks. Two of Tucson's top dance clubs, Ain't Nobody's Bizness, 2900 E. Broadway Blvd. at N.

Some lofty perches

You can catch the sun dipping down beyond the horizon at **The Flying V Bar and Grill,** Loew's Ventana Canyon Resort, 7000 N. Resort Dr. (☎ **520-299-2020**). Sip champagne while watching the rays turn pretty colors at **Soleil,** 2001 E. Sunrise Dr. at Campbell (☎ **520-299-3345**), which boasts a variety of bubbly cocktails. Its name lays no false claims: **The Lookout Lounge,** Westward Look Resort, 245 W. Ina Rd. west of First Avenue (☎ **520-297-1151**), has forever views of the sunset and the city lights. And you can't get much mellower than seeing the clouds turn pink and purple against the Santa Catalinas while quaffing a cocktail at **The Desert Garden Lounge,** Westin La Paloma, 3800 E. Sunrise between Campbell and First Avenue (☎ **520-742-6000**).

Stewart Ave., Central (☎ 520-318-4838), and It's About Time, 616 N. Fourth Ave., near the UA (☎ 520-882-3053), cater to gays and nonhomophobes who like to let loose. If you're a line-dancing fool, see also the Country and Western clubs in the preceding section; all have the requisite slippery floors, and all offer lessons.

Jazz and Latin

The lounge at the Arizona Inn, 2200 E. Elm St. between Campbell and Tucson Boulevard (☎ 520-325-1541), is the genuine item when it comes to cool piano riffs, and why not — the place dates back almost to the Jazz Age. Old Pueblo Grille, 60 N. Alvernon just north of Broadway (☎ 520-326-6000), alternates its nightly live music between the backroom and the patio, depending on the weather. Kingfisher and McMahon's Prime Steakhouse (see the "Dining Out" section for both) accompany their food with live jazz, generally on Thursdays, Fridays, or Saturdays. The Tucson Jazz Society (☎ 520-903-1265; `www.tucsonjazz.org`) has details.

Microbreweries

Nimbus Brewing Co., 3850 E. 44th St. at Palo Verde, South Tucson (☎ 520-745-9175), is the hippest place for hops, a funky warehouse with terrific home-brews and live music Thursday to Saturday. If you like Belgian-style white beer, Nimbus is the place (I don't, but I can vouch for the pale ale). The shining vats at Thunder Canyon Brewery, Ina and La Cholla, at the Foothills Mall, Northwest (☎ 520-797-2652), produce some mean ales and lagers; the place always bustles but especially on prime movie nights (it's near the mall multiplex).

The arts

Seek high culture in Tucson everywhere from the convention center to the University of Arizona.

Top arts venues

Most of the major companies perform at the Tucson Convention Center Music Hall, 260 S. Church Ave. at Cushing Street, Downtown (☎ 520-791-4101; www.cityoftucson.org/tcc). Centennial Hall, University of Arizona campus at University Boulevard and Park Avenue (☎ 520-621-3341), hosts the hard-to-typecast but always top-rate UApresents series (see http://uapresents.arizona.edu for a schedule). The 2004-2005 season included the Paul Taylor Dance Company, Hairspray, the Kronos Quartet, Laurie Anderson, The Moscow Philharmonic Orchestra, Ladysmith Black Mambazo, and plenty of other international talent (now if only the hall's acoustics were better . . .). Tickets range from $14–$62. When box offices are closed, you can get tickets for the more mainstream performances through Ticketmaster (☎ 520-321-1000); tickets for UApresents events are also available online.

Classical music

Tuning up successfully since 1929, the Tucson Symphony Orchestra (☎ 520-882-8585; www.tucsonsymphony.org) divides its time between the Tucson Convention Center Music Hall and the Pima Community College Center for the Arts, 2202 W. Anklam Rd., Westside (☎ 520-206-6988). Tickets range from $7 (student rush) to $35. You can get your aria fix with The Arizona Opera Company (☎ 520-293-4336; www.azopera.com) at the Tucson Convention Center Music Hall between November and March — when it's not in Phoenix. Tickets run from $25 to $90.

Dance

When Ballet Arizona (☎ 888-322-5538; www.balletaz.org) isn't pliéing or pas de deuxing in Phoenix, it's toeing the line at the Music Hall in the Tucson Convention Center (tickets from $11–$61, ages 12 and under half-price, 10% senior discount). For more contemporary movement, try OTO-Dance, 121 E 7th St at N. 7th Ave., Downtown (☎ 520-624-3799; www.orts.org). Tickets range from $8 to $14.

The great (arty) outdoors

Don't want to be an art shut-in? The **Tucson Parks and Recreation Department** airs out an excellent (free!) cultural program most weekends from late February through late June. The Tucson Pops Orchestra and OTO-Dance put in regular appearances at the De Meester Outdoor Performance Center in Reid Park, Country Club Road and East 22nd Street. The season ends with a weekend of Shakespeare under the stars. The Arizona Symphonic Winds breeze over to Morris K. Udall Park, at Tanque Verde and Sabino Canyon roads. Check the newspaper entertainment listings sections for details. The **Tucson Jazz Society** (☎ **520-903-1265;** www.tucsonjazz.org) often takes its cool sounds outside, too, most regularly to St. Phillips Plaza, at Campbell Avenue and River Road.

Theater

A class act, Arizona Theatre Company (☎ 520-622-2823; www.aztheatre.com) struts its stuff — everything from Shakespeare to Gilbert & Sullivan and avante garde playwrights — at downtown's Temple of Music and Art, 330 S. Scott Ave. at Broadway (☎ 520-622-2823). When you're not focused on the stage of the gorgeously restored Spanish Colonial/Moorish theater, browse the theatrical arts shop and the upstairs art gallery. Tickets run from $26 to $48. For less traditional — and often less expensive ($16 and up) — fare, try the Invisible Theatre, 1400 N. First Ave. at Drachman, Central (☎ 520-882-9721; www.invisibletheatre.com).

Cheer the heroes and boo the bad guys at the Gaslight Theatre, 7010 E. Broadway, just west of Kolb (☎ 520-886-9428), equally popular with kids and adults who need to blow off steam. Ticket prices ($15.95 for adults; $13.95 for seniors over 60, students, and military; and $6.95 for ages 12 and under) include free popcorn, but pizza, wine, beer, and soft drinks cost extra.

Fast Facts: Tucson

Area Code

Tucson's area code is **520.**

Doctors

Check your health insurance carrier before you leave for recommended — and covered — doctors in town, or check with the front desk or concierge at your hotel.

Emergencies

Call ☎ **911** for fire, police, or ambulance.

Hospitals

Options include Tucson Medical Center, 5301 E. Grant Rd. at Craycroft, Central (☎ **520-327-5461**), and University Medical Center, 1501 N. Campbell Ave. at Elm, Central (☎ **520-694-0111**), known for its advanced heart and cancer research.

Information

Contact the Metropolitan Tucson Convention and Visitors Bureau (☎ **800-638-8350;** www.visittucson.org).

Internet Access

You can retrieve your e-mail at Kinko's for $12 an hour or 20¢ a minute. The most centrally located of the four Tucson locations is at 2607 E. Speedway at Tucson Boulevard, Central (☎ **520-795-7796**).

Maps

The Gousha map of Tucson, available in every convenience store, supermarket, or gas station, does just fine. For more map options, visit Tucson Map & Flag Center, 3239 N. First Ave., just north of Ft. Lowell, Central (☎ **520-887-4234**), tops in Mexico and Southwest cartography.

Newspapers/Magazines

The *Arizona Daily Star* is the morning bringer of tidings; the *Tucson Citizen* comes out Monday through Saturday afternoons (on Sunday, the ad-stuffed *Star* is the only game in town). The *Star*'s Friday entertainment supplement, *Caliente,* has an "Outside" section that details hikes and other fresh-air activities along with arts and nightlife listings. The free, alternative *Tucson Weekly,* which turns up in supermarkets, bookstores, and various publication racks around town on Thursday, has the best club listings. The glossy *Tucson Guide Quarterly,* found on newsstands and, often, in hotel rooms, has useful tourist-oriented listings, as well as articles of local interest (sometimes written by yours truly).

Pharmacies

Several Walgreens (☎ **800-925-4733**) and Osco (☎ **888-443-5701**) drugstores operate 24-hour pharmacies. Type in your hotel's Zip Code when you phone and get the location nearest to you.

Police

Call ☎ **911** for emergencies; the non-emergency number is ☎ 520-791-4452.

Post Office

Call ☎ **800-275-8777** and select option 6 to punch in the Zip Code of the are in which you're staying to locate the post office nearest you. The main post office is at 1501 S. Cherry near Kino Parkway.

Restrooms

Sorry. You find public restrooms only in parks and malls. Alternatively, your best bet is to duck into a hotel or restaurant; I've never been turned down yet when I've asked to use the facilities.

Safety

For a large metropolitan area, Tucson is relatively safe. Most of the crime involves car theft rather than mugging. Be careful in large, poorly lit parking lots after dark. When leaving a movie theater or a mall late at night, know where your car is and have your keys ready so you're not wandering around, looking clueless. Strolling around downtown after attending a theater or other arts performance isn't a good idea; unfortunately, the streets are usually fairly empty after dark.

Smoking

Although Tucson imposed a full ban on restaurant smoking in 1999, the confusing laws are still being contested but, in a nutshell, smoking is allowed in bars and, if a restaurant gets more than 50% of its revenue from alcohol, it can be classified as one. In addition, smoking is permitted on restaurant terraces, if they're far enough from the restaurant's interior.

Taxes

The sales tax in Tucson is 7.6%; hotels add 11.5% to your tab, plus $1 per room per night. The car rental excises are 12.6% if you pick up your car in the city. If you get it from a counter in the airport — as most people do — the tax is 10.6% plus an 11.1% concession fee, for a whopping total of 21.7%. An additional $7 per car rental is added on wherever you get your wheels ($3.50 goes to the county, $3.50 to repaying whatever weird bonds the city has levied).

Taxis

A few of the more reliable cab companies include Allstate (☎ **520-798-1111**) and Yellow Cab (☎ **520-624-6611**). The drivers of Fiesta Taxi (☎ **520-622-7777**) speak both English and Spanish.

Time Zone

Tucson is in the mountain time zone. The state doesn't observe daylight saving time.

Transit Info

Call ☎ **520-792-9222** or log on to `www.suntran.com`.

Weather Updates

Call ☎ **520-881-3333** or go online to `www.noaa.gov/Tucson`.

Chapter 14

Going Beyond Tucson: Two Day-Trips

In This Chapter

- Checking out the cacti in Organ Pipe Cactus National Monument
- Getting celestial at Kitt Peak National Observatory
- Exploring under the dome of Biosphere 2

This chapter's day-trips from Tucson take you to some otherworldly places, from Organ Pipe Cactus National Monument, with its array of strange, multiarmed cacti; to Kitt Peak National Observatory, where peering at different galaxies is on the nightly agenda; to Biosphere 2, originally conceived as an experiment in living away from Earth. Many of the attractions in southeastern Arizona — particularly the sights along I-19 — also make fun side trips. However, that area has so many activities to offer that I devote an entire chapter to it (see Chapter 15).

Day-Trip #1: West to Organ Pipe Cactus National Monument

On this trip, reach for the stars — but not for the cacti. This excursion takes you through some of the most pristine stretches of Arizona desert, much of it belonging to the Tohono O'odham (pronounced tuh-ho-noh ah-ah-tem) people. Kitt Peak National Observatory and Organ Pipe Cactus National Monument are the high points of this trip (Kitt Peak, literally), but the old mining town of Ajo, near Organ Pipe, has a certain appeal, too. You can easily visit Kitt Peak and return to Tucson the same day. In fact, Mission San Xavier del Bac (see Chapter 13) is en route, so you can tour both (and I highly recommend a stop at the mission). But if you want to go all the way to Organ Pipe, staying overnight in Ajo is best. You won't want to rush through this serene, laid-back part of the state. Relax and enjoy the scenery.

Getting there

To reach Kitt Peak, take I-10 to I-19 south, and then get on Highway 86 (Ajo Way) west for 40 miles to Highway 386, where signs lead you to the 12 winding miles up to the observatory. To continue on to Ajo, return to Highway 86 and keep driving west to the junction of Highway 85 at Why. From here you can either go north on Highway 85 to Ajo or south on Highway 85 to Organ Pipe Cactus National Monument.

Seeing the sights

As you head west from an ugly industrial section on Tucson's south side, vacant lots, warehouses, and fast-food strips begin to give way to hills and open desert. You know you're approaching the eastern border of the Tohono O'odham reservation when you see a mountain dotted with white bumps (the observatories). Nearby, you see a striking thumb-shaped peak, called Baboquiviri (baa-buh-key-vuh-ree), which is sacred to the Tohono O'odhams. It is from this tribe that the astronomers lease their 200 lofty acres.

Funded by the National Science Foundation and representing eight major astronomical institutions, ❹ Kitt Peak National Observatory (☎ 520-318-8726; www.noao.edu/kpno; open: daily 9 a.m.– 3:45 p.m., closed Thanksgiving, Christmas, and New Year's Day; admission: $2 donation requested) has the world's greatest concentration of optical telescopes, including the world's largest solar telescope. No, you can't peer through them — in fact, computers do most of the observing for the scientists. However, the drive to the top of the 6,882-foot mountain and the low-cost guided tours (see the following section) make this destination a great place to visit during the day. In addition, the nighttime dinner and astronomy program, which must be booked in advance (see the "Dining locally" section for this day-trip), is really out of this world.

The Kitt Peak gift shop carries books, T-shirts, toys, and a selection of Tohono O'odham arts and crafts, especially hand-woven baskets. They're pricey, but remember, these baskets take a long time to create. (For more on these baskets, go to Chapter 19.) Bring a picnic; you won't find food concessions on the mountain, and the picnic tables offer wonderful views.

Some 10 miles northwest of Why, Ajo owes its growth to copper — as you can see when you pass the mountains of tailings (rock waste from mining) on your way in. Strolling the palm-lined Spanish Colonial Revival town square, laid out in 1917, is pretty much what there is to do after you visit the small ❶ Ajo Historical Society Museum, 160 Mission St. (☎ 520-387-5698). You can also drive up to the ❶ New Cornelia Mine lookout, at the end of Indian Village Road, and gaze at the gaping pit that once produced the town's wealth. For details on both sites — which are closed during the summer — stop in at the Ajo District Chamber of Commerce, 400 Taladro St. (just south of the Plaza; ☎ 520-387-7742; www.ajoinaz.com; open: mid-Sept to mid-July Mon – Fri 9 a.m.–5 p.m.;

Side Trips from Tucson

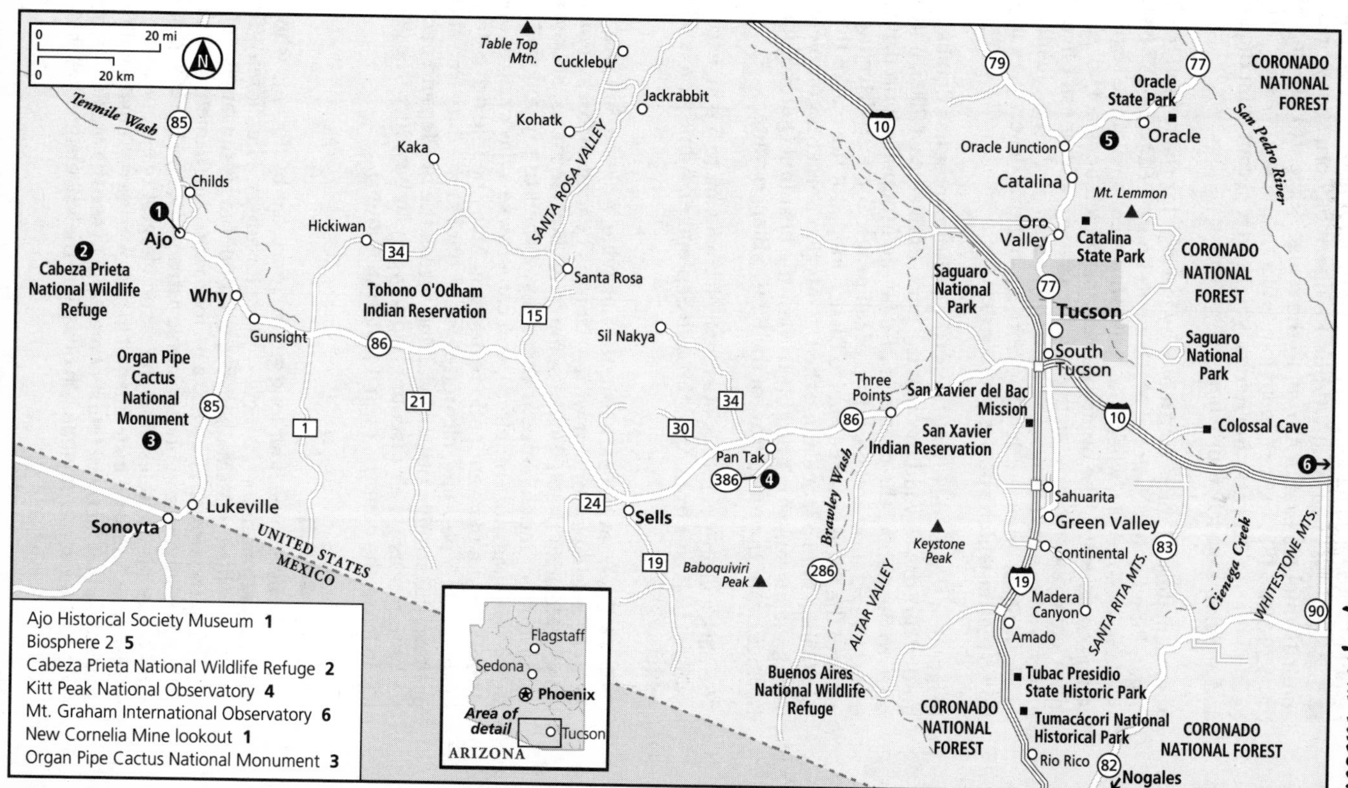

rest of the year 8:30 a.m.–12:30 p.m.) To find out about the 860,000-acre ❷ Cabeza Prieta National Wildlife Refuge, a bighorn sheep preserve about 10 minutes east of Ajo, go to the refuge office, 1611 N. 2nd Ave. (☎ 520-387-6483; `http://southwest.fws.gov/refuges/arizona/cabeza.html`). To enter the refuge, you need a permit from the office and a high-clearance, four-wheel-drive vehicle.

Approximately 24 miles south of Why is a sign for the turnoff to ❸ Organ Pipe Cactus National Monument, Route 1 (☎ 520-387-6849; `www.nps.gov/orpi`), where the multiarmed cousins of the saguaro cactus congregate. The organ pipe cactus, which does sort of resemble a pipe organ, doesn't grow as high as the saguaro and doesn't live as long. In fact, you see more saguaros here than organ pipes (and lusher stands of organ pipes grow south of the border), but this desert park is beautiful no matter which species proliferates.

In addition to several hiking trails (the visitor center has details), two graded dirt drives wind through the park. Until at least 2006, only one is open to the public: the dramatic 21-mile Ajo Mountain loop drive, with its lush vegetation and backdrop of tall peaks. You may drive the first five miles of the flatter 53-mile Puerto Blanco loop, but the rest of the drive is off limits until a fence along the U.S./Mexico border is completed — which means you won't be able to view the beautiful Quitobaquito Springs oasis, the main draw of the Puerto Blanco route.

The park's visitor center is open daily from 8 a.m. to 5 p.m. except on national holidays from April through September. Admission is $5 per vehicle.

Only 5 miles from the park exit, the Lukeville, Arizona/Sonoyta, Mexico border crossing is popular with Arizonans headed to Rocky Point, the closest Mexican beach. Unlike some other border towns, Sonoyta isn't seedy, but not much happens there. If you want to say you visited Mexico (no passport required), you can browse a few curio shops and sit outside at a pleasant patio restaurant. Many people drive down to Lukeville, buy perfume, cigarettes, or alcohol in the duty-free shop, and perform the strange ritual of walking across the border and back in order to retrieve their discount booty (you can buy duty-free goods only if you leave the country, even if just for a minute).

Taking a tour

Kitt Peak offers three hour-long guided tours, led by docents who are often amateur astronomers ($2 requested fee for adults, $1 children). The 10 a.m. tour visits the McMath-Pierce solar telescope, the largest telescope of its kind in the world. The 11:30 a.m. tour visits the (nameless) 2.1-meter telescope, a pioneer in photographic astronomy; and the 1:30 p.m. visits the 4-meter Mayall telescope, the second largest telescope in the world when it was built and instrumental in discovering dark matter. If you can't stay around for all three tours, come early to see the McMath, which collects data in the daytime. On occasion, the scientists allow visitors to observe them in their activities. Kitt Peak also offers a dinner program; see the "Dining locally" section for this day-trip for details.

Most of the tours of Organ Pipe Cactus National Monument are self-guided, but from late December through mid-April, the park rangers lead walks to points of interest. Schedules are posted daily at the visitor center.

Staying in style

Ajo has several modest motels. I've stayed at La Siesta Motel & RV Resort ($), 2561 N. Hwy. 85 (☎ 520-387-6569), which offers a pool, hot tub, and nice, clean rooms. I've also spent the night at the very pleasant Guest House Inn ($), 700 Guest House Rd. (☎ 520-387-6133; www.guesthouseinn.biz), built in 1925 to accommodate Phelps Dodge bigwigs. This friendly B&B offers attractive Arizona-city-themed rooms and generous morning meals.

If you're astronomically inclined, consider bunking on Kitt Peak. Book the Advanced Observing Program ($350 per night for one or two people, plus $55 per person for room and board), and you can gaze at the stars until the cows come home (okay, until it gets light) with your own personal astroguide, and then flop down in a dorm room. For details, see www.noao.edu/outreach/nop/advanced/info.html or phone ☎ 520-318-8726.

Dining locally

The food at Kitt Peak's nighttime program — a cold box dinner, with a deli sandwich, chips, and cookies — is just okay, but you're there for the astronomy, not the gastronomy. During the evening, you get lessons on how to use a planisphere (a flat map of a sphere), find heavenly bodies with binoculars, and peer through a 16-inch or 20-inch telescope. Programs, which start an hour to 75 minutes before sunset (you'll be told what time to arrive when you make a reservation) and last about 3½ hours, are offered nightly, except from mid-July through August. They are restricted to 34 participants and are very popular. To make a reservation, call ☎ 520-318-8726 as far in advance as possible; from November through April, call at least a month in advance, maybe longer. Costs are $36 for adults and $31 for seniors over 55, students (elementary to college), and military with current ID.

If you attend Kitt Peak's dinner program, not only do you drive down a winding, mountain road at night but, for the first ¾ of a mile or so, you are allowed to use only parking lights (so as not to interfere with the telescopes). Still, you follow a guide car so you aren't completely in the dark, and the road is wide and fully paved.

If you visit Kitt Peak in the daytime, you can buy picnic fixings at Basha's supermarket, Topawa Road (signs on Hwy 86 direct you here; ☎ 520-383-2800), in the main shopping center of Sells, the Tohono O'odham reservation's tribal capital.

Ajo isn't fine-dining terrain, but several casual options are available. My two top picks in town are both Mexican (hey, why not take advantage of being this close to the border?). I can personally recommend the combination plates dished up at Señor Sancho ($), 663 N. 2nd Ave. (☎ 520-387-6226). Locals also pile into Marcela's Café & Bakery ($), 1117 W Dorsey St. (at 2nd Ave.; ☎ 520-387-4139), which serves not only pastry but such dishes as chicken mole. Both offer a small selection of typical American fare, too.

Day-Trip #2: North to Biosphere 2

Visiting Biosphere 2 takes up a good chunk of the day, but you may want to squeeze in a stop at Catalina State Park, which is en route. You walk a good bit at Biosphere 2, so you probably don't want to go for a long trek at the state park. To save your energy, you can contact Pusch Ridge Stables (see Chapter 13) to get a friendly equine to take you around.

Getting there

Oracle Road, one of Tucson's main north-south streets, turns into Highway 77, north of town. Stay on the road's right fork at Oracle Junction and just keep heading north. You'll see signs for Biosphere 2 at mile marker 96.5, about 45 minutes from central Tucson.

Seeing the sights

5 Biosphere 2, 32540 S. Biosphere Rd. (☎ 520-838-6200; www.bio2.com), isn't featured in the news as it was in the early 1990s, when eight people of opposite genders holed up together for two years in the desert terrarium in a controversial experiment in self-contained (potentially extraterrestrial) living. Nor does it have the scientific credentials it garnered in 1995, when Columbia University took over Biosphere 2's management. Citing funding problems, the university bailed in 2003.

But Biosphere 2 is still a tourist lure, if only because of the attention it got in the past; in the mid-1990s, it was even the subject of a terrible movie, Biodome, starring Pauly Shore. And now, without scientific experimentation (real or bogus) to interfere, you get virtually unlimited access to areas that were previously sealed off to the public.

Guided tours, included in the admission price and lasting approximately an hour and a half, start out at the visitor center, where you see an introductory film. Then you walk around the big glass dome and into the famed peek-through apartments where the Biosphere 2 "crew" used to live. Next, you enter through the Biosphere's massive airlock door to view the savanna that overlooks the Biosphere's ocean (sorry, no swimming allowed) and peer at three other biomes, as the ecological units are known. The tour ends with a descent through a 200-foot-long tunnel to the Biosphere's huge "lung," which was created to control the air pressure inside the facility when it was sealed, and finally, a peek at the ocean from another perspective.

You can also walk around the facility on your own, but you miss the Biosphere 2 gossip, er, information if you do.

The visitor center is open daily from 9 a.m. to 4 p.m. except Thanksgiving and Christmas. Guided tours are offered at 9:45 a.m., 10:45 a.m., 11:30 a.m., 12:15 p.m., 1 p.m., 1:45 p.m. and 2:30 p.m. (a tour also departs at 3:30 p.m. but if you take that one, you won't be able to explore the grounds on your own afterward). Admission is $19.95 for adults, $12.95 for ages 6–12, free for children 5 and under; 10% senior, AAA, and military discounts available with valid ID.

Taking a tour

The tour offered at Biosphere 2 is described in the previous section, but if you don't have wheels, you can let Great Western Tours (☎ 520-572-1660; www.gwtours.net) transport you there for $85; the price includes admission to Biosphere.

Stargazing in southern Arizona

Southern Arizona is heaven for anyone with even the slightest interest in astronomy. In addition to Kitt Peak (detailed in the "Day-Trip #1: West to Organ Pipe Cactus National Monument" section earlier this chapter), star geeks also find bliss at the University of Arizona's Flandrau Science Center and Steward Observatory Mirror Laboratory (both in Chapter 13), the Fred Whipple Observatory on Mt. Hopkins and the Skywatcher's Inn (both in Chapter 15), and the UA's astronomy camps (see Chapter 9).

But there's more. If you're a dedicated astro-tourist, also visit ❻ **Mt. Graham International Observatory,** perched on a 10,477-foot peak some 75 miles northeast of Tucson. The observatory hosts some of the world's newest and most advanced telescopes, including the Large Binocular Telescope, a joint project of observatories in Italy, Germany, and the United States. Most Saturdays from mid-April to mid-November (when snow is unlikely to close the roads), the observatory runs daylong tours (9:30 a.m.–4:30 p.m.). The price, $40, includes a sack lunch and admission to the fun, interactive science center at **Discovery Park (☎ 520-428-6260;** www.discoverypark.com), which is also the departure point for the tours. You can listen to noises from outer space, watch lightning strike Earth, or (for an extra charge) take a virtual tour of the solar system on a high-tech flight simulator. But the biggest draw is one of the most low-tech: gazing at the night sky through a 20-inch reflecting telescope. Attendance on the Mt. Graham tours is limited to 15, and you need to reserve in advance. Get information about other activities to do in the area from the **Graham County Chamber of Commerce,** 1111 West Thatcher Blvd. (Hwy. 70), Safford (**☎ 888-837-1841;** www.graham-chamber.com), or find out more about Mount Graham International Observatory's out-of-this-world scientific projects at the Web site http://mgpc3.as.arizona.edu.

Staying in style

Biosphere 2 is only 20 minutes from Tucson and such northern resorts as the Hilton Tucson El Conquistador (see Chapter 13, so staying near the site isn't really necessary. However, spending a night in the area is a great way to experience the desert's serenity. The nearby C.O.D Ranch ($$), outside of Oracle (☎ 800-868-5617 or 520-615-3211 in Tucson; `www.codranch.com`), offers rooms with character and plenty of Old West–style diversions.

Dining locally

You find only a snack shop on the Biosphere 2 premises. On the way to Biosphere 2, Cibaria ($$), 12935 N. Oracle, at Rancho Vistoso Boulevard (in the Abco/Walgreen's shopping center; ☎ 520-825-2900), features fine light northern Italian cuisine. Stop in for lunch or plan on a terrace dinner, when you can watch the sun turn the Santa Catalina Mountains a deep pink. For a more typically Western experience, try the Lariat Steakhouse & Saloon ($$), 16666 N. Oracle Rd., Catalina (☎ 520-825-9907), where you can work off a plate of deliciously messy ribs with some Country and Western dancing (if you go at lunch time, you'll have to depend on the Biosphere 2 tour for post-rib exercise).

Part IV
Exploring the Regions

"I think we should arrange to be there for Garlic-Anchovy-Chili Bean Week, and then shoot over to the Breathmint-Antacid Festival."

In this part . . .

Ladies and gentlemen, start your engines: You're going on a major road trip. This part takes you here, there, and (almost) everywhere in Arizona, from the little cowboy towns of the south to the great — okay, grand — canyons of the north. Please, don't forget to buckle your seat belts.

Chapter 15

Southeast Arizona

In This Chapter

- Meandering along the Santa Cruz River and dipping into Mexico
- Discovering the grasslands and vineyards of eastern Santa Cruz
- Exploring the Old (and New) West in southern Cochise County
- Traveling above and below ground in northern Cochise County

If you're looking for the Old West of Spanish missions and presidios, fierce Indian battles, go-for-broke mines, and rough 'n' tumble boomtowns, you'll be hard pressed to find a better stretch of Arizona to explore than the southeast. All that history sound like a yawn? Don't cross this region off your list yet. Nature lovers, wine connoisseurs, folk-art aficionados — even die-hard duffers — find something worthwhile here. All in all, the region fits those who prefer the simple pleasures of a handsome and, in parts, surprisingly green rural region to the glamour and glitz of the state's urban centers.

You can cover a lot of this area in day-trips from Tucson, but a single day doesn't really give southeast Arizona its due, especially because of all the terrific places to stay here. A more or less leisurely three days should be plenty, because the region isn't nearly as spread out as other areas in the state. You can settle in at a local ranch and use it as a base to tour the region, or hop from one historic hotel or colorful B&B to another as you travel. The town of Bisbee has the most varied lodging options, but where you lay your head depends largely on your interests. Stargazers may seek an aerie in an astronomy-oriented B&B near Benson, while birders may want to nest near the Patagonia or Ramsey Canyon nature preserves.

This area's higher elevation allows you to escape the southern Arizona desert heat in summer. But summer is also the season when many local business people go on vacation. Expect to find some restaurants, lodgings, and shops closed, sometimes without advance notice, especially around Patagonia and Sonoita.

Along the Santa Cruz River

Jesuit missionary Eusebio Kino and, later, conquistador Juan Bautista de Anze followed the Santa Cruz River north from Nogales, Mexico, to Tucson. Today neither traveler would recognize the developed riverbanks, now roughly paralleled by I-19, but the area is still scenic — when you venture a little bit from the freeway. In a relatively short span (only 65 miles separates Tucson from Nogales, Mexico), you get a terrific sweep of Arizona history, from its Mexican roots and earliest settlements to its most recent major industries.

Of all the areas I detail in this chapter, this stretch is the easiest to cover in a day trip from Tucson. If you're pressed for time, you can squeeze in the sights that interest you most, eat in Nogales, and drive back. But if you spend the night in one of several fine lodgings in the area, you get a leisurely, more authentic experience (remember, those padres and conquistadors only traveled on foot or horseback).

Nogales, Arizona, and Nogales, Mexico, are sister towns in two separate countries. Unless I say otherwise, when I refer to Nogales, I'm talking about the one in Mexico (its U.S. sibling has little tourist appeal).

Getting there

I-19 intersects with I-10 in Tucson. Note: I-19 is one of the few U.S. highways marked in kilometers, but the speed limit — 75 for the most part — is in miles per hour. This metric/English system mix-it-up gives the illusion that you're traveling from one place to the next really, really fast. (By the way, 1 mile equals 1.6 kilometers, so 6.2 miles is 10 kilometers.)

No rail service is available to this area, but Greyhound (☎ 800-229-9429) runs buses from Phoenix and Tucson to Nogales, Arizona. Getting to Nogales, Mexico, from the Greyhound station is a hassle, though. It's too far to walk, and buses run from the depot into Mexico only about once an hour.

Spending the night

A few chain motels dot this route, but if you're not going to hole up in one of the more interesting places, you may as well stay in Tucson, where the pickin's are better. Nor does spending the night in Mexico

---

Don't discount those Tucson discounts

The **Tucson Attractions Passport** doesn't just cover attractions in the Old Pueblo; several sights in Southern Arizona — including Kartchner Caverns State Park and the Titan Missile Museum — fall under its aegis. For details, see Chapter 13.

Southeast Arizona

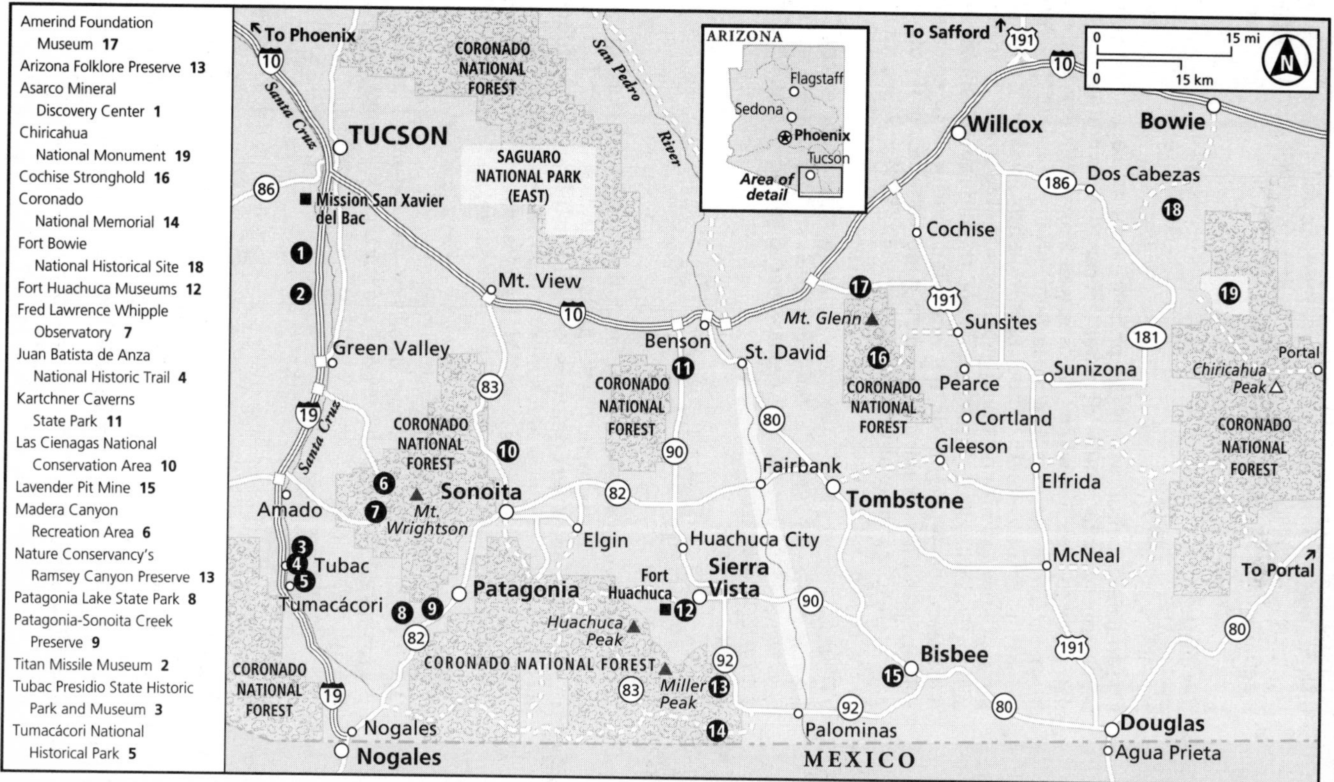

offer much advantage; best to soak up south-of-the-border color during the day, and then return to sleep on American soil. If spending the night at a B&B is more your style, see the "A stay in a B&B along the river" sidebar in this chapter.

Rex Ranch

$$ Near Amado

The journey itself is worth the price of a room. To get here, you drive across the (usually almost dry) Santa Cruz River, winding past trees that date back to the days when this area was a royal Spanish land grant. The Rex no longer functions as a guest ranch, but you can still book a horseback ride. Spa treatments and stress reduction classes are offered, too, but just lounging around this desert oasis should lower your blood pressure by several points. The grounds and the old ranch building are lovely and the rooms — fairly basic, but with such Southwest touches as beamed ceilings and tinwork mirrors — are a good value. Even if you don't stay here, consider dining at Cantina Romantica ($$$$), a meal that lives up to the restaurant's name.

131 Amado Montosa Rd. (Exit 48 from I-19, follow signs for the ranch). ☎ ***888-REX RANCH*** *or 520-398-2914. Fax: 520-398-8229.* `www.rexranch.com`. *Rack rates: Oct–May $145–$155 double, $245 casitas; June–Sept $105–125 double, $205 casitas. AE, DC, DISC, MC, V.*

Rio Rico Resort & Country Club

$$ Rio Rico

Compared with the other lodgings in this area, this thoroughly modern conference-oriented resort lacks architectural character. But the indoor public areas and guest quarters have Spanish ranch–style touches such as heavy wood armoires and leather chairs. Other pluses include a terrific location in the mountains near Nogales, lots of on-premises sports, including a Robert Trent Jones–designed golf course, and reasonable rates.

1069 Camino Caralampi (Exit 29 from I-19; follow the signs). ☎ ***800-288-4746*** *or 520-281-1901. Fax: 520-281-7132.* `www.rioricoresort.com`. *Rack rates: Jan–mid Apr: $149 rooms, $185 1-bedroom suites; mid-Apr–mid-June $139/$175; mid-June–Sept $116/$159. Oct–Dec $119/$165. Golf and tennis packages available. AE, DC, DISC, MC, V.*

Santa Rita Lodge

$ Madera Canyon

Birders and hikers who want to hole up in the woods love these simple but comfortable rooms and cabins — both types have kitchens — perched at an elevation of 4,800 feet in the Coronado National Forest. Perks include guided bird walks and nature talks in Madera Canyon (see the "Exploring along the Santa Cruz River" section for more on hiking and birding).

1218 Madera Canyon Rd. (Exit 63 from I-19; call for directions). ☎ ***520-625-8746.*** *Fax: 520-648-1186.* www.santaritalodge.com. *Mid-Feb–May cabins $98, rooms $83; June–early Feb cabins $83, rooms $73, midweek June–Sept. and Jan cabins $70, rooms 60. AE, MC, V.*

Tubac Golf Resort

$$ Tubac

You don't have to be a duffer to want to stay at this golf resort, part of Arizona's first Spanish land grant (issued in 1789) and loaded with Old West charm. When nearby Tubac sends you into retail overdrive, just kick back on the deck of your red-tile-roof casita ("little house") — some have full kitchens, others separate bedrooms — splash around the pool, hit a few tennis balls around, or gaze out at the Santa Rita mountains. A $30-million revamp, begun in 2003 and slated to be completed in 2005, is taking the resort back to the future, capitalizing on the land grant's history — for example, by having cattle graze on the golf course — while introducing up-to-date amenities such as a spa. Rates are far more reasonable than those at comparable Tucson resorts — and the serenity here is priceless.

1 Otero Rd. (Exit 40 from I-19 and drive about two miles west along the frontage road; you can't miss the arched entryway, featured in the film Tin Cup). ☎ ***800-848-7893*** *or*

A stay in a B&B along the river

This region has some terrific places to bed down — and breakfast. If you're up for bonding with others in the a.m., consider these inns (in order from north to south):

- **Mi Gatita** ($$), 14085 Avenida Haley Rd. S., about 10 miles SW of San Xavier del Bac mission (☎ **877-648-6129** or 520-648-6129; www.tucsonbirdinginn.com), offers desert digs with an artist's touch in a remote setting that's convenient both to the sights along the Santa Cruz River and to Tucson.
- **Amado Territory Inn** ($$), 3001 E. Frontage Rd. (Exit 48 from I-19), Amado (☎ **888-398-8684** or 520-398-8684; www.amado-territory-inn.com), a mid-1990s reconstruction of a late 1800 ranch house, gives you the best of both worlds: old Southwest color and new Southwest plumbing. The inn is part of a landscaped complex, so you don't feel as close to I-19 as you actually are.
- **Tubac Country Inn** ($$), 13 Burruel St., Tubac (Exit 34 from I-19) (☎ **520-398-03178;** www.tubaccountryinn.com), is a great choice if you want to forgo wheels for a while. You're in the heart of historic — and retailing — Tubac, so you can easily shop till you drop (into your room) and walk to restaurants. The hacienda-style complex and tree-shaded grounds are attractive to boot.
- **CP Ranch Bed & Breakfast** ($$), 15 Duquesne Rd., Nogales, AZ (☎ **520-287-0073;** www.cpranch.com), a colorful adobe inn a stone's throw from Mexico, is home to an appealing group of sheep-herding border collies. Bring your own dog (of any breed) for training.

520-398-2211. Fax: 520-398-9261. `www.tubacgolfresort.com`. *Rack rates: late Sept–mid-Dec $105–$140 standard double, $135–$175 casita; mid-Dec–mid-Apr $145–$175 double, $175–$195 casita; mid-Apr–early June $115–$160 double, $145–$175 casita; June–late Sept $95–$130 double, $125–$150 casita; rates lower Mon–Thurs. AE, DISC, MC, V.*

Dining locally

With a few notable exceptions, including the excellent Western-themed Stables restaurant at the Tubac Golf Resort (see the preceding section), this isn't gourmet-dining territory. It is, however, Mexican-food heaven (see the "Mexican munching on both sides of the border" sidebar). If you have a down-home American palate — and an affinity for kitsch — you'll also be satisfied at the steer-fronted Cow Palace ($–$$), 28802 S. Nogales Hwy. (exit 48 off I-19) (☎ 520-398-2201), with its huge menu of hearty egg dishes, burgers, and steaks. All the restaurants in this section are on or near the I-19 frontage road or within walking distance of recommended sights. You may also want to make a (booked in advance) detour for dinner at Cantina Romantica ($$$$) at Rex Ranch (see the preceding section), a fine-dining haven in a lovely rustic setting.

Some clichés are based on fact, and here's one you should take to heart: Drinking the water in Mexico isn't a good idea. In Nogales restaurants, stick to the bottled stuff (called agua pura), beer, or drinks without ice. On the streets, go for bottled soft drinks rather than the tempting fresh fruit drinks, often blended with ice.

Amado Café

$$ Amado SOUTHWEST/MEDITERRANEAN

The Southwest meets the Mediterranean in this cheerful light-wood dining room, where well-prepared, generously portioned dishes, such as mesquite-grilled steak and Greek chicken, always taste fresh, and the atmosphere is as warm as the regions that inspire the multicultural menu. This place tends to fill up in high season; be sure to book in advance for the weekends.

3001 E. Frontage Rd. (Exit 48 from I-19). ☎ ***520-398-9211.*** *Main courses: $14–$20. AE, DISC, MC, V. Open: Lunch Tues–Sun, Dinner Tues–Sat.*

Melio's Trattoria

$$ Near Tubac ITALIAN

White tablecloths, candles in Chianti bottles, and astounding views of the Santa Rita mountains make for a romantic ambience, in spite of the restaurant's location on the I-19 frontage road, just north of Tubac; house-made pasta makes it a magnet for Italian-food lovers. As such, you should stick with the pastas — perhaps penne topped by whiskey-seasoned cream sauce, or fettucine in a spicy tomato sauce; the meat and fish entrees are overpriced and undersize.

2261 E. Frontage Rd., (Exit 40 from I-19). ☎ ***520-398-8494.*** *Pastas: $8.50–$12.50; main courses: $13–$20. AE, DISC, MC, V. Open: Lunch and dinner Wed–Sun.*

Mexican munching on both sides of the border

When you're in the mood for Mexican food, you have lots of great options in this area — although, naturally, you have more choices on the Sonora side of the divide. My favorites (from north to south) are as follows:

Wisdoms' Café ($), 1931 E. Frontage Rd., Tumacácori (☎ **520-398-2397**), owned by members of the Wisdom family since 1944, has hosted everyone from John Wayne to Diane Keaton. Be sure to try the fruit-filled burritos. You can't miss this place: Just down the road from the Tumacácori mission, it's fronted by two large white fiberglass chickens.

Molina's Pete Kitchen Outpost ($), 555 E. Frontage Rd. (exit 8 off I-19 south; go left over freeway, take the first right and drive for about 1½ miles) (☎ **520-281-1852**), was built in the mid-1960s to resemble the ranch house belonging to Pete Kitchen, an early Arizona pioneer. Businesspeople from both sides of the U.S./Mexico divide come for the generous combination plates — say, top sirloin with a cheese enchilada, tortillas and beans, or Guaymas shrimp prepared in one of three traditional styles.

Elvira ($), Av. Obregón 1, Nogales, Mexico (cross the road after you pass through the international border and walk two blocks west [right]), (☎ **[52] 631-2-47-73**), attracts tourist by the droves because of its airy patio, its tasty, inexpensive dishes (including an impressive variety of moles) — and the free shots of tequila that arrive as soon as you sit down.

La Roca ($$), Calle Elias 91 (from the border, cross the railroad tracks and walk east [left] several blocks), (☎ **[52] 631-2-08-91**), is no great bargain, but it's worth coming here for the cliffside setting, romantically candlelit at night, informal during the day. The small but killer margaritas go well with such dishes as *carne tampiqueña* (assorted grilled meats served with a chile relleno and enchilada). Tucsonans love this spot, so you aren't the only ones *habla*-ing Ingles here; still, you're definitely off the beaten tourist track.

Exploring along the Santa Cruz River

Two of the top attractions in this area include the artisan colony of Tubac and the city of Nogales. Both are magnets for the same activity: producing friction on your plastic (skip to the "Shopping for local treasures" section, if that's your thing). Except for golf, this area's other prime draws shouldn't have a negative impact on your wallet.

The top attractions

Asarco Mineral Discovery Center

Sahuarita

Wondering about the strange, defoliated slopes you see on the west side of I-19 south of Tucson? You get the dirt (or at least see how the dirt is moved around) on this tour, operated by the American Smelting and Refining Company. Take the PR spiels about the importance of mining and its born-again environmental friendliness for what they're worth and enjoy the rare opportunity to see copper mining, one of Arizona's formative industries, in action. The tours take about an hour, but you're likely to spend another 20 minutes or so at the gift shop and exhibits in the Discovery Center, which is also where you buy the tour tickets. Unless you find the ore-extraction process endlessly fascinating, skip the free half-hour film.

See map p. 257. 1421 W. Pima Mine Rd. (15 miles south of Tucson; take I-19 Exit 80 and go west [right] from the exit ramp; you see the copper roof buildings 100 feet away on the south side of Pima Mine Road). ☎ 520-625-7513. www.mineraldiscovery.com. *Tours $6 adults, $5 seniors (62+), $4 ages 5–12, children under 5 free; other facilities free. Open: Tues–Sat 9 a.m.–5 p.m. Times and days for tours vary by season; phone ahead for information.*

Titan Missile Museum

Sahuarita

Both hawks and doves are fascinated by this museum's Cold War relic, the only one of 54 Titan II missiles in the United States — including the 18 that ringed the city of Tucson — allowed to stay intact under the terms of the SALT II treaty with the Soviet Union. In fact, this museum offers the only such exhibition of missiles in the world. Tours, which last an hour, take you down into the control center where the ground crew lived and prepared, if necessary, to fire a 165-ton rocket that held a nuclear payload 214 times as powerful as the bomb that destroyed Hiroshima. The Arizona

A one-stop shop for Fido

Perhaps your pooch needs a tasty treat or a bathroom break. Maybe you'd like to find out how to cook nutritiously for your royal dogness. Or perhaps your home could use a touch of doggie art. Satisfy all your canine needs at **The Dog Chefs of America Kitchen Headquarters** and **Oh My Dog!**, #3 Mercado Bldg., Amado Territory Ranch (take Exit 48 off I-19; it's in the complex you see immediately on the east frontage road) (**☎ 520-398-1411;** www.dogchefs.com). This combination doggie diner and art gallery is the domain of Micki Voisard, author of *Becoming the Chef Your Dog Thinks You Are* and self-styled "Master Dog Chef of America"; her husband creates many of the metal sculptures sold at the gallery. A small dog park in front of the shop is a great place for Fido to frolic or go pottie after being cooped up in your coupe.

You can pick up Voisard's dog snacks at the shop (open every day except Sun), but if you want to learn how to prepare your own, you have to plan ahead. Phone by the prior Wednesday if you'd like to attend one of the cooking-for-your-dog classes that Voisard offers every Saturday from 9–11 a.m. ($35 per human). And there's more: You and your dog can attend obedience classes in the dog park. Call **Green Valley Canine** at **☎ 520-971-6246** for details.

I left my heart in . . . Tubac?

Juan Bautista de Anza led 240 colonists across the desert from Tubac, an expedition that resulted in the founding of San Francisco in 1776. In 1859, Arizona's first newspaper was printed in Tubac, and in 1860, the town was reckoned to be the largest in Arizona.

Aerospace Foundation operates this museum, and also runs tours of the Pima Air & Space Museum (PASM) and the Aerospace Maintainence and Regeneration Center (AMARC); see Chapter 13 for details on both.

The four men who lived and worked in the cramped mission control area weren't claustrophobes (I hope!). If you're uncomfortable in somewhat small, enclosed spaces, you may want to pass on this tour. If you experience mobility problems, on the other hand, the facility can arrange special elevator tours; you aren't expected to tread the 55 steps that are involved.

See map p. 257. 1580 W. Duval Mine Rd. (about 25 miles south of Tucson; take I-19 Exit 69 west ⅒ mile past La Cañada to entrance). ☎ ***520-625-7736.*** `www.pimaair.org/TitanMM/titanhome.shtml`*. Admission $8.50 adults; $7.50 seniors, active military; $5 ages 7–12; 6 and under free. Combination Pima Air and Space/Titan Missile museums $16. Open: Nov–Apr daily 9 a.m.–5 p.m., closed Thanksgiving and Christmas; May–Oct Wed–Sun 9 a.m.–5 p.m. Tours depart every half hour; last tour at 4 p.m.; walking shoes (that is, no heels) required.*

Tubac Presidio State Historic Park and Museum

Old Tubac

Little remains of the first European settlement in Arizona or of the presidio (garrison or fortress) set up to protect it — just a portion of the original 1752 fort and an 1885 schoolhouse. You need to stop at the small museum adjoining the visitor center to get an idea of this former Spanish colony's importance. A tour of the entire complex shouldn't take you more than an hour, unless you picnic in the pleasant park.

For more action, come on Sunday from 1 to 4 p.m., October through March, when living history presentations let you chat with a frontier friar, a señora preparing tortillas, or soldiers garrisoned at the fort. Kids may be bored here the rest of the week, but they definitely like this part.

See map p. 257. 1 Burruel St. (take Exit 40 or 34 off I-19 and follow Tubac Rd into the large parking lot at the back of Old Tubac). ☎ ***520-398-2252.*** `www.pr.state.az.us/Parks/parkhtml/tubac.html`*. Admission $3 adults, $1 children 7–13, 6 and under free. Open: Daily 8 a.m.–5 p.m.; closed Christmas.*

Tumacácori National Historical Park

Tumacácori

Nearby San Xavier del Bac (see Chapter 13) may be Arizona's most impressive Spanish mission, but moody, ruined San Jose de Tumacácori is my favorite, both for the isolated beauty of its setting and the simplicity of the Franciscan structure. The visitor center/history museum takes no more than 45 minutes to tour. The timing of the rest of your visit depends on how contemplative you feel when you stroll around the mission grounds. On the third Wednesday of every month from October through April, van tours (10 a.m.–4 p.m.; $17.50) explore Calabazas and Guevavi, two other ruined missions in the historical park. The van holds only 14 people, so reserve as far in advance as you can.

The courtyard of this mission was a stand-in for Tucson in the movie Boys on the Side. The mission isn't usually as lively as it was depicted in the film, but the Christmas festivals are pretty great. (Find more on the festivals in Chapter 2.)

See map p. 257. 1891 E. Frontage Rd. (take Exit 29 off I-19 south and turn left on the frontage road; you see the mission in about a mile). ☎ ***520-398-2341.*** `www.nps.gov/tuma`. *Admission: $3 adults; 16 and under free; 62 and older with Golden Age Pass free. Open: Daily 8 a.m.–5 p.m., closed Thanksgiving and Christmas.*

More cool things to see and do

If you like to hike or ride across the landscape, tee off from it, or even leave it behind for the stars, this region has more options for you.

- Reach for the stars. Full day (9 a.m.–3 p.m.) tours of the Smithsonian Institution's Fred Lawrence Whipple Observatory on Mt. Hopkins are offered for $7 ($2.50 ages 6–12) on Monday, Wednesday, and Friday from March through November (weather and attendance permitting). You don't actually see any stars (this tour is during the daytime, remember?), but you find out about the fascinating work done here. And you don't get these great mountaintop views at night. Tour sizes are limited, so call ☎ 520-670-5707 for reservations and directions to the visitor center. See map p. 257.
- Tee off. Several golf courses in this area are open to the public. The Rio Rico Resort & Country Club, 1069 Camino Carampi (☎ 520-281-8567), was voted among the top 25 best in the state and is the site of many qualifying events for USGA and PGA tournaments (greens fees: $68 high season; $33 low season). The Spanish-style archways of the Tubac Golf Resort, 1 Otero Rd., Tubac (☎ 520-398-2211), starred with Kevin Costner and Rene Russo in Tin Cup; in fact, the lake on the 16th hole was created for the film (greens fees $75 high season, $32 low season). Kino Springs, 187 Kino Springs Dr., Nogales, AZ (☎ 520-287-8701), is on the site of a working cattle ranch once owned by married film stars Stewart Granger

and Jean Simmons (greens fees: $35 high season; $25 low season). The greens fees in all three cases include a cart but not tax, and apply to weekend mornings. Rates go down after noon, and during the week.

- Follow in the footsteps of the conquistadors. The flat 4½-mile stretch along the Santa Cruz River from Tumacácori to Tubac, popular with hikers and birders, is part of the Juan Batista de Anza National Historic Trail. Get a route map from the visitor center of the Tubac Presidio State Historic Park or Tumacácori National Historical Park (see the preceding section for both parks). Also check out the "Horsing around Santa Cruz County" sidebar for information on the "Saloon-to-Saloon" rides along this trail. See map p. 257.
- Hit the hiking or birding trail. The Coronado National Forest and the Santa Rita Mountains meet at the Madera Canyon Recreation Area, featuring about 200 miles of scenic trails and almost 250 types of birds. To get there, take Exit 63 off I-19 and go east on White House Canyon Road for 12.5 miles (it turns into Madera Canyon Rd.). Call the Nogales Ranger District ☎ 520-281-2296 in Nogales, Arizona, for information. The small, volunteer-run visitor center in Madera Canyon is only open on weekends. See map p. 257.
- Horse around. Both Rex Ranch and Rio Rico Stables offer equine adventures in this area. See the "Horsing around Santa Cruz County" sidebar in this chapter.

Shopping for local treasures

Some people — okay, me included — have been known to skip all the historical sights and just make a beeline for the shops in Tubac and Nogales. You find some similar goods in both places, especially ceramics. Prices are generally better in Mexico, but the schlep across the border is more of a hassle. In either place, avert your eyes from all those great terra-cotta planters and ceramic pots. The cost of shipping them is prohibitive, especially if you want them to arrive in one piece.

One additional shopping stop is Amado, where the Amado-Territory Ranch Inn complex hosts a few shops and galleries, including Oh My Dog! (see the "A one-stop shop for Fido" sidebar earlier in this chapter).

That's one hot tamale

The small, spice-redolent **Santa Cruz Chili & Spice Co.,** 1868 E. Frontage Rd. (just south of Tumacácori National Monument; ☎ **520-398-2591**), is salsa and chili powder central. Prices are reasonable, and you can watch the staff members make many of the products on the premises, as they have been for the past half century.

Tubac

Forget hostile Apache Indians. The biggest obstacle to reaching the old Tubac Presidio these days is getting past scores of friendly shopkeepers. The town of Tubac is adjacent to the historic park and chock-a-block with nearly 100 shops and galleries selling arts and crafts, many staffed by the artisans who created them. No one area is better for shops than another; excellent quality and schlock know no geographical boundaries. Park where you can — things can get pretty crowded on winter weekends — and just roam around.

Check out the wonderful floral metal fountains created by the artisans at Lee Blackwell Studios, 18 Plaza Rd. (☎ 520-398-2268), everything from yuccas to irises and roses. Browse the lacquered tables and hand-carved mesquite armoires sold at Rogoway Gallery, 1 Calle Baca (☎ 520-398-2913). Take the pulse of the local art scene at the Tubac Center of the Arts, 9 Plaza Rd. (☎ 520-398-2371), which hosts high-quality juried shows. Most of the work is for sale.

Nogales

As soon as you cross the border, you start seeing rows of colorful stalls and hear vendors calling out to you, "Come take a look, everything's on sale today." If you're not used to this sort of atmosphere, the sensory input may be overwhelming. Relax. Don't stop because you're being addressed, just smile and keep walking west (right) with the rest of the crowd. You soon reach Avenida Obregón, the main shopping street, where stores with doors line the street and you browse without being hassled (much). (See the "Nogales shopping tips" sidebar.) Although you can happily walk back and forth along Obregón, maxing out your credit card, good shops exist off the beaten path as well. In particular, Calle Elias (turn east [left] of the tracks rather than right as you cross the border) is fertile shopping ground.

Driving into Mexico is a hassle. The Customs line for cars is long and slow, and finding a place — safe or otherwise — to park your car is difficult. You're much better off parking on the Arizona side and walking over. When you get close to the border, you see guarded lots that cost about $4 or $5 per day. Practically all the good shopping is within easy strolling distance of the border, anyway.

Serapes and onyx chess sets abound, but you can also find high-quality crafts from all over Mexico in Nogales. Everything from cactus-stem margarita glasses and tinwork mirrors to Spanish Colonial–style wood-and-iron chandeliers are for sale. For portability's sake, brightly patterned rugs and wall hangings, tinwork candlesticks, and papier-mâché fruit are a good bet.

Farmacia facts

Nogales is known for its pharmacies *(farmacias)*. Practically every corner has one, because Arizonans make regular forays south of the border to buy discounted drugs. You may not be arrested if you sneak back a tube of Retin-A, but you're supposed to have prescriptions for all drugs, including antibiotics, that you buy in Mexico. Don't even think about trying to smuggle back pharmaceuticals that are illegal or controlled (again, unless you have a prescription) in the United States.

The following shops all offer good selections — but no bargaining. Tearing yourself away from the endless rooms of new and antique home furnishings may be tough at El Changarro (Calle Elias 93, just next door to La Roca restaurant [see "Mexican munching on both sides of the border" sidebar]). The Lazy Frog (Calle Campillo 57; you see the place before you get to Obregón) is small but has a nice array of crafts from all over Mexico; for more choices, try the much larger Nueva Maya de Mexico (Av. Obregón 150). You can find high-quality stained-glass and wrought-iron creations at Glass Alley Curios (Av. Obregón 182). Telephone numbers are far more difficult to locate than the shops — but you probably don't want the hassle of calling them, anyway.

Fast Facts: Santa Cruz River

Area Code

The area code is **520**.

Emergencies

Call ☎ **911** in the United States and try not to get in trouble in Mexico. If you do, you can find the American Embassy on Calle San Jose in the Los Alamos district (☎ **[52] 631-3-48-20**).

Hospitals

In case of a medical emergency, return to Tucson (see Chapter 13).

Information

The Tubac-Santa Cruz Visitors Center, La Entrada de Tubac shopping complex, 4 Plaza Rd. (☎ **520-398-0007;** `www.toursantacruz.com`) can inform you about all the region's towns and attractions and help you book rooms. The Nogales-Santa Cruz County Chamber of Commerce, 123 W. Kino Park, Nogales, AZ (☎ **520-287-3685;** `www.nogaleschamber.com`), doesn't have much information about Nogales, Mexico, but can answer questions about the rest of the towns and attractions in the area. Nogales, Mexico, has a small tourist information office on International Street (left of the border crossing; ☎ **[52] 631-2-02-03**).

Post Office

Locations include 2261 E. Frontage Rd., Tubac (☎ **520-398-0164**), and 1910 E. Frontage Rd., Tumacácori (☎ **520-398-2580**).

Nogales shopping tips

Shopping in Nogales, Mexico, is easy enough; however, to get the best prices, keep a few points in mind:

- **You don't need to change your dollars into pesos.** The Nogales merchants are happy to have greenbacks, and you lose money on the exchange rate if you don't end up spending all your Mexican moolah.
- **You may pay a bit more for the privilege of using plastic.** Shopkeepers pass on the hefty charges they incur from the credit card companies. Cash is a good bargaining tool.
- **Know when to haggle.** If the store has a door, you may not be able to bargain over its goods. In a stall, anything goes.
- **Know how to haggle.** Price tags on an item may or may not be an indicator of a fixed price. A merchant willing to bargain may offer you a better price if you stand around looking undecided. Asking, "Is that your final price?" doesn't hurt. Don't be rude if the shop owner says, "Yes."

When bargaining, start out by offering 50% of the vendor's asking price. You've done well if you end up meeting the seller halfway between the 50% you offer and the original selling price.

Eastern Santa Cruz County

With its fields of high golden grass waving in valleys of oak-dotted mountains, this section of Arizona falls far outside the state's scenery stereotypes. (In fact, the area doubled for prairie in the film Oklahoma.) Eastern Santa Cruz County is nevertheless rich in Arizona history, with mining and cattle shipping key industries in its past and ranching still important to its present. The (hoped for) future, however, is a product of the unusual geography: Lots of wineries crop up in this area.

Aside from a few shops, Sonoita has little to offer; this town is primarily a place to eat and sleep. However, you may easily spend a morning or afternoon poking around Patagonia, stopping into funky boutiques, and just strolling around absorbing the small-town Western flavor. If you want to tour the area's wineries, devote at least half a day. And if you're a birder — well, you're the best judge of how long you want to hang around the Patagonia-Sonoita Creek Preserve with other avian haunts, waiting for that Elegant Trogon to put in an appearance.

Getting there

I-10 east intersects with Highway 83 east of Tucson. Take 83 south to reach Sonoita, which sits at the junction of Highway 82. If you come from

I-19, take Highway 82 east from Nogales, Arizona, to Patagonia. No rail or bus service is available to this area.

Both towns pretty much consist of main streets that are easy to spot because highways change into them. In Sonoita, the highway keeps its name, Highway 82; in Patagonia, the highway becomes Naugle Avenue, and the street that runs parallel to Naugle is McKeown Avenue. Most of what happens in Patagonia — which isn't much — happens on Naugle and McKeown between Third and Fourth avenues.

Spending the night

Fans of chain hotels are out of luck here. By staying in this area, you settle for character rather than consistency. That doesn't mean giving up creature comforts by any means, but this area is rural. Even the places that offer cable TV don't necessarily get good reception.

In addition to my suggestions, you can find places with only one or two rooms through the Patagonia and Sonoita Chamber of Commerce (see the "Fast Facts: Eastern Santa Cruz County" section in this chapter). You may also consider bedding down at the Tree of Life or Phoenix Rising, both detailed in the "Exploring" portion of this section.

Circle Z Ranch

$$$ Patagonia

Sonoita Creek runs through this 5,000-acre spread in the foothills of the Santa Rita Mountains, abutting Coronado National Forest. This idyllic setting, along with cheery rooms and friendly service, explains why generations of guests come back to Arizona's oldest continuously operating dude ranch (started in 1926), year after year. No organized programs are offered for kids, but they ride and eat dinner separately (well supervised) from the adults — fun for them, even more fun for the grownups.

4 miles southwest of Patagonia (look for the ranch sign between the 14- and 15-mile markers on the west side of Highway 82). ☎ ***888-854-2525*** *or 520-394-2525.* `www.circlez.com`. *Rack rates: $975–$1,000 per adult in double room per week Oct 31–Nov 22, Dec 1–20, Jan 5–Feb 7, and Apr 26–May 15; $1,075–$1,100 Nov 23–Nov 30, Dec 21–Jan 4, Feb 8–Apr 25. Lower rates for children. Rates higher for stays under a week; 3-night minimum. Cottages, family, weekend, and birder (no riding) rates available. Rates include all meals and rides. MC, V. Closed mid-May–Oct.*

Sonoita Inn

$$ Sonoita

This unusual Kentucky-inspired A-frame once belonged to Secretariat's owner and housed the famed racehorse's triple crown — which explains all the photographs of horses and area ranches inside. Guest rooms, individually decorated in attractive Western-country style, contain all the mod-cons, including TVs with VCRs. The ones upstairs are worth the extra

Cozying up to horse country B&Bs

Who says B&Bs have to be frou-frou? These Sonoita-Patagonia-area lodgings were created to fit right in with this region's ranching roots.

The Dusquesne House ($), 357 Dusquesne Ave., Patagonia (☎ **520-394-2732;** e-mail: TheDusquesneHouse@hotmail.com), was built as a miner's boardinghouse at the turn of the last century. Pluses include separate entrances and proximity to all of Patagonia's shops — and a quirky charm that may not cut it if you're part of the Starbucks crowd.

La Hacienda de Sonoita ($$), 34 Swanson Rd., Sonoita (☎ **520-455-5308;** e-mail: reservations@haciendasonoita.com), is only a few years old but pays homage to the past with its Old West–themed rooms. Unobstructed mountain views and starry skies add to the sense of being back in another time.

Rancho Milagro ($$), 9 miles southeast of the crossroads of Hwy. 83 and Hwy. 82, Sonoita (☎ **520-455-0381;** www.ranchomilagrobb.com), is on a former ranch in the middle of nowhere — and in the heart of wine country. It doesn't get much mellower than sitting out on your patio, sipping some Callaghan cab, and watching the sun set.

charge — they're larger and offer superb views (you overlook the road if you stay in the front on either floor).

3243 Highway 82 (just east of the Highway 82/83 intersection). ☎ ***520-455-5935.*** *Fax: 520-455-5069.* www.sonoitainn.com. *Rack rates: $125 double (downstairs), $140 double (upstairs); $99 double (both floors) June–Aug. Rates include continental breakfast; wine and cheese on weekends. AE, DISC, MC, V.*

Dining locally

The good news is that this area has a few surprisingly sophisticated restaurants, offering dining quality equal to that of the big cities without big-city prices. The bad news is that eateries tend to come and go — and the ones that stick around often keep odd hours. Some places don't open every night (it's particularly tough to get fed Sunday through Tuesday nights), and many stop serving dinner at 8 p.m. In summer, all bets are off in determining when most of the restaurants decide to operate.

The dining scene also reflects the area's population mix. Rancher types get their big meat fixes at the Steak Out, 3280 Hwy. 82, Sonoita (☎ 520-455-5278) and Red's Real Pit BBQ, 436 W. Naugle Ave., Patagonia (☎ 520-394-0284). Those interested in extreme vegan eating — we're talking food that's not even cooked — dine at the Tree of Life Café (see the "Exploring eastern Santa Cruz County" section in this chapter). The restaurants listed in this section have more well-rounded menus.

Café Sonoita

$$ Sonoita AMERICAN

Come to these small, unassuming dining rooms for comfort food — especially if you find solace in the likes of cassoulet, beef tenderloin chile rellenos, or (for lunch) a filet mignon open-faced sandwich with Sonoita cabernet sauce. More traditional mood-soothers, such as meatloaf with mashed potatoes, are regulars on the ever-changing chalkboard menu. Sandwiches and burgers are the lunchtime staples, but smaller portions of the nightly specials may turn up, too.

3280 Hwy. 82 (½ mile east of the Highway 82/83 intersection). ☎ ***520-455-5278.*** *Reservations recommended for 5 or more at dinner. Main courses: $8.50–$18. Open: Lunch Fri–Sat, dinner Wed–Sat (5 –8 p.m.); occasionally open on Sun for special dinners and brunches. MC, V.*

Santos Mexican Cafe

$–$$ Patagonia MEXICAN

"Santos" means "saints," and you see several represented here. But even nonreligious fans of down-home Mexican food can find heaven in this diner-style cafe on Patagonia's main street. You can't go wrong with the huevos rancheros or cheese enchiladas with eggs at breakfast; at lunchtime, try the carne asada burros. In addition to Mexican fare, Santos is also known for its terrific fruit pies, strawberry rhubarb, blueberry . . . you name it.

328 W. Naugle St. ☎ ***520-394-2597.*** *Breakfast: $3–$5.75, lunch $4.25–$6.95. No credit cards. Open: breakfast and lunch Tues–Sun.*

Sonoita Wine Country Caffé

$$–$$$ Sonoita NEW AMERICAN

Great grassland vistas, cheerful, Mexican-tile dining rooms, and an appealing menu of creative egg dishes, sandwiches, pastas, and meat dishes make this restaurant worth a shot. But note that both food and service can be spotty. On a recent Sunday lunch visit, the roasted vegetables with feta on focaccia was terrific, while the Southwest chicken sandwich was dry and bland. Friends have also reported food and silverware delivery problems similar to the ones I've experienced.

3266 Hwy. 82 (about ½ mile east of the Highway 83 intersection, north side of the street). ☎ ***520-455-5282.*** *Main courses: $10–$18 dinner. Open: breakfast Sat and Sun; lunch Tues–Sun; dinner Thurs–Sat. AE, DISC, MC, V.*

Velvet Elvis

$–$$ Patagonia PIZZA

This combination art gallery/pizza place is as hip as its name, but the food doesn't have attitude (unless you count the fact that it's super fresh). Come here for creative, hot-from-the-oven calzones and pizzas and interesting salads, including a dynamite antipasto. (And yes, a velvet Elvis does hang on the wall.)

*292 Naugle Ave. ☎ **520-394-2102.** Reservations not accepted. Calzones $6.50–$8.25; pizzas $11–$19. MC, V. Open: lunch and dinner Thur–Sun.*

Exploring eastern Santa Cruz County

I'm almost tempted to say about eastern Santa Cruz County that there is no there, there. Except for Patagonia, this region doesn't really have a tourist center; you have to spend much of your time here roaming about.

The top attraction: Patagonia

A one-time shipping center for cattle and silver, Patagonia has managed to maintain its Western flavor. I've seen ranch hands on horseback trotting alongside traffic on the town's main drag (which flanks Highway 82). The town also attracts a variety of artsy types. You'll enjoy strolling around, looking at the old railroad depot — now the town hall — and browsing the crafts stores (see the "Shopping in eastern Santa Cruz County" section). Or check out these other nearby options.

- Go birding and hiking. The 850-acre Nature Conservancy's Patagonia-Sonoita Creek Preserve (☎ 520-394-2400; `http://nature.org`) protects a rare waterside habitat. Watchers have spotted nearly 300 types of birds here, along with plenty of less flighty creatures — everything from desert tortoises to deer. To get there, make a right on Fourth Avenue, which comes to a dead end,

Cafe country

You may be in the boonies, but you won't have to forgo such urban pleasures as good coffee and its accompaniments in this region. In fact, these are some of the most pleasant spots in the state to enjoy a light morning or midday meal.

Crossroads Café, 3172 Hwy. 83, Sonoita (☎ **520-455-5189**), serves nice breakfasts, but really shines at lunchtime with its chile- and onion-laden grilled sandwiches as well as burgers, soups, and salads. Besides coffee, liquid refreshments include smoothies, chai (tea), and Mexican hot chocolate.

Gathering Grounds, 319 McKeown, Patagonia (☎ **520-394-2097**), offers evidence of this town's nouveau artsy status by serving java made with organic shade-grown beans (it may be PC but it still has a kick). The sandwiches, baked goods, and ice cream concoctions also satisfy.

The Grasslands, 3119 S. Hwy. 83 (½ mile south of Highway 82 intersection), Sonoita (☎ **520-455-4770**), is country pretty, and the food here tastes as good as it looks. The quiches, pastas, and sandwiches use organic ingredients whenever possible, and the cinammon rolls are out of this world.

Great grapes! Southern Arizona's surprising wineries

Who wudda thunk it? Vinifera grapes seem to like the high-elevation (4,100 feet plus) valleys in Santa Cruz County. The area has lots of warm, sunny days and lush topsoil that has been compared to the (pay) dirt in Burgundy, France. Although grape growing and fermenting in this region date back centuries, scientifically based winemaking is a much more recent phenomenon.

True, Sonoma doesn't have to start sweating just yet; most of the winemakers in the area aren't quite ready for prime time. The exception is Kent Callaghan, whose **Callaghan Vineyards** (336 Elgin Rd., Elgin, call for directions, ☎ **520-455-5322**; www.callaghanvineyards.com) produces top-notch bottles (open Fri–Sun 11 a.m.–3 p.m.). But tooling around this beautiful area, stopping and sipping along the way is still fun. You find some decent wines — or at least good souvenir labels — at reasonable prices.

In addition to Callaghan, the best bets in the immediate area are **Sonoita Vineyards** (3 miles southeast of Elgin on Elgin-Canelo Rd.; ☎ **520-455-5893**; www.sonoitavineyards.com), whose founder, Dr. Gordon Dutt, reintroduced winemaking to the area (open daily 10 a.m.–4 p.m.); and **The Village of Elgin Winery** (in Elgin; ☎ **520-455-9309**; www.elginwines.com), which occupies a former (1895) bordello building and sells bottles with names such as Tombstone Red (open daily 10 a.m.–5 p.m.).

and then make a left. The paved road soon becomes dirt; take the road ¾ mile to the preserve. Admission: $5 for nonmembers. Open: Wed–Sun 7:30 a.m.–4 p.m. (an hour earlier in Apr–Sept). Guided walks: Sat at 9 a.m. (call ahead to check). See map p. 257.

- Check more birds off your list — and soak in some history. The 42,000-acre Las Cienagas National Conservation Area (best entrance: 7 miles north of Sonoita on the east side of Highway 83, around mile marker 40), (www.az.blm.gov/nca/lascienegas/lascieneg.htm) is an avian haven; you may get lucky and see a grey hawk here. No interest in winged things? Come out to see the restored 1860s Empire Ranch House (www.empireranchfoundation.org); some rooms are locked but the main entrance always stays open. For additional information about the conservation area, and for directions to the ranch house, phone the Tucson Field Office of the Bureau of Land Management (☎ 520-258-7200). See map p. 257 for both.

More cool things to see and do

If you have a bit more time in Patagonia, you may want to consider one of the attractions listed in this section. If you're a horse fan, check out the "Horsing around Santa Cruz County" sidebar.

- Hit the water. A large reservoir formed by the damming of Sonoita Creek, and subsequently stocked with fish, is the centerpiece of Patagonia Lake State Park (☎ 520-287-6965). Rowboats, paddleboats, canoes, and fishing supplies and licenses are available at the marina store (☎ 520-287-5545). You can water-ski and Jet-Ski on the western part of the lake (daily off-season, weekdays May–Sept) and swim at a sandy beach year-round. This lake isn't very tranquil on weekends or in the summertime, but it's fun.

  From October through April, more eco-oriented activities are offered by the personnel at the 5,284-acre Sonoita Creek State Natural Area (☎ 520-287-2791), a sub-unit of Patagonia Lake State Park. The natural area is closed to the public as trails and wildlife viewing areas are being developed, but it should be open by 2005. In the meantime, call ahead for information on the birding hikes, bat programs, and lake discovery tours via pontoon boat. Many are free, excluding the $1 entry fee to the natural area; the pontoon tours cost $3 per person.

  To get to the state park, take Highway 82 7 miles south from Patagonia, and then make a right at Lake Patagonia Road and drive 4 miles. Ask at the entry booth for directions to the visitor center for the Sonoita Creek State Natural Area. For locations, see map p. 257.

- Heal thyself. The serene landscape around Patagonia makes it a natural setting for spiritual health and healing centers. The Tree of Life, 771 Harshaw Rd. (☎ 520-394-2520, ext. 201; `www.treeoflife.nu`), has the most comprehensive programs, all with a healthful

Horsing around Santa Cruz County

What's ranching country without equines? **The Santa Cruz County Fair and Rodeo Association** in Sonoita (**☎ 520-455-5553;** `www.sonoitafairgrounds.com`) hosts several horsy events, including the Grass Ridge Horse Trials in mid-October, the Santa Cruz County Horse Races on the last weekend in April/first weekend in May, and the Sonoita Quarter Horse show — billed as the oldest quarter horse show in the nation — during the third weekend of May. In addition, the fairgrounds hosts the Sonoita Rodeo on Labor Day weekend, and in mid-September, the Santa Cruz County County Fair, featuring a ranch rodeo and a 4-H horse show.

Want to do your own horse-y thing? You can mount a steed at **Rex Ranch** (**☎ 520-398-2914;** see the "Spending the night" portion of the "Along the Santa Cruz River" section in this chapter) or **Arizona Trail Tours/Rio Rico Stables** (**☎ 800-477-0615** or 520-281-4122; `www.aztrailtours.com`). Options range from $25 for an hour-long ride to $1,250 for a four-day pack trip. If you like your outings accompanied by a cold one, consider the two-hour "Saloon-to-Saloon" ride along the historic Anza trail offered by Rio Rico Stables every Friday afternoon. The $50 price includes a beer at the Old Tumacácori Bar, the starting point, and another at Tubac Jack's, where the ride ends.

eating and meditation emphasis. Longer stays are encouraged, but you can just come by for a single day — or a single meal. Call ahead for reservations and information about times and prices of the surprisingly tasty vegan "live food" fare offered at the cafe.

- Go on a wine-tasting tour. See the "Great grapes! Southern Arizona's surprising wineries" sidebar for more information.

Shopping for local treasures

Sonoita has a few good shops on the strip along Highway 82. You find a nice selection of Native American jewelry at Many Horses Trading Co., 3266 Highway 82 (☎ 520-455-5545), next door to the Sonoita Wine Country Caffé (see "Dining locally," earlier in this section).

But Patagonia is definitely the place for serious retail patrols — just walk up and down the two main streets, McKeown and Naugle, which flank Highway 82 between Third and Fourth avenues. My favorites for local crafts are Mesquite Grove Gallery, 371 McKeown Ave. (☎ 520-394-2358), and Global Arts Gallery, 315 McKeown Ave. (☎ 520-394-0077), where I bought a pair of great horse earrings and a Carmen Miranda cookie jar. Fans of patchwork swoon over Quilted Creations, 317 McKeown Ave. (☎ 520-394-9000), which sells supplies as well as finished quilts and sometimes offers classes.

Living it up after dark

La Mision de San Miguel, 335 McKeown Ave. (☎ 520-394-0123), is easily mistaken for a chapel from the outside; as soon as you enter the wildly colorful, faux-rustic structure, you know it's a shrine to live music and good times (it's smoke-free too). More in keeping with the region's traditions are the Steak Out, 3280 Hwy. 82, Sonoita (☎ 520-455-5278), where good Country and Western bands play on Friday, Saturday, and Sunday nights; and the Wagon Wheel Saloon, 400 W. Naugle Ave. (☎ 520-394-2433), a local watering hole that stays open until 1 a.m. on weekends. Seeking something more uplifting? Patagonia's small Tin Shed Theater, 304 Naugle Ave. (☎ 520-394-9369), puts on an eclectic array of plays and concerts.

Fast Facts: Eastern Santa Cruz County

Area Code

The area code is **520.**

Emergencies

Call ☎ 911. The volunteer fire department and EMTs in the Sonoita-Patagonia area can be reached at ☎ **520-455-5854.**

Hospitals

The only medical facility in Sonoita is a pharmacy: Old Pueblo United Drugs, 3272 Highway 82; ☎ **520-455-0058.** Patagonia doesn't have a pharmacy, but it does have a medical center: Family Health Center, 101 Taylor St. (just off Highway 82; ☎ **520-394-2262;** open: Mon–Fri 9 a.m.–5 p.m.). In the event of a medical emergency, head for Tucson or Sierra Vista (see the "Fast Facts: Southern Cochise County" section later in this chapter).

Information

Sonoita-Elgin Chamber of Commerce, 3123 Highway 83, unit C (in Carnevale Travel) (☎ **520-455-5498;** www.sonoitaaz.com). Patagonia Visitors Center, 436 Naugle St. (☎ **888-794-0060** or 520-394-0060; www.patagoniaaz.com).

Post Office

Locations include 3466 Highway 83, Sonoita, at the intersection with Highway 82 (☎ **520-455-5500**), and 100 N. Taylor Ln., Patagonia, just off Highway 82 (☎ **520-394-2950**).

Southern Cochise County

The lower portion of Cochise County has the greatest concentration of attractions in southeastern Arizona, largely of the historical sort but also of the green variety. This area also has the widest range of places to stay, and makes a good base for side trips to the rest of the region.

In a time crunch, plan to devote at least half a day to Tombstone and another half to Bisbee. (Tombstone gets all the press, but Bisbee is equally interesting and far more scenic.) If you're not in a rush, spend a full day in each of these two towns. If you're a military history buff, allot a few hours to Fort Huachuca in Sierra Vista; if you're a nature lover, schedule some time for Ramsey Canyon and Coronado Monument, both near Sierra Vista.

Getting there

To reach Sierra Vista from Tucson, take I-10 east to Highway 90 and drive south some 35 miles to the junction with Highway 92 Business Route (also named Fry Boulevard, and Sierra Vista's main street). Tombstone is 28 miles northeast of Sierra Vista via Highway 90 or 24 miles south of Benson via Highway 80. Bisbee is 24 miles south of Tombstone on Highway 80.

Spending the night

Except for Sierra Vista and, to a lesser degree, Tombstone, this area doesn't have many chain hotels, which can make your stay difficult if you're traveling with kids. On the other hand, if you're looking for something entirely different — everything from a bordello-style B&B to a place where you can rent a vintage RV — you'll be very satisfied.

Sierra Vista's chain hotels include Best Western, Budget Inn, Comfort Inn, Marriott's Fairfield Inn, Motel 6, and Super 8. Tombstone offers a Best Western and a Holiday Inn Express, both located near the Boot Hill Cemetery, which is not in the heart of town. See the Appendix for all toll-free numbers. In addition, the Windemere Hotel & Conference Center in Sierra Vista (☎ 800-825-4656 or 520-459-5900; www.windemerehotel.com)

offers chain-style, family-friendly accommodations with amenities such as a pool and in-room refrigerators. Sierra Vista's more distinctive lodgings, in nearby Hereford, are listed below.

My Bisbee picks just skim the surface, while rooms in Tombstone are in more limited supply. In both towns, you can check with the local chambers of commerce if you need more options (see the "Fast Facts: Southern Cochise County" section later in this chapter for contact information).

Canyon Rose Suites

$$ Old Bisbee

These high-ceiling, spacious rooms in a converted historic building are not only attractive but offer lots of family-friendly conveniences, including fully-equipped kitchens and TVs with VCRs; a laundry room is on the premises, too. Other pluses: a location on a quiet street near all the town's historic sights, shops, and restaurants, as well as reasonable rates.

27 Subway St. (at the corner of Shearer St.). ☎ ***866-296-7673*** *or 520-432-5098.* www.canyonrose.com. *Rack rates: $85–$95 doubles, $120–$130 suites that sleep 3 people, $180–$200 for a duplex suite that sleeps six. DISC, MC, V.*

Casa de San Pedro

$$ Hereford

This B&B is for the birds — and for their human fans, who can hike out the back door to the nearby San Pedro Riparian Conservation Area. When you return to your nest, you can check any sightings on the software installed on the common room computer. A hacienda-style complex with colorful Southwest-style rooms, this B&B was custom-designed in the mid-1990s for travelers who like creatures but also enjoy creature comforts. The B&B offers birding tours and courses (for an extra fee) on many weekends. New to the inn in 2004: a lap-size pool, bat houses, and a butterfly garden.

8933 S. Yell Ln. (from the Highway 90/92 intersection in Sierra Vista, go south on 92 [18½ miles], north on Palominas Rd. [2 miles], and east on Waters Rd. [1 mile]). ☎ ***520-366-1300.*** *Fax: 520-366-0701.* www.bedandbirds.com. *Rack rates: Sun–Thurs $135 double, Fri–Sat $149 double; multiple nights $129. Rates include full breakfast and afternoon snacks. AE, DISC, MC, V.*

Copper Queen

$$–$$$ Old Bisbee

Host to the likes of John Wayne and Teddy Roosevelt for decades after opening in 1902, Bisbee's only full-service (three-meal restaurant, bar) hotel isn't posh enough to be a celebrity magnet anymore, but the hotel is great for local color. Although the rooms lost some Victorian charm with the addition of such amenities as private baths, phones, and color TVs, the public areas are so Old West authentic that you feel as if you should pull up in a horse-drawn carriage.

*11 Howell Ave. ☎ **520-432-2216.** Fax: 520-432-4298.* www.copperqueen.com. *Rack rates: $83–$190 double. AE, DISC, MC, V.*

Larian Motel

$ Tombstone

Of the several low-key, inexpensive motels in Tombstone's central historic district, this one stands out for its cleanliness and spacious rooms, as well as for its character. Built in 1957, it has such appealing retro touches as a stylish neon sign and rooms individually named for famous Tombstone figures like Wyatt Earp and Big Nose Kate. You get all the family-friendly basics — cable TV, foldout couches — for less than you'd pay at the chains, and you're in walking distance of most local attractions.

*410 Fremont St. (Highway 80). ☎ and fax **520-457-2272.*** www.tombstonemotels.com. *Rates: $49–$65 double. MC, V.*

Rail Oaks Ranch

$$ Hereford

This hidden gem near Sierra Vista has it all. You've got nature — you're likely to see deer, javelina, and birds frolicking among the oaks and mesquites of this gorgeous ranch spread. You've got history: The property originally belonged to Frank Weber, the inventor of the #2 pencil. You've got luxury, comfort, and privacy: The two beautifully appointed, self-contained guest houses offer full kitchens stocked with breakfast fixin's. And if hiking the area's many trails doesn't provide enough exercise, you've also have access to a small fitness room on the property.

*3248 White Lily Lane (10 miles south of Sierra Vista). ☎ **520-378-0461.*** www.railoaksranch.com. *Rates: $110–$150 double; lower weekly and monthly rates available. No credit cards accepted.*

Stay in the ultimate of '50s style

You may expect to see Wally and the Beaver emerging from one of the old trailers at **Shady Dell,** 1 Douglas Rd. (near the Highway 80 traffic circle; ☎ **520-432-3567;** www.theshadydell.com). If you're a nostalgia buff who doesn't mind close quarters — and a cemetery across the road — the period-furnished 1940s and 1950s Airstreams and Spartenettes are a kick. A 1938 Chris Craft yacht recently joined the roster of vintage accommodations. Rates range from $35 to $75, double occupancy for the trailers, $125 for the boat. The owner also operates the adjacent **Dot's Diner,** equally retro and equally fun.

Ramsey Canyon Inn Bed & Breakfast

$$ Hereford

Hummingbirds, a nature preserve, a historic home with antiques-filled rooms, and fresh-baked pies: Now that's a winning lodging combination. This native-wood-and-stone inn is adjacent to the Nature Conservancy's Ramsey Canyon Preserve. Even if you're not a birder, the hummingbirds will charm you as they feed outside the window of the breakfast nook. B&B guests do some heavy-duty feeding of their own on copious morning meals — and on the fruit pies that have become a tradition. Three creekside housekeeping suites equipped with kitchens may appeal to the more privacy oriented.

29 Ramsey Canyon Rd. (from Sierra Vista, take Highway 92 south to Ramsey Canyon Rd., turn right [west] and drive 4 miles). ☎ ***520-378-3010.*** *Fax: 520-378-0487.* `www.ramseycanyoninn.com`. *Rack rates: $130–$140 inn doubles; $150–$200 for 2 people in the self-contained suites, which sleep up to 4 (two of the suites require a 2-night minimum stay; one requires a 3-night minimum stay). Inn rates include full breakfast, suite rates don't. MC, V.*

San Pedro River Inn

$$ Hereford

This inn is the stuff of escapist fantasies, doing little more than fishing on the pond of an old dairy farm, sitting out on a front porch — just staring at a blue, cloudless sky — and barbecuing some burgers to fortify yourself for another day of doing exactly the same. The four fully equipped cottages on this lush spread next to the San Pedro Riparian Conservation Area aren't fancy, but if you want a laid-back place to bring the kids (and dog and horse), you've found the perfect getaway. One of the owners is a birding guide, and guests are welcomed to accompany him on walks to the San Pedro River (he also runs van tours of the area for an extra charge).

8326 S. Hereford Rd. (from Sierra Vista, take Highway 92 south about 20 miles past Palominas Road to Hereford Road). ☎ *and fax:* ***520-366-5532.*** `www.sanpedroriverinn.com`. *Rack rates: $105–$115 for two guests in a cottage, but three of the cottages are large enough for four to six people, which lowers rates. Rates include continental breakfast. For an extra fee, pets are boarded in an outdoor pen, and horses in corrals. Two-night minimum stay. No credit cards.*

Tombstone Boarding House

$–$$ Tombstone

Plenty of character plus a private bath in every antiques-filled room make these two joined-at-the-hip 1880s adobes my top Tombstone B&B pick. All the rooms have private entrances, so you have less of a sense that you're intruding on someone else's space. Another perk: Next door's Lamplight Room, where breakfast is served, doubles as a Continental and Mexican restaurant later in the day (see the following "Dining locally" section). Dine on margaritas and Mexican specialties on the patio or opt for sturdy New York sirloin or roasted pork loin inside.

Bisbee's colorful B&Bs

It's tough to choose from among the many colorful B&Bs in Bisbee, but, hey, it's my job. Here, then, are my favorites:

The Bisbee Grand ($$), 61 Main St., Old Bisbee (☎ **800-421-1909** or phone/fax 520-432-5900; www.bisbeegrandhotel.com) is a bit over the top, what with the high-bordello-style red wallpaper in the halls and eclectic array of rooms. You may find anything from a stuffed bird to a full-size cutout of John Wayne sleeping with you. Most guest quarters are on the second floor above a historic saloon, so serenity isn't one of this B&B's strong points.

Calumet & Arizona Guest House ($), 608 Powell St. (☎ **520-432-4815;** www.calumetaz.com), located in the quiet Bisbee suburb of Warren, was built in 1906 by Henry Trost, one of the West's famed architects. The grounds and the rooms are as lovely as the house, and breakfasts are elaborate.

Hotel La More ($–$$), 45 OK St. (☎ **888-432-5131** or 520-432-5131; http://hotellamore.com), is a good pick for those who aren't put out when a 1917 hotel has creaky plumbing. It's not your typical B&B — among other things, it sits above a saloon, and accepts "well-behaved" children and pets — but the rooms are Victorian in style and a full breakfast is included in the rate, so it more or less fits into that lodging category.

The Inn at Castle Rock ($–$$), 112 Tombstone Canyon Rd. (☎ **800-566-4449** or 520-432-7868; www.theinn.org), started its life as a miners' boardinghouse in the 1890s. Guests like its funkiness — the flooded mine shaft in the dining room, for example, and lush, overgrown gardens — as well as its hillside location, convenient to the heart of town but away from the hubbub.

The Schoolhouse Inn ($–$$), 818 Tombstone Canyon Rd. (☎ **800-537-4333** or phone/fax 520-432-2996), was built, as its name suggests, as a school in 1918. The oak-shaded grounds are perched above Old Bisbee, and the subject-themed rooms — for example, arithmetic and writing — are amusing.

108 N. Fourth St. (between Safford and Bruce, two blocks from Allen). ☎ ***877-225-1319*** *or 520-457-3716 (☎ and fax).* www.tombstoneboardinghouse.com. *Rack rates: $69–$89 double. Rates include full breakfast. AE, DISC, MC, V.*

Dining locally

Southern Cochise County has good places to sleep, but — with the exception of Bisbee — not such great eats. And even in Bisbee, full-service restaurants are rare: Several prime spots are open limited days and hours. That's the case with Café Cornucopia (14 Main St. ☎ 520-432-4820), which serves great quiches, smoothies, and other made-from-scratch fare from 10 a.m. to 5 p.m. Thursday through Monday. In contrast, Winchester's (in the Copper Queen hotel; see the preceding

"Spending the night" section) is open for three meals a day, every day, but it's been erratic over the years. Still, it's worth a try, if only to dine on its mellow deck.

Sierra Vista is the best place to get a fast food fix — as well as an Asian food hit; my favorite in the latter category is the Peacock (80 S. Carmichael St. ☎ 520-459-0095), offering authentic, well-priced Vietnamese fare. Also in Sierra Vista, Bobke's Bread Basket (355 W. Wilcox Dr., ☎ 520-458-8580) serves up terrific German pastries and overstuffed deli sandwiches. The Mesquite Tree (corner of S. Hwy 92, and Carr Canyon Road, ☎ 520-378-2758) isn't especially exciting, but it has a cozy atmosphere and a location convenient to Ramsey Canyon; the seafood is a safe bet.

In Tombstone, both Vogan's Alley Bar (487 E. Allen St., ☎ 520-457-3101) and the restaurant in Six Gun City (509 E. Allen, ☎ 520-457-3827) have decent burgers and the like. For more yuppified fare, try Gitt Wired Internet Café (505 E. Fremont St., ☎ 520-457-3250), offering espresso and deli sandwiches.

Big Sky Café

$ Old Bisbee CAFE

Whether you kick back on the patio, gazing out at the historic Art Deco courthouse, or dine inside in the airy, art-filled room, you'll enjoy the fresh baked goods, egg dishes, grilled panini sandwiches, and salads that emerge from this cafe's open kitchen. Organic ingredients are used whenever possible, and everything's fresh and tasty.

203 Tombstone Canyon. ☎ ***520-432-5025.*** *Egg dishes, sandwiches, salads: $3.50–$6.50. MC, V. Open Tues–Sun 7:30 a.m.–2 p.m.*

The Bisbee Grill

$$ Old Bisbee AMERICAN

For comfort food in a comfort setting, you can't go wrong with this upgraded coffee shop in the Copper Queen Plaza building. Caesar salads, grilled chicken sandwiches, pastas . . . everything's nice and reliable. The historic photos of Bisbee on the walls add a touch of character.

2 Copper Queen Plaza. ☎ ***520-432-6788.*** *Main courses $7–$12 lunch, $13–$19 dinner. AE, DISC, MC, V. Open daily lunch and dinner.*

Café Roka

$$–$$$ Old Bisbee ITALIAN/NEW AMERICAN

Totally out of character for hippie-ish Bisbee when it opened in the mid-1990s, Cafe Roka proved that Cochise County was ready for a sorbet palate freshener between courses. An open dining room with exposed brick walls and the original tinwork ceiling is the retro-chic setting for the food, such as artichoke and portobello mushroom lasagne, langostino and blue crab cakes, or roasted half duck, served with a small salad, cup of fresh soup — and the aforementioned sorbet.

*35 Main St. ☎ **520-432-5153.** Reservations essential; this restaurant is the region's foodie magnet. Main courses: $14–$24 (including soup, salad, sorbet). AE, MC, V. Open: Dinner Wed–Sun winter; Fri and Sat mid-June–mid-Oct (call ahead to make sure of days open).*

Lamplight Room

$–$$ Tombstone CONTINENTAL/MEXICAN

Yes, it's a tad odd for a restaurant to offer entrees like Parmesan-crusted salmon and also (on a separate menu) Mexican combination plates, but, given the dearth of good dining in Tombstone, be grateful for all the choices. You also to choose theatmosphere: Decide between a formal, antiques-filled dining room or a casual patio. If you're not sure the live flamenco guitar offered on weekend evenings goes with chicken cordon bleu, just order a few of the strong margaritas. You'll soon stop quibbling.

*108 N. Fourth St., ☎ **520-457-3716.** Reservations recommended for the fine-dining section. Main courses: $5–$8 Mexican, $12–$17 Continental. Open lunch and dinner daily. AE, DISC, MC, V.*

Exploring southern Cochise County

This area offers some of the state's best tourist stompin' grounds, with loads of stuff to do and relatively short driving distances between attractions. Enjoy, but don't try to fit too much in. Running from attraction to attraction only makes you ornery.

The top attractions

Bisbee

More of a success story than Tombstone in many ways, Bisbee is much less well known, in part because its outlaws were of the corporate sort: Phelps, Dodge & Co. was the main beneficiary of the multibillion-dollar copper lode that gave rise to this thriving mountainside town. The last mining operation didn't shut down until 1975, and if the price of copper ever goes up, Bisbee's mine may reopen. In the meantime, this one-time hippie enclave is being prospected by an increasing number of tourism-savvy entrepreneurs.

When you drive into town, take the Old Bisbee exit off Highway 80 and park your car into the first (legal, I hope) spot you find. West of Main Street is a large parking lot that fills up fast. From here, you can walk to the town's major attractions — although the town is literally uphill from here.

Bisbee sits at a mile-high elevation in the Mule Mountains, so you may find yourself especially short of breath when you walk uphill. If you have a respiratory problem, you may want to seek assistance getting around.

Stroll around Main Street, with its well-preserved Victorian buildings and interesting boutiques (see the "Shopping for local treasures" section later in this chapter). Check out the copper-trimmed Bank of America at the foot of the street (you don't have to go in). Other historic attractions include the Copper Queen hotel (see the "Spending the night" section earlier in this chapter) and the nearby Muheim Heritage House, 207 Youngblood Hill (☎ 520-432-7071), an unusual Swiss-built structure with period furnishings. Heritage House is at the top of Brewery Gulch, which was once lined with saloons and literally flowed with beer. In addition, you can find more diversions, above and below ground. For information on specific spots to ogle, pick up a copy of the Bisbee Historic Walking Tours pamphlet at the Bisbee Visitor Center (see the "Fast Facts: Southern Cochise County" section later in this section).

- Take a journey underground. Actually, the Copper Queen Mine Tour, 478 N. Dart Rd. (☎ 520-432-2071), takes you up a 30-degree grade into the mine's shaft; you just feel as if you're descending. These fascinating inter-earth journeys, which depart daily at 9 a.m., 10:30 a.m., noon, 2 p.m., and 3:30 p.m., are led by miners who once worked the Copper Queen. This tour is Bisbee's most fun attraction: In addition to everything else, you get to put on a yellow slicker and a hard hat. If you're claustrophobic, consider taking the surface tour around Old Bisbee and to the perimeter of the Lavender Pit Mine. This tour operates at the same times as the other tours (except for the 9 a.m. tour). Admission: Mine tour, $12 adults, $5 ages 4–15, under 4 free; surface tour, $7 all ages, under 4 free.
- Mine more of the town's history. The nation's first rural museum to be affiliated with the Smithsonian Institution, the small Bisbee Mining and Historical Museum, No. 5 Copper Queen Plaza (☎ 520-432-7071), gives a great overview of the town's early years. Be sure to check out the dazzling gem and mineral exhibit. Admission: $4 adults, $3.50 seniors, $1 children 16 and under. Open: Daily 10 a.m.–4 p.m.

  You can't miss the Lavender Pit Mine — it's that huge, multicolored hole off Highway 80 en route into town from the west. Something that produced 94 million tons of copper is worth more than a drive-by. Go beyond town to the intersection of highways 80 and 92 for an overlook that has a typewritten history of the mine (hey, they're not really formal in Bisbee).
- Tootle around town. Prefer to get your bearings while seated? Every day except Wednesday in high season and from Friday through Monday in summer, the Bisbee Trolley Company (☎ 520-432-7020) ferries passengers along the route of the electric rail line that linked Old Bisbee to the wealthy Warren District from 1908 to 1928. The hour-long historic tour, which departs from the Copper Queen Plaza, south of the mining museum, at 9:30 a.m., 11 a.m., 1 p.m., 2:30 p.m., and 4 p.m., is as easy on the attention span as it is on the feet. Admission: $10 adults, $7 for ages 10 and under.

Fort Huachuca Museums

Sierra Vista

Still an active military base, Fort Huachuca is the last of the famous western forts to remain operational. Many of the barracks from the 1800s are currently used as offices, and three have been turned into museums. The Fort Huachuca Historical Museum is the most interesting of the trio; among its highlights are the exhibits detailing the role that African-Americans played in the U.S. military (see the "Buffalo braves" sidebar). The historical museum's annex and Army Intelligence Museum are also worth a visit. Seeing all three museums takes about an hour or so; you need a little longer to check out the sculptures in the surrounding complex (in case you're wondering, the gold sphinx is the emblem of military intelligence — pretty apt!). Other options for activities on the base include a scenic overlook at Reservoir Hill and the hiking trails at Garden Canyon, a magnet for butterflies; the Sierra Vista Convention and Visitors Bureau (see the "Fast Facts: Southern Cochise County" section) can give you details.

See map p. 257. The main gate to Fort Huachuca is southwest of the intersection of Highways 90 and 92 (call ahead for directions). ☎ ***520-458-4716*** *or 520-533-5736 (recorded museum information).* `http://huachuca-www.army.mil/HISTORY/museum.htm`. *Museum admission: Free. Open: Mon–Fri 9 a.m.–4 p.m., weekends 1–4 p.m.*

Ramsey Canyon Preserve

Hereford

You can find out all about the unusual biodiversity of Ramsey Canyon, part of the Upper San Pedro River ecosystem in Hereford, at the Nature Conservancy visitor center. Or you can just grab a trail map and stroll around this remarkably pretty, tranquil preserve. Fourteen species of hummingbirds — more than anywhere else in the United States — stop off here. When the hummers aren't flitting around, you still see plenty of other creatures to ooh and aah over. The Miller Peak Wilderness Area in the Huachuca Mountains is honeycombed with trails, so if you're a serious hiker, consider spending all day in this area. The easy 1-mile walk from the preserve headquarters to a scenic overlook makes a good goal for a couch potato.

Buffalo braves

The 9th Cavalry, 10th Cavalry, 24th Infantry, and 25th Infantry — all four of America's black regiments — trained at Fort Huachuca. These regiments were given the respectful name Buffalo Soldiers by the Chiricahua Apaches, who were among the groups the 9th Cavalry was commissioned to fight in 1877. The Fort Huachuca Museum details the outstanding record of these African-American units. A special section devoted to the black military experience in the American West includes a rare description of Estevanico de Dorante, the African-slave-turned-conquistador who took part in the earliest European exploration of Arizona.

See map p. 257. 27 Ramsey Canyon Rd. (about 6 miles from Sierra Vista; go south on Highway 92 and take a right on Ramsey Canyon Rd). ☎ ***520-378-2785.*** *Admission $3 for members of the Nature Conservancy, $5 nonmembers. Open: Mar–Oct daily 8 a.m.–5 p.m, Nov–Feb daily 9 a.m.–4 p.m.*

Tombstone

Don't blame Tombstone for being touristy. Hollywood glamorized the "Town Too Tough to Die" so much that many visitors are disappointed if they don't get a little showmanship. Don't worry; crass commercialism (silver speculating, tourism: what's the difference?) is an old Tombstone tradition. Just relax and enjoy the Old West costume dramas.

Besides, plenty of genuine history was made here. The town's main drag and most of the town's attractions are either on or within walking distance of Allen Street. Tacky tourist shops may line the throughfare, but if you look closely, you can still see bullet holes in some of the buildings. The available activities are a mix of the truth and a past that has been, shall we say, embellished.

- Get corralled. Yes, it's touristy as all get out, but you can't leave town without visiting the OK Corral, on Allen Street between Third and Fourth streets (☎ 520-457-3456). Tombstone's most famous attraction consists of two main sections: the Historama, which screens a short background film (the fact that the late Vincent Price narrates it is an, er, dead giveaway of its vintage and historical subtlety); and the corral where you-know-what occurred. Among the historical displays in the corral, the best by far is C.S. Fly's photo gallery; Fly's famed photos of Geronimo are worth the price of admission alone. But, unless Tombstone is really quiet, don't try to schedule your day around the overpacked 2 p.m. reenactment of the shootout (an additional $2). Admission: $5.50 adults, under 6 free. Open daily 9 a.m.–5 p.m. (Historama shows run every 30 minutes from 9:30 a.m.–4:30 p.m.)

- Get the lowdown. Only a few places in town give you history that's unadulterated by hype. Among the many fascinating displays at the Tombstone Courthouse State Historic Park, Toughnut and Third streets (☎ 520-457-3311), are two diagrammed scenarios of what actually may have happened at the famous shootout between the Earps and Clantons at the OK Corral. Make this stop your first if you want some perspective on the other, more duded-up attractions. Admission: $4 per adult, $1 ages 7–13, 6 and under free. Open: Daily 8 a.m.–5 p.m. except Christmas.

  Opened in late 2003, the Tombstone Western Heritage Museum, 519 E. Fremont St. at Sixth Street (☎ 520-457-3800), is chock-a-block with well-displayed historic treasures — everything from the craps table that originally sat in the Crystal Palace and a $4 license to practice the business of "ill fame" to Doc Holliday's business card and rare editions of the Tombstone Epitaph. Like the state park, it's a must-see for Western-history buffs. Admission: $5 adults, $3 ages 12–18, 11 and under free (check this). Open: Mon–Sat 9 a.m, Sun. 12:30 p.m., closing when the last person leaves (generally from 5 to 6 p.m.).

- Read some old news. The Tombstone Epitaph Museum, 9 S. 5th St. (☎ 520-457-3456) is small, but so was the newsroom that put out the paper that created an American legend when it reported on the gunfight at the OK Corral. Come here to see the original printing presses and read 1880 news reports, including a description of the surrender of Geronimo. Admission: Free. Open daily 9:30 a.m.–5 p.m.
- See the world's largest rose tree. The Rose Tree Inn Museum, Toughnut and Fourth street (☎ 520-457-3326), holds the Guinness World Record for having the largest rose tree in the world (it's 8,600 square feet, give or take a few thorns). The 1880s period rooms also give a window on a much more genteel Tombstone than the one generally seen on the silver screen. Admission: $3 for adults, free 14 and under. Open: Daily 9 a.m.–5 p.m., closed Christmas and Thanksgiving.
- KID FRIENDLY Witness a shootout. Although the reenactment of the gunfight at the OK Corral is the best known, it's not the only showdown in town. The Six-Gun City Wild West Show (☎ 520-457-3827), held at Fifth and Toughnut streets, uses professional stuntmen for the shoot 'em ups. Admission: $4 adults, free ages 12 and under. Shows are offered throughout the day Wednesday through Sunday. The Tombstone Cowboys, another group of professional stuntmen and actors, present the Gunfight at the Helldorado (☎ 520-457-9153) in an arena at Fourth and Toughnut streets. Admission: $4 adults, $3 seniors, $1 ages 6 to 12. Shows: Mon through Fri at 12:30 and 3 p.m., Sat, Sun, and holidays, 11:30 a.m., 1 p.m., and 3 p.m. The shows are pretty similar; go for the Six-Gun City one if you're hungry, because decent food is sold on the premises. Note: Whichever you choose, don't sit near the front if you're shy; these shows are big on audience participation.
- Take to the stage. The horse-drawn stagecoach excursions run by Old Tombstone Historical Tours, Allen Street (next to Big Nose Kate's; ☎ 520-457-3018), are a fun way to pick up some information (to be swallowed with a grain of salt). Admission: $5 adults, $4 seniors, $3 ages 4–13. Tour time: Daily 9 a.m.–5 p.m.; tours last about 20 minutes.
- See treasures from the Old West. The Bird Cage Theatre, Sixth and Allen streets (☎ 520-457-3421), looks as if it hasn't been dusted since it was abandoned in 1889. Amid the debris, however, are treasures, such as the gold-trimmed Black Moriah hearse that transported the losing team at the OK Corral shootout to Boot Hill cemetery, as well as the velvet-draped "cages" where the ladies of the night plied their trade above the dance hall and casino. This is also the site of the longest poker game on record (eight years, five months, and three days). Admission: $6 adults, $5.50 seniors, $5 ages 8–18, under 8 free; $17 family rate (2 adults, 2 kids age 8–18). Open: Daily 8 a.m.–6 p.m. except Christmas.

The truth about Tombstone

Tombstone earned its name after prospector Ed Schieffelin ignored all the people who warned him that if he ventured into what was then dangerous Apache territory, all he would find was his tombstone. Instead, in 1877, he struck one of the West's richest silver veins.

Tombstone earned its "Town Too Tough to Die" nickname by surviving two major fires, an earthquake, and the rising of its water table — which caused the silver mine to literally go under.

In its silver-mining heyday, Tombstone was larger than San Francisco. But the town wasn't all bar brawls; Tombstone was also a major cultural center. Enrico Caruso, Sarah Bernhardt, and Lillian Russell were among the famous entertainers who trod the boards at the Bird Cage Theatre.

- Drink in a little history. Although the ornate mahogany bar at the Crystal Palace, corner of Fifth and Allen streets (☎ 520-457-3611), was moved from its original location, it's still the genuine item. This place is great for sipping a few beers and, on most weekends, listening to the live Country and Western sounds of pre-Shania/Dixie Chicks vintage.
- See where the bodies are buried. You must walk through a huge souvenir shop to enter the Boot Hill Graveyard, on Highway 80 (just northwest of town; ☎ 800-457-9344 or 520-457-9344), and most of the grave markers are reproductions. Nonetheless, you can't leave without visiting the town's famed 19th-century boneyard. Get the "Essential Guide" tour pamphlet for $2 to find out who's buried where and why (James Hickey, for example, was "shot in the left temple by Wm. Clayborne for his over-insistence that they drink together"). Admission: Free. Open: Mon–Fri 7:30 a.m.–6 p.m., Sat and Sun until 6:30 p.m. spring through autumn, closing one hour earlier in winter.

More cool things to see and do

This region offers more interesting ways to take in the local scenery and culture, in addition to some sunshine (don't forget the sunscreen!).

- Pretend you're a conquistador. You can see for miles and miles — all the way to Mexico — at the Coronado National Memorial, 4101 E. Montezuma Canyon Rd., Hereford (☎ 520-366-5515, ext. 23; `www.nps.gov/coro`), a 4,750-acre preserve dedicated to Spanish conquistador Francisco Vasquez de Coronado, who passed through the area in 1540. For the best views, drive the 3-mile dirt road from the visitor center to Montezuma Pass, and then walk up another ½ mile to the top of Coronado Peak (almost 7,000 feet high). This is a great place for a family visit. Kids can try on helmets and chain-link vests similar to those that the conquistadors wore, and explore a small cave (bring your own flashlight, or buy one at the visitor center, where you need to get a free permit to visit). And this is one of the prettiest places in the state to enjoy a picnic. You see a sign for the memorial 16 miles south of Sierra Vista on Highway 92. The visitor center, open daily from 9 a.m.–5 p.m., is 5 miles from the turnoff. The grounds are open from dawn to dusk. Admission: Free. See map p. 257.

- Listen to cowboy poets. I can't think of a more interesting way to spend the day than strolling around Ramsey Canyon in the morning and seeing a performance at the nearby Arizona Folklore Preserve in the afternoon. See the "Pick a peck of pickers and poets" sidebar for details. See map p. 257.
- Take a side trip to Douglas. Bordering Mexico to the east of Bisbee, Douglas was a ranching center and smelter for many of the area's most successful mines. A typical border town now, Douglas still has a few lures. You may recognize the Gadsden Hotel, 1046 G. Ave. (on the town's main street; ☎ 520-364-4481), from the Paul Newman movie The Life and Times of Judge Roy Bean; the stained-glass window of a Southwest landscape, and a Western saloon decked with rancher's brands are highlights.

  The Slaughter Ranch Museum (☎ 520-558-2474), a National Historic Landmark in Douglas, re-creates the area's ranching heyday in a remote, rural setting (bring a picnic lunch). Take 15th Street east to Geronimo Trail and follow the signs; the museum is 20 miles down a dirt road. Admission: $5 adults, children under 15 free. Open: Wed–Sun 10 a.m.–3 p.m.

- Get wet. With its computer-generated tsunamis, 150-foot indoor-outdoor tube slide, and a variety of pools for all ages and mobilities, the Sierra Vista Aquatic Center, 2900 M.L. King Jr. Pkwy. (☎ 520-417-4800; `www.ci.sierra-vista.az.us/thecove`), may be the splashiest municipal pool complex in the state. It's a huge

Pick a peck of pickers and poets

Just before you come to Ramsey Canyon, you see a sign for the **Arizona Folklore Preserve,** 44 Ramsey Canyon Rd. (**☎ 520-378-6165;** `www.arizonafolklore.com`). Dolan Ellis, an original member of the 1960s folk group the New Christy Minstrels, founded this unique performance space, research center, and bookstore. Ellis is also Arizona's official state balladeer (bet you didn't know Arizona had one). Jury-selected folk artists — from cowboy poets to storytellers, fiddlers, and bluegrass guitarists — perform each Saturday and Sunday at 2 p.m. in a small space that's part beatnik coffeehouse, part *Little House on the Prairie.* Phone ahead for reservations; schedules often shift and tickets ($10) can sell out quickly.

Birding excursions

Birders flock to Southeast Arizona — for good reason. Almost 500 migrating species use several ecologically diverse "sky islands" for migrational rest stops, and the area is considered one of this country's top five bird-watching spots. The best source of avian information is the **Sierra Vista Convention & Visitors Bureau** (see the "Fast Facts: Southern Cochise County" section), which can direct you to the nearby **San Pedro Riparian National Conservation Area** and **Environmental Operations Park;** the **Willcox Playa,** near Willcox; and **Cave Creek Canyon,** near Chiricahua National Monument, as well as to the various birding sites already mentioned in this chapter. The Sierra Vista CVB can also supply the Arizona Department of Tourism Southeastern Arizona Birding Trail map.

Want more guidance? The not-for-profit **Southeastern Arizona Bird Observatory,** based in Bisbee (☎ **520-432-1388;** `www.sabo.org`), is the top birding resource. In addition to providing a wealth of information about the best times and places for birders to visit Southern Arizona on its Web site, the organization offers year-round walks and workshops as well as seasonal hummingbird banding programs. SABO also highlights tour operators that offer more extended birding excursions, and occasionally runs its own overnight trips. Other birding associations in the area include the **Huachuca Audubon Society** (☎ **520-378-4937;** `http://has.hypermart.net`) and **Friends of the San Pedro River** (☎ **520-459-2555;** `www.theriver.com/public/fspr/fspr.htm`), both of which offer guided walks.

bargain, too, as such things as safety vests, water toys, and lockers are included in the admission price. Classes galore and entertainment (such as live bands and dive-in movies) round out the fun in summer. Admission: $5 ages 18–54, $4 ages 5–17, $3 55 up, additional fees for nighttime events. Open daily 1:30–5:30 p.m. weekdays, noon–5:30 p.m. weekends early June through Aug; open weekends only the rest of the year except spring break, Christmas week, Labor Day, and Memorial Day when summer hours apply.

Shopping for local treasures

Most of the shops in Tombstone are on Allen Street, the touristy main drag. Retail here tends toward the tacky T-shirt and souvenir shot-glass variety, but Arlene's, 404 Allen St. (☎ 520-457-3833), sells good Native American crafts and Western art. William Brown Holster Co., 302 E. Fremont St., behind the OK Corral (☎ 520-457-9208), specializes in hand-tooled reproductions of 19th-century holsters and also designs belts, saddlebags, and chaps. For Western antiques, try the Silver Lady, 515 E, Fremont St. (☎ 520-457-3800), adjoining the Tombstone Western Heritage Museum and owned by its very knowledgeable proprietors.

In Bisbee, many of the best shops are on Main Street. Tom Selleck and Faye Dunaway had themselves custom-fitted for Panama hats at Optimo, 47 Main St. (☎ 520-432-4544). Going ceramics crazy is easy at Poco Loco, 81 Main St. (☎ 520-432-7020), purveyors of wonderfully colorful dishes and other covetable housewares. My favorite of Main Street's many antiques shops, the sprawling, two-level Pentimento, 69 Main St (☎ 520-432-2752), also carries contemporary local crafts. On any given day, a flawless Czech Art Deco tea set may share floor space with kitschy Frida Kahlo shrines.

Living it up after dark

If you're seeking wine flights and other sophisticated sips, better head back to Tucson. If you like local, often historic, watering holes, however, you'll be happy in Tombstone and Bisbee.

In Tombstone, the Crystal Palace (see the "Exploring southern Cochise County" section of this chapter) gets lots of tourist traffic, but it's also where all the town's fake outlaws and real residents go to wet their whistles. Big Nose Kate's Saloon, Allen Street, between Fourth and Fifth streets (☎ 520-457-3107), which started life as the Grand Hotel in 1881, gets a similar mix of day-trippers and folks whose livelihoods depend on re-creating the characters who used to frequent the Grand.

Bisbee's past is less well known, but its bars are no less notorious: Brewery Gulch didn't get its name because the town had an abundance of tea houses. St. Elmo's, 36 Brewery Ave. (☎ 520-432-5578), is the oldest continuously operating bar in the state, and some of its patrons seem to have been imbibing there since it opened in 1902. Also in historic structures but attracting a somewhat less rowdy crowd are the Stock Exchange Bar, 15 Brewery Gulch (☎ 520-432-3317); the bar at the Hotel La More, 45 O.K. St (☎ 520-432-5131); and the saloon at the Bisbee Grand Hotel, 61 Main St. (☎ 520-432-5900). All pour Dave's Electric Ale, brewed in Bisbee.

Fast Facts: Southern Cochise County

Area Code

The area code is **☎ 520.**

Emergencies

Phone **☎ 911** for fire and police emergencies.

Hospitals

Sierra Vista Regional Health Center, 300 El Camino Real (**☎ 800-880-0088**; 520-458-2300) and the Copper Queen Community Hospital in Bisbee, 101 Cole Ave. (**☎ 520-432-5383**), offer 24-hour emergency service. Tombstone doesn't have any medical facilities.

Information

Sierra Vista Convention & Visitors Bureau is at 3020 E. Tacoma Dr. (**☎ 800-288-3861,** 520-417-6960, or 520-459-EVNT [special events hotline]; `www.visitsierravista.com`; open: Mon–Fri 8 a.m.–5 p.m., Sat 9 a.m. –4 p.m.). The Tombstone Chamber of Commerce is at Fourth and Allen streets (**☎ 888-457-3929** or 520-457-9317; `www.tombstone.org`; open: Mon–Fri 9 a.m.–5 p.m.). Tombstone's city-operated visitor Information Center is next door at 105 S. 4th St. (**☎ 520-457-3929;** `www.cityoftombstone.com`); open: daily 10 a.m.–4 p.m.). The Bisbee Visitor

Center is in the Copper Queen Plaza and Convention Center (☎ **866-2-BISBEE** or 520-432-3554; `www.discoverbisbee.com`; open: Mon–Fri 9 a.m.–5 p.m., Sat 10 a.m.–4 p.m and Sun 11 a.m.–4 p.m.).

Internet Access

In Tombstone, the Gitt Wired Internet Café, 505 E. Fremont (☎ **520-457-3250**), helps you do just what the name says. Open Mon–Fri 7 a.m.–3 p.m., Sat 8 a.m.–3 p.m.

Post Office

Locations include 2300 E. Fry Blvd., Sierra Vista (☎ **520-458-2540**); 100 N. Haskell St., Tombstone (☎ 520-457-3479); and 6 Main St., Bisbee (☎ **520-432-2052**).

Northern Cochise County

The long-awaited debut of Kartchner Caverns State Park in late 1999 continues to change the face of an area that time — and tourists — forgot. Among other things, chain motels and fast-food restaurants are cropping up in this region, which spreads south of I-10 to the east of Tucson. Benson, the town closest to the caverns, probably hasn't had this much press since the late 1880s, when three rail lines crossed here.

Benson may eventually become as convenient a base as Sierra Vista for forays into southern Cochise County, but at the moment, you won't find much reason to spend the night (with one notable exception, which I tell you about in the "Spending the night" section). Willcox, the other small town along I-10, has more Old West flavor but offers no good reason to bed down. Several lodgings outside these two main towns are great for travelers who want to bond with nature and relax in a remote setting. If you're not in this group, you can cover northern Cochise County's main attractions in a very full day trip from Tucson.

Getting there

Benson is 45 miles southeast of Tucson via I-10; continue another 38 miles on the freeway to reach Willcox. Amtrak (☎ 800-872-7245) runs trains from Tucson to Benson three times a week. Greyhound (☎ 800-231-2222) has twice daily service to both Benson and Willcox from Tucson, but you need a car to get around either town.

Spending the night

In addition to the lodgings I suggest, Benson has a Days Inn, Holiday Inn Express, Motel 6, and Super 8. In Willcox, you find links in the Best Western, Days Inn, Motel 6, and Super 8 chains. (See the Appendix for toll-free numbers.)

The two towns also offer a few low-key, nonchain motels. Choose your favorite neon sign and ask to look at a room if you want to take a chance.

Cochise Stronghold Bed and Breakfast

$$ Pearce

Its eco-conscious construction (straw bale, passive solar energy) and its spectacular setting in the Chiracahua Mountains make this B&B ideal for nature lovers of all sorts. You can enjoy vigorous hikes in the area or just sit out on one of two patios with binoculars and watch the birds flitting by during the day and the stars sparkling at night. The two lovely Western-flavored rooms are spacious enough for families but — what a treat! — you can shuttle the kids off to sleep in a well-insulated tepee and enjoy a little privacy.

2126 W. Windancer Trail, off Forest Service Road 84 (call for more detailed directions). ☎ ***877-426-4141*** *or tel/fax 520-826-4141;* `www.cochisestrongholdbb.com`. *Rack rates: $159–$189 double weekends, 10% lower on weekdays, 15% discount without breakfast. Tepee (with room rental) $79. Rates include 5-course breakfast. AE, DC, DISC, MC, V.*

Grapevine Canyon Ranch

$$$ Pearce

This guest ranch in a Western-purty setting with a working cattle ranch next door is the real deal. Cowgirl and cowboy wannabes can ride to their hearts' content and take part in round-ups and other ranching activities (May, July, Oct, and Jan only). Tenderfoots can choose to hike, swim, or soak in a hot tub. The cabins are fairly ordinary, the casitas more Southwest chic, and both types of rooms have kick-back porches or decks along with city slicker amenities, such as refrigerators, coffeemakers, and hairdryers. Casitas can sleep up to five people, depending on the unit, while cabins sleep only two people.

Highland Rd. (beyond Sunsites, off Highway 191; call for directions). ☎ ***800-245-9202*** *or 520-826-3185. Fax: 520-826-3636.* `www.gcranch.com`. *Rack rates: All per person based on double occupancy, June, July, Dec 1–15, Jan 15–30 $148 casitas nightly, $908 casitas weekly, $128/$788 cabins nightly/weekly; Feb, Aug–Sept $168/$1,038 casitas nightly/ weekly, $148/$918 cabins; Mar–May, Oct–Nov, Dec 16–Jan 14 $188/$1,158 casitas nightly/weekly, $168/$1,038 cabins. Rates include three meals, riding, and most ranch activities. Three-night minimum. Ages 12 and over only. AE, DISC, MC, V.*

Muleshoe Ranch

$–$$ Muleshoe Ranch Cooperative Management Area

How does holing up in a cabin near a natural hot spring in a nature preserve in the middle of nowhere sound to you? Clawfoot tubs, Mexican tile, and woodstoves are among the appealing details of these Nature Conservancy–run casitas, some of which date back to the late 1800s. All the units have kitchens or kitchenettes — crucial in this fast-food-barren wilderness. The surrounding land is owned and jointly managed by the Nature Conservancy, the Bureau of Land Management, and Coronado National Forest.

30 miles northwest of Willcox (call for directions). ☎ ***520-507-5229.*** www.muleshoelodging.org. ***Rack rates: $95–$158 double. AE, MC, V. Closed June–Aug.***

Skywatcher's Inn

$$ Benson

The Skywatcher's Inn is stellar. What other B&B do you know that has a private observatory and a rent-an-astronomer service? This place abounds in techno-gismos, including a classroom with mineral displays and science videos. Rooms are by no means geeky, however, and lovely rural vistas can be seen from the wraparound porch. This place is great for a family vacation, whether you're seeking earthly comforts or have your head in the clouds.

Astronomers Road (2 miles southeast of I-10 at Exit 306; call for directions). ☎ ***520-586-7906****; fax 520-586-1123.* www.skywatchersinn.com. ***Rack rates: $85–$119 double, $175 suite. Rates include full breakfast. Supervised observation programs from $59–$130 for up to 5 people; telescope rental available. MC, V.***

Dining locally

Northern Cochise County is no gourmet stompin' grounds; chain restaurants and modest cafes are pretty much all the area has to offer when chow time comes. I've driven out of my way for an apple pie from Stout's Cider Mill in Willcox (see the "Exploring northern Cochise County" section), but I haven't detoured for any other eats.

If you need to eat in Benson, I like two places on the town's main drag. The Old West diner atmosphere makes the Horseshoe Café ($–$$), 154 E. Fourth St. (☎ 520-586-3303), my favorite Benson chow down spot. The cafe duded up its menu a bit for tourists, but the green-chile burgers and fries are as good as ever, and they can never take the neon horseshoe off the ceiling — at least not if they don't want to change the restaurant's name. Ruiz Restaurant ($), 687 W. Fourth St. (☎ 520-586-2707), is fine for a down-home Mexican meal in an unpretentious setting.

In Willcox, the Desert Rose Café ($–$$), 706 S Haskell Ave. (☎ 520-384-0514), has a surprisingly sophisticated menu, including the likes of coconut shrimp and beef teriyaki. I can only personally attest to the high quality of the burgers and steak sandwich, though. Near the Rex Allen Museum, Rodney's a.k.a. "The Spot" ($–$$), 118 N. Railroad Ave. — such a hole in the wall that it doesn't have a phone — serves great barbecued pork sandwiches, with daily specials that may include ribs, shrimp, and catfish plates.

Exploring northern Cochise County

Life existed in northern Cochise County before Kartchner Caverns, but you'd never know it these days; most of the tourist action seems to have gone underground. The area's more remote natural attractions, particularly Chiricahua National Monument, are equally striking — not to mention less pricey — and Willcox hides some Western color behind its I-10 sprawl.

The top attractions

Amerind Foundation Museum

Dragoon

A stark Texas Canyon setting, a lovely Spanish colonial–style building, and a wide-ranging collection of American Indian (thus the name) artifacts make a visit to this middle-of-nowhere museum in Dragoon a unique experience. The historical materials contributed by founder William Fulton, an amateur archaelogist, are complemented by contemporary work in the same tradition. The museum is small, but allow 45 minutes to do the collection justice. If pressed for time, you can zip through the nice, but fairly traditional, Southwest art gallery next door.

See map p. 257. Dragoon Rd., 1 mile southeast of I-10 (Exit 318). ☎ ***520-586-3666.*** `www.amerind.org`. *Admission $5 adults, $4 seniors, $3 ages 12–18, 11 and under free. Open: Sept–May daily 10 a.m.–4 p.m., June–Aug Wed–Sun 10 a.m.–4 p.m.*

Chiricahua National Monument

Dos Cabezas Route

This natural monument is one of my favorites in Arizona — or anywhere. The volcanic rock outcroppings impossibly balanced against each other define the term "rugged western terrain." The Chiricahua Apaches, who spent a lot of time trying to keep white settlers out of the area, called this site the Land of the Standing-Up Rocks. But eroded boulders aren't the whole story. A huge variety of plant and animal species, many of which are more typically found in Mexico's Sierra Madres, make this area a great place to hike and bird-watch. A free 8:30 a.m. shuttle goes to a trailhead where you have a choice of descending via a 4-mile or 7½-mile route. Call ahead to check about the ranger-led tours of the Faraway Historic District, which includes a homestead turned guest ranch; they're subject to staff availability. The park has no services. Gas up and stock up on picnic supplies in Willcox.

See map p. 257. Take I-10 to the first Willcox exit and drive through town to Highway 186, where signs will direct you to the visitor center. ☎ ***520-824-3560.*** `www.nps.gov/chir`. *Admission: $5 per person, ages 16 and under free. Visitor center open daily 8 a.m.–4:30 p.m., closed Christmas.*

Kartchner Caverns State Park

Near Benson

A quarter of a century, secrecy to match the CIA's (on its good days), and about as much effort as was devoted to preserving Egypt's pyramids led to the public opening of this state park. The fascinating story of how the caverns were discovered by two Tucson cavers in 1974 is detailed in the visitor center. Despite the hype, don't get your expectations up too high if you're visiting between mid-April and mid-October. The Rotunda-Throne Room sections of Kartchner that are open to tours year 'round aren't nearly as large as those areas in other cave systems and — call me a cynic — I find the sound-and-light show at the end of the tour tacky (others tell me the display has moved them to tears). In contrast, the Big Room, which opened up to the public in late 2003, won't disappoint: This part of the caverns hosts many of the system's strangest and most colorful rock formations. Unfortunately, the bats like visiting this area, too; in order not to disturb them, visitors can't enter during the months when they're hanging around here.

The Rotunda-Throne tours lasts a little more than an hour; the Big Room tour about an hour and a half. You may want to spend another half hour or so in the visitor center; the 20-minute introductory film is definitely worth viewing. And the grounds are a great place to picnic. Pack a picnic

Ghost riding in southeast Arizona

Southeast Arizona's roads are scattered with the remains of once-bustling mining towns — some far more moribund than others — but the 35-mile back road from Pearce to Tombstone has been officially labeled the "Ghost Town Trail." A sign for the route can be seen on Highway 191 about 5 miles west of its junction with Highway 181, just beyond the town of Sunsites.

Of the three towns straddling the trail, **Pearce** is the liveliest, comparatively speaking. Grown rich on gold in the 1890s but largely abandoned in the 1930s, the town still has several intact buildings, including the stiflingly small adobe jailhouse. You also find a few functioning shops, including the old general store, a pottery shop, and **Udder Delight,** 1547 E. Old Pearce Rd. (☎ **520-826-1118;** closed Sun and Mon), which sells handcrafted goat milk soaps — and even has a soap museum!

If you're concentrating on avoiding the many ruts in the road, missing **Courtland,** some 12 miles south, is easy. The town consists of the upright shells of two buildings — one of them a jail — and a few other, less intact ruins. You can also glimpse remains of the copper mine that operated here from 1909 to 1920, when more than 2,000 people were in residence.

Gleeson, originally called Turquoise, was never as large as Courtland — the population topped out at about 500 — but it has held up a bit better. You can identify the town by its cemetery, the ruins of another lockup, and several ramshackle houses, a few of them occupied (they're easily recognizable by the "NO TRESPASSING" signs). If you'd rather add to your collection of weird souvenirs than poke around the past, follow the signs on Gleeson Road to **John & Sandy's Rattlesnake Crafts** (☎ **520-642-9207**), where purses, belts, eyeglass cases, coasters . . . about 150 rattlesnake skin items, total, are sold.

Although the packed dirt Ghost Town Trail — the signs for which disappear not far beyond Pearce — is usually maintained by Cochise County, driving a high-clearance vehicle here is best; definitely don't follow this trail in the rain otherwise. And don't come here expecting Hollywood-style ghost towns replete with rickety sidewalks — or even historical markers. You need a good imagination to appreciate the Old West aspect of this route, though not its solitude and desert scenery.

basket (only vending machines are on the grounds), and plan to spend another leisurely hour gazing at the surrounding mountains and desert, perhaps taking a short hike.

As a result of big publicity for relatively small-capacity cave tours, Kartchner Caverns books up well in advance. If you don't want to be disappointed, make reservations (yes, I'm shouting at you, but it's for your own good). Call Monday through Friday from 8 a.m. to 5 p.m., but be prepared to be patient; the line is often busy. The cavern staff sets aside 100 tickets for the Rotunda-Throne Room tours each day for people who haven't reserved, and the tickets go on sale at 7:30 a.m. and are usually sold out within 45 minutes. Because these tickets are for staggered tour times, you may have to wait around or come back much later for your assigned tour.

See map p. 257. Highway 90, 9 miles south of I-10, Exit 302. ☎ ***520-586-CAVE*** *(reservations).* `www.pr.state.az.us/Parks/parkhtml/kartchner.html`. *Admission for access to park grounds and Discovery Center (cave exhibits and visitor center): Rotunda-Throne tour (year-round) $18.95 adults, $9.95 ages 7–13, 6 and under free. Big Room tour (Oct 15–Apr 15): $22.95 adults, $12.95 ages 7–13, 6 and under not permitted to enter. Open: Daily 7:30 a.m.–6 p.m.; cave tours run approximately every 20 minutes from 8:30 a.m.–4:30 p.m. Closed Christmas.*

Willcox

These days, more trucks than trains stop at Willcox, formerly one of the country's major cattle shippers. The town still has some Old West kick left, however, especially in the Railroad Historic District, where you can see the restored Southern Pacific Willcox Historical Depot and the Willcox Commercial, Arizona's oldest department store. In addition to ducking into those two Railroad Avenue icons, you have a few other options.

Sunday isn't a good time to visit. Many of the town's attractions — including the depot and the Commercial — take this as day of rest.

- Improve your knowledge of movie cowboys. The Rex Allen Arizona Cowboy Museum and Theater, 155 N. Railroad Ave. (☎ 520-384-4583), displays the spangly costumes and other memorabilia from the many films that Willcox's favorite son made in the 1940s and 1950s. The Willcox Cowboy Hall of Fame, in the museum's back room, pays tribute to the area's less melodic ranchers and rodeo stars. Admission: $2 per person, $3 per couple, and $5 per family (talk about family values!). Open: Daily 10 a.m.–4 p.m., except Thanksgiving, Christmas, and New Year's Day.

  The ashes of the "last of the silver screen cowboys" were scattered in Railroad Park, just across the Rex Allen Museum. And Allen's mount, Koko (1940–1967), is buried in this park next to a bronze statue of his loyal human companion. (Allen thus spared Koko the fate of his fellow equestrian thespian, Trigger, who was stuffed and displayed in the Roy Rogers Museum.)

Whoop-de-do, Western style

Rex Allen Days, held the first weekend of October, continue despite the fact that Rex Allen, Sr., isn't around any longer to attend the festival that bears his name. (He died in Tucson in 1999.) For details about these four days of Western-style celebrations, including everything from turtle races and all-you-can-eat pancake breakfasts to a rip-roarin' rodeo, call the Willcox Chamber of Commerce (see the "Fast Facts: Northern Cochise County" section at the end of this chapter).

- Buy a big apple pie. Strange, but true: At an elevation of nearly 4,200 feet, Willcox is Arizona's apple center. And of the many local places to apple polish your trip, Stout's Cider Mill (☎ 520-384-3696) rules. The mill is across the parking lot from the Chamber of Commerce (see the "Fast Facts: Northern Cochise County" section later in this chapter). Don't try to pretend you're there for anything else but the famous pie, with a crust about 5 inches high and — the baker boasts — more apple-packed than any other.
- Trace the region's roots. Housed in a 1920s hardware store, the Chiricahua Regional Museum, 127 E. Maley, off Railroad Ave. (☎ 520-384-3971), focuses on the area's early ranching, railroading, and mining history. Especially noteworthy are the Apache Indian artifacts, including some belonging to Geronimo and Cochise. Admission by suggested donation: $2 singles, $3 couples, and $4 family. Open: Mon–Sat 10 a.m.–4 p.m., except holidays.

More cool things to see and do

From ancient rock art to 19th-century battlegrounds and current Arizona literature, you can find out about the state's past and present in this region.

- Find a hideaway. At Cochise Stronghold (☎ 520-364-3468; `www.cochisestronghold.com`) you see why it took so long for the U.S. Cavalry to capture Cochise and Geronimo. This natural granite fortress south of Dragoon is in a remote, rugged rock region that's great for hiking. To get here, take Exit 331 from I-10 to Highway 191; look for the sign for Cochise Stronghold at Ironwood Drive, near Sunsites. You have to drive nearly 9.1 miles on a fairly rough dirt road (Forest Rte. 84), which includes five stream crossings (don't try this in wet weather). You know you're there when you see some picnic tables, campsites, and restrooms. Admission: $3 day-use fee per vehicle. See map p. 257.
- Get fortified. You drive down a graded dirt road and trek 1½ miles to reach Fort Bowie National Historical Site (☎ 520-847-2500; `www.nps.gov/fobo`). Little is left of the 1862 fort or of the Butterfield Stage Station it guarded, and no evidence remains of the many

skirmishes between the Chiricahua Apaches and the U.S. Cavalry that took place here, but markers along the route and a serene setting render this site a good way to combine a little exercise — the hike's easy — with some history. To get here, take any of the I-10 Willcox exits to Highway 186. Drive 22 miles south; signs point you to the site. Admission: Free. Open: Grounds, daily dawn to dusk; visitor center and bookstore, daily 8 a.m.–4:30 p.m., closed Christmas. See map p. 257.

- Get bookish. A top-rate selection of books about Arizona plus a unique ranch setting make the Singing Wind Bookshop, Singing Wind Road (☎ 520-586-2425), worth the search. From Tucson, take I-10 Exit 304, just beyond Benson, and turn left. In about 2¼ miles, you see a red signpost at the bookstore turnoff. Prepare to stop and open the large green gate. Open: daily 9 a.m.–5 p.m.

Fast Facts: Northern Cochise County

Emergencies

Head to Benson Hospital, 450 S. Ocotillo (☎ **520-586-2261**), or Northern Cochise Community Hospital in Willcox, 901 W. Rex Allen Drive (☎ **800-696-3541** or 520-384-3541). For police or fire emergencies, call ☎ **911.**

Information

Benson Visitors Center, 249 E. Fourth St. (☎ **520-586-4293;** www.bensonchamberaz.com; open: Mon–Sat 9 a.m.–5 p.m.); Willcox Chamber of Commerce and Agriculture, 1500 N. Circle I Rd. (☎ **800-200-2272** or 520-384-2272; www.willcoxchamber.com; open: Mon–Sat 9 a.m.–5 p.m., Sun 10 a.m.–2 p.m.).

Internet Access

In Willcox, Motherlands Antiques/Postman Espresso, 116 S. Railroad Ave. (☎ **520-384-2875**), offers Internet access on its one computer from Mon–Sat 7:30 a.m.–8 p.m., Sun 10 a.m.–6 p.m.

Post Office

Locations include 250 S. Ocotillo Rd., Benson (☎ **520-586-3422**), and 200 S. Curtis Ave., Willcox (☎ **520-384-2689**).

Chapter 16

Central Arizona

In This Chapter

- Taking in Sedona and the Verde Valley: Red rocks, good vibes, and ancient sites
- Exploring Prescott: From Victorian row houses to Whiskey Row
- Going out Wickenburg Way: Dudes and ranches

Central Arizona has its ups and downs: Like much of the rest of the state, this region is on a geological roller coaster. Sedona, perched at 4,400 feet, and Prescott, nearly a mile high, are prime summer retreats for Phoenicians and out-of-staters alike, who are drawn year-round by the stunning red-rock vistas and charming Victorian neighborhoods. Wickenburg, Arizona's self-proclaimed dude-ranch capital, nestles at about 2,000 feet in the Hassayampa Valley. Wickenburg is nice and warm in winter, spring, and fall, but a bit too hot for most people in summer.

The towns in central Arizona are as different in personality as they are in elevation, but each offers loads of Western color and eye-catching vistas. With its no-holds-barred scenery and upscale lodging, dining, and shopping, Sedona has the highest profile in this generally low-key region. You can base yourself here for three or four nights, making trips to the Grand Canyon, Prescott, and Verde Valley, but you'd better be feeling pretty flush. Sedona isn't only the most expensive place to stay in central Arizona; it ranks with Scottsdale as the priciest in the entire state. Although much more economical, Prescott is a slightly less central base: The Grand Canyon is about 40 miles (round-trip) farther from Prescott than from Sedona. Wickenburg is fine for hops to Prescott and Phoenix, but many folks just like to settle in for a spell with a three-meal-a-day-plus-all-the-Western-style-relaxation-you-can-take guest-ranch package.

Prescott, Sedona, and Wickenburg are fairly close together, but the roads between them aren't straight. The Highway 89A/89 route from Sedona to Prescott to Wickenburg has long stretches of mountain road switchbacks. Much of the scenery is spectacular, but if you find this kind of driving as stressful as I do, you may not be able to enjoy the view.

Sedona and the Verde Valley

John Wayne meets the New Age in Sedona, a much-filmed Western landscape where, some people believe, powerful energy centers called vortexes enhance your well-being and creativity (in other words, your basic good vibes). The area definitely attracts artists, and visitors do tend to take on a mellow attitude, but that may also be because they're eyeballing incredible red-rock scenery and downing potent margaritas. Stretching out below Sedona, the Verde Valley gets far less press; most people stop by to see the Native American ruins and Jerome, a funky, far-from-moribund ghost town.

Sedona is an end, not a means, to other places, as its abundance of rooms, restaurants, and shops attest. But again, Sedona isn't cheap. Nor is it especially peaceful: In high season, the town can get annoyingly crowded with tourists (not you — all those other people). Still, Sedona has the best places to eat in the region, and I can see why you'd want to spend as much time in this gorgeous setting as possible.

Getting there

Sedona doesn't have commercial air service from Phoenix, but at each of the baggage claim areas at Phoenix Sky Harbor International Airport, you can pick up the Sedona-Phoenix Shuttle (☎ 800-448-7988 in Arizona or 928-282-2066; `www.sedona-phoenix-shuttle.com`). The shuttle departs eight times a day from 10 a.m. to 8 p.m., with hourly departures until 2 p.m., and the cost is $40 one-way and $65 round-trip. You may, however, want to skip the shuttle and head straight for the car rental counter. Although several car rental agencies operate in Sedona, you have more flexibility if you rent a car at the Phoenix airport (you're not likely to save money, however, because of the high taxes levied on cars rented at Sky Harbor).

From Phoenix, take I-17 to Highway 179 (exit 298). From the airport, the drive is about 119 miles, mostly on the freeway. Although curvy for stretches, I-17 is wide enough that you can drive the right lane at your own pace, letting the NASCAR racers zoom past.

The Coconino Yavapai Shuttle (☎ 888-440-8929 or 928-775-8929) makes regular runs to Sedona from Prescott and Flagstaff ($25 one-way from Prescott to Sedona or from Flagstaff to Sedona, $40 round-trip). You can pick up the shuttle at the Flagstaff Visitor Center (see Chapter 17) at 8 a.m., or call ahead and reserve door-to-door service.

The lay of the land

Before you set out on your own, get to know the lay of the land, which isn't as simple as you may think. The town known as Sedona really consists of four distinct areas.

Central Arizona

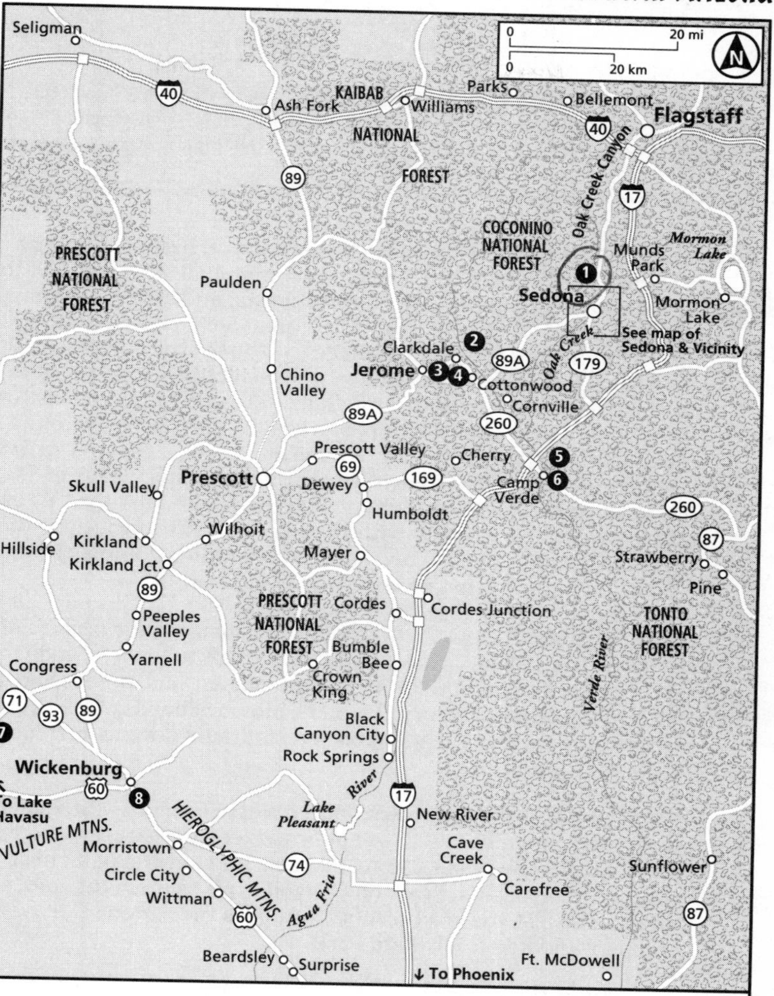

Seligman
40
Ash Fork
KAIBAB
NATIONAL
FOREST
Williams
Parks
Bellemont
Flagstaff
Oak Creek Canyon
89
17
COCONINO
NATIONAL
FOREST
Mormon
Lake
Munds
Park
PRESCOTT
NATIONAL
FOREST
Paulden
Sedona
Mormon
Lake
See map of
Sedona & Vicinity
Oak Creek
Clarkdale
Jerome
89A
179
Cottonwood
Cornville
Chino
Valley
89A
260
Prescott Valley
Cherry
69
Prescott
Skull Valley
Dewey
169
Camp
Verde
Humboldt
260
87
Hillside
Kirkland
Kirkland Jct.
Wilhoit
Mayer
Strawberry
Pine
89
PRESCOTT
NATIONAL
FOREST
Cordes
Cordes Junction
TONTO
NATIONAL
FOREST
Peeples
Valley
Yarnell
Bumble
Bee
Crown
King
Verde River
Congress
71
93
89
Black
Canyon City
Rock Springs
Wickenburg
60
To Lake
Havasu
River
17
Lake
Pleasant
New River
VULTURE MTNS.
HIEROGLYPHIC MTNS.
Morristown
Circle City
Wittman
74
Agua Fria
Cave
Creek
Carefree
Sunflower
60
87
Beardsley
Surprise
To Phoenix
Ft. McDowell
0
20 mi
0
20 km
N

Fort Verde State Historic Park 6
Hassayampa River Preserve 8
Jerome State Historic Park 3
Montezuma Castle National Monument 5
Robson's Mining World 7
Slide Rock State Park 1
Tuzigoot National Monument 4
Verde Canyon Railroad Depot 2

A tasty detour

Flying into Phoenix and driving toward Sedona around feeding time? Don't hassle with trying to find a place to eat in the big city. Get on I-17 and then stop in at the **Rock Springs Café and Bakery** (see Chapter 12), about a half hour north of the airport.

Coming in from Phoenix on Highway 179, you first encounter the Village of Oak Creek, which has a designer outlet mall with an IMAX theater; a few decent, reasonably priced restaurants; and several lodgings, many of the motel variety. It also has a U.S. Forest Service/Chamber of Commerce information center — a good place to stop for tourist information and a Red Rock Pass (see "The scenery's free — but the parking isn't" sidebar in this chapter) because it's much less crowded than the visitor center in Sedona. Continuing north past a rapidly shrinking stretch of undeveloped land, you see a sign for Sedona and several upscale strip shopping centers on your left. When you spot the shopping village of Tlaquepaque (ta-la-ka-pa-kee) on your right, you know you're near the "Y," as the usually crowded intersection with Highway 89A is known (even though, with the addition of a Hyatt time share and shopping complex in the early 2000s, the intersection now looks more like an "X").

Take a right on Highway 89A to get to the main visitor center and the touristy drag called Uptown Sedona, where you have to wade through a lot of schlock to find the gems. Several restaurants, hotels, and galleries fall into the latter category. Beyond Uptown Sedona is Oak Creek Canyon. Woodsy lodges and a few laid-back restaurants dot this extremely scenic route to Flagstaff.

If you go left at the Y, you encounter West Sedona — the real people's town, with amenities such as supermarkets, drugstores, and movie theaters. Most of Sedona's top restaurants and several of its best places to stay are here as well. Boynton Canyon is off to the right, and, as you continue along 89A toward Prescott, you pass the Sedona Cultural Park arts complex and Red Rock State Park.

The stretch of Highway 179 between the Village of Oak Creek and the Y has some of the worst traffic in the state. This winding, two-lane road is lined with businesses (maybe including your hotel) but has few turn lanes. Moreover, many people spend the afternoon or evening sipping margaritas on the outdoor decks of restaurants along this route. During the day, the road is usually too congested for much harm to be done, but watch out at night, when both the traffic flow and the booze flow accelerate.

Spending the night

Sedona is chock-a-block with rooms with a view and guest quarters that ooze character. Economical lodgings, on the other hand, are as rare as traffic-free crossings at the Y intersection. In this section, I give you a

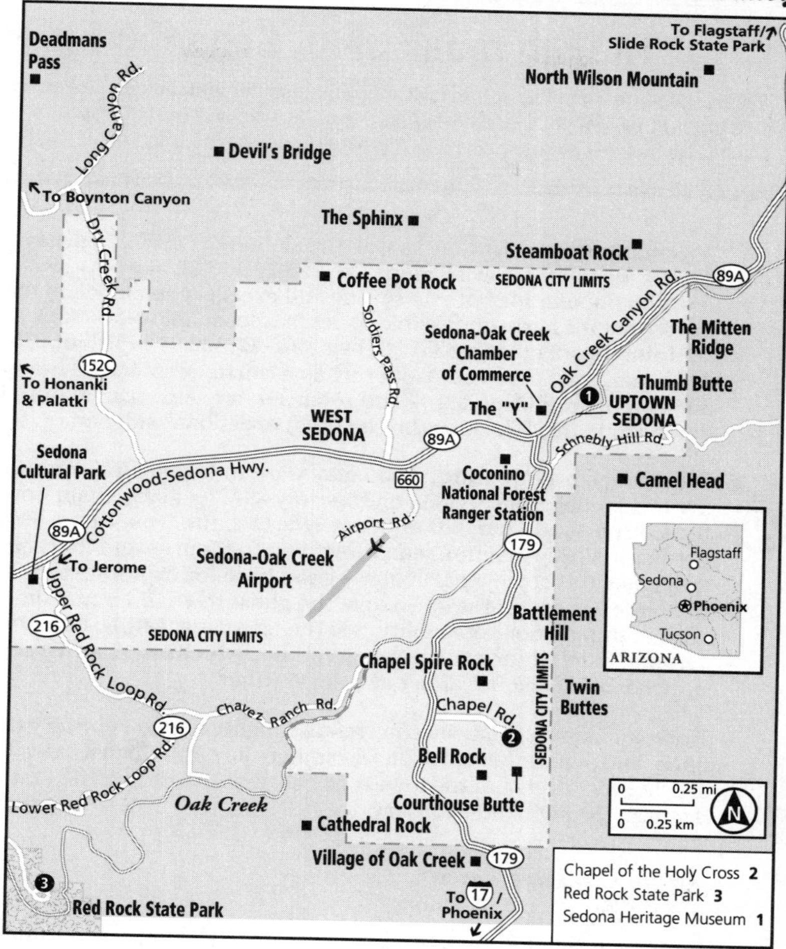

wide range of choices in the hotel and resort categories as well as in the "The inns (but no outs) of Sedona" sidebar. The town also has several chain hotels, which tend to be priced higher than their counterparts in other locations. Contact the Sedona–Oak Creek Chamber of Commerce (see the "Fast Facts: Sedona and the Verde Valley" section) for a complete listing of lodgings and reservation services.

Almost all the places I list are in areas that afford the best proximity to the red-rock vistas for which Sedona is renowned. If you're up for a more woodsy experience, consider the following creekside lodgings in verdant Oak Creek Canyon: Don Hoel's Cabins ($$), 9440 N. Highway 89A (☎ 800-292-HOEL or 928-282-3560; www.hoels.com), fairly rustic but clean and

The red rocks of . . . Schnebly?

When Theodore Schnebly, a Pennsylvania Dutch settler who bought 80 acres near Oak Creek in 1901, applied for a post office permit, he was told that his proposed name, "Schnebly Station," was too long. Luckily, his wife had a nice, short name: Sedona.

reasonably priced; Garland's Oak Creek Lodge ($$$$), Highway 89A, 8 miles north of Uptown Sedona (☎ 928-282-3343; www.garlandslodge.com), so popular for both its setting and excellent (included in the rates) meals that it's fairly impossible to get in (closed mid-Nov–Mar); and Junipine Resort ($$$), 8351 N. Hwy. 89A. ☎ 800-742-PINE or 928-282-3375; www.junipine.com), offering an assortment of family-friendly one- and two-bedroom condos — and room service. Also read about the Briar Patch Inn in the "The inns (but no outs) of Sedona" sidebar.

If economy is a top priority, you may want to hole up in Cottonwood, about 15 miles from Sedona on Highway 89A. Its many chain hotels — the Cottonwood Chamber of Commerce (see the "Fast Facts: Sedona and the Verde Valley" section) can direct you to them — and its central location make this town a particularly good base for exploring the region. On the opposite end of the spectrum, the ghost town of Jerome has lodgings with nothing if not personality. See the "Sleeping, eating, and drinking in Jerome" sidebar for my hotel suggestions, which aren't as luxurious as options in Sedona but aren't as pricey, either.

Note: In Sedona, "high season" refers roughly to mid-February through June, and September through December; July and August rates tend to be slightly lower, and the lowest prices of all are during the first week of January through mid-February.

Amara Creekside Resort

$$$–$$$$ Uptown Sedona

If you're tired of Southwest-style rooms but don't like the frilly fluffiness found in some B&Bs, you'll appreciate the pared-down design of this property, opened in 2003. The creekside setting, red-rock views, and creative cuisine are further pluses, and rates are lower than those at other resorts. On the other hand, this property doesn't offer the recreational amenities of the higher-priced places: You have to make do with a small pool and a basic exericise room.

310 N. Highway 89A. ☎ ***866-455-6610*** *or 928-282-4828;* www.amararesort.com. *Rack rates: low season $179–$259 doubles, $389 suites; high season, $259–$339 doubles; $429 suites. AE, DC, DISC, MC, V.*

Enchantment Resort/Mii amo

$$$$$ West Sedona

A knockout Boynton Canyon setting, rooms done in the height of Southwest chic, and a nice array of facilities have always put Enchantment on the top of my Arizona lodging list. I admit that I love the envy factor: Other people have to travel to reach the spectacular hiking trails that are here at your doorstep, and you have dibs on the drop-dead-view tables at the Yavapai Room. Stay at Mii amo, a separate destination spa on the property with Zen-chic guest rooms, and you get the edge on the hottest spa treatments in town and access to a terrific health-food restaurant that's off limits to the hoi polloi.

525 Boynton Canyon Rd. ☎ ***800-826-4180*** *or 928-282-2900. Fax: 928-282-9249.* `www.enchantmentresort.com` *(resort) or* `www.miiamo.com` *(spa). Enchantment rack rates: high season $420 double; low season $315 double; summer $295 double; suites from $420 in low season. All-inclusive Mii amo packages start at $1,685 for three nights, the minimum stay, in low season. AE, DC, DISC, MC, V.*

Hilton Sedona Resort & Spa

$$–$$$ Village of Oak Creek

The most family-friendly resort in Sedona, the Hilton has something for everyone, including a great pool complex (for the kids) and a well-equipped spa and proximity to one of the town's top golf courses (for parents). The spacious, nouveau Southwest-style suites, featuring microwaves and separate sleeping quarters for the young 'uns, are a boon to grownups, too, as is the property's coin-op laundry. No one minds the great red-rock views, either.

90 Ridge Trail Dr. ☎ ***877-2RED-ROCK*** *or 928-284-4040. Fax: 928-284-6940.* `www.hiltonsedona.com`*. Rack rates: $179–$239 rooms, $219–$319 1-bedroom suites high season, $99–$169 rooms, $129–$239 suites; 2-bedroom suites from $199 in low season. AE, DC, DISC, MC, V.*

L'Auberge de Sedona Resort

$$$$–$$$$$ Uptown Sedona

So what if this hillside resort feels more European than Southwest? When you cozy up in your luxurious bed, listening to the musical sounds of Oak Creek, you're in Romance World, anyway. L'Auberge offers two types of accommodations: appealing quarters in a main lodge building, and brookside cabins, all with jetted tubs and wood-burning fireplaces. Although the property seems tucked away, you're close to all the Uptown Sedona tour operators and shops — not to mention the resort's lovely French restaurant, which often has food to match the setting.

301 L'Auberge La. (½ mile west of the Y, off Hwy. 89A). ☎ ***800-272-6777*** *or 928-282-1661. Fax: 928-282-2885.* `www.lauberge.com`*. Rack rates: The Lodge: low season $265–$305 double; high season $305–$365 double. Cottages: $305–$365/$425–$525. Gourmet, romance, golf, and adventure packages available. AE, DC, DISC, MC, V.*

Getting creek-y

Keep in mind that central Arizona has two Oak Creeks. (Well, actually, just one body of water but two areas near Sedona with that name.) The Village of Oak Creek on Highway 179 is a rather nondescript town with some amazing red-rock backdrops. Oak Creek Canyon is the lovely gorge that Highway 89A winds through en route to Flagstaff. If you don't distinguish between the two when you ask for directions, you could be . . . well, up a creek.

Los Abrigados Resort & Spa

$$–$$$$ Near the Y

Although this resort operates as a time share, it has plenty to offer its many temporary guests, including a great spa and exercise facilities, in-your-pocket proximity to Sedona's famed Tlaquepaque shopping village, several lively restaurants and a sports bar, and even a new educational eco-center. The best part: suites comfortable enough for long-term stays and at rates that are relatively economical, for Sedona. The nine studio rooms near the tennis courts are a real deal. Although smaller, they have coffeemakers, microwaves, and minifridges, as well as a quieter location. Just be prepared to ignore the hard sell if you bed down anywhere on this property.

160 Portal Lane (next to Tlaquepaque shopping village; south of the Y). ☎ ***800-521-3131*** *or 928-282-1777. Fax: 928-282-2614.* www.ilxresorts.com. *Rack rates: $110 studio rooms; $225–$285 one-bedroom suites. AE, DISC, DC, MC, V.*

Radisson Poco Diablo Resort

$$–$$$ Between the Village of Oak Creek and the Y

Regular revamps haven't eliminated the motel-like look of the rooms in this resort, one of the town's older properties, but lush landscaping, a nice nine-hole golf course, several tennis courts, and a racquetball court — not to mention some terrific deals — definitely help compensate.

1752 S. Hwy. 179. ☎ ***800-333-3333*** *or 928-282-7333. Fax 928-282-9712.* www.radisson.com/sedonaaz. *Rack rates: $139–$209 double. AE, DISC, DC, MC, V.*

Sedona Reál

$$–$$$ West Sedona

For a reasonable price, you get airy, well-equipped suites that feature TVs, VCRs, refrigerators, and microwaves (some also offer fireplaces and two-person spas); free local phone calls and a complimentary Continental breakfast also add value. Best of all, you don't have to fight traffic to get into your room. Family-harmony extra: Some suites have two TVs, and you can get microwave popcorn and movies at the front desk.

Highway 89A West at Arroyo Piñon Drive (across from the movie theater). ☎ ***800-353-1239*** *or 928-282-1414.* www.sedonareal.com. *Rack rates: high season $135–$215*

1-bedroom suites; low season $105–$185 1-bedroom suites. Children under 12 stay free. AE, DISC, MC, V.

Sky Ranch Lodge

$–$$ West Sedona

I can't vouch for the existence of the vortex that's purportedly on Airport Mesa, this hotel's perch, but I can guarantee you a feeling of great well-being if you book a room here. The grounds, with old-growth trees and gardens, are lovely; the rooms, although simple, have touches that add character (some offer decks and/or fireplaces). You have access to a pool and hot tub, and you get some of the most spectacular red-rock views in town for some of the most reasonable rates.

The inns (but no outs) of Sedona

When it comes to some of Sedona's more intimate lodgings, the "bed-and-breakfast" label is misleading. True, they offer personalized service and a generous morning meal, but the following accommodations, all of which have at least eight guest units, bear a much stronger resemblance to boutique inns than they do to host homes. Expect such perks as privileges at local health clubs and on-call massage therapists. None of these inns has enforced communal dining, either, so you can be as friendly — or as antisocial — as you want to be in the a.m.

Adobe Village Graham Inn ($$–$$$ for B&B rooms and $$$$ for casitas), 150 Canyon Circle Dr., Village of Oak Creek (☎ **800-228-1425;** fax: 928-284-0767; `www.sedonasfinest.com`), offers attractive, standard B&B lodgings, but the drop-dead-gorgeous casitas, in a Spanish village–style complex, are the real reason to stay here.

Alma de Sedona ($$–$$$), 50 Hozoni Dr., West Sedona (☎ **800-923-2282;** `www.almadesedona.com`), takes Southwest luxury to the limit, offering beautifully decorated rooms in a dramatic pueblo-style building with stunning red-rock vistas.

Briar Patch Inn ($$–$$$), 3190 N. Hwy. 89A, Oak Creek Canyon (☎ **888-809-3030** or 928-282-2342; fax: 928-282-2399; `www.briarpatchinn.com`), features lovely 1930s cottages with spiffy Southwestern facelifts. During the summer, let live classical music soothe you at breakfast, along with the rushing waters of Oak Creek. More rustic than the rest, this B&B is also less pretentious.

El Portal ($$$$), 95 Portal Lane, south of the Y (☎ **800-313-0017;** fax 928-282-1941; `www.innsedona.com`), is the latest entry in Sedona's luxury inn sweepstakes, and the hands-down winner — if money is no object. The painstakingly detailed re-creation of a 1910 hacienda, replete with valuable period antiques, is spectacular, and the amenities (including the use of the spa at Los Abrigados Resort, next door) are endless.

The Inn on Oak Creek ($$–$$$), 556 Hwy. 179, south of the Y (☎ **800-499-7896** or 928-282-7896; fax: 928-282-0696; `www.sedona-inn.com`), counts a private creekside park, creatively themed rooms, and proximity to both Tlaquepaque's shopping and hiking trails among its many assets.

Airport Road (take Airport Road, off Highway 89A, almost to the top). ☎ ***888-708-6400*** *or 928-282-6400. Fax: 928-282-7682.* `www.skyranchlodge.com`. *Rack rates: $75–$159 double, $189 cottages with full kitchen. AE, MC, V.*

Dining locally

Sedona has fewer dining choices than lodging options, but with a population of only about 17,000, it definitely outdoes most towns its size, culinary-wise. It doesn't hurt (except in the pocketbook) that many of Sedona's transplanted residents have the sophisticated palates that often come along with high-priced real estate. Because restaurants cater more to the upscale visitors than to the New Age kind (the owners know what side their bruschetta is buttered on), hippie health-food dives are in short supply. However, most places please non-meat eaters with a variety of vegetarian choices.

In addition to the places listed, you may ask around about the chefs at the Yavapai Room at the Enchantment Resort and the restaurant at L'Auberge de Sedona (both resorts are detailed in the "Spending the night" section of this chapter). These two fine-dining rooms are ultra-romantic, with coveted views, but they're also ultra-expensive, and the food doesn't always warrant the financial outlay. Also check out the "A taste of Roma in Sedona" sidebar.

The Cowboy Club's Silver Saddle Room

$$$–$$$$ Uptown Sedona AMERICAN/SOUTHWESTERN

Who would have figured a place called the Cowboy Club in the touristy hub of Uptown Sedona would dish up sophisticated Southwest fare? The kitchen of one of Sedona's only historical structures turns out trendy appetizers, such as buffalo brochettes and entrees like pistachio-crusted halibut. The heaping plates of the more traditional ribs, steaks, and chops are deservedly popular, too.

241 Hwy. 89A (on the main street). ☎ ***928-282-4200.*** *Reservations suggested. Lunch: $8–$15; dinner: $15–$35. AE, DISC, MC, V. Open: Daily lunch and dinner.*

Heartline Café

$$$–$$$$ West Sedona NEW AMERICAN

Over the years, Sedona locals have come to depend on the Heartline not to disappoint. A friendly (but not obnoxiously so) staff serves some of the freshest, most interesting dishes in town in a cheery dark-wood dining room or on a pretty outdoor patio. The cultural mix-it-up menu includes such appetizers as sauteed lobster chunks with corn blinis, and entrees like pecan-crusted local trout with Dijon cream sauce. The vegetarian selections are similarly creative, and desserts like the fresh berry tart with hazelnut sauce are knockouts.

1610 W. Hwy. 89A. ☎ ***928-282-0785.*** *Reservations suggested. Main courses: Lunch $8–$14; dinner $15–$27. AE, DISC, MC, V. Open: Lunch Fri–Mon, dinner nightly.*

A taste of Roma in Sedona

Maybe it's because marinara sauce matches the red rocks. Or perhaps New Agers have been channeling chefs from Italy who've crossed over to the other side. Whatever the reason, Sedona has an abundance of good Italian restaurants. These are my favorites, for different prices, occasions, and locations (although West Sedona has the most options).

APizza Heaven ($–$$), 2675 W. Hwy. 89A, West Sedona (☎ **928-282-0299**), offers more than just good pizza (although it definitely has that covered). Come here for super-size heros and lasagne as cheesey and saucey as it's supposed to be.

Cucina Rustica ($$$–$$$$), 7000 Hwy. 179 at Tequa Marketplace, Village of Oak Creek (☎ **928-284-3010**), is the latest entry on the upscale Italian dining scene by the founders of Dahl & DiLuca (see the following entry). They've outdone themselves here with a gorgeous Mediterranean villa setting and a menu that sometimes puts a Southwest spin on the (mostly) Northern Italian specialties.

Dahl & DiLuca ($$$–$$$$), 2321 W. Hwy. 89A, West Sedona (☎ **928-282-5219**; `www.dahl-diluca.com`), a cozy candlelit room with hand-decorated walls, is the setting for starters such as mushrooms stuffed with mozzarella and fresh basil, followed, perhaps, by linguini in pomodora vodka sauce with prawns, all expertly turned out by Rome-born chef Andrea DiLuca.

The Hideaway ($$), 122 Hwy. 179 at Country Square, south of the Y (☎ **928-282-4204**), serves up spectacular red-rock views and decent Southern Italian food at prices below those of most restaurants in Sedona. A nice bonus: The kitchen creates its own sauces and spices.

Pietro's ($$$–$$$$), 2445 W. Hwy. 89A, West Sedona (☎ **928-282-2525**), has a sophisticated menu that includes dishes rare in cities far larger than Sedona (for example, penne salsicce, with lamb sausage and Swiss chard). The service is as big-city smart as the food.

Pizza Picazzo ($–$$), 1855 W. Hwy. 89A, West Sedona (☎ **928-282-4140**), may not serve the type of pizza you grew up with — possible ingredientsinclude hummus, jalepeños, and andouille sausage — but it's delicious, as are the (huge) creative salads that make great accompaniments or meals on their own.

Javelina Cantina

$$ South of the Y MEXICAN

The Javelina Cantina is one of Sedona's most popular — and liveliest — eateries. The specialty margaritas flow like water in this sprawling, oh-so-Southwest dining room; seats on the redwood deck with red-rock views are naturally the most coveted. The name of the game is tasty and fresh if Americanized Mexican food — tacos, tamales, enchilada combos, huge tortilla-base salads. Kids have a separate menu, and, with all the hubbub, most whining goes unnoticed.

671 Hwy. 179 (in the Hillside shopping center). ☎ ***928-203-9514.*** *Reservations suggested. Main courses: $11–$17 (a few dishes higher). AE, DC, MC, V. Open: Daily lunch and dinner.*

Oaxaca

$$–$$$ Uptown Sedona MEXICAN

What can be better than sitting on the outdoor deck of Oaxaca at sunset with a killer margarita in tow? Although it caters to the touristy Uptown Sedona crowds, this friendly Mexican restaurant never goes for the lowest common denominator. A multipage menu lists exotic items, such as grilled cactus pads (deprickled) with zesty romesco sauce — which also happens to be one of several heart-healthy selections. Said healthy choices are counterbalanced by desserts, such as the incredible deep-fried ice cream. The presentations are attractive, too. And did I mention the margaritas?

321 N. Hwy. 89A (smack in the middle of the main Uptown Sedona drag). ☎ ***928-282-4179.*** *Reservations needed for parties of more than 6. Main courses: $17–$23; most all-day Mexican specialties: $10–14; all-you-can-eat breakfast and fruit bar: $7.50 adults, $4.50 children. AE, DISC, MC, V ($20 minimum for all credit cards). Open: Daily breakfast, lunch, dinner.*

Rene at Tlaquepaque

$$$–$$$$ Just south of the Y CONTINENTAL

The Continental cuisine served in this pretty lace-curtain dining room isn't always exciting, but it's dependable. And despite nods to current trends seen in dishes like seitan tofu Wellington, it's also charmingly retro: The signature rack of lamb is carved tableside, and finishers include such immolated desserts as bananas foster.

Tlaquepaque, B-118, 336 Hwy. 179. ☎ ***928-282-9225.*** *Reservations recommended for dinner. MC, V. Main courses: $9–$14 lunch, $19–$30 dinner. Open: Daily lunch and dinner.*

Exploring Sedona and the Verde Valley

Sedona is strong on splendor and sports, but not so big on history. If you want to explore the area's rich mining and Native American past, tour the Verde Valley (which is no slouch in the scenery department, although not as showy).

If you drive up from Phoenix during daylight hours, detour off I-17 en route to Sedona to visit Montezuma's Castle and — if you're a military history buff — Fort Verde. You may enjoy Jerome, Tuzigoot, and the Verde Valley Railroad when you're red-rock sated. Keep in mind, too, that Jerome is about halfway between Sedona and Prescott on Highway 89A. If you want to visit Prescott from Sedona, build some extra time into your schedule for Jerome.

Wondering what gives Sedona's rosy rocks their color? The brightest red of the three layers of sandstone got its distinct hue when iron minerals mixed with oxygen to form iron oxide — in other words, rust.

The top attractions

Jerome

A bustling, rough 'n' tumble mining camp in the early 1900s — the population rose and fell with the price of copper, climbing up to about 15,000 in the late 1920s — Jerome earned its "ghost town" label after the last mine was shut down in 1953 and only 50 people stuck around the mountain. The town had a hippie and biker resurgence in the 1960s, and now some 450 folks, many of them artsy and craftsy, call Jerome home. Despite interesting shopping (see the "Shopping for local treasures" section later in this section) and fascinating history, another reason to wind your way some 2,000 feet up the side of Cleopatra Hill is for the views. On a clear day, you really can see forever. The Verde Valley spreads out below you, flanked by Sedona, the multihued Mogollon Rim, and the San Francisco Peaks, Arizona's highest mountains.

Jerome is about 25 miles southwest of Sedona via Highway 89A en route to Prescott. (If you're coming from Prescott, be aware that a popular Jerome T-shirt boasts that you'll be negotiating 158 curves in 12 miles.) If you want to stay in town for a while, see this chapter's "Sleeping, eating, and drinking in Jerome" sidebar. I list the hours for the town's few formal sights in this section, but don't hold me to them (except in the case of the state park). The attitude toward time in Jerome is, shall we say, relaxed. While you're here, you can:

- See how the other half lived. The mansion that's the centerpiece of Jerome State Historic Park, off Highway 89A on Douglas Road (☎ 928-634-5381), used to belong to Little Daisy mine owner "Rawhide Jimmy" Douglas. His original furniture sits among the displays, which include ore samples and mining equipment. The introductory film has a corny ghost narrator, but it's worth sitting through for the historical overview. Note: This mansion is also the town's unofficial visitor center. Admission: $4 adults, $1 children 7–13, free for ages 6 and under. Open: Daily 8:30 a.m.–5 p.m., except Christmas. See map p. 301.
- Mine more of the town's history. Among its many documents and artifacts, the Jerome Historical Society and Mine Museum, 200 Main St. (☎ 928-634-5477), includes stock certificates in mind-boggling amounts. Admission: $2 adults, $1 seniors 60 and up, 12 and under free. Open: Daily 9 a.m.–4:30 p.m. except Christmas and Thanksgivng.

  The displays at the Gold King Mine and Ghost Town, Perkinsville Road (follow the signs about 1 mile from the center of town) (☎ 928-634-0053), mix history with hype, but poking around the ruins of the town's once hugely wealthy gold mine is fun. Admission: $4 adults, $3 seniors 62–74, $2 ages 6–12, 5 and under and 75 and over free. Open: Daily 9 a.m.–5 p.m., except Christmas.

Sleeping, eating, and drinking in Jerome

For a ghost town, Jerome lays on lots of corporeal comforts. Here are my top picks for the best sleeps, eats, and drinks.

Lodging: A great location on the town's main street, antique furnishings, modern amenities, and reasonable rates all make the **Connor Hotel** ($–$$), 164 Main St. (☎ **800-523-3554** or 928-634-5006; `www.connorhotel.com`), hard to beat. Unlike many so-called historic lodgings, this place was actually built to be a hotel (in 1898). The vistas from the **Surgeon's House B & B** ($$), 101 Hill St. (☎ **800-639-1452** or 928-639-1452; `www.azjerome.com/surgeonshouse`), are therapeutic, and the generous breakfasts included in the room rate will cure whatever ails you.

Dining: The **Flatiron Cafe** ($), 416 Main St., (☎ **928-634-2733**), is the place to come for your morning latte or midday smoked salmon quesadilla. At the **Red Rooster Café** ($), 363 Main St. (☎ **928-634-634-7087**), follow a cup of fresh-made soup and Greek salad with some killer croissant bread pudding. Mellow deck views, a good bar, and hearty grilled fare make the **Haunted Hamburger** ($–$$), Jerome Avenue (☎ **928-634-0554**), a local dinner favorite. The most upscale eatery in town (white tablecloths and everything!), the **Asylum Restaurant & Lounge** ($$$), 200 Hill St., at the Jerome Grand Hotel (☎ **928-639-3197**), serves good versions of such dishes as steamed artichokes with aioli and grilled Australian lobster trails. (See also the "Fast Facts: Sedona and the Verde Valley" section for Reynard: A CyberCafé.)

Nightlife: Jerome's rowdy days are far from over. Bikers, hippies, and yuppies all pile into the **Spirit Room**, Main Street and Highway 89A (☎ **928-634-8809**), and **Paul and Jerry's Saloon**, just down Main Street (☎ **928-634-2603**), especially on live-music afternoons and evenings during the weekend.

Montezuma Castle National Monument

Near the town of Camp Verde

You may find larger remains of early Native American living quarters in the Southwest, but few are as well preserved and as easily viewed as these two 12th-century Sinagua cliff dwellings. Beaver Creek flows through this tree-shaded area — which explains why the Sinagua built homes here and why you'll especially enjoy your visit. A leisurely stroll around the guided loop path doesn't take more than a half hour. Devote another 15 minutes or so to the small visitor center museum, which traces the history of the Sinaguas in the Verde Valley.

If you have time, get back on I-17 heading toward Flagstaff and take the next (McGuireville) turnoff. Signs direct you to Montezuma Well, which is part of the national monument (same hours, no fee). It is a huge, strikingly blue spring-fed pool, some 368 feet across and 65 feet deep. Another easy side trip from Montezuma's Castle is to Fort Verde (see the following section, "More cool things to see and do"). If you need to choose between these two side trips because of time constraints, I vote for Montezuma Well.

See map p. 301. Exit 289 from I-17 and follow the signs. ☎ ***928-567-3322.*** `www.nps.gov/moca`. *Admission: $3, ages 16 and under free. Golden Age/Golden Eagle passes accepted for free admission. Open: Memorial Day to Labor Day 8 a.m.–7 p.m.; rest of the year 8 a.m.–5 p.m.*

Sedona/Oak Creek Canyon

Few activities in or near Sedona involve taxing your brain cells — except maybe calculating how close you are to maxing out your credit cards. This town is mainly about gazing at stunning scenery. The following list includes numerous way to do just that — without expending too much energy.

- See some stately rocks. No, the rusty sandstone cliffs that fall under the aegis of Red Rock State Park, 4050 Lower Red Rock Loop Rd. (☎ 928-282-6907), are no more exciting than any of the others in this area. This spot is, however, a good place to walk along some gentle trails near Oak Creek and take one of the daily ranger-led nature walks (10 a.m. and 2 p.m. [2 p.m. walk not offered the first Sunday of each month]). Call ahead, too, for the seasonally changing schedules of bird-watching excursions. The turnoff for the park is 2 miles beyond West Sedona on Highway 89A. Admission: $6 per car with up to 4 people, $1 additional per each additional person. Open: Daily Oct–Mar 8 a.m.–5 p.m.; Apr and Sept. 8 a.m.–6 p.m.; May–Aug 8 a.m.–8 p.m. See map p. 303.

- Go slip-sliding away. The natural water slide in Oak Creek explains the name of Slide Rock State Park, 7 miles north of Sedona on Highway 89A, Oak Creek Canyon (☎ 928-282-3034). The slide — along with a volleyball net, the pizza-selling Slide Rock Market, and picnic tables — also makes this park a major summer party place and family gathering ground. After the warm weather sets in, hardly a parking spot can be found after 10 a.m. Several trailheads are in this area, too. Admission: $8 per car with up to 4 adults (13 and under are free), $1 additional each additional adult. Open: Daily summer 8 a.m.–7 p.m., winter 8 a.m.–5 p.m., fall and spring 8 a.m.–6 p.m. See map p. 301.
- Get spiritual. You don't have to subscribe to any particular creed to want to visit the Chapel of the Holy Cross (☎ 928-282-4069), built in 1956 by a protégé of Frank Lloyd Wright. Like her mentor, Marguerite Brunwige Staude knew the importance of working with her surroundings, and this simple, clean-lined house of worship seems to have sprung from the red cliffs that surround it. Look for the cross on the right side of Highway 179 as you head north toward the Y from the Village of Oak Creek, and turn right on Chapel Road. Open: Daily 9 a.m.–5 p.m. See map p. 303.
- Soak up some history. Okay, so I lied. A couple of attractions in this area do cater to people who like to revisit the past. Slide Rock State Park (described earlier in this section) was originally Pendley Homestead, an apple farm established in 1910. Rangers sometimes xrun tours (phone ahead to Slide Rock State Park), and you can walk the easy ¼ mile Pendley Homestead Trail through some of the

original apple orchards and past the homestead house, tourist cabins, and apple packing barn. Apples are for sale in season.

The Sedona Heritage Museum, 735 Jordan Rd., Uptown Sedona (☎ 928-282-7038; www.sedonamuseum.org), also gives a feel (or is that a peel?) for an era when apple-growing was a major source of income in this region. Exhibits on the lovely woods-flanked property that once belonged to pioneers Walter and Ruth Jordan include an apple packing shed and a 45-foot-long apple-sorting machine. You also find a room devoted to film — dozens of Westerns have used Sedona as a backdrop. Admission: $3 adults, ages 11 and under free. Open: Daily 11 a.m.–3 p.m., closed major holidays. See map p. 303.

- Discover rock art. If you don't mind putting a bit of wear on your tires on (more-or-less) graded dirt roads, the area's low-key Native American sites are well worth a visit. Palatki, on the west side of Sedona, features a cliff dwelling and lots of petroglyphs, some dating back 6,000 years. Three miles away but even tougher on the suspension system, Honanki has more extensive ruins but less interesting rock art. The best petroglyphs of all are at V-Bar-V Ranch, located en route to Sedona, near the junction of I-17 and Highway 179. All three sites have limited hours of access, and directions to them are a bit complicated. Because you need a Red Rock Pass (see "The scenery's free — but the parking isn't" sidebar) to visit them, your best bet is to get directions, current hours, and road conditions (these roads wash out easily) at the U.S. ranger station where you purchase the pass.

What color is your aura?

Chakras blocked? Past lives eluding you? Not to worry. Sedona has something to meet your every psychic or spiritual need. **Crystal Magic,** 2978 W. Hwy. 89A, West Sedona, sells more than just its namesake sparkly minerals; you also find healing vitamins, New Age books, meditation tapes . . . you name it. Also in West Sedona, the **Golden World Book Centre,** 3150 W. Hwy. 89A (**☎ 928-282-2688**) claims to have the largest selection of New Age books and products in northern Arizona. At the **Center for the New Age,** 341 Hwy. 179, across from Tlaquepaque (**☎ 928-282-2085**), you can have your astrological chart read or get a snapshot that shows you precisely where your aura falls on the chromatic scale.

For an excellent — and eminently sensible — exploration of Sedona's vortexes, consider a guided hike with **MetaAdventures,** 583 Circle Dr. (**☎ 928-204-2201,** www.metaadventures.com). Founder Dennis Andres, who authored *What Is a Vortex?* and *Sedona's Best Hikes,* as well as *The Insider's Guide to Sedona,* can take you to some of the spots considered most spiritual in Sedona (not by coincidence, they're also the most beautiful).

For additional resources, contact Craig Junjulas at the **Sedona Metaphysical Spiritual Association** (**☎ 928-282-8981**).

Tuzigoot National Monument

Just outside Clarkdale

The group of Sinagua Indians who lived in Montezuma's Castle (see the listing earlier in this section) went for the creekside real estate. Their kin who settled at Tuzigoot between the years 1125 and 1400 liked the hilltop property, prime both for protection purposes (enemies approaching from anywhere around the Verde Valley could be spotted from there) and for the adjacent fertile farmland that the Hohokam Indians had left behind. These days, some of the views are spoiled by a slag field left over from the mines at nearby Jerome and by a huge cement plant tower, but this spot is still scenic and a good place to soak in some local history. Doing the slightly hilly loop around the pueblo complex takes about a half hour; add another 10 minutes for the museum/visitor center.

See map p. 301. Broadway Road (off Highway 89A, between Old Town Cottonwood and Clarkdale). **☎ 928-634-5564.** `www.nps.gov/tuzi`. *Admission: $3; ages 16 and under free. Golden Age/Golden Eagle passes accepted for free admission. Open: Memorial Day to Labor Day daily 8 a.m.–6 p.m., the rest of the year 8 a.m.–5 p.m.*

More cool things to see and do

Here you have more options for spending time outdoors, whether you want to explore an old fort or play cowboy.

- Visit a historic fort. A museum and several reconstructed officers' quarters in Fort Verde State Historic Park, 125 E. Hollamon St., Camp Verde (☎ 928-567-3275), tell the story of this fairly short-lived (1871–1891) military installation. Established to protect Verde Valley from Indian raids, the fort supervised the forced displacement of the Yavapai and Tonto Apaches to reservations in Eastern Arizona. To get there, follow the signs from any of the three Camp Verde exits on I-17. (Only the first, if you're coming from Phoenix, is marked "Fort Verde," but all three lead to downtown, where the park is located.) Admission: $3 adults, $1 ages 7–13, 6 and under free. Open: Daily 8 a.m.–5 p.m., except Christmas. See map p. 301.

- Be a cowpoke. The Blazin' M Ranch, off 10th Street in Cottonwood (☎ 800-WEST-643; `www.blazinm.com`), is a replica of an Old West town. The ranch has pony rides, a shooting gallery, a mechanical horse, and souvenir shops, but most people come for the chuckwagon suppers and Western stage shows, held nightly Wednesday through Sunday (closed Jan and Aug). For $24 adults, $21 seniors, $14 ages 12 and under (3 and under free), you get a good homespun all-you-can-eat dinner and good, clean Country and Western entertainment. Kids who think they're hip don't necessarily cotton to the old cowboy ballads and Hee Haw–style comedy routines, but they do tend to like the big barn setting — not to mention eating food off a tin plate. To get there, follow the signs to Dead Horse Ranch State Park, and turn left just past the entrance.

Guided tours

All the following tours are given in Sedona. Another tour in Sedona that I mention in this chapter is the vortex/hiking tour described in the "What color is your aura?" sidebar. Also look for the "Take the last train from Clarkdale" sidebar for excursions on the Verde Canyon Railroad.

- General tours: If you want to survey the lay of the land, board the Sedona Trolley (☎ 928-282-5400; www.sedonatrolley.com). Two 55-minute tours depart from the Sedona Center in Uptown Sedona. One (10 a.m., noon, 2 p.m., 4 p.m.) goes along Highway 179 to Tlaquepaque, the Chapel of the Holy Cross, and gallery row. The other (9.a.m., 11 a.m., 1 p.m., 3 p.m., 5 p.m.) visits West Sedona, some scenic canyons, and Enchantment Resort. The cost is $9 adults ($5 ages 12 and under) for one tour or $16 ($8) for both tours.
- Air tours: Feeling a bit too grounded? Tour operators in Sedona cater to every lofty inclination. If you go for a hot-air-balloon ride, you are picked up at your hotel. If you're up for a helicopter or small plane jaunt, drive to the Sedona Airport (turn off Highway 89A west of the Y onto Airport Road and keep going up to the top of the hill).

  A helicopter may be the best bet if you're a bit afraid of heights (like I am). It's more enclosed than the hot-air balloon, and those big, whirling blades make a helicopter feel more stable than a small plane. (That's a purely personal, totally nonaerodynamically informed opinion.)

  - By hot-air balloon: What could be more heavenly than floating above the red rocks at sunrise in a hot-air balloon? (Well, maybe floating above the red rocks at sunset, so you don't have to get up before dawn, but, again, that's just my opinion.) Wind conditions permitting, Red Rock Balloon Adventures (☎ 800-258-3754; www.redrockballoons.com) can take you up, up, and away for a minimum of an hour, then reward you with a champagne picnic and proof-of-flight certificate. The $175-per-person fee also includes one free video of your trip per reservation.
  - By helicopter: Nothing compares to a whirlybird for getting up close and personal with the landscape. Prices for a 12-minute tour of Cathedral Rock, Bell Rock, and other Sedona landmarks start at $60 per person at Arizona Helicopter Adventures (☎ 800-282-5141 or 928-282-0904; www.azheli.com) and top off at $140 per person for a 35-minute buzz through various dramatic canyons.
- Jeep tours: Pink Jeep, 204 N. Hwy. 89A, Uptown Sedona (☎ 800-873-3662 or 928-282-5000; www.pinkjeep.com), is the largest and most blushingly conspicuous of Sedona's many off-road tour operators. You can choose from seven adventures ranging from a 1½-hour Canyon West jaunt ($40) to a 4-hour combination Ancient Ruin and

Take the last train from Clarkdale

Chug-a-lug amid some of the most arresting scenery in Arizona on the **Verde Canyon Railroad,** 300 N. Broadway, Clarkdale (☎ **800-293-7245** or 800-320-0718; www.verdecanyonrr.com). You ride rails that formerly transported tons of ore from Jerome's United Verde Copper Mine. The four-hour round-trip ride through a protected wilderness area in a red-rock canyon has some historical constants — the ghost town of Perkinsville and a few Native American cliff dwellings, for example — but nature puts on a different show each season. The bald eagle watch from December through March is the most renowned, but fall foliage, spring wildflowers, and summer waterfalls are pretty impressive, too. In addition to the regular runs, special starlight and wine-tasting rides are offered in the summer. Schedules vary by season; except in January, the time of most limited service, you can expect at least afternoon trains four times a week. In peak times, especially March, April, October, and November, extra rides fill the schedule. Rates are $39.95 adults, $35.95 seniors (ages 65+), and $24.95 children (ages 2–12) in coach, $59.95 for all in first class. See map p. 301.

Diamondback Gulch archaeological tour ($95). I recommend the 2.5–3 hour Ancient Ruin tour ($65), which takes you to the Honanki petroglyph site. Another option for those interested in Native American art is the 4-hour Spirit Hunters tour ($105) offered by Red Rock Jeep Tours (☎ 800-848-7728 or 928-282-6826; www.redrockjeep.com), which visits an ancient solar calendar. Want to try your hand at maneuvering a Jeep? Consider one of the Tag Along tours offered by The Adventure Company (☎ 877-281-6622 or 928-204-1973, www.sedonajeeptours.com), ranging from $95 per person (for 2 people, lower for more) on a 2.5-hour tour to $125 each for a 4-hour tour.

Tooling around off-road has become so popular in Sedona that you often end up simply bumping along, inhaling dust from the vehicle in front of you — and not just on the Tag Along tour. Ask how many jeeps will be involved in the adventure that most interests you. Your guide's knowledge also makes a huge difference in your enjoyment of the experience. Find out how long your driver has been in town (if you're taking a Pink Jeep tour, try to get on one run by Michael Peach, an excellent guide).

Staying active

Looking for even more ways to get some fresh air in Sedona? Here ya go.

- Biking: In recent years, Sedona has become a mountain-biker's mecca. You can get wired up and wheeled out at the Sedona Bike & Bean Shop, 6020 Hwy. 179, Village of Oak Creek (☎ 928-284-8210; www.bike-bean.com), a coffee bar that rents bikes and rooms near a major trailhead. Mountain Bike Heaven, 1695 W. Hwy. 89A, West

Sedona (☎ 928-282-1312; www.mountainbikeheaven.com), offers rentals by the hour, including helmet, trail map, and water bottle, with a $20 minimum. Absolute Bikes, 6101 Hwy. 179, Suite C, Village of Oak Creek (☎ 928-284-1242; www.absolutebikes.net/sedona), has the largest selection of two-wheelers, and also rents trailers and mounts as well. All three shops offer front- and full-suspension bikes, and prices range from $7.50 per hour to $40 per day.

- Fishing: Anglers of all ages have fun at the stocked Rainbow Trout Farm, 3500 N. Hwy. 89A, 3 miles north of Sedona in Oak Creek Canyon (☎ 928-282-5799; open, weather permitting: fall to spring Mon–Fri 9 a.m.–5 p.m., Sat–Sun 9 a.m.–6 p.m., summer Mon–Fri 8 a.m.–5 p.m., Sat–Sun 8 a.m.–6 p.m.). For a $2 admission fee, you get a pole with a hook and bait. After that, you pay according to the size of your catch, from $5.25–$8.25 per fish (pipsqueak specimens under 8 inches are free). You pay another 50¢ each if you want to take the fish back clean. Maximum stay: two hours.
- Golfing: The Sedona area offers only two 18-hole championship golf courses. In fall and spring, greens fees at the Gary Panks–designed course at the Sedona Golf Resort, 35 Ridge Trail Dr., off Highway 179, near the Village of Oak Creek (☎ 928-284-9355), run $99; the price drops to $69 after 2 p.m.; fees are lower in winter and summer. In high season, you pay $75 before 1 p.m. and $60 after 1 p.m. to play the Oak Creek Country Club, 690 Bell Rock Blvd., also off Highway 179 near the Village of Oak Creek (☎ 928-284-1660), where Robert Trent Jones put his hand to the grass arrangement. A quick game at the 9-hole course at Radisson Poco Diablo (see the "Spending the night" section earlier in this chapter) sets you back only $12; all-day passes are $20. The red-rock distractions at all three courses are free.
- Hiking: You'll find even more trailheads than vortexes in this primo trekking region. Some of the most popular hiking spots are Boynton Canyon and Loy Canyon in West Sedona; the trails leading to Bell Rock along Highway 179; and the West Fork Trail in Oak Creek Canyon. Check with one of the U.S. Forest Service offices (see the "Fast Facts: Sedona and Verde Valley" section) regarding the length and difficulty of the various trails. These offices can also tell you if you need to buy a Red Rock Pass (see "The scenery's free — but the parking isn't" sidebar) for the area in which you want to hike. For other hiking suggestions, see the "Exploring Sedona and the Verde Valley" section earlier in this chapter.

- Horseback riding: At Trail Horse Adventures (☎ 800-723-3538; www.trailhorseadventures.com), rates start at $48 per person for a one-hour guided ride. Excursions of two hours ($55) or longer take you through Coconino National Forest and across Oak Creek, a stream fording unique to this outfitter. Sedona Red Rock Jeep Tours, 217 N. Hwy. 89A, Uptown Sedona (☎ 800-848-7728 or 928-282-6826; www.redrockjeep.com), trade four wheels for four-legged transport for trots around a working cattle ranch that start at $54 for one hour. Both outfitters offer dinner rides with cowboy cookouts.

The scenery's free — but the parking isn't

You can view Sedona's red rocks all you like from your car, but if you want to get up close and personal with them on U.S. Forest Service land (and there's a lot of it in this area), you'll have to buy a Red Rock Pass ($5 per day, $15 per week, $20 per year). Passes are available at Sedona's visitor centers (see the "Fast Facts: Sedona and the Verde Valley" section), at various trailheads, and at many local stores and hotels. For additional information about where to buy the passes and the areas to which they afford access, call ☎ **928-282-4119** or log on to `www.redrockcountry.org`.

- Spa-ing: Okay, so this isn't exactly a way to keep active, but it's a great way to relieve sore muscles so you can get back in the saddle (or bike seat, or hiking boots). Of the several local day spas, my favorite is Sedona's New Day Spa, 1449 W. Hwy. 89 A, Ste. 1 (☎ 928-282-7502; `www.sedonanewdayspa.com`), which offers everything from conventional massage, wraps, and facials to metaphysical services such as Aura-Soma therapy.

Shopping for local treasures

Both Sedona and Jerome are prime retail stops, particularly if you covet arts and crafts of the Southwestern and Western persuasion.

Where to look in Sedona

Shoppers practice conspicuous consumption on almost every square foot of (paved) Sedona, but retail is most concentrated in two areas: Uptown Sedona and the stretch along Highway 179 from the town limit sign north to the Y. The east side of Highway 179 hosts several shopping strips, the best known and most upscale of which are Hillside Sedona, 671 Hwy. 179 (☎ 928-282-4500) and Hozho Distinctive Shops & Galleries, 431 Hwy. 179 (☎ 928-204-2257). On the west side of the road as you approach the Y is the jewel in Sedona's shopping crown, Tlaquepaque Arts & Crafts Village, 336 Hwy. 179 (☎ 928-282-4838), a replica of the shopping town outside of Guadalajara, Mexico (except you won't find bargaining — or bargains — here). Even if you don't want to buy anything, drop in to stroll around the two charming plazas of this red-tile-roof complex. Tlaquepaque even has a small wedding chapel.

Large parking lots adjoin Tlaquepaque, but the places to leave your car at Hillside and Hozho are more limited. You may have to drive around for a while in a rather tight area before a space opens up.

In addition to the storefronts lining Highway 89A and the galleries along Jordan Road, Uptown Sedona features two shopping complexes: Sinagua Plaza, 270 N. Hwy. 89A (☎ 928-282-0641), and Sacagawea Plaza, 301 N. Hwy. 89A.

Two new retail centers to look out for are Tequa Festival Marketplace, 7000 Hwy. 179, Village of Oak Creek, and Shops at Piñon Pointe in the Hyatt Vacation Club complex, right at the Y. Both of these upscale complexes promise a combination of national chains (Chico's at Piñon Point, for example) and one-of-a-kind retail and dining (Cucina Rustica at Tequa).

Don't bother cruising congested Highway 89A for a spot in Uptown Sedona in the busy season. Free of charge, you can leave your car in the lot behind the Chamber of Commerce (see the "Fast Facts: Sedona and the Verde Valley" section) or in the larger, two-level one in the back of Sinagua Plaza.

What to buy in Sedona

Art galleries and Southwest-crafts boutiques dominate all the complexes mentioned in the preceding section; Hozho is particularly strong on art, Tlaquepaque on crafts. Which shops are the best? I could devote another entire book — not to mention my life's savings — to Sedona's shops. This section includes just a few suggestions to start you off. Also check out the "What color is my aura?" sidebar for shops that'll fill your spiritual needs.

One of Arizona's (and possibly the world's) best places to buy Native American weavings and other crafts is Garland's Navajo Rugs, 411 Hwy. 179 at Schnebly Hill Road (☎ 928-282-4070). For personal decoration, visit Garland's Indian Jewelry Inc., 3953 Hwy. 89A, 4 miles north of Uptown Sedona in Oak Creek Canyon (☎ 928-282-6632). The Turquoise Tortoise, The Hopi-owned and -run Art of the Hopi, Ste. A-206 in Tlaquepaque (☎ 928-204-2658), has one of the top selections of katsinas (see Chapter 19 for more on these dolls) in the state. The Turquoise Tortoise Gallery in Hozho (☎ 928-282-2262) sells beautifully crafted — and commensurately pricey — Native American art and jewelry.

Two of the biggest guns in the fine-art collecting game are Exposures International Gallery of Fine Art, 561 Hwy. 179, south of the Y (☎ 928-282-1125) and Lanning Gallery in Hozho (☎ 928-282-6865). James Ratliff Gallery, also in Hozho (☎ 928-282-1404), carries more fanciful — and sometimes less expensive — pieces by less established artists.

For distinctive women's wear with a romantic air, try the Victorian Cowgirl, 2445 W. Hwy. 89A, West Sedona (☎ 928-282-7592). If I could afford it, I'd make a big dent in the inventory of hand-woven scarves and hand-stitched jackets at Isadora, Ste. A-120, Tlaquepaque (☎ 928-282-6232).

If you like to give picture-perfect dinner parties — and aren't as klutzy as I am — browse the beautifully designed vases and stemware at Kuivato Glass Gallery, Ste. B-122, Tlaquepaque (☎ 928-282-1212), and the vibrantly patterned ceramic dishes at the Clay Pigeon, Hillside (☎ 928-282-2845). Categorizing Mother Nature's Gallery, Ste. B-218, Tlaquepaque

(☎ 928-282-5932), is tough — think Sharper Image meets the Flintstones. If a dinosaur sculpture would look good in your living room, give this place a try. (You find lots of fun science toys, too.)

The relatively small Oak Creek Factory Outlets, 6601 S. Hwy. 179, Village of Oak Creek (☎ 888-545-7227 or 928-284-2150), includes the Gap, Tommy Hilfiger, Oneida, 9 West, Bass, and more.

Where to look and what to buy in Jerome

Shopping in Jerome is easier than in Sedona: All the shops are on Main Street with some additional shops on Hull Avenue, just around the bend. The Jerome Artists Cooperative, 502 Main St. (☎ 928-639-4276), is a good spot for a general survey of some of the town's best crafts at some of the best prices (yes, even funky Jerome is going upscale). I've put in a fair share of time trying on floppy hats and colorful Southwestern clothes at Designs on You, 233 Main St. (☎ 928-634-7879). Other retailers on my regular check-in list include Nelly Bly, 136 Main St. (☎ 928-634-0255), with an unusual collection of kaleidoscopes, Raku Gallery, 250 Hull Ave. (☎ 928-639-0239), shimmering with the distinctive shiny-glaze ceramics that give the shop its name; and House of Joy, 416 Hull Ave.; ☎ 928-634-5339), a former brothel that specializes in reproductions of risqué Victorian posters, postcards, and outfits.

Living it up after dark

For many years, Sedona was dead after dark, but now the town is far less moribund when the sun sets. At the original Oak Creek Brewery, 2050 Yavapai Dr., off Highway 89A in West Sedona (☎ 928-204-1300), good suds, live music on the weekends, and a cool courtyard with a fire pit draw a party-hearty crowd. Younger sibling Oak Creek Brewery & Grill in Tlaquepaque (☎ 928-282-3300) doesn't have live sounds, but the young singles scene tends to be hopping. Relics Restaurant & Nightclub, 3235 W. Hwy. 89A, West Sedona (☎ 928-282-1593), has been boot scootin' and hootin' since the 1940s, when the Duke and other Western legends of the silver screen wet their whistles here (though under another name; it was the Rainbows End until 2004). Casa Rincon & Tapas Cantina, 2620 W. Hwy. 89A, West Sedona (☎ 928-282-4849), lays on an eclectic array of nightly entertainment, from classical Spanish guitar to funk and DJ dance parties. For a sophicated retro experience (punning name notwithstanding), stop by Olive'r Twist, a hip martini bar in the Old Marketplace complex, 1370 Hwy. 89A at Soldier's Pass Road, West Sedona (☎ 928-282-1229). In addition, Cucina Rustica, Dahl & DiLuca, and Pizza Picazzo (see the "A taste of Roma in Sedona" sidebar) are among the local restaurants that offer live music on the weekends.

Sedona's performing-arts scene is also getting livelier, largely due to the debut in 2000 of the 50-acre Sedona Cultural Park, 250 Cultural Park Place, West Sedona (☎ 928-282-0747; `www.sedonaculturalpark.org`). Its centerpiece, an outdoor amphitheater in an 80-foot-deep natural bowl flanked by the forest and red-rock buttes, hosted a variety of festivals and concerts in the first three years. The park underwent a sale and reorganization in 2004, so no events were scheduled, but phone or check the Web site before your visit; the park should be back in full swing by 2005. Although hardly as impressive as Sedona Cultural Park, The Canyon Moon Theatre Company, 1370 W. Hwy. 89A, Ste. 6 (☎ 928-282-6212; www.canyonmoontheatre.org), provides an intimate venue for Sedona's thespians and their devotees.

Fast Facts: Sedona and the Verde Valley

Area Code

The area code in Sedona and the Verde Valley is **928.**

Emergencies

For police, ambulance, or fire emergencies, call **☎ 911.** In Sedona, the nonemergency number for the police is **☎ 928-282-3100.**

Hospitals/Clinics

The Sedona Medical Center, 3700 W. Hwy. 89A, West Sedona (**☎ 928-204-3000**) has 24-hour emergency service. Sedona Urgent Care, 2530 W. Hwy. 89A, West Sedona (☎ 928-203-4813) is open for drop-ins (Mon–Fri 9 a.m.–6 p.m., Sat. 10 a.m.–5 p.m., Sun and holidays 11 a.m.–4 p.m.).

Information

If you're driving into Sedona from the south, the best place to get information is the South Gateway Visitor Center, 7000 Hwy. 179, Ste. 101, in Tequa Plaza, Village of Oak Creek (**☎ 928-284-5323;** open 8:30 a.m.–5 p.m. daily), shared by the Sedona Oak-Creek Chamber of Commerce and the U.S. Forest Service. The Uptown Gateway Visitor Center, 331 Forest Rd. at Highway 89A, Uptown Sedona (**☎ 800-288-7336** or 928-282-7722; open: Mon–Sat 9 a.m.–5 p.m., Sun 9 a.m.–3 p.m.) tends to be far more crowded. For advance information, log on to www.visitsedona.com or www.redrockcountry.org. Other local sources of information include the Cottonwood Chamber of Commerce, 1010 S. Main St, junction of Highways 89A and 260 (**☎ 928-634-7593;** http://cottonwood.verdevalley.com; open: Mon–Fri 9 a.m.–5 p.m., Sat–Sun 9 a.m.–noon). An information booth on Hull Avenue run by volunteers from the Jerome Chamber of Commerce (**☎ 928-634-2900;** www.jeromechamber.com) is often open in midday — but don't count on it. For that matter, don't count on anyone answering the Chamber of Commerce phone, either. The Web site's usually up, though.

Internet Access

If Sedona's vortexes don't transmit your e-mail psychically, try logging on at Ravenheart, 1370 W. Hwy. 89 A, West Sedona (**☎ 928-282-5777**). At Jerome's Reynard: A CyberCafé, 115 Jerome Ave. (**☎ 928-634-3230**), you can get high-speed Internet access with an apple tart, quiche, or salade nicoise (the coffee's high-speed, too). Open 7 a.m.–3 p.m. except Tues–Wed.

Post Office

Sedona's main post office is at 190 W. Hwy. 89A, Uptown Sedona (**☎ 928-282-3511**).

Prescott

Lots of resident college students and retirees, plus waves of heat-escaping Phoenicians, have given Prescott an orientation toward pleasure. The hub of north-central Arizona, the town is much more of a real-people place than Sedona. But if you're looking for a Southwest stereotype, you won't find it here: With its oak-shaded central square, Victorian houses, and temperate climate, Prescott feels almost Midwestern. That said, the rugged rocks of the nearby Granite Dells could come straight out of a John Ford film, and you find plenty of places to saddle up. If you like the outdoors, antiques, and history, you can easily spend a few days relaxing here. Prescott is also a relatively inexpensive base for exploring the Verde Valley; a day trip to the Grand Canyon from here is doable as well.

Getting there

If you drive from Phoenix, take I-17 north to Highway 69 west (at Exit 262, Cordes Junction); the trip is a quick 96 miles. From Sedona, take Highway 89A southwest (89A merges with Highway 89 5 miles north of town). This 60-mile route has some very curvy stretches. You can also take Highway 179 south from Sedona to I-17 south, and then head west on Highway 169 and 69 — less scenic, and you miss Jerome, but you may avoid white-knuckle anxiety if you go this way.

Of the various shuttles that run from Phoenix Sky Harbor Airport to Prescott, the Prescott Airport Shuttle (☎ 800-445-7978 or 928-445-5470; `www.prescottransit.com`) offers the most frequent scheduled service. The cost is $26 each way, $42 round-trip. America West (☎ 800-235-9292) flies to Prescott twice daily from Sky Harbor. Prescott isn't likely to be your sole Arizona destination, however, so renting a car in Phoenix may make more sense than using either of these options.

Greyhound, 820 E. Sheldon (☎ 800-231-2222 or 928-774-4573), runs buses to Prescott.

When Highways 69 and 89 enter town, they merge into Gurley Street, Prescott's main thoroughfare. Gurley meets Montezuma and Cortez in the town's center; add Goodwin Street, which runs parallel to Gurley, and you have Courthouse Plaza. Almost all the action in Prescott takes place on or near this large, eminently strollable town square.

High and hilly (gasp!)

Not only does Prescott sit at 5,347 feet, but the town itself is subtly hilly. Don't worry if you find yourself breathing heavily on your return to your hotel, when heading out seemed like a breeze — you may have just hit an upslope. Take it easy if you arrive directly from sea level.

Spending the night

If you like your rooms touched with a bit of history, you'll be in heaven here, whether you choose to stay in Arizona's first car-friendly hotel or get pleasantly spooked by a resident ghost in an old inn. And you won't pay an arm and a leg for the privilege, either. Don't give a hoot about haunts or the past? Prescott's got plenty of up-to-date lodgings, including one with a casino.

Modest motels, several with classic 1950s kitsch appeal, line Highway 69 and, as you get closer to town, its Gurley Street continuation. Cruise this route if you're not looking for anything special or don't feel like planning ahead. Chains represented in town include Best Western, Comfort Inn, Days Inn, Holiday Inn Express, Hampton Inn, Motel 6, Quality Inn & Suites, and Super 8 (see the Appendix for the toll-free numbers). The chain most convenient to the center of town is SpringHill Suites by Marriott ($$) 200 E. Sheldon St. (☎ 888-287-9400 or 928-776-0998; `www.travelsouthwest.com/prescott`), which also has excellent facilities. Check also with the Prescott Chamber of Commerce (see the "Fast Facts: Prescott" section) for a list of the many good B&Bs in town.

Hassayampa Inn

$$ Prescott

Prescott's premier historic hotel, the Hassayampa Inn first introduced porte cocheres to the state in 1929. It has a great Western Art Deco lobby and attractive rooms to match. This hotel is also a good deal: A generous order-from-the-menu breakfast at one of the town's best restaurants, the Peacock Room, is included in the rate (see the following "Dining locally" section) and several packages bring costs down even more. Not all the accommodations are large, and some get traffic noise from the main square (request a room in the back), but these are minor tradeoffs when you consider the character and the prime location.

122 E. Gurley St. (one block east of Courthouse Plaza). ☎ ***800-322-1927*** *or 928-778-9434. Fax: 928-445-8590.* `www.hassayampainn.com`. *Rack rates: Jan–Mar and Nov, Sun–Thur $99–$109 double, weekends, holidays, and special events $119–$139 double; Apr–Oct, and Dec $119–$139/$139–$169; year-round suites from $139–179. Rates include full breakfast. AE, CB, DC, DISC, MC, V.*

Hotel St. Michael

$ Prescott

These Whiskey Row digs, around since 1900, are a great base for a bar crawl (and, these days, a shopping spree). The rates are great, too. But if you need quiet to sleep off your hangover, you're not going to get it here, and the rooms are more funky than functional.

205 W. Gurley St. (on Courthouse Plaza). ☎ ***800-678-3757*** *or 928-776-1999. Fax: 928-776-7318.* `www.stmichaelhotel.com`. *Rack rates: $59–$69 Sun–Thurs; $69–$89 weekends. DISC, MC, V.*

Love on the rocks — a good thing

Some of the state's most civilized quarters meet some of its most ruggedly beautiful scenery at **Rocamadour** ($$), 3386 N. Hwy. 89, 4 miles north of Prescott (☎ **888-771-1933** or 928-771-1933; $139–$189 doubles; AE, DISC, MC, V). Furnishings from the owners' former inn in Burgundy, France, have been transported to the Granite Dells, a region of huge, strangely eroded boulders just outside Prescott. All the individually decorated rooms feature beautiful antiques and artwork. Plush robes, fresh flowers, TV/VCR, and private entrances — and in two cases, a private deck with a spa — complete the romantic picture.

Hotel Vendome

$–$$ Prescott

A cross between a hotel and a B&B, the Vendome has the privacy of the former (including your own bath and remote-control TV) and the character of the latter (including a ghost). A wine bar, convenience to Courthouse Plaza, and a cheerful veranda on each floor are other pluses. This pleasant, reasonably priced place was built in 1917 but extensively revamped in the mid-1990s.

230 S. Cortez St. (1½ blocks south of Courthouse Plaza). ☎ ***888-468-3583*** *or 928-776-0900. Fax: 928-771-0395.* `www.vendomehotel.com`. *Rack rates: Sun–Thu $79; suites from $119; Fri–Sun and holidays $99–$139 double; suites from $159. Rates include continental breakfast. AE, DISC, MC, V.*

Prescott Resort Conference Center and Casino

$–$$ Prescott

Not historic and nowhere near Courthouse Plaza, the Prescott Resort has one unique feature: a casino. The property also offers a recently spiffed-up restaurant, tennis and racquetball courts, a health club, and a spa. The vistas from the rooms' balconies are unbeatable.

1500 Hwy. 69 (on the eastern edge of town). ☎ ***800-967-4637*** *or 928-776-1666. Fax: 928-776-8544.* `www.prescottresort.com`. *Rack rates: Nov–Mar $79–$125 doubles, $99–$145 suites; Apr–Oct $89–$145 doubles, $109–$165 suites. AE, CB, DC, DISC, MC, V.*

Dining locally

Prescott College, Yavapai Community College, and Embry-Riddle Aeronautical University are all in this area, which means that Prescott has a nice, college-casual dining scene. Although a number of restaurants do cater specifically to student budgets and tastes, you find enough places to satisfy sophisticated professorial and postgraduate palates. Most of the top choices are on or near Courthouse Plaza.

If you're up for a romantic dinner in a formal atmosphere, consider, too, the Peacock Room ($$$) at the Hassaymampa Inn (see the preceding "Spending the night" section). On the opposite end of the spectrum, the Palace ($–$$; see the "Living it up after dark" section) serves good food along with its brews. You get historic settings as a bonus at both.

Belvedere's Bistro

$$–$$$ Prescott COUNTRY FRENCH/CREOLE

A recent (2003) addition to the town's fine-dining scene, this restaurant combines the casual air of a French cafe with a sense of special occasion. At lunchtime, the chef has a nice, light touch with crepes and salads; for dinner, the French Creole entrées, such as a creamy saffron bouillabaisse and shrimp étouffé, are deeply satisfying. Desserts like the terrific crème caramel are made on the premises. A bonus: Belvedere is BYOB, with a no corkage-fee policy.

125 N. Cortez St. (one block north of Courthouse Plaza). ☎ ***928-443-8587.*** *Main courses: lunch $8–$11, dinner $12–$22. AE, CB, DISC, MC, V. Open: Mon–Fri lunch, Thur–Sat dinner.*

Gurley St. Grill

$–$$ Prescott AMERICAN

Bustling and offering plenty of kid-friendly food, this spot also attracts business types who stop in for a quick lunch in the central dining room. Haute hippie cuisine — generous, reasonably priced food that's creative without being fussy — mingles on the menu with basic burgers, pizzas, salads, and sandwiches. My top picks include the asiago chicken and toasted cheese ravioli.

230 W. Gurley St. (one block west of Courthouse Plaza). ☎ ***928-445-3388.*** *Main courses: $6–$15. AE, DISC, MC, V. Open: lunch and dinner daily.*

Murphy's

$$–$$$ Prescott AMERICAN/CONTINENTAL

This restaurant's great popularity eludes me somewhat, but locals — and several friends with good taste — swear by this sprawling place. The setting — an 1890s building with lots of its original fittings — and a good mesquite grill help explain Murphy's success, as do the 60-item beer list, the extras that come with dinner, and (I'll concede) stellar desserts.

201 N. Cortez. St. (one block north of Courthouse Plaza). ☎ ***928-445-4044.*** *Reservations recommended for large groups. Main courses: $14–$28. AE, DISC, MC, V. Open: Lunch and dinner daily, Sun brunch.*

Prescott Brewing Company

$–$$ Prescott AMERICAN/PUB

Prescott may have fancier places, but I love kicking back here with a Prescott Pale Ale, some hot beer pretzels (the horseradish dipping sauce is killer), and a Sonoran chicken salad. The food is pub grub raised to a higher level: Everything's made from fresh ingredients and nicely spiced, and you get lots of veggie and white-meat selections. And who could resist a place that has one of northern Arizona's largest single malt scotch selections and a kids' menu with dinosaur-shaped nuggets?

130 W. Gurley St. (Bashford Shopping Center on Courthouse Plaza). ☎ ***928-771-2795.*** *Main courses: $6.75–$18. AE, DC, DISC, MC, V. Open: Lunch and dinner daily.*

The Rose

$$$–$$$$ Prescott CONTINENTAL

The food at the Rose — with entrées such as cherry brandied duck or julienne chicken with sweet sausage — is generally worth the price, and the wine list is well selected. The placement of the tables in the tiny dining rooms verges on personal-space invasion, however. Best to come when the outdoor areas are open and you can dine outside.

234 S. Cortez St. (one block south of Courthouse Plaza). ☎ ***928-777-8308.*** *Main courses: $16–$33. AE, DC, DISC, MC, V. Open: Wed–Sun dinner.*

Zuma's Woodfire Café

$$–$$$ Prescott SOUTHWEST/NEW AMERICAN

Choosing the bigger crowd-pleaser — the designer pizzas, pastas, and grilled dishes or the two outdoor patios with blazing fire pits — is hard to do. You may be tempted to fill up on the generously portioned main courses — chicken on spinach fetuccine with tequila cream sauce, say — but try to save room for a dessert of wood-fired s'mores. (Where else are you going to find that?) Live music and a huge selection of beers and tequilas add to the always-festive atmosphere.

124 N. Montezuma St, (½ block north of Courthhouse Plaza). ☎ ***928-541-1400.*** *Reservations recommended on weekends for four or more, on weekdays for six or more. Main courses: Individual pizzas $7–$10, dinners $9–$22. AE, DISC, MC, V. Open: Lunch and dinner daily, Sun brunch.*

Great Scott! (not)

Named for William Hickling Prescott, an East Coast historian, Prescott is pronounced *presk*-it, the second syllable rhyming with "biscuit." Why? According to local historian Melissa Ruffner, Prescott came from Boston, which was big on renouncing its colonial English roots — pronunciations included. Whatever the derivation, if you pronounce the "scott," you're announcing loud and clear that you're an out-of-towner.

Exploring Prescott

You're likely to spend much of your time in Prescott on Courthouse Plaza, the downtown square bounded by Goodwin and Gurley streets to the north and Montezuma and Cortez streets to the east and west, respectively. Two of the town's most popular activities, shopping and bar-hopping (see the "Shopping for local treasures" and the "Living it up after dark" sections later in this chapter), dovetail on Montezuma Street, the town's historic Whiskey Row. History and Western-art fans have a few other options.

- Step back in time. If you want to explore the city's many beautifully restored Queen Anne–style houses (some 525 buildings are listed on the National Register of Historic Places), take Goodwin Street east of Courthouse Plaza to Mount Vernon Street and stroll north. The three blocks between Goodwin and Sheldon streets brim with turrets, shingles, and gingerbread trim. For some more rough-hewn historic sites, see the hiking suggestions in the "Staying active" section.
- Find Old West artifacts in a museum. I've spent hours poking around the Sharlot Hall Museum, 415 W. Gurley St., two blocks west of Courthouse Plaza (☎ 928-445-3122; `www.sharlot.org`), a complex of buildings and gardens named for protofeminist, poet, and historian Sharlot Hall. Its centerpiece is the rustic pine cabin that served as the first territorial governor's mansion, but 15 other stations lead you through Prescott's past. Displays include everything from a mummified mouse, found during the mansion's excavation, to a small Wells Fargo stagecoach that squeezed some 31 people in with its bundles of mail. Admission: Free, suggested donation $5 per adult over 18. Open: May–Sept Mon–Sat 10 a.m.–5 p.m. and Sun 10 a.m.–2 p.m., Oct–Apr Mon–Sat 10 a.m.–4 p.m.
- Research the region's Native American past. The architecturally striking Smoki Museum, 147 N. Arizona St., about ¾ mile east of Courthouse Plaza via Gurley Street (☎ 928-445-1230), was built in 1935 out of native stone and wood in the shape of a pueblo. Some rare Native American pots and baskets from the region are on permanent display, and rotating exhibits are always interesting. Admission: $4 adults, $3 seniors, $2 students, ages 12 and under free. Open: Apr to Dec Mon–Sat 10 a.m.–4 p.m. and Sun. 1–4 p.m., Jan to Mar Fri, Sat, and Mon 10 a.m.–4 p.m. and Sun 1–4 p.m.
- Get artsy. Fans of Western art enjoy the small Phippen Museum, 4701 Hwy. 89, about 7 miles north of downtown (☎ 928-778-1385; `www.phippenartmuseum.org`), perched on a hill near the Granite Dells. The work (including that of George Phippen, a member of the Cowboy Artists of America) tends toward the traditional and representational, but the quality is sufficiently high so that those who have more contemporary tastes can also appreciate the shows. Admission: $5 adults, $4 seniors, ages 11 and under free. Open: Mon–Sat 10 a.m.–4 p.m., Sun 1–4 p.m., closed Mon Jan–Memorial Day.

Guided tours

Melissa Ruffner takes her Prescott Historical Tours (☎ 928-445-4567) very personally — she's descended from some of the town's pioneers. Ruffner's excursions through the town's past, done in Territorial-era costume, cost $7 per person if a minimum of ten people signs on. Two people can book a $40 tour package that includes an autographed copy of Ruffner's Prescott: A Pictorial History.

If you want to find out about the area's history — natural as well as human — at your own pace, pick up a copy of the Yavapai Heritage Foundation's excellent "Forests and Grasslands" self-guided driving tours, available at the Sharlot Hall Museum (see the preceding section) or at the Chamber of Commerce (see the "Fast Facts: Prescott" section later in this chapter). The tabloid format publication (cost: $5) has four itineraries (The Bradshaw Mountains, Walnut Grove, Williamson Valley, and Limestone Canyon) and includes everything from road conditions to a suggested reading list. All tours start out at Courthouse Plaza.

Staying active

Want to spend your time here outdoors? Prescott offers lots of options for fresh-air enthusiasts.

- Golfing: Prescott always ranks high in the surveys of America's best retirement towns, which may explain why it's getting to be a duffer's destination. The greens fees noted here are for high season — prices are often considerably lower from October through March or April — and unless otherwise indicated they include a cart.

  It's hard to beat the prices at Quailwood Greens Golf Course, 11750 E. Hwy. 69 in Dewey, 14 miles east of downtown Prescott (☎ 928-772-0130). At this par-70 public course, you pay $28 in the morning ($18 if you're willing to forgo a cart), $20 ($11) after noon. The city-owned Antelope Hills, 1 Perkins Dr., 7 miles east of downtown near where Highways 69 and 89 split (☎ 928-776-7888 or 800-972-6818 in Arizona), has panoramic views of the Granite Dells and the Mogollon Rim on its two 18-hole courses (one is a Gary Panks' creation). Greens fees are $55. A dramatic Bradshaw Mountain backdrop makes the 18-hole Prescott Golf & Country Club, 1030 Prescott Country Club Blvd., 13 miles southeast of Prescott off Highway 69 (☎ 928-772-8984), a duffer's dream. Greens fees for nonmembers are $55 during the week, $47 after noon; add $5 more Friday through Sunday. The semiprivate Prescott Lakes Community Golf Course, 315 E. Smoke Tree Lane, 3 miles north of downtown (☎ 877-643-3501 or 928-443-3500), opened in 2000, boasts state-of-the-art clubhouse facilities — not to mention 15 acres of lakes. On weekdays, the fee is $80 to tee off at this Hale Irwin–designed course; during the week, you pay $100. The newest on the greens scene, Stone Ridge, 1602 North Bluff Top Rd., 5 miles southeast of downtown Prescott (☎ 928-772-6500), was designed by Randy Heckenkemper to take advantage of the area's ups and downs — and natural beauty — while appealing to all levels of expertise. Greens fees are $49 during the week, $59 one weekends, $39 after 2 p.m. on the weekends or after 1 p.m. during the week.

Come summer, several hotels run "Stay and Play" packages, which throw in a golf game for two with the price of a room.

- Hiking: Some 450 miles of trails, covering a wide range of landscapes, crisscross Prescott National Forest. The 1¾ mile (round-trip) hike up to Thumb Butte, Prescott's best-known landmark, is fairly steep, but you're rewarded with spectacular vistas of the entire region, including (on clear days) the San Francisco Peaks. Reaching two historic sites in the piney Lynx Lake area is easier: the Lynx Creek Indian ruins, where you can wander among the remains of a prehistoric Indian pueblo; and Charcoal Kiln, a large brick dome used to create charcoal from wood in the 1800s. The dramatic boulders of the Granite Dells near Watson Lake Park attract rock climbers as well as hikers.

The Bradshaw Ranger District of the Prescott National Forest, 344 S. Cortez St. (☎ 928-771-4700), is the best place to get information on these and other trails. The office is only open Monday through Friday from 8 a.m. to 4:30 p.m., so if you want to hike on the weekend, plan ahead. You may also stop into the Chamber of Commerce (see the "Fast Facts: Prescott" section later in this chapter) for information on the less complicated hikes.

- Horseback riding: The guided rides given by Granite Mountain Stables, 2400 W. Shane Dr., some 7 miles northeast of Prescott (☎ 928-771-9551), start at $35 an hour. Two-hour sunrise and sunset rides ($90 each) are available, too, as are overnight pack trips ($175 a day per person).
- Mountain biking: Prescott's varied terrain lets fat-tire enthusiasts choose their level of ride. If you're a beginner, you may like a flat route with views of Granite Mountain such as the Peavine Trail, converted from an old rail line; if you're more advanced, you should enjoy the up-and-down adventures offered by the Granite Basin Recreation Area near Watson Lake. Ironclad Bicycles, 710 White Spar Rd., (☎ 928-776-1755; `www.ironcladbicycles.com`), rents standard front suspension ($10 per hour, $30 for a full day) and high-end dual suspension ($15 per hour, $50 per day) mountain bikes, and can provide maps for six different routes.

Shopping for local treasures

Prescott's many antiques shops sell everything from top-notch Victorian cabinets to cowboy-kitsch pitchers, and at pretty good prices — one reason that Phoenicians like to weekend here. Of course, if you fly into Arizona, the shipping costs on large pieces may wipe out any savings, but who knows? You may find something portable — or actually worth the shipping expense. Antique shops are all around town, but the best pickings are on Cortez Street, just north of Courthouse Plaza between Gurley and Sheldon. Ask at the Chamber of Commerce (see the "Fast Facts: Prescott" section later in this chapter) for the "Antiques Shops Guide" pamphlet.

Crafts and Western knickknack shops line Courthouse Plaza, particularly Montezuma and Gurley streets. You can concentrate your retail search in two good arcades, Bashford Courts, 130 W. Gurley St. (☎ 928-445-9798), and St. Michael's Plaza, 205 W. Gurley St. (☎ 928-776-1999). For local crafts, visit Arts Prescott Gallery, 134 S. Montezuma St. (☎ 928-776-7717), a high-quality co-op. Just down the street, Newman Gallery, 106-A S. Montezuma St. (☎ 928-442-9167), showcases the fun, funky creations of Dave Newman and friends, including colorful candle holders, painted step stools and handcrafted jewelry. My favorite boutique, though, is slightly off the square, tucked among all the antiques shops on Cortez Street: Ogg's Hogan and Maggie Manygoats, which share a space and phone number — 111 N. Cortez; ☎ 928-443-9856 — are a two-fer treat. Ogg's concentrates on exquisite Native American crafts and Old West collectibles, while Maggie carries creative Western-style clothing (including high-quality vintage) and fun home furnishings. The gift shop of the Smoki Museum (see the "Exploring Prescott" section) is another good hunting ground for Native American arts and crafts.

Prefer more contemporary venues? At Prescott Gateway Mall, Highway 69 and Gateway Boulevard on the outskirts of town (☎ 928-443-0067), with anchors Dillard's, Sears, JC Penney, and Barnes & Noble and numerous specialty shops. Historical photos of Prescott filling this shopping center provide an interesting contrast between old and new.

Living it up after dark

Not as exciting as it once was in the early 1900s, when some 20 saloons and brothels lined Whiskey Row (Montezuma St.), Prescott's nightlife still thrives, thanks in part to the town's many higher drinking (er, learning) institutions. The ornate mahogany bar at the Palace, 120 S. Montezuma St. (☎ 928-541-1996), is a huge tourist magnet. Just upstairs from the Palace, Jersey Lilly, 116 S. Montezuma St. (☎ 928-541-7854), offers a somewhat more refined atmosphere and good views of Courthouse Square from on high. Matt's Longhorn Saloon, 112 S. Montezuma St. (☎ 928-778-9914), lays on live Country and Western sounds. A block north of Courthouse Plaza, Lyzzard's Lounge, 120 N. Cortez St. (☎ 928-778-2244), books good alternative bands. Drop by to see the bar, manufactured in the 1880s in Chicago, shipped down the Mississippi and around Cape Horn to San Francisco, and transported to Prescott by covered wagon.

One of Prescott's most popular nightspots, Bucky's Casino in the Prescott Resort and Conference Center (see the "Spending the night" section earlier in this chapter), is far from Whiskey Row. But who needs history when you have lots o' slots?

Highbrow highlights include tastings at the Wine to Vine Cellar, 110 S. Montezuma St. (☎ 928-443-8932), accompanied by a variety of live sounds on the weekends. As its name suggests, 129½: An American Jazz Grill, 129½ N. Cortez St. (☎ 928-443-9292), features jazz nightly. Sax fiends might also call the Prescott Jazz Society (☎ 928-925-1422) for information on its members' performances. Find out what's happening at all kinds of venues in town by reading The Daily Courier on Thursday and Friday.

Fast Facts: Prescott

Area Code

Prescott's area code is **928.**

Emergencies

For police, ambulance, or fire emergencies, call ☎ **911;** the nonemergency police number is ☎ **928-778-1444.**

Hospitals/Clinic

Yavapai Regional Medical Center, 1003 Willow Creek Rd. (☎ **928-445-2700**) has 24-hour emergency room service.

Information

Go to the Prescott Chamber of Commerce, 117 W. Goodwin St. (☎ **800-266-7534** or 928-445-2000; www.prescott.org; open Mon–Fri 9 a.m.–5 p.m., Sat–Sun 10 a.m.–2 p.m.).

Internet Access

You can check your e-mail at **Mudd Hole Espresso,** 239 N. Marina St. (☎ **928-445-0951**), open Mon–Thurs 7 a.m.–8 p.m., Fri and Sat 7 a.m.–10 p.m., Sun 8 a.m.–4 p.m.

Post Office

The post office is located at 101 W. Goodwin St. (☎ **928-778-7411**).

Wickenburg

Located on the northwestern edge of the Sonoran Desert, Wickenburg resembles Phoenix and Tucson, meteorologically speaking, more than higher-elevation towns such as Prescott and Sedona. Like Tucson, Wickenburg sits at approximately 2,000 feet. But the resemblance ends at the weather. When you visit Wickenburg, you get a glimpse of what Arizona's two largest cities may have been like a century ago — give or take a few cars and a Spanish fortress or two.

Incorporated in 1863, Wickenburg is the oldest town north of Tucson and the fifth oldest in the state. Namesake Henry Wickenburg, a Prussian prospector, discovered gold in the surrounding hills. The town began mining a widespread interest in warm winters and the Old West during the 1920s and 1930s, when it became known as "The Dude Ranch Capital of the World." Most of the dude ranches have been shuttered, and the "dudes" are now called "guests," but the ranches that remain are still the town's main tourist draw. So, although you don't need more than a day to explore little Wickenburg, the average visitor spends about five days of determined relaxation here.

Keep in mind that most of the town — dude ranches included — shuts down from May to October. Come in summer, and you may be disappointed, not to mention hot and sweaty.

Getting there

Wickenburg is 53 miles northwest of Phoenix via I-17 to Highway 74 to Highway 93/60, a level but wonderfully scenic route, lush with thick stands of saguaro cactus and other high-desert vegetation. The town is 61 miles south of Prescott via Highway 89, which connects to Highway 93 just outside of town — a more dramatic but also more harrowing drive through the mountains.

You can book the Wickenburg Airport Express (☎ 928-684-2888) to take you from the Phoenix airport to town in about 1½ hours ($75 for up to two people). But unless you plan to hunker down and never leave your dude ranch of choice, renting a car in Phoenix is best. Wickenburg has only one car rental company, Jones Ford-Mercury (☎ 928-684-5481), so the rates aren't likely to be very competitive.

When Highway 60 enters town, its name changes to Wickenburg Way. When Highway 93 comes through, it becomes Tegner Street. These two main thoroughfares cross in the old historic downtown district; the stoplight where they meet is often used as a directional reference. (The town has one more stoplight, but when people tell you that something is "two blocks east of the stoplight," they mean this one.)

Spending the night

Most people come to Wickenburg to relax at one of the town's remaining three guest ranches. All have different personalities — and accordingly different rates. All include meals but not booze in their room rates, and only the Kay El Bar includes riding; Flying E and Rancho de Los Caballeros offer equine time à la carte or as part of a package. All are great for family vacations, although only Rancho de los Caballeros has

Du-du-dudeo

From December through April, the guest ranches take turns hosting monthly "dudeos." These friendly inter-ranch dukeouts don't have bull riding, calf roping, or other dangerous activities — just a lot of good, clean (okay, good *dusty*) fun. Events like the horseback relay races draw mostly kid participants, but if enough qualified older riders are interested, the grown-ups get to play, too.

regularly scheduled kids' activities and programs. And although all three, by definition, have loads of Southwest character, the Kay El Bar really shines in that department.

The town has plenty of other places to bunk besides guest ranches. Low-key motels, including a Super 8 and a Best Western (both of which have more Western charm than usual), line the main drags, Tegner Street, and Wickenburg Way (see the Appendix for the chains' toll-free numbers). Comfortable, contemporary Southwest-style rooms and a nice pool make Los Viajeros Inn ($–$$), 1000 N. Tegner St. (☎ 800-915-9765 or 928-684-7099; www.wick-web.com/viajeros) another good motel pick. In spite of its name, Rancho Casitas Guest Ranch, 56550 Rancho Casitas Rd., 5 miles north of town (☎ 928-684-2628; open Oct — May only), doesn't have horses or other cowpoke activities, but it does offer attractive one- and two-bedroom units with kitchens — not to mention a swimming pool, hot tub, and a prime hilltop location. An offbeat (and definitely off-the-beaten path) place to stay is Robson's Mining World (see the "Exploring Wickenburg" section later in this chapter).

Guest Ranches

Flying E

$$$ Wickenburg

Families and friends come back year after year to the Flying E, the only working cattle ranch of the lot (although guests can't get involved with any of the round-up-related activities, which take place in summer while the ranch is closed). The views of the Bradshaw mountains from the ranch's Yarnell Hill perch are spectacular, and the place has a nice down-home feeling. However, Flying E isn't as luxurious as Rancho de Los Caballeros, and it doesn't have as much historic appeal as the Kay El Bar. Still, rooms are comfortably rustic, and fun stuff abounds, including a guest "branding" with traffic line paint.

2801 W. Wickenburg Way (4 miles west of town, via Highway 60). ☎ ***888-684-2650*** *or 928-684-2690. Fax: 928-684-5304.* www.flyingeranch.com. *Rack rates: $245–$310, based on double occupancy; 2-night minimum Nov–Dec, 3-night minimum Jan–Apr, 4-night minimum all holidays. Rates include all meals for two people. Closed May–Oct. No credit cards.*

Kay El Bar Ranch

$$$ Wickenburg

Ceiling planks taken from a gold mine, antique Monterey furniture, a hot tub made of old adobe brick . . . talk about soaking in Old West history! If you want to experience what dude ranching must have been like in its heyday, this 12-room ranch, opened to guests in 1926 and listed on the National Register for Historic Places, is for you. Kay El Bar is also the place for serious riders. All riders are evaluated and matched with an appropriate horse and trail pardners, so you're never going to go faster or slower than you'd like. The gorgeous grounds have lots of old-growth tamarisk and eucalyptus along with lush stands of saguaro.

Rincon Road (take Highway 93 2 miles past the junction with Highway 60, turn right onto Rincon Rd. and drive 1½ miles). ☎ ***800-684-7583*** *or 928-684-7593. Fax: 928-684-4497.* www.kayelbar.com. *Rack rates: $335–$380 based on double occupancy, $2,250–$2,500 weekly rate. 10% discount on rack rates Dec 1–19 and Jan 18–31. 15% gratuity added to all bills. Different rates for the two all-women bonding/riding weeks; check Web site for details. Rates include all meals and horseback riding for two people; children must be at least 7 to ride. Two-night minimum stay Oct 12–Feb 14; four-night minimum stay all holidays and Feb 15–May 1. Closed May 2–Oct 11. MC, V.*

Rancho de Los Caballeros

$$$$ Wickenburg

Los Cab, as it's known locally, is the poshest of the horse resorts: Lots of spiffy new suites and an excellent golf course cater to corporate retreaters. But the original dining room and lobby ooze Old West charm, as do the rooms in the original ranch house, which even cost a bit less (they'd be my first pick). The ranch has been in the same family since 1948, so the owners have a continued personal stake in making guests feel welcome and well cared for. A free kids' program for ages 5 to 12 keeps the young 'uns happily playing together from 8 a.m. to 1:30 p.m. and from 6 to 9 p.m. The tennis is free, too.

1551 S. Vulture Mine Rd. (off Highway 60 on the west side of town, 1½ miles from the Vulture Mine turnoff). ☎ ***800-684-5030*** *or 928-684-5484. Fax: 928-684-2267.* www.SunC.com. *Rack Rates: Oct–Jan, May $362–$414 based on double occupancy, $448 suites; Feb–Apr $416–$482/$542. Rates include all meals for two people; ask about lower weekday rates and packages. 15% gratuity added to all bills. Closed mid-May to mid-Oct. No credit cards.*

Dining locally

Most people who come to Wickenburg don't do much dining out because the rates of the major guest ranches include meals, but several good independent restaurants cater to day-trippers or to dudes who want to branch out from the ranch. And nonguests may book a meal at the Rancho de Los Caballeros dining room; the all-you-can-eat lunch buffets are justly renowned, and dinners — more gourmet than you'd expect — are super, too.

The only other places I can personally recommend are both in the historic downtown district. The sprawling Gold Nugget ($$), 222 E. Wickenburg Way (☎ 928-684-0648), serves good comfort food (if you find comfort in chicken fried steak and Yankee pot roast, that is). A dimly lit local favorite, the Rancho Bar 7, 111 E. Wickenburg Way (☎ 928-684-5484), hasn't changed much since opening in 1937. The cheese-smothered Mexican combination plate is great at lunchtime; for dinner, you can't go wrong with the prime rib, roast pork, or any of the nightly specials. I get lots of good reports about a German restaurant, House of Berlin, 169 E.

Wickenburg Way (☎ 928-684-5044), also in the historic downtown district. I've peered in, and it's a charming, lace-curtain room, but I just never find myself feeling sufficiently in the mood for schnitzel to eat here.

Exploring Wickenburg

Wickenburg's small historic district is more or less bounded by Tegner Street on the north, Frontier Street on the south, Yavapai Street on the east, and Highway 60/Wickenburg Way on the west. Although it resembles a set for a Western flick (especially Frontier Street), this is the genuine item, with several buildings dating back to the 1890s. Stop in at the Old Santa Fe depot on Frontier Street, now home to the Chamber of Commerce (see the "Fast Facts: Wickenburg" section later in this chapter), for a map of a self-guided walking tour. A few other things to see and do include the following.

- Get some Western culture. The Desert Caballeros Western Museum, 21 N. Frontier St. (☎ 928-684-2272; www.westernmuseum.org), has it all — Remingtons, Russells, antique cowboy gear (more than 500 items in the Hays "Spirit of the Cowboy" collection), Native American pottery, glowing minerals, and period rooms that re-create several of the town's businesses down to the last dry goods details. The special exhibits, covering topics from the town's dude ranch history to bola ties (see Chapter 19), are always top-rate, too. Admission: $6 adults, $4.50 seniors, $1 ages 6–16, ages 5 and under free. Open: Mon–Sat 10 a.m.–5 p.m., Sun noon–4 p.m. Closed Easter, Thanksgiving, Christmas, New Year's Day and Sundays July–Aug.
- Mine Wickenburg's mining past. All the artifacts are real in Robson's Mining World, about 27 miles from Wickenburg (take Highway 93 to Highway 71 South and drive 12 miles), ☎ 928-685-2609; www.azoutback.com); most of them just never had anything to do with each other in the past. This re-creation of an old Arizona mining town, replete with chapel, saloon, and ice cream parlor, is well done, however, and car buffs will be riveted by the antique trucks and fire engines. Admission: $5 adults, $4.50 ages 55 and over, free ages 10 and under. Open: Oct–May 1 Mon–Fri 10 a.m.–4 p.m., Sat and Sun 9 a.m.–5 p.m. See map p. 301.

  A B&B ($$) done in the style of a timbered frontier hotel is on the premises. Rooms aren't fancy and they have no TVs or phones, but they're attractively decorated in Victorian rustic style. If you're looking for a great star- or bird-watching spot, this is it.
- Go natural. The Nature Conservancy runs the Hassayampa River Preserve, 49614 Hwy. 60, 3 miles southeast of town near mile marker 114 (☎ 928-684-2772; www.hassayampa.org), one of the few places where the Hassayampa River puts in an above-ground appearance. The water attracts some 230 species of birds, as well as salamanders, lizards, and other local wildlife. A desert garden outside the visitor center, itself a converted 1860s ranch, identifies the more typical local plants. Admission: $5 suggested donation for

A leafy jail and a tall tale

Two of Wickenburg's strangest, most colorful attractions are quick takes. Stop by Tegner and Wickenburg Way, right next to the Circle K, to see the 200-year old mesquite that's called the **Jail Tree** because, from 1863 to 1890, outlaws were chained to it instead of being locked up. In the late 1800s, Wickenburg residents used to exaggerate the town's wealth to the point that the word "Hassayamper" was coined to describe people who had a tendency to play fast and loose with the facts. From there came the legend that anyone who drank from the waters of the **Hassayampa River** would never utter a word of truth again. A plaque next to the Old Wishing Well, on the north side of the Hwy. 60/93 bridge across the Hassaympa River (just past Apache St. if you're coming from downtown), tells the tale — all true — in verse.

those who aren't Nature Conservancy members. Open: Sept 16–May 14 Wed–Sun 8 a.m.–5 p.m., May 15–Sept 15 8 a.m.–5 p.m. Fri–Sun. See map p. 301.

- Saddle up. Just because you're not duding doesn't mean you can't get on a horse. Rides with Trails West Horseback Adventures (☎ 928-684-2600) range from $20 for 1 hour to $130 for a full day with lunch. Breakfast and dinnertime encounters with equines are an option, too. Rides available from November to May only.
- Go on a Jeep jaunt. The off-road adventures offered by B.C. Jeep Tours (☎ 928-684-7901 or 928-684-4982; `www.bcjeeptours.com`) include trips to a variety of destinations around Wickenburg, including Box Canyon, Vulture Mine, and Congress Graveyard. They're a good way to learn about the flora and fauna of the area, as well as its history. Prices are $50 per person (with a minimum of two people) for up to three hours, the typical trip; you'll pay an additional $10 per person per hour if you want to keep going. Trips are offered year-round; from May through October, you'll head out in in the early morning or the evening.

Shopping for local treasures

The historic downtown area can keep you happily browsing for a couple of hours. Ben's Saddlery & Shoe Repair, 174 N. Tegner St. (☎ 928-684-2863), deals in tack (in the horse sense of the term). Come here to watch saddles being made or to buy a Western belt or boots. The Gold Nugget Gallery, 274 E. Wickenburg Way (☎ 928-684-5849), is worth a visit for its historic 1863 adobe building alone, but the wide-ranging selection of paintings, pottery, jewelry, and furniture — everything from traditional Western landscapes to raku plates — is what you're really here for.

My favorite places to shop are a short drive from downtown, however. Double D, 955 W. Wickenburg Way (☎ 928-684-7987), has an excellent selection of Western wear, including terrific women's shirts. I could happily fill my home with the colorful dishes, faux-rustic furniture, and other Western wares from Renderings, 30220 Hwy. 60 (☎ 928-684-0112). Right next door, Rustiques, 30358 Hwy. 60 (☎ 928-668-1070), buys and sells stuff that's hung around for a while — everything from fossils and stuffed lizards to antique Mexican bureaus. All three stores are large; be prepared to be overwhelmed.

Living it up after dark

Not much happens in Wickenburg after dark besides the sky filling up with stars, but a few spots may divert you. The Rancher Bar, 910 W. Wickenburg Way (☎ 928-684-5957), owned by former rodeo cowboy Stubb Hill, offers live Country and Western jam sessions on Wednesday and Saturday nights. On Saturday nights, La Cabaña, 132 E. Wickenburg Way (☎ 928-684-7671), features local bands, usually playing rock or Country and Western. Right across the street, Rancho Bar 7 (see the "Dining locally" section earlier in this chapter) has — count 'em — two historic bars where you can kick back with a longneck.

The more high-culture-inclined may want to check out the programs at the Del E. Webb Center for the Performing Arts, 1090 S. Vulture Mine Rd., on the campus of Wickenburg High School (☎ 928-684-6624; `www.delewebbcenter.org`). You may hear music from country swing and bluegrass to classical and New Age, and performances from cowboy poetry to Broadway shows.

No bridge too far

No, it's not the punchline of a joke involving waterfront property in Arizona or being gullible enough to buy the Brooklyn Bridge: The London Bridge really was transported, piece by piece, from England to **Lake Havasu City,** a desert town near Arizona's border with California. (The lake is an import, too, created when Parker Dam was built in 1938.) Come summer, Lake Havasu often turns up on the News at 10 for having the country's high mercury peak, but it's pleasant enough in winter, spring — except when the college break hordes descend — and fall. The town is a popular stop on the southern (I-10 to I-95) route from Arizona to Las Vegas, although it's really not a convenient day trip from anywhere covered in this book. If you take Hwy. 60 west from Wickenburg to Hwy. 95 north, you'll get there in about three hours.

Activities mostly center around the bridge (gaping at it, browsing the souvenir shops that line the waterfront) and Lake Havasu (boating, fishing, parasailing, kayaking . . . you name it). Chain hotels abound, as do Ye Olde England–themed lodgings; for something entirely different, try the **Agave Inn** ($$–$$$),1420 McCulloch Blvd. N. (☎ **866-854-2833** or 928-854-2833; `www.agaveinn.com`), a hip boutique hotel on the waterfront.

For more information about what to see and where to stay and eat, contact the **Lake Havasu Visitor and Convention Bureau** (☎ **800-2-HAVASU;** `www.golakehavasu.com`).

Fast Facts: Wickenburg

Area Code

Wickenburg's area code is **928.**

Emergencies

For police, ambulance, or fire emergencies, call ☎ **911.** The nonemergency number for the police is **928-684-3152.**

Hospitals/Clinics

Wickenburg Regional Medical Center, 520 Rose Lane (☎ **928-684-5421**), offers 24-hour emergency care.

Information

Wickenburg Chamber of Commerce, 216 N. Frontier St. (☎ **800-942-5242**, 928-684-5479; `www.wickenburgchamber.com`), is open Mon–Fri 9 a.m.–5 p.m., Sat 9 a.m.–3 p.m., Sun 10 a.m.–2 p.m. (hours may be shorter in summer).

Post Office

The post office is located at 2029 W. Wickenburg Way (☎ **928-684-2138**).

Chapter 17

The Grand Canyon and Northwest Arizona

In This Chapter

- Checking out trains, volcanoes, and ski lifts: lower Northwest Arizona
- Exploring the Greatest Hole on Earth, Part I: The Grand Canyon's South Rim
- Exploring the Greatest Hole on Earth, Part II: The Grand Canyon's North Rim

The Grand Canyon may be the most celebrated natural attraction in the United States. And with good reason: Gazing (or better yet, walking) into the famous abyss is an unforgettable experience. You won't be the only one wanting to enjoy the canyon, so it's a good idea to plan your trip with care. I can't do your packing, but I can help with just about everything else. And — more good news — the rest of northwest Arizona doesn't just exist to deliver tourists into the vast maws of the canyon god. This part of the state offers plenty of other interesting (and less crowded) activities, especially in and around Flagstaff, northern Arizona's largest town.

The length of your stay in this area depends on the part of the canyon you visit and what you want to do. If, like most visitors, you just straddle the edge of the South Rim, a full day at the national park is enough. If, however, you dip in — say, by hiking, river rafting, or mule riding (and I definitely recommend that you do) — plan on at least two days; add another two to do the rest of the region justice. The more remote North Rim, a destination rather than a drop-in, requires more of a time commitment. No matter what you do when you get there, you need to allot at least a day of traveling each way.

Where you bunk also depends on your touring style. If you like to be close to the action or want to explore the park early in the morning before the tourists descend, by all means spend a night or two in the national park or as close to it as possible (that's more of a given if you're going to the North Rim). I like staying in Flagstaff when I visit the South Rim, if I'm not planning any major hikes. The one-hour drive to the canyon is easy, and the town has many more places to stay, eat, and play after dark. And Flagstaff makes a great base for travel to other places, including central Arizona (see Chapter 16) and northeastern Arizona (see Chapter 18).

Lower Northwest Arizona

A pretty, piney region financed by lumber and railways before the Grand Canyon became a growth industry, lower northwest Arizona has a lot going for it. The San Francisco Peaks, the state's highest mountains, were uplifted by a not-so-ancient volcano, which also left behind soil so fertile that several Indian civilizations came to this area — the proof is in Walnut Canyon and Wupatki National monuments. Route 66, which helped speed tourists toward the abyss, left a legacy of cool neon signs, while the establishment of Northern Arizona University gave Flagstaff a youth boost. Snowbowl, on one of the San Francisco Peaks, boasts the best skiing in the state — although I admit that's not saying all that much.

You may initially think that Flagstaff never met a hotel or restaurant chain it didn't like. Don't be put off by first impressions. Behind all the fast-food restaurants and hotel strips sits a friendly, alpine (altitude: 6,902 feet) college town with the best nightlife in the area (okay, so maybe that's not saying a whole lot, either). Inexpensive hotel rooms, abundant restaurants, and a central location make Flagstaff a great base for visiting the Grand Canyon and other area attractions, but the city itself also deserves some attention — at least a day. Devote another one to Walnut Canyon, en route to the Petrified Forest National Park (see Chapter 18) or Sunset Crater and Wupatki, if you can. Woodsy Williams is even closer to the Grand Canyon, but slightly farther from the other sights. (You can pretty much cover the town in a morning or afternoon.) If you ride the Grand Canyon rails or want to stay in a cozy, small town, Williams is a good place to plant yourself for a bit.

Getting there

If you're like most people who come to Arizona, you fly into Phoenix and rent a car at Sky Harbor International Airport (see Chapter 11). Flagstaff is 134 miles from Phoenix via I-17, a divided four-lane highway, somewhat curvy in spots, with a speed limit of mostly 75 miles per hour. I-40, the main east-west road through Flagstaff, Williams (30 miles west), and northern Arizona, is about as fast and flat as they come.

Open Road Tours (☎ 800-766-7117; `www.openroadtours.com`) runs five shuttle buses a day from Phoenix's Sky Harbor Airport to Flagstaff's Amtrak station (which doubles as the visitor center). The price is $31 one-way or $56 round-trip for adults, and $21/$39 for children under 12 with an adult. Northern Arizona Shuttle and Tours (☎ 866-870-8687; `www.nazshuttle.com`) offers a similar service three times a day in high season, twice a day in low season for the same price, except that children's round-trips aren't discounted. Both companies require advance reservations.

The Grand Canyon and Northern Arizona

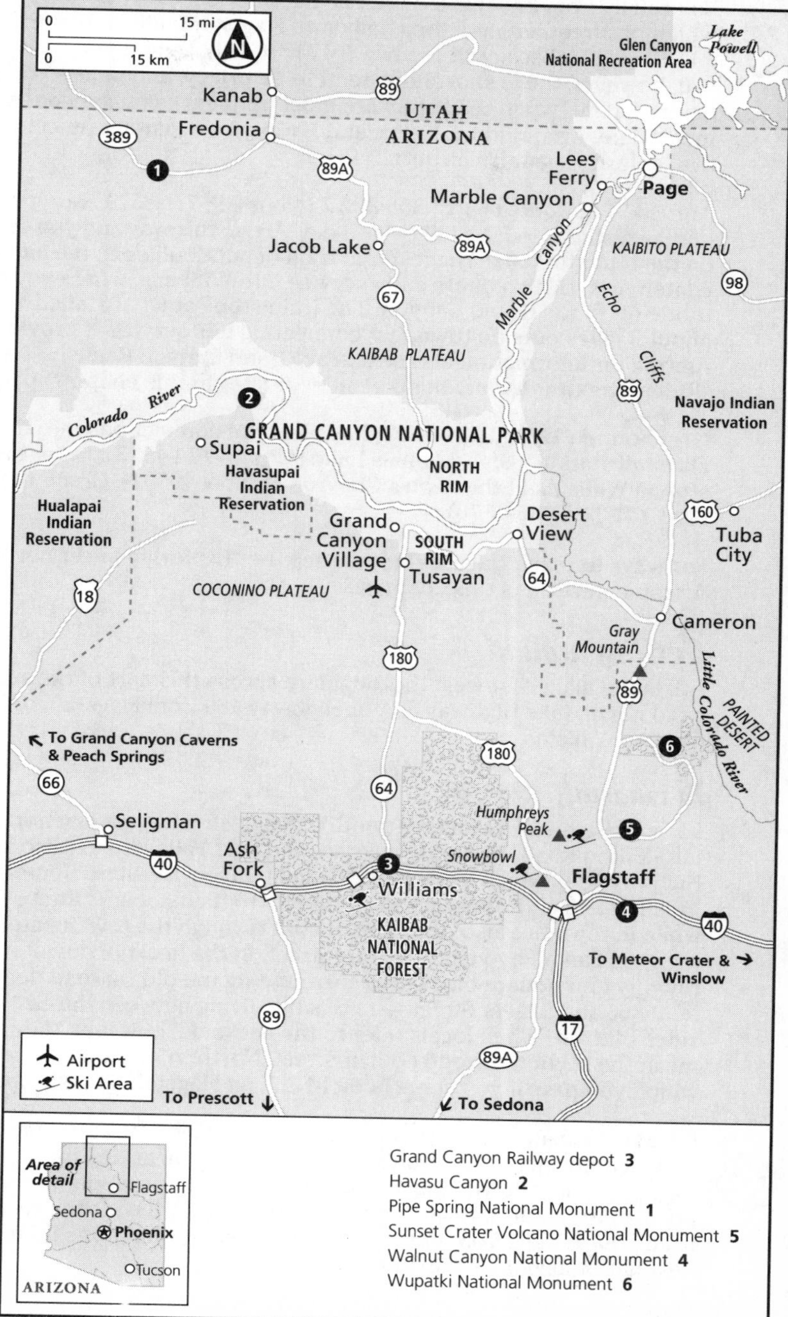

You can fly from Phoenix to Flagstaff via America West (☎ 800-235-9292), which has frequent nonstops daily into Flagstaff Pulliam Airport (☎ 928-556-1234), 3 miles south of town (I-17 Exit 337). Unless you catch a special, however, these short hops tend to be pricey, and unless you arrive before 2 p.m. (when the flights are most frequent), you may not save much time. Avis, Budget, Hertz, and National car rental agencies are available at Flagstaff's airport.

Amtrak, 1 E. Route 66 (☎ 800-872-7245 or 928-774-8679; `www.amtrak.com`), whistles into Flagstaff twice a day. Arrive this way and you get a jump on the other tourists: The restored train depot doubles as the information center. Amtrak also offers daily service into Williams, where you can tootle off to the Grand Canyon. The train stops at an unstaffed station about 3 miles outside town, but connecting bus service is provided. Call Amtrak for information about Amtrak/Grand Canyon Railway (see the "Riding the Grand Canyon rails" sidebar later in this chapter) packages.

Greyhound (☎ 800-231-2222) has plenty of connections into the Flagstaff station, 399 S. Malpais Lane (☎ 928-774-4573); fewer buses stop in Williams at the town's Chevron Station, 1050 N. Grand Canyon Blvd. (☎ 928-635-0870).

For ways to reach Havasu Canyon, see the "Exploring lower northwest Arizona" section in this chapter.

Getting around

I-40 is the main east-west thoroughfare across this part of the state. To head north, take Highway 89A or Highway 180 from Flagstaff, or Highway 64 from Williams.

In Flagstaff

I-17 and Highway 89A merge south of Flagstaff and, heading north, turn into Milton Road, Humphreys Road, and Fort Valley Road (also known as Highway 180), which leads to the Grand Canyon. Business Route 40, which parallels I-40 and runs east-west, reverts to its old name, Route 66, for a while in town but also does a brief stint through the town center under the alias Santa Fe Avenue. Leroux Street, in the heart of downtown — the roughly four-square-block area surrounding the old railroad depot at Old Route 66 and Beaver Street — marks the divide between the east and west sides of town. When locals refer to the east side, however, they generally mean the section beyond Fourth Street. Northern Arizona University, which you pass if you come in on I-17, is on Flagstaff's south side.

Because of name changes and lack of a grid, Flagstaff's streets can be really confusing. Unless you stop at a gas station, asking for directions won't generally do you much good because half the people you encounter are also from out of town. Pick up a good map at the visitor center or from your hotel's front desk (call your hotel for directions if finding your destination becomes difficult).

Flagstaff

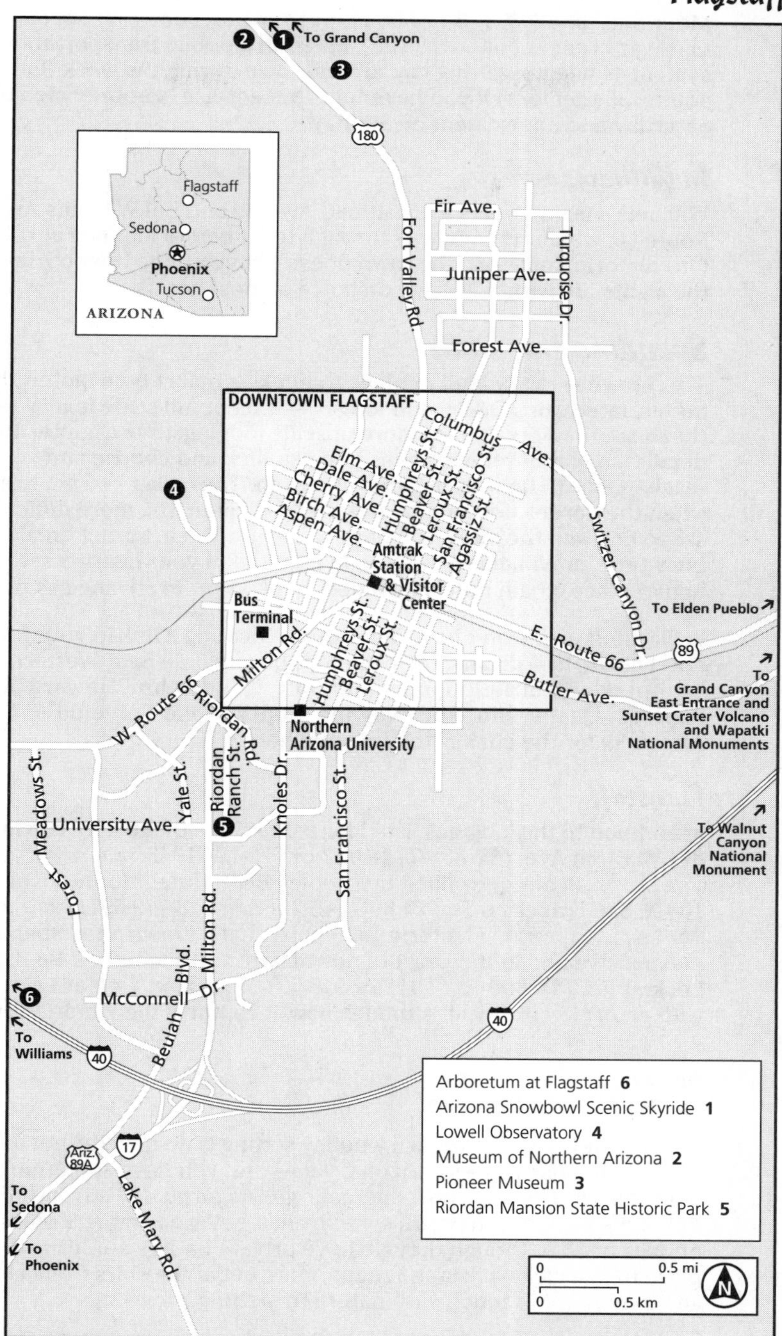
To Grand Canyon
180
Flagstaff
Sedona
Phoenix
Tucson
ARIZONA
Fir Ave.
Fort Valley Rd.
Turquoise Dr.
Juniper Ave.
Forest Ave.
DOWNTOWN FLAGSTAFF
Columbus Ave.
Elm Ave.
Dale Ave.
Cherry Ave.
Birch Ave.
Aspen Ave.
Humphreys St.
Beaver St.
Leroux St.
San Francisco St.
Agassiz St.
Switzer Canyon Dr.
Amtrak Station & Visitor Center
Bus Terminal
Milton Rd.
E. Route 66
89
To Elden Pueblo
Butler Ave.
To Grand Canyon East Entrance and Sunset Crater Volcano and Wapatki National Monuments
W. Route 66
Riordan Rd.
Northern Arizona University
Meadows St.
Yale St.
Riordan Ranch St.
Knoles Dr.
San Francisco St.
University Ave.
To Walnut Canyon National Monument
Forest
Beulah Blvd.
Milton Rd.
McConnell Dr.
40
To Williams
Arizona 89A
17
Lake Mary Rd.
To Sedona
To Phoenix
Arboretum at Flagstaff 6
Arizona Snowbowl Scenic Skyride 1
Lowell Observatory 4
Museum of Northern Arizona 2
Pioneer Museum 3
Riordan Mansion State Historic Park 5
0 0.5 mi
0 0.5 km
N

Mountain Line (☎ 928-779-6624; http://co.coconino.az.us/commservices/mountainline), Flagstaff's public transportation system, is fine for getting you around town during the week (fare: 75¢ adults, 35¢ seniors) if you have time, but service is abbreviated on Saturday and nonexistent on Sunday.

In Williams

Williams's main streets are Railroad Avenue and Bill Williams Avenue/Route 66, which run one-way through town before merging at both ends into historic Route 66. The town doesn't have public transportation, but the sights are within walking distance of most hotels.

Spending the night

This area has every kind of place to bunk — resort-type motels, historic hotels, interesting B&Bs, and lodges — except full-scale luxury resorts (head south to Sedona for more upscale lodgings; see Chapter 16 for details). A glut of rooms means you can pick and choose and get some real bargains to boot during the off-season. The closer you get to summer, when the hordes descend on the Grand Canyon, the more difficult rooms are to find and the more you have to pay for them. Spring break is also a busy time, in Williams as well as in Flagstaff. If your heart is set on a particular place, chain hotels included, book as far in advance as possible.

In Flagstaff, you won't have any trouble locating a link in your favorite hotel chain. In Williams, the chain options include Best Western, EconoLodge, Fairfield Inn by Marriott, Holiday Inn, Howard Johnson Express, Quality Inn, Rodeway Inn, Super 8, and Travelodge. See the Appendix for the chains' toll-free numbers.

Flagstaff

In addition to the lodgings listed here, I also like the Birch Tree Inn ($–$$), 824 W. Birch Ave. (☎ 888-774-1042 or 928-774-1042; www.birchtreeinn.com), an antiques-filled but homey B&B; Hotel Monte Vista, ($–$$), 100 N. San Francisco St. (☎ 800-545-3068 or 928-779-6971; www.hotelmontevista.com), a historic 1926 hotel that's grown a tad shabby but is inexpensive and in the heart of downtown; and Jeanette's B&B, 3380 E. Lockett Rd. (☎ 800-752-1912 or 928-527-1912; www.jeanettesbb.com), with an Art Deco appeal. Although new, it captures the Victorian era to a T.

Arizona Sled Dog Inn

$$ South of Flagstaff

A rustic and elegant B&B in a woodsy setting is no novelty, but add a team of Siberian huskies — in Arizona, yet — and you have something to write home about. The pups no longer take guests on guided adventures as they did in the past, but they still serve by just being adorable. Rooms have no phones or TVs (though they do have private baths), so this is the perfect place to just kick back in the sauna, stare out at the stars from a hot tub — and maybe get in touch with nature by petting a few dogs. . . .

10155 Mountainaire Rd. (6 miles south of Flagstaff). ☎ **800-754-0664** *or 928-525-6212.* www.sleddoginn.com. *Rates: $105–$149 double; $160–$185 2-bedroom suites (up to 4 people). AE, DISC, MC, V.*

Comfi Cottages

$$ Near Downtown

Great for a family or group of friends traveling together, these eight rental cottages near downtown Flagstaff give you that warm, homey feeling in addition to privacy. All are country cute but with modern facilities. Even if you're not big on antiques or frills, you appreciate the fully equipped (and stocked for breakfast) kitchens, cable TVs, picnic tables, and backyard barbecues. The term "cottages" is a bit misleading, because these spacious units, especially the one with three bedrooms; they're all definitely "comfi," though.

1612 N. Aztec (reservations office). ☎ **888-774-0731** *or 928-774-0731. Fax: 928-773-7286.* www.comficottages.com. *Rack rates: $120–$175 for 2 people, depending on the size of the house; $230–$260 for 6–8 people (larger houses for up to 8 people). DISC, MC, V.*

The Inn at 410 Bed and Breakfast

$$–$$$ Downtown

This inn is the classiest lodging act in Flagstaff, hands down — so don't be surprised that it's also the priciest. Each room and suite of this restored 1907 banker's house gets its chosen theme down to the last detail — a hand-painted French Impressionist screen in the Monet's Garden room, say, or clean-lined Craftsman pieces, such as those found in historic lodges, in the Canyon Memories room. The lovely decor, plus such details as whirlpool tubs and/or fireplaces in several units, make this inn a great romantic getaway. Rooms come equipped with TVs and DVD players, too.

410 N. Leroux St. at Dale. ☎ **800-774-2008** *or 928-774-0088. Fax: 928-774-6354.* www.inn410.com. *Rack rates: $145–$205 double. 2-night minimum weekends April–Oct, 3-night minimum some holidays. Rates include full, outstanding breakfast. Phone in breakfast room only. MC, V.*

The Inn at NAU

$ South side

Northern Arizona University has one of the best hotel and restaurant management training programs in the country. Stay at this on-campus inn — formerly the university president's home — and be part of the guinea pig, er, educational, process. The large, well-designed rooms (some available for those with allergies or environmental sensitivities) come equipped with all the goods: hair dryers, refrigerators, coffeemakers, large desks, and safes. And such a deal when it comes to meals — not only is breakfast free, but the seven-course gourmet dinners served Friday nights at the Garden Terrace dining room cost just $24.95. Don't worry, the students are carefully supervised and graded on how well they treat you.

San Francisco St., on the NAU campus (call for directions). ☎ **928-523-1616.** *Fax: 928-523-1625.* www.nau.edu/~hrm/inn. *Rack rates: June–Sept Sun–Thu $89 double, Fri–Sat $99 double; Oct–May $69/$79 double; occasional $59 weekend specials available. No taxes apply and rates include breakfast. AE, MC, V.*

Little America Flagstaff

$$ Eastside

My all-time favorite motel, and here are a few reasons why: It has a 1970s-style coffee shop with phones at the tables (they're for truckers, not international financiers); a retro-swank cocktail lounge; a 24-hour deli; a great gift shop (open until midnight on the weekends); a laundry room; 2-mile hiking trail, exercise room, large heated pool . . . even a gas station? Rooms are huge and, oddly, French Provincial style (too pretty to be kitsch), with large-screen TVs, refrigerators, coffeemakers, and high-speed Internet access. This link in a small western chain is near I-40 but shrouded in a 500-acre Ponderosa pine forest.

2515 E. Butler Ave. (at I-40 Exit 198). ☎ **800-FLAG-FUN** *or 928-779-7900. Fax: 928-779-7983.* www.littleamerica.com/flagstaff. *Rack rates: May–Oct and major holidays, $119–$129 double; Nov–April $89–$99 double. AE, DC, DISC, MC, V.*

Radisson Woodlands Hotel Flagstaff

$–$$ Westside

This is the closest thing Flagstaff has to a fancy hotel, what with its Euro-chic lobby, good Japanese restaurant, and such facilities as a steam room, heated pool, and spa. It's also one of the few places in town with business perks like room service, valet service, and complimentary airport transfers. But the good news is that you won't pay fancy hotel prices — or suffer from the snooty attitude that sometimes comes with upscale properties.

1175 Route 66 (at Milton Avenue). ☎ **800-333-3333** *or 928-773-8888. Fax: 928-773-0597.* www.radisson.com/flagstaffaz. *Rack rates: May–Oct $89–$179 double, Nov–Apr $69–$159 double; Internet specials available. AE, DC, DISC, MC, V.*

Snowbowl Skilift Lodge

$–$$ North of Flagstaff

Flagstaff's last call for lodging en route to the Grand Canyon via Highway 180. Located at the foot of the Snowbowl ski resort, near the Flagstaff Nordic Center, the lodge has nothing but miles of undeveloped land to its north. In summer, guided horseback rides and cowboy cookouts take up the activity slack. Originally part of a 1930s Western set, dismantled and trucked here from Sedona, this motel (sorry — surrounding trees do not a lodge make) has rooms with gas-burning log stoves, pine walls, and little front porches. All rooms are equipped with TVs, but no phones.

6355 Hwy. 180 (7 miles north of Flagstaff). ☎ **800-472-3599** *(in AZ & CA) or 928-779-1951.* www.arizonasnowbowl.com. *Rack rates: Memorial Day through Labor Day Sun–Thu $60 double or $75 B&B rate (includes skyride and breakfast for two),*

Fri–Sat $80 double/ $95 B&B rate; $49 double the rest of the year. Downhill and cross-country ski packages available, snow permitting. AE, CB, DC, DISC, MC, V.

Williams

In addition to the lodgings listed in this section, if you're traveling with kids, you may also consider the Canyon Caboose Bed & Breakfast, 1900 Rodeo Rd. (☎ 800-482-3955 or 520-635-9371; `www.thegrandcanyon.com/canyoncaboose`). The decor is nothing special, and the quarters are cramped, but how many chances do you get to sleep in a railroad car that doesn't move?

Grand Canyon Railway Hotel
$$ Williams

A 1990s tribute to the original 1908 Williams depot, this hotel is part of the Grand Canyon Railway complex, which includes a gift shop, Max & Thelma's restaurant (okay, but nothing special), Spenser's bar/casual eatery, an indoor pool, exercise room, hot tub, and a railway museum. The Southwest contemporary–style rooms don't have as much character as the grand public areas, but they're perfectly pleasant and comfortable.

235 Grand Canyon Blvd. (at the railway station; just follow the tracks). ☎ **800-843-8724** *or 928-635-4010. Fax: 928-773-1610.* `www.thetrain.com`. ***Rack rates:*** *Oct 15–Mar $79 double, Apr–Oct 14 $129 double. A variety of train packages, most with buffet breakfast, available. AE, DISC, MC, V.*

Sheridan House Inn
$$–$$$ Williams

A tough act to top: This inn has the hominess of a B&B, the privacy and (many) amenities of a hotel, and great food served in large quantities. Rooms in the main and adjoining house all have cable TVs, VCRs, and CD stereo systems. A guest laundry, hot tub, pool table, and wooded decks are on-site. The Sheridan House is pricier than most lodgings in this part of Arizona, but the huge breakfasts and gigantic happy-hour buffets (with open bar!) should eliminate the need to spend extra money on food if you're tooling around Williams for the day.

460 E. Sheridan Ave. (at the end, off Grand Canyon Boulevard). ☎ **888-635-9345** *or 928-635-9441. Fax: 928-635-1005.* `www.thegrandcanyon.com/sheridan`. ***Rack rates:*** *$160–$220 double. Rates include breakfast and social hour/dinner. AE, DISC, MC, V.*

A Terry Ranch
$$ Williams

Built expressly as a B&B, A Terry Ranch is your basic Victorian inn — except that it's a two-story log cabin. The four airy rooms are country pretty, with claw-foot tubs/showers and high-quality antiques. All rooms have fireplaces and access to a wraparound veranda — plus TV/VCRs, if you get bored bonding with each other. The smell of fresh-baked breads lures guests to the large wooden table in the morning for a huge breakfast.

701 Quarterhorse (at Rodeo Dr.). ☎ **800-210-5908** *or 928-635-4171.* www.terryranchbnb.com. *Rack rates: $125–$155 double. Rates include breakfast. AE, DISC, MC, V.*

Dining locally

Students, as much as tourists, drive the dining scene in Flagstaff. Fast food rules, but a few gourmet options and plenty of good ethnic and down-home restaurants exist, too. (You didn't really come here to dress up for dinner, did you?) As you may expect, smaller Williams offers proportionately fewer places to refuel, none upscale.

Flagstaff

In addition to the top picks listed here, I also like Pasto's ($$–$$$), 503 N. Humphreys (☎ 928-779-3400), an intimate Italian trattoria that would be more romantic if the dishes weren't so garlic heavy; and Stromboli ($–$$), 1435 S. Milton (☎ 928-773-1960), a low-key, family-friendly spot with good pizzas and calzones. I also enjoyed the Southwestern stew in a bread bowl that I had at the recently opened Altitudes Bar & Grill ($$), 2 S. Beaver St. (☎ 928-214-8218), a ski-themed restaurant in the heart of downtown, but I can't personally vouch for the other dishes.

Beaver St. Brewery

$–$$ Downtown BREW PUB/AMERICAN

The sprawling, ever-popular Beaver Street Brewery isn't just hopping because of its hops. Creative salads, wood-fired designer pizzas, and hearty burgers also draw the hungry hordes. The Bramble Berry beer gets raves, but I prefer my fruit in a bowl and instead hail the Derail Pale Ale.

115 S. Beaver St. (at Cottage Street). ☎ **928-779-0079.** *Reservations not accepted. Individual pizzas $7.50–$8.75, salads $6.50–$7.95, sandwiches $7.50–$8.65. AE, DISC, MC, V. Open: Daily lunch and dinner.*

The best little whorehouse in Arizona

A former bordello that served railroad roughs and their pals, the **Red Garter,** 137 Railroad Ave. (☎ **800-328-1484** or 928-635-1484, www.redgarter.com), now caters to the (theoretically) more respectable B&B crowd. Owner/innkeeper John Holst is happy to talk about his terrific restoration of the house — he kept the original graffiti in one of the "girls'" rooms, for example, but added private baths. You have to walk up a flight of stairs to get to your room, but the exercise is good for you because the free continental breakfast includes your pick of pastries made in the connecting bakery. Rack rates: $85–$120 double (Web booking and February discounts available). DISC, MC, V.

Cottage Place

$$$–$$$$ Between downtown and NAU CONTINENTAL

A cozy, candlelit classic, Cottage Place offers good if traditional Continental fare, an award-winning wine list, and service that's attentive without being in your face. Rack of lamb and pork schnitzel are typical of the specialties, but vegetarians are never ignored — or bored.

126 W. Cottage Ave. (at Humphries). ☎ **928-774-8431.** *Reservations suggested in high season, essential weekends. Main courses: $21–$30. AE, MC, V. Open: Tues–Sun dinner.*

Jackson's Grill at the Springs

$$–$$$ En route to Sedona NEW AMERICAN

Call me a big city snob, but I was bowled over to find this quality of contemporary cooking in Flagstaff. I've never had better spinach-artichoke dip; my starter spinach salad, with crisp bits of parsnip, candied pecans, and blue cheese, was as tasty as greens get; and my ahi tuna with bok choy and wasabi mashed potatoes was perfectly prepared. Enjoy the rustic elegant dining room or a patio with a view of neighboring llamas. (Don't worry. The llamas are too far away for spitting.)

7055 S. Hwy. 89A. ☎ **928-213-9332.** *Reservations recommended, especially weekends. Main courses: $12–$25. AE, DC, DISC, MC, V. Open: Dinner nightly, Sunday buffet brunch.*

Josephine's

$$–$$$ Near Downtown NEW AMERICAN

A recent addition to Flagstaff's fine-dining scene, this modern American bistro in a pretty stone cottage offers some of the most delicious and imaginative food in town. Dishes that may emerge from the open kitchen include cauliflower cheddar soup, portabello mushroom risotto, and lemon tarragon roasted chicken. You won't regret indulging in desserts like the apple-cranberry crisp with an oatmeal crust and cinnamon ice cream.

503 N. Humphreys (at Vine). ☎ **928-779-3400.** *Reservations recommended, especially weekends. Main courses: $15.50–$22.50. AE, DISC, MC, V. Open: Lunch and dinner daily except Sunday.*

Williams

For additional places to eat in Williams, see "The Mother Road mother lode" sidebar in this chapter.

Pancho McGillicuddy's Mexican Cantina

$$ Williams TEX-MEX/AMERICAN

Okay, so it ain't totally authentic (what did you expect with a name like Pancho McGillicuddy?), but the tortillas and chips are made fresh, the patio is pretty, and it's fun to down a cold one in an 1893 saloon.

141 Railroad Ave. (at Grand Canyon Boulevard). ☎ **928-635-4150.** *Main courses and combination plates: $6.50–$14.50. AE, DISC, MC, V. Open: Lunch and dinner daily.*

Pine Country Restaurant

$ Williams AMERICAN

Locals pile into this blue-curtained storefront dining room for huge slices of home-baked pies, gravy-smothered biscuits, hefty burgers, and crispy fried chicken (prepared in canola oil, the menu says; now can't you just feel your cholesterol count dropping?).

107 N. Grand Canyon Blvd. (at Railroad Avenue). ☎ **928-635-9718.** *Main courses: $6.95–$11.95 (sandwiches $4.95–$6.25, breakfasts $2.50– $5.75). AE, DISC, MC, V. Open: Daily breakfast, lunch, dinner.*

Bean there, done that

What's a college town without coffeehouses? In addition to links in you-know-what Seattle chain, Flag offers the following local favorites:

- **Café Espress,** 16 N. San Francisco St. at E. Aspen Ave., downtown (☎ **928-774-0541**), is your quintessential college chow house: lots of tofu and veggies, and elaborate espresso drinks made with organic, fair-trade, bird-friendly coffee. But the bakery turns out some tasty pastry, and the student-budget-geared prices are pretty sweet, too.
- **Campus Coffee Bean,** 1800 S. Milton Rd., #24, in a strip shopping center near NAU (☎ **928-556-0660**), offers live music or poetry readings most nights. The menu stretches beyond coffees, *chais,* and Italian sodas to include some sandwiches and sweets.
- **Jitters,** 3504 E. Route 66, at Fanning, eastside (☎ **928-526-6964**), serves freshly made soups, gourmet sandwiches, and a tempting array of cakes and pies. Great selection of offbeat greeting cards, too.
- **Late for the Train,** 107 N. San Francisco St. at Aspen Ave., downtown (☎ **928-779-5975**), features the requisite black-clad barristas with attitude preparing requisitely strong espresso. Possibly the hippest of the bunch. Also on 1800 N. Fort Valley Rd., west side (☎ **928-773-0308**); and 2880 S. Milton, #300, south side (☎ **928-213-8500**).
- **Macy's European Coffeehouse and Bakery,** 14 S. Beaver St., just south of the railroad tracks/Santa Fe Ave (☎ **928-774-2243**), is far more Californian than European (what self-respecting cafe on the continent would serve veggie lasagna with tempeh, a soy product?) and hippie chic with its bright-red coffee roasters and infinite java riffs.

Rod's Steak House

$$–$$$$ Williams STEAKHOUSE/AMERICAN

The kitschy red Fiberglas steer on Rod's roof has heralded good corn-fed, mesquite-broiled beef since 1946. The atmosphere is low-key, but the meat is high profile, with a house specialty prime rib that weighs in from the 9-ounce "ladies' lite" to a 16-ounce "cattleman's hefty."

301 E. Route 66 (at Flagel, east end of town). ☎ **928-635-2671.** *Main courses: $9–$28.50. AE, DISC, MC, V. Open: Daily lunch and dinner. Closed Jan 4–20, Sun Nov–March.*

Exploring lower northwest Arizona

You may be surprised by the many different — as in both varied and strange — things you see around here, from volcanic fields to observatories to mansions made of logs. Many of the attractions in this chapter involve being outdoors, but I put the activities primarily designed to keep you moving — as opposed to activities where moving is just a necessary adjunct — into the "Staying active" section. (You don't even have to look at that section if you feel lazy, honest.)

Flagstaff

Beyond its motel and fast-food-frenzied facade, Flagstaff has sights that track back to its roots as a railroad and lumber center and to its Route 66 glory days. Stop in at the visitor center at the old Santa Fe depot (see the "Fast Facts: Lower Northwest Arizona" section in this chapter) to pick up a self-guided map of the many turn-of-the-19th-century masonry buildings in the Downtown Historic Railroad District, or, in summer, to find out about the free 90-minute walking tours of downtown led by local historians dressed in period costumes (call ☎ 928-774-8800 for more information). Other sightseeing options follow.

- Study the culture of the Plateau. The Museum of Northern Arizona, 3101 N. Fort Valley Rd. (Highway 180 north, 3 miles north of Flagstaff; ☎ 928-774-5213; `www.musnaz.org`), which highlights the arts, culture, and geology of Colorado Plateau, would be a standout anywhere, but it's a must-see if you're in this area; the 1928 native stone building is worth the trip alone. Greatest hits include the Navajo and Hopi textile collection and, in a terrific Western-design wing, ceramics and paintings (look for the work of Mary-Russell Colton). Kids especially like the life-size Dilophosaurus, a dino-carnivore that stomped this region when it was a swamp. (Also check out the "Shopping for local treasures" section in this chapter.) Admission: $5 adults, $4 seniors, $3 students, $2 ages 7–17, 6 and under free. Open: Daily 9 a.m.–5 p.m., closed Thanksgiving, Christmas, New Year's Day, and Easter. See map p. 345.
- Check out the lifestyles of the timber rich and famous. Tour the Riordan Mansion State Historic Park, 1300 Riordan Ranch St., on the NAU campus, off South Milton Road (☎ 928-779-4395), to see

what you get when you mix a lot of tree money and a little eccentricity. The 40-room native log-and-stone mansion, built in 1904, was the domain of two lumber-baron brothers who married sisters. Along with the more typical rich-people trappings are one of the best collections of Craftsman furniture in the country and photo transparencies of the Grand Canyon that double as window panes. You can also see Paul Bunyan's baby shoes (it's a long — and tall — story). Call for West Wing hours. Guided tours given on the hour, one-half hour after the park opens (reservations recommended). Admission: $6 adults, $2.50 ages 7–13, 6 and under free. Open: Grounds and visitor center, May–Oct daily 8:30 a.m.–5 p.m., Nov–April daily 10:30 a.m.–5 p.m., closed Christmas. See map p. 345.

- See the stars. Interactive astronomy exhibits and fascinating guided tour programs make the Lowell Observatory, 1400 West Mars Hill Rd. (☎ 928-774-3358 or 928-774-2096 [after hours]; `www.lowell.edu`) terrific enough during the day, but peak science geek time is after dark when you can peer through the facility's telescopes. Viewing schedules depend on weather and planetary alignments, ranging from two star gazings, total, from January through February to six viewings per week June through August. The telescopes are in an open dome, so dress for an evening outdoors. Call for directions and night-viewing program schedule. Admission: $5 adults, $4 seniors and college students, $2 ages 5–17; 4 and under free. Open: Nov–March daily noon to 5 p.m., April–Oct daily 9 a.m.–5 p.m. See map p. 345.
- Ride up to the sky. Even with no chance of snow on Mt. Agassiz, one of the San Francisco Peaks, you can get lofted to the top via the Arizona Snowbowl Scenic Skyride, Snowbowl Road, off Highway 180, about 15 miles north of town (☎ 928-779-1951; `www.arizonasnowbowl.com`). Riding the lift is the high point of a Flagstaff visit — 11,500 feet, to be precise — and on a clear day, you can see forever (well, at least to the North Rim of the Grand Canyon). Admission: $10 adults, $8 seniors, $6 ages 8–12, ages 7 and under and 70 and over ride free. Open: Memorial Day to Labor Day daily 10 a.m.–4 p.m., after Labor Day to mid-Oct Fri–Sun 10 a.m.–4 p.m. See map p. 345.
- See flora and fauna. Tour the Arboretum at Flagstaff, 4001 S. Woody Mountain Rd (☎ 928-774-1442; `www.thearb.org`), and find out all about the landscape of the Colorado Plateau, including herbs believed to ward off vampires (you won't see any here, so clearly the plants work) and to keep parishioners awake during church services. The lovely woods and meadows (190 acres) encompass 10 gardens, four demonstration habitats, some 2,500 species of flora, plus lots of fauna, from butterflies to elk. Hour-long guided tours, which depart daily at 11 a.m. and 1 p.m., are included in the admission fee. Admission: $4 adults, $3 seniors, $1 ages 6–12, 5 and under free. Open: April 1–Dec 15 daily 9 a.m.–5 p.m., closed Dec 16–March 31. See map p. 345.

- See artifacts from Flagstaff's past. The Arizona Historical Society's small Pioneer Museum, 2340 N. Fort Valley Rd. (Highway 180, north of W. Fir Ave.; ☎ 928-774-6272), housed in Coconino County's first (1908) hospital for the poor, has a few grim displays, such as an old iron lung, but the museum is generally upbeat about Flagstaff's early days. A "Playthings of the Past" exhibit opens every winter, and a couple of railroad cars always sit out front. Admission: $3 adults, $2 seniors and students, ages 12 and under free. Open: Mon–Sat 9 a.m.–5 p.m., closed Easter, Thanksgiving, and Christmas. See map p. 345.

Havasu Canyon

If you want to see some of the state's most spectacular scenery and visit an Indian reservation, this canyon, south of the central part of the national park, fills the bill. Home to some 500 Havasupai people, Havasu Canyon is famous for its astonishingly turquoise water and for the 200-foot waterfalls that cascade down vivid red sandstone cliffs into limpid pools. Swimming in said pools — and for some people, hiking into and out of the canyon — is pretty much all you can do there; the village consists of fairly run-down homes. If you can stand being forced to relax in a beautiful spot, though, this area may just be your place. Keep in mind that Havasu Canyon is a more than a little bit off the beaten path; you must hike, ride, or book a helicopter flight to enter, and you must reserve in advance.

From Williams, take I-40 west 44 miles to Seligman, where the road splits; continue on Highway 66 west for 26 miles and turn north on Indian Route 18 (if you reach Peach Springs, you drove 6 miles too far). Drive 60 miles to Haulupai Hilltop, where the 8-mile-long Hualapai Trail, a fairly precipitous, winding route (at least for the first mile; it levels off after that) descends into Supai, Havasu Canyon's only settlement and home to the Havasupai Tourist Enterprise (☎ 928-448-2121; www.havaspaitribe.com). A limited number of people are allowed in (fee $20 per person), so you must contact the tribe, even if you're just planning to hike. The Havasupai Tourist Enterprise isn't always easy to reach by phone, but keep trying.

If you don't want to hike down, contact the tourist enterprise and arrange for a pack horse or mule to take you and your luggage (round-trip rates are $150 from Hualupai Hilltop to the campground). Again, be sure to contact the trip in advance to make arrangements.

Alternatively, Papillon Grand Canyon Helicopters (☎ 800-528-2418 or 928-638-2419; www.papillon.com) runs daily excursions to Havasu Canyon from the Grand Canyon Airport in Tusayan. For $505 per adult ($50 less if you book on the Internet), you get a round-trip helicopter ride plus a guided horseback ride to Havasu Falls (but no meals), returning the same day. If you want to helicopter in and stay overnight at Havasupai Lodge (see the paragraph that follows), you have to contact Papillon at least two weeks — preferably a month — in advance, as rooms book up quickly.

Pseudo sunset, pseudo moon

When the iron and sulfur in the lava that flowed from Sunset Crater during its last eruption (around A.D. 1250) oxidized, it gave the volcano rim a red and yellow "sunset" glow — and a perpetually molten, about-to-blow look. Fast forwarding ahead some seven centuries, the lava flow at Sunset Crater looked so much like the moon's surface that NASA sent Neil Armstrong and other astronauts over to practice their rock specimen collecting (Armstrong must have passed the rock test; he was the first man to walk on the moon).

The Havasupai Lodge in Supai (☎ 928-448-2111) has comfortable, air-conditioned rooms, but no TVs or phones (doubles $80).

For the location of Havasu Canyon, see map p. 343.

Sunset Crater Volcano and Wupatki National Monuments

A double-header. When Sunset Crater erupted in A.D. 1064–1065 (that's just about the time William the Conqueror was taking over Europe), the Sinagua Indians abandoned their fields and fled — only to return a few decades after the action cooled down because the eruption had enriched the soil and improved farming conditions. Sunset Crater and Wupatki national monuments, connected by a 36-mile loop road, not only give you a chance to witness the aftermath of a fiery natural phenomenon but also take a look at the ancient civilizations directly affected by it.

You can take a 1-mile, self-guided walk around the base of the 1,000-foot-high Sunset Crater, a study in red- and black-dotted pines, but the cone itself is off-limits. If you enjoy climbing, ask at the visitor center about ascending Lenox Crater or Doney Crater at Wupatki. Wupatki is interesting enough for its well-preserved structures, but what makes it really unusual is that three different native cultures — the Kayenta and the Cohonina peoples, along with the Sinagua — coexisted here. Don't miss the high-rise pueblo for which the national monument is named (take the short trail from the back of the Wupatki visitor center) and the Maya-like ball court with its barometer-like blow hole.

See map p. 343. Sunset Crater visitor center (14 miles northeast of Flagstaff, off Highway 89; **☎ 928-526-0502;** `www.nps.gov/suc`*). Wupatki visitor center (20 miles north of the Sunset Crater visitor center along Sunset Loop Road;* **☎ 928-679-2365;** `www.nps.gov/wupa`*). Admission to both: $5 per adult, ages 16 and under free. Open (visitor centers): summer 8 a.m.–6 p.m., winter 8 a.m.–5 p.m., closed Christmas; gates open year-round sunrise to sunset.*

Walnut Canyon National Monument

Move this spot to the top of your must-see list. This beautiful canyon is worth visiting for its lush ponderosa pine, juniper, and Douglas fir forest alone, but you also can see — and even enter — some well-preserved cliff dwellings built by the Sinagua people between 1125 and 1250. No one is exactly sure why these dwellings were left behind by 1300. They were protected over the years by limestone overhangs and the area's dry climate — only to be threatened by 19th-century picnickers, who destroyed some of them.

If you're in good shape, the steep 185-foot Island Trail down to the ruins from the visitor center shouldn't be a problem. But remember, you're at 6,690 feet — which makes breathing hard to begin with. If you suffer from respiratory problems or have bad knees, go for the easier ½-mile Rim Trail. You can still look out at the cliff dwellings, and explore prehistoric pit houses.

See map p. 343. 10 miles southeast of Flagstaff (take I-40 7½ miles east to Exit 204, then drive 3 miles south on Walnut Canyon Rd.). ☎ **928-526-3367.** *Admission: $5 adults, ages 16 and under free. Open: Memorial Day through Labor Day daily 8 a.m.–5 p.m.; the rest of the year daily 9 a.m.–5 p.m. The Island Trail closes 1 hour before the park closes; the Rim Trail closes 30 minutes before the park closes.*

Williams

A town entry sign and the tourist brochures all hail Williams as the "Gateway to the Grand Canyon," but the town also has a life, thank you — or at least a past. In its logging and railroad heydey, this alpine outpost bustled with brothels, bars, and opium dens. The population (around 3,000) is about the same now as it was then, but it's nowhere near as wild. At one time, the town became a popular Route 66 stopover. Along with hiking the woods or strolling the streets, you may want to visit before or after you ride the Grand Canyon rails.

- Ride the rails. Even if you're not too-too-tootling away, the Grand Canyon Railway depot (just west of Grand Canyon Blvd., north of the tracks) is the most happening place in town. The entertainment includes staged cowboy hijinks at 9 a.m. (before the train departs). A free museum devoted to Grand Canyon hospitality is open the rest of the day; a steam locomotive and coach car are among the items on display. See the "Riding the Grand Canyon rails" sidebar later in this chapter. See map p. 343.

- Talk to the animals. The Grand Canyon Deer Farm is 8 miles east of Williams (Exit 171 of I-40; ☎ 800-926-3337 or 928-635-4073; `www.deerfarm.com`). This place is great for kids to get up-close-and-personal with Bambi — as well as with llamas, miniature horses, pygmy goats, wallabies, turkeys, buffalo, and more. Admission: $6.75 adults, $5.75 seniors, $3.95 ages 3–13; the corn-and-pellet feed mixture costs extra. Open: Nov–Feb daily 10 a.m.–5 p.m. weather permitting, Mar–May and Sept–Oct 9 a.m.–6 p.m., Jun–Aug 8 a.m.–7 p.m.

Staying active

Home to Northern Arizona University's High Altitude Sports Training Complex for Olympic athletes, surrounded by forest, and flanked by the

Double billing

Williams was named for mountain man Bill Williams (1787–1849), a fur trapper and pathfinder famed for his survival skills (the result of being saddled with the same first and last names?).

highest mountains in the state, Flagstaff is outdoor adventure central for northern Arizona. Williams is no slouch either, when it comes to playing outside.

- Climbing: Flagstaff Mountain Guides (☎ 928-526-4489), can help you scale the heights. Rappelling classes start from full-day beginner instruction ($175) and go up from there in length and cost. Mountaineering classes are available, too. You can also prepare for on-the-rocks action at Vertical Relief Climbing Center, 205 S. San Francisco St. (☎ 928-556-9909; `www.verticalrelief.com`), which claims to have the tallest indoor walls in the Southwest (who measures these things, anyway?). Costs run $14 to play for a day, $8 to rent equipment.
- Golfing: Elephant Rocks, 2200 Country Club Dr. (3 miles west of downtown Williams; ☎ 928-635-4935; `www.thegrandcanyon.com/golf`), had to give up its title as the self-proclaimed "No.1 9-hole golf course in Arizona," when Gary Panks, the original course architect, made it into an 18-holer not too long ago. But the course has other lures to compensate — a pretty ponderosa pine setting and low greens fees ($45 weekends, $36 weekdays with cart). This well-maintained municipal course is open from mid-April to mid-November.
- Hiking: Locals head for glen and dale (whatever a dale is) in the San Francisco Peaks and Coconino National Forest when the white stuff isn't covering up the trails. Taking the Arizona Snowbowl ski lift up Mt. Agassiz (see the "Exploring lower northwest Arizona" section earlier in this section) and hiking back down is especially fun. Get trail maps and advice about the best trekking spots from the Peaks Ranger District office, 5075 N. Highway 89 (☎ 928-526-0866; open: Mon–Fri 7:30 a.m.–4:30 p.m.), or the Coconino National Forest office, 1824 S. Thompson St. (☎ 928-527-3600; `www.fs.fed.us/r3/coconino`; open: Mon–Fri 7:30 a.m.–4:30 a.m.).
- River rafting: If you don't have time for a weeklong Grand Canyon rafting trip but want to get your toes into the chilly Colorado River, consider an excursion with the Haulapai River Runners (☎ 928-769-2219). Trips, which cost $265 per person for a full day, depart from Peach Springs (see Havasu Canyon in the "Exploring lower northwest Arizona" section earlier in this section) on the Hualupai reservation. Expect a combination of white and calm waters and

lots of wonderful scenery. Bookings get you discounted rates at the tribe's affiliated Hualapai Lodge ($$), 900 Rte. 66 in Peach Springs. For more details about both river activities and lodging, contact the tribe (☎ 888-255-9550 or 928-769-2210; www.grandcanyonresort.com/rr/rr.html).

- Skiing: It's all downhill at the Arizona Snowbowl (☎ 928-779-1951 or 928-779-4577 [snow report]; www.arizonasnowbowl.com), where you can rent anything snow-oriented, including snowboards and the latest in parabolic skis. The 32 slopes (2,300 vertical feet, total) have a nice mix of beginner, intermediate, and advanced runs. Lift tickets range from $27 for a half-day midweek pass to $42 for a weekend all-day pass (adults). Ages 8 to 12 pay $19 for a half day, $24 full day, no matter what day of the week. This ski area has always been weather dependent because no ground water was available for snow making on Mt. Agassiz, an extinct volcano, but in 2004 the National Forest Service began exploring the possibility of using reclaimed water to create the white stuff.

At 30 acres, the Williams Ski Area, 10 minutes south of town (take Fourth St. to the Kaibab National Forest; ☎ 928-635-9330; www.williamsskiarea.com), may be the smallest in the state, but the area's fun for snow-bonding families who can also rent sleds and inner tubes for a sledding hill. When enough white stuff falls (usually starting in December), the ski area stays open Thursday through Monday from 9:30 a.m. to 4:30 p.m. (also open Christmas week, except Christmas day). Lift tickets are $25 adults and $20 ages 12 and under all day weekends and holidays, and $20 adults and $15 ages 12 and under all day weekdays. Lower half-day (1 p.m. and after) and beginner rates are available.

Cross-country-ski aficianados have a couple of options. The Flagstaff Nordic Center, operated by Snowbowl, 15 miles north of Flagstaff on 18400 N. Highway 180 (☎ 928-779-1951, ext. 195; www.arizonasnowbowl.com), has 40 kilometers of groomed track. All-day trail passes cost $10. Other options include snow-shoeing and skijoring, a cross between dog sledding and cross-country skiing (you can rent the skis but it's BYOD — bring your own dog — to haul you along on them). The Mormon Lake Ski Touring Center, 28 miles south of Flagstaff on Lake Mary Rd. (☎ 928-354-2240), has more than 21 miles of groomed ski trails; $5 buys you an all-day trail pass. Both ski centers rent equipment.

Second childhood? Enjoy!

At Snowbowl and at Flagstaff Nordic Center, skiing is free for ages 70 and over — and for ages 8 and under. At the Williams Ski Center, kiddies have to pay to play in the snow, but seniors 65 and up schuss without charge.

The Mother Road mother lode

Williams was the last Route 66 town to be bypassed by the freeway: Not until 1984 was the stretch of I-40 that replaced the famous road — dubbed the "Mother Road" by writer John Steinbeck — completed here. As a result, it's tough to find a store on Williams's main streets that doesn't hawk Route 66-o-bilia. The best place to find the stuff en masse, however, is the **Route 66 Road Store,** 320 W. Route 66 (☎ **928-635-0700**), where you can buy books and mementos that run the gamut from Zippo lighters to James Dean T-shirts. An entire wall is devoted to Betty Boop, and a life-size version of the cartoon glamorpuss greets shoppers at the door. A vintage car museum is also being developed in an adjoining garage.

Prefer your Route 66 nostalgia edible? Stop by **Cruisers,** 233 W. Route 66 (☎ **928-635-2445**), for a cheeseburger in a renovated service station, and then head over to **Twisters,** 417 E. Route 66 (☎ **928-635-0266**), for a root-beer freeze or banana split. Both places have cool classic cars out front.

Shopping for local treasures

This region is rich in Native American jewelry and crafts and Route 66 memorabilia, among other things.

In Flagstaff, downtown is the most fertile retail ground; sporting goods, crafts, and nostalgia are among the bestsellers. The creative home furnishings and gifts sold at Zani, 9 N. Leroux (☎ 928-774-9409), are entirely up-to-date, but the 1911 brick house's long-dead owner apparently likes to come back and browse. The Artists Gallery, 17 N. San Francisco St. (☎ 928-773-0958), represents more than 40 locals who work in genres ranging from stained glass and calligraphy to sculpture. Check out some of the outstanding jewelry. At the Black Hound Gallerie, 120 N. Leroux, near Aspen, in the Old Town Shops (☎ 928-774-2323), you find funky clothes, hip greeting cards, posters, and games — and, during sales events, staff who dress up in costumes (they were all superheroes when I visited).

From late May through September, Zuni, Navajo, and Hopi artisans come from all over the Southwest to show — and sell — their work at the huge annual Celebration of Native American Art at the Museum of Northern Arizona (see the "Exploring lower northwest Arizona" section earlier in this chapter). Other times of the year, you can make do with the extensive selection at the museum gift shop.

In Williams, a somewhat slim selection of crafts and antiques shops are located downtown, along historic Route 66; also check out "The Mother Road mother lode" sidebar in this chapter.

Living it up after dark

Artsy types and night owls throughout northern Arizona flock to Flagstaff after dark. Williams has far less to offer — but in summer, you don't have to go bed directly after dinner; a little night music is the ticket at several spots in town.

In Flagstaff

Flagstaff offers both an arts and a nightlife scene, and they're not half bad either. Check the weekend nightlife/arts insert of the Arizona Daily Sun or the free Live! listings tabloid for details of what's on during your visit.

Summer's the high culture pinnacle, with various Native American festivals, marketplaces, exhibits, and lectures at the Museum of Northern Arizona (see the "Exploring lower northwest Arizona" section earlier in this chapter, and check `www.musnaz.org` for a schedule). But the Flagstaff Symphony Orchestra, 113A E. Aspen Ave. (☎ 888-520-7214 [tickets] or 928-774-5107; `www.flagstaffsymphony.org`), a fine regional ensemble that has been around since 1949, stays tuned up year-round. The recently restored and reopened historic Orpheum Theater, 15 W. Aspen St. (☎ 928-556-1580; `www.orpheumpresents.org`) offers an eclectic mix of plays, film festivals, and concerts. In addition, Theatrikos, Flagstaff Playhouse, 11 W. Cherry St. (☎ 928-774-1662; `www.theatrikos.com`), can satisfy your basic thespian needs in all seasons.

The club scene changes constantly but you usually find something happening at downtown's two historic hotels. Charley's, at the Weatherford, 23 N. Leroux (☎ 928-779-1919), mostly hosts rock bands, while the Monte Vista lounge, 100 N. San Francisco St. (☎ 928-779-6971), brings in a variety of local and national acts. Handcrafted-beer lovers find their bliss in downtown Flagstaff: In addition to the fairly ferny Beaver Street Brewery (see the "Dining locally" section earlier in this chapter), check out the funky Mogollon Brewing Company, 15 N. Agassiz St. (☎ 928-773-8950), where a chain saw hangs over the pool table and the pale ale wins accolades. Somewhere in between the two, the Flagstaff Brewing Company, 16 E. Route 66 (☎ 928-773-1442), compensates for a lack of

Two-steppin' and taxidermy on Route 66

Never mind the name: The **Museum Club,** 3404 E. Route 66, Flagstaff (**☎ 928-526-9434**), is anything but stuffy (although lots of things that look down from the walls at you are stuffed). Nicknamed "the Zoo" because it was built in 1931 to house a taxidermy collection, this huge log cabin does attract the usual bar stiffs, but comes to life each night with the best Country and Western sounds in town. If you can't get here after dark, check it out during the day.

strong suds personality with an impressive array of single malts and small batch bourbons. A slightly older, more sophisticated set tends to frequent the Wine Loft, 17 N. San Francisco St. (☎ 928-773-WINE); it's on the second floor and easy to miss but keep looking. Macy's and Campus Coffee Bean (see the "Bean there, done that" sidebar in this chapter) often host low-key acoustic groups.

In Williams

In summer, you find live music somewhere in town most nights, either at Pancho McGillicuddy's (see the "Dining locally" section earlier in this chapter), at Cruisers (see "The Mother Road mother lode" sidebar in this chapter), or at the Mountainside Inn, 642 E. Route 66 (☎ 928-635-4431). You can also wander over for a drink at Spenser's Lounge in the Grand Canyon Railway Hotel (see the "Spending the night" section earlier in this chapter). The gorgeous carved-wood 19th-century bar was shipped over to the hotel from Ireland where, the story has it, the architect agreed to build the bar in exchange for free drinks for the rest of his life. Because he was still putting them away well into his 80s, it turned out to be a pretty good deal — for him.

Fast Facts: Lower Northwest Arizona

Area Code

The area code for this entire region is **928.**

Emergencies

For police, ambulance, or in case of fire, call **☎ 911.**

Hospitals/Clinics

Services include Flagstaff Medical Center, 1200 N. Beaver St. (**☎ 928-770-3366**), and Williams Health Care Center, 301 S. Seventh St. (**☎ 928-635-4441**).

Information

You can't miss the Flagstaff Visitors Center, One East Route 66, at the corner of Beaver Street (**☎ 800-842-7293** or 928-774-9541; www.flagstaffarizona.org); just follow the tracks to the train depot. The center is a great source of area information — as well as a prime people-watching spot because it's always bustling with hapless Grand Canyon–bound travelers, many from other countries. Hours are daily, 8 a.m. to 7 p.m. Another former railroad depot, the Williams–Grand Canyon Chamber of Commerce/Kaibab National Forest Visitors Center, 200 W. Railroad Ave. (**☎ 800-863-0546** or 928-635-1418; www.williamschamber.com), is also an excellent resource, dispensing information, as its weighty monicker implies, on the town, the forest, and the great gorge; lots of excellent books on the region are available here. Open daily from 8 a.m. to 6:30 p.m. in high season, closing earlier in winter.

Internet Access

Check your e-mail in Flagstaff at Biff's Bagels, 1 S. Beaver St. (**☎ 928-226-0424**); or Bookman's, 1520 S. Riordon Rd. (**☎ 928-774-0005**).

Post Office

You find post offices in Flagstaff, 2400 N. Postal Blvd. (☎ **928-714-9302**), and Williams, 120 S. 1st St. (☎ **928-635-4572**).

Road Conditions

Call ☎ **888-411-7623.**

Weather

Call ☎ **928-774-3301.**

The South Rim of the Grand Canyon

Even if seeing the Grand Canyon isn't your sole reason for going to Arizona, you probably still have to visit. If you don't, you spend more time explaining why you didn't go than you spend getting there. (I'm exhausted even thinking about it.) But that's fine. The Grand Canyon doesn't disappoint; it deserves all the press it gets. (One of the most amazing things about the canyon is that it seems to appear out of nowhere. You drive around this pleasant but fairly ordinary pine forest and then — wham!)

The commercialism and crowds that surround the South Rim may, on the other hand, put you off, as they do me — which is why I show you how to get the most out of your experience, whether you just go for the day or make a bigger time commitment.

I'm going to beg you to please come during the off-season if you can. Summer, spring, and fall are the busiest months. You're much happier here from November through February (the crowds are minimal, and if snow falls, the bonus of seeing the Grand Canyon dusted by all that pretty white stuff is worth the trip). But if you can't — and I forgive you — book hotel rooms and popular tours, such as river rafting and mule rides, well in advance (more on that in the "Inside the park" section later in this chapter), so you get to do everything that you really want to do. Reserving some attractions in advance during the quieter months is also important; I let you know which ones, honest.

See map p. 365 for locations of accommodations, services, and attractions in or near Grand Canyon Village.

Getting there

In Arizona every type of transport takes you to the state's top tourist attraction.

By car

The Grand Canyon Village on the South Rim is 59 miles north of Williams via Highway 64 from I-40 and 78 miles northwest of Flagstaff via Highway 180. If you take the scenic route from the east from Cameron (Highway 89 to Highway 64), the distance is 107 miles from Flagstaff. See the "Arizona

Driving Times and Distances" map on the Cheat Sheet at the front of the book for details about getting to the Grand Canyon from other popular points in and around the state.

Although it may be a while before a plan to ban cars from the Grand Canyon goes into effect, don't wait until driving is verboten. During high season, when parking lots are maxed out but all the in-park transit systems are running full gear, consider leaving your wheels in Tusayan and taking a shuttle or taxi (see the "Getting around" section).

By plane

The Grand Canyon National Park Airport (☎ 928-638-2446) is 6 miles south of the Grand Canyon in Tusayan. Most flights into the airport are via Las Vegas with tour operators, such as Air Vegas (☎ 800-255-7474; www.airvegas.com) and Scenic Airlines (☎ 800-634-6801; www.scenic.com). You can buy just transportation (about $230 round-trip), but purchasing a sightseeing package is more economical ($254, including a coach tour). Only Westwind Aviation (☎ 888-869-0866; www.westwindaviation.com) runs regular air tours from Phoenix to the Grand Canyon. Approximately $350 per person buys a same-day round-trip flight, bus tour, and lunch. Again, booking a flight alone is more costly. You can taxi or shuttle to Grand Canyon Village from the airport (see the "Getting around" section).

Riding the Grand Canyon rails

Train travel to the Grand Canyon was hot when it was introduced in 1901, but by 1927 it was already passé. Automobile fever had taken hold of the country, and more people wanted to drive than to ride the rails. In 1968, rail service was suspended for lack of interest; only three passengers rattled around the train on the last national park run.

But that was then. In the last couple of decades, after people began to realize that car exhaust probably wasn't all that good for the canyon, the **Grand Canyon Railway** (**☎ 800-THE-TRAIN;** www.thetrain.com) came back by popular demand — and in close to its original form. Every day (except December 24 and 25) the train leaves from the Williams depot at 10 a.m. on a 2¼-hour (each way) sentimental journey. Restored locomotives — one dating back to 1906 — pull the refurbished Pullman cars while cowboy balladeers and "outlaws" entertain the passengers.

The five classes of service range from Coach ($72 adult round-trip, $27 ages 2–16 round-trip) to Luxury Parlor Car ($169/$125, including entrance fees to the Grand Canyon). (I suggest you ride Coach; the extra hors d'oeuvres and beverages and, in some cases, vistas, in the higher classes aren't worth the added expense.) All kinds of packages, most of them involving a stay at the Grand Canyon Railway Hotel (see the "Williams" section of "Spending the night" earlier in this chapter), are available. Call for details or click on the "PACKAGES" box on the train's Web site.

Grand Canyon Village

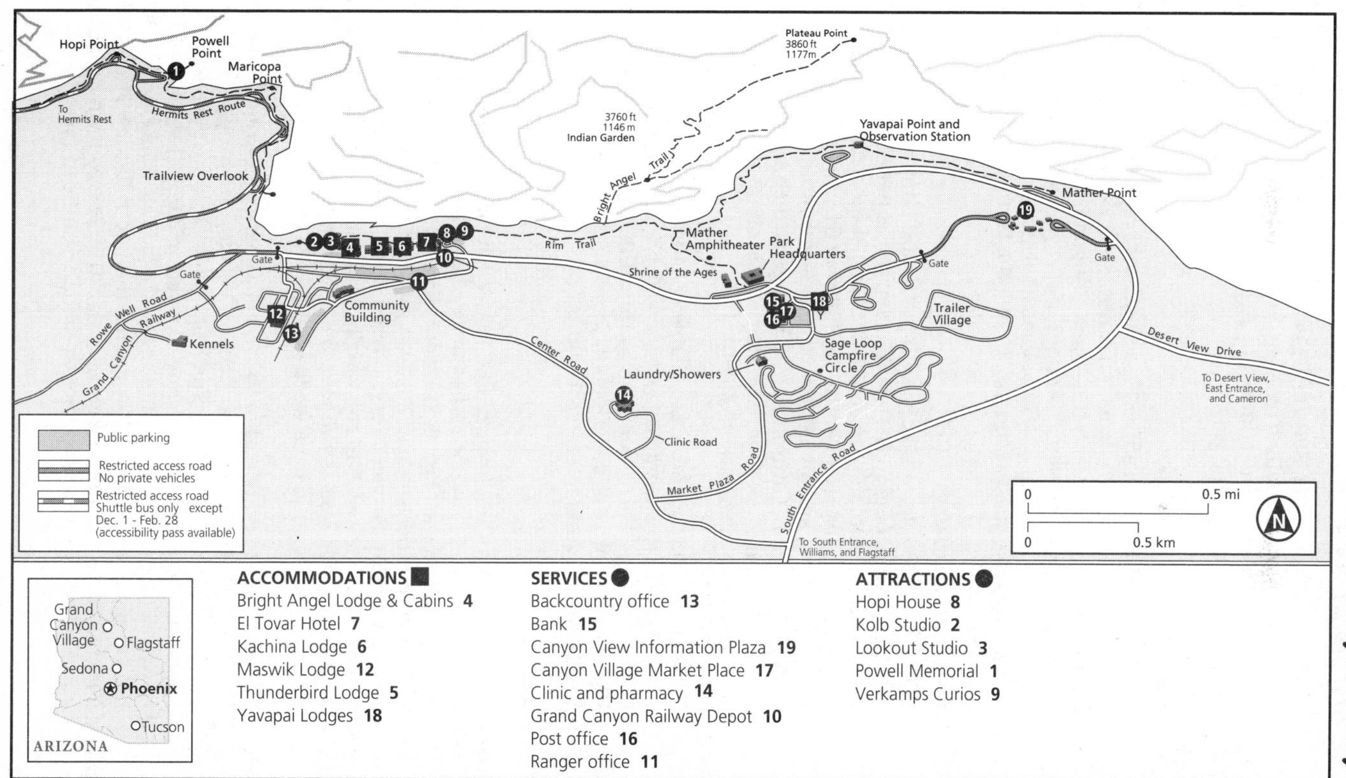

By shuttle bus

Open Road Tours (☎ 800-766-7117 or 602-997-6474; www.openroadtours.com) makes daily trips year-round to the Grand Canyon via Flagstaff ($20 each way adults, $15 ages 12 and under); round-trips are double the price of one-way.

By train

Amtrak (☎ 800-872-7245; www.amtrak.com) runs into downtown Flagstaff and also stops near Williams (an Amtrak bus takes you the rest of the way). You can shuttle into the Grand Canyon from both towns (see the preceding "By shuttle bus" section), but if you come this far by train — and even if you don't — by all means continue on into the park via the Grand Canyon Railway (see the "Riding the Grand Canyon rails" sidebar).

Getting around

If, like most people, you approach the Grand Canyon from the south, the first place you come to is Tusayan, a national park feeder (and sleeper) town with a glut of mostly chain motels, fast-food restaurants, and tour operators. Another mile north on Highway 64 you find the park entryway/fee station, and an additional 6 miles from the entryway you see the park's visitor hub, Grand Canyon Village (which is not, however, where the visitor center is — more on that in this chapter's "And it doesn't have a canyon view, either" sidebar).

If you arrive via Cameron and Highway 64 east, you pay your fee 25 miles back and take the scenic Desert View Drive before reaching Grand Canyon Village. The other main route within the park is the Hermits Rest Route; both are described in more detail in the "Exploring the South Rim" section later in this chapter.

By shuttle

Grand Canyon Coaches (☎ 866-RIM-VIEW or 928-638-0821; www.grandcanyoncoaches.com) provides service between the Grand Canyon Airport in Tusayan and the Maswik Transportation Center in Grand Canyon Village, making four other stops in Tusayan. Buses run most frequently from June through August. Service is also offered April, May, September, and October. The fare for adults is $10 round-trip; children 16 and under accompanied by an adult ride free. If you take the coach in, you also get a bargain park entry fee of $8, good for a week — a reward for not taking your car.

Free shuttles operate within the national park year-round. The Village Route circles through Grand Canyon Village, also stopping at Yavapai Point and the visitor center. The Hermits Rest Route goes to eight canyon overlooks west of the Bright Angel Lodge, making all stops westbound but only two on the way back; and the Kaibab Trail Route provides transportation between the visitor center, the South Kaibab Trailhead, and Yaki Point. An early morning Hikers Shuttle leaves from Bright Angel and Maskwik lodges to the South Kaibab Trailhead (see the "Active views: Getting down in the canyon" section in this chapter). The Hermits Rest shuttle doesn't operate in winter (when Hermit Road is open to private cars), but the other two shuttles remain in service the entire year.

But don't worry: You don't have to remember any of these times. The park service publication called The Guide (see the "Entering the park" section later in this chapter) tells you everything you need to know about routes and schedules (which change month by month). The information is also available on the Grand Canyon National Park Service Web site: `www.nps.gov/grca`.

See the "Getting there" section in the "The North Rim of the Grand Canyon (and More)" section later in this chapter, for details on the Transcanyon Shuttle.

By taxi

Strange but true: You can cab it to the canyon. The Fred Harvey Transportation Company (☎ 928-638-2631, ext. 6563) runs round-the-clock taxi service from Tusayan to Grand Canyon Village and nearby — $5 per person, with a $10 minimum.

Grand Canyon car talk

In order to ensure a safe drive around the canyon:

- **Make sure your car is in good shape.** The **Grand Canyon Garage,** east of the Grand Canyon National Park Lodges' General Offices, in Grand Canyon Village (**☎ 928-638-2631,** ext. 6502), is open for repairs from 8 a.m. to noon and 1 to 5 p.m. and has 24-hour emergency service, but it's the only game in town; you never know how long it'll take for your part to come in.
- **Always carry an extra set of car keys** with you (they're not much help inside your hotel room). The canyon doesn't have a resident locksmith.
- **Fill 'er up before you enter.** Gas stations aren't exactly clustered on every canyon corner. Only one station, **Desert View Chevron,** is inside the national park near the eastern park entry and it's not always open in winter. A service station is available in Tusayan, and you find others just outside the south entrance to the park near Apache Stables and in Cameron.
- **Carry water,** especially in summer when your car — and you — are more prone to overheat.
- **Don't even think about trying to park at the popular spots** like the El Tovar Lodge. Alternatives include the lot near the supermarket/deli at Market Plaza near Yavapai Lodge (cars tend to move in and out of here frequently) and the lot near the Backcountry Information Center. You can pick up shuttle buses from all the parking lots.

Entering the park

The cost is $20 per vehicle to enter the park, $10 per person for bikers and walkers. If you plan to visit other national parks anyway and come in high season, I suggest you invest $50 (in advance) in a National Parks Pass. Not only does the pass get you and your family into all the National Parks for an entire year, but buying one lets you thumb your nose at the other cars as you breeze through the express lane for seasonal pass holders (sometimes the wait on the other lines can be as long as 30 minutes). To order a pass, call ☎ 888-GO-PARKS between 6 a.m. and 8 p.m., Pacific standard time, every day or go online to www.nationalparks.org. You must pay an additional $3.95 for regular mail service (8–13 business days), $11.95 if you need the pass to arrive within 5 to 7 business days.

As soon as you pay your park fee, the gate attendant hands you a copy of The Guide, which has maps of the park, transportation schedules, lists of daily programs, warnings about all the dire things that can happen to you if you go hiking unprepared . . . your basic Grand Canyon bible. If your guide isn't coffee-stained and half-shredded by the end of the day, you aren't consulting it enough.

Spending the night

Beauty doesn't always come easy (as any cosmetician can tell you): The closer you want to be to the canyon, the harder it is to get a room. But if you want to gaze out at the canyon as soon as possible after you wake up, the view is definitely worth the effort. If staying in the park is not important to you, plenty of options, from bare bones to luxury, are available; see the "Outside the park" section.

And it doesn't have a canyon view, either

The National Park Service made a bit of a blooper when it designed the **Canyon View Information Plaza** (☎ **928-638-7888**) near the Grand Canyon's west (main) entrance at the beginning of the new millenium. Located about 150 feet from Mather Point, this orientation center was intended to be the terminus for a public transportation system that has been put on hold indefinitely. No parking lot adjoins it. The closest place to put your car — although no sign tells you so — is at the Mather Point overlook. If you don't find parking at Mather Point (and doing so is tough in high season), you need to drive farther into the park and take one of the free shuttles back to C-VIP. You can also get oriented at the Yavapai Observation Station.

If you drive in from the east, you pass the **Desert View Contact Station,** which is staffed by volunteers and doesn't always keep regular hours in winter. But between the trading post, cafeteria, service station, and bookstore in the Desert View Complex, you can find out whatever it is you need to know.

Inside the park

If you visit anytime from April through October and want to have a bed inside the national park, don't wait until the last minute to book. The best rooms at the El Tovar and Bright Angel Lodge sell out as much as a year in advance. You have a decent chance of getting something in Tusayan, the tourist village just south of the park, on short notice, but don't push your luck.

However, if you don't mind living on the edge — or maybe I should say really want to — snagging last-minute accommodations isn't impossible. Emergency cancellations and no-shows (from 15–30 a day in summer) always occur. Either call the park's same-day lodging switchboard at ☎ 928-638-2631 in the morning, or go to the front desk of the hotel you're interested in around 2 or 3 in the afternoon. By then, hotels know who has decided to check out a day early. Or, if you tried well in advance and couldn't get the hotel you had your heart set on, try again a month before you want to come: Large groups are required to cancel 30 days in advance in order to get their deposits refunded, so a block of rooms may suddenly open up.

You must book all the accommodations inside Grand Canyon National Park through the official parks concessionaire, Xanterra Parks & Resorts (☎ 888-29-PARKS or 303-29-PARKS; `www.grandcanyonlodges.com`). Most of the lodges cluster on the western portion of Grand Canyon Village. For locations, see the Grand Canyon Village map, in this chapter. AE, MC, DISC, and V are accepted for rooms.

Other options inside the national park perimeters include Thunderbird and Kachina lodges ($$) (on the rim), which just underwent a major renovation. Shell out the extra $10 for a second-floor "canyon view"; you won't necessarily see the rim, but you won't look out on a parking lot. At the east end of Grand Canyon Village, the two Yavapai Lodges ($$) are a mile from the historic canyon district, but plenty of parking, a tour desk, a cafeteria, and a gift shop compensate. Rooms at Yavapai East are larger and more pleasant than those at Yavapai West. For locations of all, see map p. 365.

With the exception of Maswik and Yavapai lodges, which have different winter room tariffs, rates listed apply year-round. Check the Xanterra Web site for seasonal specials and packages — most of them occurring in winter, naturally.

Bright Angel Lodge & Cabins

$–$$ On the rim

My top pick inside the park. Designed in 1935 by Mary Colter, who was responsible for several of the park's most striking buildings, Bright Angel is a beauty (even if you don't stay here, drop in to look at the geologic fireplace and the wooden thunderbird over it). The rates are also a bargain. You get a room in the main lodge with a private or shared bath (some of these rooms have only a sink, while others have both sink and toilet but no shower) or an individual cabin; four have rim views (as you can imagine, these accommodations get snapped up very fast). Furnishings are rustic but not shabby, and they suit the piney setting. This hotel isn't exactly serene during the day — it has a wildly busy tour desk, a museum, a coffeeshop, a steakhouse, and a soda fountain — but you're not going to be hanging around your room much, are you?

See map p. 365. Rack rates: $55–$67 double, some with shared bath; $84–$105 cabins.

El Tovar Hotel

$$ On the rim

The public areas of this 1905 native stone-and-pine building, a cross between a hunting lodge and a Norwegian villa, are wonderful, and the fine-dining room has the best food on the South Rim (see the following "Dining locally" section). I've always been underwhelmed by the guest rooms, though: The standard rooms are small, and the Victorian furnishings, faithful to a historic era when people liked to keep nature safely at bay, seem fussy now. Although the lodge sits near the rim, few rooms have canyon views and you face crowds every time you venture beyond the corridor. Still, this hotel is the great historic South Rim lodge, so staying here may be worth it just to say you did.

See map p. 365. Rack rates: $123–$139 standard double, $179 deluxe double, $204–$289 suites.

Maswik Lodge

$–$$ West end of the village

You're not going to get rim views here — Maswik is in the woods, about 10 minutes from the edge. However, you do get a good choice of rooms and price ranges. Many of the units in Maswik North, built in the 1960s but with fresh carpets and updated furniture, have balconies looking out on the ponderosa pine forest. Those rooms in the slightly older Maswik South are less expensive because they're smaller and, in general, viewless. Least expensive of all are the rustic 1940s cabins — the furnishings are basic and the locations are closest to the road and therefore noisier. Conveniences include a transportation center, a decent cafeteria, and a sports bar/lounge.

See map p. 365. Rack rates: $66 cabins, $77 Maswik South double, $119 Maswik North double; $68 for Maswik South and North doubles in winter.

Outside the park

Two other places worth considering are the Anasazi Inn Grey Mountain ($), 40 miles north of Flagstaff on Highway 89 (☎ 800-678-2214 or 928-679-2214; www.anasaziinn.com), neither close to the activities of Flagstaff nor in as scenic a setting as Cameron but offering decent inexpensive rooms and convenient access to the Grand Canyon's eastern approach; and the family-friendly Holiday Inn Express Hotel and Suites ($$),

Tusayan, with large, well-equipped (microwave, coffeemaker, refrigerator, VCR) suites designed around such fun themes as Route 66 or Wild Bill Hickock.

Best Western Grand Canyon Squire Inn

$$$ Tusayan

Okay, so maybe this hotel doesn't have the cachet of the older park lodges, but, hey, it has a bowling alley — not to mention a video arcade, billiards, coffee shop, restaurant, lounge, beauty salon (with massage room and tanning bed), pool, hot tub, sauna, tennis courts, exercise room, gift shop, guest laundry . . . even a small cowboy museum. The spacious, contemporary Southwest-style rooms come equipped with coffeemakers, too. If you like creature comforts nice and close to nature, this inn is the place.

Highway 64. ☎ **800-622-6966** *or 928-638-2681. Fax: 928-638-2782.* www.grandcanyonsquire.com. *Rack rates: $140–$159 double high season; $90–$120 double winter. Children 12 and under free. AE, DISC, MC, V.*

The Cameron Trading Post Motel

$$ Cameron

This motel complex isn't all that close to the Grand Canyon — or to anywhere else in the world, for that matter — but its isolated Little Colorado Canyon location is part of its considerable appeal. Other parts include a Native American fine-arts gallery; the largest modern trading post in northern Arizona, with room after room brimming with crafts and Western goods; a historic restaurant serving primo Navajo tacos; and rooms arranged among lovely terraced gardens (the staff handcrafted most of the

Miles to go before you sleep

When people complain that it's a hike to their rooms, they're usually talking about an extra-long walk from the parking lot. But to get to **Phantom Ranch**, you either have to trek 9 miles to the bottom of the Grand Canyon, raft down a river, or get a mule to carry you. Lodgings, in wood-and-uncut-river-stone cabins designed by Mary Colter (these cabins are mostly reserved for mule riders), or in newer gender-separated hiker dorms, are booked as much as a year in advance.

One-night mule trips to Phantom Ranch (and back . . .), including three meals, run $361 per person, $642 for two people. Hiker cabins cost $75 for two people, $12 for an additional person; dorm bunks run $27 per person. Meals need to be reserved, too: $15 breakfast, $9 box lunch, $18 to $27 dinner (the price depends on the entree). Like all the other national park bookings, these reservations must be made through Xanterra (☎ **888-29-PARKS** or 303-29-PARKS; www.grandcanyonlodges.com). Incidentally, Colter named the ranch for a phantom that, according to Havasupai legend, emerged from the underworld at this spot and definitely liked what he saw.

furnishings). The only drawbacks: You can't have a beer (or any other booze) because you're on the Navajo reservation, and you run the risk of never making it to the Grand Canyon because you need "just five more minutes" in that trading post.

Highway 89 (¼ mile north past the junction with Highway 64). ☎ **800-338-7385,** *ext. 414 or 928-679-2213. Fax: 928-679-2350.* www.camerontradingpost.com. *Rack rates: Feb 1–March 1 $49–69 double, March 2–May 31 $69–79 double, Jun 1–Oct 15 $89–119 double, Oct 16–Jan 31 $69–$89 double; $129–159 suites. AE, CB, DC, DISC, MC, V.*

Grand Canyon Quality Inn and Suites

$$ Tusayan

A skylit atrium with a dining room, an 18-foot spa, and a lounge lends an open, relaxed feel to these canyon-area digs. The earth-tone guest rooms are restful, too. Daily breakfast, lunch, and dinner buffets fortify you for (or replenish you after) a hard day of sightseeing, as do the outdoor pool and hot tub.

Highway 64. ☎ **800-221-2222** *or 928-638-2673. Fax: 928-638-9537.* www.grandcanyonqualityinn.com. *Rack rates: Jan–March and Oct 20–Dec 31 $79 double, April 1–Oct 19 $129 double; $124/$179 suites. AE, DC, DISC, MC, V.*

Grand Hotel

$$$ Tusayan

Old West trappings plus modern plumbing — what could be bad? Tusayan's newest hotel was designed to resemble the national park lodges, with a high-ceiling lobby, lots of Native American rugs, wrought-iron lamps, antler chandelier — you get the picture. Guest rooms have beamed ceilings and, in some cases, small balconies (although you don't see much from them but the parking lot). The hotel serves good Southwestern food and offers live cowboy singing and Native American dancing in a dining room/lounge done up like a traditional Navajo hogan. Other pluses: an indoor pool and spa.

Highway 64. ☎ **888-63-GRAND** *or 928-638-3333. Fax: 928-638-3131.* www.gcanyon.com. *Rack rates: May–Oct $149 double, Nov–April $79–$129 double. Ages 18 and under free in parent's room. AE, DISC, MC, V.*

Dining locally

Although the Grand Canyon isn't a complete void, food-wise, the park doesn't exactly have a glut of good restaurants. Still, you can expect good, hearty fare at reasonable prices in both the Grand Canyon Village and Tusayan.

Among the casual restaurants inside the park, my favorite is the Delicatessen at Marketplace ($) in Market Plaza, which serves fresh pizzas, calzones, salads, and healthful sandwiches. The Canyon Café ($), the cafeteria at Yavapai Lodge, also in Market Plaza, has something for everyone, including inexpensive, tasty Tex-Mex selections. The food at the Bright Angel Coffeehouse ($–$$) is nothing to write home about, but the view, if you're lucky enough to snag a window table, is. All are open for breakfast, lunch, and dinner (an early one, in the case of the deli). All take major credit cards, but no reservations.

In Tusayan, chains such as McDonald's, Wendy's, Taco Bell, and Pizza Hut help maintain family harmony, but the best full-service — notice I didn't say slow-food — restaurants are the Coronado Dining Room ($$$), in the Best Western Canyon Squire Inn, and the Canyon Star ($$), at the Grand Hotel (see the "Spending the night" section earlier in this chapter for both). The former has an eclectic, fairly upscale menu, ranging from enchiladas and vegetarian dishes to prime rib and game entrees, while the latter offers more casual, Southwestern-inspired fare. Both dining rooms accept major credit cards.

Arizona Room

$$–$$$ Grand Canyon Village STEAKHOUSE/AMERICAN

The crowds come as much for the Grand Canyon views as for the meat, although the open-kitchen preparations of prime rib, chicken, steaks, and the like are good (I can't always say the same for the service). Come a few minutes before the 5 p.m. opening to avoid a long wait and to be settled in for the sunset; the lines start forming around 5:30, and tables aren't really worth the wait after dark.

In the Bright Angel Lodge. ☎ **928-638-2631.** *Reservations not accepted (they have a waitlist in peak hours). Main courses: $13–$23. AE, DC, DISC, MC, V. Open: Dinner nightly; closed Jan and mid-Feb.*

Cameron Trading Post Dining Room

$–$$ Cameron AMERICAN/NAVAJO

You won't know where to look in this historic trading post dining room: at the ornate pressed-tin ceiling, the huge antique sideboard, the colorful Navajo rugs on the wall, the splendid sandstone-and-sky views from the window? The (eventual) arrival of your food should solve the problem. The American dishes are fine, but why not go local with the Navajo tacos (similar to Mexican tacos, only the toppings are on fry bread rather than tortillas). They're among the best anywhere, and they're huge, so unless you're training for a sumo wrestling match, I suggest you share.

Highway 89 (just north of the junction with Highway 64). ☎ **928-679-2231.** *Reservations not accepted. Main courses: $6–$15. AE, CB, DISC, DC, MC, V. Open: Daily breakfast, lunch, and dinner.*

El Tovar Restaurant

$$$ Grand Canyon Village CONTINENTAL/SOUTHWESTERN

You'd want to eat here even if it didn't involve the possibility of staring out at the Grand Canyon from huge picture windows: The rustic-elegant room with a soaring ceiling is drop-dead impressive and the food is (generally) a knockout, too. Rather than just catering to the lowest culinary common denominator, the menu mixes familiar Continental dishes, such as flame-broiled beef tournedos, with more adventurous Southwestern fare like rainbow trout with apple-pumpkin seed salsa. Some people book a table with their room reservation; if you want to dine at a time you like, phone as soon as you know you'll be at the Grand Canyon.

In the El Tovar Hotel. ☎ **928-638-2631,** *ext. 6432. Reservations required at dinner, not accepted for breakfast or lunch. Main courses: $17–$25. AE, DC, DISC, MC, V. Open: Daily breakfast, lunch, dinner.*

Exploring the South Rim

You can hover over the canyon in a helicopter, run a rim-to-rim marathon — or go for something in between the two; you're the best judge of the touring style that suits you. In general, the approaches to the canyon in the "Overviews: Driving around the canyon" section are designed for day-trippers; many of the activities in the "Active views: Getting down in the canyon" section require a much greater time commitment.

No matter what you do, don't be surprised if you feel headachy and sluggish your first day in the Grand Canyon, especially if you don't spend any time beforehand in Flagstaff or Williams. Adjusting to the altitude (7,000 feet) takes a while.

Ode to erosion: Some Grand Canyon stats

The erosive action of the Colorado River formed the Grand Canyon, which continues to be shaped by the river, along with rain runoff, and snow melt. One of the world's seven natural wonders, the canyon racks up some pretty impressive numbers:

- Grand Canyon National Park covers more than a million acres (1,218,375.54, to be exact).
- The canyon is 277 miles long, as the Colorado River flows.
- The distance between the South Rim and the North Rim at Grand Canyon Village is 10 miles, as the crow (or other bird of your choice) flies.
- At its lowest point from the rim, the canyon dips 6,000 vertical feet, but it's by no means the deepest canyon in the world — deeper ones include the Copper Canyon in Mexico and Hell's Canyon in Idaho.
- The oldest rocks exposed at the bottom of the canyon are close to 2 billion years old — which is only about half as old as the oldest rocks in the world. The canyon itself is a mere babe, just 5 or 6 million years old.

A (forgettable) Kodak moment

In 1937, Harold Anthony of the American Museum of Natural History decided to boldly go where he thought no man had ever gone before: to Shiva Temple, which he believed was completely isolated from the rest of the canyon. Rather than the independently evolved animal species he and his expedition expected to find there, however, they discovered only an empty Kodak film box.

One final point before you take the plunge (as it were): The park rangers always have activities organized, even in winter — everything from geology talks to guided nature walks and grab-bag question-and-answer sessions. Check The Guide's schedule of programs as soon as you get a copy so you don't find yourself leafing through it in late afternoon and muttering, "Darn, that sounded good."

Overviews: Driving around the canyon

Rim drives are a great way to take in some of the canyon's best views. I highlight the two most popular drives — along the Desert View and Hermits Rest routes.

Of the two paved drives that radiate to the rim from Grand Canyon Village, the Hermits Rest Route is the shorter and, off-season, the more popular. During high season, March 1 to December 1, this route is closed to private cars, and you must board a free shuttle to tour it. At this time, the Desert View Drive, which is open to cars, becomes the more popular route — which means you may have to wait to park your car at the various lookout points.

- Driving the Hermits Rest Route: (Remember, this route can be driven only in December, January, and February, but the lookout points remain the same year-round, so these descriptions may help you decide where to get off the shuttle bus). This 8-mile drive was first laid out in 1912, when horse-drawn buggies still outnumbered automobiles. The first stop is Trailview Overlook and Trailview Overlook II, which look down on the Bright Angel and Plateau Point hiking trails, and, in a lush cottonwood grove, Indian Gardens campground. The soaring San Francisco Peaks lie to the south, and if you gaze in you-know-which direction, you can also glimpse the North Rim. Look out from Maricopa Point to spot the remains of the 1893 Orphan Mine, which yielded a high grade of copper and, later, uranium — neither of which turned out to be very easy to transport, although the mine stayed open until 1966. The Powell Memorial at Powell Point pays tribute to one-armed Civil War veteran John Wesley Powell, who, in 1869, set out to document the then-uncharted canyons and creeks of the Colorado River (which, ironically, you can't see all that well from here). You can, however, get a good look at the river from Hopi Point, where you can also stare out at exotically named formations, such as the Tower of Ra and Osiris, Isis, and Shiva temples.

During a lull in the whirring of the videocams at Mohave Point, you may be able to hear the rushing waters of the Hermit Rapids. You can also see the Granite and Salt Creek rapids from here, along with the 5,401-foot-high Cheops Pyramid. Although the other overlooks have you concentrating on the panoramic vistas, The Abyss lives up to its name by demonstrating the utter sheerness of the cliffs — specifically, the Great Mohave Wall, which drops 3,000 feet (definitely a handrail gripper). At Pima Point, you can see the remains of Hermit Camp, a tourist complex built by the Santa Fe Railway in 1911. The camp got its supplies via aerial tramway — which was also once used to ship a Ford to the bottom of the canyon.

The drive ends at Hermits Rest, named for Louis Boucher, a French-Canadian prospector who wasn't nearly as reclusive as his nickname suggests. Views of Hermit Rapids and the Supai and Redwall cliffs compete for your attention with a striking log-and-stone structure, designed by Mary Colter, which sells souvenirs and snacks — and has the drive's only restrooms.

A leisurely round-trip drive of the Hermits Rest Route, with a rest stop at Hermits Rest itself, takes no more than 1 hour — unless you plan to set up a tripod at each stop.

The Hermits Rest Route doesn't exit the park; you have to retrace your journey. Because access to the overlooks is easy from both sides of the road, save half the stops for your return trip.

- Driving the Desert View route: Most of this 23-mile drive is open to cars year-round except its first stop (if you're departing from Grand Canyon Village), Yaki Point, which is closed to traffic from March through December. If you want to see the Point during this time, you need to take a shuttle, which many hikers do in order to pick up the South Kaibab Trail, one of the three routes to the Inner Gorge. Wotan's Throne, an imposing flat-topped butte, is the lookout's most distinctive landmark. Large stands of oak, juniper, and ponderosa and piñon pine flourish at Grandview Point, which sits at a higher elevation than most of the Desert View route. From there you can see Horseshoe Mesa, where, in the 1890s, the Last Chance Copper Mine and the Grand View Hotel both thrived. Painter Thomas Moran was especially fond of the light from Moran Point, which was named after him because his illustrations of the journals of John Wesley Powell helped convince Congress to establish the Grand Canyon as a national park. The free Tusayan Museum, built in 1932, explains the significance of the remains of the small pueblo nearby — one of 2,000 prehistoric Native American sites in the park.

Take the time to walk around here for a bit. The museum provides a nice, educational break from the old drive-stop-stare routine.

From the canyon's widest vista, Lipan Point, you get a fix on both geologic and human history. Views include colored strata of sedimentary rock and the Unkar Delta, farmed by the ancestral Puebloan peoples (often called Anasazi) around 800 years ago.

Spanish conquistadors tried to get down to the Colorado River from Navajo Point in 1540 but couldn't manage the trip (then again, they couldn't find the seven gold cities that originally brought them to the area, either). The last, and arguably most dramatic vista of both drives, is Desert View. Pay a quarter to climb the 70-foot-high Watchtower and you see the Painted Desert, San Francisco Peaks, Marble Canyon, and the Colorado River spread out before you. But don't worry if you don't want to climb the tower's steps: You're at the highest point of the South Rim, 7,522 feet, so the views from the ground are nothing to sneeze at, either. The first stop when you enter from the east, the Desert View complex includes an information center, cafeteria, and (not open in winter) a gas station. Top-quality Native American paintings and crafts are sold in the rough-hewn Desert View building, shaped like a sacred ceremonial chamber. Mary Colter (see the "Grand Canyon architecture: A woman's touch" sidebar in this chapter) designed both Desert View and the Watchtower.

Most people drive the Desert View route one way, either on the way into or out of the park. Assuming that you make 30-minute stops at both the Tusayan Museum and at Desert View, the drive takes at least 1¾ hours one-way; 2½ hours if you retrace the path (you can't drive quickly on these roads, both because of speed limits and a need to watch out for drivers mesmerized by the canyon views).

Guided views: Bus and jeep tours

If you'd rather let someone else take the wheel, consider a Fred Harvey Transportation Co. bus tour (☎ 928-638-2631), departing mornings and afternoons (schedules depend on the season) from the Bright Angel, Maswik, and Yavapai lodges — which is also where the transportation desks for booking them are located. Rates are $16 per person for a

Rock stars

The tilted stratum of bright red, black, and white rocks at Lipan Point is part of a sedimentary rock sequence called the **Grand Canyon Supergroup.** The stratum goes back about a billion years (even longer than the Rolling Stones). And talk about your rebels: The supergroup's relation to the straighter sandstone layer that hangs over it is called the Great Unconformity.

And the sundown winner is . . .

Because it juts out into the canyon, **Hopi Point** gets my vote as the best spot on the Hermits Rest Route to watch the sun set. On the Desert View Route, it's **Lipan Point,** with views that extend all the way west. Check *The Guide* for the right time to arrive.

Hermits Rest tour (two hours); $28 for a Desert View tour (four hours); and $35 for a combination of the two. Children under age 16 are free with adults.

Less herdlike, more off-road, and (weather permitting) more open-air — as well as more expensive — the Grand Canyon Jeep Tours & Safaris (☎ 800-320-JEEP or 928-638-JEEP; www.grandcanyonjeeptours.com) possibilities include a two-hour Canyon Pines Tour ($48 adult, $35 ages 12 and under) through the Kaibab National Forest to the rim via an 1880s stage coach trail; the Grand Sunset Tour (three hours; $59 adults, $45 child), another forest-rim combo; and the 1½-hour Indian Cave Paintings Tour ($40 adult, $30 child), which never leaves the trees, but gives you a close-up view of ancient art. You can mix and match these tours as well.

Bird's-eye views: Flying over the canyon

Your comfort level with small planes and helicopters — not to mention with spending lots of cash in a flash — determines whether an air tour is for you. Plane crashes have occurred in the years since flights over the canyon started, but the overall safety records are good. Helicopters are twice as expensive as small planes, but the relative smoothness and stability of the flights may make it worth the extra cost for you. All flights depart from the Grand Canyon Airport in Tusayan.

Virtual views: The canyon without parking problems

I've heard rumors that people watch the film Grand Canyon — The Hidden Secrets at Tusayan's Grand Canyon IMAX Theater (☎ 928-638-2203; www.grandcanyonimax.com) and never bother going to the national park, something I'm still scratching my head over. Nonetheless, the six-story-high surround-sound film is a good adjunct to the genuine item if you want simulated adventure (the ride on the rapids feels stomach-churningly real). The 34-minute film is screened every hour on the half hour 365 days a year (Mar–Oct 8:30 a.m.–8:30 p.m., Nov–Feb 10:30 a.m.–6:30 p.m.); tickets cost $10 adults, $7 ages 6 to 12, 5 and under free.

Active views: Getting down in the canyon

Not content with admiring the canyon at a distance? Travelers who prefer the up-close-and-personal approach have a few options, from hiking to riding to rafting.

- Hiking: You don't necessarily have to spend the night in the canyon in order to appreciate it (although some people may disagree with me). If you're in good shape, though, I urge you to at least attempt a short trek below the rim, both to escape the crowds and to get up close and personal with some of the fauna and flora (don't worry, unless you're near the bottom, it won't be cactus).

  If you want to sleep down deep, contact the Backcountry Reservations Office, Grand Canyon National Park, P.O. Box 129, Grand Canyon, AZ 86023 (☎ 928-638-7875 [call between 1–5 p.m., Mountain standard time, Mon–Fri], or 928-638-7888 [automated information line, with a long, complicated phone menu]; Fax: 928-638-2125; www.nps.gov/grca/backcountry), to request an overnight permit ($10 per permit, plus $5 per person per night), required unless you're booked at Phantom Ranch. Call to have back-country information mailed to you or check the national park's Web site. Don't wait until the last minute — eager backpackers typically snap up many of the limited amount of permits four months in advance. If you arrive without a permit, but want to take a shot at getting one, head over to the Backcountry Information Center (open: Mon–Fri 8 a.m.–noon and 1–5 p.m.), at the Maswik Transportation Center, and sign on to the daily waiting list.

Whirlybird or puddle-jumper? Photo op pros and cons

Helicopters fly 500 feet lower than small planes and have large bubble windows all around, which means excellent visibility for photographers. Helicopter hovering — as opposed to plane banking and dipping — provides better shots, too. But not everyone in a helicopter is guaranteed a window seat, something passengers on small planes (which have windows designed to minimize glare) enjoy. Ultimately, if you're not shy about leaning over someone should you be seated in the middle, the helicopter will probably allow you to take your best shot.

Air Grand Canyon (☎ **800-247-4726** or 928-638-2686; www.airgrandcanyon.com), **Grand Canyon Airlines** (☎ **800-528-2413** or 928-638-2407; www.grandcanyonairlines.com) both offer comparably priced small plane tours, starting at about $80 adults ($50 children 12 and under) for a 45-minute flight.

Tours with **Grand Canyon Helicopters** (☎ **800-541-4537** or 928-638-2764; www.grandcanyonhelicoptersaz.com), **AirStar Helicopters** (☎ **800-962-3869** or 928-638-2622; www.airstar.com), and **Papillon Grand Canyon Helicopters** (☎ **800-528-2418** or 928-638-2419; www.papillon.com) run from around $100 for a 25- to 30-minute flight to $200 for a 50-minute flight, with varying reduced rates for children. AirStar generally has the best prices.

Grand Canyon architecture: A woman's touch

Sure, you come here to bond with nature, but you can gaze into the middle distance only for so long. The **Grand Canyon Village Historical District,** with its wonderful architecture from the classic High Tourist era — otherwise known as the first three decades of the 1900s — is definitely worth a wander-through. Pick up a self-guided tour brochure at the visitor center to find out about the nine artfully rustic structures: Hotels, curio shops, photography studios, and the 1909 railway depot, which is back in use. Verkamps Curios, opened in 1898 as the Grand Canyon's first trinket shop, still looks pretty much as it did in 1905, and the Kolb studio, built between 1904 and 1926, was the domain of two brothers who captured early shots of the mule-passengers.

Hopi House, Bright Angel Lodge, and Lookout Studio are prime examples of the work of architect Mary Colter, who was also responsible for Hermits Rest, Desert View, and Watchtower. Her designs, which mesh beautifully with the landscape, were ahead of their time — as was the very fact that Colter was a designing woman: Females were not issued architect's licenses in those days, so Colter didn't have one.

- Easy hikes: A level 10-mile-long trail runs along the edge of the canyon from the Yavapai Observation Station (northeast of Grand Canyon Village) west to Hermits Rest. If you want to plan your walk, check The Guide for the distances between the various lookout points. The short and mostly flat rim trek around the historic buildings of Grand Canyon Village is also easy and scenic; see the "Grand Canyon architecture: A woman's touch" sidebar in this chapter for more details. The Canyon View Information Plaza can clue you in about other short hikes, including options along the Greenway, a network of walking, cycling, and eventually, horseback riding trails being developed in and around the national park.
- Hard hikes: Originally a bighorn sheep path and later used by the Havasupai Indians, Bright Angel Trail is the most popular route into the canyon. Almost 8 miles long, the trail descends 4,460 feet from the trailhead near Grand Canyon Village to the river at Phantom Ranch. From May through September, drinking water is usually available at the 1.5- and 3-mile resthouses — good goals for a 3- and 6-mile hike, respectively. The 4.6-mile point (Indian Garden) always has water. The 9-mile-long Hermit Trail begins beyond Hermits Rest and drops more than 5,000 feet to Hermit Creek. This trail is steep, non-maintained, and waterless; don't try it unless you're a serious hiker (it's 5 miles round-trip to Santa Maria Spring, 6 miles round-trip to Dripping Springs). Also strenuous (and waterless) but rewarding for its terrific views

is the South Kaibab Trail, which you can pick up at Yaki Point; it's a 7-mile trek from the trailhead to the Colorado River (where the trail crosses a suspension bridge and runs on to Phantom Ranch). The 3-mile round-trip to Cedar Ridge, which has portable toilets but no water, is a good goal for a decent day's hike.

Remember, the only way to get to Yaki Point most of the year is by shuttle. If you miss the shuttle, however, you can call the Fred Harvey taxi service (see the "Getting around" section earlier under the "The South Rim of the Grand Canyon" section) to come and retrieve you. You find a pay phone at the South Kaibab trailhead (even if you have a cellphone, a signal is difficult to get).

- Mule rides: For many, visiting the Grand Canyon without riding a mule would be like visiting Yellowstone without seeing Old Faithful (of course, for others, riding a mule into the canyon would be like sitting and getting soaked in Old Faithful for 6 hours). If you think you're in the former category, plan ahead. For some summer dates, rides get booked up as much as a year in advance.

  Your choices include a seven-hour, round-trip ride to Plateau Point, with lunch at Indian Gardens ($133 per person). For the 5½-mile ride down to Phantom Ranch, with a 4½-mile return the next day, see the "Miles to go before you sleep" sidebar in this chapter. For advance

Some hiking tips

You may be surprised how many generally sensible people leave their common sense behind when they descend into the canyon. To avoid discomfort — and worse — here are a few basics to keep in mind.

- **Remember, what goes down must come up:** And that means you. For every hour you hike downhill, allow two hours (and lots of huffing and puffing, if you're out of shape) for the return.
- **Wear comfortable shoes with good traction:** Hiking boots are best, but rough-soled sneakers or walking shoes are okay, too.
- **Always carry enough food and drink:** In summer, 2 quarts of electrolyte replacement fluid is minimum, and 1 gallon is recommended for every eight hours of hiking. Munch on nutritious, high-carb, salty snacks every 20 to 30 minutes.
- **Layer your clothing:** The temperature climbs up the farther down you go; be prepared for rain and snow in winter.
- **Check your copy of *The Guide* before you attempt a hike:** The 4-H list of hiking hazards (heat stroke, heat exhaustion, hyponatremia [water intoxication], and hypothermia) may send you running to the IMAX theater for a virtual descent, instead.

reservations, contact Grand Canyon National Lodges (☎ 888-29-PARKS or 303-39-PARKS; www.grandcanyonlodges.com). If you didn't book but decide at the last minute to give mule riding a shot — occasionally folks don't show up — call ☎ 928-638-2631 or stop by the Bright Angel Transportation desk to put your name on a waiting list for the next day's ride.

Be aware that you aren't allowed to ride a mule if you:

- Weigh more than 200 pounds
- Are less than 4'7" tall
- Are pregnant
- Don't speak English
- Are rude to the tour operators (just checking to see if you're paying attention, although who knows?)

And, don't ride if you

- Are afraid of heights
- Are afraid of large animals (the mule is the love child of a female horse and a male donkey, and it's often bigger than a horse; don't confuse it with the smaller burro)
- Have heart or respiratory problems
- Don't think you can sit in a saddle for at least six hours, or go 2½ hours without a bathroom break

- Horseback rides: Less stressful and less expensive than the mule tours, rides run by Apache Stables, Highway 64 (just before the south entrance to the park; ☎ 928-638-2891; www.apachestables.com), don't dip into the canyon; most, in fact, don't even enter the national park. You trot around Kaibab National Forest during the one-hour ($30.50), two-hour ($55.50), and campfire ($40.50 by trail, $12.50 in a wagon) rides. Age and weight restrictions apply, except for the campfire wagon ride. The stables are usually open from March to early December, but sometimes close earlier or open later, depending on the weather. Both mules and horses are used, so when you get home you can say you rode a mule at the canyon, which is essentially true, if you don't get hung up on phrases like "down into" as opposed to "around."
- River rafting: The options for getting wet 'n' wild on the Colorado River are almost as dizzying as the rapids you're bound to encounter. You can do everything from paddling your own canoe to zipping along on a motorized raft on trips ranging from three days to almost three weeks. You may be happy to discover that not every Joe Schmo with an air pump can run river trips into the Grand Canyon;

The canyon for kids

If your kids can't relate to nature that's not on a screen, don't worry — they get into it soon enough (just give that mouse hand a little time to stop twitching). Some quick ways to get the Internet set on line with the canyon include the following:

- **Have them take part in the Junior Ranger program.** This program gears its activities to everything from finding animal tracks to recycling aluminum cans. The program is available to three age groups — 4 to 7, 8 to 10, and 11 to 14. Kids who successfully complete five steps get a Junior Ranger Patch ($1.50 to offset the price of the program). Be sure to start early to give kids time to complete the program. Ask at the visitor center for details.
- **Buy them a disposable camera.** Beware: You may create a photography monster.
- **Take them to watch the mules set off in the morning.** The mules begin their journeys (8 a.m. in summer, 9 a.m. in winter) from the corral just west of Bright Angel Lodge (and yes, let them tell ca-ca jokes).
- **Bring them to one of the kid-oriented ranger talks and walks.** These activities are offered daily in summer, less frequently off-season; check *The Guide* for meeting times.
- **Put them on horseback.** The Apache Stables, just before park's south entrance, has gentle animals that are used to kiddie ways.
- **Take them to the IMAX.** Hey, if you can't beat 'em (and you really shouldn't), join 'em.

the National Park Service authorizes only outfitters with good credentials. You can get the most current listings by writing ahead for the Trip Planner (for the address, see the following "Fast Facts: The South Rim" section) or by clicking on `www.nps.gov/grca/river`.

Most of the outfitters run trips from April to October and most depart from Lees Ferry near Page, although some start or finish at Phantom Ranch. Expect to pay anywhere from around $700 (including meals and tent) for a two-day trip to approximately $4,800 for three weeks on the water. Book as far in advance as possible; the rafts fill up fast and not too many people bail after they sign on.

Don't do white water? See Chapter 18 for smooth-water trips from Glen Canyon Dam in Page to Lees Ferry. If, on the other hand, you want to do make the trip all on your own, contact the River Permits Office, Grand Canyon National Park, P.O. Box 129, Grand Canyon, AZ 86023 (☎ 800-959-9164 or 928-638-7843; Fax: 928-638-7844) or go to the "PRIVATE" or "NONCOMMERCIAL" link of `www.nps.gov/grca/river`.

Fast Facts: The South Rim

Area Code

The area code for this entire region is **928.**

ATMs

ATMs at the South Rim are located at Maswik Lodge and at the Bank One at Market Plaza (in the post office complex near Yavapai Lodge).

Emergencies

Call ☎ **911** for fire, police, and ambulance.

Hospitals/Clinics

The Grand Canyon Clinic (☎ **928-638-2551**) is open weekdays from 9 a.m. to 7 p.m., Saturday from 10 a.m. to 4 p.m., with after-hours care and 24-hour emergency service.

Information

Before you go, call Grand Canyon National Park at ☎ **928-638-7888** to order a copy of the free *Trip Planner,* which includes camping, hiking, and activity details, plus plenty of general advice. Get the same information electronically by logging on the National Park Service Web site, `www.nps.gov/grca`. The commercially sponsored `www.AmericanParkNetwork.com` is another useful pre-trip site, and you can pick up its affiliated publication, *Grand Canyon Magazine,* gratis, when you get near the park. See the "Entering the park" section in this chapter, for places to obtain information within the park.

Internet Access

Kiosks at Camper Services, Bright Angel Lodge, Kachina Lodge, Yavapai Lodge, and Maswik Lodge all let you log on the Internet with the swipe of a major credit card.

Park Fees

$20 per vehicle to enter the park, $10 per person to enter by foot or bicycle. Passes are good for seven days, and can be used at both rims. Sorry, no rain (or snow) checks.

Pharmacies

The closest pharmacy to the Grand Canyon is at the Safeway supermarket in Williams (see the "Fast Facts: Lower Northwest Arizona" section in this chapter).

Post Office

In Market Plaza, between the general store and the bank, the post office is open Monday through Friday from 9 a.m. to 4:30 p.m., Saturday from 11 a.m. to 3 p.m. Access to lobby stamp machines available from 5 a.m. to 10 p.m.

Road Conditions and Weather

Call ☎ **928-638-7888** (on the automated system, press selection 3, then selection 1 [road conditions] or selection 2 [weather]).

Safety

The safety concerns in the Grand Canyon are less linked to crime than to people ignoring the fact that they're in nature, not Disneyland. (If you want to read all about the various stupidity- and testosterone-driven deaths, pick up a copy of *Over The Edge: Death in the Grand Canyon.*) Although theft may not be a major problem, don't put your expensive camera down and walk away or amble around with your purse open. In short, don't leave your common sense at home.

The North Rim of the Grand Canyon (and More)

Let me hit you with a few statistics. The North Rim of the Grand Canyon gets only about one-tenth of the visitors of the South Rim. That doesn't mean you find yourself entirely alone — I'm talking one-tenth of 4.5 million, and it's estimated that each year, 5% more visitors descend on this side of the great northern Arizona divide than the year before (I'll let you do the math; it was never my best subject).

Why the disparity in the number of people visiting the different national park sections? One simple reason: The North Rim is harder to reach than the South Rim. This means that fewer services and hotel rooms are available after you arrive, so you have to plan ahead. But the North Rim views are as good as those at the South Rim, so if you prefer bonding with nature to bonding with (or bouncing off) your fellow Homo sapiens, the effort is worth it, no question.

You won't find a whole lot to do in the remote, starkly beautiful region that you drive through en route to the North Rim, nor in the Arizona Strip, the even more remote area to the west of the canyon. However, a few stops make good diversions.

Plan to linger a bit in this area — a minimum of two nights to make it worth the trip. If your pulse gets pumping at the idea of river rafting or if you're hooked on fishing, spend some more time at Lees Ferry, the departure point for the Colorado River adventures.

The North Rim doesn't have any ATMs inside the park. Credit cards are accepted at most of the park's facilities, but having a little of the green stuff is always good, so stop for cash at Jacob's Lake if you're short. More important, the closest pharmacy to the national park is in Kanab, Utah, so come prepared with any medications you may need.

The North Rim is open for overnight stays only from mid-May to mid- or late October (day use continues through November — or until the first heavy snow).

Getting there

Except for the shuttle from the South Rim — more on this subject in the "By shuttle" section — the North Rim doesn't have public transportation.

By car

The distance from Flagstaff to the North Rim is 210 miles: Take Highway 89 north to Bitter Springs, then Highway 89A to the junction of Highway 67 at Jacob Lake, and take Highway 67 south to the North Rim. The drive is spectacular.

Northern exposure: Getting to know the "other" rim

Some things are worth going out of your way for — among them, the Grand Canyon's North Rim. Just so you know what you're getting (or at least looking) into:

- At about 8,000 feet, the North Rim is approximately 1,000 feet higher than the South Rim.
- The North Rim receives about 27 inches of rain or snow annually, compared to 15 inches for the South Rim.
- Europeans took 236 years longer to find the North Rim than to find the South Rim: 1776 versus 1540.
- The land that the North Rim sits on was hotly contested by Utah and Arizona. A journalist named Sharlot Hall helped convince Arizonans to go to bat for the abyss.

Flying into Page (see Chapter 18) is an even better option if you can afford the airfare: A scenic 25-mile drive south on Highway 89 gets you to Bitter Springs/Highway 89A, hooking you up with the Flagstaff route sketched above.

You can also get here from Las Vegas via I-15 north to Highway 9 west, and Highway 67 south — a total of 263 miles.

By shuttle

From mid-May to October, the Transcanyon Shuttle (☎ 928-638-2820) makes one round-trip a day between the North and South rims. Vans depart the North Rim's Grand Canyon Lodge (or the campground or a trailhead if you put in a special request) at 7 a.m., arriving at the South Rim's Bright Angel Lodge at noon; the return shuttle leaves at 1:30 p.m., reaching the North Rim at 6:30 p.m. The one-way fare is $65 per person; round-trips cost $110. Reservations are required.

Getting around

You mostly have to rely on your own wheels to get around the park. The exception is the hiker shuttle to the North Kaibab trailhead, which leaves from the front of the Grand Canyon Lodge every day at 5:30 a.m. and 7:30 a.m. You need to buy tickets in advance from the lodge's front desk; the cost is $5 for the first person, $2 for each additional one.

Spending the night

You're not exactly spoiled by choices when it comes to rooming near the North Rim. Only one place is available in the park itself; two more lodging options are within a 30-mile radius; and an additional three are near

Lees Ferry — all are detailed in the following section. Rooms in this area are modest, but that goes for the prices, too. And these lodgings, especially the ones in Lees Ferry, tend to generate outpost-style camaraderie; don't be surprised if you make new friends here.

Inside the park

Grand Canyon Lodge

$–$$ On the rim

The Grand Canyon Lodge is the only game in this part of the national park, but you'd want to play even if it weren't. Of the variety of lodging configurations available here, the Western cabins are closest to the rim and the most luxurious (the four that actually look into the canyon are usually booked two years in advance). The Pioneer and Frontier cabins, although the most rustic, are right near the Transept Trail. The motel rooms are standard issue and farthest from the lodge, but all have queen-size beds (the others have doubles and singles). But you won't spend much time in your room. When you're not out exploring the canyon, you'll want to hang around the historic log-and-limestone lodge, where a high-ceiling dining room serves surprisingly sophisticated food that (almost) competes with the rim views from its huge windows. The bar, cafeteria, gift shop, and transportation desk are the other prime congregating spots.

Reservations: Xanterra Parks and Resorts, 14001 E. Iliff, Suite 600, Aurora, CO 80014. ☎ **888-29-PARKS** *or 303-29-PARKS. Fax: 303-297-3175.* www.grandcanyonnorthrim.com. *Hotel switchboard:* ☎ **928-638-2611.** *Rack rates: $92 Frontier cabins, $91 double motel rooms, $102 Pioneer cabins, $111 western cabin. AE, CB, DC, DISC, MC, V. Closed mid-Oct to mid-May.*

Outside the park

You come across a few low-key motels in Fredonia, Arizona, and Kanab, Utah (30 and 37 miles west of Jacob Lake, respectively), but they're a bit out of the way if you're not heading north. Page, near Lake Powell, offers plenty more beds (see Chapter 18), but doing a single-day round-trip to the park from there isn't very relaxing — and kicking back and smelling the pine cones is what the North Rim is all about. If you're not staying at the Grand Canyon Lodge, the following places offer good alternatives.

Cliff Dweller's Lodge

$ Lees Ferry/Marble Canyon

The rooms are fine — the newer, blander, slightly pricier ones have bathtubs, the older ones have only showers but more character — but the Vermilion Cliff and Echo Cliff surroundings make this place a knockout. Not surprisingly, most of the action happens outside; you can book a hiking tour in summer, or go next door to a river outfitter to plan a water adventure. If you don't feel like socializing with the river runners in the good bar and restaurant (see the following "Dining locally," section), you can stock up on booze and snacks in the hotel's convenience store.

Highway 89A (9 miles west of Navajo Bridge). ☎ **800-433-2543** *or 928-355-2228. Fax: 928-355-2271. Rack rates: $69–$74 double. AE, DISC, MC, V.*

Kaibab Lodge

$–$$ Near the park entrance

A huge stone fireplace, sometimes lit in spring and early fall, makes a cheery gathering spot for guests at this homey 1926 lodge. Most of the rooms, located in (rather thin-walled) pine-paneled cabins, are motel plain and offer only bare-bones facilities; a couple of newer, larger units have modern conveniences like refrigerators and microwaves. But the real draw is the setting, near the national park and the edge of the large DeMotte Park meadow. Other perks include a restaurant, lounge (beer and wine only), and gift shop.

Highway 67 (5 miles from entrance to Grand Canyon's North Rim). ☎ **800-525-0924** *(outside AZ) or 928-638-2389; off-season* ☎ *928-526-0924.* `www.canyoneers.com/KL.html`. *Rack rates: $80–$130 double. DISC, MC, V. Mostly closed mid-Oct–mid-May (some services remain open).*

Jacob Lake Inn

$–$$ Jacob Lake

This inn is where the action — if you can call it that — is en route to the North Rim. Everyone heading for the national park stops here for groceries, gas, Native American crafts, a hot chicken sandwich, or fresh baked cookies and milkshakes (hey, you need fortification for the long ride). Spend the night and either bunk in a shabby cabin with a private porch or in one of the nicer drive-up motel units. The complex sits on 5 acres of Kaibab Forest, but many of the rooms look out on a highway. If you want a good night's sleep, ask for accommodations behind the lodge.

At the junction of Highways 67 and 89A. ☎ **928-643-7232.** *Fax: 928-643-7235.* `www.jacoblake.com`. *Rack rates: May–Nov $72–$83 double in cabins, $91–$93 double in rooms; Dec–Apr $55–$59 rooms (cabins not rented in winter). AE, DISC, DC, MC, V.*

Lees Ferry Lodge

$ Lees Ferry/Marble Canyon

This place is a little fishy — it's where the Lees Ferry anglers tend to congregate — but the views of the Vermilion Cliffs from the garden patios are completely on the up and up (and up). Rooms in this 1929 native-stone-and-wood building sit close to the road — but, no, 89A is not exactly the Santa Monica freeway — and the plumbing is a bit noisy, but they have plenty of nice touches. See the Vermilion Cliffs Bar & Grill in the following "Dining locally" section.

Highway 89A (3½ miles west of Navajo Bridge). ☎ **800-451-2231** *or 928-355-2231. Fax: 928-355-2371.* `www.leesferrylodge.com`. *Rack rates: $56–$77 double. AE, MC, V.*

Marble Canyon Lodge

$–$$ Lees Ferry/Marble Canyon

Zane Grey and Gary Cooper were among the many celebs who bedded down at this appealing hotel, opened the same day that the Navajo Bridge was dedicated in 1929. The newer units across the road are less interesting than the units in the original lodge, which have brass beds and hardwood floors, but an apartment there sleeps up to eight. You can ease your Learjet down onto the landing strip, or just settle for gassing up your car. A restaurant, gift shop, and coin-op laundry are other on-site perks.

Half mile west of Navajo Bridge on Highway 89A. ☎ **800-726-1789** *or 928-355-2225. Fax: 928-355-2227. Rack rates: $64–$143 double. AE, DISC, MC, V.*

Dining locally

You pretty much eat where you sleep near the North Rim (I don't mean that literally, unless you take your munchies to bed. The North Rim definitely isn't room-service country). That's not generally a bad thing, though. This area is too remote for the fast-food franchises, so most of the chow is of the hearty, home-cooked variety. The best — also the only — gourmet food in the area is at the dining room of the Grand Canyon Lodge ($$–$$$), where classic American fare is sometimes given a Southwestern spin (chiles, blue corn). You have to make a reservation to eat there; call as soon as you book a room. Among the low-key eateries in the area, the standouts are the Canyon Dreamers Cafe ($$) at the Cliff Dweller's Lodge, which makes its desserts and soups from scratch and brews a mean espresso; and the Vermilion Cliffs Bar & Grill ($$–$$$) at Lees Ferry Lodge, where the beer is cold, your steak is cooked the way you order it, and the fish is fresh from the river. I haven't dined on anything but cookies at the Jacob Lake Inn, but I hear the jagerschnitzel is good.

Exploring the North Rim

Without the glut of concessionaires that converge on the South Rim, exploring the chasm's northern reaches is a much more personal, and usually more tranquil, experience. No helicopters hover here and few tour operators are around to guide you — it's just you, your car, and a few road signs.

As soon as you drive up to the entry kiosks and pay your park fee — the same as that on the South Rim, and nada if you've already paid in that busier part of the park less than a week ago (see the "Entering the park" section earlier in this chapter) — a gate attendant hands you a North Rim version of The Guide. Use it early and often. The park rangers and Grand Canyon Association employees at the North Rim Visitor Center, near the Grand Canyon Lodge (☎ 928-638-2611), can probably answer any other questions you may have. The center is open from 8 a.m. to 6 p.m. daily, sometimes longer in summer.

Rim drives

About 8 miles to the north of the Grand Canyon Lodge, the only road in the area forks off in two directions. Veer right (a sign reminds you) and drive another 3 miles to Point Imperial, the highest vista point on either rim at 8,803 feet. From there you can see the Painted Desert to the east, the Vermilion Cliffs to the north, Utah's Navajo Mountain to the northeast, and the Little Colorado River gorge to the southeast.

Turn left at the fork to reach Cape Royal, a total of 23 miles from the Grand Canyon Lodge. From the parking lot at the road's end, Cape Royal is a short (0.3 mile each way), piñon-pine-lined walk to some of the most awe-inspiring vistas in the park. Angel's Window, a giant, erosion-formed hole, is carved into a rock outcropping along the rim. Peer through the opening below the formation to catch a slice of the lower canyon, including a ribbon-like Colorado River. (For a nice walk from here, see the Cliff Springs Trail under the following section.) En route, stop at the Wallhalla Overlook to see the remains of two ancestral Puebloan villages, and at Roosevelt Point, where you get an angle on the spot where the Little Colorado River gorge and the Grand Canyon converge.

Hikes

The North Rim has fewer maintained hiking trails than the South Rim, but, then, you won't have to share them with as many other people. Check with the visitor center — see the "Fast Facts: The North Rim" section at the end of this chapter — for other suggestions. Before attempting the longer walks, see the "Some hiking tips" sidebar, earlier in this chapter.

- Easy hikes: The most popular North Rim hike because it starts just behind the Grand Canyon Lodge (pick it up at the corner of the east patio), the ½-mile (round-trip) walk to Bright Angel Point is also one of the most breathtaking — literally. You stroll along a skinny peninsula that divides Roarings Springs and Transept canyons, with sheer drops just a few feet away on either side (don't worry if, like me, you get weak-kneed just thinking about that; you can grab onto metal railings at the narrowest parts).

  Bright Angel Point seems to deprive some shutterbugs of their common sense. Don't climb any dangerous ledges to try for your best shot — it could be your last.

  Feel like a walk in the woods? The spot where you picked up the Bright Angel Point trail also marks the start of the 3-mile (round-trip) Transept Trail. This one edges the rim for a bit before plunging into the ponderosa pine forest, winding past a small ancestral Puebloan ruin, and ending up at the North Rim Campground and General Store.

  You also see signs of the canyon's earlier inhabitants — the ones who preceded Homo hikus — on the Cliff Springs Trail, the 1-mile (round-trip) path through a forested ravine that begins at Angel's

Window Overlook: About ¼ mile from the trailhead are the remains of an ancient granary. Narrow and precipitous where it hugs the north side of the Cliff Springs Canyon (if you're scared of heights, pass this one up), the trail winds beneath several limestone overhangs before reaching Cliff Springs (and no, you can't drink the water).

- Hard(er) hikes: The only maintained trail to the bottom of the canyon from the North Rim, the North Kaibab Trail, which hooks up with the South Kaibab Trail (see the "Exploring the South Rim" section earlier in this chapter), is 14.4 miles long each way and descends nearly 6,000 feet before it reaches the Colorado River. Unless you're on the Olympic hiking team (is there even such a thing?), you won't be able to finish this trail in a day, but hiking part of it is a great way to dip below the rim and see Roaring Springs and Bright Angel canyons, among other things.

The drive is just 1½ miles round-trip to Coconino Overlook, a sandstone clearing in a thick forest of aspen, Douglas fir, and gambel oak, but this stretch has lots of switchbacks. Supai Tunnel, about 2 miles from the trailhead, is an ideal turnaround point if you're more ambitious but don't want to push yourself; you find water and restrooms here. You'd better be in really good shape — almost Olympic hiking team material — and head out very early if you want to reach Roaring Springs, the water source for both rims, and back. The 10-mile (round-trip) hike can take up to 8 hours.

Spending the night down in the canyon requires a backcountry permit; see the "Exploring the South Rim" section earlier in this chapter for details.

If you want to trek with experts, check out Canyon Rim Adventures (☎ 800-897-9633; www.canyonrimadventures.com), the only National Park Service–sanctioned tour operator specializing in the North Rim. They bring camping equipment, food, Dutch oven, and, if desired, mountain bikes. You bring your enthusiasm and your checkbook (prices range from $575 per person for a three-day adventure to $795 for four days around and beneath the rim).

Mule rides

They're not as famous as their South Rim siblings — partly because of the area's lower profile, partly because they don't go the distance (to the bottom) — but the mules at the North Rim give the folks who hire them a good run (or at least trot) for their money. And the menu of options at Grand Canyon Trail Rides, at the Grand Canyon Lodge (☎ 435-679-8665, ext. 222 preseason; 928-638-9875 after May 15 and until the North Rim closes in late fall), is larger. Every day from May 15 until the North Rim closes, options include: one-hour rim rides (for ages 7 and older) for $30; half-day trips — one stays on the rim, the other goes down to Supai Tunnel on the North Kaibab Trail — for $55 (minimum age 8); and full-day trips (minimum age 12) down to Roaring Springs for $105, lunch

> **Some restrictions apply**
>
> In addition to the age minimums for the North Rim mule riders (I think different ones probably apply to the mules), weight and language rules apply. You can't weigh more than 220 pounds if you want to go around the rim or more than 200 if you'd like to dip into the canyon, and you have to speak English (sorry, the mules aren't bilingual).

included. These rides don't need to be booked as far in advance as the rides on the South Rim, but they're popular. Call or go to the transportation desk of the lodge as soon as you decide when you want to ride.

Touring beyond the North Rim

The road to the North Rim may be less traveled, but it's definitely not boring. The scenery is amazing, and you can get in some fishing if you're so inclined. Also beautiful is the Arizona Strip country, northwest of the national park. Two small towns (Fredonia and Colorado City), the Kaibab-Pauite reservation, and a national monument (the only place to do anything, really) punctuate this isolated area.

En route to the North Rim

As you drive north from Flagstaff on Highway 89, you see the Painted Desert, windswept plains and mesas colored with every pastel in the spectrum, to the east. The sandstone Echo Cliffs, with a more limited palate (soft pink to burnt umber), start putting in an appearance about 30 miles beyond the Cameron Trading Post (see the "Spending the night" section in "The South Rim of the Grand Canyon section earlier in this chapter). You can't miss them: Some are more than 1,000 feet tall. But the views get even grander. Keep going west from Navajo Bridge rather than detouring to Lees Ferry and you encounter the bright Vermilion Cliffs, topping off at more than 3,000 feet and with boulders surreally balanced on eroded columns of soil. Stop at the San Bartolome Historic Site overlook to read about the 1776 Domínguez-Escalante expedition through this area or just to look at the scenery standing still (you, not the scenery). After you're on the road again, you begin to see forest rather than desert; you know you're climbing the Kaibab Plateau, more than 9,000 feet at its highest point.

Other high (and low) points of this region include the following:

- Spanning the canyon: Listed on the National Register of Historic Places, the 834-foot-long steel Navajo Bridge, built in 1929, was the first — and, until the bridge at Glen Canyon Dam was built in 1959, the only — way to get across the Grand Canyon. Before this time, no other bridge crossed the Colorado River for the 600 miles from Moab, Utah, to the Hoover Dam. You can find out all about the bridge at the Native American-staffed Navajo Bridge Interpretive Center (☎ 928-355-2319). Keep an eye out for the building on your right, just beyond the new bridge (that's the one you drive across; the old one is pedestrian-only now). The building is hard to see because the native sandstone structure blends in beautifully with the Vermilion Cliffs backdrop. Pick up topographic maps, postcards, and books about the Grand Canyon, Lake Powell, Lees Ferry, and other area attractions at the center (admission: free; open: May 15–Oct 15 daily 8 a.m.–5 p.m.). Outside, vendors usually sell Native American jewelry.

- Trouting around: On a sharp bend in the Colorado River where the Echo Cliffs break — look for the turnoff just beyond Navajo Bridge on Highway 89A — Lees Ferry was long known as the river crossing for Mormon pioneers. Now Lees Ferry is famed for being mile zero — the coordinate from which all distances on the river system are measured. Straddling Glen Canyon upstream and Marble Canyon (the beginning of the Grand Canyon) downstream, Lees Ferry is also the point of departure for most Grand Canyon river rafting trips. Serious trout-fishers like to spend time here because trophy-sized specimens often take the bait. You can pick up fishing gear and a guide at Lees Ferry Anglers, Marble Canyon, 3 miles west of Navajo Bridge (☎ 800-962-9755 or 928-355-2261; `www.leesferry.com`); Marble Canyon Outfitters, Marble Canyon Lodge (☎ 800-533-7339 or 928-355-2245); and Ambassador Guide Services, Inc., located next to Lees Ferry Lodge (☎ 800-256-7596; `www.ambassadorguides`); see the "Spending the night" section for the last two locations. Rates range from about $280 for one person to $450 for three people for a full day. Prices may be lower if you meet the guide by the river rather than at the outfitter's shop.

- Oh, give me a home: Arizona's largest herd of American bison roam around the House Rock Buffalo Ranch, operated by the Arizona Department of Game and Fish's wildlife division (☎ 928-774-5045). On Highway 89A, about 17 miles west of Marble Canyon, is the turnoff for the 23-mile dirt road that leads to the ranch house (which is private, and has no interpretive center or other public facilities). Don't be disappointed if you don't see any buffalo, however. The ranch is huge (58,000 acres), and the 200-odd shaggy

Some flighty California transplants

Don't be surprised if you see a California condor in the Vermilion Cliffs area. Several pairs of the endangered birds were released in this area from 1996 through 1997 — no doubt because they look just mahr-velous swooping against those cliffs (and, okay, because they lived here in prehistoric times). You can find out who's mating with whom, which chicks have flown the coop, and get other condor news online at `www.peregrinefund.org`, in the "Notes from the Field" section.

behemoths don't always cooperate by coming within photo-op distance of your car (which can be a good thing: those babies are big but move fast and en masse). You're likely to see antelope, mule deer, and jackrabbits, though. Note: This drive isn't a good idea if you don't have a high clearance or four-wheel-drive vehicle, especially in the rain or snow. And the buffalo are, literally, fair game — public hunts have been held at the ranch since the 1920s — so don't phone the authorities if you should spot someone aiming a rifle at them (you may phone if the rifle's aimed at you, however).

West of the North Rim

If you don't turn south toward the North Rim at Jacob Lake junction — okay, so I'm being very hypothetical; why else would you drive all the way up there? — you head into the Arizona Strip, the 12,000-square-mile spread of northwest Arizona that has been dubbed the American Tibet, and not because yaks live there. You can see hundreds of miles in all directions on this lunar landscape, where lava outcroppings and cinder cones rise up among the more familiar (by now) red-rock and sandstone cliffs. The area is beautiful, but desolate; only some members of the Kaibub Paiute tribe and a few Mormon families live out here. The area's sole two sightseeing possibilities:

- Discover water: Pipe Spring National Monument, 45 miles west of Jacob Lake on Highway 389, Fredonia (☎ 928-643-7105), makes a good, if surreally Midwestern-looking, break from all that surrounding desert. The site's natural spring is one of the area's few consistent water sources. The Mormons built a fortress here in 1871, but it soon became a dairy farm and Arizona territory's first telegraph station. Summer mornings feature living history exhibits. Admission: $4 per adult; ages 16 and under free. Open: Memorial Day to Labor Day 7 a.m.–5 p.m., rest of the year 8 a.m.–5 p.m. See map p. 343.
- Make rock reservations: During the busy season, members of the Kaibab Paiute tribe, who have a small reservation in the Arizona Strip, offer easy, guided hikes to nearby petroglyph sites for $10 per person; in theory they're offered regularly on weekday mornings, by advance arrangement on the weekends. Reaching the tribal office by phone (☎ 928-643-7245) isn't always easy, however; your best bet is to stop in at the office, which is on Highway 389, just before the turn off to Pipe Spring National Monument (see the preceding bullet).

The original love boat

After ferry service was established at Lees Ferry (you knew the place had its name for a reason, didn't you?) in 1873, the landing became part of the Honeymoon Trail, followed by Mormon couples who had tied the knot in Arizona but wanted their union sanctified at the Temple of Latter-Day Saints in St. George, Utah.

Fast Facts: The North Rim

Area Code

The area code for this entire region is **928.**

ATMs

The closest ATM to the national park is at Jacob Lake.

Emergencies

For an ambulance, to report a fire or to get the police, call ☎ **911.**

Garage/Gas Station

The Chevron Service Station on the access road to the North Rim Campground (☎ **928-638-2611**) sells gas and does minor auto repairs. The next nearest gas is 5 miles north of the park boundary, at the Country Store & Gas Station; you can also get tanked up at Jacob Lake.

Information

You can order the free *Trip Planner,* which includes general information, by calling Grand Canyon National Park at ☎ **928-638-7888.** The planner is also available electronically at the National Park Service Web site, `www.nps.gov/grca`. The North Rim Visitor Center, near the Grand Canyon Lodge (☎ **928-638-7864**), is open from 8 a.m. to 6 p.m. daily, sometimes longer in summer. The Kaibab Plateau Visitor Center at Jacob Lake, 30 miles north of the park boundary (☎ **928-643-7298**), is open May 15 to late October daily from 8 a.m. to 5 p.m.

Internet Access

Sorry, you'll have to do without e-mail at the North Rim. Not even the Grand Canyon Lodge has Internet access yet.

Medical

Park rangers are trained in emergency medical procedures; contact the Grand Canyon Lodge (☎ **928-638-2611**) for help or call 911. The nearest pharmacy is in Kanab, Utah.

Post Office

The Grand Canyon Lodge complex has a post office, open Monday through Friday 8 a.m. to noon, 1 to 4:30 p.m., and Saturday 9 a.m. to 1 p.m.

Road Conditions and Weather

Call ☎ **928-638-7888.**

Chapter 18

Northeast Arizona: Hopi and Navajo Country

In This Chapter

- Touring flooded canyons, Hollywood buttes, and more: Navajo Nation Northwest
- Finding more canyons (dry) and a trading post: Navajo Nation East
- Enjoying a triple (mesa) treat: The Hopi Heartland
- Exploring some dead wood, an artful desert, and more: Old Route 66

The landscape of the Arizona northeast — of vast open spaces and eerie rock formations — is the Arizona you see in your mind's eye, if, like many, you've been raised on classic Western flicks. But this region is more than just the rugged, photogenic face of a John Ford movie. Home to the Navajo and Hopi and their ancestors, northeastern Arizona is also the spiritual heart of the Southwest. Sound a little too somber for you? Not to worry. You can play as hard here as anywhere else in the state, whether you're water-skiing on Lake Powell, hiking to see a cliff dwelling at Navajo National Monument, or horsing around at the bottom of Canyon de Chelly. And a key way to experience local culture, of course, is shopping.

The only two places where you're likely to want to linger are the Page/Lake Powell area and the Canyon de Chelly region. Otherwise,

Time after time

Arizona is on a strange time trip: It's in the Mountain time zone, but it doesn't observe daylight saving time like most states. And time tracking gets even weirder in Northeast Arizona. The Navajos do observe daylight saving time (which is only logical because their reservation crosses into New Mexico and Utah), while the neighboring Hopi do not. If you go from Page to Monument Valley to the Hopi Mesas, you theoretically have to switch your watch three times. (You probably won't have any pressing engagements to worry about, though.)

You don't need a passport, but . . .

Traveling on an American Indian reservation is similar to visiting a foreign country. The Navajo Nation is the largest sovereign, self-governing community within U.S. boundaries. Both the Navajos and the Hopis have their own customs, laws, and even languages. (Relax; you won't need an interpreter — but don't be surprised if you hear the Navajo language spoken.) For example, you don't see any street addresses, because there's no house-to-house postal delivery; everyone retrieves mail from a P.O. box. When in doubt about directions, just ask; locals are happy to help. You, in turn, are expected to behave politely. (See the "Native American etiquette: Some reservation do's and don'ts" sidebar in this chapter.)

your sleepovers may pretty much be limited to one-night stands, although I can see spending two nights at Goulding's, a historic trading post/hotel near Monument Valley. That said, you can easily stay at least a week in this spectacular, spread-out region. Just prepare to forgo some luxuries during your visit.

Navajo Nation Northwest

This part of the state has some of the country's weirdest and most wonderful scenery, including the series of wet 'n' wild canyons that comprise Lake Powell; the skinny, strangely convoluted Antelope Canyon; and the mounds and spires of Monument Valley that set the scene for Westerns ranging from The Searchers to Thelma and Louise. The area is also rich in cultural sites like the cliff dwellings at Navajo National Monument and assorted historic trading posts. Plan on spending a minimum of three days to give this area its due. In fact, if you enjoy playing on the water and/or if you detour to the Grand Canyon's North Rim (see Chapter 17), you may decide to spend your entire vacation here.

Getting there

Traveling from Flagstaff to Page couldn't be easier: Just keep driving north on Highway 89 for 138 miles. When you reach Bitter Springs, where Highway 89A branches off from Highway 89, continue on Highway 89; Page is just 25 more miles up the road. The scenery along the way is eye-popping (see Chapter 17 for details on the route to Bitter Springs). About 5 miles beyond the Bitter Springs turn-off, at mile marker 527, you come to the Big Cut. Pull off the road to gaze at the sweeping vista of the Vermilion Cliffs and the Colorado River canyon on the Marble Plateau spread out below.

America West (☎ 800-235-9292) offers two flights a day from Phoenix to Page Municipal Airport (1 mile east of town on Highway 98; ☎ 928-645-2494). Great Lakes Aviation (☎ 800-554-5111) has three flights a

Northeast Arizona

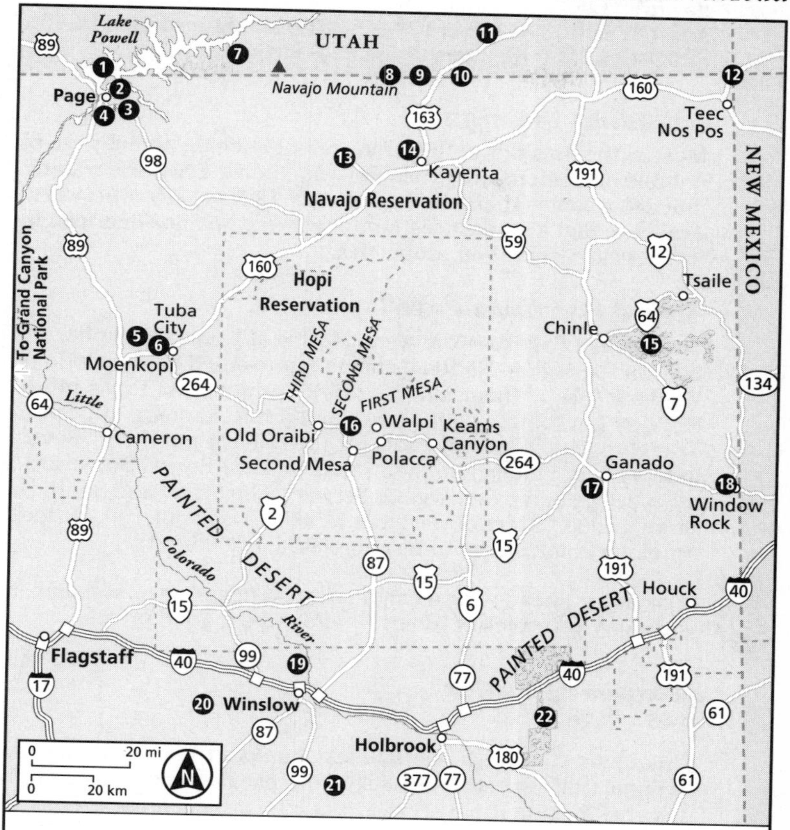

Antelope Canyon Navajo Tribal Park **3**
Canyon de Chelly National Monument **15**
Dinosaur Tracks **5**
Four Corners Monument Navajo Tribal Park **12**
Glen Canyon Dam **2**
Glen Canyon National Recreation Area **1**
Goosenecks **11**
Goulding's Trading Post Museum **9**
Homolovi Ruins State Park **19**
Hopi Cultural Center Museum **16**
Horseshoe Bend **4**
Hubbell Trading Post National Historic Site **17**
John Wesley Powell Memorial Museum **2**
Meteor Crater **20**
Monument Valley Navajo Tribal Park **10**
Navajo Cultural Center **14**
Navajo National Monument **13**
Navajo Nation Museum **18**
Navajo Village Heritage Center **4**
Olijato Trading Post & Museum **8**
Petrified Forest National Park **22**
Rainbow Bridge **7**
Rock Art Canyon Ranch **21**
Tuba Trading Post **6**

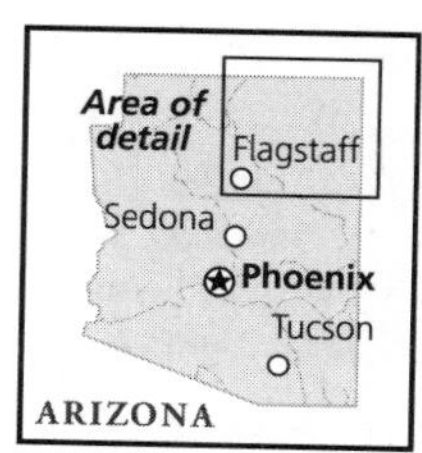

day from Phoenix to Page and offers regular service to Page from Denver. Avis (☎ 800-331-1212 or 928-645-2024) and Enterprise (☎ 800-261-7331 or 928-645-1449) rent cars at the Page airport.

Spending the night

Most of the lodgings in this area are of the chain persuasion, but several notable exceptions are available — including a historic trading post and moveable rooms that aren't on wheels. Unless I say otherwise, you may expect to find a modest restaurant serving Navajo/American fare on all the Navajo reservation properties.

Around Page/Lake Powell

The town of Page and Wahweap Marina at Lake Powell offer the best beds in the region. National chains represented here include Best Western (two of them, side by side), Comfort Inn, Day's Inn & Suites, Holiday Inn Express, Motel 6, Quality Inn, Ramada Inn, Super 8, and Travelodge (see the appendix for the toll-free numbers). Several modest independent motels join their ranks on Lake Powell Boulevard, Page's main drag, and on 8th Avenue between Elm Street and South Navajo Drive, called "Street of the Little Motels." Look out, too, for lodgings at Antelope Point, slated to be completed in 2006.

Book as far ahead as you can if you visit in spring or summer. In winter, you enjoy your pick of rooms — and at very good prices.

Courtyard by Marriott

$–$$ Page

This chain hotel has the fanciest bunks in Page and the Lake Powell National Golf Course in its backyard. Upscale perks not generally found in this area include room service (until 9 p.m.), laundry, exercise room, and a spa — plus the requisite pool. The big, comfy rooms have coffeemakers, hair dryers, and ports for computer hookups. Rooms with views of the golf course and/or Lake Powell cost extra. The on-site Peppers restaurant ($$) is a local favorite for buffet breakfasts, including a make-your-own Belgian waffle bar.

600 Country Club Dr. (at Lake Powell Blvd. and Highway 89). ☎ ***800-851-3855*** *or 928-645-5000. Fax: 928-645-5004. Rack rates: June–early Oct $99 double ($109 for a view room); Jan–Mar $59/$69; Apr–May $69/$79, mid-Oct–Dec $49/$59; golf packages available. AE, DC, DISC, MC, V.*

Uncle Bill's Place

$ Page

Ideal if you're coming with an entourage or feeling friendly, these pleasant, economical quarters are designed for longer stays. You can rent everything from a single room in a house with a communal bath to your own suite; all accommodations offer kitchens. Uncle Bill's place is modest but not austere, with sculptures and paintings indoors, and a nice garden outside. Other perks: laundry facilities, barbecues, and picnic tables.

117 8th Ave. (between Elm St. and N. Navajo). ☎ ***888-359-0945*** *or 928-645-1224. Fax: 928-645-3937.* `www.canyon-country.com/unclebill`. *Rack rates: $36–$45 rooms in guest house; $49–$79 1-bedroom suite; $69–$149 3-bedroom Garden Apartment. MC, V.*

Wahweap

$$ Wahweap Marina

The closest digs to Lake Powell without actually being on it. (See the "Here, B&B means bed and boat" sidebar in this chapter.) The rooms are no big deal; a touch of Southwest styling puts them a cut above a standard motel. What you're paying for is (for better or worse) being in the heart of the watersports and tour boat action at Lake Powell's biggest marina. In some rooms, you're able to gaze out at the lake. A casual restaurant (in season), gift shop, and tour desk cater to your material needs, but the vistas from the Rainbow Room restaurant (see the following "Dining locally" section) and the adjacent bar and deck soothe your soul.

100 Lakeshore Dr. (4 miles north of Glen Canyon Dam). ☎ ***800-528-6154*** *or 928-645-2433.* `www.lakepowell.com`. *Rack rates: June–Oct $160–$170 double, $248 suite; mid-Oct–April $89–$109 double; $179 suite. B&B and touring packages available. AE, DC, DISC, MC, V*

Near Navajo National Monument

Anasazi Inn at Tsegi

$ Tsegi

This spot is convenient to both Navajo National Monument and Monument Valley. The rooms are small, basic, and phoneless, but if you get one in the back, looking out at soaring Tsegi Canyon, you may not mind the lack of amenities. And you can't beat the off-season rates.

Highway 160 at Tsegi Canyon (about halfway between Navajo National Monument and Kayenta). ☎ ***928-697-3793.*** *Fax: 928-697-8249.* `www.anasaziinn.com`. *Rack rates: mid May–Oct $60–$80 double; Nov–early May $40–$50 double. AE, DC, DISC, MC, V.*

In Monument Valley

The closest town to Monument Valley (23 miles south) and the largest (which isn't saying much) in this region, Kayenta isn't exactly quaint but it does have dueling gas stations, a supermarket, several casual restaurants, and three motels. In addition to the two accommodations I list, a Holiday Inn and Best Western are also available (see the Appendix for toll-free numbers). For a unique accommodation in this area, see also the "Hogans' (that's hoh-gahns) heroes" sidebar in this chapter.

Here, B&B means bed and boat

If you want to tour Lake Powell without straying more than a few feet from your fridge, go ahead — join the houseboating hordes. Don't worry if the closest you usually come to things nautical is riding the Staten Island Ferry. These babies are easy (and fun) to steer, and you get plenty of training before anyone lets you go sliding away from the slip.

For a long time, **Lake Powell Resorts and Vacations** (☎ **800-528-6154** or 928-645-1111; www.lakepowell.com) was the only houseboat game in town. The company still offers the most choices for sleeping on the lake. In high season 2004, prices ranged from $1,658 for three days (the minimum) on a 44-foot standard class houseboat (sleeping up to eight people) to $8,897 for a week on a luxurious 75-foot Admiral class model (which sleeps up to 12).

But in the summer of 2004, the new **Antelope Point Marina** (☎ **800-255-5561** or 480-998-1981 (in Scottsdale), www.lakepowellhouseboating.com) introduced two super-luxurious houseboat models to Lake Powell. We're talking a GPS tracking system, large-screen color TVs with DVD players in each room, and a wet bar and hot tub on the upper deck. Rates in high season range from $3,295 for a three-day stay on the 59-footer (sleeps up to 10) to $7,495 for a week on the 70-foot model (sleeps up to 12).

For both companies, rates go down considerably in winter — but, unless you like playing in cold water, so do your activity and comfort levels. Also, the more space you share, the lower the per-person cost. Just make sure all of you really want to spend that much time on a boat together.

Goulding's Lodge

$$ Monument Valley

Director John Ford's former stomping ground is still a Hollywood magnet. If you see a pickup truck commercial on TV with a big sky/big rocks background, odds are good that the film crew and actors from the shoot bunked at Goulding's. The rooms are comfortable, with freshened-up Southwest-rustic decor and all the mod-cons. An on-site museum details the history of this former trading post, and a gift shop still has plenty of Native American goods for sale. Other pluses include great craggy-cliffs views from the balconies of many rooms, a tour desk, coin-op laundry, gas station, and an airstrip (where else would Hollywood types land their Learjets?).

On Indian Route 42 (intersects at Highway 163 about 27 miles north of Kayenta; take Indian Route 42 west [left] 2 miles). ☎ ***435-727-3231.*** *Fax: 435-727-3344.* www.gouldings.com. *Rack rates: Mar 15–Mar 30 $108 double, Apr 1–Nov 15 $135–$160 double; Nov 16–Mar 14 $68–$78 double. AE, DC, DISC, MC, V.*

The Hampton Inn

$$ Kayenta

This is Kayenta's most pleasant sleep stop, offering the freshest, most attractive rooms (light-wood furniture, Navajo print bedspreads), a good restaurant with room service, plus a nice outdoor heated pool. A tour-bus haven near two highway crossroads, the location isn't terribly peaceful, but you're right next to the Navajo Cultural Center (see the "More cool things to see and do" section) and the Burger King with the code talker displays (check out the "Hogans' [that's hoh-gahns] heroes" sidebar).

Highway 160 at Highway 163 (next door to the Burger King). ☎ ***800-Hampton*** *or 928-697-3170. Fax: 928-697-3189.* www.hampton-inn.com. *Rack rates: summer $115–$125 double, winter $75–$95 double. Rates include continental breakfast. AE, DC, DISC, MC, V.*

Dining locally

Page has the area's greatest number of fast-food franchises (Kayenta has a couple, too). In addition, Page is the only town in the region that even makes a stab at gourmet cuisine (but don't expect to find mixed baby mesclun greens dressed with a nicely aged raspberry vinaigrette).

Around Page/Lake Powell

Peppers in the Courtyard by Marriott (see the preceding "Spending the night," section) is a good place for breakfast; I also like to start my day at the Ranch House Grille ($), 819 North Navajo Dr. (☎ 928-645-1420), a low-key local hangout. Lunchtime in Page you can find me either at Stromboli's ($–$$), 711 N. Navajo Dr. (☎ 928-645-2605), with good pizza and calzones and a terrific deck, or The Sandwich Place ($), 662 Elm St. (☎ 928-645-5267), where the pastrami burger is super. The following are my favorite dinner spots. See the "Exploring Navajo Nation Northwest" section that follows for information regarding dinner at the Navajo Village Heritage Center.

Dam Bar & Grill

$$–$$$ Page AMERICAN/ITALIAN/SOUTHWEST

The dam theme dominates only the front section of this cavernous restaurant, but the fun atmosphere (and the puns) prevails throughout. The menu is fairly eclectic — ranging from fish and chips, burgers, and pizza to top sirloin and rotisserie chicken marinated in red chile apple cider — but everything tastes fresh, and portions are more than generous.

644 N. Navajo (in the Dam Plaza). ☎ ***928-645-2161.*** *Reservations recommended in summer. Main courses: $9–$19, pizzas, burgers, and sandwiches $6–$12. AE, MC, V. Open: Dinner nightly.*

Ken's Old West

$$–$$$ Page STEAKHOUSE

This is your quintessential wood-front steakhouse. Prime rib rules, but you find huge steaks — as rare as you want 'em — too. Seafood and chicken entrees and a salad bar are available for red-meat avoiders, and a children's menu and friendly staff make this a good choice for families. Stick around for the live Country and Western music (weekends only in winter, nightly in summer).

718 Vista Ave. (behind the Best Western at Lake Powell). ☎ ***928-645-5160.*** *Reservations suggested on high-season weekends. Main courses: $10–$22. AE, DISC, MC, V. Open: Dinner nightly.*

The Rainbow Room

$$–$$$ Wahweap Marina AMERICAN/SOUTHWEST

Circular shape aside, all resemblance to Manhattan's swank dinner palace begins and ends with the name. That's okay. You don't have to dress to the nines to eat here, you won't exceed your credit limit, and you enjoy amazing lake views from this room's panoramic windows. The food and the service have their ups and downs, but the buffets are dependable, and at dinner you're safe with the house specialty: pine nut–crusted trout.

Wahweap Lodge, 100 Lakeshore Dr. ☎ ***928-645-2433.*** *Reservations not accepted (and you may face a wait in summer if you want to eat anywhere near a normal hour). Main courses: $12–$23. AE, DISC, MC, V. Open: Daily breakfast, lunch, and dinner.*

In Monument Valley

The restaurants in the Monument Valley area aren't vastly different from one another. Expect reasonable versions of casual American dishes and a few good Mexican and Navajo selections in Kayenta's three motel restaurants and at the Haskéneini dining room (named after an early-20th-century Navajo leader) in Monument Valley Navajo Tribal Park. Haskéneini has great views but it's small and gets really crowded in summer. The dining room at Goulding's is a cut above the rest in terms of selection, quality, and view (although not necessarily service).

The entire Navajo Nation is dry; you can't buy or bring any booze (including beer and wine) onto the reservation.

Exploring Navajo Nation Northwest

You can easily spend a week in this area, which has tons of things to see and do. Look for activities that involve a deliberate expenditure of energy in the "Staying active" section later in this chapter.

The top attractions

Monument Valley Navajo Tribal Park

Near Kayenta

The deep rust sandstone buttes, mesas, and spires of the 50-square-mile Monument Valley are the ultimate icons of the West, perhaps because they seem to exist on a different planet than urban and suburban America. The rock formations are strangely shaped to begin with — they're named after everything from mittens to elephants — but what makes them even more striking is that they rise up suddenly from a practically flat stretch of plain.

It used to be possible to tool around Monument Valley on your own via a 17-mile unpaved and unmaintained loop drive. Because of damage to the sites and concerns about visitor safety — tourists with low-clearance vehicles frequently got stuck in the road and stranded — those self-guided tours were phased out in 2004.

Now the only way to tour Monument Valley is with an on-site guide. Tours range from 1½ hour tours via Jeep or large, open vehicle to overnight hikes (check out the "Seeing Navajo Nation Northwest by guided tour" section later in this chapter for some options). Frankly, tooling around Monument Valley has never been one of my favorite things to do, especially in summer when the place is packed: I'd rather appreciate the scenery at a distance than bump down ungraded, dusty roads. That said, the formations are sacred to the Navajos, and several of them let visitors view petroglyphs from earlier cultures. If this is one of your main stops in Indian Country, you'll definitely benefit from going with a local guide and getting the lore behind the rocks.

See map p. 399. 3 miles off Highway 163; take Highway 160 to Kayenta and drive north 27 miles until you see the sign on the right side of the road. ☎ ***435-727-5870;*** *Admission: $5 per person, ages 9 and under free. Open: May–Sept daily 8 a.m.–7 p.m., Oct–Apr daily 8 a.m.–5 p.m., Thanksgiving 8 a.m.–noon, closed Christmas. National Park passes not accepted.*

Navajo National Monument

Between Tuba City and Kayenta

Navajo National Monument is a dazzler, with two sets of wonderfully preserved cliff dwellings in a sublime high-desert setting of soaring ochre cliffs punctuated by thick stands of fir and aspen trees. This site is now on Navajo land, but the people who settled in the two communities preserved here, Betatakin (beh-tat-uh-kin) and Keet Seel — from about A.D. 950 to A.D. 1300 and A.D. 1250 to A.D. 1300, respectively — are forebears of the Hopi. (These people are often referred to as the Anasazi, which likely means "ancient enemy" in Navajo, but archaeologists now prefer the term "Ancestral Puebloans.") Because Navajo National Monument isn't as well known as some of the other ancient sites in the Southwest, crowd control isn't a problem — another reason this is one of my top picks in the region.

The 1-mile Sandal Trail loop that leads to a spectacular overlook of Betatakin involves a bit of an upward slope on the return trip. If you take the trail slowly, you shouldn't have a problem, even if most of your hiking is done from the TV to the refrigerator. (For harder treks, see the "Staying active" section later in this chapter.) The Sandal Trail loop takes about 45 minutes to complete. Allot another 45 minutes if you also want to hike the short but steep Aspen Forest Overlook trail, which branches off from the Sandal Trail. And — I admit — I always end up spending at least 15 minutes at the great gift shop (see the "Shopping for local treasures" section) next to the visitor center.

See map p. 399. On Highway 264, 9 miles north of the Highway 160 turnoff. ☎ ***928-672-2366.*** `www.nps.gov/nava`. *Admission: Free. Open: Daily 8 a.m.–5 p.m., except Christmas, Thanksgiving, and New Year's Day.*

Page/Lake Powell

Page was started in 1956 as a construction site for Glen Canyon Dam, built to harness hydroelectric power from the Colorado River. The dam's secondary result was a bit more splendid: After 17 years of slowly flooding nearly 100 dramatic sandstone canyons (most of them in Utah), the huge reservoir known as Lake Powell was created. Stretch out its 1,960 miles of shoreline, and you end up with more waterfront property than exists on the entire West Coast of the United States.

Because of drought conditions in recent years — and because a certain amount of water is committed to different entities — the lake's water levels have hit record lows. In 2004, Lake Powell was at 42% capacity, the lowest it has been since 1970, when the canyons were still being filled. Still, it's by no means low enough to interfere with most aquatic activities.

The lake is only a small part of the huge Glen Canyon National Recreation Area. Three smaller marinas on Lake Powell offer recreation, but Wahweap, 6 miles north of Page, is watersports central. Antelope Point, an $80-million marina and hotel complex that broke ground in 2003, is aiming to catch up with Wahweap, but it won't be fully operational until 2007 (for progress reports, go to `www.azmarinas.com`).

Lots of folks spend their time hanging off the sides of their rented houseboats or getting wet in other ways (see the "Staying active" section later in this chapter). If you're a landlubber — or just want to dry out for a bit — you have a few other options.

- Give a dam. You don't have to care about hydroelectric energy to be impressed by the gigantic Glen Canyon Dam, Highway 89, 2 miles west of Page (☎ 928-608-6404; `www.nps.gov/glca/damindx.htm`); only Hoover Dam is taller (by 16 feet). You enjoy great Lake Powell views at the Carl Hayden Visitor Center, where a small bookstore stocks information about the area's many natural attractions. Free 45-minute-long guided tours of the dam are offered year round on a first-come, first-served basis. The schedule ranges from four tours daily in winter to nine daily in summer; call ahead for times. Note: Security at the dam has been tight since 9/11. Leave any large bags in the car and be prepared to go through a metal detector. Admission: free. Open: Daily Memorial Day through Labor Day 7 a.m.–7 p.m., rest of year daily 8 a.m. to 5 p.m.; closed Thanksgiving, Christmas, and New Year's Day. See map p. 399.
- Explore an explorer (and a dinosaur). The John Wesley Powell Memorial Museum, 6 N. Lake Powell Blvd. at N. Navajo Dr. (☎ 928-645-9496; `www.powellmuseum.org`), celebrates the life and journeys of the one-armed Civil War hero who led the first (1869) river expedition along the entire length of the Grand Canyon. He named the canyon and many other landmarks in the area and, in turn, had several places — including Lake Powell — named after him. In 2004, the museum started displaying the nearly intact skeleton of a plesiosaur, a marine dinosaur that swam around the Colorado Plateau some 93 million years ago (Lake Powell is a

puddle compared to the sea that once covered this region). Measuring some 20 feet, with six-foot-long paddle arms and four-foot-long jaws with 100 teeth, the plesiosaur is a major crowd pleaser. The museum doubles as a visitor center. Admission: $2 adults, $1 ages 5–12. Open: Mon–Fri 9 a.m. to 5 p.m.; closed mid-Dec to mid-Feb. Call ahead, however, because the museum is hoping to stay open additional days and hours. See map p. 399.

- Dine with the Diné. At the living-history museum run by the Navajo Village Heritage Center, 531 Haul Rd., about a mile south of Page between Highways 89 and 98 (☎ 928-660-0304), you find out a lot about the traditions of the Diné — as the Navajo call themselves. Tours of several different Navajo structures (for example, a sweat lodge and two types of homes) take place during the day from 9 a.m. to 3 p.m. (by donation). The dinner program includes a dance performance, talks, and demonstrations such as weaving. The full program, from 4 to 8 p.m., costs $49.95 for adults, $34.95 for children ages 6 to 13. I recommend the two-hour program, beginning at 5 p.m. and 6 p.m., which includes dancing and shorter presentations along with a Navajo taco dinner; costs are $34.95 adults, $24.95 children. Buy tickets at the Page/Lake Powell Chamber of Commerce (see the "Fast Facts: Navajo Nation Northwest" section) if you're interested in enjoying this unique experience, because programs are only offered when a minimum of four people commit to attending. See map p. 399.
- Go over the rainbow. The world's largest natural arch (height: 290 feet, span: 275 feet), the spectacular sandstone Rainbow Bridge (`www.nps.gov/rabr`) is Lake Powell's most famous landmark. Long held sacred by the area's native peoples, the bridge is in a remote canyon at the foot of Navajo Mountain, some 50-lake miles north of Wahweap Marina. The hike is 26 miles round-trip from the nearest land point and you need a permit, so you probably want to go most of the way by boat (see the "Guided tours" section). If you want to find out more about this marathon-length hike, check with Navajo Nation Parks and Recreation (☎ 928-871-6647; `www.navajonationparks.org`) for details. See map p. 399.
- Get the skinny. In Lower Antelope Canyon, sand dunes from an ancient sea solidified over millennia into what are variously known as skinny caves, wind caves, slot canyons, corkscrew canyons . . . well, you get the picture — and so does every professional or aspiring shutterbug. The narrow beams of light that stream into the caves from above offer a great photo op. The entrance station to Antelope Canyon Navajo Tribal Park is about 3 miles east of Page on Highway 98 at milepost 299 (☎ 928-698-3384 or 928-698-3285). You can't visit the canyon unaccompanied, but you can hire a Navajo guide at the gate; it's $15 adult, plus a $6 entrance fee, for a one-hour tour. You can also book a tour from Page (see the "Guided tours" section later in this chapter), a more reliable option because the entrance gate tours operate irregularly. Gates usually open

The X-Files

It's not as long as the world-famous Antelope Canyon, and doesn't have quite as many whorls and swirls. But Canyon X — a pair of slot canyons linked by a more traditional canyon rich with plant and animal life — is plenty spectacular nevertheless. And if you're looking for a unique experience, as well as the cachet of being able to say that you boldly went where few men and women have gone before, consider a visit to this remote spot. It's about 6 miles upstream from Antelope Canyon, but a world away from the tourist hordes.

Canyon X also has mystery going for it. Among the strange phenomena that led Jackson Bridges, a photographer and tour guide, to allude to the other-wordly phenomena of *The X-Files* TV show when giving Canyon X its name are the perfect circles that appear on the canyon walls. "Several scientists have visited with me," Bridges says, "But they can't explain these circles away with science."

Canyon X has only been open to the public since 2000, and only one tour operator, Overland Tours (see "The top attractions" section), has access to it: The canyon is on Navajo land that belongs to the aunt of Harley Klemme, Overland Tours' owner. The company offers photographic, hiking, and sightseeing excursions into the canyon, ranging from $95 to $135 per person. All require some agility, as you have to climb down a rocky slope to get to the canyon floor. But the tours are not out of the realm of most people's physical abilities and more than reward any huffing and puffing you may experience.

between 8 a.m. and 9 p.m., and close at around 5 p.m.; the last tour departs at around 3 or 3:30 p.m. For another slot canyon option, see "The X-Files" sidebar. See map p. 399.

- Take a scenic toss. To reach Horseshoe Bend, a stunning overlook of the Colorado River that makes a — what else? — complete horseshoe bend around a soaring sandstone butte, take Highway 89 about 5 miles south from the Carl Hayden Visitor Center. A little before mile marker 545 and just beyond the large "P" on the opposite side of the road, turn west onto a paved pullout (it's unsigned, and thus easy to miss), drive about ¼ mile, and park at the base of the hill. The hike to the overlook is only about ¾ of a mile, each way, but much of it is through soft sand, and you'll be walking almost entirely uphill on the way back. That said, the breathtaking scenery definitely compensates for the energy expenditure. See map p. 399.

More cool things to see and do

Great views, Navajo history, and dinosaur footprints — the Navajo Nation Northwest has much more to offer visitors.

- Drive the Goosenecks. Drive north on Highway 163 from Monument Valley and then turn west on Highway 161 (4 miles past Mexican Hat, Utah) to reach the overlook for the wildly convoluted, erosion-created San Juan River canyons called Goosenecks. During the week, especially off-season, you often find no one at this remote outlook point except perhaps a jewelry vendor or two. See map p. 399.

- Trade on the past. The Goulding's Trading Post Museum (see the "Spending the night" section earlier in this chapter), in the store that Harry Goulding established in the 1920s, includes Native American artifacts and mementos from director John Ford's films. Upstairs, you can visit the Gouldings's former living quarters. Admission: $2 suggested donation. Open: April–Oct daily 7:30 a.m.–9 p.m., more limited hours Nov–Apr. Some 14 miles beyond Goulding's — take the same road west around Hoskininni Mesa — the remote Oljato Trading Post & Museum (☎ 435-727-3210; `www.a-aa.com/monumentvalley`; open daily 8 a.m.–6 p.m. in winter, 8 a.m.–7 p.m. in summer) is on the National Register of Historic Places. Established in 1921, the trading post has shelves stocked as they were in the old days; entry to the small museum/bookstore is free. At the Tuba Trading Post (on the corner of Main and Moenave streets in Tuba City; ☎ 928-283-5441; open Mon–Fri 8 a.m.–6 p.m., Sat 8 a.m.–5 p.m., Sun 9 a.m.–5 p.m. high season, shorter hours in winter), built in 1906 in the shape of a six-sided Navajo hogan, locals still trade crafts for necessities. Along with jewelry, belts, rugs, and the like, you find creative T-shirts and books about the Southwest. See map p. 399.
- Discover more about Navajo history. In Kayenta, the unmanned Navajo Cultural Center, on Highway 160, between the Burger King and the Hampton Inn (no telephone), includes several traditional structures — two hogans (the hexagonal buildings that serve as both homes and ceremonial chambers), a sweat house, and a shade house with signed displays about Navajo customs and religious beliefs; sometime crafts or dance exhibitions are offered. Also check out the "Hogans' (that's hoh-gahns) heroes" sidebar in this chapter for information on displays at the adjacent Burger King. See map p. 399.
- Track down some dinosaurs. In the first stretch of Highway 160 beyond Highway 89 (just beyond mile marker 316), a turnoff for Dinosaur Tracks takes you to one of only two sets of dilophosaurus footprints ever found — and the other set is in China. The dilophosaurus, or "running dinosaur," got some pretty bad press in the movie Jurassic Park, where it had a nasty habit of spewing venom before polishing off its prey. No proof exists that the dilophosaurus was either poisonous or that it spat (I think there were dino laws against spitting in public places.) See map p. 399.

A local Navajo child likely will approach you in the parking lot and ask whether you want a tour. If you agree — though there's really not a whole lot to tour — you're expected to tip a dollar or two.

Hogans' (that's *hoh*-gahns) heroes

The secret code devised by a group of Navajos for the United States in World War II was the only code that the Japanese never broke. Introduced at Iwo Jima, the system of encryption — based on, but not exactly the same as, the complex Navajo language — helped the Allies win a victory that many consider the war's turning point. By the end of WWII, the Navajo Code Talkers, as this unit of soldiers was called, numbered some 425. About 150 are still alive today.

The fact that the code wasn't declassified until 1968 is one reason these heroes remained relatively unsung. That changed in 2002, when filmmaker John Woo's World War II thriller *Windtalkers*, starring Nicholas Cage, highlighted this historic episode.

Three small displays on the Navajo reservation detail the Code Talkers' story with less glitz and more accuracy. You'll find them at Kayenta's Burger King, Highway 160, just west of the Highway 160/163 intersection; at the Junction restaurant at the Best Western Canyon de Chelly Inn (see "Spending the night" in the "Navajo Nation East" section of this chapter); and at the visitor center of Monument Valley (see the "Exploring Navajo Nation Northwest" section). All feature photographs, memorabilia, and articles about the Code Talkers; you'll also see World War II uniforms, weapons, and Japanese souvenirs.

Guided tours

Whether you prefer to tour by air, boat, Jeep, or even horse, you're sure to find an option that suits you. Also check out the "Staying active" section later in this chapter, for guided hikes to Navajo National Monument and for river-rafting trips in Page.

If you want to hover above the crowds at Rainbow Bridge, see spectacular formations that aren't accessible by boat or road, or just save some time, consider taking an air tour. American Aviation (☎ 866-525-3247 or 928-608-1060; www.lakepowellairtours.com) and Westwind Air (☎ 800-245-8668 or 928-645-2494; www.westwindaviation.com) offer trips out of Page Airport to Lake Powell, Rainbow Bridge, Lees Ferry, Monument Valley, the Grand Canyon, and southern Utah sights. Times range from ½ hour to 3 hours, costs from $95–$250 per adult (less for children).

Four different concessionaires afford you Antelope Canyon entry and guidance: Antelope Canyon Adventures, 104 S. Lake Powell Blvd. (☎ 866-645-5501 or 928-645-5501; www.jeeptour.com); Antelope Canyon Tours, 22 S. Lake Powell Blvd. (☎ 928-645-9102 or 928-660-0739 [cell]; www.antelopecanyon.com); Grand Circle Adventures, 48 S. Lake Powell (☎ 928-645-5594; www.antelopeslotcanyontours.com); and Overland Canyon Tours, 695 N. Navajo (☎ 928-608-4072; www.overlandcanyon.com). All charge $20 for adults and $10 for children (plus $6 for a Navajo Nation entry fee, waived for ages 7 and under) for their basic 1½-hour tours. The first two tours operate in open-sided four-wheel drive vehicles while the latter two use enclosed SUVs; you decide whether you like the wind in your hair or prefer air-conditioning. Other distinguishing features: Both Antelope Canyon Tours and Overland Canyon tours are Navajo-run, giving you an insider's take on the area, and all except Grand Circle offer longer tours for photographers, who get to stand around endlessly, waiting for the light to shift. Overland Canyon is the only one that runs tours to Canyon X (see "The X-Files" sidebar in this chapter).

Lake Powell Resorts & Marina (☎ 928-645-1070; `www.lakepowell.com`) offers a variety of boat trips from Wahweap Marina. Those trips on the company's two-deck cruisers include full-day excursions to Rainbow Bridge ($99 adult, $79 ages 12 and under; includes a box lunch); and shorter trips to Antelope Canyon and Navajo Canyon ($49–$29 for a 3-hour tour, $28–$21 for 1½ hours). In summer, you can also book a one-hour cruise via the Wahweap Bay Paddlewheeler ($13 adults, $10 children), or enjoy a dinner cruise on the Canyon King paddlewheeler, a 19th-century riverboat ($61 adult and children). With the exception of the paddle-wheeler and dinner cruises, all excursions are offered year-round, but schedules change seasonally, so check ahead.

Trip times can vary up to 45 minutes, depending on lake levels and water traffic And when water levels are low, boats can't come very close to Rainbow Bridge; in 2004, a 1¼-mile hike to and from the site was required

Navajo-led tours around Monument Valley range from 1½-hour Jeep jaunts (around $20 per person) to overnight horseback excursions ($160). You also find hiking tours to Mitchell Mesa that last 3½ hours ($65); full-day tours that divide their times between Monument Valley and Mystery Valley, where you can see cliff dwellings and petroglyphs ($115); sunrise ($35) and sunset ($30) tours on four wheels or four feet; and tours where photography is the main focus (from $30 an hour). About a dozen tour operators have kiosks at Monument Valley. I haven't done any comparison touring, but can definitely recommend Simpson's Trailhandler's Tours (☎ 435-727-3362; `www.trailhandlerstours.com`). All the guides in the company are Navajos who have grown up in the Monument Valley area, and their expertise about the site's landscape and lore is invaluable.

When you drive to the dirt parking area just past the Monument Valley visitor center, you see rows of concessionaire's booths. Don't make yourself crazy by comparison shopping. The park superintendent fixes the prices for all the tour groups so the sellers can't go above the advertised rates (they can dip a little below). In addition, I suggest that you decide in advance what kind of tour you want to take, in what kind of vehicle — or nonvehicle. (Incidentally, if it's a choice between an enclosed Jeep and a seat on an open-air truck, I'd spend the extra money on the Jeep to avoid the dust.) Establishing your preferences gives you a sound basis for choosing a guide service.

Staying active

I cover horseback riding and hiking in Monument Valley in the preceding section. Except for hiking in Navajo National Monument, all the following activities take place in the Page/Lake Powell area:

- Fishing: Lake Powell, like hell, never freezes over — which makes the lake an angler's heaven. Large- and small-mouth bass, striped bass, catfish, carp, walleye, and crappie abound year-round. Because Lake Powell straddles both Arizona and Utah, unless you stay on one side of the lake or the other, you need two licenses (fees for nonresidents: \$12.50 in Arizona, \$12 in Utah for one day; prices go down the longer the license length). You can get all your paperwork and buy tackle and bait at Wahweap Marina (☎ 928-645-1136), where you can also rent a boat (see the "Watersports" bullet later in this section).

  Bubba's Guide Service (☎ 888-741-2822 or 928-645-3506; www.bubbasguide.com) can lead you to all the prime angling spots, including the tight ones, on sleek, fast bass boats. The price — \$400 for a 9-hour day for the first two people, \$50 each additional person — includes everything except ground transportation and licenses.

- Golfing: The 27-hole Lake Powell National Golf Course, 400 N. Clubhouse Drive (behind the Marriott; ☎ 928-645-2023; www.lakepowellgolf.com), is one of the most stunning places in the state to tee off — the lush, rolling greens contrast with the surrounding red and buff sandstone and startling blue-green lake. Green fees are reasonable, too: \$45 for 18 holes, including cart. Off-season and twilight specials lower rates even more.

- Hiking: Hikes to the major ruins at Navajo National Monument are always offered between Memorial Day and Labor Day, and are usually available in spring and fall. Rangers lead the difficult five-hour treks to Betatakin, departing every morning at 8 in summer, less frequently off-season. These hikes are on a first-come, first-served basis and limited to 25 per group. To get up close and personal with Keet Seel, you need to reserve a backcountry permit and take the 17-mile (round-trip) trek on your own (well, okay, you can go with a friend). This hike, restricted to 20 people a day, is very popular, so call as soon as you know when you're going to visit. Reservations are taken up to two months in advance by the visitor center at Navajo National Monument (☎ 928-672-2366).

  For a shortish hike near Page, you can't do better than Horseshoe Bend. In addition, the Carl Hayden Visitor Center (see the listing for Page/Lake Powell under "Exploring Navajo Nation Northwest," earlier in this chapter, for both) is a great source for trail information, and can tell you which new areas are hikeable as a result of the receding lake levels. You can pick up a map of the 8-mile hiking, biking, and jogging trail that surrounds the mesa on which Page sits at the Page–Lake Powell Chamber of Commerce (for the chamber's address, see the "Fast Facts: Navajo Nation Northwest" section in this chapter).

- River rafting: Open water without the fear, but not without the excitement. From mid-May to mid-September, Wilderness River Adventure, 50 S. Lake Powell Blvd. (☎ 800-528-6154 or 928-645-3279; `www.riveradventures.com`), runs smooth water-rafting trips from Glen Canyon Dam to Lees Ferry. You float along an undeveloped section of the Colorado River past sandstone cliffs and Native American petrogylphs. From mid-May to mid-September, two half-day trips head out at 7:30 a.m. and 1:30 p.m. ($59 adults, $49 ages 12 and under). The weather is too cold for boat floating from November to February but from mid-September to October and March to mid-May, one half-day trip departs at 11 a.m.
- Watersports: Lake Powell is not exactly serene in summer. Every motorized or human-powered contraption you can imagine zips in and out (and sometimes under) every inlet and cove.

If you can't beat the throngs, join 'em at the Wahweap Marina (☎ 928-645-1111) where you can rent your favorite water toy: Sea Doos, which are kind of like water motorcycles ($163–$271 a day, for two people, depending on the season); wakeboards ($39 per day year round); ski tubes ($24); or trampolines ($167). A 14-foot power boat that holds up to five people costs $17 to $28 per hour or $83 to $138 a day; the rate is $41 to $69 per hour and $198–330 per day for a 19-foot craft that holds ten. A one- or two-person kayak runs you from $4–$6 per hour, $15–$25 per day. A two-hour minimum applies on all hourly rentals.

Except for power boats, renting your watersports equipment in town is cheaper. At H2O Zone, 136 6th Avenue (☎ 928-645-3121, `www.powellzone.com`), for example, a Sea Doo will run you $125 per day, year round. But — and it's a big but — the toys are large and you must get them to the water. Still, even adding on the cost of renting a truck from the shop ($45), you can save money in high season.

Shopping for local treasures

Native American crafts, especially those crafts made by the Navajo, are sold all over Page, but you're better off going directly to the source: the reservation. You aren't automatically guaranteed high quality or low prices there, but at least you don't pay extra for a middleman's commission. Also, keep in mind that if you buy from one of the open-air vendors near practically every natural attraction, you don't pay extra for real-estate overhead.

Impromptu outdoor markets are hit and miss. Sometimes you see goods that look (and are) mass-produced from China, other times you find treasures (I once bought a prized and unique key chain at the bottom of the Canyon de Chelly). Bargaining is acceptable; just find the comfort zone between not wanting to be taken advantage of and not being the

Health — check? Car — check?

The Navajo and Hopi reservations are not ideal destinations if you or your wheels aren't in shipshape condition. A few modern medical facilities and up-to-date car repair or parts shops exist, but the region is large and remote, so assistance isn't always quick. For the locations of medical facilities and road-service providers, see also the "Fast Facts" sections in this chapter for Navajo Nation Northwest, Navajo Nation East, and the Hopi Mesas.

one who's taking advantage. Remember, you're likely to pay a lot more for these crafts at home.

In Kayenta, the hotel gift shops carry a good array of Navajo-made items; also, you find a branch of the cooperative Navajo Arts and Crafts Enterprise (☎ 928-697-8611) on Highway 160, east of the intersection with Highway 163 (just beyond the Thriftway supermarket). The gift shop in Navajo National Monument carries items you're not likely to see anywhere else on the reservation, created by Native American artists from all around Arizona and New Mexico, and three historic trading posts still sell interesting crafts; see "Exploring Navajo Nation Northwest," in this chapter for information on all these spots.

Fast Facts: Navajo Nation Northwest

Area Code

Dial **928** for Arizona listings in this chapter; for those in Utah, dial **435.**

ATMs

Page is the best place to find money machines, but Wells Fargo has branches with ATMs in Kayenta and Tuba City.

Emergencies

Call ☎ **911** for fire, police, and ambulance.

Hospitals

Page Hospital, 501 N. Navajo Ave. (☎ **928-645-2424**), is your best bet in case of a medical emergency. On the Navajo reservation, U.S. Public Health Service Indian hospitals in Tuba City (☎ **928-283-2501**) and Kayenta (☎ **928-697-3211**) are available; locate these hospitals via the blue "H" road signs (or ask locally). Only Native Americans get free medical care, but others are welcome to use the hospitals' services; many insurance plans are accepted.

Information

Page/Lake Powell Chamber of Commerce, 644 N. Navajo Dr., Suite B (☎ **888-261-7243** or 928-645-2741; `www.pagelakepowellchamber.org`), open high season Monday through Saturday 9 a.m. to 6 p.m., Sunday 10 a.m. to 6 p.m., shorter hours in winter; or Page's John Wesley Powell Museum and Visitor Center (☎ **888-597-6873** or 928-645-9496; `www.powellmuseum.org`), open Monday through

Friday from 9 to 5 p.m.; closed December 15 through February 15 (call ahead; hours are likely to expand.) For advance information, log on to the Official Navajo Nation Visitor Guide (`discovernavajo.com`).

Internet Access

In Page, you can check your e-mail at DigitalLands, 40 S. Lake Powell Blvd. (☎ **928-645-2241**), for $3 per half-hour.

Police

In Page, call ☎ **911**; in Kayenta, ☎ **928-697-5600**; in Tuba City, ☎ **928-283-3111.**

Post Office

You find a post office in Page at 44 6th Ave. at Elm (☎ **928-645-2571**). On the reservation, ask for the nearest mail depot. In many towns, postal services operate out of convenience stores.

Navajo Nation East

This remote area doesn't have many landmarks or attractions, but those it does have are terrific. In addition to Canyon de Chelly (one of my all-time favorite spots) and the Hubbell Trading Post (a wonderfully preserved and still functioning historic retail hub), this region encompasses Window Rock, the Navajo Nation's capital, and the Four Corners Monument, a place you should visit — once.

You may spend two leisurely days at the Canyon de Chelly — hiking, four-wheeling, horseback riding, and perhaps taking a short side trip to Window Rock — or choose to see the canyon in a very long morning or afternoon by just driving along one of the two rim routes. The Four Corners Monument isn't on the way to anywhere in Arizona, so you need to detour to get there (unless you're heading to Colorado). The Hubbell Trading Post, on the other hand, is en route to almost everywhere you're likely to visit, requiring just a few miles of backtracking. All in all, if you're on the move, you may cover the entire area comfortably in about 1½ days. Plan to spend the night near Canyon de Chelly, not only because the area is beautiful, but also because it offers the nicest lodgings on the Navajo reservation.

Getting there

If you come from the north (from around Monument Valley), take Highway 160 east. The distance from Kayenta to Mexico Water is 40 miles. Turn south onto Highway 199 and drive 60 miles to reach Chinle, the closest town to Canyon de Chelly. (Alternatively, keep going another 40-odd miles on Highway 160 beyond Mexico Water and you arrive at the Four Corners Monument. If you're thinking of going there, now's the time!) You journey another 30 miles south on Highway 191 from Chinle to the Highway 264 turnoff to reach Ganado, home of the Hubbell Trading Post. This stretch is actually a 6-mile interruption in Highway 191, which you take south another 38 miles to get to I-40.

The intersection of Highway 191 and I-40 is 140 miles east of Flagstaff. If you approach via the southern I-40 route, just follow these instructions backward. (You won't discover any hidden references to Satan if you repeat them at high speed, I promise.)

Spending the night

The best place to hole up in this part of Arizona is around Chinle. The accommodations aren't fancy, but they're very pleasant, and you wake up in or very near to the wonderful Canyon de Chelly. In addition to their various amenities, all the hotels in Chinle offer tours desks.

Around Window Rock (see the "More cool things to see and do" section later in this chapter), you find the modest Navajo Nation Inn ($), 48 W. Hwy. 264 at Highway 12 (☎ 800-662-6189 or 928-871-4108, www.navajonationinn.com), which is clean and reasonably efficient, and a newer, better equipped Day's Inn (see the Appendix for the toll-free number).

Best Western Canyon de Chelly Inn

$ Chinle

The farthest from the canyon of the three hotels recommended here (but still less than 4 miles from the park entrance) and without much distinct character, this motel compensates with an indoor pool, sauna, and hot tub; an on-site bakery; and rooms that have a bit of Southwest flair. The Junction Café is a local hangout, and features a small Code Talker display (see the "Hogans' [that's hoh-gahns] heroes" sidebar).

On Indian Route 7, about ¼ mile east of the junction with Highway 191. ***☎ 800-327-0354*** *or 928-674-5875. Fax: 928-674-3715.* www.canyondechelly.com. *Rack rates: May–Oct $99 double, Nov–April $69 double. AE, DISC, MC, V.*

Holiday Inn Canyon de Chelly

$$ Chinle

Built in 1992, this Holiday Inn holds on to a bit of Old West history: The main lobby incorporates the trading post built on this site in the 1880s. The hotel restaurant and gift shop go way beyond generic, too. Rooms, on the other hand, are pastel bland, but have all the modern requisites. The hotel sometimes hosts outdoor music and dance performances, and although you're not inside the park, you're actually closer to the start of both rim drives than you are at the Thunderbird Lodge.

Indian Route 7, about 3 miles east of the junction with Highway 191 (½ mile from the park entrance). ***☎ 800-23-HOTEL*** *or 928-674-5000. Fax: 928-674-8264.* www.ichotelgroups.com. *Rack rates: May–Aug $94–$114 double, Sept–April $79–$99 double. AE, DC, DISC, MC, V.*

The Thunderbird Lodge

$$ Canyon de Chelly

You have it all here — history, nature, and shopping. The only roofed bunk within the park's boundaries, this one-time trading post sits nestled in a

Oh, give me a hogan

Staying in a hogan is camping raised to an art — and cultural — form. You sleep in a traditional six-sided log, dirt, and cement structure with a small hole in the center (in Manhattan, it's called a skylight). Smoke from a wood-burning stove escapes through the opening. You glimpse the stars while you're lying on a cot, sleeping bag, or sheepskins. (Sorry, no indoor plumbing — another reason this experience is like camping.)

Coyote Pass Hospitality (☎ **928-724-3383**; www.navajocentral.org/cppage.htm) introduced this type of accommodation to the Navajo reservation in the 1990s. Among the three hogans offered by Coyote Pass to guests is one at Tsaile, not far from the Canyon de Chelly. In recent years, various other Navajo concessionaires, including **Simpson's Trailhandler's Tours** (☎ **435-727-3362**; www.trailhandlerstours.com) at Monument Valley, have jumped on the stay-in-a-hogan bandwagon. Ceremonies and tours of the area may be bundled with these accommodations in a "Native experience" package. For information about other Navajo B&Bs, contact **Largo Navajoland Tours** (☎ **888-726-9084**; www.navajolandtours.com). Expect to pay anything from $85 per person for lodging and breakfast alone to $150 per person with dinner and tour options.

lovely cottonwood grove. Rooms, in pink pueblo-style buildings, are updated rustic with all modern amenities. Other perks include a great gift shop and a Navajo rug–draped dining room in the original 1896 building.

Off Indian Route 7 (South Rim Drive), inside Canyon de Chelly (about ½ mile southwest of the visitor center). ☎ ***800-679-2473*** *or 928-674-5841. Fax: 928-674-5844.* www.tbirdlodge.com. *Rack rates: Apr–Oct $106–$111 double, $151 suite; Nov–May $75 double, $96 suite. AE, DC, DISC, MC, V.*

Dining locally

You don't find much in the way of fine dining in this region, but you enjoy lots of local flavor around the Canyon de Chelly. (Remember that the Navajo Nation bans alcohol.) Food in the Thunderbird Lodge restaurant ($–$$) — the original trading post building lined with old photos — is served cafeteria style, which works well if you're a vegetarian, because you get a nice choice of side dishes and desserts (it also hastens the food acquisition process, which can be slow in the area's other eateries). Garcia's ($$) in the Holiday Inn is the closest this area comes to fine dining, with Navajo-inspired dishes such as blue-corn-breaded trout offered along with American standards. Locals, who have little other choice, except for a few fast-food places, frequent both of these restaurants. The low-key Junction Café at the Best Western, serving decent American, Mexican, and Navajo coffee-shop grub, gets the lunch and breakfast townie regulars. You'll be hard pressed to spend more than $10 here.

Fans of Tony Hillerman's mysteries may want to check out the restaurant in Window Rock's Navajo Nation Inn, where fictional Navajo police detectives Joe Leaphorn and Jim Chee drink endless cups of coffee. The standard American/Navajo fare is pretty good.

If you buy a snack from one of the vendors near the Four Corners Monument (corn dogs or fry bread, for example), you can pig out in four states. Now you can't say I never tell you how to have a good time!

Exploring Navajo Nation East

You should find something to satisfy your interests here, whether you crave rug buying, canyon hiking, or splaying yourself around four states.

The top attractions

Canyon de Chelly National Monument

Chinle

The Grand Canyon (see Chapter 17) is, well, grander, but cold and remote compared with the softer, more accessible grace of these gorges. In the Blessing Way ceremony, the Navajo speak of walking in beauty. Those words often come to my mind when I visit the Canyon de Chelly (de-shay) and gaze at the soaring red sandstone cliffs rising from canyon floors laced with gently flowing streams and dotted with cottonwoods. In addition to its natural allures, the area is also rich in culture. Many dwellings and petroglyphs of the ancestral Puebloans are found here, as are sites important to the Navajo, who resisted relocation by the U.S. Military by holing up at the canyon's Fortress Rock. The Navajos still farm and graze sheep on the canyon floor. A bonus: Inviting as the area is, it's relatively uncrowded.

You may choose from two rim drives: a 37-mile round-trip South Rim drive with seven dramatic overlooks into the Canyon de Chelly (the name of one of the three gorges that meet here, as well as the name of the national monument); and a 34-mile North Rim drive with four vistas overlooking the adjoining Canyon del Muerto. Both drives branch off from the same road (Highway 64/Indian Route 7) just beyond the visitor center. The South Rim drive takes at least two hours when you add in the time you spend gazing from each viewpoint. Because the North Rim drive has fewer viewpoints, the drive's a bit shorter; you can cover it in about 1½ hours.

Have time for only one? If you're most interested in the vistas, choose the South Rim drive with spectacular overlooks like Spider Rock. The North Rim, with sites such as Antelope House and Massacre Cave, is ideal for history buffs. Get details on both routes from the visitor center, where you can also check out the available activities, such as the ranger talks given in the hogan.

The only unescorted hike you may take into the Canyon de Chelly is on the 2½-mile round-trip White House Ruin trail, which leads from the White House overlook on the South Rim to the White House Ruin. It's a moderately difficult trek, with a winding descent of 600 feet to the canyon floor, where you can see a two-level ancestral Puebloan cliff dwelling dating back to around A.D. 1060.

For other hikes, as well as horseback rides and Jeep tours, you need a Navajo guide (see the "Guided tours" section later in this chapter).

See map p. 399. At Indian Route 7 and Highway 64 (3 miles east of Highway191). ☎ ***928-674-5500;*** www.nps.gov/cach. *Admission: Free. The visitor center is open daily Oct–Apr 8 a.m.–5 p.m., May–Sept 8 a.m.–6 p.m. except Christmas You may drive along the paved canyon rims any time, weather permitting — you just don't see anything in the dark.*

Hubbell Trading Post National Historic Site

Near Ganado

I'm happy when I can merge two of my prime interests — history and retail — so I'm in hog heaven here. John Lorenzo Hubbell purchased this trading post in 1878, and the Hubbell family operated it until 1967, when the family sold it to the National Park Service. Although not-for-profit now and managed by trader Bill Malone, the post still looks (and works) much the same as it did a century ago.

You can browse Southwest crafts of all types here, but the specialty is Navajo rugs, both new and antique. Unless you're planning on buying a rug, which can take half the day, you'll probably spend more time here in summer, when lots of events are slated, than in winter. Call ahead — especially during the off-season — to get a schedule for the Hubbell home tours, weaving demonstrations, lectures, or tours of the 160-acre grounds. All the activities are interesting — and free. A 30-minute house tour plus the standard amount of rug and craft ogling takes about 1 to 1½ hours.

See map p. 399. One mile west of Ganado, on Highway 264. ☎ ***928-755-3475.*** www.nps.gov/hutr. *Admission: Free. Open: Daily summer 8 a.m.–6 p.m., winter 8 a.m.–5 p.m. Closed Thanksgiving, Christmas, and New Year's Day. Tours of the Hubbell home are given on the hour (usually every hour) during the summer, less frequently in winter.*

More cool things to see and do

A couple of oddities — one natural, one man-made — may also be of interest.

- Get a window on Navajoland. Window Rock is the hole-y sandstone cliff that gave the Navajo Nation's capital its name. Find the formation 2 miles north of Highway 264, near the government administration center. Besides this sandstone cliff, take time to see the modern Navajo Nation Museum, at Highway 264 and Post Office Loop Road (☎ 928-871-7941). The museum is still a work in progress as the permanent collections evolve and expand. Expect to see everything from historic photographs to contemporary Navajo art. Admission: Free. Open: Mon 8 a.m–5 p.m., Tues–Fri 8 a.m.–8 p.m., Sat 9 a.m.–5 p.m. See map p. 399.

- Survey a cartographic quirk. Did you know that Native Americans own the piece of the United States where Arizona, New Mexico, Utah, and Colorado meet? Officially called Four Corners Monument Navajo Tribal Park, ¼ mile north of Highway 160 (6 miles beyond the Highway 164 junction at Teec Nos Pos; ☎ 928-871-6647), the site isn't much more than a bronze plaque on a concrete slab with four state seals, but you have to come, if only to see people splay their arms and legs in awkward positions in order to be photographed in four states — and to get yourself snapped in a similarly compromising pose. You find snack and souvenir stands here and also restrooms (you'll be literally relieved because by the time you arrive at this site you'll have been driving around the middle of nowhere for ages). Admission: $3. Open: May–mid-Aug daily 7 a.m.–7 p.m., late Aug–Apr 8 a.m.–5 p.m.; closed Thanksgiving, Christmas, New Year's day. See map p. 399.

Guided tours

All the following guided activities take place in the Canyon de Chelly. Also check out the "Exploring Navajo Nation East" section for information on guided tours of the Hubbell Trading Post.

Be sure to reserve all these tours ahead of time. In summer, tours fill up fast, and in winter, many tours operate only if a minimum number of people sign on.

- Hiking: On all Canyon de Chelly hikes, except the White House Ruin trail, a Navajo guide is required. At the visitor center (☎ 928-674-5500), you find members of the Tsegi Guide Association, who take you (and 14 others, max) trekking for $15 per person, per hour (minimum of 3 hours). Destinations depend on your interests and the hiking ability of the group. Sometimes you get to view the canyon's rock art; other times you may follow the Tunnel Trail to see a ruin.

  Don't be macho (or macha). If you don't hike much, make that clear to your guide. A hike that is easy for your guide, who may run up and down the canyon to visit relatives routinely, may be very difficult for you. If you have a fear of heights (or, more accurately, edges), discuss that concern, too. (I didn't think to ask, and I found myself terrified by the sheer rock ledges involved in the descent.)

- Four- (or six-) wheel tours: The Thunderbird Lodge (see the "Spending the night" section earlier in this chapter) runs tours of the canyon in six-wheel-drive flatbed trucks outfitted with padded seats. A full-day version of these tours is available from spring to late fall, road conditions permitting ($65 adults and children, including lunch). Half-day tours are available year-round, departing at 9 a.m. and 2 p.m., depending on the season ($40 adults, $31 children under 12).

  De Chelly Tours (☎ 928-674-3772 or 674-5000; `www.dechellytours.com`) offers a variety of four-wheel excursions into the

Native American etiquette: Some reservation do's and don'ts

Forgive me if you think I'm stating the obvious, but you may be surprised how many people seem to leave their manners — and sense — back home.

- **Don't enter a home uninvited.** How would you feel if someone wandered into your living room or knocked on your door, asking for a tour?
- **Don't enter any areas marked off-limits.** In addition, stay on designated trails or routes unless a Native American tour guide accompanies you. Driving or hiking back roads or trails on your own is forbidden.
- **Don't litter.**
- **Don't bring alcohol, drugs, or firearms onto the reservation.**
- **Observe outdoor as well as indoor privacy.** On the Navajo reservation, ask for permission to photograph, videotape, sketch, or audiotape any event or person. (If you are granted permission, you're expected to tip the grantee a dollar or two.) On the Hopi reservation, no photography and other types of reproduction — either personal or commercial — are allowed. Period.
- **Make sure your attendance at a ceremony is permitted.** Just because an event is held outside doesn't necessarily mean that it's open to the public. And if you're granted permission to attend, stand politely in the back unless you're invited to do otherwise. (Imagine attending an outdoor wedding where strangers shove in front of the immediate family to get a better view of the ceremony.) And don't applaud.

canyon. Tours cost $125 for three hours in a Jeep Wrangler that holds three passengers (plus a guide) and $150 (for the first four people) to $175 (for five to seven people) for an eight-person capacity vehicle. In all cases, an additional $30 per hour (per vehicle) is charged if you want to tour longer than three hours. These tours, which include Antelope House and the White House Ruin, depart twice daily in high season, less frequently in winter.

Similar Jeep tours with similar rates are run by the similarly named Canyon de Chelly Tours; they can be booked at the gift shop of the Holiday Inn (see the "Spending the night" section earlier in this chapter) or by contacting the company directly at ☎ 928-674-5433 or `www.canyondechellytours.com`. Three-hour tours in a Unimog army truck that cost $47 per person ($32 for children) theoretically depart twice daily, but these tours operate only if all 12 spaces are filled.

You still must follow a Navajo leader if you drive your own all-terrain vehicle, but the tour is less expensive. Canyon de Chelly and De Chelly Tours and the Tsegi Guide Association (see the "Hiking" bullet earlier in this list) lead you (and up to four more vehicles) for $15 to $20 per hour (three-hour minimum).

- Horseback tours: Justin's Horse Rental, South Rim Drive near the park entrance (☎ 928-674-5678), and Totsonni Ranch, South Rim Drive 1.3 miles east of the Spider Rock turnoff, where the pavement ends (☎ 928-755-6209; www.totsoniiranch.com), both charge $10 per person horse rental, plus an additional $15 per hour charge for the guide. Rides generally run from two to six hours, although overnight pack trips are available, too.

Shopping for local treasures

You don't have to go beyond the area's two main attractions to shop. At the Canyon de Chelly, the Thunderbird Lodge and the Holiday Inn run excellent gift shops; the latter is smaller, but has some unusual, high-quality pieces. And although rugs are its specialty, you can find pretty much any type of craft you're looking for at the Hubbell Trading Post. If you're visiting Window Rock, check out the Navajo Arts & Crafts Enterprise, Highway 264 and Route 12 (☎ 928-871-4090), and the gift shop at the Navajo Nation Museum (see "More cool things to see and do" section earlier in this chapter), which has a huge collection of Native American tapes and CDs that you may listen to before you buy.

Fast Facts: Navajo Nation East

Area Code

Dial **928** for Arizona listings in this chapter; for those in Utah, dial **435.**

ATMs

Page is the best place to find money machines, but Wells Fargo has branches with ATMs in Kayenta and Tuba City.

Emergencies

Call ☎ **911** for fire, police, and ambulance.

Hospitals

A hospital is available in Chinle (☎ **928-674-7001**), but Sage Memorial Hospital in nearby Ganado (☎ **928-755-3411**) has better facilities.

Information

The visitor center of the Canyon de Chelly and the Hubbell Trading Post are your best resources. In Window Rock, the Navajo Nation Visitor Center in the Navajo Nation Museum is open Monday–Friday 8 a.m.–5 p.m. For all three locations, see the "Exploring Navajo Nation East" section earlier in this chapter.

Police

In Chinle, call ☎ **928-674-2111** or 928-674-2112; in Window Rock, call ☎ **928-871-6113** or 871-6114.

The Hopi Mesas

Navajo land entirely surrounds the small Hopi reservation, but the size of their real-estate holdings isn't the only thing that distinguishes the two nations. The Navajo, who migrated from Canada in the 15th century, are relative newcomers to this area, whereas ancestors of the Hopi have been in the Four Corners region since prehistoric times. The Hopi established the village of Old Oraibi in the 12th century, when upstart settlements like Boston or even St. Augustine, Florida, weren't even gleams in European explorers' eyes.

The Hopi reservation has no Safeways, McDonald's, or Holiday Inns. One of the villages, Walpi, isn't even wired for electricity. And, although the pueblos (villages) and the three mesas on which they perch are picturesque, they offer few natural or archaeological attractions. Why come here, then? For a glimpse of an ancient culture's living traditions.

Tourism is a mixed blessing for the Hopi, simultaneously an economic necessity and, at times, a pain in the neck (see the "Native American etiquette: Some reservation do's and don'ts" sidebar earlier in this chapter).

Strolling around the villages and browsing the shops takes you no more than a half to a full day. The one hotel on the reservation isn't exactly hopping after dark. If you're up for a peaceful evening, spend the night; otherwise, make the Hopi mesas a day visit.

Getting there

Highway 264, which extends from Tuba City to the Arizona/New Mexico border, links the Hopi reservation with the outside world, Highway 191 is its easternmost link. The southern roads connecting Highway 264 with I-40 are Highway 77 (just east of Holbrook); Highway 87 (at Winslow); Highway 99; and Indian Route 15 (both Hwy. 99 and Indian Route 15 hook up with Indian Route 2 at Leupp).

If you're en route from (or to) Flagstaff, Indian Route 15 to Indian Route 2 is a scenic shortcut that takes you right into the heart of Hopi land, between the Second and Third Mesas.

In addition to linking the Hopi reservation with the outside world, Highway 264 is also the route you take through it; the road runs through the entire Hopi reservation, from Keams Canyon on the east to Moenkopi on the west; all the small, unnamed roads that lead to the three Hopi mesas branch off from Highway 264.

Spending the night

To say your choice of lodgings is limited is an understatement; the reservation offers one motel, period. If you don't choose to bed down there, your next best bet is Winslow (see "Staying the night" in the "Along Old Route 66" section later in this chapter), some 70 miles away.

The Hopi Cultural Center Motel

$$ Second Mesa

How can you resist a motel that lists as its location "the Center of the Universe?" The hotel is definitely at the center of the Hopi tourist world, with the best restaurant on the reservation (see the following "Dining locally" section), a museum that doubles as an informal visitor center, and the only lodging available. The guest rooms are modest but clean, and have some nice Native American design touches, as well as TVs and phones.

On the north side of Highway 264, west of the junction with Highway 87. ☎ ***928-734-2401.*** *Fax: 928-734-6651.* `www.psv.com/hopi.html`. *Rack rates: March 15–Oct 15 $95–100 double, Oct 16–March 14 $65–$70 double. AE, DC, DISC, MC, V.*

Dining locally

In the Keams Canyon shopping center, a coffee shop dishes out burgers, sandwiches, and Native American dinner fare (although the fry bread pileup isn't called a Navajo taco here, as it is elsewhere). But unless you're really hungry, best hold out for the Hopi Cultural Center restaurant ($) on Second Mesa. There, you find everything from BLTs to Philly cheese steaks on the menu, but go for the local dishes such as Nöqkwivi (a lamb and hominy stew served with green chiles), which comes with blue-corn fry bread.

Remember, no alcohol is permitted on the Hopi reservation.

Exploring the Hopi Mesas

Most of the Hopi villages cluster on three mesas that are about 10 miles apart from each other and which extend, fingerlike, from the huge Black Mesa to the north. The town of Moenkopi, 40 miles west of Third Mesa, and Keams Canyon, an administrative center 15 miles east of First Mesa, offer little to interest the visitor.

Although physically close, the three mesa villages have different histories and governing bodies. You can't necessarily expect someone on Third Mesa to give you information about First Mesa. You can stroll around all the villages except Walpi — accessible by guided tour only — but you don't find bronze "HISTORIC LANDMARK" plaques on the old houses and small shops (nor do you find signs with town names, for that matter). Don't worry, getting lost isn't a problem; each mesa has only one road, and you can figure a cluster of houses is a village. Be courteous and park outside the towns, not on the narrow streets.

Make your first stop at the Hopi Cultural Center on Second Mesa, where you're introduced to Hopi traditions and can browse the posted notices about the events on the different mesas. After that, drive over to Walpi on First Mesa for one of the daily tours and finish off with a stroll around Old Oraibi on Third Mesa. Alternatively, if you want to arrive in time for lunch at the Hopi Cultural Center, begin your day with the Walpi tour, a good initiation into Hopi culture. Perhaps the best — if most expensive — option is to book an individual guide (see the "Guided tours" section later in this chapter) before you arrive. Hopi is far more difficult than the Navajo reservation for outsiders to enjoy unassisted. Without guidance, it's easy to leave here as mystified as you were before you arrived — and to miss interesting archaeological sights that are otherwise off-limits to visitors.

The Hopi are renowned for their elaborate religious ceremonial dances — but don't be disappointed if you don't get to see one. Because of visitors' disrespectful behavior in the past, the famous snake dances are completely barred to outsiders, and access to the katsina dances is restricted; only katsina dances on Second and Third mesas are occasionally open to non-Native Americans now.

Katsina dances are very elaborate, colorful religious ceremonies, with masked and costumed dancers representing the katsina spirits. The Hopi hold the dances most weekends from December to July, but even the locals don't know until a day or two in advance exactly where and when these dances occur. If you're determined to see a dance, your best bet is to show up on a weekend during katsina season, find out if a dance is scheduled, and ask permission to attend. (And if you do get to go, behave yourself!)

First Mesa

At the foot of First Mesa you find Polacca, a town founded in the late 1800s as an offshoot of Walpi. Walpi is the most interesting of this mesa's towns, both for its old sandstone homes and its amazing views. Established on the side of the mesa as early as A.D. 900, Walpi moved to the hilltop for protection purposes after the 1680 Pueblo Revolt against the Spanish. The steep road that snakes up to Walpi also passes Sichomovi and Hano/Tewa, both established after the 1680 revolt, the former by the people of Walpi, the latter by two successive groups of non-Hopi Puebloan peoples.

Second Mesa

The Hopi Cultural Center Museum, on the north side of Highway 264, about 5 miles west of the junction with Highway 87 (☎ 928-734-6650), is the main draw of Second Mesa. The museum is open Monday to Friday from 8 a.m. to 5 p.m. (admission $3). The oldest village on the mesa is Shungopavi, which lies to the south of Highway 264, on the road west of the Hopi Cultural Center. Sipolauvi and Mishongnovi, on a paved road that heads north from Highway 264 just east of the cultural center, were both created soon after the 1680 Pueblo Revolt. You see the Corn Rock shrine, a natural monument, just below the edge of the mesa in Mishongnovi.

Third Mesa

Old Oraibi, founded around 1100, claims to be the oldest continuously occupied town in the United States. You see the ruins of a Spanish mission, as well as several ancient houses intermingled with newer ones.

(If you plan to wander around, you may want to do the locals the courtesy of politely introducing yourself at the shop called Hamana so'oh, which is an informal visitor center.) All the other Third Mesa towns derive from Old Oraibi: Hotelvilla was formed after an internal clan schism in 1906; Bacavi was a 1907 offshoot of Hotelvilla; and Kykmostmovi, at the base of the mesa, was founded soon afterward by villagers who wanted to be closer to the main road. Kykmostmovi is the home to the Hopi Tribal offices (see the "Fast Facts: The Hopi Mesas" section later in this chapter). Although 40 miles to the northwest, Moenkopi is also a satellite town of Oraibi and considered part of Third Mesa.

Guided tours

Guided walking tours of Walpi on First Mesa run from 30 to 45 minutes and are given daily between 9 a.m. and 5 p.m. in summer, 9:30 a.m. and 4 p.m. in winter, except when religious ceremonies are being held ($8 adults, $5 ages 5–17). No set starting times are scheduled for the walks; tour guides wait at the First Mesa Visitor Center in Sichomovi (☎ 928-737-2262) — just keep driving up the hill until you see the sign for the center — until about ten people gather or until the guides determine that no one else is going to turn up.

On the tour, the guides ask whether you want to visit any artisans' houses. You may decline but, if you say yes, you're under no obligation to buy anything. However, you may have a tough time walking away empty-handed, especially because many of the artists are poor. Don't let guilt be your guide. If you don't like what you see at the first home, you're bound to find something you really want to purchase later.

Bertram Tsavadawa, an Oraibi native, tours visitors around his village and around a petroglyph site called Dawa Park. He charges $15 per person per hour, and the excursions generally take around two hours. Leave a message for him at ☎ 928-734-9544 or call him on his cellphone at ☎ 928-306-7849. The guided tours run by Gary Tso at Left Handed Hunter (☎ 928-734-2567; E-mail: `lhhunter58@hotmail.com`) are more extensive — and accordingly more expensive, starting from $125 for two people for a half day tour that includes a visit to a Hopi artist and a tour of Old Oraibi and the petroglyphs.

Shopping for local treasures

Many of the shops on the Hopi mesas are literally mom-and-pop operations: Residents sell crafts out of their homes (look for signs that say something like, "Pottery sold here"). Log on to `www.hopimarket.com` for a preview of goods and prices. See also Chapter 19 for information on Hopi katsina dolls and overlay silverwork.

Among the more traditional shops, my favorite is Tsakurshovi, Second Mesa (1½ miles east of the Hopi Cultural Center on Highway 264; ☎ 928-734-2478), with a great collection of high-quality and unusual crafts. The staff is extremely knowledgeable — and this shop is the only place to find owner Janet Day's original "Don't Worry, Be Hopi" T-shirts and bumper stickers. Look for the blue signs to locate Hopi Market, on Highway 264 between First and Second Mesas (☎ 928-737-9434; `www.hopimarket.com`); if you don't find it, you can always order from its excellent selection of silver inlay jewelry and other crafts on line. The Hopi Silver Crafts Cooperative, just west of the Hopi Cultural Center (☎ 928-734-2463), has a large selection of belt buckles, jewelry, and other decorative items. A non-Hopi business but owned by traders long respected on the reservation, McGee's Indian Art in Keams Canyon (☎ 928-738-2295) is a good place to shop for katsina dolls and other crafts.

Fast Facts: The Hopi Mesas

Area Code

The area code on the Hopi reservation is **928.**

Hospitals

The 24-hour Hopi Health Care Center, on Hwy. 64 between First and Second Mesas (**☎ 928-739-2211**), administers basic health care and stabilizes emergency cases, who are usually evacuated to hospitals in Flagstaff or Phoenix.

Information

The Hopi Tribal Council (**☎ 928-734-3000** [main switchboard]) and the Hopi Cultural Preservation Office (**☎ 928-734-2244,** 734-6636) are both in Kykotsmovi on Third Mesa. The official Hopi Web site is `www.hopi.nsn.us`.

Police

Call **☎ 928-734-3700** (Hopi police) or 928-738-2233 (Bureau of Indian Affairs Police) for emergencies. For nonemergencies, **☎ 928-738-2234.**

Along Old Route 66

When you drive the stretch of I-40 that borders southern American Indian country from its intersection with Highway 191 to its eastern approach to Flagstaff, the journey itself — or, more precisely, the road — is the attraction. With the exception of Petrified Forest National Park and Meteor Crater Natural Landmark, this area's main draw is old Route 66, which runs roughly parallel to I-40, the highways that bypassed the road in 1965.

The first highway stretching from Chicago to California, Route 66 represented the lure of the West to many. John Steinbeck dubbed this early freeway the "Mother Road." Lined with neon signs and classic kitsch storefronts, Route 66 embodies tourism nostalgia.

The region's two main towns, Holbrook and Winslow, straddle Old Route 66, and make good, economical bases for exploring American Indian Country (in Holbrook, Route 66 is called Hopi Drive; in Winslow, the Mother Road goes under the name 2nd Street).

You may cover this area in a single day if you just want to hit the main sights, but Winslow's La Posada Hotel (see the "Spending the night" section later in this chapter) is itself a good reason to make this an overnight stay.

You're off the reservations here. All the usual rules apply.

Getting there

Pretty much everything you want to see in this area is off an I-40 exit ramp. See "The Hopi Mesas," earlier in this chapter, for the roads that feed into I-40 from the north.

From Phoenix, Highway 87, the old Beeline Highway, is the most direct route northeast to Winslow. This scenic road, which winds through the piney White Mountains, is not for the faint-of-heart in some stretches. If you take Highway 87, be sure to stop at Tonto Natural Bridge State Park.

Route 66 was also a major rail route for the old Atcheson, Santa Fe, and Topeka line, and Amtrak (☎ 800-872-7245; www.amtrak.com) now stops at the original station in Winslow, next door to the terrific La Posada Hotel. Prefer the bus? Greyhound (☎ 800-231-2222; www.greyhound.com) offers service from Phoenix to Winslow. If you arrive by train or bus, you may rent a car at Winslow Ford (☎ 928-289-3354).

Spending the night

Motel franchises replaced most of the funky Route 66 lodgings in Holbrook and Winslow, although some great old neon signs announce some not so great (I suspect) old rooms for $19.99 per night. The chains in Holbrook include two Best Westerns, Budget Inn, Comfort Inn, Day's Inn, Econo Lodge, Holiday Inn Express, Motel 6, Ramada Limited, and Super 8. In Winslow, Best Western, Day's Inn, Econo Lodge, Holiday Inn Express, Super 8, and Travelodge are available. See the Appendix for the chains' toll-free numbers.

The towns are only about 25 minutes from one another, so your choice may depend on which of the following two lodgings appeals most to you (though there's a bit more to do in Holbrook).

La Posada

$–$$ Winslow

Charles Lindbergh and Clark Gable were among the glitterati who bunked at this grand Spanish rancho–style hotel, which Mary Colter designed in 1930 for the Santa Fe Railway (see Chapter 17). The individually decorated rooms (several with fireplaces), gardens, and ornately detailed lobby have been beautifully restored, and the place just keeps getting better and better. Fast becoming a destination for far-flung history buffs, La Posada also draws locals to its excellent restaurant (see the following "Dining locally" section), retro-chic martini lounge, and great gift shop. And La Posada is a bargain; it's tough to get this much character for these prices anywhere else.

*303 E. 2nd St. at Highway 87. ☎ **928-289-4366.** Fax: 928-289-3873.* www.laposada.org. *Rack rates: $89–$109 double, $99–$129 deluxe theme rooms and suites. Complimentary continental breakfast on Mon when restaurant is closed. AE, DC, DISC, MC, V.*

Wigwam Village Motel

$ Holbrook

A Route 66 classic, this 1940s holdover has small, pointed-ceiling units — but what do you expect when you sleep in a wigwam? The rooms are inexpensive, cheerful, and clean, and each one is fronted by a classic car. You won't have a phone, but you can tune in to cable TV.

*811 W. Hopi Dr. ☎ **928-524-3048.*** www.galerie-kokopelli.com/wigwam. ***Rack rates: $42–$48 double. MC, V.***

Dining locally

You don't have a lot of options, but fans of down-home Mexican food will be happy in Holbrook, while gourmands have a great getaway in Winslow. I haven't had a chance to eat at Holbrook's Butterfield Stage Co. ($$–$$$), 609 W. Hopi Dr. (☎ 928-524-3447), but I like the Old West atmosphere and hear the steak is good. Plenty of fast-food places are available in both towns, so finding kiddie eats is no problem.

Romo's Cafe

$ Holbrook MEXICAN

This down-home Mexican restaurant — in a building constructed in 1931 as a Chevron station — benefits from Holbrook's proximity to New Mexico: Many of the combination plates offer a choice of tasty red or green chile sauces and come with sopaipillas (delicious puffy fried bread) on the side. If, like me, you love generously portioned Mexican food with a bit of a kick at low prices, you'll be in heaven.

*121 W. Hopi Dr. ☎ **928-524-2153.** Reservations not needed. Combination plates: $6–$10. AE, MC, V. Open: 10 a.m.–8 p.m. Mon–Sat.*

The Turquoise Room

$$–$$$$ Winslow AMERICAN/SOUTHWEST

A foodie outpost in northern Arizona, the rustic elegant dining room at La Posada (see the preceding "Spending the night" section) is by no means elitist. You can get duded up and enjoy the likes of filet mignon or chile cherry duckling, or come casual with the family and chow down on a cheeseburger. Whatever you order, start with the signature cream of corn swirled with black bean chile soup: It's a knockout.

*La Posada Hotel, 303 E. 2nd St. at Highway 87. ☎ **928-289-2888.** Dinner reservations suggested on high season weekends. Main courses: $12–$24. AE, DC, DISC, MC, V. Open: Breakfast, lunch (seasonally), and dinner Tues–Sun; closed Mon.*

Exploring along Old Route 66

Although the road is the main attraction, you also have a few good reasons to use the exit ramps.

The top attractions

Holbrook

You come to this classic Route 66 town, with one of the country's few remaining wigwam motel courts (see the "Spending the night" section earlier in this chapter), miles of neon, and towering dinosaur replicas on its main drag, to ogle the kitsch and browse the shops selling rocks, petrified wood, and Mother Road-o-bilia (see the "Shopping for local treasures" section later in this chapter). The town's one real sight is, conveniently, also its visitor center: a free historical museum in the 1898 Navajo County Courthouse, containing replicas of an early drugstore/soda fountain and a jail cell replete with prisoner graffiti. The courthouse is also the place to pick up a free self-guided-tour pamphlet detailing the other historical buildings in Holbrook. On summer weekday nights, Indian dances are performed in front of the courthouse from 6:30 to 8:30 p.m.

Holbrook Chamber of Commerce, Old West Courthouse: 100 E. Arizona. ☎ ***800-524-2459*** *or 928-524-6558.* `www.ci.holbrook.az.us`. *Open Mon–Fri 8 a.m.–5 p.m., Sat–Sun 8 a.m.–4 p.m., closed Christmas.*

Meteor Crater

West of Winslow

I find it annoying that this privately owned hole-in-the-ground is fronted by a cheesy rock shop and costs $12 to see. But nowhere else do you get such a graphic view of what could — and did — happen if a meteorite were to strike Earth. Talk about deep impact: The mega-million-ton hunk of rock that hurtled down at a speed of 45,000 mph about 50,000 years ago left a hole 570 feet deep and wide enough to fit 20 football fields. NASA used this place to test moonwalks, as the films and exhibits at the museum and visitor center show. You can't enter the crater but you may take a 45-minute-long guided hike along the rim trail (daily 9:15 a.m.–2 p.m., weather permitting) and peer at the crater through telescopes.

See map p. 399. 20 miles west of Winslow (Exit 233 of I-40). ☎ ***800-289-5898*** *or 928-289-2362.* `www.meteorcrater.com`. *Admission: $12 adults, $11 seniors (over 60), $6 ages 6–17, 5 and under free. Open: Daily, Memorial Day–Labor Day 7 a.m.–7 p.m., rest of the year 8 a.m.–5 p.m.; closed Christmas.*

Petrified Forest National Park

East and souteast of Holbrook

Reality check: Don't expect to see a turned-to-stone version of Redwood National Forest (like I did the first time I visited). The petrified wood is in

You wooden, wood you?

Despite the posted warnings and the testimonials from people who claim that cadging wood from the Petrified Forest ruined their lives — check out the wonderful collection of cautionary "I've been hexed" letters in the Rainbow Forest Museum's "Guilt Book" — some 12 tons of fossilized wood are stolen from the Petrified Forest every year. Resist the temptation. You can buy as much hard wood as you like in Holbrook, hex-free.

log form and it's laying on the ground. And, although this park has magnificent vistas of the Painted Desert at its north end, this area isn't the only place that offers you views of that multihued sandstone wonderland. The Painted Desert begins east of the Grand Canyon; if you come from that direction, you experience great stretches of it.

That said, if you leave behind unreasonable expectations, you should enjoy this 93,500-acre park, as remarkable for its past as for its present. At the Rainbow Forest Museum and Visitor Center, you see vestiges of the days when the park was a forest primeval roamed by dinosaurs. "Gertie," an ancestor of the tyrannosaurus, about the size of a crocodile, is one of the three, kid-pleasing, Triassic period dino skeletons on display, along with fossils of other animals and plants. The area's human history, dating back more than 2,000 years, is evident at sites like Newspaper Rock, with its large concentration of petroglyphs, and the Puerco Pueblo, home to many rock artists until A.D. 1400. And the Painted Desert Inn, built in 1924 and a favorite spot for motorists tooling Route 66, is slated for restoration, as is a remnant of the Mother Road itself.

A 28-mile road with more than 20 overlooks connects the park's two visitor centers. If you're on a mission, you can complete the drive in less than an hour. If you can spare a bit more time and arrive in the morning, start out from the south end. Peruse the Rainbow Forest visitor center and museum, stroll the three easy self-guided trails, and stop at the scenic overlooks. By the time you reach the Painted Desert Visitors Center in the north, you're ready for lunch at the cafeteria or a picnic at nearby Kachina Point (where you can also visit the museum in the Painted Desert Inn). Alternatively, start out at lunchtime on the north side and end at the south visitor center's snack bar in the late afternoon. Hikers may easily spend an entire day in the nearby wilderness areas; campers need to obtain a free overnight permit from either of the visitor centers.

See map p. 399. North entrance: Exit 311 off I-40 (30 miles east of Holbrook). South entrance: off Highway 180 (19 miles southeast of Holbrook). ☎ ***928-524-6228.*** `www.nps.gov/pefo`. *Admission: $10 per vehicle, $5 per person on foot or bicycle (good for seven days). Park open: Daily summer 7 a.m.–7 p.m., winter 8 a.m.–5 p.m.; closed Christmas. Visitor centers and museum close about 15 minutes before park closes.*

Is that a flute, or are you just happy to see me?

Like the howling coyote, Kokopelli, the hunchbacked flute player, is ubiquitous in Southwest shops, appearing on everything from candlesticks to chandeliers. In fact, he's such a cliché by now that the more times he turns up in a store, the tackier it's likely to be. But many of the ancient rock art versions of Kokopelli found throughout the region show him to be no innocent piper. A fertility symbol, he's often depicted with a phallus nearly as prominent as his flute.

Winslow

This town's stretch of Route 66 doesn't offer nearly as many nostalgia-inducing shops and signs as Holbrook's, but you have a couple of ways to spend your time.

- Take it easy. So many people asked about the fictional Winslow intersection immortalized by the Eagles in the song "Take It Easy" that the "Standin' on the Corner" park was dedicated at 2nd and North Kinsley streets in 1999. Highlight: John Pugh's trompe l'oeil mural, complete with a girl in a flatbed Ford, permanently slowed down to take a look at you.
- Get your kicks. Much of the Route 66 stuff missing from the streets of Winslow seems to have ended up at the free Old Trails Museum, 212 N. Kinsley St. (☎ 928-289-5861; Open: Apr–Oct Tues–Sat 1–5 p.m., Nov–March Tues, Thurs, Sat 1–5.p.m). You also see artifacts from the town's heydey as a hub for the Santa Fe Railway, much of it derived from La Posada Hotel (see the "Spending the night" section earlier in this section). Even without all its original plates and cutlery (many of which are on display at the museum), La Posada is also well worth touring; pick up a self-guided pamphlet in the lobby ($2).

More cool things to see and do

In this part of the world, you may enjoy being between a rock and a windy place.

- See an array of rock art. You can visit an incredible array of pictographs and petroglyphs at Rock Art Canyon Ranch at Chevelon Canyon, about 15 miles south of I-40 between Holbrook and Winslow (☎ 928-288-3260). The ranch also has the last remaining bunkhouse of the Hashknife Outfit, the largest U.S. ranching operation in the 19th century, as well as museums featuring 19th-century farm implements and ancestral Puebloan artifacts. Call in advance to get a brochure with a map and to arrange to meet owner Brantley Baird at the ranch house. He points out the highlights of the canyon, which you can explore on your own (you must be accompanied on tours of the ranch museums). Prices depend on the number of people coming on a particular day and what they're interested in seeing (if it's only two, say, who just want to go directly to the canyon, you may pay $10 a person). See map p. 399.

- Get windswept in the ruins. You may explore more than 300 remains of ancestral Puebloan dwellings at Homolovi Ruins State Park, 3 miles northeast of Winslow (☎ 928-289-4106; `www.pr.state.az.us/parks/parkhtml/homolovi.html`). It's hard to imagine that people lived on this rather bleak plain, where the winds always seem to howl. Several hiking trails lead through the ruins, which include prehistoric pit houses, 14th-century pueblos, and a variety of petroglyphs. To get to the park, take I-40 to Exit 257; then go 1.3 miles north on Highway 87. Access to the ruin sites is available 365 days a year during daylight hours; the visitor center open daily 8 a.m–5 p.m. except Christmas Day. Fees, which run around $5 per vehicle for up to 4 adults for day use, are subject to change; call ahead. See map p. 399.

Shopping for local treasures

Petrified wood, fossils, and Route 66 memorabilia are Holbrook's specialties. Julien's Roadrunner, 109 W. Hopi Dr. (☎ 928-524-2388), carries lots of good Mother Road T-shirts and road signs, and Jim Gray's Petrified Wood Company, 147 E. Highway 180 (☎ 928-524-1842), carries an excellent selection of — well, I don't really have to tell you, do I? For high-quality Native American jewelry, baskets, and other crafts, don't miss McGees, 2114 E. Navajo Blvd. (☎ 928-524-1876). In spite of its shlocky-looking road signs and tacky tee pees out front, Geronimo Indian Store, exit 280 off I-40 (☎ 928-288-3241) sells a tasteful array of jewelry and petrified wood crafts — along with items like entire fox skins. Jack Rabbit Trading Post, near Joseph City between Winslow and Holbrook (take Exit 269 off I-40, ☎ 928-288-3230), is loaded with more Route 66 kitsch and more rocks. Get yourself photographed with the giant namesake rabbit in the parking lot. In Winslow, Moore's, 1020 W. 3rd St., (☎ 928-289-3871), a combination (used) hardware store and pawnshop, offers a great selection of turquoise-studded Navajo bracelets and necklaces. Roadworks, 101 W. 2nd St. (☎ 928-289-5423), is the town's central repository for Route 66 items, including lots of "Standing On a Corner" stuff.

Fast Facts: Along Old Route 66

Area Code

The area code in this region is **928.**

Hospitals

Holbrook doesn't have a hospital; for medical emergencies, go to Winslow Memorial Hospital, 1501 N. Williamson Ave. (☎ **928-289-4691**).

Information

Holbrook Chamber of Commerce, Old West Courthouse, 100 E. Arizona (☎ **800-524-2459** or 928-524-6558; www.ci.holbrook.az.us/Chamber), is open Mon–Fri 8 a.m.–5 p.m., Sat–Sun 8 a.m.–4 p.m., closed Christmas. Winslow Chamber of Commerce and Visitor Center, 300 W. North Rd. (☎ **928-289-2434**; www.winslowarizona.org), is open Monday through Friday from 8 a.m. to 5 p.m. year-round.

Police

Call ☎ **911.**

Post Office

Post office locations include: 100 W. Erie St., Holbrook (☎ **928-524-3311**), and 223 N. Williamson Ave., Winslow (☎ **928-289-2131**).

Part V
The Part of Tens

"Of all the stuff we came back from Arizona with, I think these adobe bathrobes were the least well thought out."

In this part . . .

The parts of this book are like children — you pour your heart into getting them to be the best they can, and then they go out into the world (the ingrates!) — so I don't like to play favorites, but suffice it to say this one has loads of personality and is very organized to boot. It consists of three fun topics — crafts, local quirks, and food — presented in a "top ten" format. What's not to like?

Chapter 19

The Top Ten Crafts to Buy in Arizona

In This Chapter

- Getting Native American goods
- Wrangling Western wares
- Seeking out south-of-the-border stuff

Shopping for crafts is one of Arizona's great recreational activities, but don't let anyone try to tell you that it doesn't involve skill. Identifying the best items to buy and the best places to find them takes savvy sleuthing — or scanning the following list. What did it take for a craft to make my top ten list?

- Provenance: I concentrate on items either indigenous to Arizona or — if nothing like it is made in the state — to immediate neighbors New Mexico and Mexico. (Sorry, nothing from Nevada; I figure you have enough fuzzy dice.)
- Portability or shipability: Why buy something special that's not going to arrive home intact or is prohibitively expensive to send safely?
- Value for money: Some of the items I recommend are quite costly, but these are investments both in works of art and continuing traditions.

In general, if you want to be sure that a Native American craft is genuine rather than mass-produced or a cheap knockoff, look for the artisan's name on the piece or ask the seller, who should be able to tell you. Small irregularities are also a tip-off that an item is handmade.

For a preview of Hopi crafts and their prices, log on to `www.hopimarket.com`. For a quick introduction to Navajo rugs, check out `http://navajo-arts.com/navojo-rugs.html`. Guide to Southwest Indian Arts and Crafts by Susanne and Jake Page (Random House) is an excellent all-around resource, and Phoenix's Heard Museum (see Chapter 11) is the best single stop in the state if you're interested in Native American crafts. To find out more about goods created south of the border, get a hold of Arts and Crafts of Mexico by Chloë Sayer (Chronicle Books).

Hopi Katsina Dolls

To the Hopi people, katsinas (pronounced kat-see-nuhs, and less accurately termed (kachinas) are the spiritual aspect of all material phenomena, including plants, animals, rain — you name it. More than 400 different kinds exist. Naturally, when in spirit form, you can't see them, but their representations are made visible through such items as ceremonial masks, headgear, costumes worn by katsina dancers, and, most famously, dolls. Katsina dolls were (and still are) used as toys and teaching tools for young girls, but craftspeople now make many katsinas to be sold to outsiders as well. Hopi katsinas are intricately carved and painted and always made of cottonwood root; knockoffs are generally cruder and created from other materials. Buy these dolls on the Hopi mesas (see Chapter 18), either directly from the artisans or at one of the small shops, in order to guarantee authenticity and good prices. The smallest katsina dolls start around $50, and you may pay $500 or more for larger, more detailed figures.

Hopi Overlay Silverwork

A relatively new craft (originating in the mid-1950s), Hopi overlay silverwork is just what is sounds like: intricate designs are cut with a fine tool out of a flat layer of silver, which is soldered onto a second layer that is approximately the same size but slightly thinner. Both layers are oxidized, but only the top layer is polished, which makes it stand out in contrast with the black layer below. The back may be (but isn't always) stamped with a personal hallmark — usually the artist's name or clan symbol — and you can expect to find a "sterling" stamp (unless of course, the item is made of gold, which some of the younger artists are now using). This double-layered silver is fashioned into decorative items — everything from earrings to watch bands and belt buckles — as varied as the Hopi universe-oriented designs. The Hopi mesas (see Chapter 18) are the best places to buy this work, but you can find good pieces throughout the state. Prices start around $15 for a simple pair of earrings and go up from there.

Navajo Rugs

The 300-year history of Navajo rugs is long and complicated. In the 19th century, western traders influenced the design of the rugs, encouraging the Navajos to create patterns that would sell well to Anglos. Many of the distinct designs you find today — for example, Two Grey Hills, Crystal, and Ganado Red — are named for the trading posts where they originated. The colors used in Navajo rugs vary widely, and most of the patterns are abstract and purely decorative. Some rugs weave tall, skinny figures into their designs representing yeis, supernatural healers. Other rugs show yeibichais (look for the uplifted feet), Navajo dancers dressed as yei spirits. Rugs with pictorial scenes depict life on the reservation; details may include anything from pickup trucks to soda machines. You pay a lot for the genuine item — rugs start around $350 and go well into the thousands. Large, antique rugs fetch upward of $25,000. Ironically, now that the rugs are becoming prized for their great artistry, few skilled artisans are left. Most of the younger Navajos abandoned weaving for more potentially lucrative professions.

You can trust the authenticity of anything you buy at the Hubbell Trading Post in Ganado (see Chapter 18) and at Garland's Navajo Rugs in Sedona (see Chapter 16), both of which have wide selections of contemporary and antique pieces.

Navajo Silverwork

Navajo silversmithing began in the mid-19th century as a vehicle for incorporating much-prized pieces of turquoise — traditionally a lucky, healing stone — into decorative items such as necklaces and belts. These days, many pieces, especially wide bracelets, belt buckles, and squash blossom necklaces (the ones with the horseshoe-shaped pendants), still incorporate the blue stone, although coral is used, too. You may also find intricate designs on plain silver concha (shell-style) belts, earrings, and bracelets. Navajo silverwork is single layer, unlike that of the Hopi. Braided silver is common, too, especially in antique pieces. You find good pieces at trading posts and crafts shops all over the Navajo reservation (see Chapter 18). Some of the older, heavily turquoise-studded ones are sold near the reservation in towns such as Flagstaff, Winslow, and Holbrook. Some of the most creative work is exported to Native American crafts boutiques in Greater Phoenix (see Chapter 11) and Tucson (see Chapter 13). Prices range widely, starting at about $20 for small earrings and going up to the thousands for the larger items. For newer work, check for markings (sometimes in ink) with the artist's name and for a stamp that says, "sterling." Antique work may not have those signs of authenticity.

Zuni Carvings (Fetishes)

A fetish is a kind of talisman or personal charm. All tribes in the Southwest make use of fetishes, but the Zuni, a New Mexico Puebloan people closely related to the Hopi, are particularly renowned for their skill at carving these small figurines. According to legend, certain animals — mountain lions, bears, badgers, wolves, eagles, and moles — serve as protectors, as healers, and as messengers to and from the spirit world. The Zuni people wear small stone representations of these sacred animals, believed to contain their spirits, for protection from harm and to assure success. The stones made for sale to non-Indians (the Zunis allude to them as "carvings" rather than fetishes) aren't imbued with any religious significance. The Zunis make these crafts out of a variety of carvable, colorful stones, including such semiprecious ones as turquoise, alabaster, and lapis. Because they're not native to Arizona, you don't find Zuni carvings in any particular place in the state; most reputable Native American crafts shops sell them, however. Prices start around $15 and rarely go beyond $40.

Tohono O'odham Baskets

The Tohono O'odham (pronounced tuh-ho-noh ah-ah-tem) people, whose reservation near Tucson is the second largest in the United States (after that of the Navajo), are the most prolific basket makers in the Southwest. Their traditional coiled baskets are prized for their artistry as well as for the complicated process involved in making them. To collect the natural materials used — willow, yucca, devil's claw (for the black color), and bear grass, to name a few — the Tohono O'odham often travel far and in different seasons. The labor is careful and painstaking, too, so don't be surprised that small baskets start around $200. The "Man in the Maze" design, which depicts a small figure at the head of a circular labyrinth, is the main tribal symbol. You may find several other patterns, including linked friendship dancers and a variety of desert plants and critters (even scorpions and snakes look charming when they're woven).

Locating these baskets is easiest in Tucson (see Chapter 13), at shops selling Native American crafts, and at San Xavier Plaza. San Xavier Plaza is directly across from the San Xavier Mission, built for the Tohono O'odham people centuries ago and still their prime place of worship. The largest selection, however, is at the gift shop at Kitt Peak National Observatory (see Chapter 14), which leases its lofty plot from the tribe.

Bola Ties

Arizona can't lay claim to having invented such standard Western items as cowboy boots or saddles — most of them are actually of Spanish/ Mexican origin — but the state can take credit for the classic Western string tie. In Wickenburg in 1949, as the story goes, Vic Cedarstaff caught a glimpse of his cowboy hat's "stampede strings" lying across his shoulders. He fixed the strings around his neck with an oval clasp of turquoise and silver and called his tie a "piggin' necklet," but for obvious reasons, the name didn't catch on. Then he changed the name to "bola" — short for boleadora, a rope contraption used for reigning in cattle in South America — and a trend was born. Turquoise and silver remain the most popular fastener materials, although styles vary from copper to plastic and designs include everything from corporate logos to replicas of the state of Texas (where they no doubt claim they invented the tie). The bola was declared Arizona's official state neckwear in 1971.

Bola ties make great gifts for both men and women (worn with a simple, tailored shirt, a bola makes a nice stand-in for a necklace). You find these ties at every Western store and practically every Native American crafts shop in the state; both the Hopi and Navajo fashion bolas with elaborately designed silver clasps. Prices start around $15 for mass-produced ones and go up from there depending on the materials used and artistry involved. Just don't buy one anywhere that uses the spelling "bolo" — you need to draw the line in the sand somewhere.

Western-Style Leatherwork

Unless you own a horse, you probably won't want to tote a saddle home. You're unlikely to use a full set of chaps (except maybe at some leather bars with a cowboy bent), but other hand-tooled, stitched, studded, and stamped leather items say "West" in a way most people can use. Belts, wallets, purses, and briefcases are the most obvious choices. If you're looking for purely decorative items, you may consider a holster. Factory-made leatherwork is sold all over the state. If you want the real thing, follow the horse trail — although not literally, that could get messy — to places like Wickenburg (see Chapter 16), Tucson (see Chapter 13), and southeast Arizona (see Chapter 15) where ranching still goes on. Check out William Brown Holster Co. in Tombstone (see Chapter 15) and Ben's Saddlery in Wickenburg; elsewhere, check the Yellow Pages under "Leather" and look for places that have "saddlery" in their names. Secondhand or antiques stores can also be a good source of leatherwork if you don't mind it a bit worn (just call it "broken in"). Estimating prices is difficult; these items are labor intensive, and good leather doesn't come cheap. Expect to shell out at least $35 for something small — and without studs — like a wallet.

Mexican Tinwork

For inexpensive gifts, especially around the holidays, you may be hard-pressed to find anything as pleasing as Mexican tinwork. The colorful painted ornaments are a particularly good choice. They come in delightful, sometimes surprising shapes: angels, tropical fish, cactus, parrots, armadillos, cheerful Day of the Dead skeletons engaged in all manner of activities — most not overtly religious in subject matter. In Nogales, Mexico (see Chapter 15), where practically every shop sells the tinwork, these ornaments cost about $1.50 each, but at even twice or quadruple the price in crafts stores in Tucson (see Chapter 13) or Greater Phoenix (see Chapter 11), they're still a bargain. Also interesting and very transportable are the unpainted tin ex-votos (votive offerings) called milagros (literally, "miracles"). These small, charmlike representations of arms, legs, eyes, hearts, and other body parts that may be cured through divine intervention are often sold inexpensively in bins for about 75¢ each. You may also find milagros incorporated into works of devotional folk art in Mexico and southern Arizona.

Piñatas

Dating back to the days of the Aztecs, piñatas have been a mainstay at Hispanic celebrations for centuries. These hollow papier-mâché sculptures, stuffed with candy and toys, are great energy releasers for children. The kids are blindfolded and spun around, and then they try to whack the piñata open with a stick. Piñatas are increasingly popular with other cultures, too (even Hallmark puts out a line now, and at www.pinatas.com, you can find Hanukkah-themed versions). If you want the authentic item, go to the source: Mexico, or the Mexican-American communities in southern Arizona. Just comb the stalls in Nogales (see Chapter 15) or check Phoenix and Tucson Yellow Pages under "Party Supplies."

Piñatas come in a variety of shapes — from the traditional donkeys to the latest cartoon characters — and can be custom designed. (I once saw a piñata version of a pink 1957 Chevy convertible.) The Guinness Book of World Records lists one that's 27-feet high and weighs 10,000 pounds, but most are a lot more portable and affordable. Prices start around $8 in Mexico and $15 in the states — of course you pay considerably more for something like that Chevy. Piñatas can be a bit bulky, but smallish ones are available. And what other item can you promise the kids they can break just as soon as they get home?

Chapter 20

Arizona's Top Ten Desert Denizens

In This Chapter

- Discovering Arizona's desert dwellers
- Getting to know the good, the bad, the ugly, and the creepy-crawly

The Sonoran and the Chihuahuan deserts, which spread across southern Arizona, are home to all kinds of creatures that love the hot, dry climate or have adapted over the years to live here. This chapter presents ten of the more exotic critters you're likely to encounter — although not necessarily up close and personally and almost definitely not in your hotel room. Want to know more? One of the best places (aside from frat bars) to learn about local animal life is Tucson's Arizona-Sonora Desert Museum (see Chapter 13), where you can view the creatures described here in their habitats — and at a safe distance.

Coyotes

The coyote — a type of wild dog roughly the size of a German shepherd — is the speedster of the canid species: It can sprint up to 40 miles per hour and cover several hundred miles in a single night. Coyotes are social, often traveling in packs, and they're domestic: They mate for life, and the pups often hang out with their folks for more than a year. In addition, the coyote is very intelligent and has a larger, more sophisticated vocabulary than that of any other type of dog, communicating through growls, whines, yips, barks, and howls, as well as such body language as tail wagging, lip curling, and mock fighting. The most distinctive of the coyote's calls — a series of barks and yelps followed by a drawn-out howl and a few short, sharp yaps — is used to gather group members together before or after a hunt. Its verbal nature has earned the coyote the name "song dog" in several Native American languages.

These animals keep to themselves during the day, so you may not see any, but you're very likely to hear them at night. And, no, coyotes don't wear bandanas.

Hummingbirds

Southern Arizona is hummingbird heaven; nowhere else in North America can you find such a wide variety — as many as 22 species. These adorable birds flit and hover, helicopter-like, around flowers — but what they're actually doing is pigging out. With the highest metabolic rate of any warm-blooded vertebrate, hummingbirds eat all day long to keep from starving.

Jackrabbits and Desert Cottontails

You're most likely to see jackrabbits and their cousins, the desert cottontails (the latter's ears are smaller, and they have cute, fluffy tails), hopping around at dawn or dusk. Both types are constant noshers; they nibble voraciously on a variety of plants, including cacti.

Javelinas

Also called collared peccaries, these animals resemble small wild boars — although they're not actually in the pig family (or related to spears, for that matter). Their closest relative is, oddly enough, the hippo. Javelinas are the desert version of raccoons: They like to root through the garbage in the more remote housing developments. Several resorts in Greater Phoenix and Tucson have resident javelina families. They're cute, but my, what big teeth they have (the better to nibble cactus, prickles, and all, my dear), so steer clear.

Lizards

Small, pinkish, and delicate geckos are notable for the round pads on their fingers and toes — helpful in climbing the walls, literally. These lizards are far more common — you may be relieved to hear — than the two-feet-long, black-and-orange-striped Gila monster. The largest native lizard in the United States, the Gila monster is the only venomous animal protected by state law. Don't be deceived by its placid, sluggish demeanor; Gila monsters can bite with a vise-like grip. Pick one up, and you may need to pry it off with a screwdriver, and then head for the nearest emergency room. Gila monsters aren't considered deadly to humans, but you don't really want to test that theory.

Quails

These chubby, plumed birds tend to cross the road together in family groups called coveys. The mother quail shepherds her babies on outings. These birds may also turn up on your dinner plate — but I won't discuss that here.

Rattlesnakes

Arizona public relations people like to point out that rattlers are present in nearly every state in the United States. However, said PR people aren't likely to mention the fact that the Southwest has more species of rattlesnakes than does any other single region in the Americas. The good news: Rattlers don't really want to tussle with you; that rattling sound means "go away." Nor do they want to waste venom on you — you're too large to kill and eat. If you do get bit, chances are 50/50 that the bite is dry (nonpoisonous). The bottom line: Watch where you step in the wild, but don't make yourself miserable with worry. You're 20 times more likely to be struck by lightning than to be bit by a rattlesnake.

Roadrunners

I spotted one of these large (about two-feet-long), crested birds sprinting across the parking lot of my accountant's office in Tucson. I've never seen one being pursued by a coyote, however, or heard one go "beep, beep." — and neither will you. Roadrunners eat rattlesnakes whole, they prefer to run rather than fly, and they can sprint as fast as 15 miles per hour.

Scorpions

These miniature lobsters like to hang out in dark, dry spots. All varieties are nearly invisible in the dark (although they glow under ultraviolet light). If your shoes have been under your bed all night, shake them out before sticking your feet back into them. The scorpion's bite is painful, but not dangerous. Their sting is venomous, but they only sting humans in self-defense, and most species' stings just cause a painful swelling. The exception (out of the 30 species common to Arizona) is the small bark scorpion, which can cause convulsions and, occasionally, heart failure. Log on to `http://ag.arizona.edu/urbanipm/scorpions/scorpions.html` to find out about its distinguishing characteristics.

Spiders

Big, hairy tarantulas are the most conspicuous of the desert spiders, but they're harmless — honest; some people even keep them as pets. The spiders you really want to give a wide berth are the much smaller, but far more poisonous black widows. A black widow spider's bite can be deadly, but, fortunately, they're not aggressive; just don't go poking your fingers in their faces or into dark corners. You can recognize the venomous females by the bright red, hourglass-shaped markings on their chests.

Chapter 21

Arizona's Top Ten Food Groups

In This Chapter

- Chowing down in Arizona
- Making the most of Mexican ingredients
- Savoring Southwest favorites

The beans are black; the corn is blue. Arizonans sometimes eat cacti and prepare their steaks dry — on purpose. No wonder the local cuisine, with its strong Native American and Mexican influences, may occasionally seem a little strange to outsiders. But familiarity breeds contentment when it comes to food; you're likely to enjoy Arizona specialties, too, once you figure out exactly what you're eating.

Beans

Beans play a large role in northern Mexican and cowboy cooking alike (the famous campfire scene from Blazing Saddles may come to mind). Arizona has beans in any form you can imagine. Kidney beans are cooked in tangy barbecue sauce and served with ribs, chicken, and the like in casual steakhouses. Chic New Southwestern restaurants embrace the rich, smoky-flavored black bean (also known as the turtle bean) for soups and dips. Frijoles — the Mexican-menu bean of choice — are more commonly called pintos and turn up as refritos, which are refried and topped with cheese.

Beef

Arizona does steaks in all cuts and sizes — this was, after all, cattle country not so long ago — with preparations ranging from roadside pan-fried to big-city butter sautéed. The most common (and most delicious) way to get your big meat fix, however, is mesquite-grilled.

In the days before ice cube–dispensing refrigerators with double freezers, dried meat was a staple of the Southwest diet. That tradition lives on in statewide convenience stores, where beef jerky sits next to the cash registers. And dehydrated beef also comes in a much more palatable, Mexican variety: Carne seca, which is sun-dried, shredded, and spiced before being sautéed, often fills tacos, burritos, and enchiladas.

Bread

Forget sourdough, wheat, or doughy white. Sure, Arizona has those breads, but what the state does best is tortillas (mostly corn and flour, although yuppie whole-wheat versions have snuck in) and Indian fry bread (flat discs of deep-fried dough served with a variety of toppings). When lettuce, cheese, tomatoes, and ground beef are piled on fry bread, you have a Navajo taco — similar to the Mexican variety, only flat. Another Native American specialty is piki bread, a delicate, flaky variety made from blue cornmeal (see "Corn," below) and baked over a hot stone. Piki bread is generally only available on the Hopi reservation.

Cacti

No, Arizonans don't eat all kinds of cacti, and we don't eat the spines, but pretty much everything else is fair game on the prickly pear cactus. The plant's tender young pads, called nopales, turn up on Mexican menus in southern Arizona, mostly sliced and diced and scrambled with eggs. Occasionally, nopales are roasted or served marinated in salads. Supermarkets also sell them as nopalitos — small pickled strips. Nopales don't really have a strong taste; they're similar to okra (which they resemble in texture, too, unfortunately). The good news: Nopales are loaded with vitamins, minerals, antioxidants, and amino acids, and they're even touted as diet aids because their fibers slow down digestion. The sweet, kiwi-size fruit of the prickly pear, filled with seeds, is called a tuna (although nothing's fishy about it). Ranging in color from pale pink and lavender to deep red, tunas are made into jams, jellies, marinades, and sweet syrup (often used to create a colorful margarita).

Chiles

First things first: There's no such thing as a chile pepper. According to chef Mark Miller's The Great Chile book, the mix-up dates back to Christopher Columbus, who thought he had brought a new type of black pepper to the Old World; he actually introduced a plant of an unrelated genus, capsicum. Second, the chile plant is spelled with an e, not an i. Chili, the stew made of meat and (sometimes) beans and usually containing chiles, is a whole other food group — but not an Arizonan one. (Talk to Texans if you want to talk chili.) Third, not all chiles are hot.

The chiles you most often come across in Arizona are the fairly mild anaheims and poblanos, which tend to turn up stuffed (relleno). Anaheims are also dried and strung together in chile strings known as ristras. The medium-hot jalapeño (called chipotle when it's dried and smoked) is used in a lot of recipes, too. You sometimes find dishes that include serranos, farther up still on the heat scale (they've got a bit of an after-kick), but you rarely encounter the incendiary habanero, estimated to be 30 to 50 times hotter than the jalapeño. Frankly, much as I hate to admit it, Arizonans are generally wusses, chile-wise — especially when compared with diners in New Mexico. No need to be scared of your salsa here.

Chimichangas

As opposed to Tex-Mex or New Mexican, Arizona's version of Mexican cuisine isn't all that distinct from the hearty, cheese-smothered fare of northern Mexico. Although filling and tasty, Arizona's Mexican-inspired edibles are not wildly exciting. This state did, however, originate two excellent south-of-the-border spinoffs: the chimichanga and the topopo salad (see the "Topopo Salad" section later in this chapter). The chimi — as it's known to its fans — consists of a large flour tortilla filled with meat, deep-fried, and topped with guacamole, cheese, and salsa. Can anything be more fattening — or yummy? Like that of the Caesar salad and of the fajita, the exact genesis of the chimi is widely disputed, but El Charro restaurant in Tucson stakes a pretty strong claim.

Cilantro

The herb derived from the lacy leaves of the coriander plant, also called Chinese parsley, and related to the American kind, definitely rules. Nothing says Mexican/Southwest like cilantro. Don't be surprised if you come across a menu item like crabmeat enchiladas with jalapeño-cilantro pesto sauce, for example.

Some people absolutely despise cilantro, which is hard for the many who adore its fresh, bracing taste to understand. Turns out, just as folks have allergies to peanuts, dairy, and other foods, the body chemistry of some people reacts with the herb so that it literally tastes like soap. If you fall into this group (you'll know the first time you try anything with cilantro) and you dine at a Mexican or New Southwest restaurant, be sure to ask your server if cilantro is included in a dish that you order.

Corn

Another New World food, corn is a staple of both American Indian and Mexican diets. Corn turns up in everything from tortillas and piki bread to soups and stews that use hominy (corn from which the hull and germ have been removed). Even the husks (think tamales) are used by both cultures.

The so-called Indian corn, with its multicolored kernels, is mostly decorative these days, although one native corn hue has become synonymous with Southwest food — blue. Grown by many Pueblo tribes and important to the Hopi for whom it is part of a creation myth, blue corn isn't eaten on the cob, but is dried and ground into a cornmeal. This blue cornmeal is somewhat more flavorful — and definitely more attractive — than the regular kind. Chic Southwest chefs adore blue corn because it exemplifies two key cooking tenets: drawing on local traditions and providing aesthetic pleasure. Expect to find blue corn tortilla chips or blue corn taco shells on some of the state's priciest plates.

Topopo Salad

No one's exactly sure where the name came from, how the salad turned up in Tucson, or why you won't find topopo salad anywhere else. But everyone pretty much agrees that the topopo salad is a treat. This dish comes in several variations, but generally, you can expect a crispy corn tortilla spread with refried beans and topped with lettuce, tomato, chicken, cheese, and often, sour cream (yep, this pig out is one you can rationalize by saying, "But I only had a salad"). Most of Tucson's South Fourth Avenue Mexican restaurants list the topopo on their menus.

Vegetables

Lettuce is probably the most popular vegetable in the state. In fact, Yuma, Arizona, is the country's largest producer of the much-maligned iceberg variety. Lettuce is particularly prized in its shredded form as a garnish for cheese and beans in Mexican dishes. But squash is the darling of New Southwest chefs, in part because it's indigenous to the Western hemisphere and in part because so many types of squash are unpronounceable. For example, two favorite squashes are calabaza, a yellow variety similar in sweetness and firmness to butternut squash, and chayote, the mild-tasting (think cucumber), pear-size gourd that was a principal food of the Aztecs and the Mayas. Another veggie star is jicama (that's heek-uh-muh), a member of the root family most often used raw in salads. Jicama has the crunchy consistency of a water chestnut but with a sweeter taste.

Appendix

Quick Concierge

This handy section presents a wrap-up of the practical information you need to plan a stress-free vacation — from A-to-Z facts to a phone list of airlines and hotel chains — plus, if you're an over-achiever, some additional resources to consult. Another bonus: You don't need to tip this concierge.

Fast Facts

AAA

For emergency road service, call ☎ **800-AAA-HELP** (800-222-4357). To locate the AAA offices in Arizona — most are in Greater Phoenix, but two are also in Tucson and one in Prescott — phone ☎ **800-352-5382** or log on to www.aaa.com.

ATMs

Automatic teller machines are everywhere in Arizona — including, in some places, drive-throughs — and all the major ATM networks are represented. Locations for branches in the **Cirrus** (☎ **800-424-7787;** www.mastercard.com) and **Plus** (☎ **800-843- 7587;** www.visa.com) networks can be found by calling the toll-free numbers or checking the Internet.

Business Hours

Business hours vary throughout Arizona and are often more relaxed — as in "I feel like closing my store this afternoon, so I will" — than in other parts of the country, but you can use the following as a guideline. Note, too, that business tends to be conducted on the early, rather than the late side: You're likely to have better luck reaching someone in an office at 8 a.m. than finding that person at his or her desk a few minutes before 5 p.m. Banks: Monday through Friday from 9 a.m.–5 p.m. (in Greater Phoenix and Tucson, many banks are also open on Saturday from 9 or 10 a.m. to noon or 1 p.m.). Retail stores: Monday through Saturday from 9 or 10 a.m.–5 or 6 p.m.; malls usually stay open Monday through Saturday until 9 p.m., and operate Sundays from 10 a.m., 11 a.m., or noon until 6 p.m. Bars: Most places don't open their doors until 11 a.m. or noon, but drinking establishments are legally allowed to let customers in Monday through Saturday from 6 a.m.–2:30 a.m., Sunday from 10 a.m.–2:30 a.m.

Credit Cards

MasterCard's general information number is ☎ **800-307-7309.** For Visa, call ☎ **800-847-2911.**

Driving

The Arizona Department of Transportation (ADOT) provides a handy number for you to call to find out about road conditions throughout the state: ☎ **888-411-7623.**

Less handy when you're on the road but useful when you're heading out is the roadway conditions section of the ADOT Web site www.az511.com. See the "AAA" listing earlier in this section for the numbers to call for emergency road service.

Emergencies

In most parts of the state, call ☎ **911** to report a fire, contact the police, or get an ambulance. The numbers for emergency services on the Indian reservations are given in the Fast Facts sections of Chapter 18, but you're not likely to remember where to find them in a hurry so just call *0* and have the operator connect you.

Health

I can't emphasize it too much: Wear sunscreen and drink lots of water when you're traveling in Arizona. The sun is surprisingly strong, even in the north, and getting sunburned and dehydrated in no time is easy. The major metropolitan areas have excellent and plentiful medical facilities; however, that's not the case on the Native American reservations in northeast Arizona, where health centers are infrequent and less modern. See Chapter 10 for additional details on health-related matters, including what to do in case of medical emergencies.

Information

See "Finding More Information," at the end of this appendix.

Internet Access and Cybercafes

You can access your e-mail at most Kinko's locations (check the telephone directory) in Tucson and the Valley and at cybercafes in several of the smaller cities; See Chapter 10 and the Fast Facts sections in the destination chapters for locations. In addition, the public libraries in most towns allow visitors to use their computers for Internet access, gratis.

Liquor Laws

The legal age for buying or consuming alcoholic beverages is 21. Hours to purchase booze are the same as those of bars: You can't buy alcoholic drinks Monday through Saturday between 2:30–6 a.m. and Sunday between 2:30 and 10 a.m. Liquor stores tend to have the most specialized selections, but you can get the hard stuff as well as wine and beer at most major supermarkets and drugstores. Convenience stores generally only sell beer and wine coolers.

Mail

To find the address and hours of operation of the U.S. Post Office nearest you, phone ☎ **800-275-8777.** Be prepared to know what zip code you're calling from.

Maps

Most gas stations, convenience stores, and supermarkets sell maps, and they tend to be better than the ones you can get at the local tourist offices, although those often indicate the popular tourist sights. If you're a member of AAA, you can also get excellent maps in advance at your local AAA office. Mapquest, www.mapquest.com, can plot your route from point A to point B. Mapquest is a good online resource if you know exactly where you're coming from and where you're going, but it's no help for the clue- or computer-less.

Newspapers/Magazines

See "Where to Get More Information," at the end of this appendix.

Safety

You need to take the usual common sense precautions for your personal safety and that of your belongings as you would anywhere else in the United States. In Arizona, you also have to think about the road — and the elements. See Chapter 7 for details about driving around Arizona, and see the individual destination chapters for tips relating to touring desert or high-altitude areas.

Smoking

Arizona may look like Marlboro Country, but not as many people light up in the state as they did in the past. Some businesses and public buildings ban smoking entirely, and restaurants tend to have separate smoking areas or restrict puffing to outdoor terraces. That said, only Tucson, and, in Greater Phoenix, Tempe, and Mesa have blanket laws against smoking in restaurants or, in the case of Mesa and Tempe, all public places, including bars. Everywhere else, smoking policies are set on a business-by-business basis.

Taxes

The state sales tax is 5.6%, and all the individual counties and towns tack additional tariffs on your purchases. You usually won't pay more than 8½% on anything you buy, however. Not so for car rental taxes, which range from 10% to more than 20%, or hotel room taxes, which run from around 6% to 14% (depending on which pet projects each city decides to have tourists help finance — but don't say you read that here).

Time Zone

You gotta love a state ornery enough to just say no to daylight saving time (DST) — hey, the one thing we have more than enough of is daylight — but bucking the temporal tide does wreak havoc with our time zones. Arizona is on mountain standard time, but when most of the country goes on DST, the state is, in effect, on pacific standard time. To compound the confusion, the Navajo reservation does observe DST, while the Hopi reservation, which it encircles, doesn't.

Weather Updates

For the best weather reports online — replete with satellite pictures and loads of other great trivia for meteorological junkies — log on to the National Weather Service Web site at `www.wrh.noaa.gov`. Cable subscribers may also get the Weather Channel, one of the more soporific stations on TV when you tune in to Arizona, where you usually find gradations of sunny, sunnier, and sunniest. There's no central number for state weather reports; see the Fast Facts sections of the destination chapters for your preferred prognostication.

Toll-Free Numbers and Web Sites

Airlines

Aeromexico
☎ 800-237-6639 in U.S.
☎ 01-800-0214010 in Mexico
www.aeromexico.com

Air Canada
☎ 888-247-2262
www.aircanada.ca

Alaska Airlines
☎ 800-426-0333
www.alaskaair.com

Aloha Airlines
☎ 800-367-5250 in Continental U.S. and Canada
☎ 808-484-1111 in Oahu; 244-9071 in Maui; 935-5771 in Hilo and Kona; 245-3691 in Kauai
www.alohaairlines.com

American Airlines
☎ 800-433-7300
www.aa.com

American Trans Air
☎ 800-225-2995
www.ata.com

America West Airlines
☎ 800-235-9292
www.americawest.com

British Airways
☎ 800-247-9297
☎ 0345-222-111 or 0845-77-333-77 in Britain
www.british-airways.com

Continental Airlines
☎ 800-525-0280
www.continental.com

Delta Air Lines
☎ 800-221-1212
www.delta.com

Great Lakes Airlines
☎ 800-554-5111
www.gpair.com

Hawaiian Airlines
☎ 800-367-5320

Mexicana
☎ 800-531-7921 in U.S.
☎ 01800-502-2000 in Mexico
www.mexicana.com

Midwest Express
☎ 800-452-2022
www.midwestexpress.com

Northwest Airlines
☎ 800-225-2525
www.nwa.com

Southwest Airlines
☎ 800-435-9792
www.southwest.com

Sun Country
☎ 800-359-6786
www.suncountry.com

United Airlines
☎ 800-241-6522
www.united.com

US Airways
☎ 800-428-4322
www.usairways.com

Car Rental Agencies

Advantage
☎ 800-777-5500
www.advantagerentacar.com

Alamo
☎ 800-327-9633
www.goalamo.com

Avis
☎ 800-331-1212 in Continental U.S.
☎ 800-TRY-AVIS in Canada
www.avis.com

Budget
☎ 800-527-0700
www.budget.com

Dollar
☎ 800-800-4000
www.dollar.com

Enterprise
☎ 800-325-8007
www.enterprise.com

Hertz
☎ 800-654-3131
www.hertz.com

National
☎ 800-CAR-RENT
www.nationalcar.com

Payless
☎ 800-PAYLESS
www.paylesscarrental.com

Rent-A-Wreck
☎ 800-535-1391
www.rentawreck.com

Thrifty
☎ 800-367-2277
www.thrifty.com

Major Hotel and Motel Chains

Baymont Inns & Suites
☎ 800-301-0200
www.baymontinns.com

Best Western International
☎ 800-528-1234
www.bestwestern.com

Clarion Hotels
☎ 800-CLARION
www.clarionhotel.com or
www.hotelchoice.com

Comfort Inns
☎ 800-228-5150
www.hotelchoice.com

Courtyard by Marriott
☎ 800-321-2211
www.courtyard.com or www.
marriott.com

Days Inn
☎ 800-325-2525
www.daysinn.com

Doubletree Hotels
☎ 800-222-TREE
www.doubletree.com

Econo Lodges
☎ 800-55-ECONO
www.hotelchoice.com

Fairfield Inn by Marriott
☎ 800-228-2800
www.marriott.com

Four Seasons
☎ 800-819-5053
www.fourseasons.com

Hampton Inn
☎ 800-HAMPTON
www.hampton-inn.com

Hilton Hotels
☎ 800-HILTONS
www.hilton.com

Holiday Inn
☎ 800-HOLIDAY
www.basshotels.com

Howard Johnson
☎ 800-654-2000
www.hojo.com

Hyatt Hotels & Resorts
☎ 800-228-9000
www.hyatt.com

La Quinta
☎ 800-531-5900
www.laquinta.com

Marriott Hotels
☎ 800-228-9290
www.marriott.com

Motel 6
☎ 800-4-MOTEL6 (800-466-8356)
www.motel6.com

Omni
☎ 800-THEOMNI
www.omnihotels.com

Quality Inns
☎ 800-228-5151
www.hotelchoice.com

Radisson Hotels International
☎ 800-333-3333
www.radisson.com

Ramada Inns
☎ 800-2-RAMADA
www.ramada.com

Red Lion Hotels & Inns
☎ 800-RED-LION
www.redlion.com

Red Roof Inns
☎ 800-843-7663
www.redroof.com

Residence Inn by Marriott
☎ 800-331-3131
www.marriott.com

Ritz-Carlton
☎ 800-241-3333
www.ritzcarlton.com

Rodeway Inns
☎ 800-228-2000
www.hotelchoice.com

Sheraton Hotels & Resorts
☎ 800-325-3535
www.sheraton.com

Sleep Inn
☎ 800-753-3746
www.sleepinn.com

Super 8 Motels
☎ 800-800-8000
www.super8.com

Travelodge
☎ 800-255-3050
www.travelodge.com

Vagabond Inns
☎ 800-522-1555
www.vagabondinn.com

Westin Hotels & Resorts
☎ 800-937-8461
www.westin.com

Wyndham Hotels and Resorts
☎ 800-822-4200 in Continental U.S. and Canada
www.wyndham.com

Where to Get More Information

Still want additional data — after all my hard work? Okay, this book isn't designed to cover everything, so this section shares a few more resources. Now enough reading already. Start packing!

Tourist information

Call or write the Arizona Office of Tourism, 1110 W. Washington, Ste. 155 Phoenix, AZ 85007 (☎ 866-275-5816; www.arizonaguide.com), for a copy of Arizona Official State Visitors Guide, a glossy publication that details attractions, activities, and lodgings throughout the state. You can also phone with specific questions. If the friendly representatives can't tell you what you want to know about the state, they can refer you to someone who can. The office of tourism's Web site is the prime source of online information, with links to Arizona cities and regions and to lots of special interest sites (for example, one for families traveling with kids, another for scenic routes). See also the Fast Facts sections of the destination chapters for the local tourism offices and for additional useful Web sites.

Newspapers and magazines

If a peek at Arizona Highways magazine doesn't make you want to visit the state, nothing will; finding more spectacular photography anywhere would be hard (of course, the landscape lends a hand by being incredibly photogenic). See Chapter 9 for information on photo workshops run by the magazine. Single copies are available at newsstands and supermarkets in Arizona, or you can opt for a subscription; call ☎ 800-543-5432 for current rates ($21 for 12 issues in 2004). You can also find an online teaser of the magazine at www.arizonahighways.com. Newspapers and magazines relating to Greater Phoenix and Tucson are detailed in the Fast Facts sections of Chapters 11 and 13.

State guides

Frommer's Arizona (Wiley Publishing, Inc.) is a great complement to this book, covering destinations that aren't included in these pages and offering additional details on many that are. Another excellent resource is www.frommers.com, which is full of travel tips, online booking options, and a daily e-mail newsletter filled with bargains and travel advice.

Index

• A •

• B •

• C •

• D •

• E •

• F •

• G •

• H •

• I •

• J •

• K •

• L •

• O •

• Q •

• R •

• S •

• U •

• V •

• W •

• Z •

JSINESS, CAREERS & PERSONAL FINANCE

-7645-5307-0 0-7645-5331-3 *†

Also available:

- Accounting For Dummies † 0-7645-5314-3
- Business Plans Kit For Dummies † 0-7645-5365-8
- Cover Letters For Dummies 0-7645-5224-4
- Frugal Living For Dummies 0-7645-5403-4
- Leadership For Dummies 0-7645-5176-0
- Managing For Dummies 0-7645-1771-6
- Marketing For Dummies 0-7645-5600-2
- Personal Finance For Dummies * 0-7645-2590-5
- Project Management For Dummies 0-7645-5283-X
- Resumes For Dummies † 0-7645-5471-9
- Selling For Dummies 0-7645-5363-1
- Small Business Kit For Dummies *† 0-7645-5093-4

)ME & BUSINESS COMPUTER BASICS

-7645-4074-2 0-7645-3758-X

Also available:

- ACT! 6 For Dummies 0-7645-2645-6
- iLife '04 All-in-One Desk Reference For Dummies 0-7645-7347-0
- iPAQ For Dummies 0-7645-6769-1
- Mac OS X Panther Timesaving Techniques For Dummies 0-7645-5812-9
- Macs For Dummies 0-7645-5656-8
- Microsoft Money 2004 For Dummies 0-7645-4195-1
- Office 2003 All-in-One Desk Reference For Dummies 0-7645-3883-7
- Outlook 2003 For Dummies 0-7645-3759-8
- PCs For Dummies 0-7645-4074-2
- TiVo For Dummies 0-7645-6923-6
- Upgrading and Fixing PCs For Dummies 0-7645-1665-5
- Windows XP Timesaving Techniques For Dummies 0-7645-3748-2

)OD, HOME, GARDEN, HOBBIES, MUSIC & PETS

-7645-5295-3 0-7645-5232-5

Also available:

- Bass Guitar For Dummies 0-7645-2487-9
- Diabetes Cookbook For Dummies 0-7645-5230-9
- Gardening For Dummies * 0-7645-5130-2
- Guitar For Dummies 0-7645-5106-X
- Holiday Decorating For Dummies 0-7645-2570-0
- Home Improvement All-in-One For Dummies 0-7645-5680-0
- Knitting For Dummies 0-7645-5395-X
- Piano For Dummies 0-7645-5105-1
- Puppies For Dummies 0-7645-5255-4
- Scrapbooking For Dummies 0-7645-7208-3
- Senior Dogs For Dummies 0-7645-5818-8
- Singing For Dummies 0-7645-2475-5
- 30-Minute Meals For Dummies 0-7645-2589-1

TERNET & DIGITAL MEDIA

-7645-1664-7 0-7645-6924-4

Also available:

- 2005 Online Shopping Directory For Dummies 0-7645-7495-7
- CD & DVD Recording For Dummies 0-7645-5956-7
- eBay For Dummies 0-7645-5654-1
- Fighting Spam For Dummies 0-7645-5965-6
- Genealogy Online For Dummies 0-7645-5964-8
- Google For Dummies 0-7645-4420-9
- Home Recording For Musicians For Dummies 0-7645-1634-5
- The Internet For Dummies 0-7645-4173-0
- iPod & iTunes For Dummies 0-7645-7772-7
- Preventing Identity Theft For Dummies 0-7645-7336-5
- Pro Tools All-in-One Desk Reference For Dummies 0-7645-5714-9
- Roxio Easy Media Creator For Dummies 0-7645-7131-1

eparate Canadian edition also available

eparate U.K. edition also available

ilable wherever books are sold. For more information or to order direct: U.S. customers
: www.dummies.com or call 1-877-762-2974.
customers visit www.wileyeurope.com or call 0800 243407. Canadian customers visit
v.wiley.ca or call 1-800-567-4797.

SPORTS, FITNESS, PARENTING, RELIGION & SPIRITUALITY

0-7645-5146-9 0-7645-5418-2

Also available:

- Adoption For Dummies 0-7645-5488-3
- Basketball For Dummies 0-7645-5248-1
- The Bible For Dummies 0-7645-5296-1
- Buddhism For Dummies 0-7645-5359-3
- Catholicism For Dummies 0-7645-5391-7
- Hockey For Dummies 0-7645-5228-7
- Judaism For Dummies 0-7645-5299-6
- Martial Arts For Dummies 0-7645-5358-5
- Pilates For Dummies 0-7645-5397-6
- Religion For Dummies 0-7645-5264-3
- Teaching Kids to Read For Dummies 0-7645-4043-2
- Weight Training For Dummies 0-7645-5168-X
- Yoga For Dummies 0-7645-5117-5

TRAVEL

Italy For Dummies

0-7645-5438-7 0-7645-5453-0

Also available:

- Alaska For Dummies 0-7645-1761-9
- Arizona For Dummies 0-7645-6938-4
- Cancún and the Yucatán For Dummies 0-7645-2437-2
- Cruise Vacations For Dummies 0-7645-6941-4
- Europe For Dummies 0-7645-5456-5
- Ireland For Dummies 0-7645-5455-7
- Las Vegas For Dummies 0-7645-5448-4
- London For Dummies 0-7645-4277-X
- New York City For Dummies 0-7645-6945-7
- Paris For Dummies 0-7645-5494-8
- RV Vacations For Dummies 0-7645-5443-3
- Walt Disney World & Orlando For Dummies 0-7645-6943-0

GRAPHICS, DESIGN & WEB DEVELOPMENT

0-7645-4345-8 0-7645-5589-8

Also available:

- Adobe Acrobat 6 PDF For Dummies 0-7645-3760-1
- Building a Web Site For Dummies 0-7645-7144-3
- Dreamweaver MX 2004 For Dummies 0-7645-4342-3
- FrontPage 2003 For Dummies 0-7645-3882-9
- HTML 4 For Dummies 0-7645-1995-6
- Illustrator CS For Dummies 0-7645-4084-X
- Macromedia Flash MX 2004 For Dummies 0-7645-4358-X
- Photoshop 7 All-in-One Desk Reference For Dummies 0-7645-1667-1
- Photoshop CS Timesaving Techniques For Dummies 0-7645-6782-9
- PHP 5 For Dummies 0-7645-4166-8
- PowerPoint 2003 For Dummies 0-7645-3908-6
- QuarkXPress 6 For Dummies 0-7645-2593-X

NETWORKING, SECURITY, PROGRAMMING & DATABASES

0-7645-6852-3 0-7645-5784-X

Also available:

- A+ Certification For Dummies 0-7645-4187-0
- Access 2003 All-in-One Desk Reference For Dummies 0-7645-3988-4
- Beginning Programming For Dummies 0-7645-4997-9
- C For Dummies 0-7645-7068-4
- Firewalls For Dummies 0-7645-4048-3
- Home Networking For Dummies 0-7645-42796
- Network Security For Dummies 0-7645-1679-5
- Networking For Dummies 0-7645-1677-9
- TCP/IP For Dummies 0-7645-1760-0
- VBA For Dummies 0-7645-3989-2
- Wireless All In-One Desk Refere For Dummies 0-7645-7496-5
- Wireless Home Networking For Dummies 0-7645-3910-8

ꞮEALTH & SELF-HELP

-7645-6820-5 *†

0-7645-2566-2

Also available:

- Alzheimer's For Dummies 0-7645-3899-3
- Asthma For Dummies 0-7645-4233-8
- Controlling Cholesterol For Dummies 0-7645-5440-9
- Depression For Dummies 0-7645-3900-0
- Dieting For Dummies 0-7645-4149-8
- Fertility For Dummies 0-7645-2549-2
- Fibromyalgia For Dummies 0-7645-5441-7
- Improving Your Memory For Dummies 0-7645-5435-2
- Pregnancy For Dummies † 0-7645-4483-7
- Quitting Smoking For Dummies 0-7645-2629-4
- Relationships For Dummies 0-7645-5384-4
- Thyroid For Dummies 0-7645-5385-2

DUCATION, HISTORY, REFERENCE & TEST PREPARATION

0-7645-5194-9

0-7645-4186-2

Also available:

- Algebra For Dummies 0-7645-5325-9
- British History For Dummies 0-7645-7021-8
- Calculus For Dummies 0-7645-2498-4
- English Grammar For Dummies 0-7645-5322-4
- Forensics For Dummies 0-7645-5580-4
- The GMAT for Dummies 0-7645-5251-1
- Inglés Para Dummies 0-7645-5427-1
- Italian For Dummies 0-7645-5196-5
- Latin For Dummies 0-7645-5431-X
- Lewis & Clark For Dummies 0-7645-2545-X
- Research Papers For Dummies 0-7645-5426-3
- The SAT I For Dummies 0-7645-7193-1
- Science Fair Projects For Dummies 0-7645-5460-3
- U.S. History For Dummies 0-7645-5249-X

Get smart @ dummies.com®

- **Find a full list of Dummies titles**
- **Look into loads of FREE on-site articles**
- **Sign up for FREE eTips e-mailed to you weekly**
- **See what other products carry the Dummies name**
- **Shop directly from the Dummies bookstore**
- **Enter to win new prizes every month!**

ꞩeparate Canadian edition also available
ꞩeparate U.K. edition also available

ailable wherever books are sold. For more information or to order direct: U.S. customers it www.dummies.com or call 1-877-762-2974.
K. customers visit www.wileyeurope.com or call 0800 243407. Canadian customers visit vw.wiley.ca or call 1-800-567-4797.